Information Systems for Managers

With Cases
EDITION 3.1

Gabriele Piccoli
Louisiana State University

Federico Pigni
Grenoble École de Management

Prospect Press

Edition 3.1
Edition 3.1 includes necessary updates and and a few minor corrections to
Edition 3.0. As of October 31, 2016, all URLs in the text have been checked
and updated. For a detailed list of the changes, see the Student Resources page
at http://www.prospectpressvt.com/titles/piccoli-3e/student-resources/.

Founded in 2014, Prospect Press serves the academic discipline of Information
Systems by publishing innovative textbooks across the curriculum including
introductory, emerging, and upper level courses. Prospect Press offers
reasonable prices by selling directly to students. Prospect Press provides
tight relationships between authors, publisher, and adopters that many
larger publishers are unable to offer. Based in Burlington, Vermont,
Prospect Press distributes titles worldwide. We welcome new authors to
send proposals or inquiries to Beth.golub@prospectpressvt.com.

Cover Photo: © istock/aykuterdogan
Cover Design: Maddy Lesure
Production Management: Rachel Paul, Scribe Inc.
Editor: Beth Lang Golub

E-book (with cases), ISBN: 978-1-943153-04-6
Printed paperback (with cases), ISBN: 978-1-943153-05-3

To Margaret, the finest teammate I could have asked for.
To Laura Jean and Erik, who always help put it all in perspective.

GP

To Paola, who teaches me how life is beautiful every day.

FP

Contents

Preface

The Philosophy of This Book

This book is inspired by the notion that today, 40 years into the "information age," general and functional managers must be able to *actively* and *knowledgeably* participate in discussion and decisions about information systems and information technology. I have designed this book from the ground up, based on what has worked and proven useful to advanced undergraduate, master of management, and executive management students I have taught over the past 15 years in the United States and in Europe. Thus the topics this book covers; its writing style; and the examples, minicases, and full-length cases I use are all carefully chosen to be both *relevant* and *engaging* to an audience of students who may or may not plan to become information systems specialists.

I have found in my interactions with executives of large and small firms that both general and functional managers in modern businesses need to be able to do two things when it comes to information systems decisions:

1. Evaluate the plethora of modern information technology and trends—from a strategic not a technical standpoint—in order to be able to identify and use the technology/technologies that will generate value for the organization.
2. Become effective partners of the information systems function. To this end, they need to be familiar with those areas where they will have to come in contact with information systems professionals.

The main foci of this book are therefore the strategic role of information systems in the modern firm and the design and implementation of IT-dependent strategic initiatives. Over the years I have come to believe that masters and executive MBA students, as well as undergraduates who concentrate in information systems, need less of a "breadth book" that offers an overview knowledge of technology and technology issues and much more of an "analytics tools-focused" book that offers them frameworks and tangible guidance on how to ensure that their firms benefit from information systems and technology efforts. I designed and wrote this book to provide such a toolkit for them.

Thus this is not a text *about* IT and *how IT works*. This is a book about the information system and information technology resource and how these should be optimally deployed to achieve an organization's objectives. In other words, this book treats IT like any other organizational resource—an asset that general and functional managers alike need to understand enough to be able to plan for, select, deploy, and effectively manage with a keen eye to its strategic potential so as to be able to create and appropriate value for their organizations.

How This Book Is Organized

The book follows a progression designed to engage skeptical students while creating a sound long-term basis for decision making. I have been particularly sensitive to the audience with both the expository approach and content selection. The book uses a more colloquial and engaging writing style than traditional textbooks, with many examples and quotes centering on decision making by both general and functional managers. My students, as well as many of my colleagues' students, have told us that this book has the colloquial style of a consulting report rather than the dry writing style of a textbook. This is important feedback for me, as it confirms my hunch that once the "dry reading" obstacle is removed, students can see what the course is really all about: a critical subject matter for modern managers delivering a set of tangible and practical skills that will help them be an asset for their organization. The opening minicases, written from the perspective of functional or general managers, reinforce this approach by clearly showing the relevance of the chapter's content while helping foster discussion and generate momentum at the start of class.

The book's content is organized into four sections, four stepping-stones that build upon one another in a sequential manner. Part I covers essential definitions and provides the conceptual foundation for the following chapters. Part II describes how new technologies have changed, and continue to change, the competitive landscape and social environment, thus creating both opportunities and new threats for established firms and start-ups. Part III carries the defining content of this book, offering actionable frameworks to help managers envision how to develop value-adding IT-dependent strategic initiatives and to gauge whether they can be protected so as to reap benefits in the long term. Part IV concludes the text by focusing on how to create and implement information systems at the core of any initiative. It also discusses common systems and major trends as well as security, privacy, and ethical considerations.

Finally, the book provides a number of full-length end-of-chapter cases, written by myself and colleagues, that were expressly designed to use the frameworks and debate the issues covered in the chapter. This tight parallel between content and cases has worked very well in my classes because students immediately see the applicability of the theories and concepts covered.

New for the Third Edition

For this third edition, I wanted Federico to join as coauthor of the book. With him, we developed the current edition, causing the text to undergo a major—and probably timely—update.

The world has changed rapidly since the previous edition I wrote four years ago, shaped by the ever increasing pervasiveness of IT. It has never been so compelling for students to understand the opportunities IT provides for creating new strategic initiatives.

With this edition, we account for these changes at the same time, respecting the plan I drew since the first installment of the book. All chapters underwent a careful update, and several new and current examples are introduced to engage students in critically reviewing the discussed concepts. Chapters 3 and 12 are those that underwent the most changes. We now cover themes such as big data and cloud computing and discuss emerging trends such as the Internet of Things, wearable computing, digital manufacturing, and advanced analytics.

We further introduced three new case studies, phasing out those that we felt lost their appeal and welcoming the suggestions from the second edition's adopters. Thus, to complement Chapter 3, you find a brand new cloud-opportunity case—"eLoanDocs: Riding the Tide of Technology without Wiping Out." To support Chapter 8, we have now a new case discussing the design, development, and platform opportunity of a custom-made strategic customer relationship management system—"H-GRM: Bringing Back High Touch Hospitality." For Chapter 9, we provide the case of a cloud-based revenue management system impacting, and probably changing, an entire industry—"Duetto: Industry Transformation with Big Data."

With this new edition, you will "feel at home" if you already used this book. We believe you will find the new content engaging for your students and supportive of a successful learning journey.

Supporting Resources

For this book, we have developed an extensive set of support resources, all available on the book's website (http://www.is4managers.com). We really recommend you to join. You will find the standard set of materials, including the following:

- PowerPoint presentations for each chapter
- A test bank (to supplement the study questions at the end of each chapter)
- An instructor's manual containing teaching notes for each of the opening minicases, along with tips and suggestions on how to use them to jump-start class with a high-energy discussion
- Links to videos and other interactive materials

Moreover, we invite you to share your experiences and discuss how you use the book. We have grown a vital user base engaged in constantly improving the teaching materials that will provide a unique value for this edition.

Information on pricing and ordering the different versions of the text can be found at the publisher's website: http://www.prospectpressvt.com/titles/piccoli-3e/.

Acknowledgments

While there are only two names on the cover of this book, and while we take responsibility for any errors or inaccuracies, a book like this one is really a joint effort. The ideas and concepts, teaching philosophy, pedagogical approaches, tools, and techniques covered came about through observation of and discussion with the many colleagues we have had the good fortune of interacting with over the years. Among the most influential, we want to acknowledge Roy Alvarez, Kathryn Brohman, Blake Ives, Dick Moore, Erica Wagner, and Rick Watson. Each of them has helped us in shaping the courses we have taught and ultimately the content of this book.

We would also like to acknowledge the contribution of the many students over the last fifteen years who have brought a positive attitude and an open mind to the Information Systems Management course, those who have challenged our own understanding of the concepts in this book, as well those who pushed us to find better ways to introduce and discuss them. We would also like to acknowledge the many companies, their management and employees, who recognize that we can't have relevant education without their full engagement and support. These people have kindly volunteered their time to discuss many of the ideas explored in this book with us. Many have also agreed to allow their companies' examples and experiences serve as case studies and welcomed my colleagues and us to share their knowledge.

We would also like to thank the colleagues who took time from their busy schedules to review the first and second editions of the manuscript and to offer valuable and constructive feedback. From the first edition,

Louis Beaubien, Providence College
Ed Christensen, Monmouth University
John Kohlmeier, DePaul University
Blake Ives, University of Houston
Roberto Mejias, Indiana University
Graham Peace, West Virginia University
Cynthia Ruppel, Nova Southeastern University
Paul Licker, Oakland University
Richard McCarthy, Quinnipiac University
Paul Pavlou, Temple University
John Scigliano, Nova Southeastern University
Michael Wade, IMD Lausanne
Erica Wagner, Portland State University
Ted Williams, University of Michigan, Flint

From the second edition,

Patrick Becka, Webster University, Louisville
Leida Chen, Creighton University
J. Michael Cummins, Georgia Tech
F. J. DeMicco, University of Delaware
David Dischiave, Syracuse University
Rassule Hadidi, University of Illinois, Springfield
Raymond Henry, Cleveland State University
Jeff Howells, University of Georgia
Shin-jeng Lin, Le Moyne College
Rodger Morrison, Troy University
Barbara Ozog, Benedictine University
Jeffrey Pullen, University of Maryland
Malu Roldan, San Jose State University

We also wish to thank the colleagues who provided input for the development of the new Edition 3.0. These include the following:

Michael Bliemel, Dalhousie University
Sophie Buer-Chemin, Grenoble École de Management
Mark Cecchini, University of South Carolina
Mitchell Church, Coastal Carolina University
Michael Cummins, Georgia Tech
Pierre Dal Zotto, Grenoble École de Management
Greg Dawson, Arizona State University
Patrick Fan, Virginia Tech
Alberto Francesconi, University of Pavia
Robert Gordon, Molloy College
Iris Lui, Ming Chuan University
Brandi N. Guidry Hollier, University of Louisiana at Lafayette
Alex Heckman, Franklin University
Paul Licker, Oakland University
Efrem Mallach, University of Massachusetts, Dartmouth
John Muraski, University of Wisconsin, Oshkosh
Mark Rosso, North Carolina Central University
James Stewart, Syracuse University
Andrew Walker, Grenoble École de Management

Last, but certainly not least, I would like to acknowledge Beth Lang Golub, who originally saw the opportunity for this book to be written and constantly supported its development.

Foreword

There tend to be two major approaches to teaching information systems. The technology perspective instructs students about hardware and software, and the focus is very much on information technology. The transformative approach assists students in identifying how information systems can transform an enterprise's relationships with its key stakeholders, such as customers and suppliers. Under the transformative approach, the emphasis is on the information systems an enterprise can create and the value they can then unleash. Anyone can buy information technology, but it takes skill, vision, and persistence to create a transformative information system that can radically change an enterprise and even a society.

Gabe is a key member of the transformational school of information systems. His academic research and work with practitioners, the results of which are incorporated in this book, are directed at understanding and exploiting the transformative power of information systems. He has studied many examples of transformation, as you will find when you read some of the insightful cases in this book and the highly useful frameworks he presents. As you read this book, you will discover why information systems have been the major change engine for many enterprises and economies over the last five decades. Nothing else has had anywhere near the same influence on the way we live today.

As you develop your managerial skills, it is important that you realize that to become an organizational leader, you will need to demonstrate that you can design, lead, and execute transformational projects. Most of the morphing assignments you take on will require an intimate understanding of technology in organizations. Irrespective of which particular field is your area of concentration, you will find that at some point you will need to become deeply steeped in understanding how you can exploit one or more information technologies to create a new information system to generate a competitive advantage or superior customer experience. How well you integrate people, procedures, and information technology to create an information system will determine your success. This book is about developing your skills to successfully participate in, and possibly lead, an information systems–enabled project to create new opportunities for customer service and organizational growth. Read the book carefully, reflect on the frameworks and cases, incorporate the key insights into your model of the world, and above all, apply the knowledge gained to improve your organization's performance.

Richard T. Watson
Rex Fuqua Distinguished Chair for Internet Strategy
University of Georgia
Athens, GA

As we all know, the required master level information systems course is a very difficult one to teach. I always admire the few faculty teaching this course who can transcend the reluctance, prejudice, and general disinterest too many of us confront from our students. Gabe is one of the talented few. He has enjoyed significant success teaching the required information systems course over the years, receiving teaching awards for his work with both masters and executive MBA students. In my foreword to the first edition, I said, "Hopefully, this book will arm the rest of us with some of Gabe's teaching magic." Now that we are in edition 3.0, I can report that I have talked to a number of colleagues who teach required MBA, executive MBA, and upperclassmen in undergraduate courses who have confirmed that this book has worked quite well for them.

I can now be confident in saying that this book will be a great addition to your arsenal, allowing you to leverage the enthusiasm of students already interested in the material, while energizing those who come in the door with a negative bias toward an "IT course." This book can make your course more compelling to your students thanks to Gabe's very approachable writing style, the wealth of examples he uses, the opening minicases that quickly create excitement and buzz, and the unique full-length cases in the full version of this textbook (several of which we wrote together). Most helpfully, Gabe has identified both the foundation and cutting-edge content that is most relevant to management students. With this book, you will find it much easier to demonstrate the relevance of information systems to your students and to create a positive learning environment in your classes.

Blake Ives, PhD
C. T. Bauer Chair in Business Leadership
C. T. Bauer College of Business
University of Houston

FOUNDATIONS

In Part I, we lay the foundations for the study of information systems (IS). Although the press and commentators devote much attention to information technology (IT) and the (often substantial) IT investments that organizations make, modern general and functional managers don't have the time, or often the inclination, to become IT experts. After all, that's why organizations hire and pay IS and IT professionals.

Yet with information technology becoming pervasive in both business and society at large, modern general and functional managers can no longer abdicate their obligation to make decisions about this crucial organizational resource. The good news is that you can be an effective manager without knowing a huge amount about IT, without knowing in detail how the technology works, and without having to keep up with the barrage of new technologies that are constantly being commercialized. To be an effective general or functional manager, a proficient user of IT resources, and a productive partner of the firm's information systems and technology professionals, you need a strong grounding in the fundamentals of IS management and decision making.

As we describe in Chapter 2, information systems are sociotechnical organizational systems that encompass technology, the people who will be using such technology, and the business processes they execute to accomplish their daily tasks and carry out business activities. User-managers can rely on IT professionals when it comes to choosing among programming languages or the appropriate structure of a new database being implemented, but general and functional managers must be able to design the appropriate information systems for their organization, plan and budget for the use of IT resources, and analyze whether or not a given information system creates a competitive advantage that can be protected.

This is not a book about IT and how it works. This is a book about information systems and the IS decisions that general and functional managers are routinely called on to make. In Part I, we lay the foundations upon which you will build your information systems knowledge.

- *Chapter 1: Information Systems and the Role of General and Functional Managers.* The first chapter defines some basic terms and makes the case for why general and functional managers must be intimately involved in information systems decision making.
- *Chapter 2: Information Systems Defined.* The second chapter defines what an information system is (the central concept in this book), places this definition in the organizational context, and draws the crucial distinctions between IT and IS.
- *Chapter 3: Organizational Information Systems and Their Impact.* The third chapter categorizes the different information systems found in modern organizations and provides the vocabulary you need in order to communicate with other managers and the information systems professionals in your firm. This chapter also provides you with a foundation to consider the impact of various types of information technology on the organization.

1

Information Systems and the Role of General and Functional Managers

What You Will Learn in This Chapter

This chapter focuses on the role that general and functional managers play in the organizational use and management of information systems (IS). The chapter also describes the meteoric rise to prominence of information technology (IT) and the role advanced IT plays in the modern organization.

Specifically, this chapter will

1. Define the terms *general manager*, *functional manager*, and *end user* and articulate the differences among these concepts.
2. Define the role of the modern chief information officer (CIO).
3. Identify organizational and information technology trends that have led to the current popularity of IT-based information systems.
4. Explain why it is important for general and functional managers to be involved in IS decisions.
5. Identify the risks that arise when general and functional managers decide to abdicate their right (and duty) to make important information systems decisions.

MINICASE: Facing Termination?

The silence was beginning to become uncomfortable as you searched for words to answer the question from your chief executive officer (CEO). The boardroom had never looked so big, and it seemed as if her words were still echoing: "How could it get to this? You sat here telling us how this new software program would dramatically improve our marketing efficiencies and customers' repurchase frequency. It has been over two months, and the bloody thing isn't even working!"

As you searched for the right way to respond, the events leading up to this moment flashed through your mind. It was more than two months ago when you sold the board on the benefits of a new sales force automation tool. You had just been promoted to vice president of marketing, taking over from Tom

Vecchio. Tom was an old-fashioned salesperson, with a huge personality and an incredible memory. He was employee number four when the company launched back in 1982, and he had been instrumental in its early growth via personal networking—phone calls, rounds of golf, and birthday calls. He had surrounded himself with very similar people. You understood that culture, you had been one of the young guns a few years ago, and now you had replaced the master.

But things had changed in your industry, competition was much tougher, and markets were now global. "How could a firm the size of this one run sales and marketing without any IT support?" you wondered once promoted. How ironic that you'd be the one to usher in the "new IT-enabled world." You had managed to never concern yourself with all that techie computer stuff. You were a pretty good user: e-mail, web, Word, PowerPoint, some Excel . . . the usual. But now your bonus depended on the performance of the whole function, not just the number of contracts you closed, and it seemed as if you had been getting all the heat about efficiencies that they could not put on Tom . . . they could scream all they wanted—he was untouchable. But you weren't!

It all seemed to have fallen into place when you went to the National Convention of the Sales Executives Association. At one of the booths, you had seen VelcroSoft and the sales force automation product VelcroSFA. There was a lot of buzz around the product both at the conference and in the press. The attendant at the booth told you about all the great features of VelcroSFA: automated recording of information at each stage in the sales process, automated escalation and approval, contact management, lead sharing for team selling, and in-depth reporting. It could even integrate with human resource systems for immediate computation of commissions, reduced data entry, and increased speed.

After you returned to the office, you read some more material about VelcroSFA and called a couple of friends who had implemented it in their organizations. It seemed to be the right application. You showed the website demo to some of the best-performing salespeople. They did not seem impressed, and they raised a bunch of issues. Joe, one of the old-timers, said, "The Rolodex did wonders for me throughout my career; what do I need a computer for?" Joe never liked you anyway since you had taken Tom's spot, you thought. Amanda, a younger associate, seemed more positive: "I'm willing to give it a shot, but it seems quite convoluted. I'm not sure I need all those functionalities." You recall thinking that they would change their minds once they saw their commissions go up because the software would allow them to spend more time with customers. You did not like computers, after all, but you liked the software more as you found out more about it. They would, too.

Jenny Cantera, the IT director, had pledged her help with the implementation and, after looking at the brochure, had said, "Should take a weekend to have this application running and write the interface to the HR system. I'm busy with the implementation of the new accounting system for the next three or four weeks, but I should be able to do this afterward." You had some doubts about Jenny. She was very smart and technically gifted, but she was the very first IT director in your firm, and she had little experience in the position.

The board had been sold pretty easily on the purchase, even though at $55,000 it was a sizable investment for your firm. You had used the return-on-investment (ROI) calculations provided by VelcroSoft. Granted, VelcroSoft personnel were very aggressive with assumptions underlying their calculations, but with a bit of effort on everyone's part, you truly believed you could achieve strong results. As soon as you got the go-ahead, you contacted the vendor and obtained the installation package. Everything had gone perfectly up to that point, but your fortune seemed to turn right after.

First, you had the software license codes sitting on your desk for more than a month. Jenny was running into unexpected trouble with the accounting application. Once she finally got around to implementing your product, she took one weekend to complete the implementation and created the user accounts. The interface to the HR application was not operational yet—something about an "XML parser," which you did not quite understand. However, you pressed on. Over the following week, you had encouraged your sales rep to "play around with the applications." You had even sent an e-mail with the subject line "Up and running in the brave new world of sales force automation!" But the response had been cool at best. Only a few accounts had been accessed, and overall, the people you spoke to said they were too busy and would look at the software once the quarter closed.

Last weekend, when Jenny wrote the interface to the HR systems, all hell broke loose. On Monday (yesterday), the HR database was locked and the HR system was down. Jenny was scrambling to bring it back up, and she was now saying she might have to reinitialize the software. She had already removed VelcroSFA, and at this point, it looked like the application would not be a priority for a while. You did not really mind; you had bigger fish to fry . . . you were concerned about getting fired.

Discussion Questions

1. Who do you think is to blame for the current state of affairs?
2. What do you think is the most critical mistake you made over the last two months? What were the principal mistakes made by others involved?
3. How could these mistakes have been avoided, if at all?
4. Should you take this opportunity to say good-bye to everyone and resign now? If not, what should you say in response to the CEO's question?

Introduction

It is hard these days to escape the hype and publicity surrounding information technology (IT) and its business applications. IT has become more affordable and pervasive than ever before; just think about the wide array of technologies that you use for work and pleasure on any given day. You may own an iPad, a Microsoft Surface, or a Galaxy Tab; most likely you own a laptop and a smartphone; and perhaps you even have a game console, such as the Microsoft Xbox One or Sony PlayStation 4.

At work, you are likely a heavy user of word processing and spreadsheet programs, as well as some more specialized applications such customer relationship management or business intelligence software. You may even have been talented enough to create your own Android apps (Figure 1.1) or launch your own start-up.

More generally, for business, not-for-profit, and governmental organizations, IT has become a critical resource that draws significant investments. The recent recession put pressure on spending, but expenditures remained significant, particular in some sectors. As Gartner reported, from a cross-industry perspective, IT spending per employee is increasing (Figure 1.2),[1] supporting the fact that now "the success of every enterprise, department, function and employee depends increasingly on IT. Everyone in the organization must have a role in determining how IT resources are used to achieve business results." In other words, "every budget is an IT budget."[2] As important as technology is to today's general and functional managers, don't be misled—this is not a book about IT and how it works. Nor is this a book written exclusively for IT professionals. This book is written from the standpoint of, and to serve the needs of, the modern manager.

FIGURE 1.1. The Android operating system
Source: Copyright © 2015 The Android Open Source Project, licensed under the Apache License, Version 2.0

General and Functional Managers

A manager is a knowledge worker of modern business and not-for-profit organizations who is in charge of a team, a functional area (i.e., functional managers), a business unit, or an entire organization (i.e., a general manager). These individuals are typically trained in management schools and, particularly in larger organizations and entrepreneurial ventures, often hold a master's degree in management or business administration.

General and functional managers have, through schooling and on-the-job experience, developed strengths in business areas such as operations, marketing, finance, human resources, accounting, and the like. Those of you who plan on a career in business consulting will develop a similar set of functional expertise. However, with the unrelenting pace of IT innovation and its widespread adoption in organizations, the personal success of managers and of their areas of responsibility increasingly depend on these managers making optimal decisions about the use and management of information. Information is a critical organizational resource. As Thomas Watson Jr., the legendary chairman of IBM, recognized more than 50 years ago, "All the value of this company is in its people.

---

1. Gartner Inc. (2011, January 25), *IT metrics: IT spending and staffing report 2011*, retrieved from https://www.gartner.com/doc/1528717/it-metrics-it-spending-staffing

2. Gartner Inc. (n.d.), *IT cost optimization*, retrieved from http://www.gartner.com/technology/topics/it-cost-optimization.jsp

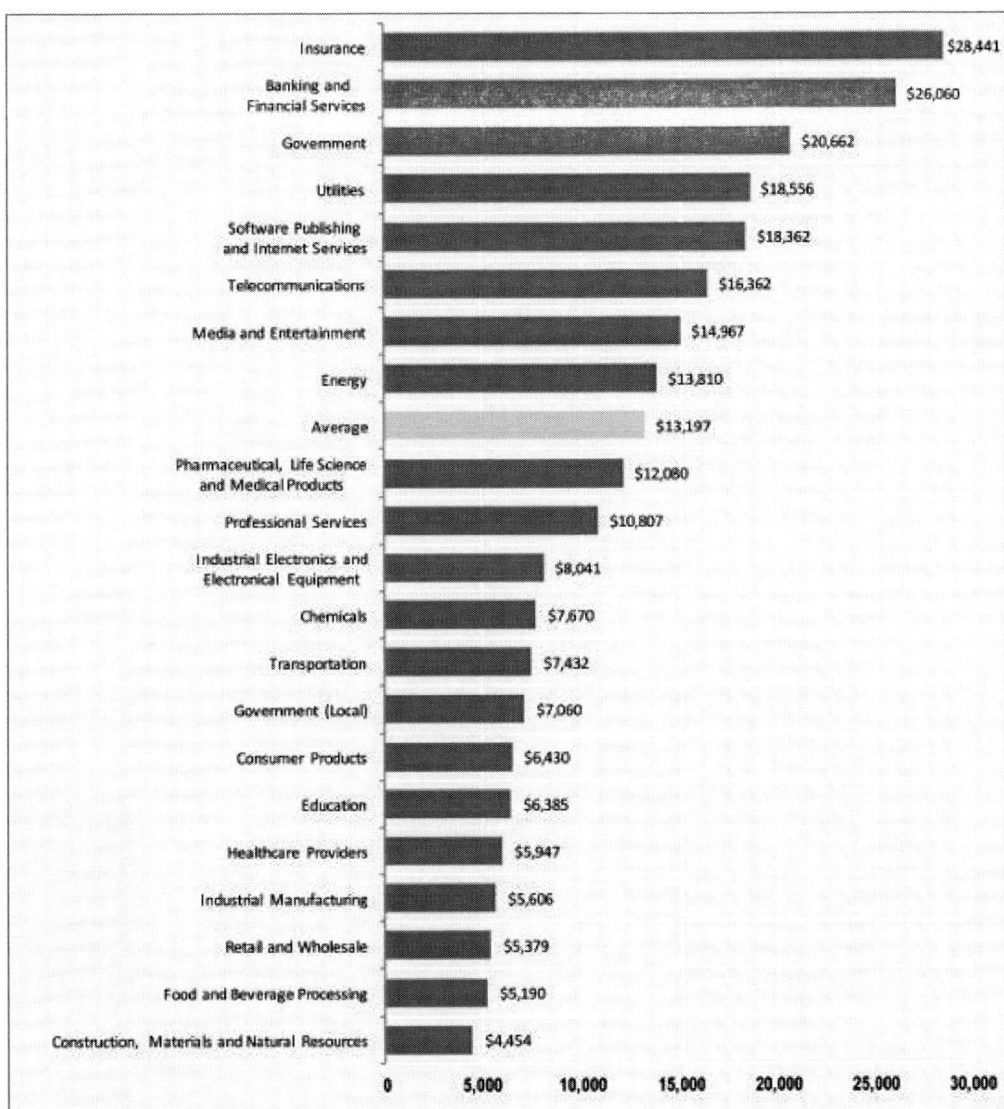

FIGURE 1.2. IT spending per employee by industry
Source: Gartner ITKMD (2013)

If you burned down all our plants, and we just kept our people and our information files, we should soon be as strong as ever."[3]

To manage information effectively, the modern firm must adopt and use information systems and information technology resources. Selecting, designing, and managing these resources are no longer exclusively the job of the technology professional but are now the shared responsibility of all modern and functional managers. Bill Gates neatly captured this point when he stated, "Information technology and business are becoming inextricably interwoven. I don't think anybody can talk meaningfully about one without the talking about the other."[4] As a consequence, general and functional managers must

3. Quinn, S. B. (1992), *Intelligence enterprise: A knowledge and service based paradigm for industry*, New York, NY: Free Press, p. 244.

4. Gates, B., & Hemingway, C. (1999), *Business @ the speed of thought*, New York, NY: Warner Books.

work in partnership with information systems and technology professionals—those individuals with substantial technical training and education in management information systems, computer science, and engineering—when it comes to carrying out these decisions. *Partnership* is the key word here; it is no longer acceptable for general and functional managers to claim ignorance of IT and delegate all IT decisions to technologists. As Douglas Merrill put it when he was serving as the chief information officer (CIO) of Google Inc., "The distinction between technology and business is antediluvian—it's gone."[5] The notion that the IT function needs to cater to its internal customer—"the business" (as if the IT function was not part of "the business"!)—no longer represents reality. So many managerial and organizational decisions depend heavily on information systems to be successfully implemented, and new information technology constantly opens up new possibilities for innovation in strategy, products, processes, and organizational design. The success of an organization in today's environment depends on the interplay of the information systems and information technology with the other organizational resources (e.g., labor, brand, capital).

Let's look at examples of what happens when this partnership works well:

- Consider Zara, the world's largest apparel retailer. The root of its success can be traced back to the shared vision of Inditex founder Amancio Ortega Gaono and José Maria Castellano, a former IT manager. Both believed that computers were critical for building a responsive supply chain. The company profited from this unique blend of IT competencies and business visions for making "fast fashion" a reality—a sought-after chimera since the 1980s, consisting of the continuous design of affordable and fashion-inspired apparel. Zara gained the flexibility required to adapt its designs to the ever-changing preferences of customers by putting IT at the core of its store and supply chain coordination efforts. The 6,500 stores in 88 different countries receive new deliveries twice a week, and new products just take between two and three weeks to reach the store from the design table. For competitors, this generally takes months. The ability of the company to sense the market starts in stores, where sales data are generated and complemented with store managers' accounts of shoppers' preferences. Again, IT supports the supply chain coordination effort of the company to determine the best-performing products in each region, manufacture them, and deliver them as quickly as possible. Interestingly, Zara spends less than one quarter of other brands in the industry.

- As it became clear that the Internet would be a viable channel for economic transactions, Michael Dell, founder and CEO of Dell Computers Inc., challenged his team to take advantage of the opportunity. The Internet offered Dell the chance to sell directly to the consumer (not just to business accounts) without having to compromise its direct model. In charge of the efforts was 30-year-old Scott Eckert, a recent master of business administration (MBA) graduate. Working closely with the information systems and technology group, Eckert developed Dell Online, the online store, and an application that allowed customers to configure their machines. As they say, the rest is history. Fueled by the staggering growth rates of the Internet itself, the online store generated $1 million in revenue per day in six months, $2 million a day in nine months, and $3 million a day in a little more than a year since opening for business. Dell Computers is now one of the largest computer makers in the world, and the Dell Online initiative was instrumental in helping the firm achieve this result.

- The Hotel Lugano Dante is a four-star hotel in Lugano, Switzerland, that is part of a small two-property chain. While the Lugano Dante is a nice hotel, there is nothing intrinsically unique about it in terms of location, facilities, or any other structural characteristic. In the age of the Internet, where competition is only a click away, Carlo Fontana, the hotel's general manager, feared that his property could quickly become a commodity—an undifferentiated good that would be dragged into one price war after another. Believing in the power of

5. Weiss, T. R. (2008, March 10), Google CIO: Online success rests on talking with, not to, customers, *Computerworld*, retrieved from http://www.computerworld.com/article/2537599/internet/google-cio--online-success-rests-on-talking-with--not-to--customers.html

differentiation through service, Fontana set out to enable his staff to create superior and highly personalized experiences for guests by providing attention to detail and catering to the unique needs of individual customers—far superior to the standard four-star service. Working closely with Davide Bernasconi, the director of IT, Fontana conceptualized and built a comprehensive system that provides accurate, real-time operational and guest data and disseminates it to each guest-facing employee. Staff members have personal iPads that allow them to produce and receive the necessary information to provide outstanding service. After a year of operation, the system has contributed to make the Lugano Dante the number-one hotel in its market based on customer reviews on TripAdvisor, with a 99% approval rate by customers that helps both differentiate the hotel and ensure above-average loyalty.

The preceding examples highlight a few critical lessons for prospective general and functional managers:

- The general and functional managers in the examples, while not IT experts, were making educated decisions about the deployment of information systems in their organizations.
- The objective of IT deployment was business driven. In other words, the new technology was brought in to serve the growing or changing needs of the organization. The people who perceived and understood the need for this new way of doing things were the general and functional managers.
- These general and functional managers were not IT professionals and had no specific training in technology, but they worked in close partnership with the IT professionals in their organizations to ensure the successful deployment of the needed information systems and technology functionalities.
- The general and functional managers did not use the new technologies firsthand once introduced. Rather, other employees, the end users, had direct contact with the hardware and software programs that had been introduced.

The last of the preceding points is important, as there is a clear difference between the roles of general and functional managers and end users.

General and Functional Managers versus End Users

End users are those individuals who have direct contact with software applications as they use them to carry out specific tasks. For example, I am an end user as I use word processing software (i.e., Microsoft Word) to write this book. You, as a student, are an end user as you engage in spreadsheet analyses using Microsoft Excel in your statistics, operations, or finance courses.

Most general and functional managers in modern organizations are also end users. They use software programs to improve their own personal productivity—from the very basic, such as e-mail and calendars, to the most advanced, such as mobile management dashboards designed to keep a real-time pulse of the business's performance. Although being a sophisticated end user is an important asset for the modern manager, because effective use of software programs can lead to increased productivity, it is far more important for modern managers to have the skills and knowledge to make appropriate information systems decisions at the organizational level.

It should now be clear why this book is not an IT training book and its focus is not on end-user skills. This book is expressly designed for current and future managers, for those individuals who have general management and/or functional management responsibility, and for those who serve, or will one day serve, on the board of directors of an organization. The promise of this book is that to be an effective manager, you need not know an inordinate amount of information about IT or how technology works, even though some of this IT-specific knowledge undoubtedly helps.

Rather, you really need to have and feel confident with knowledge of information systems and the role that IT plays in them. (See Chapter 2 for definitions.) You need to know how to identify opportunities to use information technology to your firm's advantage; how to plan for the use of information systems resources; and how to manage the design, development, selection, and implementation of information systems. As Michael Dell, chairman and CEO of Dell Inc., says, "The instinct when something new shows up is to say, 'How do we bolt this on to the old way we were doing it and deliver some incremental improvement?'" That's the wrong way of approaching the challenge, he explains: "What you really have to do is rethink the problem and say, 'Now that we have all these new tools and new techniques, how can we solve the problem in a fundamentally different way?'"[6] These are the skills that separate effective modern managers (those who can be productive partners of the information systems function) from ineffective ones (those who delegate critical IT decision making and, more often than not, live to suffer the negative consequences of their decisions). In the words of Rob Solomon, senior vice president of sales and marketing for Outrigger Hotels and Resorts, "Every manager must have an IT strategy. You can't delegate to technologists and only worry about your allocated cost or what training your employees need. You must understand how to be master of your own destiny and make IT work best for you. Too many managers still don't get that."[7]

The Next Wave of CIOs

Another interesting trend that makes this book relevant to management school students is the increasing permeability of the boundaries of the IT function—that is, the CIO position is increasingly seen not as the endpoint of a career but as a stepping-stone to the chief executive officer (CEO) or president posts. The old joke "CIO stands for Career Is Over"[8] no longer rings true. Examples of CIOs being promoted to the role of CEO or to other executive-level positions now abound. For example, David Bernauer, former CIO at the pharmacy chain Walgreens, was promoted to chief operating officer (COO) after four years in the top IT post and later to CEO and chairman of the board. Andrew Rashbass, IT director at *The Economist*, became the CEO of Economist.com, then chief executive of *The Economist*, and more recently chief executive of Thomson Reuters and then chairman of *Euromoney*. Maynard Webb, CIO at Gateway Computers, was hired as COO by online auction giant eBay and later as chairman at Yahoo! Kevin Turner, former CIO of Walmart, became CEO at Sam's Club and later COO at Microsoft Corporation. Dawn Lepore, former CIO of the Charles Schwab company, took the CEO position at Drugstore.com in 2004. Philip Clarke made the jump from the head of IT to CEO of Tesco in 2011.

Two primary reasons are fueling this trend:

- The increasing prevalence of IT and the consequent need for those who serve on the executive teams and the board of directors to have some understanding of how to use this crucial resource. In the words of a British headhunter, "CIOs are the only ones with a helicopter view of the business and they have a great deal of operational experience of the business."[9]
- The fact that the prevalence of IT and information systems throughout the organization gives CIOs a broad view of operations, business processes, interorganizational coordination challenges, and opportunities and a broad understanding of how the firm is positioned to execute its strategy. As Tom Murphy, former CIO of Royal Caribbean Cruise Lines and current CIO of pharmaceutical supply chain services provider AmerisourceBergen, put it, "Information technology is everywhere; we touch almost every process in the firm. We must intimately understand operations to enable them; from my CIO post I have a complete view of the organization and its operations."[10]

6. PwC (2015), Creating new value in new ways through digital transformation, *18th Annual Global CEO Survey*, retrieved from http://www.pwc.com/gx/en/ceo-survey/2015/assets/pwc-18th-annual-global-ceo-survey-jan-2015.pdf

7. Piccoli, G. (2005), Outrigger Hotels and Resorts: A case study, *Communications of the Association for Information Systems, 15*(5), retrieved from http://aisel.aisnet.org/cais/vol15/iss1/5

8. There is even a forum for technology leaders jokingly titled *career is over*!

9. Weisinger, D. (2012, April 10), Cloud computing: Adoption as Rorschach—Perspectives on the CIO psyche, *Formtek*, retrieved from http://formtek.com/blog/cloud-computing-adoption-as-rorschach-perspectives-on-the-cio-psyche/

10. Personal communication with authors.

On the flip side, forward-looking firms no longer view the IT function as the province of technologists who speak a foreign language that nobody else understands. Individuals with strong technical skills still represent irreplaceable assets, of course, but the information systems function is increasingly staffed with employees with business or humanities training who share an excitement for the potential of technology to solve business problems and who are relatively well versed in information systems issues and vocabulary. For example, Douglas Merrill, former Google CIO, majored in psychology, while Tom Murphy, who held the CIO post at Royal Caribbean Cruise Lines and AmerisourceBergen has an English literature degree! The modern IT function increasingly finds in its ranks business analysts, system analysts, project management specialists, and even CIOs who don't have engineering or computer science backgrounds and yet complement software designers and developers, IT architects, and other professionals with more technical profiles.

Modern CIOs are required to exhibit many of the skills of their executive counterparts while maintaining priorities that are focused on keeping the lights on and IT operations running. They need to be well versed in business while not losing sight of the delivery of information services that enable the organization to operate effectively (Table 1.1).

The digital transformation firms are undergoing requires CIOs and senior business executives to lead together. As Frédéric Oudéa, CEO of Société Générale—a top European bank—said, "This is not a technology challenge as much as it is an understanding that our business model is changing and that our teams have to change to be efficient and proactive in this transformation. [. . .] We are trying to move forward and accelerate the cultural change, to make everyone aware of how to deal with clients in a different way with new tools and much more on a real-time basis, as well as at a lower cost."[11]

Consider this as you begin this course: As much as you might think you will never be an integral part of the IT group, the truth is that you may soon find yourself becoming involved in information systems selection, development, or implementation projects. This is a very common occurrence, as younger members of the workforce often are (or are assumed to be!) tech savvy and comfortable with information technology. It is therefore natural for your more senior colleagues to think of you as the right person to represent your organizational function on the design and implementation of new information systems. Participating in such projects is an opportunity to showcase your talent . . . and perhaps to discover that a career in information systems is for you. Whether you are trying to position yourself for this career path or just looking to be a successful general or functional manager, this book is written for you.

Table 1.1. Top 10 business and technology priorities in 2015 according to Gartner and KPMG

Top 6 CEO strategic priorities	Top 10 CIO priorities
Developing new growth strategies	Business intelligence and analytics
Stronger client focus	Infrastructure and data center
Geographic expansion	Cloud
Reducing cost structures	Enterprise resource planning
Greater speed to market	Mobile
Fostering innovation	Digitalization and digital marketing
	Security technologies
	Networking, voice, and data communications
	Customer relationship and experience
	Industry-specific applications

Source: Adapted from Gartner CIO Agenda Report (2015) and KPMG Global CEO Outlook (2015)

---

11. KPMG (2015), *Global CEO outlook 2015*, p. 6, retrieved from http://www.kpmg.com/Global/en/IssuesAndInsights/ArticlesPublications/ceo-outlook/Documents/global-ceo-outlook-2015-v2.pdf

Fundamental IT Trends: The Staying Power of Moore's Law

Information systems—those organizational systems that enable the processing and management of an institution's information—are the backbone of organizational operations. These information systems are powered by more or less advanced IT at their core in all but the smallest of firms. Understanding the drivers and the trends that shape the evolution of IT is important for you as a general or functional manager because new technologies constantly enable new strategies, new initiatives, and the effective management and use of greater and greater amounts of data and information.

The popularity and growing importance of IT-based information systems is self-evident in the 21st century. For those in need of further convincing, we only need to show statistics that capture the breathtaking rates at which IT has become, and continues to grow into, a critical tool for modern organizations, consumers, and individuals alike. For example, in 2015, the number of people with access to the Internet was estimated to exceed the three billion mark—around 40% of the world's actual population.

Another source of evidence is the precision that has characterized Moore's law over the 40 years since its announcement by Dr. Gordon Moore. In 1965, Dr. Moore, who three years later cofounded Intel Corp., commented at a conference that if the current rate of improvement in the production process of transistor-based microprocessors continued, the number of transistors that could be etched on an integrated circuit (i.e., a microchip) would double every one to two years. What is remarkable about Moore's law is not so much how Dr. Moore arrived at it but rather how precisely it has held true over the last 50 years (Figure 1.3) and the fact that it is expected to continue to hold true for a decade or two more.

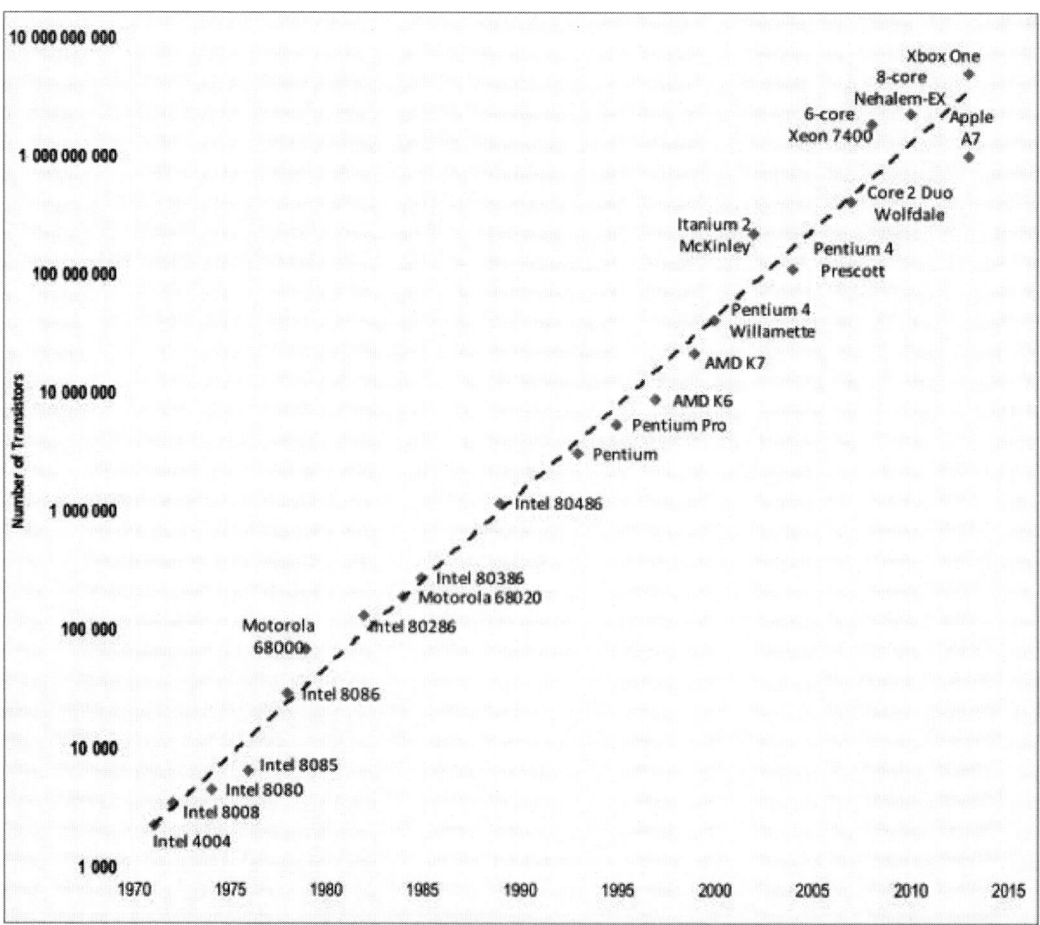

FIGURE 1.3. Number of transistors in different generations of commercial microprocessors
Source: Data from Wikipedia

The unrelenting pace of performance improvement in microchip design and production processes has a number of important managerial implications, which we discuss in detail below. At a more general level, it is this unflagging progress that enables continued innovation and the reinvention of processes, strategies, products, and services. It is critical to recognize, however, that the responsibility for taking advantage of this continuous technological progress in modern organizations falls squarely on the shoulders of general and functional managers.

Processing Power and Memory Has Increased

As stated by Moore's law, the processing power of microprocessors has experienced exponential growth. Because a transistor is the basic unit of computational ability of a microprocessor, more transistors equates to greater computational power in any device that uses a microchip—your personal computer, of course, but also your music player, your cellular phone, your digital camera, your car, and even your microwave and your refrigerator. Not only has the programmable computational capacity available to us increased exponentially over the last two decades, but it also has proliferated to a multitude of devices, from game consoles to mobile devices (Figure 1.4).

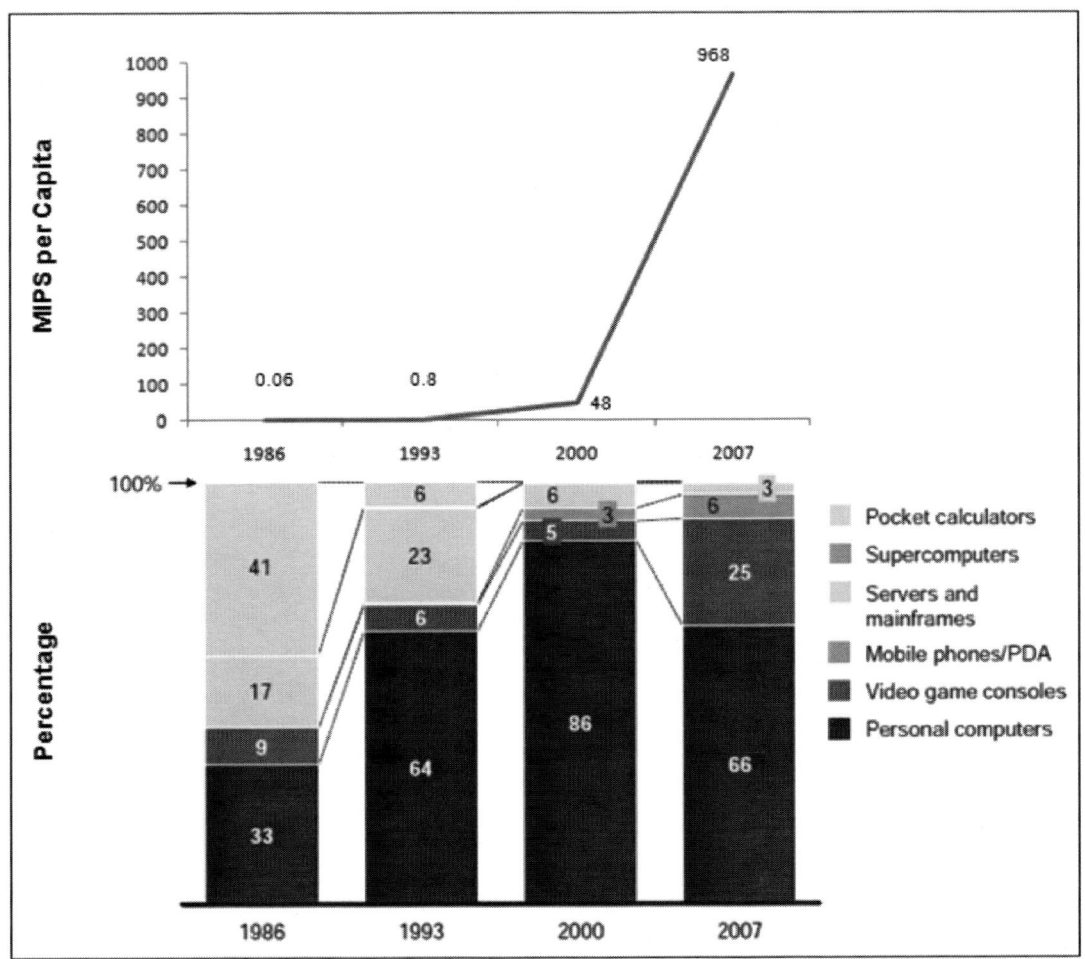

FIGURE 1.4. Estimated worldwide general-purpose computational capacity (MIPS per capita)
Adapted from McKinsey Report (2011), *Big data: The next frontier for innovation, competition, and productivity*, retrieved from http://www.mckinsey.com/insights/business_technology/big_data_the_next_frontier_for_innovation. Estimations and data from Hilbert, M., & Lopez, P. (2011, April 1), The world's technological capacity to store, communicate and compute information, *Science*, 60–65.

The storage capacity of memory chips has also increased exponentially. With transistors also serving as the basic component of memory chips, a higher density of transistors makes for increased memory capacity and performance, thus providing the necessary complement to increasing the computational ability of microprocessors. A similar pattern of evolution has occurred with respect to secondary storage capacity (i.e., hard disks, tapes), which has grown exponentially, shifting decisively to the digital format (Figure 1.5).

Costs of Computing Power Have Declined

The cost of computing power and storage has declined at breathtaking rates as Moore's law has shown its effects. By some estimates, all the power of a mainframe that cost more than $10 million in 1965 had been incorporated into a $7 chip by 2002. The cost of that same chip is projected to drop to about one cent in 2017.[12] It is this amazing combination of power and affordability that has led to the spreading of "intelligence"—here defined as computational ability—in products ranging from the more advanced (e.g., smart cameras that can recognize human faces) to the more mundane (e.g., a hotel minibar that can recognize when items are consumed).

While the number of transistors on microchips has steadily increased, chip manufacturers have been able to contain energy requirements through innovative designs. This trend, coupled with continued improvements in battery technology, has enabled the development of countless new portable devices based on digital computer architecture. Familiar examples are iPads and other tablets, smartphones, smartwatches, Fitbits, and other wearable devices. In parallel, we have seen the computerization of products that exhibited little or no intelligence before, such as cars and appliances, and the transformation of plastic cards and labels into smart cards and radio frequency identification (RFID) tags. This

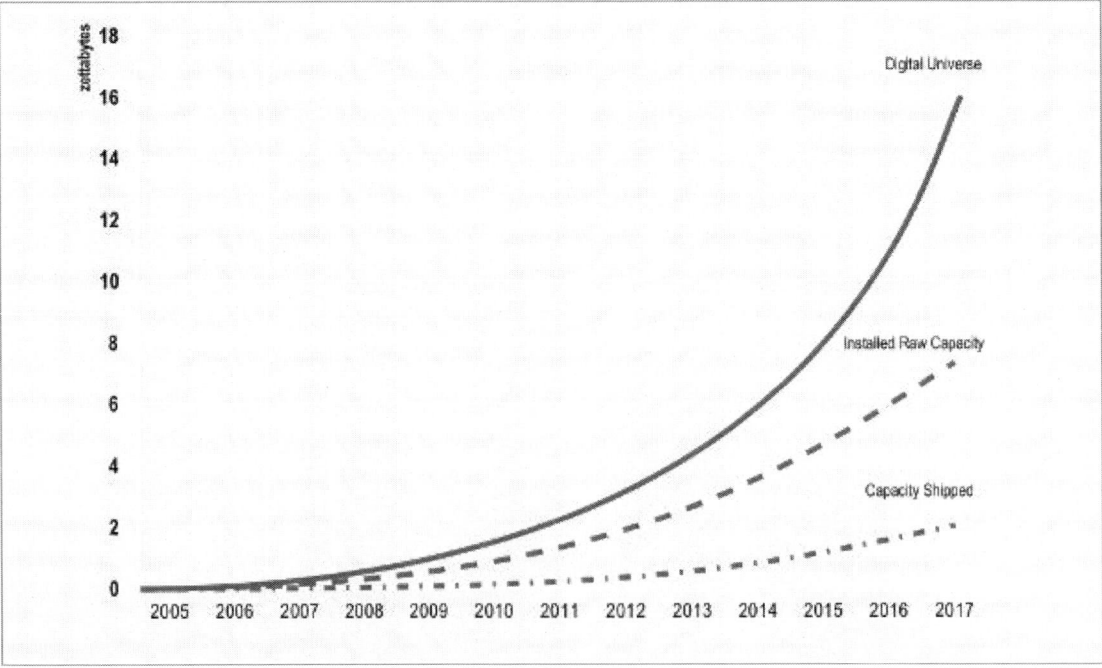

FIGURE 1.5. Estimated worldwide storage capacity per capita in PB
Source: IDC (2013), *Where in the world is storage? Byte density across the globe*, retrieved from http://www.idc.com/downloads/where_is_storage_infographic_243338.pdf

---

12. McFarlan, F. W. (2003), *The new strategic weapon: Information technology*, Faculty Seminar Series, Boston, MA: Harvard Business School Press. CD-ROM.

trend, sometimes called *pervasive computing* or the *Internet of things*, is poised to spur significant innovation in the years to come (Chapter 12).

Computers Have Become Easier to Use

One remarkable characteristic of the evolution of IT is that as computers have become more powerful and more internally complex, they have also become easier to use. This is an interesting side effect of Moore's law and one of the most intriguing characteristics of information technology. Because software is extremely malleable, as computers become more powerful and are able to process more and more operations in a unit of time, they can be asked to do more work on behalf of and for the user. If you had the (sometimes painful) experience of using computers before the arrival of graphical user interfaces, then you know how difficult it can be to memorize a command (with perfectly correct syntax!) in order to have the computer perform a task. For example, in MS-DOS, in order to copy a file from the CD-ROM to the hard disk, you had to issue a command with the following structure:

COPY [/Y|-Y] [/A][/B] [d:][path]filename [/A][/B] [c:][path][filename] [/V]

Failing to remember the appropriate syntax would yield a cryptic error message and, typically, little hint as to how to go about fixing the error. Conversely, when using modern graphical user interfaces, copying a file from one location to another is as simple as identifying the right icon and dragging it to the target location. Voice-recognition interfaces are also becoming more common, and we can envision a world in which we will increasingly issue commands to a computer by simply telling it what to do or, as with modern multitouch interfaces, by manipulating objects to convey our intentions to the machine.

The simplicity of user interfaces is just one example of how IT, as it becomes more sophisticated and complex, becomes easier to use. Another example is offered by the many software-enhanced objects we come into contact with regularly. Modern cars are quite difficult to service and quite powerful in terms of the number of software instructions that their controllers and control units can process. However, while all this software and hardware makes the car more internally complex, modern automobiles are easier and safer than ever to drive, with features like night vision systems, rearview cameras, automatic brakes that activate if you get too close to the vehicle in front of you, and alert systems that can detect if you fall asleep at the wheel.

As more powerful computers can process more and more sophisticated software code, they are able to interact with humans in ways that are closer and closer to our natural behavior—such as the interpretation of visual cues and the use of vocal commands (e.g., Apple Siri, Google Now, or Microsoft Cortana)—and support us in unprecedented ways in an incredibly varied array of tasks. It is not a coincidence that senior citizens represent a sizable, and growing, portion of the online population. Note that these are individuals, age 65 and older, who often claim to be unable to program a thermostat, yet they are connected to the Internet; e-mailing, chatting, and videoconferencing with their grandkids; sharing pictures; and organizing trips and cruises. Why? Because modern computing devices offer the things they want (e.g., keeping in touch with family), are affordable, and shelter them from much of the complexity of the machine's inner workings.

Other IT Trends of Managerial Interest

Beyond the lasting effects of Moore's law, there are other IT trends that are critical for general and functional managers to recognize.

Declining Storage Costs

The cost of computer storage has plummeted at ever-increasing speeds. It took 35 years from the shipping of the first hard disk by IBM to the introduction of the 1 gigabyte (GB) hard disk. It took 14 years from there to reach 500 GB and only two more (in 2007) for the 1 terabyte (TB) hard disk to be introduced by Hitachi. By some estimates, 1 GB of storage cost more than $600 in 1993, about $5 in 2003, $0.39 in 2007, and reached a cost of $0.03 cents in 2015 (Figure 1.6).

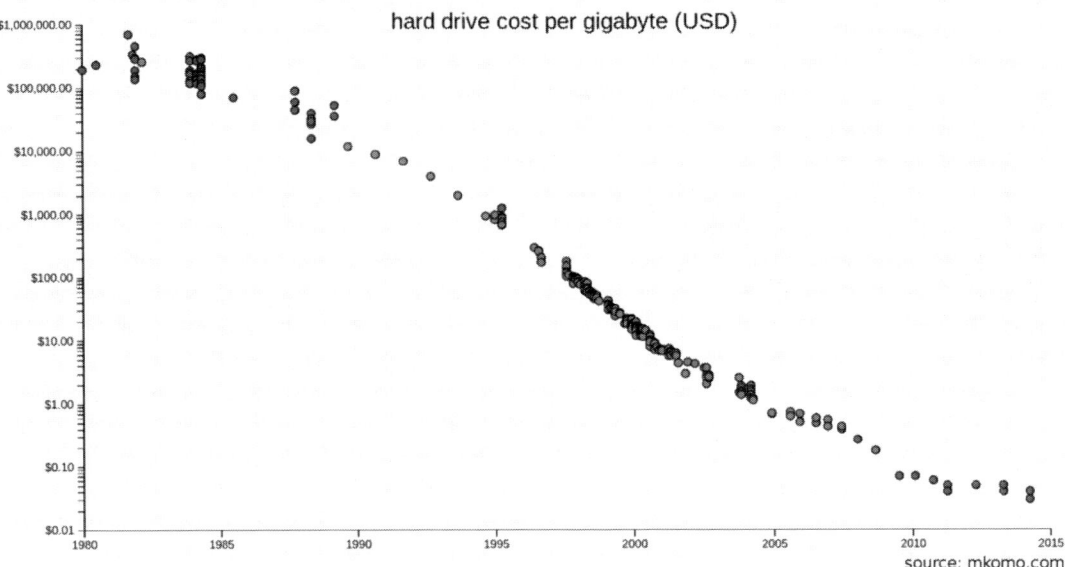

FIGURE 1.6. The decreasing cost per GB
Source: mkomo.com (2014, March 9), *A history of storage cost: Update*, retrieved from http://www.mkomo
.com/cost-per-gigabyte-update

While the exact numbers are of secondary relevance, as a manager you should realize that this trend has enabled the emergence of a whole host of strategic initiatives predicated on the collection and analysis of significant amounts of data. Consider the example of Kayak.com, the travel search engine that has the ability to make suggestions about *future* airline prices. While many sites can tell you what the lowest fare is today for a Paris to New York flight, only Kayak.com can tell you whether you should purchase today or wait for fares to decrease. How do they do it? They use a proprietary forecasting model based on the analysis of years of multiple daily searches for airline tickets and hotel reservations to identify patterns of fare and hotel room rate changes. Cheap storage is a critical enabler for the Kayak.com's service.

Ubiquitous Network Access

Ubiquitous networks are now a reality. In the early 1990s, the Internet, and its most visible services, such as the World Wide Web and electronic mail, took the world by storm. "The Internet changes everything" was the rallying cry that spurred the emergence of new business models and sent billions of dollars through the hands of venture capitalists and into those of high-tech entrepreneurs all over the world.

The *dot-com era*, as it is sometimes called, has now come and gone. What remains is the Internet: a global network of networks relying on distributed ownership and openly available standards and communication protocols. Access to the Internet is increasingly pervasive, with wireless and cellular network access having eliminated the final obstacle to "always on" connections. We are approaching a world in which we won't wonder whether we'll have access to a high-speed Internet connection when we travel; we will assume so—just like we do today with access to electricity in many parts of the world.

Network access is not only becoming ubiquitous, but the costs of data transmission are becoming negligible. The convergence of these trends is spurring an amazing array of initiatives. Consider the recent trends of enabling cell phones to receive notifications when your bus is approaching your stop (no more waiting in the cold!) or enabling apps to pay bus fares and vending machines through NFC[13]

---

13. *Near field communication* (NFC) refers to a set of technologies enabling close-range data exchange between two devices. Contactless payment systems are available for Android and iOS smartphones.

(no more being thirsty due to a lack of correct change!). Some start-ups, along with innovative established players, are positioning themselves to capitalize on ubiquitous network access.

Ubiquitous Computing and Digital Data Genesis

As IT costs and storage costs have plummeted, and as global data networks have become widely available, more and more devices are now intelligent (i.e., able to store and process data) and connected (i.e., able to communicate with other devices). The smart home is now a reality, with smart appliances like the refrigerator that can tell you what's inside, alert you when food is going bad, suggest recipes that use ingredients you have on hand, and even order food (Figure 1.7); smart heating systems that you can control over the Internet from your office; and bathtubs that will allow you to start running a bath before you get home. For the aging population, the availability of cost-effective sensors enables people to remain independent in their homes longer than ever before.

Modern automobiles often pack as much computing power as your personal computer, and through satellite networks and telemetry technology, some can self-diagnose and e-mail you alerts about preventive maintenance and potential trouble you may experience down the road. Moreover, the presence of intelligent devices enabling or monitoring events and human activity implies that data are generated by those activities in digital form. This digital data genesis dramatically reduces the barriers to data collection and analysis. While there are serious implications to be considered—for example, privacy—digital data genesis enables further innovation (see Chapter 12).

The trends discussed in this chapter, summarized in Figure 1.9, have had a few direct and indirect effects. First, computing devices are smaller and increasingly embedded in everyday products (Figure 1.8). As a consequence, digital content and services have increased dramatically and will continue to increase over time, along with the convergence of multiple devices. Chances are you already carry a smartphone that doubles as a planner, a digital still camera, a digital video camera, an e-mail client, a music player, a GPS, a compass, and who knows what else.

Second, the rapid proliferation of easy-to-use computing equipment has spurred more and more digitization—the method by which content and processes become expressed and performed in digital form. Digital data genesis is a clear example of digitization, as is this book if you are reading it on a book reader or listening to it in the form of a podcast. Finally, as computing devices become increasingly easier to use and more interconnected, they become pervasive. These trends have important implications for the manager of the future.

FIGURE 1.7. Smart appliances
Photo by LG Electronics / CC BY 2.0

FIGURE 1.8. A stark example of miniaturization

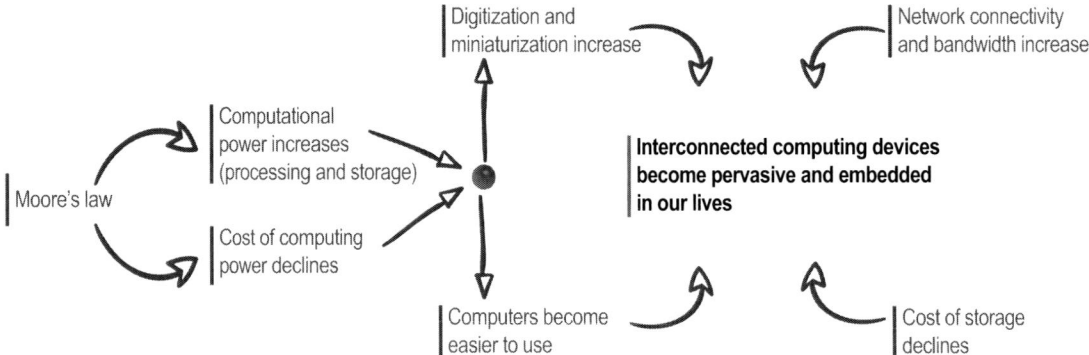

FIGURE 1.9. Interconnected trends

How Do These Trends Affect Today's Managers?

The discussion in the previous section depicted the world in which you, as a modern general and functional manager, will operate. You will increasingly be challenged to devise strategies and implement processes that enable your organization to take advantage of these trends and better serve your increasingly IT-savvy customers.

But perhaps the most important implication of the pervasiveness of computing for today's management is to be found in the sheer size of organizational investments in IT equipment, software, and services. The ever-increasing amount of money being spent on IT is largely due to one of the most interesting characteristics of software. Software is extremely malleable and can be molded into almost anything. Through the infinite combinations in which software code can be written by talented engineers and programmers, digital devices can morph into an infinite number of applications, many still left to invent! Vinton Cerf, coinventor of the TCP/IP protocol, said in a 2007 interview, "Specifically for young people pursuing careers, software is an endless frontier. There isn't any limit to what you can do. I can confidently argue that maybe only 1% or 2% of the possible applications have already been implemented or thought of."[14] And, considering the proliferation of smart devices (see Chapter 12), you may consider that number conservative: "I think we are going to be surrounded by smart devices. There's something really magic, to be able to assume, that any device you have that has some programmability in it could be part of a communications network, and could communicate with any other random, programmable device. When you assume that's the norm, you have almost no limit to the kinds of ideas you can come up with," Cerf recently commented.[15]

As a consequence, the number of opportunities for innovation and business success that depend on the appropriate use of IT is literally skyrocketing. If you think for a moment about the different types of software you come in contact with daily, you'll see that they support a huge variety of tasks.

For example, we use e-mail, instant messaging, and Voice over IP (VOIP) applications such as Skype to communicate with our friends, family, and colleagues. With these applications, IT acts as a communication device, replacing our traditional telephone or penned letters. Many of us listen to streaming radio and watch videos on our personal computers or mobile phones; we play video games and organize our pictures using websites such as Flickr or Picasa. With these applications, our IT behaves like an entertainment device, replacing our radio, stereo, television, and scrapbooks. We use word processing, spreadsheets, and presentation software to carry out our work. With these applications, our IT takes on the role of a productivity tool for the office, replacing typewriters, calculators, and flipcharts. Finally, and most important for you as a manager, IT can embed intelligence and decision-making capabilities previously required of employees or organizational functions. For example, modern check-in kiosks used by airlines and hotels replace the work of front-line employees; forecasting software and automatic inventory reorder software used in retail embed some of the intelligence and the decision-making abilities of skilled inventory managers; and automated sprinkler systems in modern greenhouses monitor and analyze the state of the soil and decide when to turn on or off and even what and how much fertilizer to add to the water.

Beyond replacing earlier ways of doing business, new technology creates a constant stream of new possibilities. For example, it is now possible for you to virtually try the latest Ray-Ban styles by simply using their Virtual Mirror application. This augmented reality software (see Chapter 12) overlays the digital model of the latest sunglasses onto the video feed of your camera, allowing you to virtually try their extensive catalog.

Why Can't We Just Hire Good IT People?

One of the most enduring results of research in information systems has been the degree of discomfort that executives exhibit when it comes to making decisions about information systems and information technology. The great number of acronyms (increasing daily, it seems), the pervasiveness of technical language, and the unique blend of skills that are required to understand computing can be very intimidating. As a consequence, we often hear executives wonder why it isn't enough to hire "good" IT professionals and let them worry about all the IT stuff.

This stance immediately raises the question "How do you know if an IT professional is indeed good without knowing a minimum amount about what IT professionals do?" More important, "How can you establish a good partnership with your firm's IT group if you are not equipped to prove useful in the relationship?" Just as most general and functional managers are not trained in the design and implementation of IT the way computer scientists and engineers are, most computer scientists and engineers are not trained in marketing, management, finance, or accounting.

This diverse training leads to a great deal of communication difficulty. Because the skills and knowledge of general and functional managers are complementary to those of the information systems

---

14. King, J. (2007, July 30), The grill: Google's Internet evangelist Vint Cerf on the hot seat, *Computerworld*, retrieved from http://www.computerworld.com/article/2552965/networking/the-grill--google-s-internet-evangelist-vint-cerf-on-the-hot-seat.html

15. Park, B. (2014), Wisdom from the father of the Internet—Vint Cerf, *Startup Grind*, retrieved from https://www.startupgrind.com/blog/wisdom-from-the-father-of-the-internet-vint-cerf/

professionals in the organization, communication and a good relationship are critical to the firm's success.

As a simple example, imagine being the vice president of marketing for a retail chain (e.g., Ikea) that wants to be able to measure customer spending patterns precisely and rank shoppers based on the customer lifetime value[16] they contribute to the firm. Business intelligence technology and techniques (discussed in Chapter 3) will enable this strategy. However, how can your IT group build the appropriate infrastructure, track all the relevant data, perform accurate analyses, and best segment the customer base unless you and your marketing team are intimately involved in the design and development of this technology and analytical infrastructure? The IT professionals in your organizations are not as familiar as you are with the retail operations, and they are certainly not well versed in marketing segmentation and customer valuation techniques.

The only recipe for success in this case is to have a productive partnership. You contribute the marketing-specific knowledge and make decisions about the critical requirements and capabilities of the initiative and the information systems. The information systems and technology professionals make decisions about platforms, interfaces, programming languages, and hardware performance. Together, you ensure that organizational processes are accurately redesigned and that data models used are coherent with business operations and comprehensive.

While you clearly should not delegate information systems decisions to technologists, there is good news. You need not know an inordinate amount of IT-specific information to be a good user of the information systems and technology resources or a good partner of the IT function. The sheer size of the information technology expenditure, however, commands the attention of today's managers. This ever-increasing budget means that as you join the workforce, you will find yourself making decisions that have an increasingly large IT component. Moreover, as IT becomes an increasingly important business tool, you will find that a larger and larger stake of your function's (and your personal) success rides on making good decisions when it comes to investing in and using, or not investing in and not using, information systems and IT.

Summary

This chapter laid the groundwork for this book by identifying the managerial and technology trends that make it imperative for the modern general and functional manager to get involved in decision making pertaining to information systems and information technology (IT). In this chapter, we learned the following:

- General and functional managers, those individuals in organizations who have the responsibility to lead a functional area or a business, can no longer abdicate their right, and duty, to be involved in information systems and IT decisions. They should act in partnership with the firm's information systems and technology professionals.
- The information systems skill set required of the modern general and functional manager pertains to decisions about identifying opportunities to use IT to the firm's advantage; planning for the use of information systems resources; and managing the design, development, selection, and implementation of information systems. While end-user skills (i.e., the ability to use computers proficiently) are an important asset for any knowledge worker, the critical skills for modern managers relate to the organizational, not personal, uses of information technology.
- Chief information officers (CIOs), the leading figures in the information systems and technology function, are increasingly being selected from the functional and managerial ranks rather than from the technology ranks.

---

16. Customer lifetime value is a metric used to estimate the value of a customer over the complete history of his or her interaction with the firm.

- The enduring effects of Moore's law have led to increasingly powerful yet cheaper computing strength, declining costs of computer memory, and a dramatic improvement in the ease and breadth of use of digital devices. Moreover, increasingly available network connectivity and storage capacity, improved battery life for portable devices, and the proliferation of intelligent devices have contributed to dramatically change the business and social landscape.

Study Questions

1. Define the following terms: *general manager*, *functional manager*, *CIO*, and *end user*. Explain how these roles differ and the skill set each role requires.
2. Explain why it is critical to the success of modern firms that general and functional managers be directly involved in information systems and technology decision making.
3. Explain why modern firms are increasingly selecting CIOs from the managerial ranks rather than from the technology ranks.
4. Describe Moore's law and its direct and indirect effects on organizations.

Further Readings

1. HBR Analytic Service. (2014). *Driving digital transformation: New skills for leaders, new role for the CIO*. Boston, MA: Harvard Business School Press.
2. Hilbert, M., & Lopez P. (2011, April 1). The world's technological capacity to store, communicate, and compute information. *Science*, 60–65.
3. Huff, S. L., Maher, P. M., & Munro, M. C. (2006). Information technology and the board of directors: Is there an IT attention deficit? *MIS Quarterly Executive*, 5(2), 1–14.
4. Hunter, R., and Westerman, G. (2009). *Real business of IT: How CIOs create and communicate value*. Boston, MA: Harvard Business School Press.
5. Leavitt, H. J., and Whisler, T. L. (1958, November–December). Management in the 1980s. *Harvard Business Review*, 41–48.
6. Nolan, R., & McFarlan, F. W. (2005, October). Information technology and the board of directors. *Harvard Business Review*, 83(10), 96–106.
7. Ross, J. W., & Weill, P. (2002, November). Six IT decisions your IT people shouldn't make. *Harvard Business Review*, 84–92.

Glossary

- **Chief information officer (CIO):** The individual in charge of the information systems function.
- **Digitization:** The process by which content and processes become expressed and performed in digital form.
- **End users:** Those individuals who have direct contact with software applications as they use them to carry out specific tasks.
- **Information system:** Formal, sociotechnical, organizational system designed to collect, process, store, and distribute information.

- **Information technology (IT):** Hardware, software, and telecommunication equipment.
- **IT professionals:** Those employees of the firm who have significant technical training and are primarily responsible for managing the firm's technology assets.
- **Manager:** A knowledge worker of modern business and not-for-profit organizations who is in charge of a team, a functional area (i.e., a functional manager), an entire organization, or a business unit (i.e., a general manager).
- **Polymediation:** The process of convergence of multiple digital devices into one.

CHAPTER 2

Information Systems Defined

What You Will Learn in This Chapter

This is one of the most important chapters of this book because it defines the key concepts that we will use throughout. Specifically, this chapter will

1. Define the terms *information system (IS)* and *information technology (IT)* and articulate the difference between the two concepts.
2. Define the terms *information system success* and *information system failure*.
3. Discuss the principal reasons modern firms create and deploy information systems.
4. Discuss the influence of the firm's context and the external environment in which it is embedded on organizational information systems.
5. Identify the four components that make up an information system and the manner in which they interact.
6. Explain how to design successful information systems and how to troubleshoot problematic information systems implementations.

MINICASE: iPad Menus at McDonald's

As you get settled in your office for another day of work at WizConsult, the consulting firm you have recently joined, you sip your morning coffee and start your computer. Surprisingly for this early hour, your boss walks in and asks you to follow him immediately. You take one last sip of your coffee and go. Your boss is on the phone with a large McDonald's franchisee who operates 42 restaurants in the upstate New York area. They quickly bring you up to speed: McDonald's has been quietly evaluating whether to join the iPad bandwagon. The corporate office is investigating the option of rolling out iPad-based menus that would allow patrons to walk in and immediately sit at a table and then order using the device available at the table. They could place orders, customize them to their tastes, and then submit it. When their numbers are called, guests could then pay for and pick up their orders as they normally would.

Such iPad menus are becoming popular in restaurants around the world, such as Mundo Global Tapas in Australia or Stacked in Torrance, California, and the approach that McDonald's is considering is very similar to the one introduced by Delta Airlines in its terminals at JFK and Minneapolis airports. Coincidentally, you were at JFK last week (Figure 2.1)! At these restaurants, patrons sit down and use one of hundreds devices to order directly from a graphically pleasing and interactive menu. As they wait for their food to be delivered, they can play games, check flight information, read the news, and surf the web. As Rick Blatstein, the chief executive officer (CEO) of OTG, the management company behind the concept, put it, "We are giving travelers a one-of-a-kind experience. [. . .] By combining cuisine with innovative seating and ordering technology, we are offering a truly unique airport travel experience."[1]

---

1. Robbins, K. (2010), At JFK airport eateries, iPad will be your server, *Delish*, retrieved June 6, 2011, from http://www.delish.com/food/recalls-reviews/at-jfk-airport-eateries-ipad-will-be-your-server/

FIGURE 2.1. iPads available for ordering and surfing in concourse G at the Minneapolis airport
Photo by Andrea Pokrzywinski / CC BY 2.0

Your client explains that McDonald's doesn't expect to earn money initially from this service. He quotes a conversation he had with Ron Jonson, president of McDonald's Northeast Division: "What we're banking on is that more customers will visit McDonald's. Moreover, your customers may stay longer as they can surf the Internet and read the news right on the iPad, and therefore increase their consumption." The program seems to be gaining strong support at corporate, but your client, the franchisee, has heard mixed feedback on the idea from his fellow franchisees attending a recent conference. He does not want to miss out on making extra revenue, as every bit helps. However, he does not want to waste money on the latest high-tech gizmo just for the sake of staying on trend.

As a knowledgeable and enthusiastic early adopter of technology, you are now on the hot seat as your boss and the franchisee turn to you for a recommendation.

Discussion Questions

1. Drawing on your own experience at JFK airport last week, do you think that iPad menus will work well at McDonald's restaurants? Justify your answer.
2. Given your answer to Question 1, can you see exceptions or do you believe your answer applies to all restaurants? What about McDonald's restaurants in other countries?
3. What do you suggest WizConsult's client should do tomorrow?

Introduction

Despite the well-documented challenges associated with achieving a satisfactory return on information technology (IT) investments, modern organizations around the world continue to spend significant amounts of money on IT, lured by its promise to yield efficiencies and improved competitive positioning. With IT spending on the rise, there is little doubt that being able to wring value from these investments is critical for the modern organization. However, a narrow focus on IT investments alone is problematic. Instead, you should focus on information systems (IS) and their design. To do so, we must first cover some important background information and introduce some key definitions.

Information Systems: Definition

In order to refocus our attention from the IT investment perspective to a more comprehensive IS design perspective, we need to first define the concept of the information system and separate it from IT.

IS, Not IT

Without a doubt, information technology engenders a plentitude of confusing lingo, technical terms, and acronyms—a problem compounded by the many half-prepared, fast-talking individuals using terminology incorrectly.

Recent buzzwords, such as big data, data science, and analytics, present no exception. And we can already see this phenomenon affecting emerging trends such as wearables, augmented reality, and the Internet of things (IoT). Two quick examples will drive this point home:

- *Drones everywhere*. Strictly speaking, in computing and mechanical engineering, a *drone* is an unmanned aerial vehicle (UAV). Its defining characteristic is the use of artificial intelligence (AI) to enable autopilot features. A drone without the ability to autopilot is not a drone (Figure 2.2); it is a radio-controlled aircraft. However, with the explosion of interest in quadcopters for recreational and commercial uses, the drone label is quickly losing its original meaning.
- *Holograms in the box*. Strictly speaking, a *hologram* is a three-dimensional rendering of an image that humans can perceive with the naked eye without the use of special glasses or any other apparatus. With the increasing interest in augmented reality, more and more vendors are referring to superimposed objects viewable by users through their devices as holograms. Most recently, Microsoft even launched a product, HoloLens (Figure 2.3), that bakes this misguided use of terminology right into the product name.

Of all the potentially confusing terms, none is more insidious than the term *information system*, usually abbreviated IS. In this context, information system is often used as a rough synonym for information technology. But there is a critical difference between IT and IS!

Consider a simple example. The famous Ricasoli Winery is the oldest family-owned winery in Italy, producing wine in the heart of the Chianti region since obtaining ownership of the Brolio Castle (Figure 2.4) in the year 1141. It is to one of the members of the Ricasoli family, in fact—Baron Bettino Ricasoli—that we owe the formula of the "sublime wine," the Chianti. Bettino Ricasoli perfected the blend in 1872 after years of studies and experiments at a time when his estate was exporting wine all over Italy and beyond. Did the Ricasoli estate have an information system when the baron perfected the Chianti recipe?

The answer is yes, of course. The Ricasoli Winery's information system allowed the firm to take orders, track payments, organize activities around the farm, manage its inventory of aging wines, and help the baron collect information about the blends and treatments that enabled the wine to maintain its organoleptic characteristics when shipped far from the Brolio Castle. Using books and ledgers, the technology of the time, the estate was able to keep track of all data and information necessary to its proper operations and longevity.

Yet the first-known implementation of digital computing did not occur until World War II, and digital computers did not begin to enter business organizations until the postwar years. However, all kinds of organizations—from car manufacturers to laundry services, from banks to soft drink makers—had been conducting business for decades (in some cases, as the example of the Ricasoli estate shows, even centuries!). Clearly, while IT is a fundamental component of any *modern*

FIGURE 2.2. A US military drone
Photo by Marion Doss / CC BY SA 2.0

information system, we can see from these examples that IT and IS are separate concepts.

Information Systems as Sociotechnical Systems

Information systems are formal, sociotechnical, organizational systems designed to collect, process, store, and distribute information. Within this book, we primarily concern ourselves with formal organizational information systems—those that are sanctioned by a company, not-for-profit endeavor, or government entity. While as students you are likely very familiar with various *informal* information systems—for example, the valuable "grapevine" at your school that you tap into for networking contacts and to find out the scoop about a professor or a class—such informal systems are beyond the scope of this book. Snapchat, the app that lets you send "self-destructing snaps" to your friends, is another example of such an informal information system (Figure 2.5).

The key aspect of our definition is the notion of a sociotechnical system. Sociotechnical theory has a long tradition of research dating back to work done at the Tavistock Institute in London, England. Sociotechnical theory questioned overly optimistic predictions about the potential benefits of new technology and suggested that the impact of new technologies on work systems was not a direct one but depended on the interplay of technology with other aspects, or components, of the work system.

FIGURE 2.3. Microsoft HoloLens headset prototype
Photo by Microsoft Sweden / CC BY 2.0

FIGURE 2.4. The Ricasoli estate: The Castle of Brolio
Photo by Darold Massaro

The Four Components of an Information System

While sociotechnical theory is general in nature and applicable to any work system, it has been successfully applied to IT-based information systems. Specifically, we can represent any formal organizational IS as having four fundamental components that must work together to deliver the information processing functionalities that the firm requires to fulfill its information needs.

The four components of an IT-based information system are IT, people, processes, and structure (see Figure 2.6). They can be grouped into two subsystems: the technical subsystem and the social subsystem. The technical subsystem, comprising IT and processes, is that portion of the information system that does not include human elements. The social subsystem, comprising people and people in relation to one another (i.e., structure), represents the human element of the IS.

As a general and functional manager, you will be called on to make information systems decisions as they

FIGURE 2.5. Snapchat for your self-destructive snaps
Photo by Adam Przezdziek / CC BY SA 2.0

Social System   Technical System

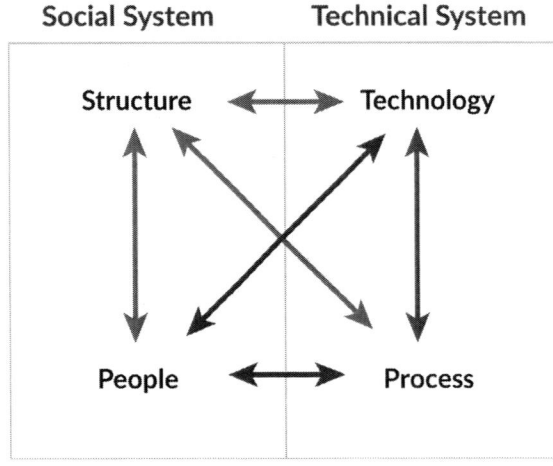

FIGURE 2.6. Information system components

impact your sphere of influence (e.g., your department or functional area). In order to make appropriate decisions in this realm, you will need to have a solid understanding of each of the four components and how they interact with one another.

Information Technology IT is defined here as hardware, software, and telecommunication equipment. The IT component is a cornerstone of any modern IS, enabling and constraining action through rules of operation that stem from its design. For example, if you choose to collect and analyze data using spreadsheet software such as Microsoft Excel rather than using a relational database management system such as Microsoft Access (Figure 2.7), you are limited by the design of the spreadsheet software. Microsoft Excel cannot create meaningful associations among separate data elements. The result is substantial duplication of data, leading to redundancy, inconsistencies, and inefficient data management. This is because the design of Microsoft Excel is focused on computations and formulaic calculations, not on efficient data management.

In addition, it is important to remember that software design, still as much an art as a science, is driven in large part by the choices and opinions of the developers and programmers who create it. InfoWorld columnist Bob Lewis put it well when he said, "Every piece of software is an opinion." Software, particularly custom-developed applications, represents the developers' viewpoint on how the data should be represented, organized, and manipulated.

To relate to Lewis's quote, you need only think about the last time, on the phone with a customer service representative, you heard the phrase "The system won't allow that." In such a circumstance, the software design team, knowingly or unknowingly, restricted the functionality of the software to enforce a given behavior. Note, however, that this ability to enforce rules through software is a double-edged sword. For example, some car rental companies do not allow a rental contract to print unless the customer provides two distinct phone numbers. The design of the software seeks to ensure that the customer can be easily contacted if needed and that valuable customer contact data can be tracked. However, those customers who do not have (or do not want to provide) more than one number and rushed employees trying to move quickly through the queue of waiting customers find it easy to produce "phantom" phone numbers—thus defeating the very purpose of creating the restriction in the software.

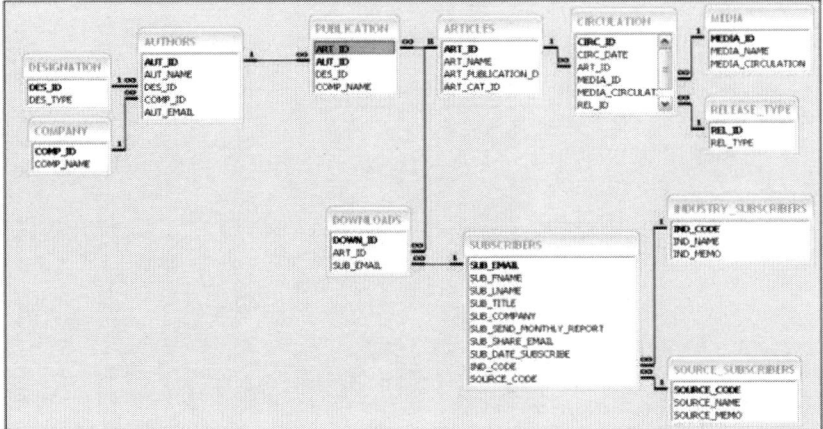

FIGURE 2.7. A relational database management system enables connections among data elements

Process The process component of an information system is defined here as the series of steps necessary to complete a business activity. Consider the job of a small, family-owned grocery store manager and the process he engages in when restocking inventory. The store manager must (1) check the inventory and identify the needed items; (2) call individual suppliers for quotes and delivery dates; (3) compare the various quotes; (4) select one or more suppliers for each of the needed items based on the terms of the agreement (e.g., availability, quality, delivery); (5) call these suppliers and place the orders; (6) receive the goods upon delivery, checking the accuracy and quality of the shipped items; and (7) pay the suppliers.

Note that the same activity may be performed using a variety of different business processes. Note as well that gaps can exist between the official business process that forms the basis of training programs and customer service protocols and the informal ways in which these processes are actually performed. This discrepancy is due to the fact that while many business processes are codified in procedure manuals and training materials, ultimately they are enacted by people. Consider again the case of the rental car company mentioned previously. While the stated business process calls for the collection of two separate customer phone numbers, you can imagine an employee—who sees a long line and is attending to a customer who is unable or unwilling to provide two numbers—typing in a fictitious number rather than wasting time arguing.

This potential discrepancy between the business processes as designed by the organization and the manner in which it is actually enacted is often the root cause of IS failure. When designing a new IS or when confronted with IS failure, it helps to think about what possible obstacles exist that may make it difficult for employees to accurately follow the business process.

People The people component refers to those individuals or groups directly involved in the information system. These individuals—whether they are end users, managers, or IT professionals—have their own set of skills, attitudes, preconceptions, and personal agendas that determine what they are able to do and what they will elect to do as part of the IS. A genuine understanding of the people involved, including their skills, interests, and motivations, is necessary when designing and implementing a new IS or when troubleshooting an existing IS that is not performing as expected.

Consider the example of a national government intent on rationalizing and improving communication between the local administrations (e.g., school districts) and the central institutions (e.g., ministry of education). As part of this initiative, e-mail addresses are produced for the school district superintendents and each school's principal and assistant principal. You quickly realize that this simple initiative is more likely to be successful today than it was 10 or 15 years ago, when computer skills were scarce and computer anxiety was high even among highly educated individuals.

Structure The organizational structure component (or "structure" for short) refers to the organizational design (hierarchy, decentralized, loose coupling); reporting (functional, divisional, matrix); and relationships (communication and reward mechanisms) within the information system. Understanding the structure component is crucial because user resistance, incentive systems, and relationships are often silent enemies of IS success that go undetected before, and sometimes even after, IS failure becomes apparent.

Consider the famous case of a large IT consulting firm. The firm, with global operations, recognized the potential for knowledge sharing among its consultants. "If we introduce a knowledge management system," the thinking went, "we can create repositories of knowledge to which our consultants will contribute upon completing a project. This will enable us to surface and share best practices, rather than having to reinvent the wheel with similar projects just because they are in different regions and involve a different team of consultants. Moreover, we will be able to identify subject matter experts to whom we will direct questions on specific topics. The outcome of this IS implementation will be increased turnaround time on projects, better quality results, and more satisfied clients."

A few months after the rollout of the system, it became clear that usage was spotty at best. Upon careful analysis, the firm realized that there was little incentive for consultants to contribute to the knowledge base. In the fast-paced world of IT consulting, the road to success was the "billable hour," which was gained by spending productive time working on client projects. Moreover, the organizational culture embodied in the existing reward mechanisms was such that individual behavior and superior skills were valued over teamwork and knowledge sharing. The inevitable conclusion was that in order for the knowledge management systems to reap the expected benefits, the tangible reward structure and the traditional mentality of the organization would need to change.

Systemic Effects

It should be clear from the preceding discussion that all four components are necessary to ensure that the information system is successful and delivers the functionality it was intended to provide. Imagine dropping any one of the four components in any of the preceding examples: the system would not work. More subtly, the four components of an information system don't work in isolation but instead interact with one another—as noted by the arrows in Figure 2.6. This notion of the interdependence of the components goes by the name *systemic effects*, indicating that changes in one component (e.g., the introduction of a new software application, a process redesign, a new organization chart, or turnover among employees) affect all other components of the system and, if not properly managed, its outputs. Mark Hedley, the former chief information officer (CIO) of Wyndham International, perfectly captured this notion: "Many companies rush out, buy software solutions, install them quickly, and then can't understand why the system failed. You have to look at what business issues exist, what people and processes pertain to that business issue, and what those people do. Technology won't solve [a problem] by itself—other components have to be part of the solution."[2]

Because of systemic effects, when called upon to design a new IS or to modify an existing one, you should focus not on optimizing the technology (i.e., adopting the most innovative and cutting edge IT) or any other component individually; rather, you should optimize the IS as a whole (i.e., selecting components that create the best chance to deliver the needed information processing functionality when working simultaneously with the other components). This focus on information systems design, rather than IT investment decisions, also suggests that there are multiple ways to achieve the same information systems goal—as demonstrated by the many different ways in which similar organizations meet their information processing needs.

Understanding the importance of systemic effects is critical not only when designing a new system but also when troubleshooting an existing one that is underperforming, in order to diagnose the root causes of the failure and to devise the appropriate intervention. Consider a large telecom firm that introduced advanced IS to improve service quality at the call center. Instead of having call center managers listen in on a small sample of calls to offer coaching to the associates in individual one-to-one meetings, the new system applies speech recognition to automatically analyze every call and produce a standard report that each associate is required to read with automated recommendations to implement. Call center managers must review all reports but only meet face to face with severely underperforming associates. The system is met with discontent and rejection by the call center managers, who complain about the fact that the system is not intuitive, is difficult to use, and limits their ability to make good decisions. How would you solve this problem if you were the head of the analytics project? There may be a number of options here:

- You could deem the new system a failure and cut your losses by reverting to the previous face-to-face approach.
- You could ascribe the failure to the quality of the user interface of the reporting application and then negotiate with the provider to improve the reports in order to make them more intuitive. This solution focuses on IT.
- You could ascribe the failure to the quality of the user interface of the reporting application but choose a different solution. You could work with both call center managers and associates

---

2. Piccoli, G. (2007), Career isn't over: How CIOs are reaching new heights, *Cutter Benchmark Review*, retrieved from https://www .cutter.com/journal/career-isnt-over-how-cios-are-reaching-new-heights-486016

to convince them that the system is not as awkward as it seems and that a bit of training will solve all their issues. This solution focuses on people.

- You could ascribe the failure to the fact that your staff comprises mostly old-fashioned managers who rose through the rank of the call center at a time when personal relationships, motivational cheers, and team spirit were the norm to improve service quality. They are not equipped to make the transition to data-driven decision making and evidence-based management. You could then turn over your staff, replacing all management with younger, tech-savvy, data-loving types. This solution also focuses on people.

- You could ascribe the failure to human inertia and your staff's resistance to change. You could then call a meeting and inform both management and associates that the speech-recognition system is going to stay and that the next person who complains is going to be fired. (You may offer incentives if you are more of the positive-reinforcement management type.) This solution focuses on structure.

Why Do Organizations Build Information Systems?

Now that we know what an information system actually is, we should step back and question why organizations build them in the first place. Simply put, a firm's objective when introducing IT-enabled information systems is to fulfill its information processing needs. Sometimes external requirements, such as financial reporting, safety, or tax regulations, mandate the introduction of a new IS. More typically, an organization introduces information systems in an effort to improve efficiency[3] and effectiveness.[4]

In order to fulfill its information processing needs, an organization must capture relevant data that are then manipulated, or processed, to produce an output that will be useful to the appropriate users, either internal or external to the firm (e.g., customers). These data and information are typically accumulated, or stored, for future retrieval and use (see Figure 2.8). Thus, while not a component of the information system per se, information itself plays a critical role in modern organizations.

Note that while the focus of this book is on IT-enabled information systems, the processing of information does not necessarily require IT support in order to happen. Consider the last time you contributed to the in-class discussion of a case study. In order to produce valuable comments for the class, you gathered substantial information (i.e., you read the case, you read assigned articles and other class materials, you actively listened to the professor setting the context for the discussion, and you listened attentively to your classmates' comments). You then processed the information (i.e., during preparation, you thought about the case issues in the context of the information presented in the readings, and during class discussion, you thought about how your classmates' comments supported or contradicted your point of view). Finally, you produced some output—your insightful analysis for the whole class to hear. In other words, you engaged in significant information processing without ever using a computer.

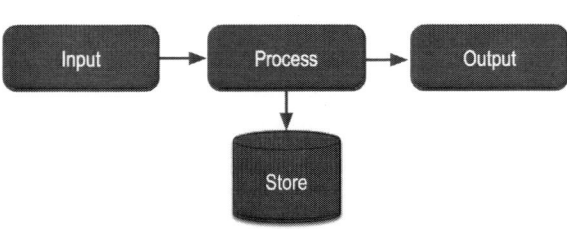

FIGURE 2.8. Information processing in an IS

IT is not to be downplayed, as all but the most trivial of today's organizational information processing requirements cannot be fulfilled in a reliable and cost-effective manner without IT. However, IT can only be successfully leveraged as an integral part of an information system, not in isolation. Moreover, while managers often focus on the financial results produced by the design and

---

3. *Efficiency* is defined as the ability to limit waste and maximize the ratio of the output produced to the inputs consumed. In other words, a firm is more efficient when it produces more with the same amount of resources, produces the same with fewer resources, or produces more with fewer resources.

4. *Effectiveness* is defined as the ability to achieve stated goals or objectives. Typically, a more effective firm is one that makes better decisions and is able to carry them out successfully.

introduction of a new IS, there are nonfinancial outcomes, both planned and unexpected, that you need to be aware of as well.

Successful Information Systems

Any information system should be built according to an explicit goal (or a set of goals) designed to fulfill the specific information processing needs of the implementing organization.[5] Examples of typical IS goals include the following:

- For a large retail store (e.g., Walmart, Carrefour)—To increase the efficiency and speed of customer checkout, perhaps using self-checkout stations.
- For a high-end car manufacturer (e.g., BMW)—To improve customer service by allowing individual customers to select finishings and accessories on their cars and quote real-time price changes and delivery date changes.

Consider the choice faced by McDonald's franchisees in 2003 who had to decide whether or not to offer Wi-Fi connectivity in their restaurants—taking a page out of Starbucks' approach. While a cursory examination may suggest that Wi-Fi simply does not fit with McDonald's strategic positioning, a more careful analysis would indicate that for some customers (e.g., busy parents, truck drivers) and in some locations (e.g., tourist areas), connectivity may be highly valued. This lack of clear fit led to McDonald's failing to develop a clear Wi-Fi strategy. After testing the program in 2003 with a $4.95 charge for two hours of use, the firm lowered the charge to $2.95 in 2004, allowing franchisees to decide whether they wanted to join the program. In 2009, Wi-Fi connectivity became a standard, available in every one of the more than 32,000 restaurants in the world free of charge.

One of the difficulties that McDonald's executives faced was in clarifying for franchisees what the primary objectives of the program were. While at first they suggested that the program would increase consumption, the benefits weren't very clear. At the very least, if customers felt that McDonald's plastic seats were too uncomfortable to sit on for more than 15 minutes and that the food was too messy to fumble with their laptops during or after the meal, the systems would be largely unused, hence delivering little benefit to the franchisee that paid for it. When the program became a brand standard, it became clear that the value of Wi-Fi at each McDonald's was in attracting more customers to the stores with the added benefit that they could quickly check their e-mail while on the road. Whichever the best objective is in this particular case, it is important to note that establishing a clear aim for the system is a critical prerequisite. Table 2.1 highlights some high-profile failures.

Information Systems Success: Definition We can unequivocally deem an information system a failure if it is abandoned (i.e., the design and implementation phase is never concluded) or not used (i.e., the information system is completed only to be rejected by its intended users). In either case, the system is a failure because, due to nonuse, it will yield none of the promised benefits (e.g., efficiency improvements).

Beyond nonuse, discriminating successful information systems from failed ones requires an evaluation of whether, and to what extent, the system has delivered the expected results. This is why it is so important to articulate information system goals during the design and justification phase. Yet for as thorough a job you may do in defining the intended IS goals, there are many situations when unintended results, both positive and negative, will emerge. The celebrated SABRE reservation systems pioneered by American Airlines, the best-known strategic information system, was originally introduced simply to enable inventory control in response to a very tangible operational problem: American Airlines found itself unable to manage and sell the increasing number of seats it supplied in response to mounting consumer demand for commercial air flights.

---

5. Note that while the IS goals should fit with the firm's strategic goals, the IS cannot ensure that the correct business objectives have been chosen. In other words, an IS is deemed successful when its information-processing goals are achieved—even in the face of business failure due to the pursuit of a flawed strategy.

Table 2.1. Some noteworthy systems failures in the recent history of business computing

Year	Company	Outcome
2013	French Ministry of Defense	Expected to enter service in 2017, Louvois—Logiciel unique à vocation interarmées de la solde—was supposed to simplify and unify the payment system for the French army's 130,000 members. The system was scrapped in November 2013 after consuming €346 million.
2013	NHS Connecting for Health (U.K.)	Originally expected to cost £2.3 billion over three years, in June 2006, the total cost was estimated to be £12.4 billion over 10 years. The system was abandoned in September 2013 despite already costing taxpayers £10 billion.
2012	Royal Bank of Scotland Group (U.K.)	A failed upgrade to the payment processing system left customers without access to their accounts for two weeks and disrupted customers' payments either incoming (i.e., wages) or outgoing (i.e., bills payments). The company was later fined £56 million over the accident.
2011	Allied Irish Banks (AIB)	AIB sued Oracle Financial Services Software for €84 million, plus damages and lost profits, claiming it wasted the money on a failed implementation of a new retail banking system.
2011	U.S. Federal Bureau of Investigation (FBI)	In 2001, the FBI started work on a criminal case management system called Virtual Case File. The project was scrapped four years (and $170 million) later. The project was restarted under the name Sentinel and, as of May 2011, was unfinished after five years in (and $400 million) in development.
2010 (2007)	AXA Rosenberg, a privately owned investment management company (U.S.)	A "coding error" led to underrepresented investing risk factors and resulted in investors losing a total of $217 million.
2010	Electronics retailer Dixons (U.K.)	Reiterated difficulties with its new eCommerce system were blamed for £15 million in lost revenue.
2009	Government of Victoria (Australia)	A smartcard ticketing system (called Myki), contracted in 2005 with AU$500 million budgeted, was rushed into operations (current cost: AU$1.3 billion) with limited functionality and still causes significant operational problems.
2009	Britain's National Health Service (NHS)	NHS scaled down its "Connecting for Health" program, designed to create the national electronics health record system, after investing an estimated £12 billion since the project began in 2002.
2008	Centrica, the largest utility supplier of gas to domestic U.K. customers	Centrica sued Accenture for £182 million in damages stemming from a collapse of customer service levels and loss of more than one million customers attributed to the failure of a "best-of-breed" customer billing system.
2008	J. Crew (U.S.)	Shares of the company fell more than 7% after the announcement of persistent website performance, order fulfillment, and call center performance problems leading to slowing sales trends, lower gross margins, and $3 million in unanticipated costs.
2007	LA Unified School District (LAUSD) (U.S.)	LAUSD discovered that, due to ongoing payroll system problems, it overpaid 36,000 employees by a total of $53 million.

Table 2.1. Some noteworthy systems failures in the recent history of business computing (continued)

Year	Company	Outcome
2007	Palm Beach County (U.S.)	Palm Beach County evaluated scrapping a $13.6 million upgrade to its computer systems that took three-and-a-half years to develop (six months originally budgeted) due to an inability to operate with it.
2006	Child Support Agency (CSA) (U.K.)	The CSA was shut down in part due to the problem-ridden deployment of a £456 million IT system built by EDS.
2005	Hudson Bay Co. (Canada)	Problems with inventory system contributed to a $33.3 million loss.
2005	U.K. Inland Revenue	Software errors contributed to a $3.45 billion tax-credit overpayment.
2004	Avis Europe PLC (U.K.)	An enterprise resource planning (ERP) system was canceled after $54.5 million was spent.
2004	Ford Motor Co. (U.S.)	A purchasing system was abandoned after deployment, costing approximately $400 million.
2004	J Sainsbury PLC (U.K.)	A supply chain management system was abandoned after deployment, costing $527 million.
2004	Hewlett-Packard Co. (U.S.)	Problems with an ERP system contributed to a $160 million loss.
2003–2004	AT&T Wireless (U.S.)	Customer relations management (CRM) upgrade problems led to a revenue loss of $100 million.
2002	McDonald's Corp. (U.S.)	The Innovate information purchasing system was canceled after $170 million was spent.
2002	Sydney Water Corp. (Australia)	A billing system was canceled after $33.2 million was spent.
2002	CIGNA Corp. (U.S.)	Problems with a CRM system contributed to a $445 million loss.
2001	Nike Inc. (U.S.)	Problems with a supply chain management system contributed to a $100 million loss.
2001	Kmart Corp. (U.S.)	A supply chain management system was canceled after $130 million was spent.
2000	Washington, D.C. (U.S.)	A city payroll system was abandoned after deployment, costing $25 million.
1999	United Way (U.S.)	An administrative processing system was canceled after $12 million was spent.
1999	State of Mississippi (U.S.)	A tax system was canceled after $11.2 million was spent; the state received $185 million in damages.
1999	Hershey Foods Corp. (U.S.)	Problems with an ERP system contributed to a $151 million loss.
1998	Snap-on Inc. (U.S.)	Problems with an order-entry system contributed to a revenue loss of $50 million.
1997	U.S. Internal Revenue Service	A tax modernization effort was canceled after $4 billion was spent.
1997	State of Washington (U.S.)	A Department of Motor Vehicle (DMV) system was canceled after $40 million was spent.

Year	Company	Outcome
1997	Oxford Health Plans Inc. (U.S.)	Billing and claims system problems contributed to quarterly losses; stock plummeted, leading to a $3.4 billion loss in corporate value.
1996	Arianespace (France)	Software specification and design errors caused a $350 million Ariane 5 rocket to explode.
1996	FoxMeyer Drug Co. (U.S.)	A $40 million ERP system was abandoned after deployment, forcing the company into bankruptcy.
1995	Toronto Stock Exchange (Canada)	An electronic trading system was canceled after $25.5 million was spent.
1994	U.S. Federal Aviation Administration	An Advanced Automation System was canceled after $2.6 billion was spent.
1994	State of California (U.S.)	A DMV system was canceled after $44 million was spent.
1994	Chemical Bank (U.S.)	A software error caused a total of $15 million to be deducted from 100,000 customer accounts.
1993	London Stock Exchange (U.K.)	The Taurus stock settlement system was canceled after $600 million was spent.
1993	Allstate Insurance Co. (U.S.)	An office automation system was abandoned after deployment, costing $130 million.
1993	London Ambulance Service (U.K.)	A dispatch system was canceled in 1990 at $11.25 million; a second attempt was abandoned after deployment, costing $15 million.
1993	Greyhound Lines Inc. (U.S.)	A bus reservation system crashed repeatedly upon introduction, contributing to a revenue loss of $61 million.
1992	Budget Rent-A-Car, Hilton Hotels, Marriott International, and American Airlines (U.S.)	A travel reservation system was canceled after $165 million was spent.

Source: Adapted from *IEEE, BusinessWeek, CEO Magazine, ComputerWorld, InfoWeek, Fortune*, the *New York Times*, and the *Wall Street Journal*

Information Systems Outcomes

Beyond efficiency and effectiveness improvements and the associated financial considerations, information systems have other direct and indirect effects on people within and outside the firm (e.g., employees, customers, suppliers). These effects can be positive, including empowering employees' and widening the scope of their responsibility, or negative, resulting in deskilling (i.e., reducing the scope of an individual's work to one, or a few, specialized tasks), loss of responsibility, and the creation of a monotonous working environment.

Another important outcome of information systems use pertains to their effect on future opportunities available to the firm. The introduction of a new information system may enable or constrain future information systems and strategic initiatives available to the organization. This is due to the fact that future systems typically rely on, or connect with, preexisting ones. Consider the example of social networking sites like Facebook. As the user base grows larger and each individual member has more connections within the social network, Facebook and third-party developers have the opportunity to develop applications that leverage these data. Social games like *Candy Crush Saga* or *Farmville*, and applications such as *Where Have I Been*, could not have been easily created without the underlying Facebook social graph.

Beyond an appreciation of their goals and outcomes, successfully designing and implementing information systems requires recognition that any information system that you envision or propose exists in a unique and very specific organizational context.

Information Systems in the Organizational Context[6]

Consider the cultural differences between Ritz-Carlton, the operator of 87 luxury hotels in 27 countries, and Duetto Research, the cloud-based big data revenue strategies provider with offices in San Francisco, Las Vegas, Singapore, and London. Both firms are in the lodging sector of the tourism industry, but they could not be more different. At the Ritz, the mantra is "Ladies and Gentlemen serving Ladies and Gentlemen." Bellhops still wear white gloves and the organization is very formal. At Duetto, the dress code is Adidas sweatshirts, and every employee has direct access to the cofounders. Imagine that management in each organization heard about the potential for virtual teaming and collaboration at a distance. At the hotel company, executives pushed to have general managers from each of the locations work together as a team to share best practices and help one another respond to emergencies, such as the massive blackouts that affected Brazil in 1999 and North America in 2004 or an approaching hurricane. At the startup, the objective is to enable programmers and the customer support team in the four locations to share their knowledge and help each other share customer success best practices. Both firms introduce a groupware solution supporting the following functionalities: a shared calendar, a contact manager, personal e-mail, a discussion forum and chat functions, resources and content management system, a file manager, a knowledge-base engine, and a shared whiteboard. Will the same system yield comparable results in each of these firms? Where will the "virtual teaming" vision most likely come to bear?

Every Organization Is Unique

The simple example just described should clarify that organizations are unique in many respects. This is true not only of companies in different industries but also of otherwise similar firms that compete head to head. Microsoft and Apple Computers were the two most recognizable names in the software industry throughout the 1990s, vying to establish their respective operating systems as the dominant platform. Yet the two firms had dramatically different images and cultures. Even starker is the difference between two of today's London-based airlines—British Airways and EasyJet.

At the highest level of abstraction, a firm is characterized by its strategy, its culture, and its current infrastructure, stemming from the organization's history, size, product line, location, values, and so on.

Firm Strategy A firm's *strategy* represents the manner in which the organization intends to achieve its objectives. In other words, understanding a firm's strategy tells us what the firm is trying to do and what course of action it has charted to get there.

Consider two other head-to-head competitors: Dell Computers and Hewlett-Packard (HP), who battled for supremacy of market share in the personal computer industry during the late 1990s. At the time, Dell and HP were the number-one and number-two makers of personal computers, respectively. While the market share rivalry between the two is still going on, the two manufacturers had drastically different strategies. On the one hand, Dell focused on highly customizable, made-to-order devices that were assembled upon receipt of orders directly from consumers and business clients. Conversely, HP historically focused on producing standardized devices to be sold through a wide distribution channel (e.g., Best Buy, Media World). Similar examples of direct competitors in the same industry with very different strategies abound.

Firm Culture A firm's *culture* is defined as the collection of beliefs, expectations, and values shared by the organization's members. The firm's culture, a broad representation of how the firm does business, is an important characteristic of the organization because it captures the often unspoken and informal way in which the organization operates. Practices that are deemed appropriate in one organization may not be in another one.

---

6. The following discussion is largely influenced by Silver, M. S., Markus, M. L., & Beath, C. M. (1995, September), The information technology interaction model: A foundation for the MBA core course, *MIS Quarterly, 19*(3), 361–390.

Consider the 2004 merger between software titans Oracle Corp. and PeopleSoft Inc. Announcing the merger, the *San Francisco Chronicle* posed the question, "What do you get when you combine a company run by an Armani-clad executive known for take-no-prisoners tactics with a firm led by a fatherly founder who hands out bagels and lets his workers wear flannel to work? . . . For the merger to succeed, Oracle faces the tough task of creating a cohesive company out of two firms with distinct, even contradictory, cultures." Quoting a Forrester Research analyst, the article concluded, "Pretty quickly, the PeopleSoft employees are going to divide themselves into those who say 'I think I can work for Oracle' and 'I don't ever want to work at Oracle.'"[7]

Infrastructure When it comes to making information systems decisions, it is also important to consider the current IT infrastructure of the firm. The existing IT *infrastructure*, defined as the set of shared IT resources and services of the firm, constrains and enables opportunities for future information systems implementations.

The example of checkout scanners at grocery stores highlights this point. Once the infrastructure is in place, the grocery store can consider future initiatives that rely on it, such as automatic inventory reordering, but also checkout coupons (i.e., the ability to print coupons at checkout based on the items the customer bought), frequency shopper cards, and basket analysis (i.e., the ability to identify correlations among items purchased by the same customer).

The External Environment Organizations themselves don't exist in a vacuum but instead are embedded in the external environment that encompasses regulation, the competitive landscape, and general business and social trends (e.g., outsourcing, customer self-service).

Consider three competitors, such as the Sony Corporation, Philips Electronics, and Samsung Group, headquartered in Tokyo, Amsterdam, and Seoul, respectively. While these three firms compete, at least in part, in the world market for consumer electronics, they have to contend with widely different local labor and taxation laws, governmental incentives, and so on. The external environment is fairly removed from day-to-day operations, yet these factors have an influence on the firm and, as a consequence, on the type of information systems the firm will need to introduce.

Bringing It All Together

The previous discussion of the outcomes associated with information systems use and information systems in context is summarized in Figure 2.9.

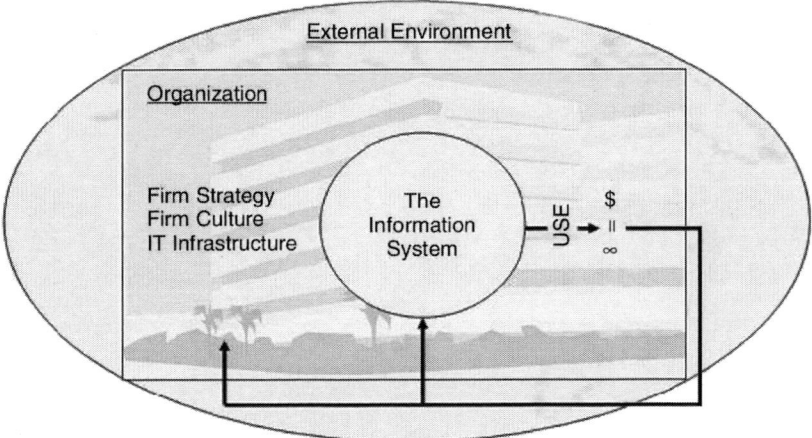

FIGURE 2.9. Information systems in an organizational context

The model in Figure 2.9 indicates that the immediate effect of information systems is whether or not they are used. If they are used, then intended and unintended outcomes ensue, including financial results, effects on people, and effects on the future opportunities and constraints available to the firm. The model also shows that information systems do not exist in a vacuum but are embedded in a specific organizational context, defined by the firm's strategy, culture, and IT infrastructure. Moreover, the organization itself does not exist in isolation but is embedded in the external environment, including social and competitive forces. The feedback loops represented by the solid, bold line remind us that the outcomes produced by the information system, whether positive or negative, will affect organizational characteristics and future information systems decision making.

This model is important for you as a general or functional manager because it draws to your attention all the external influences that will aid in or undermine information system success.

Information Systems and Organizational Change

An understating of organizational change and the issues associated with it completes the discussion of information systems design and successful implementation. As a general or functional manager, you must pay close attention to organizational change. With the widespread adoption of IT by modern organizations, increasingly this organizational change is brought on by the introduction of new IT. Defining information systems as sociotechnical systems can be instrumental in helping you better manage organizational change. Specifically, we can identify three levels of organizational change brought about by the introduction of new IT.

First-Order Change: Automate

The simplest order of change ensuing from the deployment of technology is automation. This level of change involves technology and processes but does not affect the sphere of the social subsystem (Figure 2.10). First-order change occurs when an IT innovation is introduced that modifies how an existing process is performed.

Consider those online banking tasks previously executed through a touch-tone phone interface—such as checking balances or transferring money between accounts. Many of us now perform those same tasks through a web interface or a smartphone. What has changed with the move to the web is the manner in which these processes are performed, not the tasks themselves or the individuals involved (e.g., customers). With the introduction of the web as a customer interface, the process has become simpler and more intuitive.

Managing first-order change The limited scope of first-order change makes it relatively easy to envision, justify, and manage. General and functional managers understand how the new technology impacts the firm's operations, and the project is straightforward to justify because the financial benefits of the change, in terms of the return on investment, can be estimated with some precision. Thus first-order change requires little executive sponsorship and involvement.

Second-Order Change: Informate

Second-order change has major implications for the "people" component of the information systems as well as IT and

FIGURE 2.10. First-order change

processes (Figure 2.11). With second-order change, not only the manner in which the process is performed changes, but also those individuals who perform it, are affected by the change—either their role is modified or a different set of people is now involved. Moreover, the manner in which people interact with the technology also undergoes modification. This level of change typically occurs when the information intensity of the process being performed changes substantially due to the introduction of new IT. For this reason, this level of change is called *informate*.

A good example of second-order change is IT-enabled customer self-service. Consider airline check-in kiosks. Traditionally, as an airline traveler, you'd have to go to the airport, line up, and interact with an agent, who would

FIGURE 2.11. Second-order change

authenticate you by checking your ID card and then provide you with a seat and boarding passes. The advent of check-in kiosks, and now online check-in, has dramatically changed this process. First, it is now the machine that authenticates you—using your reservation number, a credit card, or frequent flier card. Then you can proceed to select a seat and print the boarding passes (see Figure 2.12).

For anyone who is very tall and used to implore the agent for an exit row seat, the kiosk has opened up a wealth of new possibilities. More important, the kiosks have had a dramatic impact on the agents themselves, who now serve in more of a training and troubleshooting role, helping travelers solve any problems they encounter with the system rather than completing the check-in process on behalf of the travelers.

Managing Second-Order Change The primary impact of second-order change is on the "people" dimension of the sociotechnical system. As such, second-order change provides much more of a challenge to managers who seek to implement it than does first-order change. Those affected may include employees as well as customers. Thus providing appropriate training and overcoming the human tendency to resist change are key challenges.

The objectives of second-order change are typically far reaching as well. While first-order change is focused on automating existing tasks, informate-level change is often seeks to take advantage of available market opportunities. Thus justifying this level of change is more difficult and requires a more speculative analysis.

FIGURE 2.12. Choosing a seat during web check-in

Third-Order Change: Transform

Third-order change represents the most pervasive and radical level of change—as such, it is often referred to as *transform*. Third-order change subsumes first- and second-order change while also causing organizational structure disruptions (Figure 2.13). The interaction between structure and technology is substantiated by a change in the way the organization selects, uses, and manages technology. The interaction between the organizational structure and the people generally results in a change in the reporting and authority structure of the organization. A flatter or more permeable organizational structure usually emerges after the technology implementation. The interaction between the organizational structure and tasks manifests itself in a novel way of task accomplishment or a new set of tasks.

FIGURE 2.13. Third-order change

Consider a familiar example: Wikipedia. Wikipedia, the free online user-written encyclopedia, transformed the way we access and produce knowledge. Traditional encyclopedias have a strong top-down approach to content creation. Editors commission articles from individual experts who write an entry. Editors then review the entry and might share it with one or two other experts for peer review before finalizing and including it in the next release of the encyclopedia. We then buy the book and read the experts' entries. In contrast to this, thanks to the ability to easily connect any of the two billion people currently online across the globe and thanks to the capability of Wikis to allow easy, multiple editing of the same document, Wikipedia uses a very different knowledge codification and dissemination process. Anyone can contribute to an article, and the quality assurance is performed by the community of readers through a discussion page associated with each entry. As such, the people involved in content generation and the process by which knowledge is produced change dramatically. But the organizational structure of the online encyclopedia is also significantly different from its traditional printed counterparts. In fact, the very notion of an expert on a subject is lost and expertise is instead contributed by the population of readers at large.

Managing Third-Order Change   Third-order change requires significant managerial and executive involvement. Championship by the top management team is necessary both for signaling purposes and to provide the political impetus to complete the transition. Changes in organizational structure are, in fact, likely to engender political battles and resistance by those whose authority and political influence is diminished. The history of the business process reengineering (BPR) movement (see Chapter 3) provides countless examples of the perils associated with third-order change and the difficulties of managing dramatic IT-enabled change.

Culture and Information Systems[8]

Every society possesses an internal logic that enables it to run—if this was not so, that society would no longer exist. This logic is embedded in shared systems of meaning, or "culture." *Culture* is defined as the unwritten rules of the social game that are shared by the members of some group. This could be

---

8. This section has been kindly contributed by Gert Jan Hofstede. Further reading after this section could start at http://www.geerthofstede.com and be pursued in the book *Cultures and Organizations: Software of the Mind* (New York, NY: McGraw-Hill, 2010).

a firm, a family, or a society. Today, there are vast amounts of research confirming that countries tend to have distinct cultures. To be sure, there are also regional and ethnic differences within countries, and some countries have similar cultures—for instance, all the Anglo countries: the United Kingdom, the United States, Canada, Australia, and New Zealand. The unwritten rules of culture at the level of society are about basic issues of social life that need to be settled in order to divide scarce societal resources such as possessions but also social resources such as prerogatives, power, and belongingness. These unwritten rules are sometimes referred to as "deep values." People acquire them in early childhood, and after puberty they are very hard to change. Moreover, cultures have a strong continuity across generations.

National Culture

Culture is pervasive, and anyone working in a multinational environment should have a basic understanding of it, or he or she might make severe errors. A growing number of cross-nation studies have confirmed that dimensions of culture at the level of countries have bearing on the following issues:

- *Collectivism.* The degree to which members of the society feel interdependent, bound to their fixed role in society by rules of position, loyalty, and relatedness. The opposite of collectivism is individualism, meaning people consider themselves to be independent. Job-hopping, process perspective, working on contracts, and organizational change are much more typical in individualistic societies than in collectivistic ones. What is often called "the West" usually refers to individualistic societies: northwest Europe and Anglo countries worldwide.
- *Hierarchy.* The degree to which subordinate people accept their position as natural. The opposite of a hierarchical or "large-power-distance" culture is an egalitarian or "small power distance" one. Civic rights, empowerment, and shifting leadership are typical of small power distance countries, such as Anglo, Scandinavian, and Germanic ones. Asymmetric relationships, with paternalistic leadership versus obedience, are typical of large-power-distance societies, such as the BRIC countries (Brazil, Russia, India, China), whose economies are rising to prominence at the moment.
- *Aggression.* The corresponding dimension is called masculinity versus femininity. Masculinity is the degree to which society is seen as a fighting arena, and there tends to be a "winner takes all" mentality. Its opposite, femininity, corresponds with a consensus-oriented, forgiving society. Masculinity is also associated with very different emotional roles between the sexes. Typical feminine countries are the Scandinavian countries, with their taste for schooling and for having "welfare states." Masculine countries include Germanic and Anglo countries and China and India.
- *Otherness.* This dimension is about anxiety in the face of the unknown. It separates "uncertainty avoiding" societies from "uncertainty tolerant" ones. In the former, there is an emotional need for rules, even though these rules may not be followed. In the latter, rules are deemed unnecessary unless they are followed. Uncertainty-tolerant countries include China and the Anglo countries, while Latin and Slav countries are uncertainty avoiding.
- *Context: Short- versus long-term orientation.* This dimension is about the width of perspective that people take to their life events. People in long-term oriented cultures, of which the Southeast Asian countries are prime examples, consider themselves to be small entities in a large and ever-changing world. People in short-term oriented cultures, exemplified by African countries, consider themselves to be proud and living in the here and now, in which adherence to rules for good behavior, based on tradition, are important.
- *Happiness: Indulgence versus restraint.* This last dimension concerns the degree to which people feel in control of their lives and free to do as they like, as opposed to bound by duty, fate, or rules and powerless to take action. Indulgent parts of the world include Central America and, to a lesser degree, the Anglo world. Individual freedom is an important concept here. Restrained parts of the world include the Slavic countries and Southeast Asia. Duty and fate are important here.

Cross-cultural competence involves the ability to recognize one's own "deep values" and those of others and to account for the difference when interpreting others' behavior. This is usually a process that takes years of life experience that can be helped, but not replaced, by study. With globalization, and with the rise of non-Western economies, cross-cultural competence is becoming a fundamental skill for managers.

Organizational Culture and National Culture

Firms also have cultures. But the members of a firm do not need to agree on "deep values"; research has shown that firm cultures center on the shared understanding of practices. For instance, what does "empowerment" mean? What is an appropriate dress code? How bad is it to be late for a meeting? Firms like to speak about their values, but this tends to be window dressing or, in the best cases, limited to work-related practices.

Almost all business literature assumes an organizational culture that fits with an individualistic, egalitarian, uncertainty tolerant mind-set. But firms are populated by people who live the values of their own cultures. The cultural backgrounds of a firm's leaders, of its headquarters location, and of its main workforce are likely to have a strong influence on its culture. This, in turn, will strongly affect the workings of the organization's information systems. Here we focus on two culture-contingent decisions that are crucial to the operation of a firm: "Who decides what?" and "According to what process are decisions reached?" Information systems tend to include implicit or explicit assumptions about these questions that may not be in harmony with the organization's culture. For example, if the design of an information system assumes delegated authority or process perspective, but employees are acculturated to obedience and managers to nondelegation, then that system will likely fail miserably.

In practice, one dimension of culture tends to change much more readily than the others: individualism, which correlates with national wealth. It is not to be confounded with it, though. For instance, East Asian cultures tend to be much more collectivistic than Indo-European ones, even at equal prosperity. France is a case of a country with a culture that is individualistic but has a strong hierarchy.

As discussed before, firm culture contributes to the creation of the context in which the information system is embedded. As a consequence, there has to be a fit between organizational culture, which itself is a child of dominant national cultures in the firm, and the IS design. This requirement is particularly significant and particularly challenging to multinational or transnational organizations that wish to have one unified information systems architecture based on standardized technology (e.g., enterprise systems).

How Culture Impacts Structure

Business terminology changes its meaning when you travel. I once asked a number of European telecommunications managers to define *strategy*. A German said, "Bringing order into elements." A Brit smilingly countered, "Letting ideas bubble up into the organization," upon which a Dane said, "Yes, but realistic ideas." Two Spaniards had been silent and when prompted said, "A sense of direction." And similar variability holds for the social subsystem of any information system.

There is method in this madness, and the above-mentioned six dimensions can help show that method. When it comes to the implicit structure of the social system in a company, plotting two of them against one another has good predictive value. For example, plotting uncertainty avoidance and power distance (Figure 2.14) provides information about how organizations of that country, or business leaders socialized in a particular country, are likely to think about decision making and organizational structure.

In the upper left "market" quadrant, we find egalitarian, uncertainty-tolerant countries. Here, organizations resemble markets. Managers, or indeed anyone, can come up with generalistic ideas; others can "buy into" these ideas; ad hoc task forces can be created or consultants hired; and projects can be started. This quadrant fits with attaching importance to marketing, to change, and to strategic use of IT.

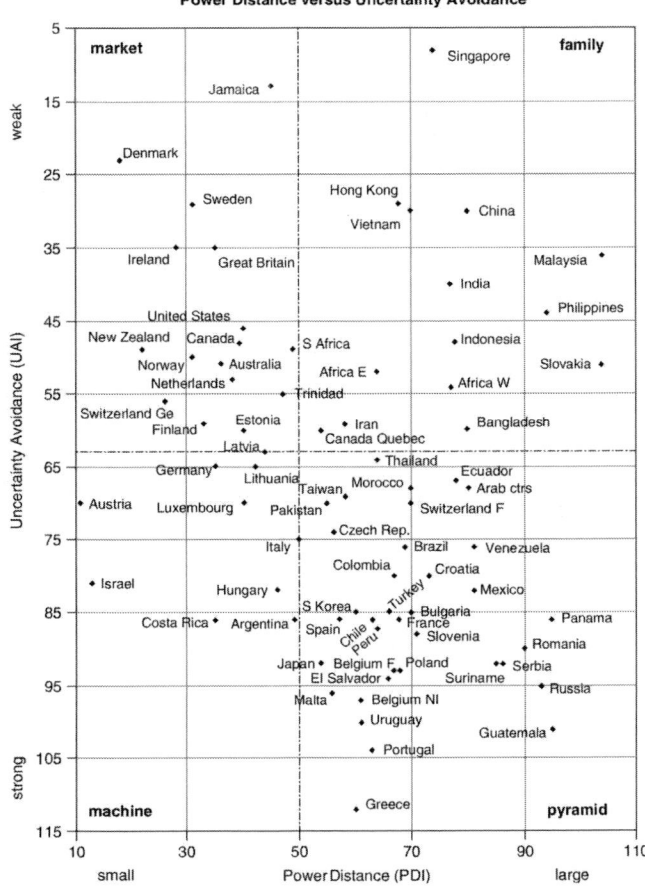

FIGURE 2.14. Plotting uncertainty avoidance and power distance
Source: Hofstede, G., Hofstede, G. J., & Minkov, M. (2010), *Cultures and organizations: Software of the mind*, revised and expanded ed., New York, NY: McGraw-Hill. Used with permission.

In the lower left "machine" quadrant are countries with organizations that are organized as well-oiled machines. The overall structure is more important than any part, detailed descriptions are preferred, and predictable behavior is important. These countries tend to be good at precision production. When it comes to IT, they favor enterprise requirements planning (Chapter 3) software and other applications that structure the internal organization of the firm.

In the right-hand side "family" and "pyramid" quadrants, we find countries where person-bound power prevails over structural power. Here, bosses can be expected to disregard any rules that might hold, if the fancy—or a good idea—strikes them. The top half is the family quadrant, where there are few rules except a great respect for authority. The bottom half is the pyramid quadrant, where there is respect for specialism and there tends to be a great deal of red tape.

The upshot of all this is that no multinational can escape culture, and no leader in a multinational organization can afford to be ignorant of it. Consider the fictitious case in the Sidebar 2.1 as an example of an all-too-common discrepancy in the interpretation of the same situation by managers from different cultures.

SIDEBAR 2.1. INFORMATION SYSTEMS AND THE NEED TO RECONCILE DIVERSE CULTURAL PERSPECTIVES[9]

Wei Liu was frustrated. It had seemed so nice: a joint venture of his Chengdu glass manufacturing company with a British partner, opening up new sales channels in high-quality markets. But in the 10 years that he'd been involved with the British, he had never been able to build up a good relationship with one of them. It was no use; if for once there was a decently behaved manager, that person would be gone the next year. The Brits were creative and good at investing in plants, but they had no sensitivity for the needs of Chinese personnel, who usually came from rural areas to feed their families and needed a fixed contract and a company-provided place to sleep. He regularly had to calm down personnel or local officials. The only sure thing about the Brits was that they had a fetishist reliance on their ERP systems—in particular, the quarterly reports. Two years ago, they had appointed a Brit to enter data into the ERP in Chengdu—this person was just a dead weight, costing money but not bringing in a yuan. Worse, the Brits made him harass his Chinese business partners, with whom he had excellent *Guanxi* (influence), for immediate payment before the end of the quarter. There was no way he could convince them that his good-Guanxi relationship was worth far more than today's cash flow. Was it time to say good-bye to the Brits?

Meanwhile, in London, Chris Westrup was being instructed by his predecessor, James Oldman, as CIO of the joint venture. James was obviously glad to be rid of the job. "Chris," he said, "I've done this for two years now and I tell you, you just cannot trust these Chinese. They do not care about data; they do not care about transparency. They'll enter any old figures into the ERP, and when you call them to task, they just sit there and nod politely but take no action whatsoever. That's why I appointed our own man in Chengdu, so that we have decent control of our operations. But the worst thing is, they do not care about cash flow; you've got to be at their heels all the time. It's oral promises all along, all of it in Chinese!" Chris grinned—with a master's in international business and in Chinese, he was game. "Yes, and good luck," said James. "I'll talk to you again in a year, when you have been driven crazy too. You know what it is? They just cannot work according to any plan. All they ever do is improvise, change, and deal. How they get so much done is still a mystery to me. I sometimes wonder if this whole joint venture is worth the trouble." Chris thought that it was time for James to retire and for someone like himself to take over and take the collaboration to a new level.

Implications

From the preceding definitions of information systems and IS success and the discussions of the roles of systemic effects and organizational context, a number of implications of interest to general and functional managers follow.

Don't Put the Cart before the Horse

We often receive inquiries from former students or other managers asking our opinion about one or the other IT solution (e.g., what is the best CRM software?). However, you may now recognize that asking such questions is equivalent to putting the proverbial cart before the horse by letting technology drive decision making.

While it is common for strategy to be inspired by the functionalities of a powerful software product, the selection of a specific IT product should not be the point of departure but rather the point of arrival of your information system design effort. When asked to express an opinion about a software program or other technology, you should always start by asking, Why are you investigating this software program (i.e., what is the firm strategy)? What are you attempting to do with the software (i.e., what is the IS goal)?

In our opening minicase, the firm's intention was to be able to improve its volumes (i.e., increase the number of customers and their level of consumption). This can be classified as the strategic goal.

---

9. This vignette is inspired by the following: Westrup, C., & Liu, W. (2008), Both global and local: ICTs and joint ventures in China, *Information Systems Journal, 18*, 427–443.

From this goal, the firm should derive a precise set of IS goals that specify what information processing functionalities are needed to achieve the strategic objective (e.g., to create a comfortable space for restaurant patrons to more conveniently place orders at the table and to access the news and other relevant information). Once the goals are set, the IS design team can identify, shape, and deploy the appropriate components of the system, of which IT is one.

The Rock in the Pond

As in any other system, the components of an IS mutually influence one another (systemic effects). Similar to the ripples resulting from the act of throwing a rock into a pond, changes to one or more IS components impact, sooner or later, all other components. This influence may be significant or limited. However, when you are called upon to participate in IS design and implementation, you should try to contribute to your team's successful introduction of a new IS by anticipating these ripple effects and proactively managing them before they become a cause for concern.

Let's return to the example of airline check-in kiosks. When kiosks are installed, the business process of identifying travelers and assigning them seats must change for those customers who prefer this method. The role, and the skills required, of check-in agents is modified as a result of the change in the business process—at a minimum, they must be able to explain the kiosks' operation and provide helpful support as customers learn to use them. In this case, the new technology significantly impacts both process and people, while the effect on structure is negligible. However, the more precise you can be a priori in estimating what the effects will be, the better able your firm will be to proactively manage the changes.

Information Systems Are in Flux

An information system is not designed "once and for all" as if it were a static artifact. Business strategy and the external environment evolve continuously. This evolution calls for a constant reevaluation of IS goals and needed information processing functionalities. In turn, this reevaluation will at times engender the need for changes to the design of an existing information system.

The design and use of an IS should be seen as an iterative process involving the cyclical evaluation of individual IS components and the assessment of how different organizational systems work together to support the business. The synergy among IS components, as well as among discrete organizational information systems, can be maintained over time only if there is a willingness to modify aspects of this IS configuration as needed. Any time a major change occurs, the current IS design must be reevaluated and the system must be optimized once again.

Optimize the Whole   As mentioned earlier, you should never lose focus of your objective: to optimize the information system rather than any of its constituent parts. Optimizing the system as a whole often requires that one or more components be de-optimized (i.e., they are not as powerful or cutting edge as they could be). This fundamental insight is one that is often forgotten when managers get caught up in the IT investment mentality—the most effective information system need not comprise all the best parts.

To the contrary, examples abound of firms that deployed cutting-edge technology where there was no need for it to deliver the desired information processing functionalities. In some cases, the adoption of cutting-edge technology in fact reduces the effectiveness of the IS as a whole, making the achievement of the needed information processing functionalities more difficult.

Conclusion

Like all frameworks, those presented in this chapter are valuable because of their ability to support a systematic and disciplined analysis of specific issues (e.g., software selection, IS design, system failure diagnosis). They don't offer cookie-cutter answers, but they provide the support necessary for a disciplined and thorough analysis. By using them to guide your thinking, you can be sure to complete a comprehensive analysis rather than being tempted to stop upon identifying the first or second most obvious explanations—perhaps those communicated by the most vocal members of your organization.

Furthermore, working with the models challenges conventional wisdom and management fads and fashions that may lead you to reach simplistic conclusions that, while true, often only reveal part of the story (e.g., "You must train your employees when new software is introduced"). The alternative—being driven by a best-practice mentality, benchmarking your organization against the performance of competitors—is a risky strategy, and you should always be wary of so many buzzwords in one sentence! As a manager, you must always consider how new IT fits within the context of your own company. Does it suit the unique people, processes, and structures of your firm? If not, is it a wise strategy to make changes to these components in order to fit with the IT? Or do you need different IT? All too often, when selecting a system, considering change initiatives, or troubleshooting underperforming information systems, the focus is on IT and system functionality. The frameworks presented here challenge you to think in terms of overall IS design instead—perhaps a more difficult task, but certainly a more appropriate and productive one.

Summary

This is a critical chapter in the book because it provides fundamental definitions and sets the stage for the discussion in the next chapters. The chapter defined information systems as sociotechnical systems composed of four components: information technology (IT), people, processes, and structure. This definition and its implications provide the basis for this book.

Specifically, in this chapter we learned the following:

- Information systems are designed and built with the objective of improving the firm's efficiency and effectiveness by fulfilling its information processing needs. Successful information systems are those that are used and that achieve their intended goals.
- Information systems exist in an organizational context, characterized by the firm's strategy, culture, and IT infrastructure. The organization itself is subject to the influences of its external environment, including regulatory requirements, social and business trends, and competitive pressures.
- Information systems are subject to *systemic effects*, defined as the notion that the different components of a system are interdependent and that changes in one component affect all other components of the system. Thus, when designing a new information system or troubleshooting an underperforming one, you can devise multiple ways to achieve the system's goal.
- Increasingly, in modern firms, organizational change stems from the introduction of new information technology. Depending on the objectives and reach of the new system, we identify three levels of change—first-, second-, and third-order change—each requiring different levels of commitment and sponsorship to be successfully managed.

Study Questions

1. Describe the difference between information systems and information technology. Provide an example of each.
2. Provide an example of two organizations in which you think a similar information system would engender two very different outcomes. Explain why.
3. Provide two examples, from your personal experience, of information systems that generate positive and negative unintended results.
4. Define the concept of systemic effects. Explain why it is important for you as a general or functional manager to be aware of this concept.
5. Describe first-, second-, and third-order organizational change induced by the adoption of new IT. Provide an example, real or imagined, for each of these three levels of change.

Further Readings

1. Glass, R. L. (1997). *Software runaways: Monumental software disasters*. Upper Saddle River, NJ: Prentice Hall.

2. HBR Analytic Service. (2012). *Innovation from efficiency: Unlocking the value in IT systems*. Boston, MA: Harvard Business School Press.

3. Hofstede, G., Hofstede, G. J., & Minkov, M. (2010). *Cultures and organizations: Software of the mind*. Revised and expanded ed. New York, NY: McGraw-Hill.

4. O'Hara, M. T., Watson, R. T., & Kavan, C. B. (1999). Managing the three levels of change. *Information Systems Management Journal*, 16(3), 63–70.

5. Zuboff, S. (1988). *In the age of the smart machine: The future of work and power*. New York, NY: Basic.

Glossary

- **Effectiveness:** The ability to achieve stated goals or objectives. Typically, a more effective firm is one that makes better decisions and is able to carry them out successfully.

- **Efficiency:** The ability to limit waste and maximize the ratio of the output produced to the inputs consumed. In other words, a firm is more efficient when it produces more with the same amount of resources, produces the same with fewer resources, or produces more with fewer resources.

- **External environment:** The world outside the firm that creates influences, such as regulation, the competitive landscape, and general business and social trends (e.g., outsourcing, customer self-service).

- **Firm culture:** The collection of beliefs, expectations, and values shared by the members of an organization.

- **Firm strategy:** The manner in which the organization intends to achieve its objectives.

- **Information system:** A formal, sociotechnical, organizational system designed to collect, process, store, and distribute information.

- **Information technology (IT):** Hardware, software, and telecommunication equipment.

- **IT infrastructure:** The set of shared IT resources and services of the firm, forming a firm's technological backbone, that constrains and enables opportunities for future information systems implementations.

- **Organizational structure:** The organizational design, reporting, and relationships within the information system.

- **Process:** The series of steps necessary to complete an organizational activity.

- **Systemic effects:** The notion that the different components of a system are interdependent and that change in one component affects all other components of the system.

Organizational Information Systems and Their Impact

What You Will Learn in This Chapter

This chapter completes our introduction to the foundations of information systems (IS). In Chapter 1, we made the case for this book's value to general and functional managers. In Chapter 2, we provided important definitions. In this chapter, we discuss the vocabulary and concepts that will enable us to categorize different types of information systems and to communicate with other managers and IS professionals.

Specifically, this chapter will

1. Categorize systems according to the hierarchical, functional, and process perspectives. You will learn the rationale for each perspective and its limitations.
2. Discuss the underlying principles and applications of business process reengineering (BPR), as well as its advantages and disadvantages.
3. Evaluate the integration trend and the role of integration principles in the modern firm. We will explore the pressures toward integration and the challenges integration creates. We will also discuss business and systems integration trends and the relationship between the two.
4. Explain the genesis of the enterprise systems (ESs) trend and why so many companies are employing or introducing them. You will also learn to articulate the principal benefits and risks associated with these systems.
5. Explain what is meant by supply chain management and the role that supply chain management applications play in modern organizations.
6. Clarify what is meant by knowledge management, categorize the different types of knowledge commonly found in organizations, and explain why organizations feel the need to employ knowledge management applications.
7. Evaluate the business intelligence (BI) trend and explain the components of the BI infrastructure. You will learn how to identify and describe the role of the technologies that compose a modern BI infrastructure.
8. Evaluate the big data trend and gain insight on consolidated technologies and practices.
9. Define customer relationship management (CRM) and articulate both its benefits and its limitations. You will also learn how the CRM and BI trends relate to one another.
10. Explain what is meant by cloud and the role cloud computing plays in shaping modern IS.

MINICASE: Integration at BigPharma Inc.

As you walk out of the boardroom, still shaking your head in disbelief, you mumble to yourself, "Boy, that was fun! They were really going at it today!" As you get to your desk, though, it hits you—you have to make sense of what just happened in there.

As the executive assistant to the CEO at BigPharma Inc., the second largest pharmaceutical firm in the United States, you have had the luxury of attending all the executive team meetings and sometimes participating in decision making with your analyses without any of the responsibilities that come with making those decisions. However, far from what you had imagined the glamour of boardroom discussions to be, most meetings of the executive team were pretty boring. Not today!

Surprisingly, you had predicted this one to be a real snoozer. A pretty safe bet given the topic: the need to gain efficiencies by better integrating across functional areas. The meeting took a turn toward the exciting right out of the gates when Laura Jean Polly, your boss, announced that at PharmaMed (the premier industry trade event of the year), she had drinks with the senior VP of business development of BigCoSoft, the second largest vendor of enterprise systems.

She said that BigCoSoft was interested in breaking into the pharmaceutical market and was seeking to sign up a high-profile customer. They looked at this contract as a mutually beneficial partnership that would lead to lots of press and advantages for both firms. The client would be a "showcase customer," featured on the website and in case studies. BigCoSoft was willing to waive licensing fees for the first three years. "But the biggest advantage," the senior VP had said, "is that with you on board, we will attract more customers. With critical mass, we can put huge development resources into this product."

At this point you were thinking, "Yep, snoozer! I was right." Two seconds later, the first salvo was fired. Jane Pinket, the senior VP of finance, said, "Everyone

knows that BigCoSoft's strength is manufacturing. Their financial package stinks. They will surely want to reuse that code, and I am going to have to take the hit. We can cut the same deal with LargeCoSoft. They already have an enterprise system for pharmaceutical firms, and their financial module is top notch."

"Another option could be to write a bolt-on," chimed in Erik Dino, the chief operations officer (COO). "That should take care of the missing finance functionalities." "But the human resource module of BigCoSoft also leaves much to be desired," interjected Joe Cole, the senior VP of human resources. "Plus, we just spent $12 million on the overhaul of the benefits management system; am I going to get hit with more information systems service charges for an upgrade I don't need?"

This is about the time confusion set in, and the story became fuzzy as you got lost in the ping-pong volleys of comments, questions, and responses. With a heated topic on the agenda, it was painfully clear that the people in the room were more used to being listened to than to listening.

You were snapped back to attention when Ms. Polly closed the meeting by calling your name. She said, "Well, it looks like I underestimated how much my staff cared about systems! I will need a report with an investigation of the top three most viable options; the need to integrate is not going away, so we have to do something. I told BigCoSoft I would get back to them in three weeks."

Discussion Questions

1. Even as the lowly executive assistant to the CEO, it was apparent to you that there was some group-think going on here. Was buying an enterprise system the only option?

2. You vaguely recall this idea of best-of-breed applications from your information systems class two years ago. Could that approach work here?

Introduction

In Chapter 2, we formally defined information systems (IS) as those sociotechnical organizational systems designed to collect, process, store, and distribute information. We identified the four components of an IS and introduced the notion of systemic effects to represent the mutually interdependent relationships among the four components. We also discussed how information systems fit within the organization in which they are embedded and within the larger external environment.

In this chapter, we rely on those definitions to explore the organizational impacts of information systems. This chapter is important for two main reasons. First, information systems pervade the modern organization, so understanding how they are classified and organized is a prerequisite to becoming a successful manager and being able to navigate the infrastructure of the modern firm. Second, because you are ultimately responsible for the success of your company or the organizational function that you oversee (e.g., finance, marketing), it is critical that you optimally manage organizational change when it occurs. Increasingly, the impetus behind organizational change comes from the introduction of new information technology (IT) and the implementation of information systems. Moreover, even when IT is not providing the impulse for change, organizational change calls for information systems adaptation. It is therefore paramount that you have the appropriate vocabulary to join the conversation and that you have a solid understanding of what classes of software programs underpin information systems in modern organizations.

Categorizing Systems

Since Leavitt and Whisler popularized the term *information technology* in the business literature in 1958,[1] researchers have advanced a number of approaches to classify and describe the role that IT plays in organizations. These efforts focus on categorizing the software applications as the point of departure for understanding the function and functionality of the information systems built around them.

Classification models are useful for two reasons. First, they provide you with a vocabulary to interact with your colleagues and with IS professionals—a vocabulary that today is taken for granted in modern organizations and in the business press. Second, the models described below provide the basis for you to develop your own thinking about the role that technology plays in your organization and on how to best manage its impacts.

Hierarchical Perspective

The hierarchical perspective recognizes that decision making and activities in organizations occur at different levels. At each level, the individuals involved have different responsibilities, make different types of decisions, and carry out different types of activities (see Table 3.1). As a consequence, the type of information systems introduced to support each level must take these differences into account.

Operational Level   The operational level of the organization is mostly concerned with short-term activities, typically those that occur in the immediate term. Operational personnel are focused on performing the day-to-day activities that deliver the firm's value proposition. For example, in a grocery store, operational personnel concentrate on keeping the shelves stocked, keeping the store clean,

Table 3.1. Activities by hierarchical level

Activity	Time horizon	Hierarchical level	Characteristics
Strategic	Long-term	General management Functional management	Externally focused Ad hoc Highly unstructured
Tactical	Mid-term	Middle management	Repeatable Semistructured Recurrent
Operational	Short-term	Front-line employees	Low discretion Highly structured Transaction focused

1. Leavitt, H. J., & Whisler, T. L. (1958, November–December), Management in the 1980s, *Harvard Business Review*, 41–48.

addressing customer questions and requests in a timely fashion, and ensuring speedy transaction processing at checkout.

Decision making at the operational level is typically highly structured by means of detailed procedures, and traditionally, front-line employees enjoy little discretion. The objective here is efficient transaction processing under a limited degree of uncertainty. When referring to IT-enabled data management (e.g., in a database structure), the term *transaction* identifies a single logical operation on the data. To ensure reliable transaction processing by the software, the system must respect the atomicity, consistency, isolation, and durability (ACID) properties of every transaction (Table 3.2). Classic examples of a transaction are the withdrawal of funds at an automated teller machine (ATM) or the change of a passenger's seating assignment by an airline employee.

We refer to the information systems that support this organizational level as *transaction processing systems* (TPSs). The information technology underpinning a TPS is typically used to automate recurring activities and to structure day-to-day operations, ensuring that they are performed with speed and accuracy and as prescribed by the procedures. The scanner checkout system in the aforementioned grocery store represents a classic example of a TPS. Another example is represented by the inventory management system in any retail store.

Transaction processing can occur in a batch, when transactions are acquired and stored before being computed all at once (e.g., payroll processing), or online, when transactions are processed as they occur, in real time (e.g., credit card authentication). A typical batch process is the end-of-day reporting done by many transaction processing systems. For example, restaurant point-of-sale software will, at closing, tally up all food and beverage items sold as well as compute total revenue, number of customers, and the like. While this type of reporting could be done in real time (i.e., online processing), it is unlikely that a busy chef could consult the report while the restaurant is open. Contrast this situation with the wine inventory system at Aureole restaurant, where a 42-foot-tall (12 meter) glass tower houses the restaurant's 2,300-bottle wine list. Having real-time knowledge of the inventory is necessary for the restaurant's sommeliers to be able to make optimal suggestions.

Managerial Level The managerial level of the organization is mostly concerned with midterm decision making and a functional focus. The activities performed tend to be semistructured, having both well-known components and some degree of uncertainty. Returning to our grocery store example,

Table 3.2. ACID principles for reliable transaction processing

Atomicity	Transactions are atomic. If one part of the transaction fails, the system must cancel the transaction. For example, if while withdrawing money at the ATM, the cash dispenser jams, your balance should not be debited.
Consistency	Transactions are consistent. In other words, only valid data are committed to long-term memory and stored in the system. For example, if the airline seat assignment system requires only letters in the first-name field, no transaction with numbers in the field is accepted.
Isolation	Transactions are nonconcurrent. If the system has yet to store the results of a transaction while writing the results of a second transaction, its database may end up holding invalid data. For example, if you are withdrawing money from an ATM while your sister is moving money electronically at home, the resulting balance may be invalid unless the system maintains isolation of the two transactions.
Durability	Transactions are durable when they can be recovered in the face of system failure. In other words, once the system has successfully processed the transaction, it will no longer lose it. For example, once the agent has changed your seat, the change is recorded in a transaction log. If anything were to go wrong with the database, the current state could be re-created by reprocessing the transactions from the log.

consider the job of the store manager. Store managers in large chains are typically responsible for selecting that portion of the inventory that experiences regional and local demand. The store manager therefore must be able to monitor demand for these products, forecast future demand, and make inventory management decisions. In a manufacturing context, such as a chemical plant or a factory, middle management is charged with decision making that pertains to optimizing plant operations (e.g., inventory management, production schedules, labor utilization) given the overall production goals.

Decision making at this level is typically semistructured but characterized by repeatable patterns and established methods. The focus is on tactical decision making characterized by some discretion. The objective is to improve the effectiveness of the organization, or one of its functions, within the broad strategic guidelines set by the executive team.

The information systems that support this organizational level are typically called *decision support systems* (DSSs).[2] DSSs provide the information needed by functional managers to engage in tactical decision making. The objective is to produce recurring reports (e.g., daily sales reports, monthly customer service reports) and exception reports (e.g., reports of items that are running low and may cause a stockout). DSSs typically focus on internal operations, and the data they use for analysis stem from the firm's TPS (Figure 3.1).

Executive Level   The executive echelon of the organization is concerned with high-level, long-range decisions. Executives are focused on strategic decision making and on interpreting how the firm should react to trends in the marketplace and the competitive environment. Continuing the example of the grocery store chain, the executive team is focused on judgments such as where to locate new stores, what to do with underperforming stores, and what long-term contracts to sign with suppliers and at what price.

Decision making at this level is highly unstructured, often ad hoc, and reliant on internal as well as external data sources. The objective is, as much as possible, to predict future developments by evaluating trends, using highly aggregated data and scenario analyses. Little structure and few formal methodologies exist for activities at this level.

We refer to the information systems that support this organizational level as *executive information systems* (EISs). A recent development in EISs is offered by the use of software applications known as *executive dashboards*. These tools enable rapid evaluation of highly aggregated organizational and trend data while still providing drill-down features that enable executives to view detailed information. (See Figure 3.2 for an example.)

Evolution of the Hierarchical Perspective   The hierarchical perspective has proven very useful over the years in enabling

FIGURE 3.1. Hierarchical perspective

FIGURE 3.2. Executive dashboard

2. There is some confusion about terminology at this level, with some sources referring to information systems in support of middle management as management information systems (MISs). The term *MIS* can be misleading, as it is often used to refer to the collection of all the information systems used by the firm. We therefore use the term *DSS*.

FIGURE 3.3. Partial organizational chart

managers and IS professionals to easily identify the main characteristics and purpose of information systems and the information technology products designed to support them. However, this perspective is becoming increasingly less representative due to the recent organizational trend toward the adoption of flatter hierarchies with fewer layers between front-line operations and strategic decision making. Moreover, we witnessed a trend toward the empowerment of operational personnel who increasingly enjoy decision-making discretion.

Another limitation of the hierarchical model stems from the fact that it is difficult to separate information systems into clear-cut categories. For example, the defining characteristic of TPSs is their operational focus on day-to-day transaction processing. However, the software applications that support many modern TPSs provide extensive reporting functionality, increasingly giving these systems the traits and functionality that characterize DSSs.

Functional Perspective

As the post–World War II years created a significant impetus for the growth of American businesses, the centralized organizational forms could no longer cope with the increasing managerial complexity brought on by size and diversification. As a consequence, there was a trend toward decentralization, with organizations creating business units and distinct functional areas within them (e.g., accounting, finance, human resources).

This decentralized management structure was very successful because it solved the coordination problems brought on by increasing size. Each unit was able to maintain its operations to a manageable degree of complexity while the corporation as a whole grew larger. The functional organization within business units is typically represented in the form of the organizational chart. (See Figure 3.3 for an example.) With every function managing its own budget independently and having unique information processing needs, functional information systems emerged.

Functional Systems Functional systems are expressly designed to support the specific needs of individuals in the same functional area (see Figure 3.4). Functional systems are based on the principle of local optimization, which suggests that information processing needs are unique and homogeneous within a functional area. Thus the optimal systems are tailored to those highly specific needs and use a language that is familiar to the professionals in that area. As a result, today there is a vast software industry catering to the information processing needs of every functional area in almost any industry sector. The functional perspective, in conjunction with the hierarchical approach (see Figure 3.5), worked reasonably well for a number of years, until the recession of the late 1980s put pressure

FIGURE 3.4. Functional perspective

FIGURE 3.5. Functional systems

FIGURE 3.6. Silos on a farm
Photo by Arjan / CC BY 2.0

on U.S. firms to both increase efficiency and offer superior customer service.

Process Perspective

The primary limitation of the functional and hierarchical perspectives is their lack of integration among separate systems and the introduction of considerable redundancy. This redundancy often created inefficiency, with duplication of similar efforts in separate business units, and substandard service, with customers often being referred to different representatives of the same organization for support. From a technology perspective, the functional approach led to the development of silo applications. Like silos used in farms to store and keep different grains separate (Figure 3.6), these applications would serve a vertical (i.e., functional) need very well but made it difficult to enable communication across different functional areas.

Consider the case of Johnson & Johnson (J&J), the highly diversified health care products maker, with product lines ranging from beauty-care goods to medical and diagnostic devices. After engaging in some internal research, J&J found that a number of its customers (e.g., drug stores) would purchase products from as many as seven different business units. Customers began to ask why they could not interact once with a single J&J representative for all their needs. This change would make it easier for the customer to do business with J&J, and it would also enable them to negotiate volume discounts, coordinate shipments, and experience superior customer service.

Business Process Reengineering Business process reengineering (BPR) emerged in the early 1990s as a way to break down organizational silos in recognition of the fact that business processes are inherently cross-functional. Since its inception, BPR has evolved under a number of labels (e.g., business process redesign, business transformation), and it has now become a standard approach to efficiency improvement in organizations. A business process is defined here as the series of steps that a firm performs in order to complete an economic activity (see Figure 3.7).

BPR is a managerial approach that employs a process view of organizational activities. BPR was codified as a methodology for achieving internal business integration using a top-down approach to business process redesign and seeking dramatic performance improvements through rationalization of activities and elimination of duplication of efforts across separate functions and units. As Michael Hammer put it in the *Harvard Business Review* article that first popularized the term *BPR*, "We should 'reengineer' our business: use the power of modern information technology to radically redesign our business processes in order to achieve dramatic improvements in their performance."[3] The poster child for BPR was Progressive Insurance, an American car insurance company that, under pressure from larger insurers, conceived a process called *immediate response* claim handling. With this novel approach, Progressive had claim adjusters who worked out of vans, rather than

FIGURE 3.7. Process perspective

offices, and were able to inspect a vehicle within 9 hours of a customer call. Before the reengineering effort, Progressive was much closer to the industry standard of 7 to 10 days. Moreover, aided by information systems, the adjuster was able to produce an on-site estimate of the damage and even cut a check to the insured driver. By completely rearchitecting the claim payment process, the firm dramatically improved its speed of operation and quality of service—resulting in a sales growth from $1.3 billion annually in 1991 to $9.5 billion in 2002.

As the Progressive Insurance example suggests, the BPR methodology focuses on activities internal to the firm and requires that managers in charge of the redesign effort question old assumptions regarding how the business should operate (e.g., claim adjusters must work in an office). Such redesign should be driven by a process focus—defined as a way of organizing work that centers on the steps necessary to create value for customers (e.g., speed of claim processing)—without regard for what functional areas would traditionally be responsible for the process steps (Figure 3.8). Proponents of BPR suggest that it is this process focus that enables the firm to eliminate the redundancy and inefficiency associated with

---

3. Hammer, M. (1990, July/August), Reengineering work: Don't automate, obliterate, *Harvard Business Review*, 104–112.

FIGURE 3.8. Reengineering schematic of a product development process

the multiple handoffs of tasks from one area to another. The firm should therefore reorganize its work in a series of processes designed around the intended outcomes. In charge of each process is a processes champion, who oversees things from start to finish. Finally, the BPR methodology is radical in nature, requiring total disregard for existing processes to make room for the redesigned ones. Only with this approach can the firm "stop paving the cow paths"[4] and achieve drastic performance improvements.

The Dark Side of Reengineering   As with any far-reaching transformation process, there are significant risks associated with BPR efforts. First, radical third-order change (see Chapter 2), as required by BPR efforts, engenders significant resistance by those involved. Changes in an individuals' scope of work, responsibility, and position within the organizational structure require abundant retraining and careful planning. People tend to be very comfortable with the way they operate, and changes in their job role, scope, or responsibility require the development of new sets of skills and training. This often engenders confusion.

Second, despite its obvious importance, operations (and consequently business processes) are not "glamorous" or highly valued. Consider for example the excitement that surrounds a successful high-profile merger and the clout of the executives who conclude it. Compare that with the typical "excitement" surrounding the reduction of claim processing time.

Third, BPR initiatives are very expensive because they often require the firm to retire its legacy systems and develop a costly integrated technology infrastructure. Applications that had been developed to enable a functional perspective rarely can be adapted to support a process perspective. BPR's rise to prominence was seized by the software industry and spurred the development of a number of integrated applications. New classes of software programs, such as enterprise systems and supply chain management systems (see below), built to support a process focus, emerged at this time. However, such complex and expensive initiatives require significant managerial commitment and executive sponsorship. And securing such commitment is often difficult, as executives focus on strategic planning, budgeting, capital allocation, and the like.

Finally, the BPR methodology developed a bad reputation after the initial excitement because of its complexity and the fact that for many organizations, BPR led to significant downsizing and layoffs.

The Role of IT in Business Process Reengineering Efforts   The main catalyst for BPR efforts is modern information technology; technological innovation typically enables the firm to question old assumptions that constrain current operations. For example, while traditionally firms have waited to receive invoices from a supplier before issuing payment, the advent of affordable and comprehensive networks has enabled the development of secure extranets (see Chapter 5). Such extranets have allowed the redesign of billing processes, with many organizations installing networked computers at receiving docks, where employees can check the accuracy of a shipment as it is received. If the goods are found to be acceptable, payment can be issued immediately, dramatically reducing the number of handoffs required to complete the process and, consequently, its cost.

As organizations and technology evolve over time, traditional business processes may become obsolete and need to be reevaluated. The interplay of new technologies, and the opportunities they afford, with the redesign of business processes to take advantage of these technologies, has the potential to yield substantial performance improvements. Note that while BPR was developed as an internal methodology to the organization, the same idea has been extended to interorganizational relationships.[5]

The Information System Cycle

When discussing the various categories of systems found in modern organizations, we described transaction processing systems as those concerned with automating routine, day-to-day activities that happen in the present. But attentive managers have long recognized that, while the implementation of these

---

4. Hammer, M. (1990, July/August), Reengineering work: Don't automate, obliterate, *Harvard Business Review*, 104–112.

5. Hammer, M. (2001, September), The superefficient company, *Harvard Business Review*, 82–91.

systems is typically justified by arguments focused on efficiency improvements, the value of the data that they capture should not be underestimated.

The information systems cycle portrays the progression of business data from their inception in transaction processing systems, to their storage in data repositories, and finally to their use in analytical tools (Figure 3.9). Data are typically produced as a byproduct of daily operations and transactions (e.g., shoppers purchasing items at a retail shop, fans walking through the turnstile at a stadium) that the firm completes as it handles business in the present. Such

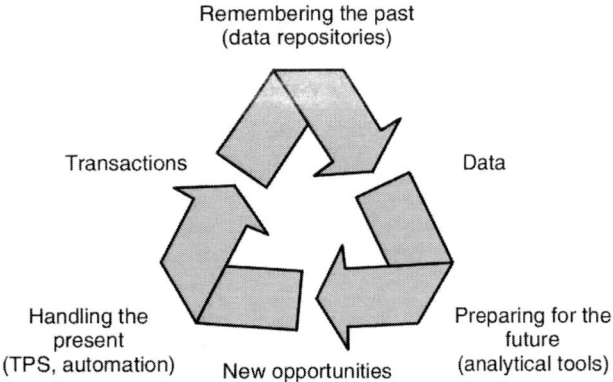

FIGURE 3.9. The information systems cycle

organizational data, when not disposed of, can be accumulated in data repositories and create a record of past transactions (i.e., the data are used to remember the past). Using analytical tools, the firm can then make sense of the accumulated data to find patterns, test assumptions, and more generally enable decision making in an effort to better prepare for the future.

Often these decisions directly impact the firm's information systems with the introduction of new systems (i.e., new IT, new people, new processes, new structures) or the modification of existing ones in an effort to position the firm to achieve its future objectives in an ever-changing, competitive environment. Consider again the example of a grocery store. As customers come and go, a wealth of transactional data is generated. This information is necessary for the store to manage its daily operations (i.e., to handle the present). Customers need to find shelves stocked with popular items. Managers must optimize inventory in order to minimize working capital and spoilage of perishable items. Correct billing, taking into account promotions and discounts, must be generated at checkout. All these instances describe events that happen during the normal course of business in the grocery store. When customers leave, and the present has been handled, all the data generated that are not subject to legal requirements may then be thrown away.

Alternatively, the store can create data repositories that catalog and hold this information—now historical in nature. This act of "remembering the past" is of course only meaningful if the data can be used at a later stage to prepare for the future (e.g., gain beneficial intelligence through analysis of the data). For example, management may commission basket analyses seeking to identify items that sell well together and, based on the results, change the product mix or the location of some items. Management may also use inventory data to optimize reorder schedules and limit chances of stockouts.

The Integration Imperative

The emergence of the process perspective, and the promise it held for streamlining business operations and thereby creating substantial efficiencies and effectiveness improvements, was at the heart of the impetus behind integration efforts during the previous two decades. It was during that time that we saw the popularization of the term *enterprise systems* (see below) and the proliferation of large-scale integrated applications designed to answer the call for business process integration.

Defining Integration

The Merriam-Webster online dictionary defines the act of integrating as to "form, coordinate, or blend into a functioning or unified whole" or "unite." Thus integration is the process that an organization, or a number of organizations, goes through in order to unify, or join together, some of its tangible or intangible assets. The term *assets* here represents physical possessions, such as computer networks and applications, or intangible resources, such as data, knowledge, or business processes.

The overarching goal of integration is to organize, streamline, and simplify a process or an application. Alternatively, the firm's integration effort seeks to modify processes, applications, or assets so that they better represent the realities of the organization and are more closely aligned with the current business objectives and strategic orientation of the firm. Consider, as an illustration, what may happen the next time you rent a car. Major car rental companies are able to share renter's billing information with the firms that process camera-enforced speeding and traffic-light violations. When a camera identifies a rental car violating traffic laws (e.g., speeding), it can immediately query the rental car company's database and identify the driver on record at the time of the violation, charge the person's credit card, and provide a receipt that will be issued to the driver upon return of the car. While it is understandable if you prefer not to experience this situation, you will recognize this as a great example of business process integration across companies!

The Dimensions of Integration

We can categorize integration efforts on two dimensions: their locus and object. The locus of integration can be internal or external. In the first case, the firm is seeking to unify and coordinate owned assets that reside within the boundaries of the firm. For example, a bank may take loan applications at a branch, by phone, or by asking customers to fill out paper-based applications and mail them to the bank. Once an application has been collected, it is checked for accuracy and sent to the bank's administrative office for processing. There, a clerk collects any documentation still needed, such as the applicant's credit score, and passes the application on to a loan officer, who makes a decision.

Using an expert system and networked computers, such a process can be redesigned to achieve dramatic improvements in speed. The application can be completed online or input directly into a computer application by an agent if the applicant prefers to call or visit a branch. Its accuracy can be immediately enforced by rules in the software application that do not allow the process to continue without the needed data. The system, connected to the credit rating agency, can immediately obtain credit scores and any other relevant information. For the majority of loan applications, where decisions are fairly straightforward, this is typically all that is needed to issue a recommendation, and the expert system can do so in real time. More complex applications can be escalated to an experienced loan officer, who, accessing the information through a networked computer, makes a decision.

In the second case, the assets being integrated are not all owned by the firm, and interorganizational integration efforts are involved. Consider the example of General Mills and Land O'Lakes, two companies with different product lines but a similar customer base of grocery stores and similar needs for refrigerated warehousing and transportation. Realizing the potential for synergies and efficiencies, the two firms now coordinate their logistics efforts. As a consequence, General Mills warehouses Land O'Lakes products and delivers them with fuller trucks that make fewer stops. Integrating their distribution and logistics has proven beneficial to both firms.

The second dimension of interest is the object of integration (i.e., what assets the firm is looking to unify or combine). With respect to the object of integration, we distinguish between business integration and systems integration.

Business Integration   Business integration refers to the unification or the creation of tight linkages among the diverse, but connected, business activities carried out by individuals, groups, and departments within an organization. The outcome of business integration is the introduction of cohesive, streamlined business processes that encompass previously separate activities.

Consider the experience of a large computer manufacturer describing how its financing processes have recently changed: "The last thing we want to do is make customers fill out paperwork and [then] call them at a later date to say, 'you are not qualified.' [. . .] This is no longer a satisfactory way to deal with the customer—we need to qualify the customer on the spot."[6] This degree of responsiveness can only be achieved through an integration of the sales and financing processes.

---

6. Brohman, M. K., Piccoli, G., Watson, R., & Parasuraman, A. (2005), NCSS process completeness: Construct development and preliminary validation, *Proceedings of the Thirty-Eighth Hawaii International Conference on System Sciences*, Hawaii.

Business integration is considered critical to the survival of the modern firm. Many observers have suggested that in order to stay competitive, today's business ventures must be able to present one face to the customer, provide solutions, and achieve global inventory visibility.

Presenting One Face to the Customer   Increasingly we hear that organizations must organize around their customers' needs rather than in functional areas or around product lines. With the continuous speeding up of competition, organizations must be able to react and respond quickly and effectively to customer requests and make it as easy as possible for customers to work with the firm. The development of mobile commerce and the increase of customer touchpoints add to this challenge the need to provide a consistent customer experience across the different channels. A request by the firm to call a different department or a different location to have questions addressed is increasingly met with discontent by consumers. Barnes & Noble and other retailers with both online and offline channels are attempting to better integrate their diverse channels of distribution. As customers, we have come to expect the ability to shop online but still check to see if an item of interest is available at the local store. When we have an item to return, we don't understand why we can't simply drop it off at the local store rather than having to fumble with packaging and the postal service. If these are different channels of distribution for the same company, we argue, why can't we work seamlessly with the one that makes it easiest for us at the time?

Providing Solutions   Companies are now expected to provide solutions, not an array of products or services. Hotels, for example, are increasingly defining their business as "travel support" rather than lodging. This redefinition of the firm's value proposition from a product to a solution creates a wealth of opportunity for creating new services, like airline check-in and baggage pickup at the hotel. The sporting goods store Finish Line provides another example for solving a nagging problem: shoes on sale often are missing some of the sizes. At Finish Line, customers who are eyeing a nice pair of sneakers at the right price but find out that their size is missing are not at a loss. Finish Line associates can look up the availability of the same item at other stores affiliated with the chain. If they do find it, they charge the customer and issue a request for direct shipment of the item to the customer's address. This initiative recasts the inventory clearance process from a local store affair to a coordinated, chain-wide, integrated process. Incidentally, the initiative not only leaves customers more satisfied but also moves old inventory more quickly by increasing the reach of the sale—a happy note for the company itself.

Global Inventory Visibility   With the increasing rate of speed at which business moves, customers are also progressively coming to expect fast and precise responses to their questions about customization and modification of the firm's products. This trend, perhaps more typical of manufacturing industries and business-to-business relationships, rewards firms that have achieved global inventory visibility. Global inventory visibility represents the knowledge of current inventories and the ability to instantly estimate price and delivery schedule changes in response to requests for customization. At the now-famous Dell Online store, you can customize your new computer system and receive a precise estimate of the date you will receive it—such a delivery date will change based on the actual components you request in your machine.

Systems Integration   With the business integration imperative taking center stage, information systems professionals and the software industry have sought ways to enable integration. It is evident that without information systems and technology infrastructure to support them, business integration strategies cannot be feasibly implemented.

The term *system integration* refers to the unification or tight linkage of IT-enabled information systems and databases. The primary focus of systems integration is the technological component of the information systems underpinning business integration strategies. The outcome of system integration is a collection of compatible systems that regularly exchange information or the development of integrated applications that replace the former discrete ones. More precisely, when the systems integration effort seeks to enable communication among separate software programs, we speak of *application integration*. When the systems integration effort seeks to enable the merging of data repositories and databases, we speak of *data integration*.

Internal integration pertains to the unification or linkage of intraorganizational systems, while *external integration* pertains to interorganizational ones. Internal and external systems integration substantiates itself in custom-developed applications or off-the-shelf commercial products and tools with names that you have probably heard before: enterprise resource planning (ERP), enterprise systems, business intelligence (BI) tools, supply chain management software, and the like. Because of their importance and pervasiveness, we discuss some of these systems in detail here.

Enterprise Systems

Organizations have historically designed and custom developed software applications to support their unique work activities and business processes. This approach was necessary as computers became a staple of operations in large organizations in the 1970s and 1980s, when a stable software industry had yet to emerge. These custom-developed applications were typically designed and implemented at the departmental or functional level, giving rise to what we have termed the functional perspective.

Once organizational computing became prevalent, as software entrepreneurs identified more and more areas where operations of organizations could be automated using standardized software programs, the software industry grew dramatically. Today, the worldwide software industry is a large and diverse one, estimated to net more than $400 billion in revenue in 2013 and projected to surpass the $600 billion mark in 2016[7]—a testament to its continuing tremendous growth.

In the late 1980s and early 1990s, the proliferation of stand-alone applications began to highlight the limitations of the functional approach, giving rise to the process perspective, business process reengineering methodologies, and the integration imperative. The missing piece in the quest for integrated operations was a class of standardized software applications that would enable and support integrated business processes. Such applications are now known as enterprise systems (ESs).

The Genesis of Enterprise Systems

While enterprise systems have been a dominant trend in organizational computing over the last decade and a half and continue to garner significant attention, their roots reach as far back as the 1960s, when computing resources began to be applied to manufacturing problems. At that time, manufacturing organizations employed information technology for the optimization of inventory control, quickly realizing that in order for inventory to be efficiently managed, it would have to be linked to production schedules. Thus the material requirement planning (MRP) approach was born, and manufacturing firms wrote software designed to automatically translate master production schedules into requirements for subassemblies, components, and raw materials.

Under pressure to be increasingly efficient, in the 1980s, manufacturing organizations introduced manufacturing resource planning (MRP-II), a concept that extended MRP to encompass the entire factory production process. At that time, software houses like German-based SAP began to seek integration of activities that had a bearing on manufacturing processes but spanned other functional areas as well, such as human resources, engineering, and project management. So what did they ultimately call the software application that extends the MRP concept to support integrated management beyond the manufacturing function and encompasses other functions across the enterprise? ERP, of course! It's quite a confusing label that only makes sense based on its genesis and its history.

With the relentless pursuit of efficiency by manufacturing firms, the steadily declining cost of information technology assets, and the emergence of the client/server model, which made complex software applications such as ERPs accessible through user-friendly personal computer terminals, the stage was

---

7. Gartner Inc. (2014, March 31), *Market share: All software markets, worldwide*, retrieved from https://www.gartner.com/doc/3019720/market-share-software-markets-worldwide; and Bartels, A., with Burris, P., & LeClair, A. (2015, January 7), The global tech market outlook for 2015 to 2016, *Forrester*, retrieved from https://www.forrester.com/The+Global+Tech+Market+Outlook+For+2015+To+2016/fulltext/-/E-RES115771

set for ERP (or enterprise systems, as they were later renamed) to become mainstream. The final push for commercial success of enterprise systems came from the fear that 20- and 30-year-old legacy applications[8] would suddenly stop running on January 1, 2000 (known as the Y2K bug).

While much early development in this area was focused on functionalities (i.e., what the software applications could do), the parallel development of the business process reengineering (BPR) methodology, which called for a process focus and the use of IT to integrate activities across the organizational functions, led

FIGURE 3.10. Boeing's factory shop floor in Seattle
Photo by Jetstar Airways / CC BY SA 2.0

to increasing attention to changing the way activities in the enterprise were performed. At this time, ES vendors began focusing on incorporating "best practices" into their applications with the objective of offering a ready-made set of menus of business processes native to the application. Today, the label "best-practice software" is a pervasive and highly inflated one.

As enterprise systems have continued to mature, the list of top vendors reads like a who's who of the software industry, and significant consolidation has occurred, with Oracle in particular swallowing many former competitors. The top five vendors control almost 53% of the market (Figure 3.11).

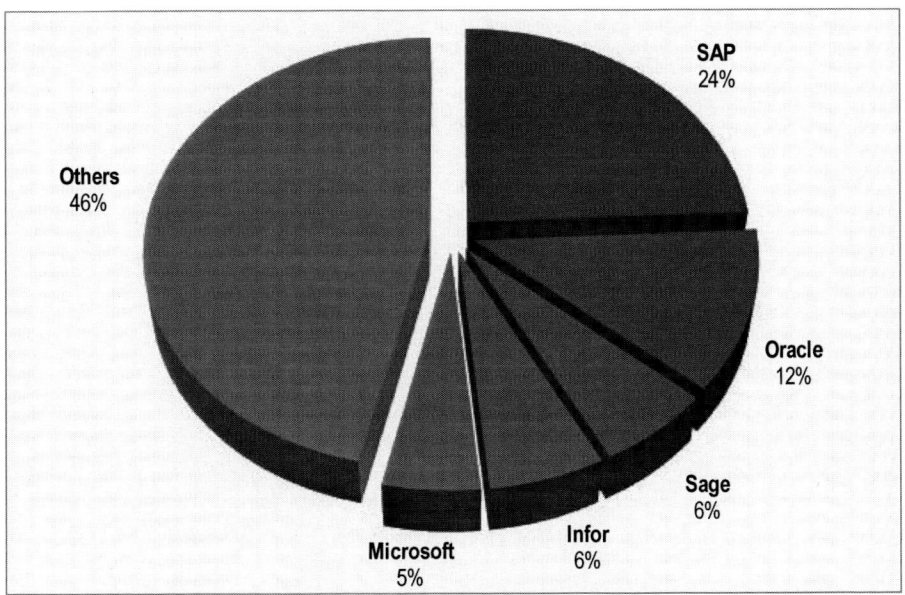

FIGURE 3.11. Market share of the top five ERP vendors
Source: Data from Gartner (2013), Market Share: ERP Software, Worldwide

---

8. *Legacy* is a term that does not have a precise definition in information systems. It is typically used to refer to older functional applications based on traditional programming languages (e.g., COBOL) that run on mainframes.

Competition is now fierce; with the market for larger Fortune 1000 organizations close to saturation, the main vendors have developed enterprise systems aimed at small and medium enterprises (SME).

As a consequence of the commercial success of enterprise systems, as you enter the workforce, you will be managing either in an organization that already has an ES or in a smaller firm that is evaluating such a purchase. In either case, you will need to understand the characteristics of these applications—with the advantages and risks they engender—and their impact on the surrounding information system and the organization at large.

Enterprise Systems: Definition

It is clear from the genesis of modern enterprise systems that their defining features are native integration and an effort to support all components of the firm's IT infrastructure. We define an enterprise system as a modular,

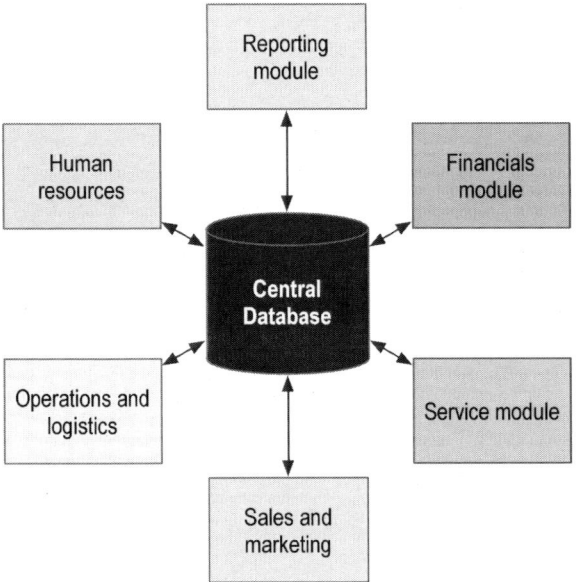

FIGURE 3.12. Enterprise system modules

integrated software application that spans (all) organizational functions and relies on one database at the core (Figure 3.12). An organization can theoretically build its own ES in house. For example, in 2003, Hilton Hotels unveiled OnQ, a custom-made enterprise system estimated to cost more than $50 million. Describing it, Tim Harvey, chief information officer (CIO) of Hilton at the time, stated, "OnQ is comprised of six major business functions; the idea was to take all the business functions required in a hotel and make them all work together as one system so it's highly integrated."[9]

Some custom development notwithstanding, the great majority of firms will purchase an ES from one of the dominant vendors in an effort to capitalize on the economies of scale associated with off-the-shelf software applications (see Chapter 11). The principal characteristics of enterprise systems are modularity, application and data integration, and configurability.

Modularity   Enterprise systems are modular in nature, thus enabling the organization that purchases one to decide which functionalities to enable and which ones not to use. The modularity of enterprise systems is a necessity dictated by their size and scope. For as much as ES vendors strive to code comprehensive menus of configuration options and "best practices" into their applications, no single vendor can be the best at each module. For example, PeopleSoft (now owned by Oracle) has historically been known for the strength of its human resource module, while SAP's ERP is known for the strength of its manufacturing module. (See Table 3.3 for sample ES modules and functionalities.)

Modularity enables customers of enterprise systems to exercise some flexibility with respect to the components of the application they intend to purchase and those that they don't need (and should not pay for). In the extreme, modularity also enables a firm to pick and choose individual modules from competing ES vendors, even though this approach defeats the very driver of ES implementations.

Application and Data Integration   Native integration is the defining characteristic of enterprise systems. More specifically, ESs enable application integration. With application integration, an event that occurs in one of the modules of the application automatically triggers an event in one or more of the other separate modules.

9. Shein, E. (2003, July 15), Hilton Hotels CIO talks "OnQ," *CIO Magazine*, retrieved June 6, 2007, from http://www.cioupdate.com /insights/article.php/2235231/Hilton-Hotels-CIO-Talks-OnQ.htm

Table 3.3. Sample ES modules and functionalities

Financials	Operations and logistics
Accounts receivable and payable	Inventory management
Asset accounting	Material requirements planning
Cash management and forecasting	Materials management
Financial consolidation	Plant maintenance
General ledger	Production planning
Product-cost accounting	Routing management
Profit-center accounting	Shipping

Human resources	Sales and marketing
Payroll	Order management
Personnel planning	Pricing
Travel expenses	Sales management
	Sales planning

Consider the following example: A Paris-based sales representative for a U.S. computer manufacturer prepares a quote for a customer using an ES. The salesperson enters some basic information about the customer's requirements into his laptop computer, and the ES automatically produces a formal contract, in French, specifying the product's configuration, price, and delivery date. When the customer accepts the quote, the sales rep presses a key; the system, after verifying the customer's credit limit, records the order. The system schedules the shipment; identifies the best routing and then, working backward from the delivery date, reserves the necessary materials from inventory; orders needed parts from suppliers; and schedules assembly in the company's factory in Taiwan.

The sales and production forecasts are immediately updated, and a material-requirements-planning list and bill of materials are created. The sales rep's payroll account is credited with the correct commission, in euros, and his travel account is credited with the expense of the sales call. The actual product cost and profitability are calculated in U.S. dollars, and the divisional and corporate balance sheets, the accounts-payable and accounts-receivable ledgers, and the cost-center accounts are all automatically updated. The system performs nearly every information transaction resulting from the sale.[10]

The above example, a sort of sales pitch for the perfect world of ES, neatly highlights the notion of application integration. A number of modules—inventory, production, logistics, human resources, and financials—are all engaged by one simple event: the sales rep presses the enter key to confirm the order.

Data integration focuses on the information that is stored by the ES, instead of the processes it supports. ESs rely on one logical database at the core—that is, while there may be multiple physical data stores and locations where information resides, they will be treated as one, thus ensuring data integration. This feature is a critical selling point of ESs because one logical database ensures a high degree of data integrity (i.e., data are accurate), a limitation of data redundancy (i.e., data are not repeated unnecessarily), and the enforcement of one data schema (i.e., all modules define the same piece of data—say, customer—in the same way).

Configurable Enterprise systems are parameterized. That is, because they are intended to serve the needs of a wide range of different organizations in an industry, ESs come with configuration tables that enable the adopting firm to choose among a predefined set of options during the implementation of the application. For instance, your firm may prefer to account for inventory on a last-in first-out (LIFO)

10. Davenport, T. H. (1998, July/August), Putting the enterprise into enterprise system, *Harvard Business Review*, 121–131.

basis, while another firm that purchased the same ES needs to use the first-in first-out (FIFO) method. During the implementation, you and your competitor will simply configure the application differently by choosing different options.

Enterprise systems also allow the firm to extend the capabilities of the standard application by creating "bolt-on modules." Bolt-on modules, typically written using a programming language that is native to the ES (e.g., ABAP in SAP), are used to further tailor the ES to the specific needs of the organization. While this tailoring of a standardized application may seem counterintuitive, the development of add-ons to supplement the functionality of the package has represented a fairly common occurrence.[11]

The Advantages of Enterprise Systems

At this point, there is considerable literature describing the advantages of adopting enterprise systems, including efficiency improvements through direct and indirect cost savings, responsiveness, knowledge infusion, and adaptability.

Efficiency   Perhaps the biggest selling point of enterprise systems to an executive audience is their promise to rein in complex, generally hard-to-manage legacy IT infrastructures. Because of their support for business and data integration, ESs have the potential to dramatically reduce direct costs, such as those associated with the need for entering the same data in multiple applications. ESs also promise improved efficiency through the reduction of indirect costs achieved by streamlining business processes and operations.

Responsiveness   As the scenario presented earlier shows, one of the advantages of application integration is a dramatic improvement in the firm's ability to respond to customers and market demands. With up-to-date information available in the field, the sales representative in the example was able to quote a delivery date and price on the fly. Moreover, application integration confirmed the order seamlessly and immediately engaged all processes necessary to fulfill the contract.

Knowledge Infusion   As with most off-the-shelf applications, enterprise systems enable the infusion of knowledge into the adopting firm—that is, the application is thought to embed the state of the art in industry practice so that it can be used as a vehicle for updating business processes and operations within the firm. The appeal of knowledge infusion has traditionally been one of the primary selling points of enterprise systems because ES vendors have made it a cornerstone of their strategy to embed "best practices" in their software releases by vetting and selecting the parameters of the application.

ES vendors have been largely successful in these efforts, and the major vendors now commercialize ES geared toward specific verticals that make industry best practices a key value proposition. In fact, many enterprise systems implementations have been justified on the basis of senior executives' frustration with the current state of operations. In these organizations, the ES project became a means to drastically reorganize the firm's operations using business process reengineering techniques and the software to enforce the new business processes.

Adaptability   A final advantage offered by enterprise systems is their high degree of adaptability to each unique organizational context. While certainly not comparable to the adaptability of tailor-made applications, enterprise systems offer a degree of customizability rarely provided by off-the-shelf applications. The adaptability of ES is achieved through the use of configuration tables and bolt-on functionality.

Because of the size, scope, and complexity of ES, implementation and configuration processes are very complicated. For example, SAP ERP has more than 3,000 configuration tables. Beyond configuration and the development of bolt-on functionalities, an ES implementation requires migration and consolidation of data repositories. For this reason, every major vendor has a network of partners, called integrators, who have developed specific expertise in implementing the applications. Large integrators,

---

11. Ulrich, W. (2006), Application package survey: The promise versus reality, *Cutter Benchmark Review*, 6(9), 13–20.

such as IBM Global Services, Accenture, Deloitte, Infosys, and Wipro, take ownership of the installation, implementation, and adaptation processes, and their fees (rather than software licenses) make up the bulk of the cost of an ES implementation.

The Limitations of Enterprise Systems

A massive undertaking of the kind that enterprise systems implementations bring about is bound to have significant drawbacks and the potential for project failure and ensuing litigation (Table 3.4). To help managers limit some of the risks associated with such sweeping projects, there is now a comprehensive literature on the limitations of enterprise systems. The critical issues to consider are the trade-off between standardization and flexibility, the limitations of best-practice software, the potential for strategic clashes, and the high costs and risks of the implementation process.

Table 3.4. A sample of high-profile ERP failures and litigation cases

Year	ERP vendor/ integrator	ERP customer	Reason for ERP failure and/or lawsuit
2013	IBM and SAP	Bridgestone	Bridgestone's complaint alleged that "IBM's defective system lost or deleted scheduled customer orders, would not process orders, duplicated, or partially processed orders and, for those limited orders that were processed, did not complete critical corresponding business applications."
2013	Accenture and Microsoft	ScanSource	The lawsuit alleged that Avanade (Accenture subsidiary) purposely underestimated the cost of the ERP software system Microsoft Dynamics AX for $17 million in 11 months; however, "within a few months," the cost escalated to an estimated $66 million and took more than three years to complete.
2013	Infor	Buckley Powder	The system was still not operational after 18 months and "the project has been plagued by setbacks and non-performance on behalf of Infor and no reasonable solution has been presented."
2012	SAP and IBM	Avantor Performance Materials	The lawsuit alleged that IBM's proposed solution was "woefully unsuited" to its business, that the implementation brought its operations to "a near standstill," and that the project was staffed with "incompetent and reckless consultants" who made "numerous design, configuration and programming errors."
2012	Epicor	Major Brands	Major Brands alleged that the software vendor failed to deliver a satisfactory system after years of effort and significant cost overruns and then offered a solution that would force the company to install a new version that hadn't yet been completed, pushing back the original "go-live" date by four years.
2010	JDA Software (i2)	Dillard's Inc.	Dillard's alleged that i2 failed to meet obligations regarding two software-license agreements for which the department-store operator had paid $8 million.
2010	SAP and Deloitte Consulting	Marin County, California	The lawsuit alleged that Deloitte committed fraud and "misrepresented its skills and experience."

Table 3.4. A sample of high-profile ERP failures and litigation cases (continued)

Year	ERP vendor/ integrator	ERP customer	Reason for ERP failure and/or lawsuit
2010	Capgemini and SAP	Dorset County in the United Kingdom	A job that previously only took a minute is now alleged to take an hour. The system has to shut down a few days each month to allow data to be processed.
2009	Epicor Software Corporation	Ferazzoli Imports of New England	Epicor's system never worked as intended or promised. The initial budget was $184,443, and the cost to date is $224,656.
2009	SAP and Axon	City of San Diego	The city of San Diego, California, terminated its software implementation contract with services provider Axon. The project was $11 million over budget.
2009	Lawson Software	Public Health Foundation Enterprises	The ERP implementation failed.
2008	SAP	Levi Strauss	The company was forced to take shipping systems at its three massive U.S. distribution centers offline for a full week with ensuing loss of business.
2008	Oracle	Overstock.com	ERP implementation problems were blamed for losses during the 2005 Christmas season and extending into 2006.
2008	SAP	City of Portland	Portland's SAP project, budgeted at $31 million in 2006 for a 2007 go-live date, is now estimated to cost nearly $50 million.
2004	PeopleSoft	Cleveland State University	There was a faulty installation of the company's ERP applications. The lawsuit charged PeopleSoft with breach of contract and negligent misrepresentation.
2003	EDS	British Sky Broadcasting	The project was delivered late, and lost benefits amounted to an estimated £709 million.
2001	Oracle Corporation and KPMG	University of Cambridge	The ERP was project considered "faulty" after the university spent $13 million for the implementation.
2001	SAP (R/3) and Accenture	FoxMeyer Corp.	The company claimed that a botched SAP R/3 implementation in the mid-1990s ruined them, driving them to bankruptcy.
2000	J. D. Edwards and IBM	Evans Industries Inc.	The lawsuit alleged that OneWorld was "defective and failed to operate and function as promised by the defendants."

Source: Adapted and updated from Kimberling, E. (2011, February 8), ERP failures and lawsuits: It's not just for the tier I ERP vendors, *Backbone*, retrieved from http://panorama-consulting.com/erp-failures-and-lawsuits-its-not-just-for-the-tier-i-erp-vendors/

Standardization and Flexibility Despite the potential for adaptability and the support for the development of bolt-on modules, when implementing enterprise systems, organizations are highly encouraged to implement as close to a standard version of the software as possible. This "vanilla" implementation ensures that the organization capitalizes on the development economies of scale of the vendor and that implementation time and effort are kept to a minimum. Moreover, if the firm limits itself to configurations and adaptations that are native to the ES, it will find it easiest to transition when upgrading its current software during marketplace migrations.[12]

This approach is diametrically opposite to the custom development approach, where the technology is shaped to fit the unique needs of the organization. With "vanilla" enterprise systems implementations, it is the firm and its business processes that need to accommodate the characteristics of the packaged enterprise system—often requiring significant business process reengineering and change management.

The trade-off between standardization and flexibility is further amplified by the fact that there is a significant premium associated with the consolidation of a firm's IT infrastructure around one enterprise system. The high degree of application and data integration promised by enterprise systems can only be delivered if the firm is willing to standardize on one vendor and install a sufficient number of modules. Yet as the reach of the application within the organization extends (i.e., more modules are implemented), so do the limitations to the flexibility of individual units. The high degree of integration of ESs requires that the separate units learn to coordinate their efforts and negotiate their preferences.

Finally, enterprise systems are often referred to as software concrete. Concrete is very adaptable and moldable while being poured yet very inflexible and difficult to modify after it has set (Figure 3.13). In other words, while it is true that enterprise systems offer degrees of adaptability that are not typical of off-the-shelf applications, it is important to note that much of the adaptability comes from configuration tables that can only be used during the implementation process.

Is the Best Practice Embedded in the ES Really Best?

One of the critical selling points of enterprise systems is the fact that they are thought to embed industry best practices. The notion of best-practice software is predicated on the idea that it is possible to identify the technique or techniques that are optimal to delivering a given outcome and that these techniques or methods can be codified in a software program. When the application is implemented in an organization, it will "force" the firm to adapt, thus putting into practice the optimal technique.

While the notion of best-practice software is intuitively appealing, it is critical that you recognize some of its limitations. First, it is unclear how best practices are identified. In the case of enterprise systems, the best practice may simply be what the software design team deemed as the optimal set of processes necessary to complete the activity. Second, as we discussed in Chapter 2, it is not enough to implement a software program to enact a new practice. Third, and most important, the unique approach your organization has developed to carry out a given activity—your own best practice, if you will—may not be supported by the ES. This limitation of the best-practice approach can have dramatic impacts when it leads to a strategic clash.

Strategic Clash

When a firm adopts an enterprise system, it will have to choose among the set of business processes supported by the software—the best practices. Often they will be readily available within the existing set of configuration tables provided by the application (e.g., FIFO inventory management). In other cases, the established business processes of the firm may not be supported. This is not a problem when the traditional organizational processes are considered substandard. Indeed, as mentioned above, the case for ES implementation often stems

FIGURE 3.13. Statue made of concrete
Photo by Jim Burcham / CC BY 2.0

---

12. The term *marketplace migration* refers to the cyclical upgrades associated with new versions of the software.

from the need to update the firm's operations. But what if one of your unique practices, one that you think gives you a competitive edge, is not supported by the ES?

Consider the case of a spare parts manufacturer. The firm made customer service a cornerstone of its strategic positioning and was willing to shuffle the queue of orders when one of its best customers required a rush order. The firm did not advertise this "best practice," and such a practice was not coded into the ES the firm was considering implementing. Yet management thought that such a differentiating process was a source of competitive advantage. What would you do in this case?

As this example illustrates, as a general or functional manager, you must be extremely careful with enterprise systems installations. You need to identify those highly unique business processes that differentiate your organization from the competition. Such processes will likely not be codified in the ES inventory of best practices. Thus you will have to weigh each of the following options:

- Forgo the ES implementation.
- Implement the ES but build bolt-on modules to maintain support for your unique processes.
- Implement the ES without the modules that impact the unique processes and maintain the associated legacy systems.
- Implement the ES in a standard fashion (i.e., vanilla installation) and sacrifice your unique processes to seek improved efficiency and preserve integration.

The appropriate course of action will depend on the number of unique business processes you identify and their impact on the firm's performance. The important consideration here is to evaluate the decision beforehand rather than during implementation or, even worse, afterward.

High Costs and Risks   Enterprise systems have achieved a high degree of maturity, and the ES industry has consolidated around a few major vendors. Yet, over the years, ESs have had plenty of casualties. This is because enterprise systems, like most large-scale systems implementations, are costly in terms of time and money and are risky endeavors overall.

Consider the following well-documented case:

FoxMeyer Drugs was a $5 billion company and the nation's fourth largest distributor of pharmaceuticals before the fiasco. With the goal of using technology to increase efficiency, the Delta III project began in 1993. FoxMeyer conducted market research and product evaluation and purchased SAP R/3 in December of that year. FoxMeyer also purchased warehouse-automation from a vendor called Pinnacle, and chose Andersen Consulting [now Accenture] to integrate and implement the two systems. [. . .] FoxMeyer was driven to bankruptcy in 1996, and the trustee of FoxMeyer announced in 1998 that he was suing SAP, the ERP vendor, as well as Andersen Consulting, its SAP integrator, for $500 million each.[13]

An enterprise system engenders a number of technical (e.g., the migration and integration of existing databases) and behavioral (e.g., a significant degree of business process change) challenges that must be actively managed by the adopting firm with the help of a skilled integrator. While ERPs have matured as a product and there is significant expertise now available to manage ERP implementation projects, a recent survey by Panorama Consulting[14] suggests that ERP implementations remain complex and costly projects (Table 3.5) characterized by a significant degree of risk in the outcome (Figure 3.14).

---

13. Scott, J. (1999, August), The FoxMeyer Drugs' bankruptcy: Was it a failure of ERP?, *Proceedings of the Association for Information Systems Fifth Americas Conference on Information Systems*, Milwaukee, WI: Computer Society Press.

14. Panorama Consulting Solutions, *2015 ERP report: A panorama consulting solution research report*, retrieved from http://panorama-consulting.com/resource-center/2015-erp-report/

Table 3.5. Sample project metrics for recent ERP implementations

	2009	2010	2011	2012	2013	2014
Average project cost (millions)	$6.2	$5.48	$10.5	$7.1	$2.8	$4.5
Project duration (months)	18.4	14.3	16	17.8	16.3	14.3
Late projects	35.5%	61.1%	54%	61%	72%	75%
Projects over budget	51.4%	74.1%	56%	53%	54%	55%

Source: Adapted from Panorama Consulting 2011 and 2015 ERP Reports; courtesy of Panorama Consulting Solutions, http://www.panorama-consulting.com

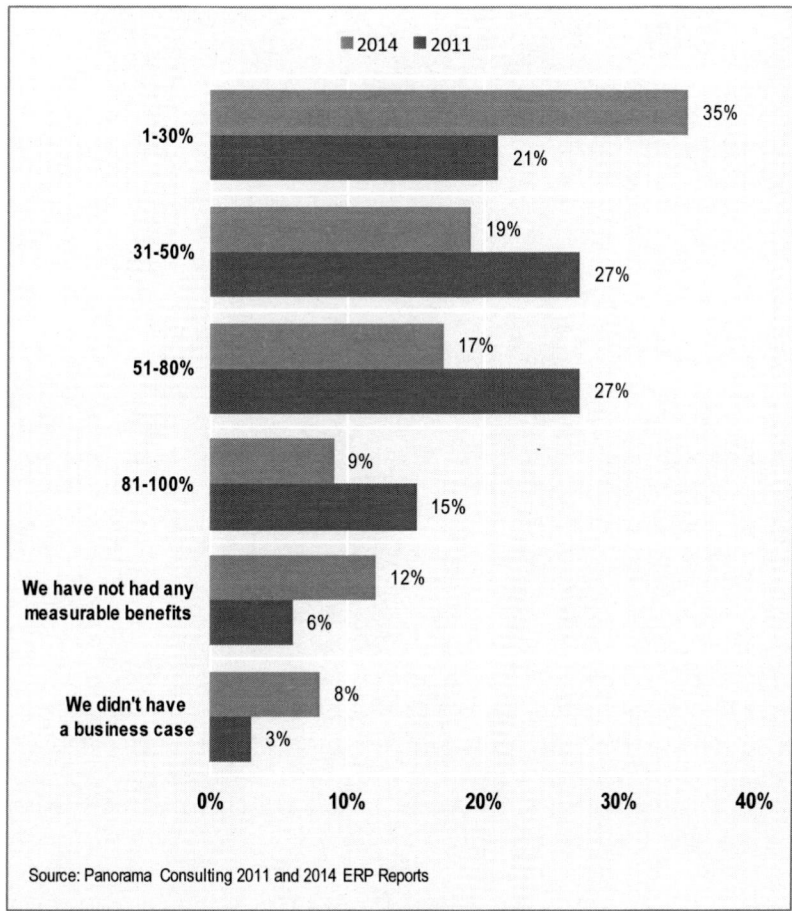

FIGURE 3.14. Estimated percentage of benefits actually realized
Courtesy of Panorama Consulting Solutions, http://www.panorama-consulting.com

Supply Chain Management

In its most general terms, a supply chain is the set of coordinated entities that contribute to moving a product from its production to its consumption. From the standpoint of a given firm, the upstream supply chain is concerned with gathering and providing the organization with the resources it needs to perform its transformation process (e.g., raw materials, energy, and equipment). The downstream supply chain is concerned with moving the outputs of the firm's production process to its intended consumers.

For instance, the supply chain of a grocery store is the complex network of firms that produces the groceries consumers purchase at individual stores (Figure 3.15). Supply chain management (SCM) is

FIGURE 3.15. Supply chain of a grocery store

the set of logistical and financial processes associated with the planning, executing, and monitoring of supply chain operations.

A Brief History of Supply Chain Management

The use of information technology to enable supply chain management has a long tradition, following a pattern of increasing integration of separate processes similar to that of enterprise systems. Software support for supply chain management emerged to capture the strong linkages between the warehousing and transportation functions of the organization (Figure 3.16). Integrated warehousing and transportation allowed firms to create efficiencies due to the joint optimization of warehouse locations, layouts, transportation routes, and related processes. Something as simple as ensuring that delivery trucks leave the warehouse full, rather than half-empty, can have dramatic impacts on a firm's profitability because of the high fixed costs of this activity.

The next step in the evolution of integrated supply chain management was marked by the recognition that further efficiencies could be created by integrating logistics processes (i.e., transportation and warehousing) with manufacturing schedules and activities (Figure 3.17). At this stage, the financial and information flows associated with the management of the supply chain (i.e., procurement and order management processes) were also integrated.

This increasing degree of integration was enabled by continued improvements in the power of IT and the functionality of supply chain management software. Those firms able to manage these activities in concert could minimize slack resources (e.g., costly slow-downs or stoppages in manufacturing due to a lack of the needed raw materials), improve logistics, and make better purchasing decisions.

Modern Supply Chain Management

The last step in the evolution of supply chains consisted in the realization that tight linkages could be established with upstream (i.e., suppliers) and downstream firms (i.e., customers). Modern supply chain management systems are therefore interorganizational systems (Chapter 2) increasingly supported by the use of the Internet (Figure 3.18). Typically a firm will establish an extranet in order to coordinate activities with its supply chain management partners. An extranet is a private network that uses the public Internet infrastructure and Internet technologies but spans the boundaries of the organization and enables secure transactions between a firm and its suppliers, vendors, customers, or any other partner.

The last stage in the evolution of supply chain management has been its integration with enterprise systems. As ERP applications have traditionally been focused on internal operations, merging

FIGURE 3.16. First-generation supply chain

FIGURE 3.17. Second-generation supply chain

with boundary-spanning supply chain management systems has been a natural evolution. Moreover, as the ES market is maturing and the majority of large organizations have deployed them, linking firms in the supply chain has become simpler. More specifically, supply chain collaboration practices supported by an ever-increasing data availability have granted a higher level of visibility of goods along the supply chains.

The increasing attention to IT-enabled supply chain management has also given rise to focused intermediaries whose value proposition is providing the tools to enable integrated supply chain management in specific industry "verticals" (i.e., industry segments). Such B2B intermediaries (see Chapter 5) facilitate coordination of the material, financial, and information flows in the supply chain.

More recently, the emergence of cost-effective radio frequency identification (RFID) chips has opened a new frontier for supply chain management. RFID relies on a set of tag readers that detect and decode information contained in RFID tags using radio frequencies. RFID has a number of advantages:

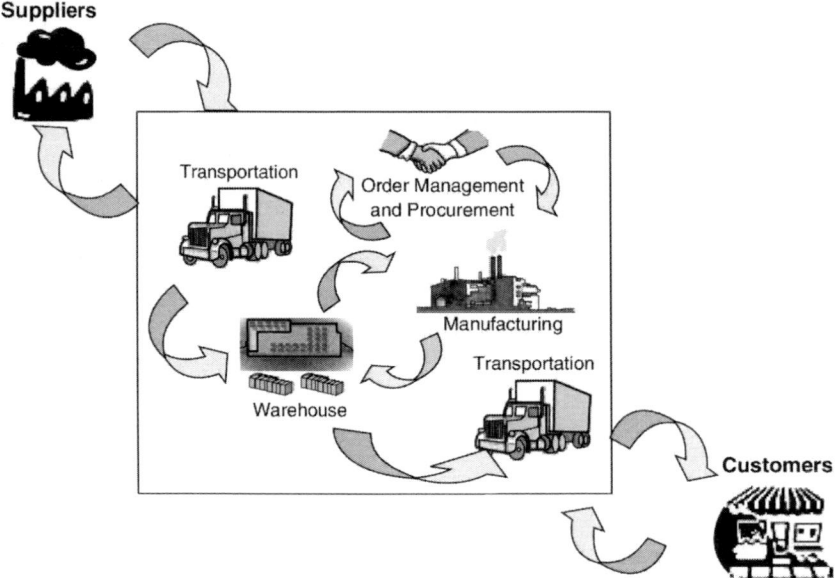

FIGURE 3.18. Third-generation supply chain

- *No line-of-sight requirements*. Because RFID tags use radio frequencies, they do not require that a tag be directly in contact with or have an unimpeded path to the transponders, as is the case with bar code scanners, for example.
- *Embedding*. Because RFID tags need no line of sight to communicate with tag readers, RFID tags can be embedded in the products they are to identify. Moreover, tags can be embedded in livestock and even humans (e.g., patients in a hospital).
- *Writing capability*. The content of RFID tags, unlike that of bar codes, can be changed over time by erasing and rewriting to the tag.
- *Storage capacity*. RFID tags are an evolving technology, but they can already contain significant descriptive information. For example, a tag may tell us when the product was manufactured, where it was manufactured, its expiration date, and so on.

RFID tags are not new. For instance, they have been used in highway toll booth payment for more than a decade. Their price point is rapidly falling to the point where it is feasible to incorporate RFID tags in a myriad of products, including consumer goods. RFID tags promise substantial efficiency improvements in the supply chain, from speeding the process of receiving and warehousing products to improving the monitoring and control of inventories. However, the true potential for RFID tags, as it is for most new information technology, may be in their ability to enable new processes and new applications. Imagine a day when cartons of milk will come equipped with RFID tags and signal to your fridge that this milk is nearing the spoil date.

Knowledge Management

Recognizing the importance of knowledge as an organizational asset, Thomas Watson, the legendary chief executive officer (CEO) of IBM, once stated, "All the value of this company is in its people. If you burned down all our plants, and we just kept our people and our information files, we should soon be as strong as ever."[15]

---

15. Quinn, J. B. (1994), Appraising intellectual assets, *McKinsey Quarterly, 2*(Spring), retrieved from https://www.questia.com/library/journal/1G1-15727095/appraising-intellectual-assets

Knowledge: Definition

Knowledge can be thought of as a blend of actionable information built over time based on accumulated experiences and the understanding of a phenomenon. We can categorize knowledge with respect to its object as follows:

- *Knowing what.* This type of knowledge is based on the ability to collect, categorize, and assimilate information. An example is the ability of a financial intermediary to articulate and explain which type of investment is best suited to the goals expressed by a given client.
- *Knowing how.* This type of knowledge is predicated on the ability to recognize or create the sequence of steps that are needed to complete a task or carry out an activity. An example is the ability of the financial intermediary mentioned above to create the portfolio of investments by completing the appropriate forms and purchasing the appropriate securities.
- *Knowing why.* This type of knowledge is based on an understanding of cause-effect relationships and the laws that govern a given phenomenon. An example is the ability of the same financial intermediary to recognize why some investments are best suited for her various clients as they progress through life and conditions change. This understanding will allow her to identify relevant changes and suggest the appropriate adjustments to each of them.

Knowledge has also been categorized with respect to its type:

- *Explicit knowledge.* Explicit knowledge can be articulated, codified, and transferred with relative ease. An example is provided by the training manual that the financial intermediary described above used to learn how to purchase securities for her clients. The manual enables the intermediary to know how to perform the transaction. She can then pass this knowledge on to her associates if necessary.
- *Tacit knowledge.* Tacit knowledge is the type of knowledge that individuals possess but find difficult to articulate, codify, and transfer. A classic example is offered by athletes who, when asked about the reasons for a specific decision during the game, often refer to instinct—an instinct that is developed through years of practice and handling of similar game situations but, as such, is hard to express in words and convey to others.

The above distinction is important because a firm that engages in knowledge management will find it easier to handle explicit rather than tacit knowledge. Whether explicit or tacit, however, knowledge is increasingly considered a critical asset for modern organizations and, as such, needs to be protected and proactively managed. Knowledge enables a firm to interpret environmental signals, process these inputs, and identify and implement appropriate responses.

Knowledge Management: Definition

Given the increasing importance assigned to knowledge assets, the last decade has seen growing attention to their active management. It is perhaps no coincidence that knowledge management became a full-fledged business trend in the mid-1990s, seemingly in response to the realization that the downsizing and "delayering" that followed the rise to prominence of business process reengineering engendered significant loss of organizational knowledge. As a consequence, business leaders—aided by consulting firms—concluded that institutional systems needed to be developed to preserve and communicate organizational knowledge in the face of change and over time.

The term *knowledge management* refers to the set of activities and processes used to create, codify, gather, and disseminate knowledge within the organization. The challenge is best articulated by the chief knowledge officer of a large, multinational consulting organization: "We have 80,000 people scattered around the world that need information to do their jobs effectively. The information they need is too difficult to find and, even if they do find it, it is often inaccurate."[16] Thus knowledge management is the

---

16. Leidner, D. E. (2006), The ongoing challenges of knowledge management initiatives, *Cutter Benchmark Review,* 6(3), 5–12.

set of activities and processes that an organization like this enacts to manage the wealth of knowledge it possesses and to ensure that it is properly safeguarded and put to use to help the firm achieve its objectives.

Information technology has featured prominently in knowledge management initiatives since the inception of this trend, giving rise to a class of applications known as knowledge management systems. However, no single software application can enable a firm to successfully implement a knowledge management initiative. Rather, a number of technologies are used in concert to enable the various aspects of a knowledge management initiative: creating, capturing and storing, and disseminating knowledge.

Creating Knowledge   Knowledge creation is the first phase in any knowledge management initiative. In this phase, the organization's employees generate new information, devise novel solutions to handle existing problems, and identify new explanations for recurrent events. Such new knowledge is potentially very valuable to others in the organization who may be facing similar problems.

Consider, for example, the genesis of the now ubiquitous "to-go" service at your local casual dining chain (e.g., Chili's Bar and Grill). A restaurant manager at Outback Steakhouse noticed a group of his customers opting not to wait for a table in the long line of people ahead of them. Rather, they would order their food from the bar and then set up a makeshift dining table in the bed of their pickup truck. Identifying an opportunity for increased sales to customers willing to trade off eating on the premises for speed, he set up a separate pickup area and began to promote the take-out service. When corporate saw what he was doing, it formalized the program and encouraged all restaurant managers to establish separate take-out operations. In many franchises, the take-out area is now a brand standard. This case exemplifies the potential far-reaching impact of locally developed knowledge.

Capturing and Storing Knowledge   The main objective of a knowledge management initiative is to consciously compile and use knowledge. The process of capturing and storing knowledge enables the organization to codify new knowledge and maintain an organizational memory. While this process may sound trivial at first glance, you need only imagine the multiple forms that organizational knowledge can take (e.g., paper documents, computer files, hallway conversations, interactions with customers, images, videos) to realize the complexity of the challenge. More insidiously, it is critical that the firm be able to create a culture that values knowledge and knowledge sharing in order to ensure that the firm's employees are willing to engage in knowledge management activities—activities that often do not have immediate and measurable impacts on the firm or individual performance.

Knowledge repositories and content management systems (CMSs) feature prominently among the technologies used to capture and store knowledge. A *knowledge repository* is a central location and search point for relevant knowledge. However, as the popularity of such repositories increases, so too does the volume of knowledge. And as the volume of knowledge increases, so too does the difficulty of finding high-quality, relevant information to address a specific problem. A CMS offers a partial solution to this. A CMS is a software program designed to organize and facilitate access to digital content such as text, pictures, and video.

Disseminating Knowledge   Knowledge dissemination is the last phase in a knowledge management initiative. It is at this stage that the investments made in knowledge creation and storage pay off. When knowledge is available in a format that is quickly searchable and readily usable for those employees confronted with a new problem, dramatic improvements in effectiveness and efficiency can be achieved.

Business Intelligence

Organizations have been managing data and information since the beginning of organized social life. You can imagine traders in Asia Minor keeping records of inventory and sales in 3000 B.C. and even before. Consider ancient Rome as a more recent example. The provinces would have to keep detailed records to account for taxes to be paid to the emperor. With the emergence of computerized information systems, databases took center stage. In technical parlance, a *database* is a self-describing collection of related records. Modern organizations manage their databases using a *database management*

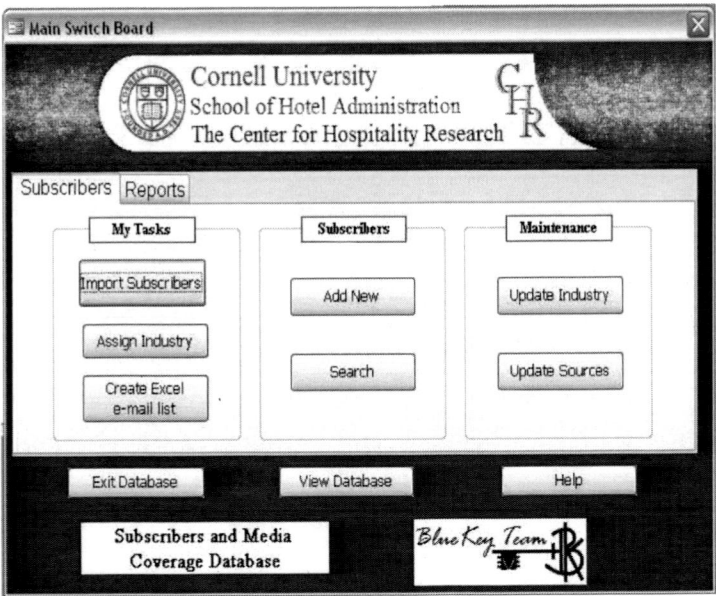

FIGURE 3.19. MS Access database application

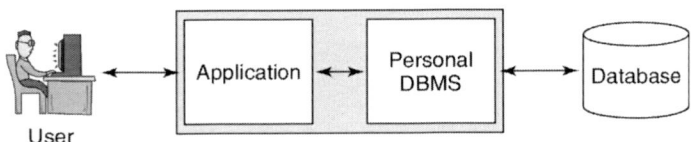

FIGURE 3.20. Individual application and DBMS

system (DBMS)—the software program (or collection of programs) that enables and controls access to the database. A DBMS equips a database administrator with the tools to manage the data (e.g., protect the data through authentication, schedule backups) and enables application/data independence—that is, when using a DBMS, applications need not store the data themselves but rather issue requests to the DBMS. The database can therefore be shared among multiple applications, and upgrades to one of the applications or the database itself can be made independently.

You are perhaps most familiar with personal DBMSs, such as Microsoft Access, that allow individuals or small groups to create and manage relatively small databases (Figure 3.19). Such a system can be confusing because typically it embeds both the DBMS and the database applications (Figure 3.20).

Now consider a large organization—say, Sabre Holdings Corporation, the parent company of Travelocity, Sabre Travel Network, and Sabre Airline Solutions. Sabre manages what at one point in time was the second largest computer system in the United States. The Sabre systems are anchored by a database that supports a huge number of users, ranging from travel agents and individuals seeking to make airline and hotel reservations, to airline check-in agents issuing boarding passes and seat assignments, to airline employees routing planes and managing their maintenance schedules. The Sabre database was once estimated to perform 8,000 transactions per second! For such large operations, and for much smaller ones like grocery stores, eCommerce websites, and the like, you will need a multiuser industrial-strength DBMS (e.g., Oracle Database 11g). A set of separate database applications makes requests to the DBMS (Figure 3.21).

While databases have been a staple of organizations' operations since their inception, data have only recently gained widespread popularity as a critical organizational resource. Referring back to the IS cycle discussed earlier, you will note that each of the examples described up to this point focuses on the

FIGURE 3.21. Multiuser database structure

first stage: handling the present. In other words, up to this point, we have only described transactional database applications.

As we described in Chapter 1, the declining cost of computing and storage, along with the increasing interconnectivity of computing devices, has given modern organizations access to more data and information than ever before. The business opportunities associated with this wealth of available information have spurred the emergence of the BI phenomenon.

Business Intelligence: Definition

Business intelligence is one of the most recent buzzwords in a long tradition of confusing lingo associated with business computing. Yet, as with many of the acronyms and jargon in business computing, it is intuitively simple when stripped to its core. Intelligence, in the connotation used—for example, in the term *Central Intelligence Agency*—represents the ability to gather and make sense of information in a given area of interest. In the case of the CIA, it is enemies and their behavior. Business intelligence is therefore the ability to gather and make sense of information about your business. It encompasses the set of techniques, processes, and technologies designed to enable managers to gain a superior insight into and understanding of their business and thus make better decisions (Figure 3.23).

Consider the example of Anheuser-Busch Inc., the parent company of beer brands such as Budweiser and Michelob. Anheuser-Busch's distributors carry handheld devices, rather than the traditional clipboard, when they visit the stores they supply. They use the device to take orders but also to gather data about competitors' products and strategy (e.g., pricing, placement, promotions). The data are immediately uploaded to Anheuser-Busch's data warehouse, where they are joined with demographic, marketing, and other external data to become available for analyses using an application called BudNet. Mapped to the IS cycle, this application shows how data progresses through it, from collection as orders are taken (handling the present), to long-term storage in the data warehouse (remembering the past), to employment for analytical purposes (preparing for the future; Figure 3.22).

As the example above shows, business intelligence encompasses transaction processing, since these transaction processing systems generate the data. However, the defining characteristic of business intelligence is a conscious focus on the analysis of the data generated.

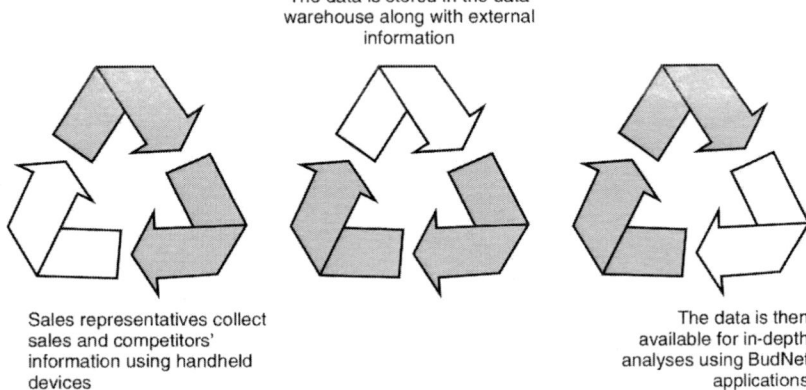

The data is stored in the data warehouse along with external information

Sales representatives collect sales and competitors' information using handheld devices

The data is then available for in-depth analyses using BudNet applications

FIGURE 3.22. Business intelligence at Anheuser-Busch Inc.

Components of the Business Intelligence Infrastructure

From our definition of business intelligence, it is clear that BI is not a technology or set of technologies. In fact, as was the case in the Anheuser-Busch example, in order to engage in business intelligence, the firm must develop an information system paying particular attention to each of the four components (see Chapter 2). Yet given the sheer volume of data and information that a firm needs to manage as part of its BI initiatives, IT is a critical component. As a consequence, business intelligence applications now represent a thriving segment of the software industry.

We use the term *business intelligence infrastructure* to refer to the set of applications and technologies designed to create, manage, and analyze large repositories of data in an effort to extract value from them. Beyond the transaction processing systems that generate the needed data, the main components of a BI infrastructure are data warehouses, data marts, query and reporting tools, online analytical processing (OLAP), and data mining.

Data Warehouse A data warehouse, or, more precisely, an enterprise data warehouse, is a data repository that collects and consolidates data from multiple source systems, both internal to the organization and external, with the purpose of enabling analysis. A data warehouse typically has the following characteristics:

- *Large in size.* Data warehouses easily span into the scale of terabytes—the rough equivalent of all the content of an academic library.
- *Large in scope.* Data warehouses draw information from a wide variety of source systems.
- *Enabling data integration.* Data warehouses compile and collect data from multiple source systems, ensuring that data are accurate and current.
- *Designed for analytics.* The defining characteristic of a data warehouse, what makes it different from a large transactional database, is its focus on analysis and analytics.

A data warehouse is typically the cornerstone of a BI infrastructure, but the repository is only valuable insomuch as the data it contains are accurate—a condition that IT professionals like to call GIGO, or garbage in, garbage out. Thus the primary driver of the complexity and cost of building a data warehouse is the need to gather and clean the data to be compiled—the extracting, transforming, loading (ETL) process, as it is known. What may appear to be a trivial process at first glance is in fact a lengthy and complex undertaking designed to ensure that redundancy, data integrity violations, and inconsistencies are kept to a minimum.

As mentioned above, a data warehouse is optimized for analysis. While traditional transactional databases enable analysis and reporting, their structure is optimized for fast data retrieval at the atomic level. For example, if you asked a gate agent to change your seat assignment as prepared to board an American Airlines flight, she would have to retrieve your individual record, make the change, and store it before issuing the new boarding pass. Such a transaction is focused on the present, accesses one record, and addresses a specific item in the record (Table 3.6).

Now consider the example of Anheuser-Busch. The firm is not interested in any one of its target customers individually (i.e., how much beer you purchase). Rather, it focuses on large groups of individuals who share some characteristics in an effort to identify patterns and draw conclusions about their collective behavior (i.e., how much, when, and how people in your neighborhood purchase a given brand of beer). Such transactions seek to access multiple (i.e., thousands of) historical records and aggregate them on several dimensions of interest (Table 3.6).

While such aggregation is possible with transactional databases and indeed it is performed every day in organizations to extract reports, as the size of the database grows, aggregating data in transactional databases can put a lot of strain on the system. There are situations where, beyond a certain size, the database will require more than 24 hours to create a report—clearly negating the possibility of daily analysis.

Using techniques such as multidimensional representations and preaggregation, an analytical database is optimized for enabling complex querying and the analysis of large amounts of data with a response time of a few seconds. For example, using OLAP tools (described below) and an analytical database, a bank analyst would be able to identify which accounts are currently overdue, organizing the results by branch, type of loan, customer type, and so on. What's more, the analyst can expect the results within a few seconds of issuing the query.

Data Mart   A data mart is a scaled-down version of a data warehouse that focuses on the needs of a specific audience. Like a data warehouse, a data mart is a repository built explicitly to enable analysis. Unlike a data warehouse, though, a data mart is designed for the specific needs of a narrowly defined community of knowledge workers (e.g., marketing group, accountants). The advantages of a data mart over a data warehouse are that the data mart is smaller in scope, and thus easier to build, and uses audience-specific data classifications and language. In very large organizations that have already created an enterprise data warehouse, data marts may be introduced to simplify and focus analysis by a department or function.

In many cases, a firm will develop data marts in order to take an incremental approach to its BI strategy. In this case, the firm will introduce one or more data marts before creating a data warehouse. These early data marts focus on areas that offer the highest potential return on the investment in data analysis. This incremental strategy can help generate buy-in from senior executives and momentum behind business intelligence initiatives. The drawback of this approach is that a proliferation of data marts creates the potential for replicating the problem that centralized data storage was designed to eliminate—data redundancy and lack of data consolidation.

Online Analytical Processing   The term *online analytical processing* (OLAP) refers to a class of software programs that enables a knowledge worker to easily and selectively extract and view data from analytical databases. The defining characteristic of OLAP tools is that they are user driven. In other words, an analyst must issue a query that specifies what data items the user is interested in. Note

Table 3.6. Transactional versus analytical databases

Transactional database	Analytical database
Atomic level	Aggregate level
Current data	Historical data
Individual record access	Multiple record access

that OLAP users need not be IT specialists; in fact, if you elect to become an analyst for a financial institution or a marketing organization, you stand a very good chance of using OLAP tools yourself.

For instance, as an analyst for Spalding, the sports equipment maker, you may be interested in viewing all the beach ball products sold in southern Spain in the month of July and comparing revenue figures from these items with those for the same products in September in the same location and/or in the south of France during the same period. The revolutionary aspect of OLAP is that you would no longer need to request such data from the IT department and wait for them to design ad hoc queries for you. Rather, you can perform the analysis on your own and receive an immediate response employing a user-friendly application.

Data Mining   Data mining is the process of automatically discovering nonobvious relationships in large databases. The recent popularity of data mining is due to the availability of powerful computer systems that can quickly search through large volumes of data contained in data warehouses. A recent example of the power of data mining is offered by Walmart, a company that built its data warehouse in the early 1990s. Using years of compiled data, Walmart analysts recently sought to identify what the best-selling items were in areas under threat of an approaching hurricane. Much to everyone's surprise, the most important item needed to prepare for a hurricane was not water, wood, or nails. It wasn't even beer, a perennial favorite in audiences confronted with this question. In fact, Walmart found that strawberry Pop-Tarts were the top sellers! While it is relatively easy to make sense of this finding once we are told about it (i.e., Pop-Tarts have a long shelf life, they need not be cooked, kids like them), it is a nonobvious and largely unexpected finding beforehand.

Like OLAP tools, data mining is used to analyze historical information. Unlike OLAP, though, data mining is more akin to a brute force approach, enabling the software to identify significant patterns by analyzing all possible combinations rather than relying on an analyst to structure a specific query. Of course, analysts are still heavily involved in data mining, as they must interpret the results. Yet, as in the Walmart example, data mining is used to seek unexpected (i.e., nonobvious) relationships among data items. The following is a list of possible patterns a data mining application may identify:

- *Associations.* Associations occur when one event can be correlated to another event (e.g., beer purchases are highly associated with chips purchases in the week leading up to the Super Bowl).
- *Sequences.* Sequences occur when one event leads to another subsequent event (e.g., a rug purchase is followed by a purchase of curtains).
- *Anomalies.* Anomalies occur when data deviate from an expected pattern (e.g., when a credit card is used in a physical store within 1 hour, one in Grenoble, France, and the other in Baton Rouge, Louisiana).
- *Classification.* Classification occurs when categories are generated from the data (e.g., customer profiles based on historical spending).
- *Forecasting.* Forecasting occurs when patterns in the data can be extrapolated to predict future events (e.g., sales forecast based on weather patterns).

The Evolution of Business Intelligence

At its core, business intelligence is about decision making and managing change. As such, organizations (and the vendors serving their needs) are constantly seeking ways to improve the timeliness of decision-making support and its capillarity. For this reason, business intelligence trends include the following:

- *Real-time BI.* Real-time BI, also called business activity monitoring, is a business intelligence approach focused on real-time situation awareness through the constant monitoring of critical business performance indicators based on event-driven sources of data.
- *Mobile BI.* With the rapidly increasing mobility of the workforce and the increasing widespread use of mobile devices in the organization, BI vendors have been trying to bring decision analysis tools to users anywhere they may need them. New form factors, such as powerful smartphones and tablets, have renewed organizations' interest in mobile BI.

From Business Intelligence to Big Data

Traditionally, BI expert have worked to answer question based on specific domain knowledge. BI systems were conceived to deliver an accurate representation of business conditions supporting executives' decision making. Armed with a deductive approach, they generally looked at the data on the basis of predefined models and precisely specified questions.

Information systems scholars generally demarcated clearly the difference among data, information, and knowledge—terms that are colloquially used as substitutes:

- *Data* is defined as codified raw facts—events, occurrences, or descriptions coded as letters and numbers and stored, increasingly, by way of digital devices.
- *Information* is defined as data in context. In other words, data become information when they have been given meaning and can therefore be interpreted by individual users or machines. It follows, then, that information is audience dependent; one person's data are another person's information.
- *Knowledge* is the capacity to identify required problem-related information and interpret it (Figure 3.23).

Reports and dashboards are examples of institutionalized decision models with the aim of generating structured and repeatable analyses. Dashboards give managers a convenient and condensed view of key business metrics, support the organization in setting goals, and monitor achievements.

Consider this example that one of us worked on. A large IT service company needed to design an integrative dashboard for measuring service performance and customer satisfaction. They wanted to complement the "hard" IT service and quality metrics (i.e., system up-time, help desk response satisfaction) with "soft" metrics assessed through surveys. Account managers were then given a scorecard dashboard to monitor and proactively take remedial action. At the base of the dashboard was a service-level measurement model we developed and tested. This is a typical *deductive* approach: previous knowledge is used to select the data and develop the algorithms necessary to extract the relevant information. It requires an a priori understanding (or the perception of such understanding) of the structure of the data, the information needed, and the decisions to be made.

But what can we do when the aim is to discover new knowledge? The obvious method would be to manually analyze and interpret the data. For example, a financial analyst could look into economic data to spot trends, make recommendations, and eventually write reports. This would be an *inductive* approach: knowledge (e.g., a new trend, a business opportunity) is derived from the data and the analysis of information. Today, interest in advanced analytics comes from the increasing capacity of IT systems to analyze data in order to discover meaningful patterns.

The pervasiveness of digital technologies and the ubiquity of the Internet allow organizations to collect and store increasing amounts of data—probably more data than they can make use of. This

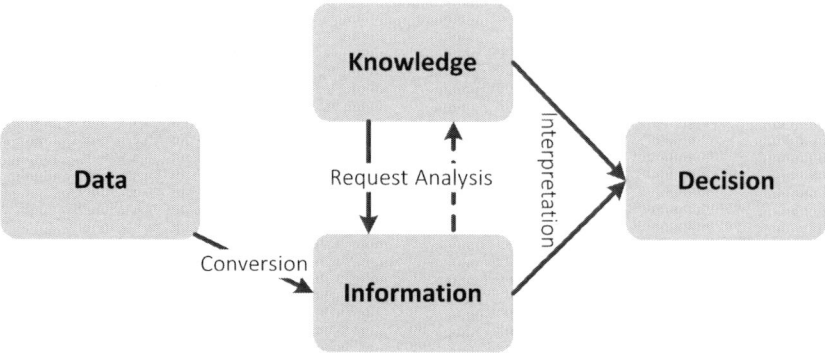

FIGURE 3.23. The relationship between data, information, and knowledge

phenomenon is generally called *big data*. The hype about big data is inescapable these days. While it is unclear what the exact genesis of the term, by some accounts,[17] it was first used in the IT industry in the mid-1990s during a lunch conversation at Silicon Graphics—now SGI. At the time, the Milpitas, California–based firm was the leading authority in computer graphics and high-performance computing and a leading supplier for Hollywood studios and NASA. The term was used to convey effectively the idea that a new IT infrastructure was emerging to cope with the growth of both data storage and processing needs. As it often happens in IT, the idea slowly grew in labs and IT shops, then caught the attention of early adopters pushing the limits of their current infrastructure, and at one point burst onto the mainstream business scene. Today, big data is an established buzzword discussed in mainstream business publications, IT vendors offer big data products, and consultants host conferences on the subject.

The current established definition of big data is credited to Doug Laney, a consultant with the IT advisory firm the META Group, who wrote a two-page 2001 report outlining emerging trends for the next five years.[18] The report was organized along three lines of data evolution: volume, variety, and velocity (3V). In 2001, there were no smartphones or social media. Web 2.0 was years in the future, and the main focus was on how to handle the proliferation of business channels brought about by the emerging eCommerce trend. Laney's report was written from a pure BI perspective, but the categorization struck a chord and became, years later, the standard way to discuss the evolution of the big data phenomenon:

- *Volume* is the amount of digital data that organizations have to store and manage. This dimension is best thought of as a trend rather than a threshold. It is not clear what would constitute "big data volume"—is it terabytes, petabytes, exabytes? What is clear, however, is that organizations have to manage increasing amounts of data (see Chapter 1) and that the new data storage architectures are required to do so. As an example, YouTube's own statistics showed that in 2015, its one billion users uploaded a total of 300 hours of video footage . . . per minute![19]
- *Velocity* is the speed of creation and use of new digital data. This dimension relates to the need to gather, process, and communicate information in real time. New data sources like sensors, RFID tag readers, video streams, clickstreams, and tweets—to just cite some of them—require modern IT architectures capable of handling streaming data. By contrast, traditional data warehousing environments were designed for batch processing and the support of online analytical processing within the predetermined confines of internal organizational data. Data velocity enables firms to sense and respond to relevant events (e.g., a market change, a competitor's move) and fuel the trend of accelerated business operations that proprietary networks created in the 1980s and the Internet consolidated in the late 1990s and early 2000s.
- *Variety* is the kind of digital data that organizations have to store and manage. You can roughly think about variety in terms of data types (e.g., text, image, video, sensor readings). More important, you should think about variety in terms of the structure of the data. If BI was the realm of structured data (i.e., data that is configured within a predefined organizing schema), a big data infrastructure must handle unexpected formats and "schema-less" data. A defining characteristic of the big data paradigm is that both the problem definition and the data model are (often) not completely known in advance.

As you can see from the above discussion, big data is not just a kind of analytics. You can think of big data as the continuation of the trends we discussed in Chapter 1. However, you should recognize

---

17. Lohr, Steve (2013, February 2), The origins of "big data": An etymological detective story, *The New York Times*, retrieved from http://bits.blogs.nytimes.com/2013/02/01/the-origins-of-big-data-an-etymological-detective-story

18. Laney, D. (2001, February 6), 3D data management: Controlling data volume, velocity and variety, *Application delivery strategies: META Group*.

19. YouTube Statistics (n.d.), *YouTube*, retrieved August 21, 2015, from https://www.youtube.com/yt/press/statistics.html

that there is a discontinuity in the trend—one that warrants our categorizing it as a new era. The volume, velocity, and variety of today's data require organizations to use new technology and a new management paradigm. A traditional BI architecture cannot cope with this change.

Big Data: Technology

We are in the midst of the big data era: both technology and management practices are evolving rapidly. However, there are some consolidated technologies and practices that form the cornerstone of an organization's big data infrastructure. Apache Hadoop is the foremost example. First devised at Yahoo! Corporation in 2005 for managing search engine data, today it is an open source framework for distributed storage and distributed processing by the Apache Software Foundation. The defining characteristics of Hadoop are the Hadoop Distributed File System (HDFS) and the MapReduce processing paradigm. It is based on the view that in the big data environment, code should move to the data and processing should occur in place (known as data locality), instead of the traditional paradigm of data being moved to the processing unit. While parallel and distributed processing are concepts that predate the big data challenge, the HDFS leverages thousands of commodity servers (Figure 3.24)[20] managing the distribution of processing, the consolidation of results, and fault tolerance procedures when servers fail. Hadoop splits files into large blocks onto the commodity servers and maintains an inventory of such data.

When processing is required, the MapReduce process manages the transfer of packaged code to the nodes so that the data they already house can be processed in place. It is not our objective for you to be an expert Hadoop programmer, but you should intuitively understand the appeal of this approach over moving massive amounts of data to be processed. As with any immature technology, Hadoop and similar approaches hold great promise, but implementation in the field is fraught with challenges. The technology infrastructure enabling the big data era is evolving rapidly, and we discuss many of the emerging trends in Chapter 12.

Customer Relationship Management

Customer relationship management (CRM) has been a dominant business trend over the last decade and a half and, like enterprise systems, is still receiving substantial attention. CRM finds its roots in the proliferation of customer data and the efforts of modern business organizations to differentiate themselves through customer service.

As with many of the business technology trends that preceded it, CRM has been co-opted by vendors, consulting firms, and various other pundits, and the term has increasingly lost a precise meaning. We define *customer relationship management* as a strategic orientation that calls for iterative processes designed to turn customer data into customer relationships through active use

FIGURE 3.24. Rack of commodity servers
Photo by D Coetzee / CC BY 1.0

---

20. Commodity servers are inexpensive standardized computers that can be easily replaced and swapped from the racks when they fail.

of, and learning from, the information collected. Thus the defining characteristics of CRM are the following:

- CRM is a strategic initiative, not a technology. Information technology is an essential enabler of all but the smallest CRM initiatives.
- CRM relies on customer personal and transactional data and is designed to help the firm learn about customers.
- The ultimate objective of a CRM initiative is to help the firm use customer data to make inferences about customer behaviors, needs, and value to the firm so as to increase its profitability.

Aspects of CRM

A CRM strategy needs to encompass front-office functionalities—termed *operational CRM*—which determine how the firm interacts with customers to create and maintain the relationship. Today, customers in most industries expect to be able to interact with firms through a multiplicity of touchpoints, such as a firm's website, stores, call center, and so on. Moreover, modern firms are increasingly expected to be able to provide consistency across these proliferating touchpoints and communication channels. As a consequence, a priority for organizations today is the integration of the transactional databases that have historically supported the different channels into one operational data store (Figure 3.25).

A CRM strategy requires that the organization be able to actively manage and strengthen its relationships with profitable customers while achieving efficiencies with (and sometimes firing!) less profitable ones. This level of precision and granularity of interactions with customers requires substantial data analysis—analytical CRM.

It should be clear at this point why it is nonsensical to be talking about a CRM system as a technology product that, once installed, allegedly enables the firm to establish and maintain relationships with customers. CRM is a highly customizable strategic initiative that will differ dramatically between

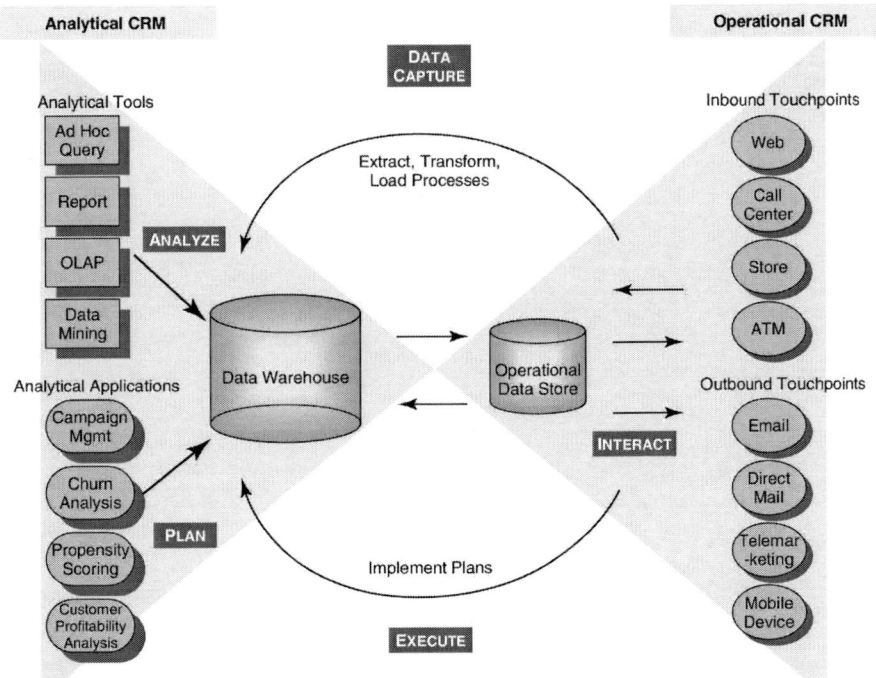

FIGURE 3.25. Example of a CRM infrastructure
Source: Goodhue, D. L, Wixom, B. H., & Watson, H. J. (2002), Realizing business benefits through CRM: Hitting the right target in the right way, *MIS Quarterly Executive*, pp. 79–94

companies. Thus, as with business intelligence, we need to talk about a CRM infrastructure as the collection of applications that support and enable the specific aspects of the firm's CRM strategy.

The Limitations of CRM

CRM is an intuitively appealing concept, but it may engender the very seed of its demise. If this is the case, companies that make it a cornerstone of their strategy may in turn be setting themselves up for failure.

CRM Is Firm Centered   One of the main limitations of current CRM approaches is that a firm's CRM strategy only relies on transactional and behavioral customer data pertaining to the interactions of the customer with the firm. Consider what is probably the most celebrated example of CRM strategy: Amazon.com's collaborative filtering initiative. When a returning customer logs on to the Amazon website, he is personally greeted and receives suggestions based on prior purchases. However, as good as the Amazon CRM initiative is, there are some problems. First, not all the products that customers purchase are for themselves; they also purchase gifts. Second, not all the products customers buy are for the same purpose; we may purchase items for work or leisure. Amazon has attempted to account for these potential problems by asking customers to qualify their purchases (i.e., shifting the burden of precise data collection to customers). Third, and most important, Amazon only knows customers' transactions with Amazon. Yet your music library may include songs you downloaded from iTunes or music directly streamed from Spotify or Deezer, and you may have purchased items from Amazon's competitors—online and in physical stores.

This limitation is rooted in the fact that the firm has access only to transactions and behavioral data that are generated in the interaction between its customers and itself. Indeed, the firm can buy demographic and other personal data about customers from companies such as Acxiom and LexisNexis, but it can't obtain customers' transactional data from competitors. Under these circumstances, the picture that the firm creates of each customer is irremediably partial, and drawing accurate inferences or producing good advice based on it is difficult at best and impossible at worst.

CRM Has Limited Predictive Ability   Even those organizations that have exclusive relationships with their customers (i.e., 100% wallet share) still face a challenge. Some events are unforeseeable and only the customer knows about their occurrence or future plans about them. Think of customers who have recently had a baby, purchased a house, gotten divorced, or been involved in a big accident. As good as the firm's inference systems may be, they rely on historical data and patterns, and unless the customer volunteers information about life-changing events, they will typically fall short on accuracy. While there are many areas, industries, and organizations that have benefited and will continue to benefit greatly from their CRM strategy, the example above highlights an endemic problem. To the extent that the objective of a CRM strategy is personalization, inference, consultation, and advice, the battle may be an uphill one and the end result not as comprehensive as hoped.

Best-of-Breed Integration

Organizations have implemented enterprise systems and integrated supply chain management applications in response to the recent emergence of the integration imperative. Both of these solutions rely on the use of a single-vendor, highly integrated, modular software program that limits the firm's flexibility. While a firm can install a subset of ES modules and use multiple vendors, this approach reduces the advantages offered by the package. Thus, in order to preserve integration, the firm typically will install modules that are not considered the best for the firm's needs.

Recognizing these limitations, a competing approach, known as best-of-breed, emerged over time. The best-of-breed approach is designed to enable the firm to retain a high degree of flexibility with respect to the applications it decides to adopt while still being able to achieve tight integration among them. As the term suggests, best-of-breed allows the firm to choose the module or application that best suits its information processing needs. As such, the best-of-breed approach enables a firm to achieve integration using applications from different vendors.

Enterprise Application Integration (EAI)

The best-of-breed approach is enabled by a new integration paradigm that focuses not on the applications to be integrated but on the linkages among them. Integration of separate systems has been traditionally achieved with point-to-point connections called interfaces. This approach engenders significant limitations as the number of interfaces grows dramatically with the number of applications that need to be connected—that is, the number of bilateral interfaces needed to connect n systems is $n(n-1)/2$ (i.e., 3 systems, 3 interfaces; 5 systems, 10 interfaces; 10 systems, 45 interfaces; and so on). Such an approach can quickly result in a messy infrastructure that is difficult and costly to maintain (Figure 3.26). Note that any time a change is made to one system, all interfaces that connect to it will need to be modified.

In order to achieve the promise of best-of-breed integration without the limitations of bilateral interfaces, the enterprise application integration (EAI) approach has recently emerged. EAI consists of "rearchitecting" existing programs so that an intermediate layer, termed *middleware*, is developed between the applications and databases (Figure 3.27). The existing applications are designed to make calls to the middleware layer rather than to one another, as with bilateral interfaces. Integrating applications and databases in this fashion provides the firm with the highest degree of flexibility when selecting applications and the ability to swap them independently when upgrades are needed.

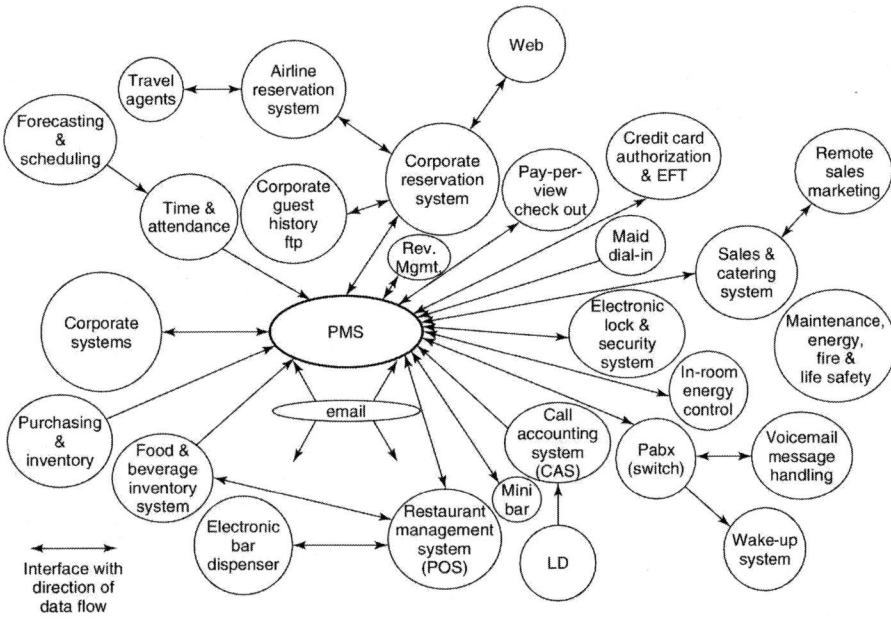

FIGURE 3.26. Best-of-breed infrastructure of a hotel

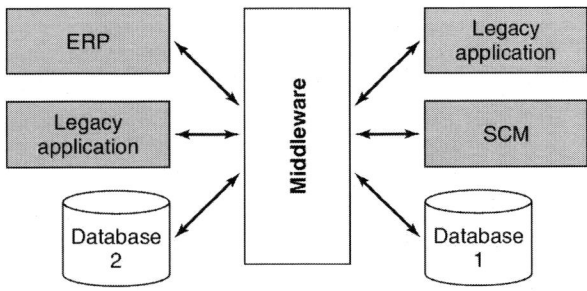

FIGURE 3.27. The EAI approach

The EAI approach also streamlines the maintenance process because changes to an application will not affect all the interfaces connected to it. Rather, as long as each application is able to make requests to and receive requests from the middleware layer, no other application needs to be modified.

Ultimate Flexibility: Service-Oriented Architecture

Business organizations are under constant pressure to become increasingly flexible and agile in order to respond to rapidly evolving customer needs and accelerating competition. IT professionals and the software industry have seized the opportunity to enable such increasing levels of agility and flexibility. The dominant solution goes under the broad label of service-oriented architecture (SOA).

SOA is a software design perspective focused on reusability of software components, interoperability, and ongoing optimization of business processes. SOA works by using standards to make independent services available on a network. These services, sometimes referred to as web services, are made available as components to be accessed and used by applications without knowledge of their underlying design or structure. In other words, SOA enables the rapid creation of applications by the combination of prebuilt services.

The SOA approach is different from EAI, even though it conceptually builds on the same ideas. EAI calls for the integration of separate best-of-breed applications through middleware. With SOA, the applications themselves, as well as the manner in which they communicate, are built using separate but interoperable components that can be modified and combined depending on the characteristics of the business process they are designed to support.

Integration: Concluding Remarks

Like many business and organizational trends that you will find yourself assessing in your position as a general or functional manager, the integration imperative has created its share of hype and buzz. As you have learned, there are a number of approaches to achieving integration, through either one solution or a blend of solutions, and the scope of the integration effort can vary significantly. While integration remains one of the most often cited business imperatives, it is, of course, no panacea; more integration is not necessarily better or advisable. Rather, the integration trend engenders trade-offs that need to be evaluated.

Benefits of Integration   An organization undertakes integration efforts because they offer a number of benefits. First and foremost, integration promises a drastic reduction in duplication of efforts and redundancy of operations. For example, once a firm integrates its receiving and inventory applications, it no longer needs data to be keyed into separate databases multiple times. This reduces not only direct costs but also the potential for errors and inconsistencies leading to further expenditures of time and money. Second, integration offers advantages in terms of access to information, speed, and response time. It also serves to increase coordination across organizational units and to enforce standardization.

Drawbacks of Integration   The advantages mentioned above come at a cost, however. Aside from the actual expense of achieving integration itself, successful integration requires that organizations bear a number of coordination costs that the decentralization movement was designed to eliminate in the first place. While modern information technology has helped reduce such costs, many of them are still significant. Let's return to the General Mills and Land O'Lakes example. Both firms clearly benefited from the integration of their logistics and distribution processes. Now, however, each firm has to coordinate with the other to ensure that the right products are warehoused and ready to go according to the agreed-upon schedule.

Moreover, the standardization advantages mentioned above also bring about limitations of flexibility that are all the more relevant for larger firms with unique local operations. With highly integrated operations, the need for change in a business unit or function must be weighed against the needs of the other units and the costs that they will have to bear to accommodate the change.

Consider the example of Barnes & Noble, which originally established its online retail unit as a separate organization. While customers may demand cross-channel integration between the physical stores and the web, this level of integration requires compromises between the units involved—a level of coordination that is harder to muster the more independently the units are run (e.g., separate profit and loss statements). For example, ensuring that a book purchased online can be returned to a store requires stores to be willing to collect and resell books that they otherwise might not carry due to a lack of sufficient local demand.

Cloud Computing

Cloud computing, named after the icon traditionally used to diagram the telecommunication network (Figure 3.28), uses the Internet to pool IT resources. In other words, applications or computational or storage components—the building blocks of IT solutions—"reside online" and are accessed by clients through the Internet infrastructure.

Consider Dropbox, a service you surely have used in the past. Dropbox provides users with cloud storage capacity to back up, store, and share files. Until recently, Dropbox was running and offering its service as a cloud solution based on Amazon's infrastructure—yes, the same Amazon that sells books! Streaming services like Netflix or Spotify, social services like Reddit, or companies like Airbnb are all running on Amazon's servers.[21]

But what's all the hype? How is cloud computing different from the venerable concept of data centers that were outsourced to large IT providers like EDS or IBM? What is unique about the modern cloud computing approach is the notion that the utilization of, and payment for, the resources used by the organization is dynamic and agile. By agile, we mean that an organization that sees a growing demand for its applications can scale the service relatively rapidly—major infrastructure providers suggest that they can scale their service in a matter of minutes. Moreover, the scalability is also flexible, allowing customers to acquire different services, like storage or processing capacity. This is significantly different from what happens in owned or outsourced data centers, where dedicated hardware is purchased for or assigned to the client and configured to run its applications.

The uniqueness of cloud computing is not only technical but also characterizes how the service is managed. A typical cloud computing provider adopts a utility billing model, whereby the user only pays for the usage of the service in a metered fashion—just like you pay for electricity, gas, and water as a function of your meter readings. Imagine a retailer's website after Christmas or the FIFA website a few days after the World Cup Finals. As demand for the company's application subsides and utilization drops, so does the cost of maintaining the service.

Cloud computing parlance is differentiated along the three main delivery modes: the application (SaaS), the platform (PaaS), and the infrastructure (IaaS) (see Figure 3.29).

Software as a service (SaaS) is when an application runs in the cloud. Salesforce, Gmail, and Dropbox are classic textbook examples of SaaS. Microsoft Office 365 is the SaaS version of the popular suite of personal productivity apps. The provider hosts the application in its data centers and the customer accesses the needed functionalities over a computer network. Thus, instead of licensing the application and requiring the customer to install it on his or her hardware, maintain it, and generally support it, in the SaaS model, the software vendor performs these tasks.

Platform as a service (PaaS) is when what is being rented from the provider is not a full-fledged application but rather a platform on which the client builds its own applications. In that case, you would be renting the use of hardware (i.e.,

FIGURE 3.28. Cloud icon typically used in computing

---

21. You can access some Amazon's customers' stories at https://aws.amazon.com/solutions/case-studies/, and you can establish a free account yourself at https://aws.amazon.com.

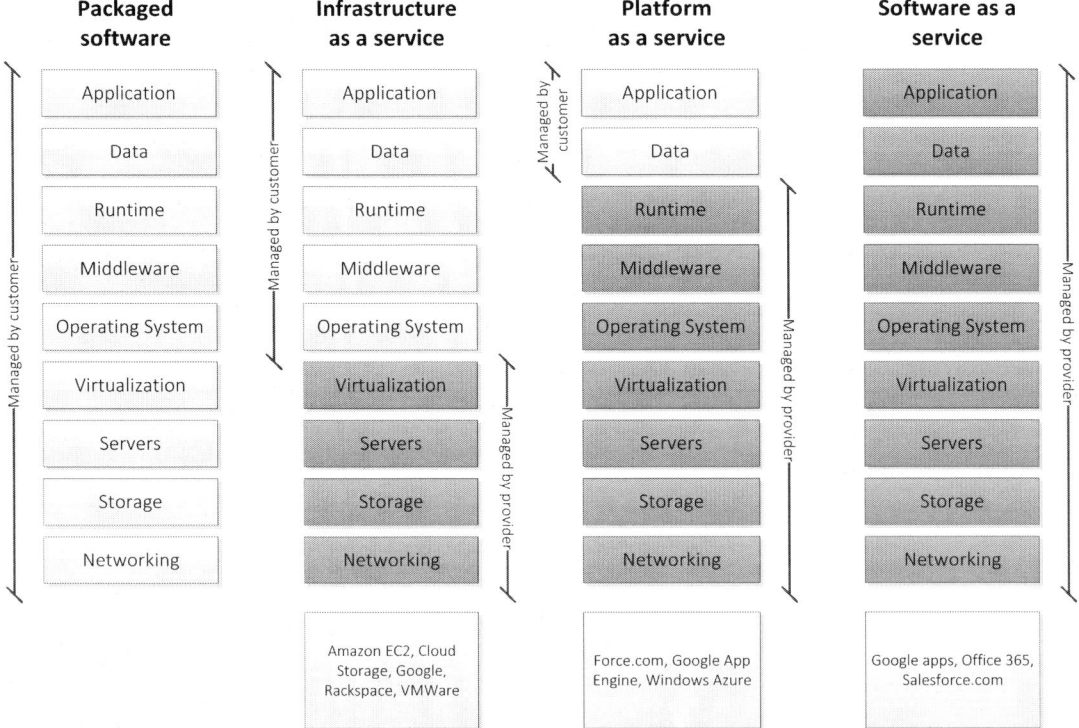

FIGURE 3.29. The elements of the Cloud: IaaS, PaaS, and SaaS
Source: Microsoft, Deploy Microsoft Dynamics AX 2012 R3 on Azure using Lifecycle Services [AX 2012], retrieved June 2015 from https://ax.help.dynamics.com/en/wiki/deploy-microsoft-dynamics-ax-2012-r3-on-azure-using-lifecycle-services-lcs/

the servers in a data center on which all this software runs) along with the functionalities of operating systems and utilities (i.e., storage, security, backup and recovery, application serving, and the like). This model is generally used for development, testing, and deployment of applications, as components are already in place. For example, companies can use the platforms components from Force.com—the developers' side of Salesforce.com—to create and deploy their own cloud applications.

Infrastructure as a service (IaaS) is the level closest to hardware. In this case, the client purchases the use of hardware functionality—in essence, computational power, storage capacity, and network connectivity. In the IaaS model, you rent just the virtualized hardware. All software—including the operating system, backup and recovery, and the like—are your responsibility. The IaaS provider takes care of the running and maintaining the infrastructure, for a fee. Like all other cloud models, IaaS platforms offer scalable resources that can be adjusted on demand. The Amazon service that powers Netflix and Airbnb, called Amazon Web Services (AWS), is another example.

Cloud Software Architectures

Cloud software architectures pertain to the way applications and software services are designed to run in the cloud. Consider a typical SaaS application, like Gmail. Each user has the impression that he or she is running a dedicated application, exactly like when you are using Outlook or any other e-mail client application on your computer. Users feel that they have exclusive access to all the applications features as well as their data. However, the underlying architecture could follow one of two approaches:

- *Single-tenant.* This is the traditional server hosting architecture where customers access their own dedicated software resources. While, strictly speaking, the hardware may be shared, through virtualization technologies, each (virtual) server is dedicated to a client and its users.

In the specific case of storage servers, the data are physically segregated in separate databases if the architecture is single-tenant.

- *Multitenant.* In a multitenant architecture, a single instance of the software serves all customers, and hardware resources are shared by all users. Despite users sharing the same application, their data are confined so that no other user can access them. However, the manner in which the data are segregated does not imply that each client has access to a separate database. In fact, in the case of multiple databases with the same structure (e.g., the client databases of different Salesforce.com users), the segregation is performed through the metadata while user data are comingled in one large database.

The multitenant SaaS approach, while significantly more complex to build, offers key advantages for both customers and providers when compared to more traditional approaches. Providers generally experience higher economies of scale for maintaining a single copy of the software and for sharing the same infrastructure among all users, thereby maximizing usage of resources. Customers enjoy the benefits of economies of scale, and their application is upgraded whenever a new version is released. Because every client is running the only copy of the application and database rather than separate instances, any improvement is immediately and automatically propagated to all users. While multitenancy sounds like one of those techie concerns that will quickly bore any executive or business manager, a minimal understanding of its characteristics, and clarity as to whether or not your vendor uses it, is a critical business concern. Multitenancy has significant implications for IT performance dimensions (e.g., deployment, scalability) that have direct impact on business performance dimensions (e.g., availability of service, customizability of the product, adaptability to customer needs).

Historical Context

Business Process Outsourcing
The idea of accessing software as a service provided by an outside firm is not new. The concept of business process outsourcing (BPO) has been around, on and off, since the mainframe era and the 1960s. In a BPO agreement, a client (say, the local independent convenience store) engages a provider to supply and manage a given business process (say, accounting and payroll).

In the traditional BPO approach, management at the convenience store would pass the provider the weekly time cards detailing hours worked by each employee as well as invoices from suppliers and cash register records. The BPO provider would feed this information into its accounting and payroll applications; compute accrued vacation, benefits, and tax withdrawals; and cut the checks for the employees. The provider would also be able to produce financial statements for the business and accounting reports. In this case, not only are the payroll and accounting software applications outsourced, but so too is the entire business process that they enable.

As the BPO model evolved over time, a number of other business processes became viable candidates for outsourcing. Today, they include accounting, human resources and payroll, call center operations, and the like.

Application Service Providers
With the emergence of the commercial Internet during the dot-com days in the mid-1990s, application service provision emerged on the wings of the slogan "the network is the computer." This slogan captured the idea that, with the availability of widespread, increasingly reliable, and cheap computer networks (i.e., the Internet), it would not matter much where computer processing happened—at the user's workstation, on the firm's premises, or somewhere else in cyberspace.

Application service provision (ASP) is a software delivery model where a provider hosts and manages a standard application—say, Microsoft Office—and enables clients to access it and use it over a computer network. This application is often purchased and licensed by the customer but managed and supported by the provider on its infrastructure. Note that the term *provider* here does not necessarily imply an external vendor. For example, a retail chain—say, Best Buy or Zara—may enable its shops to run the point-of-sale (POS) system directly from the chain's data centers using an ASP model instead of requiring each store to have a locally installed copy of the POS application. A defining feature of the ASP approach to software service provisioning is that each client will have access to a separate instance of the software application running on the vendor's remote servers. In the very early days of the ASP model, the provider would run an instance (i.e., a copy) of the application for each client on a separate server (i.e., hardware). Later, with the advent of *virtualization* techniques, whereby a physical server is able to run multiple, independent instances of a software environment, the ASP vendors began consolidating servers and running multiple instances of their client software on the same hardware. However, each client accessed a separate instance of the application, even when the same application was being provisioned.

The Cloud Today

The cloud market has greatly changed in the last few years. While the cloud computing concept has been around for some time, in 2013 firms were just starting to experiment heavily with it and develop growing confidence in the stability of the cloud approach and its providers. The focus was first on private cloud implementations—cloud computing architectures implemented within organizational boundaries.

Today, the situation has radically changed. Analysts agree that cloud services will sustain a two-digit year-over-year growth in the next few years (Figure 3.30). Cloud services are now mainstream components of the IT infrastructure, and the major software companies dominate the scene (Figure 3.31).

This growth is built on the cloud solutions' key advantages compared to on-premises implementations:[22]

- *Lower entry barriers.* Firms with limited investment capacity have access to dynamically priced enterprise-class IT resources, shifting IT costs from capital expenditures to operational expenditures. Start-ups can realize their IT project with initial investments an order of magnitude lower than in the past.
- *Faster innovation.* The immediate access to IT resources reduces time to market. Without an up-front investment, firms can deploy solutions faster, thereby facilitating innovation.
- *Higher scalability.* Solutions can easily scale and new IT resources can be allocated or reduced depending on the actual need.

Source: Cisco Global Cloud Index, 2013–2018

FIGURE 3.30. The evolution of Cloud platform delivery models
Cisco Systems Inc. (2014), *Cisco Global Cloud Index: Forecast and methodology 2013–2018*, p. 41, retrieved from http://www.cisco.com/c/en/us/solutions/collateral/service-provider/global-cloud-index-gci/Cloud_Index_White_Paper.pdf

22. Marston, S., Li, Z., Bandyopadhyay, S., Zhang, J., & Ghalsasi, A. (2011), Cloud computing—the business perspective. *Decision Support Systems*, 51(1), 176–189, doi:10.1016/j.dss.2010.12.006

The SaaS model is forecasted to be the driving force behind the cloud market's sustained two-digit growth. The success of SaaS is well represented by the wealth of providers offering software programs ranging from basic personal productivity tools to highly specialized and customized applications. The advantages and disadvantages of the SaaS model parallel those that are inherent to any type of outsourcing agreement, with the added risks and rewards associated with the delivery of the application through a network.

On the positive side, SaaS applications reduce setup time and can be up and running relatively quickly. Their pricing can be more flexible, with charges based on actual usage rather than fixed licensing fees. As with any other outsourcing arrangement, SaaS reduces the number of local staff needed to maintain and support the application.

The above advantages come at a cost, of course. The chief limitation of SaaS arrangements is the added reliability risk associated with the availability of the Internet. If the firm's Internet connection experiences an outage, the applications become unusable, even though they are actually up and running. Another limitation of SaaS is that it is more difficult to integrate remote applications with the existing IT infrastructure of the firm and with its other applications.

The success experienced by cloud solutions is making companies realize the challenges of integration with applications and middleware lying beyond a firm's premises (Table 3.7). An increasing number of business organizations departed from the centralized or "monolithic" model of traditional ERP systems, resulting in mixed environments where functionalities are delivered through a combination of on-premises and cloud solutions.

This new scenario increases the complexity of managing the current applications landscape, challenging process and databases integrity and performance. As the range of ERP solutions increases in number and the diversity of applications increases (e.g., cloud analytics, SCM, cloud CRM), integration strategies need to become more diversified, requiring specific investments in tools, methodologies, and people. The search for an ever-increasing business agility found a formidable ally in cloud applications.

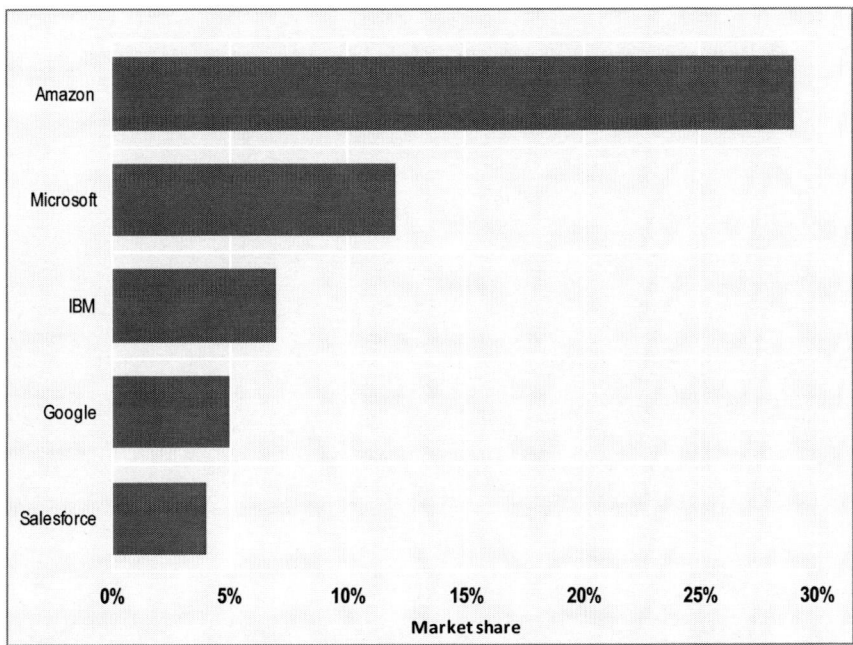

FIGURE 3.31. Major cloud infrastructure providers by market shares (IaaS, PaaS)
Source: Synergy Research Group, 2015. Data from Q4 2014, adapted from Bort, J. (2015, February 3), Amazon still dominates the $16 billion cloud market, *Business Insider*, retrieved from http://uk.businessinsider.com/synergy-research-amazon-dominates-16-billion-cloud-market-2015-2

The inherent advantage of cloud deployments is appealing to business managers, who find in these solutions applications tailored to their business needs. However, there is no free lunch, and this new trend results in higher complexity and integration difficulties.

Finally, as with any other outsourcing arrangement, the performance of the firm is directly impacted by the performance of the service provider. For example, many Salesforce.com (Figure 3.32) customers blamed the firm for lost sales when Salesforce.com experienced an outage lasting almost a whole day on December 20, 2005—during the holiday season's final days.

Summary

This chapter completed our introduction to the foundations of information systems (IS) by explaining the vocabulary and concepts you need in order to categorize different types of information systems and communicate with other managers and IS professionals. Specifically, in this chapter we learned the following:

Table 3.7. Traditional and modern ERP integration challenges

	Traditional ERP	Modern ERP			
	One ERP vendor	*Core ERP Vendor 1*	*SaaS Vendor 2*	*Public Cloud 3 Vendor 3*	*Outsourced Vendor 4*
Integration	Tight integration within the ERP solution	Tight integration remains only within the ERP solution	Integration within business application and *loosely to other apps*	Integration within business application and *loosely to other apps*	Integration within outsourced processes and *loosely to other apps*
Integration tools	ERP vendor	Possibly ERP vendor	Vendor's integration platform (cloud)	Vendor's integration platform (cloud)	Provider's integration platform (cloud); client's integration platform (cloud)
Data integrity and consistency	Inherent within suite; *client responsibility to ancillary apps*	Within suite; *client responsibility to ancillary apps*	Within business app; *client responsibility to ancillary apps*	Within business app; *client responsibility to ancillary apps*	Maintained within outsourced process; *client responsibility elsewhere*
Process integrity	Inherent within suite	Within suite; *client responsibility to ancillary apps*	Within business app; *client responsibility to ancillary apps*	Within business app; *client responsibility to ancillary apps*	Outsourced to vendor *but ancillary processes responsibility of client*
Upgrades (test and patch workload)	Major upgrade every 12–18 months	Major upgrade every 12–18 months	Multiple: 3–4 per year	Multiple: 2–3 per year	None to 3–4 per year

The italicized text indicates where more responsibility and complexity is being generated on the end-user organization.

Source: Adapted from Gartner (July 2015)

FIGURE 3.32. Salesforce.com's website on December 20, 2005

- Different organizational information systems can be characterized through a hierarchical perspective. This perspective identifies three types of systems: transaction processing systems, decision support systems, and executive information systems. These systems are designed and built to support different activities—operational, tactical, and strategic, respectively.

- Different organizational information systems can be characterized through a functional perspective. This perspective identifies vertical organizational systems focused on the specific needs of each unit (e.g., accounting, marketing, finance, receiving).

- More recently, a process perspective has emerged. According to the process perspective, the firm and its operations are seen as a set of processes rather than functional areas. The functional perspective underpins many of the most recent managerial trends, including business process reengineering (BPR) and business systems integration efforts, as well as information systems trends such as systems integration initiatives.

- BPR, defined as a managerial approach calling for a process view of organizational activities, was one of the principal management trends of the mid-1990s. While its popularity has faded somewhat, you should not forget the key lessons of BPR: firms evolve over time, as do technologies; old assumptions may no longer be valid today; and you have an opportunity to use information technology (IT) to dramatically improve the efficiency and effectiveness of the firm's business processes.

- Enterprise systems (ESs), also known as enterprise resource planning (ERP), are modular, integrated software applications that span (all) organizational functions and rely on one database at the core. The defining characteristics of ESs are their large scope (seeking to support all aspects of an organization's IT infrastructure in an integrated fashion), their modularity (enabling adopting firms to select which components they need), and their configurability (allowing adopting organizations to choose among a predefined set of options during the implementation of the application).

- While enterprise systems offer much promise in terms of efficiency improvements, increased responsiveness, knowledge infusion, and adaptability, they have some significant limitations as well, including the trade-off between standardization and flexibility, the limitations of best-practice software, the potential for strategic clash, and the high costs and risks of the implementation process.

- Enterprise systems have traditionally focused on internal organizational processes. Conversely, supply chain management applications have been introduced to enable interorganizational business processes across the supply chain. Supply chain management applications have become increasingly integrated in an effort to create efficiencies through tight relationships between suppliers and customers.
- Best-of-breed integration approaches have emerged in response to the limitations of enterprise systems. Specifically, enterprise systems limit the adopting firm's ability to maintain a flexible IT infrastructure by restricting available options. In contrast, best-of-breed, enabled by the enterprise application integration (EAI) approach, allows an organization to purchase applications from multiple vendors and integrate them with its existing legacy systems using middleware.
- Knowledge management is the set of activities and processes that an organization enacts to manage the wealth of knowledge it possesses and ensure that such knowledge is properly safeguarded and put to use to help the firm achieve its objectives. A knowledge management initiative evolves over three phases: knowledge creation, capture and storage, and distribution. While knowledge management has intuitive appeal, knowledge management initiatives are deceptively complex and prone to failure. This is due to the sheer quantity and variety of organizational knowledge and to the fact that most organizations lack a culture of knowledge sharing and management.
- Business intelligence (BI) has been one of the dominant trends in organizational computing over the last decade. It encompasses the set of techniques, processes, and technologies designed to enable managers to gain superior insight into and understanding of their business and thus make better decisions. A firm that intends to engage in business intelligence needs to create a business intelligence infrastructure that typically is centered on a data warehouse. Internal transaction processing systems and external sources feed the data warehouse. Once the data have been structured for analysis in the data warehouse, or a data mart, it can be examined using analytical tools such as online analytical processing (OLAP) and data mining.
- Customer relationship management (CRM) represents another enduring business trend of the last decade. We have defined CRM as a strategic orientation that calls for iterative processes designed to turn customer data into customer relationships through an active use of, and by learning from, the information collected. While the term *CRM* has lost much of its original meaning as of late, it is critical that you realize that CRM initiatives are unique to the characteristics and objectives of the implementing organization. Thus the set of technologies and applications the firm will use (i.e., the CRM infrastructure) to enable both the operational and analytical aspects of its CRM strategy will vary dramatically.
- Big data is the umbrella term under which the major recent trends converge. The impacts on decision making and knowledge extraction are a paradigm shift in the way management and organizations have traditionally made decisions.

Study Questions

1. Describe the principal differences among transaction processing systems, management information systems, and executive information systems.
2. Identify the three types of organizational activities. For each one, describe its typical time horizon, hierarchical level, and principal characteristics. Provide an example for each type.
3. Provide an example of functional systems. What is the defining characteristic of these systems?
4. Define the concept of BPR. Can you provide an example, real or imaginary, of a company operating under old assumptions that are no longer valid? How would you propose to redesign the firm's business processes? What information technology would you expect the firm to adopt to enable the redesigned process?

5. What are the principal limitations and drawbacks of BPR?

6. How have we defined the concepts of business and systems integration? What is the relationship between the two? Can you provide examples of each?

7. What is an enterprise system (ES)? Can you describe its genesis? Identify the principal advantages and risks that a firm considering the installation of an ES should consider.

8. What is a supply chain? Why is it important to actively manage the supply chain?

9. If you were the chief executive officer (CEO) of a hospital, would you consider using radio frequency identification (RFID) technology? If not, why? If yes, for what applications?

10. Define the term *best-of-breed integration*. Why has best-of-breed integration recently emerged as a business trend?

11. Explain how enterprise application integration (EAI) works. What are its primary advantages over competing integration approaches?

12. Define the following terms: *knowledge, explicit and tacit knowledge*, and *knowledge management*. What are the principal phases of a knowledge management initiative? Describe the essential benefits of knowledge management for modern organizations. Why are so many organizations struggling with their knowledge management initiatives?

13. Define the following terms: *business intelligence, business intelligence infrastructure, data warehouse, data mart, OLAP*, and *data mining*. What is the relationship among the various elements of BI infrastructure?

14. What are the main advantages and disadvantages of a cloud solution compared with an on-premises one?

15. Define the term *big data*. What are the main implications of the 3 Vs—volume, velocity, and variety—on current managerial practices?

Further Readings

1. Birst, S. J. (2014, August 21). The battle of business intelligence: Data discovery vs. traditional BI. *Wired*. Retrieved from http://www.wired.com/insights/2014/08/battle-business-intelligence-data-discovery-vs-traditional-bi/

2. Chen, H., Chiang, R. H. L., and Storey, V. C. (2012). Business intelligence and analytics: From big data to big impact. *MIS Quarterly, 36*(4), 1165–1188.

3. Davenport, T. H. (1992). *Process innovation: Reengineering work through information technology*. Boston, MA: Harvard Business School Press.

4. Davenport, T. H. (1998, July/August). Putting the enterprise into enterprise system. *Harvard Business Review*, 121–131.

5. Davenport, T. H. (2006, January). Competing on analytics. *Harvard Business Review*, 98–107.

6. Hammer, M. (1990, July/August). Reengineering work: Don't automate, obliterate. *Harvard Business Review*, 104–112.

7. Hammer, M. (1996). *Beyond reengineering: How the process-centered organization is changing our work and our lives*. New York, NY: Harper Business.

8. Hammer, M. (2001, September). The superefficient company. *Harvard Business Review*, 82–91.

9. Hammer, M. (2004, April). Deep change: How operational innovation can transform your company. *Harvard Business Review*, 84–93.

10. Hammer, M. (2007, July/August). Process audit. *Harvard Business Review*, 104–112.

11. Hammer, M., and Champy, J. A. (1993). *Reengineering the corporation: A manifesto for business revolution*. New York, NY: Harper Business.

12. Leavitt, H. J., and Whisler, T. L. (1958, November–December). Management in the 1980s. *Harvard Business Review*, 41–48.

13. Markus, M. L. (2000). Paradigm shifts: E-business and business/systems integration. *Communications of the AIS, 4*(10).

14. Marston, S., Li, Z., Bandyopadhyay, S., Zhang, J., and Ghalsasi, A. (2011). Cloud computing: The business perspective. *Decision Support Systems, 51*(1), 176–189. doi:10.1016/j.dss.2010.12.006

15. Senge, P. (1990). *The fifth discipline: The art and practice of the learning organization*. New York, NY: Currency.

Glossary

- **Business integration:** The unification or creation of tight linkages among the diverse but connected business activities carried out by individuals, groups, and departments within an organization.
- **Business intelligence (BI):** The ability to gather and make sense of information about your business. It encompasses the set of techniques, processes, and technologies designed to enable managers to gain superior insight into and understanding of their business and thus make better decisions.
- **Business intelligence infrastructure:** The set of applications and technologies designed to create, manage, and analyze large repositories of data in an effort to extract value from them.
- **Business process:** The series of steps that a firm performs in order to complete an economic activity.
- **Business process reengineering (BPR):** A managerial approach calling for a process view of organizational activities. The BPR methodology calls for internal business integration and seeks dramatic performance improvements through rationalization of activities and the elimination of duplication of efforts across separate functions and units.
- **Cloud computing:** The use of the Internet as gateway for pooling IT resources. In other words, applications or computational or storage components—the building blocks of IT solutions, if you will—are offered online by a provider.
- **Customer relationship management (CRM):** A strategic orientation that calls for iterative processes designed to turn customer data into customer relationships through active use of, and by learning from, the information collected.
- **Database:** A self-describing collection of related records.
- **Database management system (DBMS):** A software program (or collection of programs) that enables and controls access to a database.
- **Data mart:** A scaled-down version of a data warehouse that focuses on the needs of a specific audience.
- **Data mining:** The process of automatically discovering nonobvious relationships in large databases.
- **Data warehouse:** A software program that collects and consolidates data from multiple source systems, both internal to the organization and external, with the purpose of enabling analysis.
- **Decision support systems (DSS):** Systems designed to provide information needed by functional managers engaged in tactical decision making in the form of regular reports and exception reports.
- **Enterprise system (ES):** Modular, integrated software applications that span (all) organizational functions and rely on one database at the core. Also known as ERP.
- **Executive information systems (EIS):** Systems designed to serve the long-range planning and decision-making needs of senior managers.
- **Explicit knowledge:** The type of knowledge that can be articulated, codified, and transferred with relative ease.
- **Extranet:** A private network that uses the public Internet infrastructure and Internet technologies but spans the boundaries of an organization and enables secure transactions between a firm and its suppliers, vendors, customers, and any other partner.
- **Functional systems:** Systems expressly designed to support the specific needs of individuals in the same functional area.
- **Information systems cycle:** An analytical model that portrays the progression of business data from their inception in transaction processing systems, to their storage in data repositories, and finally to their use in analytical tools.
- **Infrastructure as a service (IaaS):** A class of cloud services where a vendor provides customers with the use of hardware functionality—in essence, computational power, storage capacity, and network connectivity. In the IaaS model, the client rents the virtualized hardware. All software—including the operating system, backup and recovery, and the like—are the client's responsibility. The IaaS provider takes care of the running and maintenance of the infrastructure, for a fee. Like all the other cloud models, IaaS platforms offer scalable resources that can be adjusted on demand.
- **Integration:** The process that an organization, or a number of related organizations, uses to

unify, or join together, some tangible or intangible assets.

- **Integrator:** A consulting firm that partners with an enterprise systems vendor and becomes a specialist in the implementation of the ES vendor's products.
- **Knowledge management:** The set of activities and processes that an organization enacts to manage the wealth of knowledge it possesses and ensure that such knowledge is properly safeguarded and put to use to help the firm achieve its objectives.
- **Multitenancy:** A software architecture where a single copy of software is instanced (runs) to serve all tenants. It is a defining characteristic of the cloud model and is behind services like Salesforce, Dropbox, or Gmail, just to cite a few.
- **Online analytical processing (OLAP):** A class of software programs that enables a knowledge worker to easily and selectively extract and view data from an analytical database.
- **Platform as a service (PaaS):** A cloud software environment a vendor provides to customers on which the client builds its own applications. This model is generally used for development, testing, and deployment of applications, as components are already in place.
- **Single tenancy:** Architecture where for each user, a single copy of the application is instanced. It is the typical model adopted by application service provision (ASP) vendors.

- **Software as a service (SaaS):** A software delivery approach in which a provider hosts the application in its data centers and the customer accesses the needed applications' functionalities over a computer network. Instead of licensing the application and requiring the customer to install, maintain, and generally support it, in the SaaS model, the provider shoulders these tasks—customers simply gain access to the needed applications in much the same way they gain access to utilities (e.g., water, electricity).
- **Supply chain:** The set of upstream firms that produces and sells the resources that an organization needs to perform its transformation process (e.g., raw materials, energy, equipment).
- **Supply chain management (SCM):** The set of logistic and financial processes associated with the planning, execution, and monitoring of supply chain operations.
- **System integration:** The unification or tight linkage of IT-enabled information systems and databases.
- **Tacit knowledge:** The type of knowledge that individuals possess but find difficult to articulate, codify, and transfer.
- **Transaction processing systems (TPS):** Systems mainly concerned with automating recurring activities and structuring day-to-day activities to ensure that they are performed with speed and accuracy.

PART II

COMPETING IN THE INTERNET AGE

The rallying cry of enthusiastic engineers, entrepreneurs, venture capitalists, investors, and just about everyone else during the late 1990s (or the dot-com era, as it became known) was "The Internet changes everything."

In such a statement there was certainly quite a bit of "the emperor has no clothes" syndrome, as Netscape Corp. cofounder Marc Andreessen described it. In other words, while most people were unsure as to how exactly the Internet was going to change everything, they did not want to miss out on it . . . in case it did. The frenzy took the NASDAQ—the tech-focused electronic equity security market—past 5,000 points in March 2000 before seeing it tumble down to a 1,400-point low. The market crash notwithstanding, the dot-com era ushered in what some have named the "network economy." It is evident now, more than a decade after the crash, that the Internet, and the many related information technologies and innovations that are built on the Internet infrastructure, dramatically changed the competitive landscape for almost every company. Today we can see a resurgence of the positive mentality that drove the growth of the Internet. The driving force is the phenomenon called Web 2.0, the cloud, as well as the now viable mobile platform (see Chapter 5). The first of the Web 2.0 darlings to go public, business-oriented social network LinkedIn, had a very successful initial public offer (IPO) on May 19, 2011, when its stock was offered at $42 but rocketed to $115 in intraday trading to settle at around $93 at closing on the second day of trading. More recently, analysts observed that the number of these new ventures entering the billion-dollar valuation has more than doubled,[1] enriching the pipeline of "ready-for-IPO" firms like Airbnb, Box, Dropbox, Pinterest, Snapchat, and Uber. These successes had many observers cheered (other feared) the return of inflated expectations that characterized the dot-com era thinking.

What is the network economy? Simply put, a network economy is one in which ubiquitous global networks drastically reduce geographic and time constraints, enabling organizations to truly compete on a global basis. This notion is at the center of the famous book *The World Is Flat*, written by *New York Times* columnist Thomas Friedman. The main thesis of the book is that the technology revolution that took place during the dot-com era has changed modern business and has enabled work to move seamlessly around the globe. The consequence is that the global competitive playing field has been leveled, leading to an unprecedented degree of globalization.

The most apparent changes brought about by the network economy took place at the front end of companies' interactions with their clients, in what is called the *business-to-consumer* space. You could not imagine running an airline or a hotel today without a professional and functional website that your

---

1. CB Insights (2015), *2015 Tech IPO Pipeline*, retrieved from https://www.cbinsights.com/tech-ipo-pipeline

customers could use to learn about your offer, book reservations, and even check in. The same goes for banks, retailers in the widest variety of sectors, publishers, newly released movies, and even celebrities, for whom a website seems to be a must! However, while the front end grabbed all the headlines, the bulk of the "Internet revolution" took place behind the scenes, within company walls, in what is termed the *business-to-business* space. This trend is captured by a quote attributed to Jack Welch, the iconic former chief executive officer (CEO) of General Electric. Welch, referring to the potential for efficiencies ushered in by the Internet: "Where does the Internet rank on my priority list? It is number one, two, three, and four. I don't think there's been anything as important or more widespread in all my years at GE."[2]

Whether or not the Internet does indeed "change everything" is really not the issue. There is no doubt that a global, affordable, digital network infrastructure for communication is a critical business enabler. Thus you as a modern general or functional manager must be able to appropriately use it to benefit your organization. In order to do so, you must be able to answer two broad questions:

1. What impacts do Internet technologies have on the competitive landscape? How do they change the environment your firm is, and will be, competing in?
2. How have the Internet and related technologies been used by organizations before? How can they be used by your firm to improve business efficiency and effectiveness?

Part II of this book is devoted to answering these two questions.

- *Chapter 4: The Changing Competitive Environment.* This chapter focuses on the first question and discusses how networks and information differ as economic entities from traditional and physical goods. With this backdrop, the chapter discusses how Internet technologies have changed the modern competitive landscape and the implications this has for strategy in the modern firm.
- *Chapter 5: Electronic Commerce: New Ways of Doing Business.* This chapter tackles the second question and provides you with a background on the Internet and related technologies. It then introduces a vocabulary with which to understand electronic commerce and electronic business trends past, present, and future. The chapter also discusses the role of the Internet and related technologies both within and outside the modern firm.

---

2. Fingar, P., & Aronica, R. C. (2001), *The death of "e" and the birth of the real new economy: Business models, technologies and strategies for the 21st century*, Tampa, FL: Meghan-Kiffer Press.

CHAPTER 4

The Changing Competitive Environment

What You Will Learn in This Chapter

This chapter focuses on the revolutionary changes that have occurred in the global economy since the advent of the commercial Internet in the mid-1990s. The networked world is widely different from the prenetworked one because networks have peculiar economic characteristics. Moreover, in the presence of pervasive networks, the amount of data and information that can be generated and transferred in real time is dramatically increasing. The successful firm, and the successful manager, must be able to design and implement strategies to take advantage of, rather than suffer from, these changes. The concepts and examples discussed in this chapter will help you do so.

In this chapter, you will become well versed in the language of network economics, information economics, and disruptive technologies. Specifically, this chapter will

1. Discuss the basic principles of network economics, including the sources of value in networks, and define physical and virtual networks. You will also learn to apply these concepts to strategy and managerial decision making.
2. Explain the concepts and vocabulary of network economics, including positive feedback, network externalities, and tippy markets. You will be able to recognize when network effects occur and what makes a market tip, as well as what market will not tip toward a dominant player.
3. Clarify the basic principles of information economics and the role that information plays in the modern competitive environment. You will be able to understand the concepts and vocabulary of information economics, including the ability to define classic information goods and information-intensive goods.
4. Explain how the advent of pervasive networks has enabled information to break the constraints imposed by traditional information carriers. You will also be able to explain what the richness/reach trade-off is and its implications for modern organizations.
5. Distinguish between disruptive and sustaining technologies. You will be able to identify each kind and draw implications for decision making in organizations faced with the emergence of disruptive technologies.

MINICASE: Airbnb and the Ghost of Start-ups Past

"You always had an entrepreneurial streak," you tell yourself with a chuckle as you reflect over a hot cappuccino at your favorite coffee shop. With an undergraduate degree in computer engineering and a soon-to-be-granted master's of management degree, a start-up sounds like a perfect way to jump back into the real world. While the global crisis during the last few years has put the squeeze on venture funding, the recent success showed that good ideas still get attention. Flipagram.com got $70 million from heavy hitters like Sequoia Capital and Index Ventures in their series B funding, and the payoff could be handsome. Or the now "textbook case" Airbnb, after totally disrupting an industry, in 6 years was able to raise $2.3 billion and be valued 10 times more. And you cannot forget that Groupon received a buyout offer of $6 billion from Google after a little more than two years in operation . . . and turned it down!

As you ponder the issue, you reflect on lessons from tech ventures of the past. One that you know quite well is eBay, having been an avid buyer and a successful seller as a teen and having followed the company over the years. In fact, you remember an interesting article from back in 2004 drawing a parallel between eBay Inc. and Amazon.com. At the time, the two firms were respectively 60th and 66th in *BusinessWeek*'s Top 100 Brands[3] and were considered the poster-children of eCommerce, having helped create the category: "EBay and Amazon.com, the Internet's top two eCommerce sites, are taking opposite approaches to growth. EBay raised its prices this month for the fourth year in a row, while Amazon renewed its pledge to keep cutting prices even if it means lower profits."[4] You recall Meg Whitman, at the time eBay's chief executive officer (CEO), saying, "The eBay marketplace is a powerhouse. [. . .] We

continue to enjoy ever-bigger, ever-faster cycles of success, fueled by the unlimited opportunity of our huge addressable market." At the time, eBay was reaching the peak of its financial achievement and growth. You recall the same article quoting Amazon's founder and CEO, Jeff Bezos: "We will, for years and years and years, consistently give back the gains we get in lower operating costs to our customers in the form of lower prices." You also recall the numbers quoted in the article: "eBay's gross profit margin—its revenue minus the cost of sales—was 82 percent. That's after subtracting the cost of running its Web site, customer support and payment processing operations. And eBay's bottom-line profit stood at 22 percent of its revenue after subtracting all other expenses, including the hefty $172 million that eBay forked over for marketing and sales expenses. Amazon's gross profit for the same quarter, by contrast, was 22 percent, and its bottom-line profit was under 4 percent."

Was Groupon applying some of eBay's lessons? Was Flipagram.com? As you ponder your next move, you cannot help but think that replicating eBay's early and sustained success is predicated on understanding these dynamics.

Discussion Questions

1. As you reflect on what you have read and your knowledge of the impact of new technology on the competitive landscape, why would Amazon and eBay act so differently?
2. What would you say are the key lessons you should draw from the eBay versus Amazon experience?
3. Would you argue that AirBnB, Groupon, and Flipagram.com are indeed applying some of the same lessons?

Introduction

Whether you believe that "the Internet changes everything," as dot-com enthusiasts vigorously maintained during the late 1990s rally of the NASDAQ, or you take a much more conservative stance, it is undeniable that the Internet and the many kinds of information technology (IT) that the global network has spawned are important tools in the strategic arsenal of the modern firm. We discuss the Internet itself as well as the many innovations it has enabled in the next chapter, while devoting the present one to some critical concepts underpinning those innovations.

---

3. The global brand scorecard (2004, August), *BusinessWeek*, 72, 2.

4. Walker, L. (2004, January 29), A study in e-commerce opposites, *Washington Post*.

Understanding how to appropriately deploy the information technology now that the Internet is a cornerstone of business infrastructure requires a basic appreciation of what the Internet is and how it works (see Chapter 5). More important for general and functional managers, being able to use the Internet and related technology requires an understanding of the economic characteristics of networks and of information, as well as their impact on the competitive landscape and the strategy of the firm. In the remainder of this chapter, we discuss each of these issues in turn.

Network Economics

Consider this question: How can a smartphone app of fewer than 10 MB of code, as useful and innovative as it may be, enable the firm that owns it to fetch one billion dollars in fewer than two years since it was released? This is what happened to Instagram, a firm that sold its business—the Instagram app—to Facebook when it had only 13 employees. How could a company create such a large valuation so quickly? Much of the answer is to be found in the economics of networks.

Anyone who has recently gotten engaged can easily rattle off key statistics about diamonds. The value of a diamond depends on its physical attributes: color, clarity, cut, shape, and, of course, size (measured by its weight in carats). Interestingly, while jewelers may try to convince you that a diamond has a soul, spirit, and personality (!?!), diamonds are cataloged and measured quite precisely by national organizations such as the Gemological Institute of America (GIA) in the United States. The price of a diamond is a fairly precise function of its physical characteristics. A quick online search reveals that as diamonds become harder to find, their value increases. For example, a superior round diamond of ideal cut, D color, and IF clarity will cost you about $2,200 for half a carat, $15,000 for one carat, $72,000 for two carats, and a cool $230,000 for three carats.

The lesson is clear: The value of diamonds is proportional to their rarity. In fact, diamonds are a great example because they have little use outside the jewelry domain. What you are paying for is indeed scarcity, which is a function of the physical characteristics that determine a diamond's beauty, brilliance, and fire. Ironically, oxygen and water are much more valuable than diamonds. After all, if you couldn't breathe or were severely dehydrated, you would hardly notice the beauty or personality of that diamond you bought! However, water is cheap and oxygen is free because they are plentiful.

To be sure, the relationship between the scarcity and the value of a resource is the rule, not the exception. Skilled labor and managerial talent, the resources you sell to your employer, are no different. While we can debate the morality of sky-high executive compensations, it is clear that they are justified with the argument that few people in the world have the talent and experience to run large, complex business operations. The same argument is used for professional athletes in popular sports—there was only one Michael Jordan who could fill seats in an arena, make people tune into the games he played, and have kids clamoring for his shoes and jerseys. Today, the likes of Cristiano Ronaldo, Lionel Messi, and Zlatan Ibrahimovic fill soccer stadiums and help earn lucrative television contracts for their teams. Like scarce diamonds, these people command a premium price for their services. In his last year with the Chicago Bulls, as the scarcest attraction in basketball, Jordan fetched the highest one-year contract in the sport—$34 million for the single 1997–1998 season.

The above examples represent the norm rather than the exception. Value is typically found in scarcity, and the heart of strategy is about being unique in a positive way (see Chapter 7).

Networks Are Different: Value in Plentitude

We suspect that you get significant value from Instagram. It is most likely not monetary value, but it is social relationships, news, and probably often entertainment value (Figure 4.1). But how much would you have been willing to pay for the very first copy of the Instagram app in October 2010? If value is found in scarcity, would you have paid hundreds of thousands of dollars for that uniquely scarce application? Probably not!

In fact, you probably would take a pass and pay nothing for it.[5] The very first copy of Instagram is valueless. The same goes for the very first fax machine, telephone, or copy of Skype or WhatsApp. On the other hand, if a business associate of yours had a fax machine too, you might consider purchasing one if the price were low enough given the amount of real-time document exchange you had to engage in with this associate. As more and more of your friends download the WhatsApp messaging app, you begin to see significant value in it and you would consider paying more and more for it. We downloaded WhatsApp to our smartphones early on, and we did not have to pay for it. As you know, now the app has become the de facto standard for simple text messaging and group communication, and it is no longer free.

Where do Instagram, fax machines, and WhatsApp draw their value from then? Not scarcity, but rather plentitude (Figure 4.2). In fact, the value in a network is proportional to the number of connected nodes. Similar arguments can be made for network technologies, like the telephone, instant messaging, railroads, and the telegraph. The insight underlying these examples is that networks differ dramatically from most other goods, as their value is tied to how many other nodes are in the network (plentitude) rather than how few (scarcity).

Physical and Virtual Networks

In the previous section, we talked about computer networks and the Internet. There are, of course, other types of networks, like the telephone network or the railroad network. We call these *physical networks*, where the nodes of the network are connected by physical links (i.e., railroad tracks, telephone wires). However, network economics also apply to "virtual" networks.[6] The defining characteristic of a virtual network is that connections between network nodes are not physical but intangible and invisible. The nodes of a virtual network are typically people rather than devices.

FIGURE 4.1. Crazy fans make for great entertainment value

FIGURE 4.2. Networks find value in plentitude

Whether tangible or intangible, network connections enable network nodes to share and communicate. In a virtual network, the people in the network can share information (i.e., share files of the same format) with other members of the same user network (e.g., BitTorrent file-sharing users), expertise (e.g., information on how to use a given software program within a certain community of practice), or just images of their friends dressed up for the game (Figure 4.1). Note that a virtual network is generally sponsored by an organization or technology that enables it, controls access to it, and manages its evolution. Apple Computer Inc., for instance, sponsors the iTunes network, while Microsoft controls the Skype network of Voice over IP (VoIP) users. Maintaining control of the network puts the sponsor in a position of advantage.

---

5. We are aware of the fact that Instagram is a free app for users, in the sense that you don't pay any money to download and use it. You are indeed paying with your time and attention, but this discussion is beside the point at this stage.

6. We adopt the term *virtual networks* following the definition used in Shapiro, C., & Varian, H. R. (1999), *Information rules*, Boston, MA: Harvard Business School Press.

FIGURE 4.3. Scribes text editor
Courtesy of LinuxLinks

Consider the writing of this book as an example. We are writing this book using Microsoft Word on a Wintel platform.[7] If you were also a Microsoft Word user, it would be easy for you to become a coauthor on our next edition. This is because we could easily exchange versions of the chapters for comments and editing. Conversely, if you used the Linux operating system and the Scribes Writer text editor it would be much harder for us to work together (Figure 4.3). Documents might not convert correctly; images might be rendered differently; we might lose special formatting in the exchange; we might not be able to easily track, approve, or reject each other's changes; and so on.

Size Still Matters   Whether physical or virtual, the value of the network for its members is a function of its size—that is, the more nodes the network has, the more valuable it is to its members. Consider the Wintel platform example again. If you are getting ready to buy a new computer, you will likely not make the decision in isolation. Rather, you will look at your immediate circle of friends and coworkers and make sure that you purchase a computer that allows you to interact with them. For example, as a student, you write papers with your classmates, you exchange spreadsheet models, you swap notes, and so on. As a consequence, if most other people at your school are using a Wintel platform or a different one (e.g., Apple Macs), then you would most likely choose the same so as not to be left out of the network.

Now consider Groupon, the deal-of-the-day website mentioned in the opening minicase. While it has number of competitors, like LivingSocial (Figure 4.4) or Groupalia, when you decide which network to join, you will be drawn toward the one with the greatest number of service providers. This is because you will have access to the greatest number of offers without having to sign up and manage multiple accounts.

Key Concepts and Vocabulary

To move beyond an intuitive level, in order to understand how networks operate and to explore their potential for firm strategy, we need to introduce some vocabulary and some fundamental concepts.

---

7. In a strict sense, a platform is a combination of a hardware architecture and an operating system. The Wintel platform refers to the dominant personal computer platform using Microsoft Windows running on machines using an Intel microprocessor.

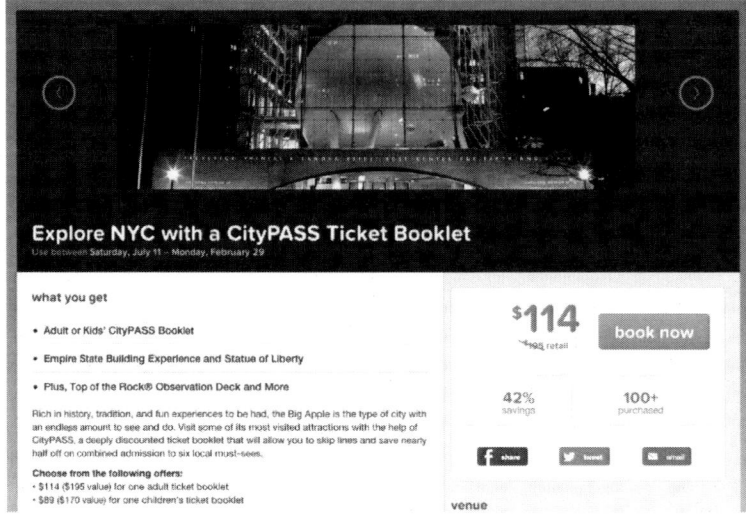

FIGURE 4.4. Daily deal on LivingSocial.com

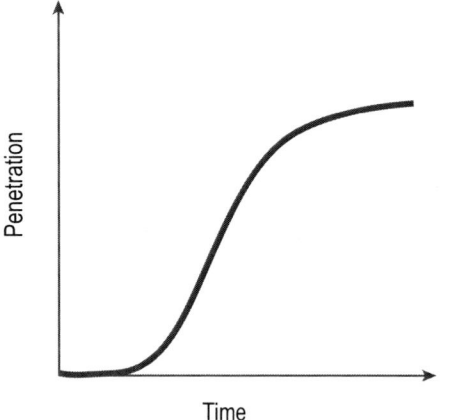

FIGURE 4.5. Classic technology adoption curve

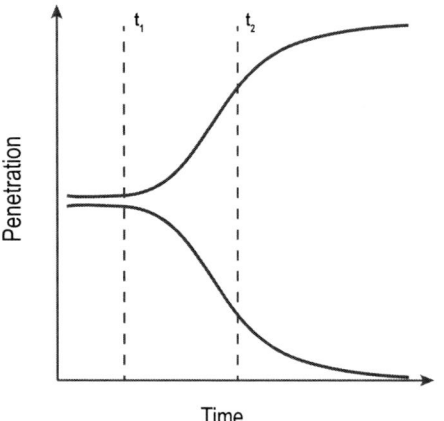

FIGURE 4.6. The dynamics of positive feedback

Positive Feedback Adoption of a new technology product or service typically follows the pattern represented by the S-curve (see Figure 4.5). Positive feedback is simply defined as that self-reinforcing mechanism by which the strong gets stronger and the weak gets weaker. It is very similar to the process by which return in a microphone quickly becomes louder and louder until it reaches a deafening volume (i.e., a high-pitched sound due to interference is picked up by a microphone and amplified, and the now louder sound is picked up again by the microphone and amplified more).

Positive feedback is a well-known economic phenomenon at the heart, for example, of economies of scale. In industries with strong economies of scale—say, automobile manufacturing—there is a significant advantage stemming from size. Imagine two car makers, one larger than the other. The larger manufacturer can spread its fixed cost across a larger volume of cars, thus being able to reduce its prices—assuming everything else is the same, including expected profit margins. With lower prices, the larger manufacturer will sell more cars, thus being able to further spread its fixed costs. With even lower prices, the cycle begins again, allowing the dominant manufacturer to further reduce unit cost and increase volumes (see Figure 4.6). Note that the smaller manufacturer, losing market share to the larger one, will see its unit cost increase as it loses market share, thus having to raise prices and seeing even lower sales. While the losing firm may still have a chance at time t_1, things look compromised at time t_2.

Positive feedback sets in motion a virtuous cycle, benefiting the larger firm, and a vicious cycle, penalizing the smaller one. Thus the stronger firm gets stronger and continues to grow while the weaker firm gets increasingly weaker. Unless the smaller firm is able to identify a profitable niche or somehow differentiate its product, it will likely fade into oblivion, unable to sustain itself as a viable business.

Negative Feedback   The above discussion should clarify that there is nothing inherently positive (i.e., good) about positive feedback—particularly for the firms on the losing side of it! In other words, positive feedback simply means that the process is self-reinforcing, not that it is beneficial.

Negative feedback is the term used to refer to the opposite dynamic. If negative feedback is at play, the stronger gets weaker and the weaker gets stronger. Negative feedback typically characterizes economies of scale and takes effect when the dominant firm has reached a significant size. After a certain size, economies of scale no longer reduce unit cost and, due to coordination costs and increasing overhead, further growth is hampered. In other words, past a certain size, the dominant firm encounters difficulties that limit further growth.

Network Effects   Positive and negative feedback play a crucial role in physical and virtual networks because the value of a network to its members is a function of the number of nodes in the same network. Positive feedback dynamics that occur in networks go under the name of network effects, network externalities, or demand-side economies of scale.

Network effects occur when a new node (e.g., a new WhatsApp user), while pursuing his or her own economic motives, creates value for all the other members of the network by making the network larger and thus more valuable. Network effects have the characteristic of economic externalities[8]—hence the name network externalities. That is, they create spillover effects that have an impact on other individuals: positive for those members of the growing network and negative for the members of the other ones.

Consider once again the example of Instagram, and ask yourself how the firm reached 300 million monthly active users in just four years from its inception and today tops 400 million. Instagram enables those who download it to share images and moments of their lives. If you are an Instagram user, a friend or colleague who had already downloaded it probably alerted you to its existence. Once you downloaded the application and started using it, you probably began to recruit your own friends and colleagues. The reason is that any one of them who downloads Instagram makes your use of the app more valuable. In other words, since you can now interact with more people, Instagram is more useful to you. The term *evangelist effect* describes this dynamic and the incentive that current members of the network have to "spread the word" and convince others to join it. A similar dynamic has fueled the growth of many other applications you may use today: Facebook, Snapchat, Waze, and the like.

Perhaps the easiest way to understand network effects is to look at the services offered by those organizations that have sought to build an explicit business model around them. Mercata, a firm backed by Microsoft cofounder Paul Allen, pioneered the "group-shopping" business model along with Mob-Shop (Figure 4.7). Groups of strangers seeking to purchase the same product (e.g., a Toshiba CD/DVD player) would come together via the Internet to form a Mercata-enabled buying group. As the number of new customers joining the buying group increased, the price for the item would decrease *for each member of the group*.

The Mercata website showed the current price and future prices available to all once targets in the number of customers were hit (e.g., $550 per item once the size of the group reaches 10, $540 at 15). The network effect at play here is clear. Every new customer who joins the buying group, while seeking

---

8. As you may recall from your introductory economics courses, an externality occurs when an economic actor, pursuing his or her own economic motives, affects other actors' economic positions. Consider the example of a large resort able to charge $500 a night. If a pig farm is opened upwind of the resort, with no intention to hurt the resort but simply to pursue a business opportunity, the resort will no longer be able to charge premium prices . . . or any price at all! This spillover effect is called an *externality*—a negative externality in this case.

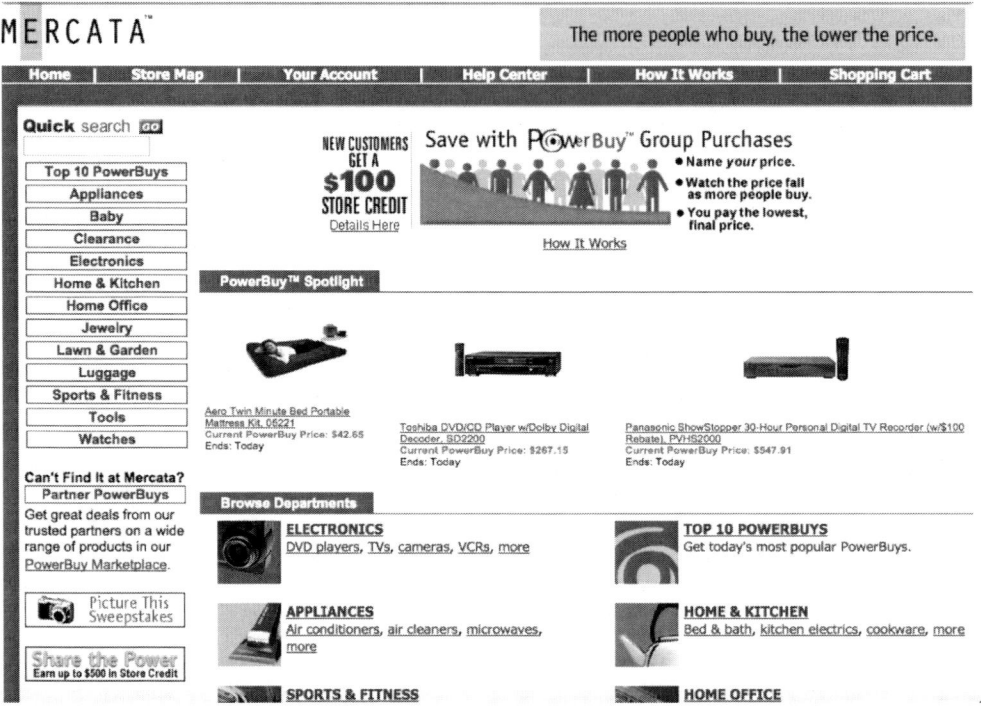

FIGURE 4.7. Mercata home page back in 2000

his or her own economic benefit, lowers the price for all. While both Mercata and MobShop were casualties of the dot-com bust, their business model offers a great example of network effects at play, and new organizations, such as Groupon (Figure 4.8) and LivingSocial, have built their businesses around the same core idea.

Positive feedback associated with traditional economies of scale typically exhausts itself well before one firm can achieve market dominance, but this is not the case for network effects. Positive feedback associated with network effects can play out, without limit, until one firm dominates the network and all others disappear—a situation typically referred to as a "winner-take-all" dynamic (see Figure 4.6).

A firm that finds itself on the losing side of network effects can survive under two conditions:

- It can become compatible with the dominant player, thus being able to connect to the dominant network and tap into its value. When Apple Computers found itself on the losing side of the battle for dominance of the personal computer platform, it was forced to seek compatibility with Wintel products—sponsor of the dominant network. However, the sponsors of the dominant network will often resist this move toward compatibility.
- It can find a niche that is different enough from the broader market and big enough to sustain the firm. Before Apple became compatible with the dominant Wintel platform, it was able to survive by offering a far superior product for designers and publishers, who found the Macintosh computer and software much better than Windows machines for their needs (Figure 4.9).

The dominant network sponsor may react by trying to either block or limit compatibility. It may also try to take over the available market niches. Its ability to do so will depend on the characteristics of the market it competes in and the demand for product variety that characterizes it.

Tipping Point and Tippy Markets   A *tippy market* is one that is subject to strong positive feedback, such that the market will "tip" in favor of the firm that is able to reach critical mass and dominate it. A tippy market is therefore a market with "winner-take-all" tendencies.

FIGURE 4.8. The Groupon model

We define a *tipping point* as the watershed of dominance. In other words, the tipping point is that moment in the evolution of a market where one organization or technology reaches critical mass and goes on to dominate it—the point of no return where winners and losers are defined. In Figure 4.6, the tipping point occurred sometime between times t_1 and t_2.

The lower the cost of production and distribution of a product, and the stronger the network effect, the quicker the onset of the tipping point (Figure 4.10).

Apps such as WhatsApp represent a good example. The active users have now passed the 800 million mark (Figure 4.11)—not bad for a company in business for six years.

Not All Markets Tip During the dot-com days, there was a prevalent misguided perception that any business that used the Internet would be able to harness strong network effects. As a consequence, many firms focused on ramping up their user base at any cost, trusting that once they reached critical mass, they would be able to dominate the market and figure out how to turn a profit.

Not all markets tip, and winner-take-all dynamics are more the exception than the rule. Consider Garmin, the maker of navigation and communication equipment (Figure 4.12). Garmin is a vertically integrated company that directly controls the design, manufacture, marketing, and sales of its products. Its automotive GPS navigators help customers plot their course, identify points of interest along the road, and receive real-time driving directions. Is Garmin in a tippy market?

FIGURE 4.9. The original Apple Macintosh
Photo by Luc Legay / CC BY SA 2.0

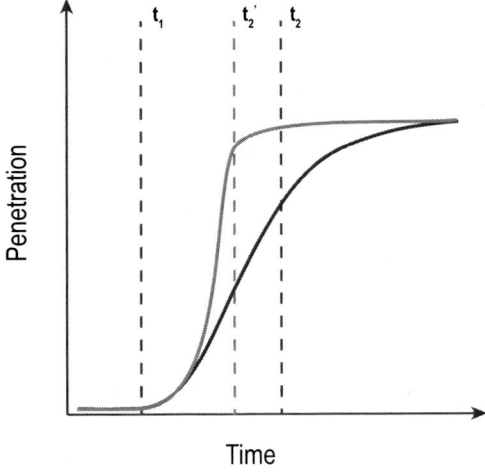

FIGURE 4.10. Adoption curve in the presence of a network effect

No, the automotive GPS navigation market is not a tippy market. If you own a Garmin device to help you find your way (i.e., you are in the Garmin network) and I purchase my own GPS navigation device, you don't stand to benefit in any way from my purchase. We both use the receiver independently to find our way. Now, imagine if the navigation device automatically uploaded the location and speed of each user to a database that computed the average speed of cars on different routes. When I seek to find the quickest way home during rush hour, the more people that are in the Garmin network uploading their speed and position, the more accurate directions I would get—thus creating strong network effects and a tippy market.

Contrast the above example with that of Resort Condominiums International, LLC (RCI). RCI is a well-established timeshare company founded in 1974 to enable "exchange vacations." In the timeshare model, customers buy the right to one or more vacation weeks in a condominium unit in a specific property and a specific location (e.g., unit 235 at the Outrigger Palms at Wailea, on the isle of Maui, Hawaii). Those who own a timeshare can enjoy it during their allotted time. Alternatively, when seeking variation in their vacation, timeshare owners can exchange the right to use their unit with others. RCI and other companies that support exchange vacations create the market and facilitate the process of finding suitable trading partners, managing credits (e.g., a week in a high-end Maui resort may be worth two weeks in a midscale Florida property), and providing the many other services necessary to enable the exchange.

RCI has a membership base of 3.7 million timeshare owners, with more than 4,000 affiliated resorts in more than 100 countries. RCI now has a website that supports many of its interactions with its

FIGURE 4.11. WhatsApp's CEO and cofounder's announcement on Facebook

FIGURE 4.12. The Garmin Vivoactive
Photo by Glory Cycles / CC BY 2.0

members and prospective timeshare owners (Figure 4.13), but it is certainly not a "network business." Is RCI's industry characterized by strong network effects?

The answer here is yes. Every new member who joins the RCI network increases the network's value for the entire current (and prospective) membership because the new member's unit increases the pool of available options. Moreover, it increases the potential pool of people interested in current members' own units—thus making current RCI members' units more likely to be requested for exchange. It follows that for prospective timeshare buyers, joining the largest timeshare exchange network offers the highest value.

How to Recognize a Tippy Market   The two examples above show that "being on the Internet" is no guarantee of being able to harness network effects and that even non-Internet businesses can benefit from network effects. How can we recognize a tippy market a priori? How can you tell if your firm has the potential to harness positive feedback?

Whether a market will tip toward a dominant technology or a dominant player depends on two factors (Figure 4.14):

FIGURE 4.13. RCI's website

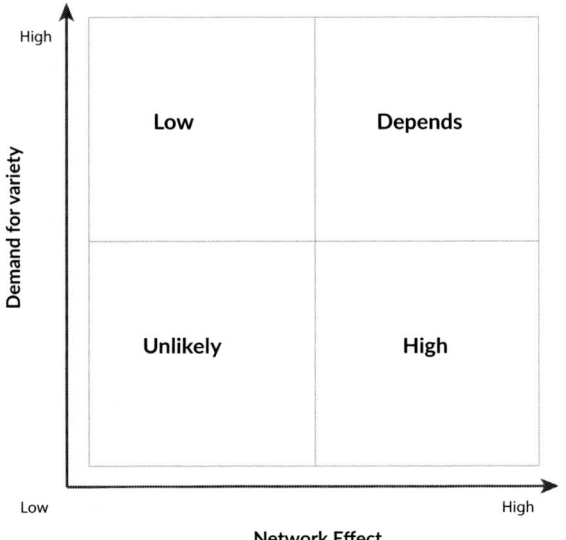

FIGURE 4.14. Likelihood of market tippiness

- *The presence and strength of economies of scale.* Strong economies of scale, whether traditional economies of scale or network effects, provide an advantage to larger firms.
- *The variety of the customer needs.* Customer demand for variety creates the potential for the development of distinct market niches that the dominant player may be unable to fulfill.

When economies of scale are significant and customer needs are fairly standard, then the conditions for market tippiness are strongest. Consider our first example, the fax machine. As we discussed, there are strong network effects in the faxing industry. Moreover, the need for fax machines is a very standardized one—customers don't need much variety in the service. It follows, then, that one dominant fax network would emerge. While more than one fax standard may have been vying for dominance in the early days, the market eventually tipped toward one. The others disappeared. A similar dynamic has played out for modems; videocassette recorders; and, more recently, in the high-definition DVD market.

When economies of scale are limited and the market has a wide range of different needs, the potential for market tippiness is the weakest. This is because not only is there a slight advantage associated with increasing size, but there are also a number of smaller niches that can support multiple smaller focused players. Consider sports cars, for instance. Typically, the top manufacturers, such as Ferrari or Lamborghini (Figure 4.15) and the like, make a limited number of cars. Thus economies of scale are small. Moreover, those who seek to purchase high-end sports cars do so partly to differentiate themselves from the crowd. Those who purchase exclusive goods seek variety—at times even uniqueness. This is therefore a market that is likely to sustain a number of relatively small players.

When economies of scale are significant and demand for variety is high, the potential for market tippiness depends on the number and size of the available market niches. The ability to tap into a sizeable market niche seeking a product with unique specifications (e.g., graphic designers) is what allowed Apple Computers to survive prior to ensuring compatibility with Microsoft-dominant products.

When economies of scale are limited, even if the demand for variety is low, the potential to create positive feedback is small and the market is unlikely to tip.

Two-Sided Networks

Now that we have discussed the dynamics of networks in their purest sense, we can complicate the picture a bit. When network effects are present, the addition of one node to the network directly creates value for all the existing members. However, positive feedback can also occur in what we term *two-sided networks*—that is, networks that have two types of members, each creating value for the other.

Consider, for example, Adobe, the firm that in 1990 invented the now ubiquitous Portable Document Format (PDF) standard. Documents that are converted to PDF are guaranteed to look exactly the same on any platform. Chances are that you are a heavy user of PDF documents, reading them with Adobe's Acrobat Reader, for which you paid exactly nothing—not because you are a user of pirated software, but because Adobe gives the software away for free. In similar fashion, Microsoft gives away its Windows Media Player, as do all other streaming audio/video makers. Why is this so? Does it make sense for a company to give away its product?

The strategy described above is sensible, particularly as the firm tries to establish its product as the standard. As you realize when you move from wanting to read PDF files to wanting to create them, Adobe Acrobat is not free. In other words, Adobe created a market for software programs that would ensure documents' cross-platform accuracy of display. Then it proceeded to establish its technology as the standard by creating a market of users, all those who downloaded and

FIGURE 4.15. The Lamborghini Aventador
Photo by Norbert Aepli / CC BY 3.0

used the free reader. As the number of users grew, fueled by some early adopters of the authoring software (i.e., PDF document makers), organizations that produce and publish documents (e.g., companies publishing manuals for their products online) decided to adopt Adobe Acrobat. In turn, the increasing number of PDF documents available for download created even more demand for the reader software, aided by the "Free: Download Acrobat Reader" link that would be placed next to it.

You immediately recognize this process as an example of positive feedback. If you tried to break into the cross-platform document maker market as of today, you would be taking on a next-to-impossible feat. On the other hand, Adobe today provides a whole family of "ePaper solutions," including, of course, the ubiquitous (and free) Acrobat Reader.

More generally, in a two-sided network, the value of the network to one type of member depends on the number of members from the other side who take part in the network. An example is offered by electronic procurement exchanges (see Chapter 5), such as Alibaba.com. In these marketplaces, whether catering to consumers or businesses, buyers are interested in the number of suppliers they will be able to reach (i.e., selection), while sellers are interested in the number of buyers they will be able to reach (i.e., potential sales volume). In this case as well, the firm that enables the marketplace (i.e., the sponsor of the network) and is first to reach critical mass (i.e., the first to pass the tipping point) will dominate the industry, leaving little room for any competitor (i.e., any competing marketplace).

Implications for General and Functional Managers

Network economics have substantial implications of managerial interest. As networks become more ubiquitous, you must take these implications into account.

Network Effects, Not Just Networks   As we have seen in the many examples provided above, network effects and, more generally, positive feedback create the precondition for winner-takes-all dynamics. Network effects occur in the presence of technology standards, like the fax machine or a computer platform, but are not restricted to the technology arena. They also occur in the presence of virtual networks and communities of interest.

Consider, for example, the great success enjoyed by dating communities, such as Match.com, or employment search sites, such as Monster.com. While these communities do not use or require their members to purchase any specific technology or buy into any technical standard, their value is directly proportional to the number of users they can attract and, as a consequence, they enjoy strong network effects. This dynamic became apparent when a recent hacker attack exposed the list of members of the Ashely Madison website. Men and women join the community, allegedly, to have an affair . . . because, apparently, life is short and we should have affairs (Figure 4.16). When the list was exposed, hackers demonstrated how the site handled its two-sided network effects strategy. A married couple affair site is a "two-sided market" with one side finding value from the prevalence of the other (i.e., men seek women, and women seek men). However, there were only 4.5 million accounts held by women—about 13% of the total.[9] But this is somewhat predictable, and in fact the firm itself claimed to have 5.5 million female members. What is more interesting is that by some analyses, the true number of accounts held by women was much smaller—with a great proportion of profiles being fake accounts operated by bots.[10] While the story is still developing at time of this writing and we can't unquestionably assume that the data released by the hackers are real, this hack makes for a great example of two-sided network

9. Ashley Madison: A final analysis of the data (2015, August 31), *BinaryEdge*, retrieved from http://blog.binaryedge.io/2015/08/31/ashley-madison-a-conclusive-analysis

10. A bot is a computer program designed to respond and interact with users in a human-like manner. More details on this alleged fraud can be obtained here: http://gizmodo.com/how-ashley-madison-hid-its-fembot-con-from-users-and-in-1728410265

FIGURE 4.16. The Ashley Madison website

strategy. If one side of your network is limited in numbers and prevents your market from tipping, you can go the Ashley Madison way and manufacture some entities to fake its existence.[11]

The Threshold of Significance   We defined the tipping point as the watershed of dominance—that moment in the evolution of a market where one organization or technology reaches critical mass and goes on to dominate it. Traditionally, the onset of the tipping point would take some time, as the dominant technology slowly gained acceptance and became adopted by more and more users. For example, in the classic battle for dominance of the videocassette recorder (VCR) market, Sony and JVC struggled to establish their standards—Betamax and VHS, respectively (Figure 4.17). The battle between these competing standards lasted more than a decade and, as we know today, was won by JVC's VHS technology.

The new generation of general and functional managers will not have a decade to monitor competitors before the onset of the tipping point. As a case in point, the recent battle in the DVD market between two technologies vying for dominance—Sony's Blu-ray and Toshiba's high-definition DVD (HD DVD)—played out much more quickly . . . and Sony came out on top this time. Particularly for digital products delivered

FIGURE 4.17. Betamax and VHS tapes

---

11. Newitz, A. (2015, August 31), Ashley Madison code shows more women, and more bots, *Gizmodo*, retrieved from http://gizmodo.com/ashley-madison-code-shows-more-women-and-more-bots-1727613924

over the Internet, the market can tip very rapidly. In some cases, by the time a competitor realizes that a technology is emerging (i.e., the new technology reaches the threshold of significance), it is too late to react. In these markets, being the innovator and the first mover may be critical.

Users Select a Network   One of the most important implications of the above discussion is that customers will pick a network, not a product or a service provider. Let's return to your decision to buy a personal computer. If all your friends are in the Microsoft Windows network, you are most likely to join them in that network. Yet while many of your friends may be using Dell laptops, you could choose a Lenovo machine or even a Mac—which now enables you to be a member of the dominant network. In other words, you will not care about what hardware or software you use, as long as it enables you to tap into the resources of your network of interest.

Controlling the Network Provides Competitive Advantage   Firms are willing to engage in standards battles and invest significant resources to achieve critical mass because sponsoring a dominant network provides the firm with a position of competitive advantage. Consider the court battle involving Facebook and Power Ventures Inc., owner of the domain Power.com, which offered a single sign-on interface to access one's social networks, including LinkedIn, Twitter, MySpace, and AOL or Yahoo! instant messaging. When Power.com, in an attempt to make good on its motto "All your friends in just one place," cached Facebook content to add the most popular social network to its list of sites, Facebook's lawyers sprang into action and sued.[12] They won the 2009 copyright infringement proceedings, and Power.com quickly faded. Why was Facebook the firm that sued Power.com, while other social networks did not? Being the dominant network, Facebook had the most to lose from participating in an arrangement that enabled compatibility across networks.

The Importance of Mutual Exclusivity   Up to this point, we have treated competing networks as mutually exclusive. This is true for many of them. Consider the high-definition standards battle once again. Very few individuals would be willing to purchase two DVD players, one using the Blu-ray standard and the other one using the Toshiba HD DVD standard. This is because not only would they need to purchase two devices that cost money and take up space, but they would also have to maintain separate movie collections with some titles in one format and some in the other.

Simply put, there are costs associated with being a member of both networks. The steeper these costs, the more valuable it is to be able to control and retain ownership of the network. Consider Skype and the VoIP market. Skype is a small piece of software that can be installed quickly and requires little configuration. Once installed, Skype runs as a service in the background until the user decides to make a call. If a competitor with very similar characteristics were to emerge, it would not cost users much to run both applications simultaneously. It is a bit of a nuisance to have to install and run two VoIP applications, but the two networks would not be mutually exclusive, and the power associated with controlling the dominant network (i.e., Skype) would be largely diminished.

The Economics of Information

As networks of interoperable digital devices have continued to expand, one of the most important results of managerial interest has been the unprecedented amounts of data and information that are being captured, stored, processed, and distributed by modern organizations. Andy Cohen, former senior vice president of sales and marketing at supply chain operator iTradeNetwork, said it best a few years back: "The information you can derive from eCommerce is as interesting as the commerce itself."[13]

---

12. Facebook Inc. v. Power Ventures Inc. (n.d.), in *Wikipedia*, retrieved from https://en.wikipedia.org/wiki/Facebook,
_Inc.,_v._Power_Ventures,_Inc.

13. Schwartz, E. I. (2002), *Digital Darwinism: 7 breakthrough business strategies for surviving in the cutthroat Web economy*,
New York, NY: Crown Business.

However, in order to be able to wring value from data and information, you must understand its economic characteristics. Information, like networks, has some interesting traits that differentiate it from physical goods. These unique characteristics of data and information have significant implications for firm strategy and competition.

Data and Information

Information systems (IS) researchers typically draw a distinction between the terms *data* and *information*. *Data* is defined as codified raw facts—things that have happened (e.g., a customer has lodged a complaint) are coded as letters and numbers and stored, increasingly, by way of digital devices (Figure 4.18).

Information is defined as data in context (Figure 4.19). In other words, data become information when they have been given meaning and can therefore be interpreted by individual users or machines. It follows, then, that information is audience dependent; one person's data are another person's information.

7975593065 HAKE4H Th, Dec 30, 2010 6:45 Th, Dec 30, 2010 18:38 DL1072 ATL MSY DR. GABRIELE PICCOLI

FIGURE 4.18. A string of data

Ticket number	Record Locator	Departure	Arrival	Flight #	Departure	Arrival	Passenger
7975593065	HAKE4H	Th, Dec 30,2010 6:45	Th, Dec 30,2010 18:38	DL1072	ATL	MSY	DR. GABRIELE PICCOLI

FIGURE 4.19. Contextualized data become information

FIGURE 4.20. Wind and waves forecast: A classic information good
Source: Windfinder.com

Classic Information Goods

The unique characteristics of information are best understood by first looking at products where information is at the heart of the value proposition. Classic information goods are those products that a customer purchases for the sole purpose of gaining access to the information they contain. Examples include software, books, music, Ted Talks,[14] and the news.

For example, this book (and any other book) is a classic information good. The only reason you purchased it was to be able to gain access to its content.[15] The same goes for movies. The only reason you go to the theater or rent a movie is to gain access to the experience that a film provides. The news represents yet another example. Whether you read the newspaper, watch television, or visit a news agency website, the only reason to do so is to acquire the information provided. Other classic information goods are stock quotes, class lectures, and the like (Figure 4.20).

A simple test for recognizing information goods is to verify whether the product can be digitized (i.e., can be encoded into bits and stored in digital format). If so, the product is an information good. You are probably holding a paper copy of this book, but the same content could be delivered online, as an e-book, or as sound if we decided to publish an audio book version. I have a version of this same book on my computer in Microsoft Word format, while the publisher has a version on their computers in Adobe InDesign.

Now consider the chair on which you are sitting as you read this book. Could that be digitized? The answer is no, of course. The plans and drawings for making the chair could be digitized (another example of an information good), but the chair itself is a physical product that you purchased not for its information content but for its ability to support you in a comfortable reading position. In the future, you may be able to send schematics for a chair anywhere in the world and have a 3D printer produce the chair, but again, the schematics are an information good, whereas the chair is not.

The Economic Characteristics of Information

The fairly specific definition of classic information goods provided above is important because information has some unique and interesting characteristics.

Information Has High Production Costs   The first copy of an information good is very expensive to create in terms of time and money. Consider this book once again. Writing this text required a substantial amount of time in front of a computer typing a first draft, editing it multiple times, selecting appropriate examples, responding to reviewers' comments, and performing further editing as necessary. More subtly, before the writing process even began, substantial time was invested in studying these ideas, learning frameworks proposed by other authors, developing the unique frameworks and analytical models that are original to this text, doing the interviews and writing up the case studies, teaching the material, and taking notes on what seemed to work well in the classroom and what did not. After the draft of the book was completed, editors from the publishing house revised it and typeset it, assistants fact-checked the information and obtained the required copyright permissions for images and quotations, and so on. While this book was a big undertaking, you can envision projects that are even more costly and time consuming. Think about the latest big budget film you have seen, a project that easily cost hundreds of millions of dollars and involved a large number of people who spent years developing their craft. All that work went into creating a less than two-hour-long entertainment experience for you to enjoy. In summary, information goods are very costly to produce. This is particularly true in relative terms, when the cost of producing the first copy is compared to the cost of producing the second one.

Information Has Negligible Replication Costs   This is where information goods begin to differ drastically from physical goods. For as long as it took to create the first copy of this book or the blockbuster movie you last saw, the second copy could be produced at a fraction of the cost. Consider software—say,

---

14. See the Ted Talks website: https://www.ted.com/talks

15. While it can convincingly be argued that we can use a book in many other ways (e.g., as a status symbol), we are focusing here on the use of books, and other information goods, in their primary function—that of conveying the author's message.

the copy of Microsoft Word we are using to write this book. By some accounts, Word is made up of millions of lines of code written by hundreds of Microsoft programmers over the years. The first copy of such a complex software program takes a significant amount of time and money to produce, but what about the second copy? Producing the second copy of Microsoft Word was essentially free. It simply took up a few gigabytes of storage space on a hard disk somewhere at Microsoft Corp.

For many information goods, the second copy, and all subsequent ones, has such a low cost of production that it is essentially free. This is not true of physical goods, such as the chair discussed above, or a car, or a meal. In a restaurant, for example, food is the second largest component of cost, second only to labor. Thus no matter how many steaks the restaurant cooks that evening, each one will consume roughly the same amount of ingredients. The second copy of a steak (i.e., a physical good) is not free.

The Information Is Not the Carrier

Consider the way you access your favorite magazines. Despite the fact that you can go online and read *The Economist* or *TIME* magazine, you might still like to receive a physical copy in the mail. However, you should realize that the paper is simply the "carrier" of the information, not the information itself. After all, you could easily access the same content through a browser on a personal computer or with a tablet or other digital reader. The authors are old enough to remember a time when pictures were physical and had to be developed by specialists, music was carried by vinyl records and cassette tapes (we are now dating ourselves), and software came on CDs (and even before, floppy disks). Today, in the post-PC era (as Steve Jobs used to call it),[16] apps are automatically downloaded onto your smartphone through wireless channels, and the CD is quickly going the way of the floppy disk (Figure 4.21) and the tape cassette.

A stark example of this inexorable transition is the end of Blockbuster, the place that we as kids visited to get movies—first on VHS tapes and later on DVDs. At its peak in 2004, Blockbuster operated more than 9,000 stores worldwide, whereas today, only fewer than 50 franchise-owned stores are still open.[17] We suspect that you don't visit Blockbuster stores and, if you are into movies, either you get them streamed through your cable provider, you have an account on Netflix, or you use one of the many alternative streaming services available on the Internet.

Information Has Negligible Distribution Costs

As with replication costs, the distribution costs associated with information goods are very low. Distribution costs are defined here as the expenditures associated with delivering the information good to the customers so that they can access its content.[18]

Consider once again the example of a big budget movie. How does the movie get to the theater for your enjoyment? Traditionally, the studios copied films onto reels—a typical movie fits on five or six reels—and shipped them in film cans to the theaters. However, strictly speaking, the cost of distributing the cans is the cost of distributing the carrier of the information, not the information itself. In fact, modern delivery systems for in-room entertainment in hotels, for example, rely on digitized movies that are downloaded onto servers that in turn stream them to the TV sets in the rooms. High-definition movie theaters also have done away with the reels.

Where the infrastructure for digital distribution has been created (e.g., the App Store for software applications in the iOS ecosystem), the distribution cost of the information goods is indeed negligible—free in practice. Information goods are therefore characterized by high fixed costs and very low marginal costs. The cost

FIGURE 4.21. 8", 5.25", and 3.5" floppy disks

---

16. Steve Jobs ushers in post-PC era (2010, June 2), *PC magazine*, retrieved September 6, 2015, from http://www.pcmag.com/article2/0,2817,2364545,00.asp

17. See the Blockbuster website: http://www.blockbuster.com/franchise.html

18. A point of confusion here is that the term *distribution cost*, for information goods like movies and music, often refers to marketing expenditures (which can be significant for information goods). In this book, the term *distribution cost* is used in its strict sense and does not include marketing expenditures.

of producing the first copy is steep, whereas the cost of making and delivering incremental copies is almost free.

Costs Are Sunk   Unrecoverable costs—those expenses that the firm has incurred to create its product or service but cannot be recuperated—are termed *sunk costs*. For example, if you are remodeling your kitchen and purchase some new flooring only to find out that your significant other hates it and vetoes your installing it, you can return the material and recover the expense, but you can't recuperate the costs (in terms of time, effort, and gasoline in this case) you spent in selecting and transporting the flooring. Your time and the gas you wasted are sunk costs. Information goods are unforgiving. If nobody is interested in reading our book after it available for sale, we will be unable to recover all the expenses associated with writing and publishing it. If you have dreams of making it big in the music industry, all the time and money you invested in making your first tracks are lost if nobody cares for your form of artistic expression.

What's unique about information goods is that the bulk of their production costs are sunk costs. It follows, therefore, that there is significant risk involved in producing information goods, and consequently a good deal of attention and research needs to be devoted to gauging and creating demand for them—incidentally, this is the reason music artists spend time touring and peddling their music and Hollywood movie actors visit talk shows.

Information Has No Natural Capacity Limits   While the creation of new information goods entails the significant risk that the investment will not be recovered, the upside is also significant. Information goods face almost no constraints to reproduction. Let's return to the example above and imagine that your songs struck a chord with the executives at Shady Records, who see in you the next big hip-hop star. When your songs make it into the iTunes music store, there is no limit to how many times they can be downloaded (i.e., how many digital copies can be generated for next to zero cost).

Information Is Not Consumed by Use   Perhaps the most intriguing characteristic of information is that it can be reused multiple times. Physical goods, like an apple or one night in a hotel room, are destroyed through their use. That is, if you eat the last apple in the room, there is nothing left for anyone else. If you occupy room 235 at the Ritz in Paris on March 19, 2016, that room, that night, will not be available for others to enjoy—unless, of course, they are traveling with you! Conversely, information goods are not consumed by use. When you are watching the FIFA world cup, there are millions of other fans around the world sharing into the same experience. All the people in the theater with you can enjoy the movie alongside you. The fact that you read the news this morning does not preclude me from learning the same facts from the nightly news . . . or even from the very same newspaper you left on the subway on your way to work.

Information Goods Are Experience Goods   Experience goods, are those products or services that need to be tried (i.e., experienced) before their quality can be assessed. All new products and services are experience goods; in fact, perfume trials and samples of shampoo have been used for decades to entice people to buy. However, information goods are experience goods every time. If you are happy with the scent of the Acqua di Giò by Giorgio Armani perfume (Figure 4.22) you sampled, you can make it your perfume of choice and purchase it over and over with confidence (or at least until the manufacturer changes the formula).

But how do you know if next week's copy of *TIME* magazine will be as good as today's? Can you be sure that the next book by Dan Brown is worth reading (assuming the first one was!) or that the BBC international newscast is worth watching tonight?

FIGURE 4.22. Acqua di Giò by Armani
Photo by Net Sama / Public Domain

Implications

The unique economic characteristics of information and classic information goods described above have some important implications for you as a general or functional manager:

- *Information is customizable.* Information goods can often be modified with relative ease. For example, movies are typically edited for different showings or different audiences. Bonus cuts and extra material are often included in DVD releases or collector's editions as a somewhat desperate attempt to entice movie lovers to own their own copies. Physical goods are typically much more difficult to customize before or after they are produced. Imagine realizing that your kitchen is too small after purchasing a new house.
- *Information is reusable.* Because information is not consumed by use, it is reusable multiple times and, because it is customizable, in multiple forms.
- *Information is often time valued.* The value of information is tied to the user's ability to employ it. Often timely use of the information is necessary to reap the potential value. Stock quotes represent a perfect example of this. Stock quotes on a 15-minute delay are useless information to a stock trader. Another example is represented by book publishers, who often release hardcover versions of popular novels and business books before releasing paperbacks that sell for much less. The cost of production of hard covers is not the reason for the price difference. Publishers are simply "versioning" their product to capitalize on the fact that some customers are willing to pay a premium to read the book as soon as it is released.
- *Information goods can achieve significant gross profit margins.* Because of their economic characteristics—high production costs and low replication and distribution—firms that produce successful information goods can enjoy vast profit margins. Microsoft Corporation has enjoyed legendary profits over the years thanks in large part to its two cash cows: Microsoft Windows, the dominant operating system software for personal computers, and Microsoft Office, the dominant suite of productivity tools.

Information-Intensive Goods

As you read the above discussion about classic information goods, you may have wondered what applicability it has to industries that don't deal directly with these goods. That is, how useful is the above discussion to executives in industries such as restaurant franchising, car manufacturing, cruise ship operations, or health care? In each of these industries, you may reason, the value proposition customers seek is a tangible product or service, not information. While this is true, a quick look "under the hood" will reveal that information plays a critical role in these businesses as well.

Authors Evans and Wurster, from their vantage point at the Media and Convergence practice of the Boston Consulting Group, claimed back in 1997 that "every business is an information business." As an example, they cited health care, an industry that offers a very "physical" service, but where one-third of its cost is "the cost of capturing, storing and processing such information as patient's records, physicians' notes, test results, and insurance claims."[19] Most industries, while not dealing directly with information goods, rely on information to create and bring to market their product or service; from research and development, to logistics, to distribution, to sales and marketing, information is the "glue" that holds together business operations. This means is that most products and services are information-intensive goods. For information-intensive goods, while information is not exclusively what the customer seeks when purchasing the products or service, information is either one of their critical components or a necessary resource during their production process.

The role that information plays could be at the periphery of the product or service (e.g., informational material about the features of a product, the brand) or could be embedded in the product itself as knowledge (e.g., R&D and product development research). Consider, for instance, McDonald's Corporation, the franchiser of the popular fast-food restaurants. Is McDonald's in the "restaurant

---

19. Evans, P. B., & Wurster, T. S. (1997, September/October), Strategy and the new economics of information, *Harvard Business Review*, 70–82.

business" or is it in the "information business"? While you may opt for the first answer, a careful analysis reveals that the second is a more accurate label. What McDonald's Corporation sells to its franchisees around the world is sales volume through customer traffic due to its strong brand (i.e., information in the consumer's mind), management know-how (i.e., information about optimal practices, ranging from pricing, to purchasing, to human resource management), and various other support services (e.g., training, bulk purchasing contracts). Thus much of what the franchisor offers is in the form of information and knowledge.

Information is also embedded in the production and organizational processes that enable the transformation of inputs into products and services to be sold. Moreover, products and services in today's economy are increasingly "augmented" by information services. As computers have become increasingly embedded in products and services are more and more computer mediated, the value proposition customers receive from these products and services is increasingly dependent on their information content. Information is also embedded in the production and organizational processes that enable the transformation of inputs into products and services to be sold.

Consider a couple of modern examples: self-driving cars (Figure 4.23) and modern hospitality revenue management. The value proposition of a self-driving car is to get you to your destination safely—many argue more safely than if you drove it yourself—without you having to devote attention to the road. In short, then, the value proposition of a self-driving car is to create extra time for the user—perhaps the most valuable commodity for busy professionals. How does the car "create time," then? Is a self-driving car an information good? Probably not, but it is certainly an information-intensive good, as its value proposition depends on the car's ability to obtain and analyze massive amounts of sensor data in order to make appropriate decisions on the road. Its "analytics engine" is as important as its internal combustion engine. The latter uses gasoline as its fuel, while the former uses digital data streams.

You can think of revenue management in the hospitality industry as a key process in the production and delivery of the hotel experience. Revenue management is the art and science of price optimization—in this case, the process designed to sell the right room, at the right rate, to the right customer at the right time. It is a price optimization process that can help a hotel increase its bottom line while ensuring that customers are satisfied because they perceive that they received good value. Duetto Research uses a cloud-based analytics engine, drawing from a number of new digital data streams, to help hotels achieve this objective.[20] While hospitality is ultimately a tangible product and no amount of data would make up for a missing bed in a hotel room, the process of creating satisfying hospitality experiences is extremely information intensive.

Because of its pervasiveness, information has become a clear source of competitive advantage. Many of the most admired modern organizations draw their advantage from a superior ability to capture, manage, and distribute (or use) information. In Chapter 8, we will discuss ways to think about how to create value using organizational data and information.

Information in Networks

As we have seen, information has unique economic characteristics. However, it has traditionally been constrained to rely on physical carriers in order to be delivered. Film reels carry movies to the theater, books carry text and images to readers, and professors carry lecture content to a class of students. The fact that information has had to rely on a physical carrier has acted as a constraint, limiting its ability to behave according to its inherent characteristics.

Consider the process of organizing your honeymoon prior to 1993, the date of the commercialization of the

FIGURE 4.23. Google's self-driving car
Photo by smoothgroover22 / CC BY SA 2.0

20. Applegate, L. M., Piccoli, G., & Pigni, F. (2015, August), *Duetto: Industry transformation with big data*, Boston, MA: Harvard Business School Press, N9-816-028.

Internet. Back then, you would likely visit a travel agency with your spouse and, after waiting in line for your turn to speak with an agent (the carrier of the information you were seeking), you would tell the agent your likes and dislikes and receive some suggestions. Based on these suggestions and your reaction to them, a skilled travel planner would narrow his or her suggestions, asking increasingly specific questions and offering advice based on his or her superior knowledge of destinations and even individual resorts.

This example suggests that when information is constrained by a carrier, such as the travel agent, it is not allowed to behave like information. That is, while information is not consumed by use and is cheap to reproduce and distribute, since it has to be delivered by a person, it has to follow the economics of the carrier—only one person can speak with the agent at a time. The travel agency could hire and train new agents to reduce the lines, but this would be a costly proposition.

Even in 1993, you could have organized your honeymoon independently. You could have collected brochures and publications (Figure 4.24), telephoned individual resorts for pricing and suggestions, called multiple airlines, and put all the information together—quite a risk for a newlywed, since independent planning would leave you unable to blame the travel agent if your spouse were to have a bad experience! More important, this would have been a time-consuming (i.e., costly) proposition on your part.

The travel agency could also reach a larger audience—for example, by creating brochures with suggestions and sample packages and distributing them by mail. Or it could purchase TV time and run some infomercials. However, such brochures and infomercials provide only limited content when compared with the personalized, interactive exchange that an experienced travel planner could offer.

The Richness and Reach Trade-Off

The travel agency example above is representative of a phenomenon known as the trade-off between richness and reach. *Richness* represents the amount of information that can be transmitted, the degree to which the information can be tailored to individual needs, and the level of interactivity of the message. *Reach* represents the number of possible recipients of the message. Traditionally, as information has been constrained by its physical carrier, a firm would have to make a trade-off decision between the number of people it wanted to communicate a message to (i.e., reach) and the depth of the message (i.e., richness).

FIGURE 4.24. Traditional travel brochures

Before the advent of widespread information networks, a firm with a fixed budget would have to decide whether it was willing to reach a smaller audience with a richer message (e.g., individual consultations with a travel agent) or use a leaner message to reach a larger audience (e.g., create a brochure and mail it to perspective travelers). This trade-off, a "compromise" that constrains information to behave like its physical carrier, is represented by the line in Figure 4.25. The line on the graph represents the frontier of optimal decisions—that is, the firm will be able to choose any point below the frontier, but the optimal decisions (those that offer the highest return in terms of simultaneous reach and richness) are those on the frontier. Because of the constraints identified above, the firm cannot go beyond this frontier.

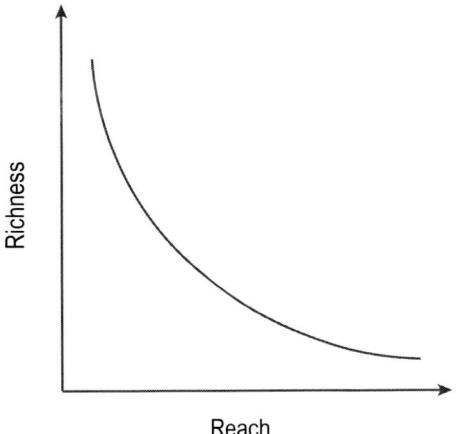

FIGURE 4.25. The richness/reach trade-off

With the advent and widespread adoption of a cheaply and easily accessible information infrastructure, such as the Internet and the services it makes available, these constraints are increasingly being lifted. Ubiquitous communication networks and powerful computers are quickly enabling firms to decouple information from the physical objects that traditionally carried it.

For example, digital music no longer needs a CD, novels and stories no longer need books, and lectures and meetings carried out on a platform like WebEx or Cisco's TelePresence no longer require the physical copresence of participants. The Internet and the technologies that leverage it have mitigated the trade-off between rich information and the reach of the message. Note that the trade-off between reach and richness has not been eliminated. There are still compromises to be made between reaching a large audience and offering a very rich exchange. However, new technology is making it increasingly possible to reach many people with more

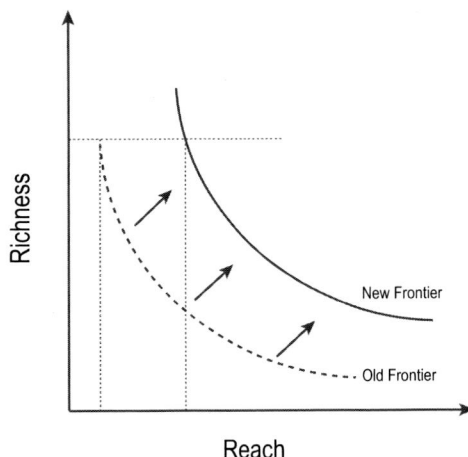

FIGURE 4.26. Technology pushing the richness/reach frontier

information-intensive, interactive, and personalized messages (Figure 4.26).

Consider the travel agency example once more. As travel products have moved aggressively to the Internet platform, you now have increasing access to 360-degree views of resorts, live chats with agents, travel blogs, communities of interest where people share their cumulative experiences (Figure 4.27), and travel products packaged by an online agency.

Yet while these technologies are increasingly pushing the reach/richness frontier and encroaching on travel agents' territory, they have yet to be able to fully replicate the face-to-face interaction and high degree of personalization that a knowledgeable, skilled travel agent can offer.

Implications

As new technology eases the trade-off between richness and reach, a number of implications emerge for you as a general or functional manager.

Continued Questioning of Traditional Business Models A number of "traditional" business models were predicated on the fact that information was constrained by its carrier. Such business models have been facing, and will continue to face, challenges from focused organizations that exploit emerging information technology. Consider the traditional travel agent business model one final time. Many travel agents do an outstanding job of providing valuable consultation and advice to prospective travelers. In the past, others based their value proposition on the fact that most travelers didn't have the ability to book their own travel. As airlines, hotels, and car rentals created their own bookable websites and travel intermediaries such as Kayak.com and Skyscanner made it easy to quickly query multiple providers, the latter kind of travel agents faced significant pressure, and many closed up shop (Figure 4.28). With technology advancing relentlessly, even those travel agents who offer valuable information and expertise will come under increasing pressure.

The effect of widespread adoption of computer networks is particularly threatening to organizations that historically bundled services, using one to subsidize the other. Consider the daily newspaper industry. By some accounts, a typical newspaper collects 20% to 25% of its revenue from the classified section. Yet the classifieds account for only 5% of the cost of operating a newspaper. As a consequence, the classifieds are subsidizing many other aspects of the newspaper business, such as reporting and editing.

With the advent of the Internet and websites such as eBay and Craigslist, newspapers have seen and continue to see a loss of revenue from the classifieds—after all, what is eBay if not a global classified ads section with an auction twist? While

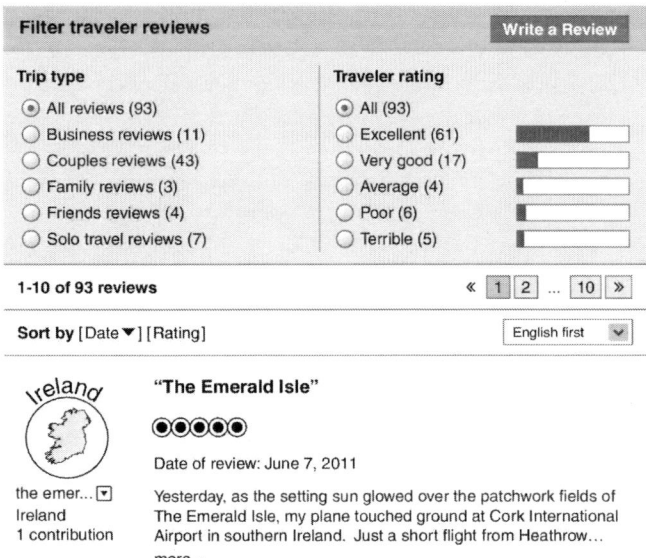

FIGURE 4.27. Online travel review

FIGURE 4.28. A travel agency gone out of business

newspapers are unlikely to become extinct any time soon, this example shows that the unbundling of information from the physical carrier can have far-reaching consequences—particularly for firms whose current business model is predicated on the need to bundle information with a physical carrier.

Consider another example: the movie rental business. With high-capacity broadband networks coming to the home in the form of digital cable, we are now able to order movies on demand and start, pause, and restart them at will—just like rentals, but without the late fees. Unbundling the information customers want (the movie) from the carrier (the VHS tape or DVD) has enabled superior convenience in the form of easy billing in a monthly statement; no late fees; and no need to leave the home, stand in line, or find that the movie we want is sold out.

The Importance of the Customer Interface   If information is increasingly allowed to travel independently of its carriers, it becomes feasible to unbundle traditional products and services (as described above) and bundle products that could never be brought together before. Consider the retail banking industry. Traditionally, a customer would purchase a bundle of services from her retail bank—say, a checking account, a savings account, certificates of deposit, mutual funds, a car loan, and a mortgage.

An important value driver of this bundle would be the convenience of one-stop shopping (i.e., being able to visit one branch to address a number of financial needs).

Today, that same customer may use Quicken or Mint.com to manage her finances, thus being able to interact directly with individual providers of each of the services she needs—even through a cell phone (Figure 4.29). She might have checking and savings accounts with the local bank, a car loan with another local provider, a mortgage through LendingTree.com, mutual funds and retirement planning with Schwab.com, and some stocks with Ameritrade. Being able to easily download monthly statements to Mint, she can keep the pulse of her financial standings and easily switch providers, as long as the new one also enables downloads to Mint. The old adage about the importance of "location, location, location" is in many industries based on information friction and is being challenged by technologies that mitigate the trade-off between reach and richness.

FIGURE 4.29. Mint on the iPhone

In the environment described in the above example, having a direct relationship with the customer, or owning the customer interface, may become critical. In the banking case, it is Mint, a software company, which is in the strongest position. Customers may become more loyal to Mint than to any of the providers of financial services in the background.

The example still seems a bit futuristic, and significant obstacles remain to the widespread adoption of these arrangements (see below), but we are beginning to see a number of organizations vying to control the customer interface. Consider Progressive insurance, for instance. In its advertisements, the firm promises that its agents will seek to find you the best insurance plan, even shopping and suggesting competitors for you. The objective of this approach is to ensure that you think about them when seeking to purchase insurance, thus allowing them to preserve control of the customer interface.

The Decreasing Value of Asymmetric Information   Perhaps the most evident implication of the emergence of technologies that ease the trade-off between reach and richness is the amount of information modern customers have available to them. This has put significant pressure on organizations that benefit from asymmetry of information.[21] If an organization bases its value proposition on the inability of individuals to obtain and use information at low costs, that position is increasingly untenable as the richness/reach frontier is progressively pushed outward. Today, for example, within a few minutes you can shop for a car online, find out the factory price from Edmunds.com, research various dealer packages, find out the value of your used car trade-in, and walk into a dealership ready to negotiate.

---

21. Asymmetry of information is the condition where one party to a transaction has more information than the other party. Purchasing a used car is a classic example, where the seller knows the history of the car, while the buyer has to rely on the seller or use other imprecise means to gauge the quality of the car (e.g., take it to a mechanic).

Obstacles

While there are many examples of industries where the effects of the easing trade-off between reach and richness are being felt, there are a number of obstacles that have been slowing and will continue to slow down this process.

New Technology Must Replace All Characteristics of the Old One   Consider again the example of newspapers. Newspapers do not offer the best platform for consuming the news; they are not as timely as the television news or the Internet, they support neither video nor high-quality images, they offer limited space, and they have many other drawbacks. Why do we still buy them and read them (albeit in fewer and fewer numbers)? Why don't we all read the news online? Most newspapers have websites anyway.

The answer is simple: With all the drawbacks newspapers have due to the constraints of printed paper, the broadsheet is still the most portable, most convenient, and easiest-to-read device for accessing the news. While e-books and tablets are increasingly challenging the dominance of paper, the newspaper will not disappear until new technology is able to supplant its advantages. The lesson is clear: old technology goes away only when the new one has replaced all its relevant characteristics. Until then, the new and old technologies tend to coexist—as do newspapers and online news today.

Retaliation from Incumbents   As we attempt to envision how new technology changes society and the competitive environment, seeking ways to create value in the new environment, it is easy to commit a critical fallacy: ignoring incumbents' retaliation. This was one of the main mistakes many observers made during the dot-com days. Retaliation can come in a number of forms:

- *Legal means*, such as those used by the music industry in reaction to the advent of digital music and the MP3 compression standard
- *Legislative means*, such as the lobbying efforts of car dealership networks to stave off direct sales by car manufacturers
- *Hybrid offers*, such as those provided by retailers with physical stores and online operations so as to leverage their existing infrastructure
- *Heightened competition*, such as that started by telecommunications companies in reaction to the offering of voice over IP solutions

While it is enticing to think about the promise of the new technology and the opportunities it offers, you always need to remember that the road from today's landscape to the future reality is paved with competitive battles.

Human Resistance to Change   Perhaps the most powerful bottleneck to some of the changes discussed above is human inertia. New technologies and new ways of doing business, while offering advantages, entail costs in the form of learning to use the new technology or simply stopping the old routine. While easily dismissed, these considerations can spell the difference between success and failure in a fledgling business. The history of IT is full of great ideas that fell prey to the "if we build it, they will come" mentality and failed to address and manage human resistance to change.

Attention Challenges   A byproduct of the unprecedented availability of information is the increasing difficulty people encounter in keeping up with it. Customers' attention is not only required for your product or service to be considered, but it is also required to educate customers about its advantages and how they can best use it. People's time and attention is perhaps the scarcest resource an organization has to deal with. The scarcity of attention leads to slow adoption rates for all but the most revolutionary of innovations.

Consider, for instance, online grocery shopping, an industry mostly remembered for having produced the largest failure of the dot-com era. Webvan, the poster child for online grocery shopping, burned through $1.2 billion in funding before it closed up shop, much to the dismay of its few but

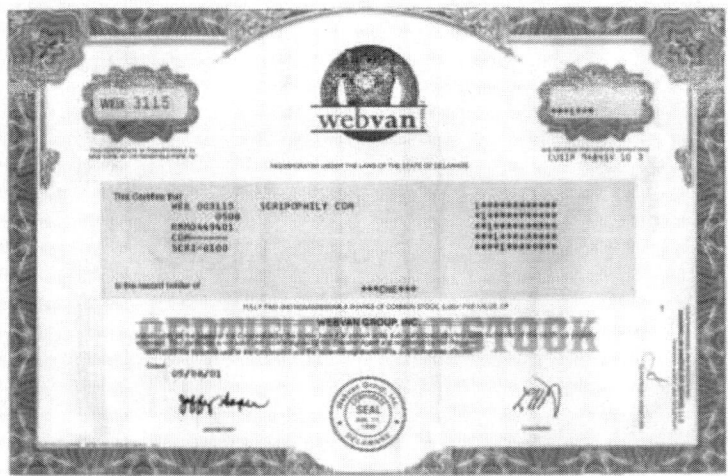

FIGURE 4.30. Webvan stock certificate
Source: Scripophily (n.d.), *Webvan.com: Bankrupt dot com brought home the bacon*, retrieved from
http://scripophily.net/webvancom.html

enthusiastic customers (Figure 4.30). Yet online grocery shopping is alive and well in many locales, the torch being carried by traditional brick-and-mortar grocery chains.[22] The lesson of the Webvan story is not so much that online grocery shopping was an ill-conceived idea but rather that the consumer adoption rate of this radically new way of performing a task that is thousands of years old was much slower than the adoption rates Webvan needed to survive as an online-only grocery operation.

A Note about Disruptive Technology

Beyond the role of the Internet in changing the competitive landscape and the role of information and network economics, as a general or functional manager, it is important that you are aware of the potential disruptive impact of new technologies. Specifically, you should be able to identify and, to the extent possible, manage the impact of emerging disruptive technologies.

Sustaining Technology

For decades, the innovation literature has investigated the characteristics of new technology. Clayton Christiansen's[23] work has identified a classification that has important implications for strategy: the differentiation between sustaining and disruptive technologies.

The defining characteristic of sustaining technologies is that they maintain or rejuvenate the current rate of performance improvement of the products and services that use them. The performance trajectory of a new product (e.g., electric cars) is typically captured visually by the use of the S-curve (Figure 4.31). The S-curve suggests that as the product is first introduced, its performance is limited. With design refinements comes a growth period where substantial improvements in performance are

---

22. Peters, K. (2003, July 2), Online grocery showing fortified strength, study says, *InternetRetailer*, from http://www .internetretailer.com/internet/marketing-conference/27475-online-grocery-showing-fortified-strength-study-says.html, retrieved January 9, 2015; How to win in online grocery: Advice from a pioneer (2014, December), *McKinsey Insights*, retrieved January 9, 2015, from http://www.mckinsey.com/insights/consumer_and_retail/how_to_win_in_online _grocery_advice_from_a_pioneer.
23. Christiansen, C. M. (1997), *The innovator's dilemma: When new technologies cause great firms to fail*, Boston, MA: Harvard Business School Press.

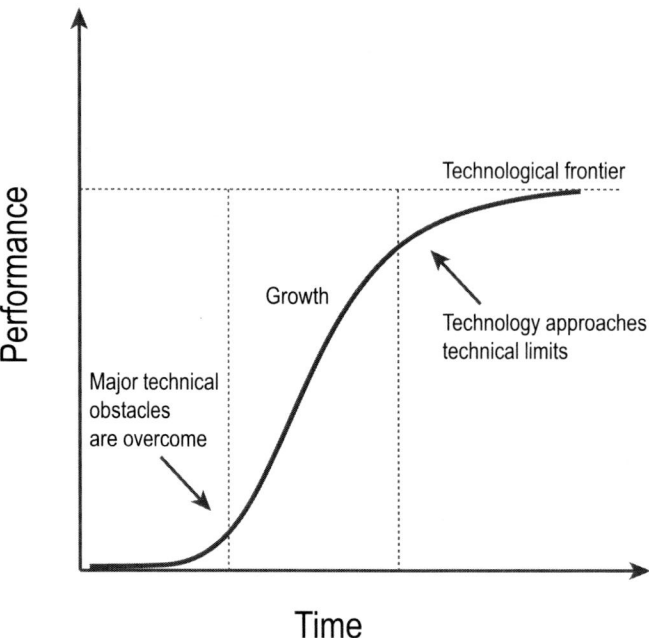

FIGURE 4.31. Product performance improvements over time

achieved until the technology underpinning product performance plateaus and further performance improvements become marginal.

Sustaining technologies are those new technologies that enable a product's performance to continue to grow—in other words, sustaining technologies extend the useful life of the product as the market demands further and further improvements (Figure 4.32). A sustaining technology will therefore be a good candidate to replace a previous generation because it offers the same set of attributes, but it yields superior performance. Thus firms that are using the existing technology in their product will find it appealing to switch to the sustaining technology as they seek to improve their products along the established performance trajectory.

Consider, for instance, the mechanical excavation industry. At the turn of the century, the tool of choice in this industry was the steam shovel. Steam shovels used a steam engine to generate the power required to pull the cables that would lift buckets full of dirt to be moved. In the early 1920s, the steam shovel began to be replaced by gasoline-powered shovels that offered superior performance on the critical performance dimension: the ability to move dirt in a fast, reliable, and cost-effective manner. This is an example of sustaining technology, since the new technology (i.e., gasoline engines) enabled manufacturers of dirt-moving equipment to improve the performance of their product on critical performance dimensions.

Disruptive Technology

Disruptive technologies are defined by the following two characteristics:

- The technology offers a different set of attributes than the technology the firm currently uses in its products.
- The performance improvement rate of the technology is higher than the rate of improvement demanded by the market (Figure 4.33).

While a disruptive technology has an inferior performance with respect to current market demands and what is delivered by existing technology, it offers two advantages: a different set of performance characteristics and a high rate of performance improvement on the critical performance dimensions.

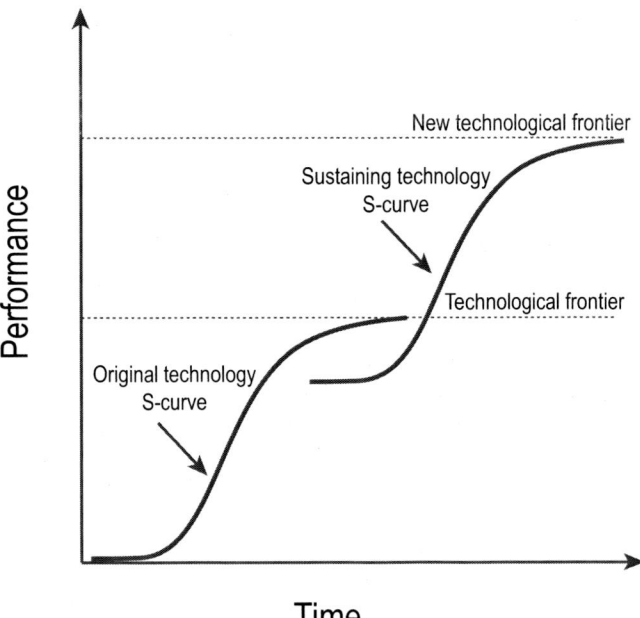

FIGURE 4.32. Performance improvements over time

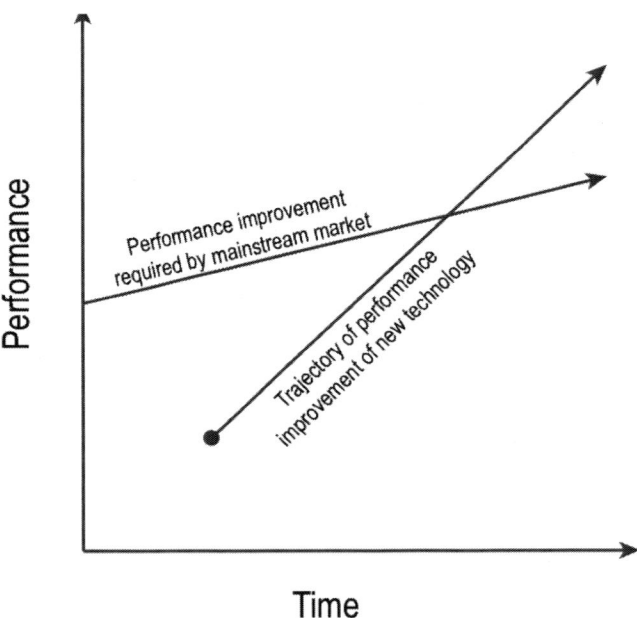

FIGURE 4.33. Market expectations for performance and new technology performance improvement over time

Consider the example of the hard disk industry. The critical performance dimension for customers of hard disk drives (i.e., computer manufacturers) is the storage capacity of the disk. With remarkable precision, hard disk drive manufacturers have been blindsided by the emergence of an architecture design that enabled smaller and smaller drives to be produced—from the original 14-inch drives, to the 8-, 5.25-, 3.5-, 2.5-, and 1.8-inch architectures. This is because these changes were disruptive in nature.

Each generation of smaller disk drives did not at first offer the same storage capacity as the established one. Yet each generation offered a performance rate of improvement on this dimension (the critical performance dimension) far superior to the speed with which computer manufacturers required greater storage capacity. As a consequence, when the storage capacity of the smaller drives reached market needs, the incumbent's mainstream customers switched to the new entrants. No longer having storage capacity concerns, they now valued the other characteristics offered by the new technology (i.e., smaller size, reduced power consumption). Many have suggested that 3D printing and digital manufacturing (see Chapter 12) may turn out to be a disruptive technology (Figure 4.34). The industry recently experienced two-digit growth and is forecasted to more than double every year between 2015 and 2018.[24] By bridging the physical and the digital worlds, 3D printing is making a new business ecosystem emerge in which digitally designed objects are shared online and locally manufactured. The technology has been around since the 1980s, but only recently has the massive drop in the cost of 3D printers made the tech-

FIGURE 4.34. 3D printer
Photo by Creative Tools / CC BY 2.0

nology affordable and personal. The story may repeat itself, and personal 3D printing may disrupt the manufacturing industry just as home and personal computers changed the IT industry forever.

Implications for Managers

Familiarity with the dynamics of disruptive technologies is important for modern general and functional managers because disruptive technologies typically blindside leading firms (i.e., the incumbents in the market), who see their position of dominance lost to those upstarts that were able to ride the disruptive technology wave.

Differential Rates of Improvements   The deadliest characteristic of disruptive technology is its rate of evolution on the currently established performance metrics. As shown in Figure 4.33, a disruptive technology begins with performance that is well below the needs of the firm's mainstream customers. Moreover, the disruptive technology will likely not improve at a rate sufficient to overcome the existing or sustaining technologies available. However, this is misleading information for a manager!

In truth, it is irrelevant whether the disruptive technology will ever outstrip the current one on key performance metrics. Rather, you should estimate whether, in the foreseeable future, the disruptive technology will catch up to market needs on the critical performance dimensions (i.e., become good enough for mainstream customers).

It is often the case that a firm, focused on its most demanding and most advanced customers, will push the performance of its products using new generations of sustaining technologies. However, such a relentless focus on the most demanding customers may end up pushing the firm to increasingly overshoot the needs of its mainstream customers. When this is the case, the incumbent firm becomes particularly vulnerable to disruptive technologies.

Different Sets of Attributes Become Relevant   As disruptive technologies close the gap between the performance level they offer and mainstream customer needs, the novel set of attributes they offer may become increasingly attractive to potential customers. In other words, as the disruptive technology closes the gap on the primary performance metrics, the technology's other characteristics may become a source of positive differentiation. At this point, customers defect from established suppliers offering the standard products and begin to adopt the new technology—but it is typically too late for established players to make the switch to the new technology.

---

24. Gartner Inc. (2014, October), Gartner says worldwide shipments of 3D printers to reach more than 217,000 in 2015, retrieved from http://www.gartner.com/newsroom/id/2887417

Listening Closely to Customers Might Spell Trouble   Conventional business wisdom suggests that a firm is well served by listening closely to its customers in an effort to develop the products and services that best serve their needs. While you should not ignore this suggestion, we add a word of caution: listening attentively to your most aggressive customers will create a bias toward prompt adoption of sustaining technology and a reluctance to buy into disruptive technology.

Your best customers are constantly pushing the envelope of your product performance. Consider again the hard drive industry. High-end computer manufacturers, seeking to outdo each other, will seek larger and faster hard disks to be included in their machines. As a consequence, they will create an incentive for you to adopt those technologies that offer improved performance on the accepted set of performance metrics. A technology that enables the development of smaller hard disks is not valued, even though these smaller devices have other interesting characteristics, such as compact size, lower energy consumption, and less need for heat dispersion. They simply are not good enough on the "important" dimensions that your best customers are clamoring for. However, if the new, smaller hard disks are a disruptive technology, their performance will soon meet the needs of your mainstream customers. When this happens, all those other characteristics may become valuable, and you'll be left with a rapidly shrinking market.

What to Do?

Those studying disruptive technology change suggest the following approach to managing organizations that face the emergence and development of disruptive technologies:

- Monitor market developments for the emergence of new technologies and determine whether they are of the sustaining or disruptive kind.
- When disruptive technologies emerge, envision the new market they would likely be best suited for. One of the greatest challenges faced by the incumbent firm is to identify which customers will likely appreciate the new blend of features and functionalities that the disruptive technology supports. While a producer of large mainframes does not care much about the power requirements and physical size of hard disks, these are critical characteristics for laptop manufacturers.
- Spin off a new division that focuses exclusively on the commercialization of products based on the disruptive technology. Separating the group that is blazing the trail for the new technology may be necessary to create the appropriate financial incentives. Disruptive technologies start off serving the needs of a small niche market. As such, it is difficult for large companies to get excited about—and, more important, divert resources to—such small markets. A separate entity, focusing on that business and competing with the other small firms in the new market, would have no difficulty creating the appropriate incentives.

Summary

This chapter provides you with a framework to understand how new technologies are shaping the competitive landscape you will encounter as you enter the job market. Specifically, in this chapter, we discussed three broad topics: network economics, information economics, and disruptive technologies.

- Value in networks—physical ones such as the telephone network and virtual ones such as eBay's online community of buyers and sellers—is created by plentitude. This value driver is the opposite of the principal value driver of most other goods and services: scarcity.
- Because the most valuable networks are the largest ones, an individual's act of joining a network creates value for the other members of the network—a phenomenon termed *network effects*. In industries subject to strong network effects, particularly when the demand for variety is low and networks are mutually exclusive, winner-take-all dynamics ensue and the market is dominated by one organization.

- Information, a prevalent resource in the modern competitive landscape, has unique economic characteristics. In its purest form, information has high production costs, which are sunk, and negligible replication and distribution costs. The production of information faces no natural capacity limits, and information is not consumed by use. As a consequence, information is infinitely reusable, highly customizable, and often time valued.
- When discussing information as an organizational resource, it is important to distinguish the information itself from the carrier of the information. Historically, information as a resource or product had been constrained by the economics of the carrier. The advent of the Internet, a global infrastructure for information exchange, has in many cases separated the two. New technology continues to push the frontier of the richness/reach trade-off and, in the process, threatens established business models in information industries and beyond.
- New technologies can be characterized as sustaining or disruptive. Sustaining technologies are those that maintain or rejuvenate the current rate of performance improvement of the products and services that use them. Conversely, disruptive technologies are those that offer a different set of attributes than the technology the firm currently uses in its products, and their performance improvement rate is higher than the rate of improvement of market needs. Disruptive technologies are particularly dangerous for established firms, which typically tend to underestimate their potential impact on the firm's current business. Proper monitoring and management of disruptive technologies by the incumbent are necessary because, due to the rate of performance improvement and the different set of features they offer, once a disruptive technology has achieved acceptable performance improvements on the traditional dimensions of performance, customers quickly defect to products that use it.

Study Questions

1. Define the term *Internet* and offer examples of its principal services. What is the difference between the Internet and the World Wide Web?
2. What do you see as the likely evolution of the Internet in the near future?
3. Explain each of the following concepts: positive feedback, network effects, and tippy markets. Explain how the three concepts relate to one another.
4. Offer an example of a tippy market and an example of a market that does not tip.
5. Differentiate physical and virtual networks and provide examples of each.
6. Explain the defining characteristics of a two-sided network and provide an example.
7. What is the defining characteristic of classic information goods? How do they differ from information-intensive goods? Provide examples of each.
8. Information, as an economic entity, behaves quite differently than traditional goods. Identify the principal economic characteristics of information and draw the primary implications for strategy.
9. Explain what we mean by the richness/reach trade-off. Why is this concept important today for general and functional managers? Provide examples of recent technologies that have pushed the richness/reach trade-off frontier farther out. What industries or organizations are under pressure as a consequence of this development?
10. Do you believe that "the Internet changes everything," or is it "just another technology"? Be sure to defend your position.
11. What is the difference between sustaining and disruptive technologies? Offer one example of each.
12. What would you advise an incumbent firm to do in the face of the emergence of new technology? For example, if you were an executive for American Airlines, what would you do about the recent introduction of very light jets (VLJ)—such as the 2,000 preordered Eclipse 500 VLJs from Eclipse Aviation, which are able to reach 300 miles per hour and a have a range of 1,125 nautical miles?[25] Is "air taxi" a disruptive technology? What should major airlines do about it, if anything?

25. Light jets promise air revolution (2006, March 31), *CNN*, retrieved January 10, 2011, from http://edition.cnn.com/2006/TRAVEL/03/31/private.jet/

Further Readings

1. Bower, J. L., & Christensen, C. M. (1995, January–February). Disruptive technologies: Catching the wave. *Harvard Business Review*, 43–53.
2. Christensen, C. M. (1997). *The innovator's dilemma: When new technologies cause great firms to fail.* Boston, MA: Harvard Business School Press.
3. Evans, P. B., & Wurster, T. S. (1997, September/October). Strategy and the new economics of information. *Harvard Business Review*, 70–82.
4. Evans, P. B., & Wurster, T. S. (1999). *Blown to bits: How the new economics of information transforms strategy.* Boston, MA: Harvard Business School Press.
5. Halaburda, H., and Oberholzer-Gee, F. (2014). The limits of scale. *Harvard Business Review, 92*(4), 94–99.
6. Porter, M. (2001, March). Strategy and the Internet. *Harvard Business Review*, 62–78.
7. Rayport, J., & Sviokla, J. (1994, November–December). Managing in the marketspace. *Harvard Business Review*, 141–150.
8. Schrage, M. (2013, December 4). Who's managing your company's network effects? *Harvard Business Review*. Retrieved from https://hbr.org/2013/12/whos-managing-your-companys-network-effects/
9. Shapiro, C., & Varian, H. R. (1999). *Information rules.* Boston, MA: Harvard Business School Press.
10. Shirky, C. (2001, March). The Internet revolution rages on. *Business 2.0.*
11. Tapscott, D. (2001, July 1). Rethinking strategy in a networked world. *Strategy and Competition*, third quarter, 1–8.

Glossary

- **Classic information goods:** Goods purchased for the sole purpose of gaining access to the information they contain.
- **Data:** Codified raw facts—things that have happened—coded as letters and numbers and increasingly stored by way of a computer.
- **Disruptive technologies:** Technologies that offer a different set of attributes than the technology a firm currently uses in its products and whose performance improvement rate is higher than the rate of improvement of market needs.
- **Information:** Data in context.
- **Information-intensive goods:** Those tangible products and services (i.e., not classic information goods) for which information is either one of the critical components or a necessary resource during the production process.
- **Internet:** A global, publicly accessible network of digital networks relying on distributed ownership and open standards.
- **Message reach:** The number of possible recipients of a message.
- **Message richness:** The amount of information that can be transmitted, the degree to which the information can be tailored to individual needs, and the level of interactivity of the message.
- **Negative feedback:** The self-reinforcing process by which the strong get weaker and the weak get stronger.
- **Network effects:** The process by which a network becomes more valuable as its size increases—that is, when a new node, while pursuing his or her own economic motives, joins the network, the network is more valuable for all the other members.
- **Network node:** Any device connected to a network.
- **Physical networks:** Networks where the nodes are connected by physical links (e.g., railroad tracks, telephone wires).
- **Positive feedback:** The self-reinforcing process by which the strong get stronger and the weak get weaker.
- **Protocol:** An agreed-upon set of rules or conventions governing communication among the elements of a network (i.e., network nodes).
- **Sustaining technology:** A technology that maintains or rejuvenates the current rate of performance improvement of the products and services that use it.
- **Tipping point:** That moment in the evolution of a market where one organization or technology reaches critical mass and goes on to dominate the market—the point of nonreturn where winners and losers are defined.

- **Tippy market:** A market that is subject to strong positive feedback, such that the market will "tip" in favor of the firm that is able to reach critical mass and dominate the market. A tippy market is therefore a market with "winner-take-all" tendencies.
- **Virtual networks:** Networks in which the connections between nodes are not physical but intangible and invisible. The nodes of a virtual network are typically people rather than devices.
- **World Wide Web:** One of the most popular services available on the Internet. It consists of "pages" and other resources that can be easily created, published, and accessed by way of uniform resource locator (URL) addresses.

CHAPTER 5

Electronic Commerce: New Ways of Doing Business

What You Will Learn in This Chapter

This chapter covers almost two decades of electronic commerce history and trends. The objective is to help you develop a solid grounding in electronic commerce concepts and vocabulary—a vocabulary that is no longer the exclusive province of Silicon Valley insiders but an integral part of the language of modern business. After laying the foundations, we look ahead to coming electronic commerce trends. Specifically, this chapter will

1. Articulate what the Internet is and discuss its principal characteristics and the services it makes available to users.
2. Broaden your definition of the Internet from a network of computer networks to an information grid connecting a staggering range of devices, both wired and wireless.
3. Compare and contrast *electronic commerce* and *electronic business* and provide examples of each. You will learn how to identify and understand the enablers of electronic commerce trends.
4. Categorize electronic commerce phenomena on a number of different dimensions, including the type of transactions taking place and the structure of the organizations involved.
5. Help you understand and apply the concept of *business model* and explain why the Internet has led to so much business model experimentation. You will learn how to identify the principal *revenue models* employed in electronic commerce and explain the dominant business model in use today.
6. Allow you to understand and evaluate the principal implications of electronic commerce for both established firms and new entrants.
7. Evaluate the *Web 2.0* phenomenon and discuss both its technological and its organizational manifestations.
8. Discuss some of the more relevant future electronic commerce and electronic business trends.

MINICASE: The Quest for Differentiation and Profits at EpicTrip.com

The phone started ringing as you arrived in the office. You picked up the receiver and immediately recognized the familiar soft voice: "Hey there, it's Steve-O!" You had not heard from him in a few months, but in a split second his whole work history flashed in your brain. Steve Yu, Steve-O as his closest friends called him, went to work for a large corporation right after college. As the executive assistant to the president of one of the largest hotel chains in the United States, he had the luxury of being involved in high-stakes strategic decisions, without much of the responsibility. But as an entrepreneur and a dreamer at heart, Steve quickly became disenchanted with the corporate lifestyle. As a former Marine, he was fond of saying, "Life's too short not to chase your dream."

The genesis of Epic Trip stemmed from Steve's interest in studying television commercials while attending college. He believed commercials told compelling stories when emotionally connecting with consumers about the possibilities of what the product could help the customer realize or achieve. About a year and half ago, Steve resigned from his job as executive assistant and founded his own firm. With one childhood friend and a lot of ramen noodles, they began developing what would soon become EpicTrip.com (Figure 5.1). An arts enthusiast, Steve brought significant design sensitivity to the team, while his partner brought the technical skills. The vision behind EpicTrip.com was to revolutionize how people purchase travel.

The Epic Trip website read: "Epic Trip is a new and unique way for travelers to know what their destinations and their hotels are all about, even before setting off. We aim to become the premiere multimedia travel search engine and social network on the web by connecting travelers with videos, virtual tours, reviews, and their experiences."

The Internet travel market was crowded with sites that focused on listing as many options as possible and finding customers the "best deals," so Steve believed there would be value in focusing on the experience of travel, even before the trip started. Through the use of rich media (videos, virtual tours, photos, and audio), Epic Trip was designed to help travelers get a feel for the unique offerings of their destination before arriving—and to dream about new ones. Epic Trip also focused on community, with tools for members to share their experiences and photos and to connect with other like-minded travelers.

Still in beta version, without any formal marketing campaign, EpicTrip.com was attracting some attention from bloggers, travel industry insiders, and travel enthusiasts. The consensus was that the Epic Trip site was visually appealing and extremely easy to navigate.

"What's up, Steve-O?" you screamed into the receiver, a bit too loud for the early hour. "I know that you've been doing some eCommerce consulting for the travel industry as of late," said Steve, adding with a chuckle, "I keep up with you, my friend." You fire back: "I've been monitoring your progress, too. I see you have launched in beta already." "We're at a crossroads," Steve said, his voice becoming serious. "We have the site up and running, and we have the partnerships in place with the major travel distributors. The site is fast, and we have rolled out the members' area and the platform for featured destinations" (Figure 5.2).

"Nice going, Steve-O!" you exclaim, excited about the progress. "Time to make some dough now, buddy," Steve replies. "As you know, we originally thought about a referral model, taking a cut when people follow a link from our site and purchase some travel product." "That's a tough business," you interject. "Exactly," Steve replies. "It appears we have people doing research on the site, but they don't go straight through. They may come back over and over, and later book or even call an agency or a hotel themselves. We don't get paid that way. In addition, we just learned that Expedia is now offering free production of virtual tours to hotels to be featured on their site."

With very limited resources, Steve knew he had to quickly come up with a solid value proposition that differentiated Epic Trip and a revenue model to approach potential investors. "You're my eCommerce guru; I need some guidance. I have some ideas, but I would love your take. I need to start monetizing this platform we've built," said Steve. "Absolutely!" you reply without hesitation. "Give me until the end of the week to study this and I'll call you with some ideas." Steve answers, "Thanks bud, I knew I could count on you. Talk to you at the end of the week."

Discussion Questions

1. What kind of information do you think you need to seek out as you formulate your recommendations for Steve?
2. How do you suggest that Epic Trip think about driving revenue? What are some of the options? How would you rank them relative to each other?
3. What would you suggest Epic Trip do to differentiate itself? How can Steve ensure the long-term viability of Epic Trip?

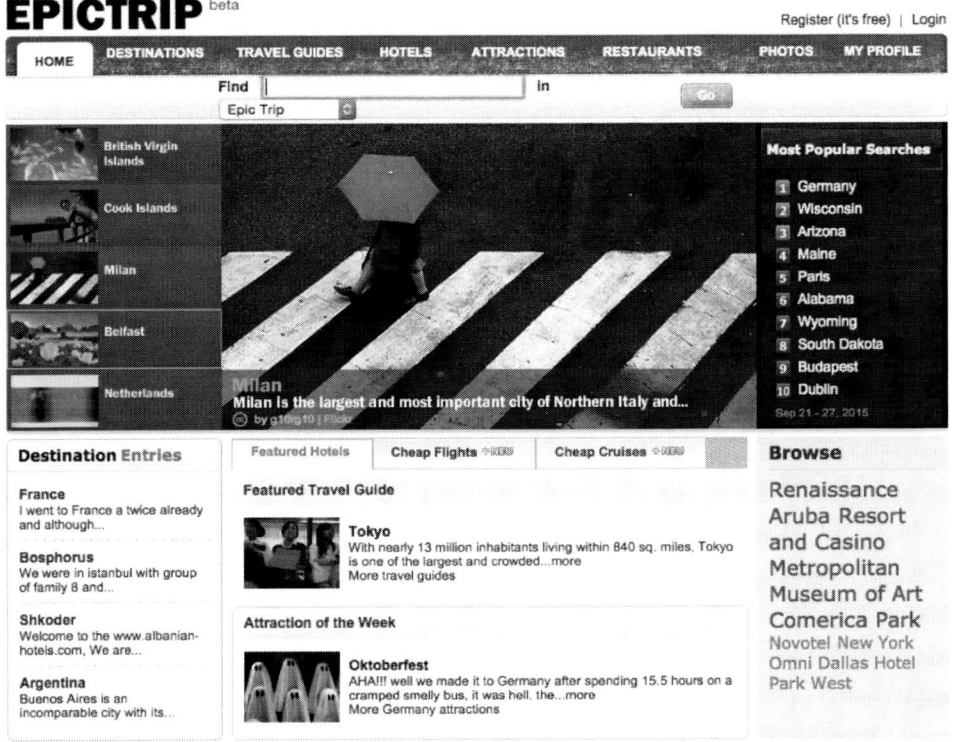

FIGURE 5.1. Epic Trip's home page

Explore Scottsdale, Arizona

featured destination

Relax in Style at Gainey Suites
Located just north of downtown Scottsdale, the Gainey Suites Hotel offers luxurious resort-suite accommodations in a tranquil, intimate environment.

Frank Lloyd Wright's Taliesin West
This magnificent complex was built as Wright's personal residence and architectural school and was created from native materials, rocks from the desert floor and sand from the washes.

Welcome HOME to the Heard Museum!
A staple on any Scottsdale itinerary, the Heard Museum is world-renowned for its outstanding collection of Native American art and artifacts.

Mike and Sandy LaBauve
Every civilization invents its own games to test skill, strength and intelligence. Indian cultures left ballfields behind. When future archaeologists uncover Scottsdale, they may conclude this society worshiped golf.

Recipes for Relaxation
According to Spa Finder, the Scottsdale area has a higher concentration of spas than anywhere else in the United States. Here you'll find facilities and treatment menus inspired by the beautiful Sonoran Desert.

1   2   3   4   5   6   7   8   9   10   11   PAUSE

Anyone who has read Zane Grey's The Call of the Canyon knows of Sedona and nearby Oak Creek Canyon, the mystical red rock and canyon country that characters Glenn Kilbourne and Carley Burch called home.

Sedona - Red Rock Crossing

VIDEO   PHOTO

FIGURE 5.2. Epic Trip's featured destination area

Introduction

In the previous chapter, we introduced concepts and techniques to understand the implications of recent technological advancements for the modern firm. We introduced the notions of network economics and information economics and discussed the role of disruptive technologies in shaping the competitive landscape. These concepts are critical for general and functional managers, who increasingly find themselves managing in the network economy. With this theoretical background firmly in hand, we now formally discuss the Internet and its associated services and then focus on the business innovations that have been spurred by the widespread adoption and rise to prominence of the Internet. Our objective here is to help you become familiar with the language, history, and manifestations of the electronic commerce phenomenon by providing useful categorizations and examples.

A basic understanding of how the Internet works and a mastery of the business vocabulary that has developed around it since its commercialization in 1993 is important because the Internet is critical to modern business. Recent studies show that the Internet is a powerful economic engine in developed economies and that its impact on economic growth has increased as the technology has become increasingly mainstream (Figure 5.3).[1] The research found that in Organisation for Economic Co-operation and Development (OECD) member countries, nearly 80% of firms have a website, more than 40% use the Internet for purchasing, and 21% receive online orders. The Internet contributes directly as a vehicle for economic activity (e.g., online sales, advertisement) and indirectly as an element of economic progress. Therefore, it follows that, aside from the fact that you may be one of those people getting an Internet-enabled job soon, at a minimum you will need to understand and leverage the opportunities for growth enabled by the Internet.

The Internet

A brief look at any information systems textbook quickly reveals that the Internet is, simply put, "a network of networks." In other words, the Internet is broadly defined as a collection of networked computers that can "talk to one another." This simple definition points to a fundamental issue: the Internet is an infrastructure upon which *services*—such as e-mail, the web, instant messaging (IM), and many others—are delivered.

Wikipedia, the free, web-based encyclopedia, provides a more complete definition:

> The Internet is a global system of interconnected computer networks that use the Internet protocol suite (TCP/IP) to link several billion devices worldwide. It is a network of networks that consists of millions of private, public, academic, business, and government networks of local to global scope, linked by a broad array of electronic, wireless, and optical networking technologies. The Internet carries an extensive range of information resources and services, such as mobile apps including social media apps, the inter-linked hypertext documents and applications of the World Wide Web (WWW), electronic mail, multiplayer online games, telephony, and peer-to-peer networks for file sharing.[2]

From this definition follow a number of observations, but before discussing them, you should carefully note that the definition of the Internet is very general and "device agnostic." In other words, as a collection of computer networks, the Internet can connect any device based on the digital computer architecture—such as a laptop, a smartphone, a face-recognition digital camera, and so on. Today there are more devices connected to the Internet than there are people with access, and analysts predict that by the end of this decade, Internet-connected devices will outnumber humans by four to one[3] (see

---

1. OECD (2015), *OECD digital economy outlook 2015*, Paris: OECD Publishing, doi:10.1787/9789264232440-en

2. Internet (n.d.), in *Wikipedia*, retrieved October 1, 2015, from http://en.wikipedia.org/wiki/Internet

3. Norton, S. (2015, June 2), Internet of things market to reach $1.7 trillion by 2020: IDC, *WSJ CIO Journal*, retrieved January 10, 2015, from http://blogs.wsj.com/cio/2015/06/02/internet-of-things-market-to-reach-1-7-trillion-by-2020-idc/

FIGURE 5.3. The diffusion of information and communications technology (ICT) services: Percentage of enterprises with more than 10 employees
Source: OECD (2015), *OECD Digital Economy Outlook 2015*, Paris: OECD Publishing, doi:10.1787/9789264232440-en

Chapter 12). Samsung's chief executive officer (CEO) BK Yoon echoed this trend in his 2015 speech at the International Consumer Electronics Show in Las Vegas: "By 2017, 90% of all Samsung products will be IoT [Internet of things] devices—and that includes all our televisions and mobile devices, and five years from now, every single piece of Samsung hardware will be an IoT device, whether it is an air purifier or an oven."[4] The extreme flexibility of the Internet protocol is what allows such scalability and variety of devices. Note as well that the general definition above does not restrict the type of channel connecting these intelligent devices across the Internet. In other words, if you are imagining an Internet made of computers and cables, you should revise this mental picture, because the channels are increasingly wireless—using radio signals, satellites, or even cellular technology.

Internet Services

As the Wikipedia definition suggests, the nodes of the Internet "carry an extensive range of information resources and services." A common misconception is that the terms *Internet* and *World Wide Web (or web)* are synonymous. This is incorrect, and it is important to differentiate the two. The Internet is the infrastructure upon which many services are made available. Typically, you will connect to the Internet, the infrastructure, to access the services you want to use (e.g., IM).

The web is a service available on the Internet and, alongside electronic mail, is the most popular. However, there are many other services that we use daily—for example, IM, Voice over IP (VoIP), blogs, Real Simple Syndication (RSS) feeds, discussion groups (asynchronous electronic discussion), chat rooms (synchronous electronic discussion), and even the old trusty File Transfer Protocol (FTP; Figure 5.4).

Distributed Ownership

The Internet is "publicly accessible," meaning that no single entity owns it, regulates its use, or otherwise controls it. In fact, the Internet has many owners but no one who centrally controls it. In other

---

4. Cheng, J. (2015, January 5), Samsung preaches harmony in "Internet of Things" push, *WSJ Digits*, retrieved January 10, 2015, from http://blogs.wsj.com/digits/2015/01/05/samsung-preaches-harmony-in-internet-of-things-push/

FIGURE 5.4. FTP client

words, different portions of the Internet (i.e., different networks connected to other networks) are owned by different entities—literally millions of them. For example, your university network, while connected to the public Internet, is privately owned by your university. Your university manages and pays for it. Similarly, if you decide to launch your start-up upon graduation and need it to have a web presence, you may decide to run your own infrastructure rather than purchase it as a service. In this case, you would maintain your own web server and your own dedicated connection to the Internet, thus becoming one of the many entities owning a small piece of the global network. Distributed ownership has been perhaps the main strength of the Internet, limiting regulation, fostering experimentation, and ensuring widespread access leading to significant growth.

Multiplicity of Devices

The Internet is a digital network consisting of millions of smaller digital networks. Each of these smaller digital networks encompasses a collection of digital devices, called nodes. The simplest digital network to visualize is perhaps a home network (Figure 5.5). Your home network may be composed of a couple of personal computers and a printer to which both computers can send documents. Using a home router, wired or wireless, and a broadband modem (e.g., cable, fiber, or DSL), you connect to the Internet. Each of these digital devices—the two computers, the printer, and the router—are nodes on your home network.

Your home network is a tiny contributor to the larger Internet. The fancier ones among us may have more cutting-edge devices, such as a connected thermostat for mastering the energy bill, a wireless media center to stream music and videos from a computer through the living room stereo or to listen to Internet radio stations, a wireless web cam to monitor the front door, a couple of tablets, and even cooler stuff! A connected car—equipped with a GPS device, the OnStar system, or a permanent Internet connection (Figure 5.6)—is another example of a networked node, as is a modern smartphone. As the price of microchips and bandwidth keeps dropping (see Chapter 1), the number and type of devices that become nodes of a network will continue to increase. In other words, the Internet is in continuous expansion.

Open Standards

The Internet relies on open technology standards and protocols. A protocol is an agreed-upon set of rules or conventions governing communication among the elements of a network (i.e., network nodes). For example, case study discussion in your class follows a (stated or implicit) protocol. Typically, the

FIGURE 5.5. A simple home network
Figure by Norrellstrange / CC BY SA 4.0

FIGURE 5.6. The Tesla Model S connected dashboard
Photo by Steve Jurvetson / CC BY 2.0

professor sets the stage for the case discussion. You listen, and when the floor is open, you might raise your hand. When you are called on, you contribute your perspective. You may disagree with the professor or classmates, but you do so in a polite manner, addressing ideas rather than individuals. Respect of the protocol by all is necessary to enable constructive communication rather than unproductive classroom chaos.

Similarly, in order to communicate, network nodes need to follow an agreed-upon set of rules. On the Internet, such a set of rules is the TCP/IP protocol mentioned in the Wikipedia definition. Nobody owns the TCP/IP protocol; as such, it is an open (i.e., freely available) standard, as opposed to a proprietary one. The same holds true for the other technologies that enable the Internet and its services, such as HTML (the language used to write web pages). While there are standard-setting bodies that decide how each of these technologies should evolve (in the case of HTML, it is the World Wide Web Consortium, or W3C), no entity can charge for their use. Thus anyone who wants to embed support for these standards in his or her applications can do so . . . and innovation continues to thrive on the Internet!

The Network: More than the Internet of Today

The definition of the Internet as a network of networks can be very misleading. It typically conjures up a vision of computers of various shapes and sizes hooked together by a maze of cables of different shapes and colors—the Internet as a bunch of interconnected computers. While this image more or less correctly captures what the Internet looked like in the past, it is more confusing than helpful when

FIGURE 5.7. New versus old portable devices

trying to understand the current state of affairs. For example, while it may not look like it at first glance, modern smartphones are full-fledged digital computers, and the cell phone network, while not a cable, is a data transmission channel. In fact, modern smartphones are way more powerful than the computers of just a few years ago (Figure 5.7).

Don Tapscott, a consultant and author, put it best when he wrote in 2001 that it is "an all-too-common mistake [to assume] that the Internet we see today—a network that connects desktop PCs—is the same Internet we will see tomorrow. This is nonsense. The Internet of tomorrow will be as dramatic a change from the Internet of today as today's Internet is from the unconnected, proprietary computing networks of yesterday." He went on to describe a vision that has, in large part, already become reality: "Mobile computing devices, broadband access, wireless networks, and computing power embedded in everything from refrigerators to automobiles are converging into a global network that will enable people to use the Net just about anywhere and anytime. No facet of human activity is untouched. The Net is a force of social change penetrating homes, schools, offices, factories, hospitals, and governments."[5]

For an example of the Internet as a force for social change, recall what happened to Lego, the notorious maker of toy building bricks, in July 2014. Greenpeace, supported by the YouTube video "Lego: Everything Is NOT Awesome," pressed the toymaker into dropping a 50-year partnership with Shell for the distribution of branded Lego sets at gas stations. At the base of the protest was Shell's intention to start oil drilling in the Arctic. The video—which made reference to *The Lego Movie* and its theme song, "Everything Is Awesome"—went viral and, despite briefly being removed from YouTube for alleged copyright infringement, was watched more than

FIGURE 5.8. Greenpeace targets Lego's deal with Shell
Source: Popularresistance.org

---

5. Tapscott, D. (2001), Rethinking strategy in a networked world, *Strategy and Competition*, third quarter.

7.4 million times. During the three-month campaign, online activists created other videos, petitions, and contents (Figure 5.8) that led to more than one million e-mails addressed to Lego. The campaign resulted in the toymaker dropping the $116 million copromotion contract with Shell, and the oil company postponed drilling operations.

Others have discussed a vision of the Internet as a pervasive network, using the word "grid."[6] The idea is that distributed intelligent devices and high-volume network connections will soon make it possible to turn computing into a utility, much like water or electricity. In the near future, the proponents of grid computing claim, we will not have to wonder whether we will have access to the Internet and all its services when we travel, just like we don't worry about whether we will have access to electricity or water now. With such a pace and magnitude of evolution awaiting you as you enter the workforce and get ready to make decisions as a general or functional manager, you must be equipped with some fundamental concepts to navigate the new environment.

The eCommerce Vocabulary

The concept of electronic commerce (or eCommerce for short) has been widely investigated since its advent in the early 1990s. We recall a quote we read in the late 1990s that suggested "in five years there will be no eCommerce, just commerce." This statement is perhaps a bit bold and certainly designed to be attention grabbing. However, history has proven it largely true. It is hard to imagine organizations today, beyond those of very small size, that would be well served by ignoring the Internet as a vehicle for commerce, whether as a tool for back-office operations (e.g., purchasing and logistics), a channel of distribution (e.g., online sales), or a complement to the customer service experience.

eCommerce and eBusiness

A number of definitions of the terms *electronic commerce* (eCommerce) and *electronic business* (eBusiness) have been proposed over the years. Perhaps the simplest definition of the term *electronic commerce* is the broadest one: an online exchange of value. A more specific one, adopted in this book, is the following: electronic commerce is the process of distributing, buying, selling, marketing, and servicing products and services over computer networks such as the Internet. This definition succinctly captures the essence of the electronic commerce phenomenon as the coming together of parties in an exchange that is mediated by networked information technology (IT).

The term *electronic business* originally referred to the digital enablement of internal organizational business processes, such as logistics and the use of Intranets. However, recognizing the increasingly interconnected nature of business operations upstream and downstream in the value chain, the term rapidly evolved to encompass interorganizational processes spanning such areas as electronic purchasing and supply chain management. Thus we broadly define the term *electronic business* as the use of Internet technologies and other advanced IT to enable business processes and operations.

Today, the definitional boundary between the terms *electronic commerce* and *electronic business* has largely blurred, and regardless of definitional differences, both phenomena rely on the same set of enablers.

The Enablers

While much of the attention-grabbing electronic commerce headlines date back to the dot-com era (1993–2000),[7] electronic commerce and electronic business concepts, as defined above, are not a new phenomenon. Electronic transactions have been completed over computer networks since their early development in the 1970s and 1980s.

---

6. Heingartner, D. (2001), The grid: The next-gen Internet?, *Wired News*, retrieved July 12, 2006, from http://archive.wired.com/science/discoveries/news/2001/03/42230

7. While there is no agreed-upon timeline of the dot-com era, we can think of it as beginning with the commercialization of the web in 1993 and ending with the crash of the NASDAQ security market in March 2000.

Consider, for example, the Minitel in France, launched in the early 1980s by France Telecom (Figure 5.9). The Minitel, introduced as a tool to check telephone directories, quickly evolved into a platform for accessing a wide range of services, from ordering flowers to purchasing train and airline tickets—even chat rooms to socialize with other Minitel users.

Another early example is offered by Electronic Data Interchange (EDI) technologies, pioneered conceptually in the late 1960s. EDI enabled the computer-to-computer exchange of structured data by two or more organizations that agreed-upon message standards to be used by their respective applications. In fact, in a business-to-business setting, electronic business has been around since the intro-

FIGURE 5.9. Minitel terminal
Photo by Joi Ito / CC BY 2.0

duction of telecommunication and networking technologies. The hospitality industry, often regarded as a technology laggard, was engaging in electronic business as early as the 1970s using proprietary networks to sell reservations.

Yet if electronic commerce and electronic business transactions have been around for such a long time, why have the last two decades been so ripe with innovation and opportunities? A number of enablers, discussed in previous chapters, are at the heart of the meteoric rise to prominence of eCommerce and eBusiness. We briefly summarize them here:

- *Affordable computing equipment.* Data from the International Telecommunication Union[8] indicate that in 2012, 41% of households in the world possessed a computer. The number increases still further when access at work or in public venues (e.g., schools, libraries, Internet cafés) is also considered.
- *Access to the Internet.* An estimated three billion people have access to the Internet worldwide (about 45% of the world's population).[9]
- *Ease of use.* Technology adoption is strongly influenced by its perceived usefulness and ease of use. The emergence of the World Wide Web created an easy-to-use, graphical method for navigation of the Internet. This tool dramatically broadened the potential audience for the Internet and its services. The trajectory toward increasing ease of use is continuing to this day with direct-manipulation interfaces (e.g., iPad) and gesture- and voice-recognition software.
- *Open standards.* Open standards—technology standards that are readily available and can be used for free—created the bedrock for the expansion of the Internet.

Categorizing Electronic Commerce Initiatives

The electronic commerce and electronic business landscape literally exploded during the dot-com era. It was a unique period of time when venture capital was plentiful and a sense of possibility pervaded Silicon Valley and other hotbeds of information technology innovation. To make sense of the seemingly endless number and type of innovations, a specific vocabulary was introduced. This vocabulary has now become part of the language of business circles, and you should therefore master it.

Note that the process of creating categories is useful in that it enables us to identify and quickly refer to different entities. However, categorizations are a simplification of reality, and as a consequence, you may find that the different categories introduced below overlap somewhat.

Categorizing Ventures by Transaction Type   The most immediate way to classify different types of electronic commerce ventures and innovations is to identify the parties involved in the transaction.

---

8. International Telecommunication Union (2013), *Measuring the information society*, p. 9, retrieved from https://www.itu.int/en/ITU-D/Statistics/Documents/publications/mis2013/MIS2013_without_Annex_4.pdf

9. Internet usage statistics: The Internet big picture (2015), *Internet World Stats*, retrieved January 10, 2015, from http://www.internetworldstats.com/stats.htm

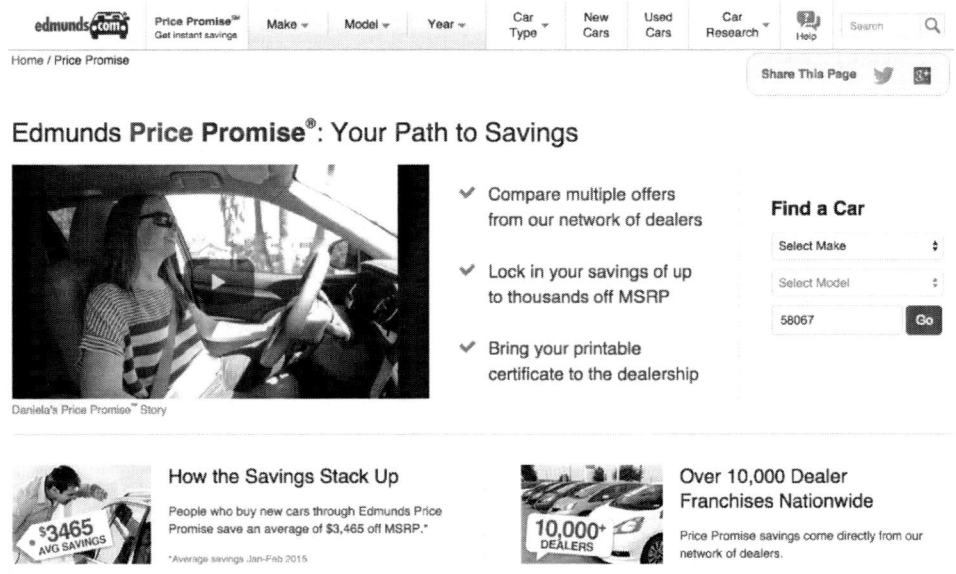

FIGURE 5.10. Edmunds.com's website

Business-to-Consumer (B2C)   Business-to-consumer transactions are those that involve a for-profit organization on one side and an end consumer on the other. This category includes online retailers, such as Amazon.com or Target.com, as well as business models where a firm offers value to a consumer without selling any physical goods. Take, for instance, Edmunds.com, which provides information and referrals to consumers seeking to purchase automobiles. Edmund's revenue model is based on referrals and advertisement revenue (Figure 5.10).

We recall a conversation with an executive at uBid.com, the online auction pioneer, who told us that the biggest question in 1995 for electronic commerce trailblazers was "whether consumers would feel comfortable providing their credit card information to a website." That question, with many similar others, has long been answered, and the B2C electronic commerce model is now a mature one, as well as the most visible kind of eCommerce.

Business-to-Business (B2B)   Businesses-to-business transactions are those in which two or more business entities take part. The transactions can range from one-time interactions, very similar to the ones described above (e.g., your company purchases printer toner through Staples.com), or they can be highly unique and tailored to the relationship between two firms. For instance, Alibaba.com is the world largest eCommerce platform targeted to business customers (Figure 5.11). In 2014, transactions totaled $248 billion. Either buyers or suppliers can access tailored services, such as inspections to assure product quality, trade assurance, secure payments, and revolving credits.

Consumer-to-Consumer (C2C)   Consumer-to-consumer transactions are those that enable individual consumers to interact and transact directly. The classic example of a firm that enables C2C transactions is eBay Inc., the marketplace that lets any one of us trade goods with other consumers. Since its inception as a pure C2C player, eBay has provided an opportunity to retail shops and other businesses to reach its large audience of buyers. As a consequence, eBay is no longer a pure example of C2C but rather employs a blended C2C/B2C model. A more recent example of C2C is offered by Etsy, a site for individuals to sell handmade and vintage items and craft supplies (Figure 5.12).

Business models built around community and social networks, such as YouTube or Facebook, fall into this category as well. For example, in 2005, Yahoo! launched Yahoo! Answers, a website where individuals can post questions that other people respond to. Interactions occur between members of the Yahoo! community, while the firm benefits from the traffic they generate.

Consumer-to-Business (C2B) Consumer-to-business transactions occur when individuals transact with business organizations not as buyers of goods and services but as suppliers. Upwork.com represents an example of this (Figure 5.13). The company enables firms to upload the specifics of a project or job they need completed and allows individuals (or other firms) to offer their services to do the

FIGURE 5.11. Alibaba.com homepage

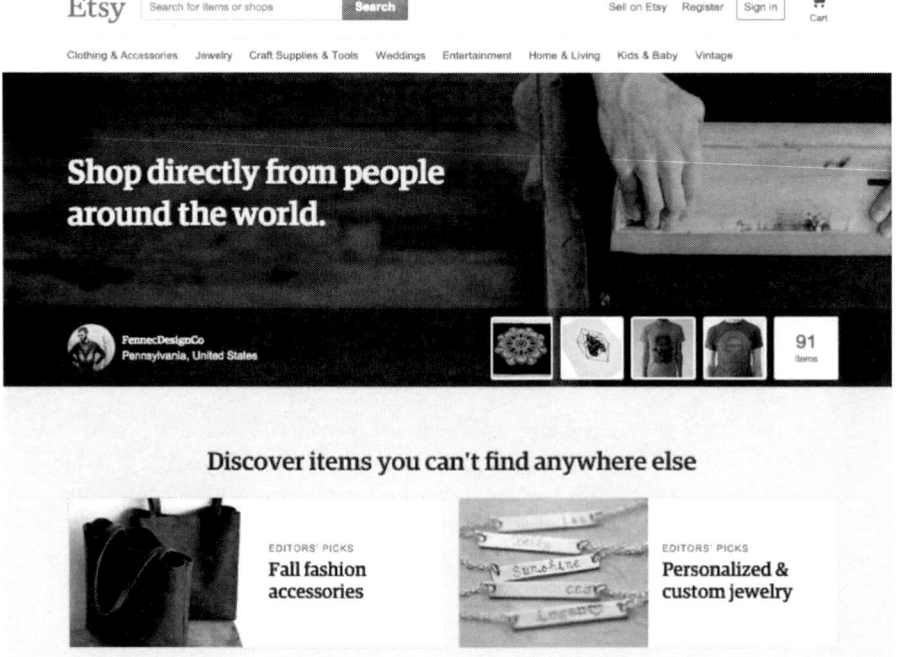

FIGURE 5.12. Etsy eCommerce website

project or job. Typical projects are those amenable to simple outsourcing and delivery, like graphic design, research, or programming, but any type of project can be posted.

eGovernment   Electronic government, or eGovernment, refers to all transactions involving legislative and administrative institutions. eGovernment transactions can occur with individual citizens, businesses, or other governments. An example of an eGovernment transaction may be electronic filing of income tax. Another example is offered by electronic voting or the use of websites to solicit public input on upcoming regulation and legislation.

Categorizing Ventures by Company Structure   Beyond the type of transaction being investigated, another way in which observers have been trying to make sense of the electronic commerce landscape is by categorizing the companies involved in it on the basis of their structure.

Brick and Mortar   *Brick and mortar* is a term used to refer to "traditional" organizations—in other words, those firms that have physical operations and locations (i.e., stores) and don't provide their services exclusively through the Internet. In the early days of the dot-com era, brick-and-mortar firms were regarded by many observers and commentators as dinosaurs soon to be swept away by nimble online firms. This prediction proved incorrect, and today most brick-and-mortar organizations have substantial eBusiness and eCommerce operations. Consider, for example, General Electric (GE), the largest company in the United States. GE is certainly a business with substantial brick-and-mortar operations. Yet, under the leadership of Jack Welch, GE moved very aggressively to incorporate the Internet into the very fabric of its operations.

Bricks and Clicks   Bricks and clicks, or click and mortar, is a label used to refer to organizations that have hybrid operations. These are typically brick-and-mortar operations that saw the potential offered by the Internet and aggressively used the new channel. Bricks-and-clicks operations evolved in one of two ways.

Some developed independent ventures to take advantage of the opportunities and capital available to online ventures. A classic example of this model is offered by Barnes & Noble, the largest bookseller in the United States. Barnes & Noble was thrust, much to its dismay, into the eCommerce limelight once Amazon.com opened its virtual doors, selling books as its very first category. In response to the online threat, Barnes & Noble developed a separate subsidiary focusing on online sales of books, music, DVDs, video games, and related products and services.

PROJECTS   HIRING   PAYMENTS   PROTECTION   FAQ   Get Started

How do I hire the right freelancer?

Start by writing a clear and concise job post. Each freelancer submits a cover letter and link to their Upwork profile covering:

- Skills, experience and portfolios
- Client feedback
- Language and communication skills

You'll get applications from independent professionals and receive our personalized recommendations within minutes. From there, just interview your strongest candidates and hire your favorite.

CEM BAYCAM
Web Developer
★ ★ ★ ★ ★

FIGURE 5.13. Hiring a freelancer on Upwork.com

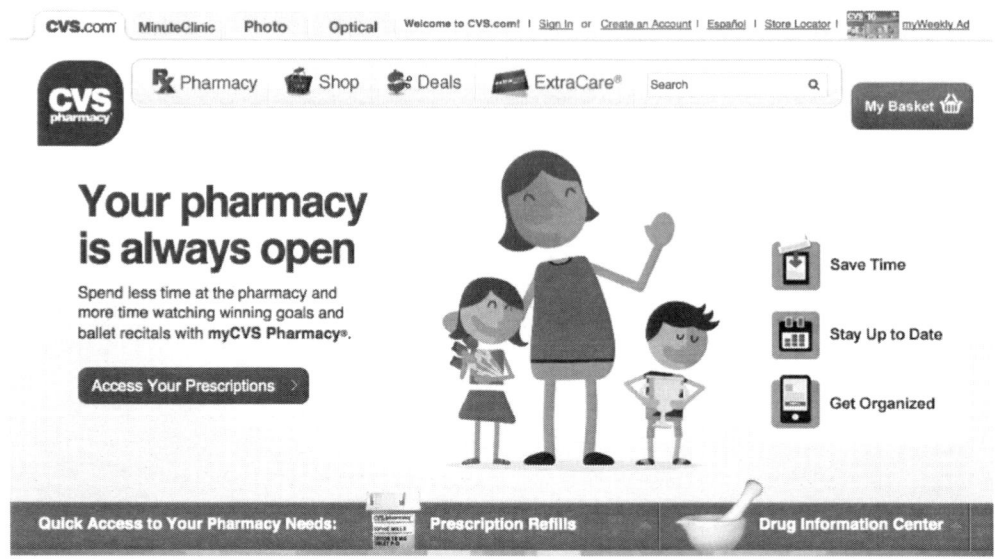

FIGURE 5.14. CVS website

Alibaba provides another example of a bricks-and-clicks strategy. In a perfect example of co-opetition,[10] the firm struck a partnership agreement with brick-and-mortar electronics retailer Suning Commerce. Alibaba was interested in the logistic capabilities of Suning and its 1,600 physical stores distributed around China. Suning benefitted from the strong online brand of Alibaba, and its presence on Tmall.com to drive consumers into physical stores: a strategy known as "online-to-offline" (O2O). O2O consists of all the different techniques and services aimed at engaging online customers in the physical retail space, with services such as product pickups, free shipping, returns, and payments. As explained by Joe Tsai, Alibaba's executive vice chairman, "You can imagine a customer going into a store using an Alibaba app, experiencing the product first hand, but operating the whole purchase online so he doesn't have to wait at the checkout counter."[11] A competing approach consists of running the online channel as part of the brick-and-mortar operations in a highly integrated fashion. An example of this strategy is offered by the drugstore chain CVS pharmacy. The firm launched CVS.com in 1999 with the objective of fully integrating the online pharmacy with store operations. Doing so enabled it to offer a seamless experience to shoppers, allowing them to interact with the firm online, offline, or (most likely) in different manners at different times (Figure 5.14).

Which approach is better for bricks-and-clicks firms is a matter of debate. On the one hand, independent operation allows the online channel to make decisions with only limited concern for the impacts on store operations. On the other hand, proponents of the integrated model point out that combining online and offline operations yields potential synergies.

Pure Play   *Pure play* is a term used to identify those organizations "born online"—that is, firms that have no stores and provide their services entirely through the Internet. Google, Amazon.com, Yahoo!, Monster.com, Match.com, and eBay are some of the traditional pure play brands. Skype, YouTube, Facebook, Airbnb, Groupon, LivingSocial, and many others have more recently emerged. Note, however, that not having stores does not equate to not having physical operations—unless the firm deals exclusively in classic information goods (e.g., Google). Amazon, for example, has its goods stored in

---

10. The term *co-opetition* is a combination of the terms *cooperation* and *competition*. It represents situations where competitors strike mutually beneficial partnership agreements.

11. Reporters, F. T. (2015, August 11), Alibaba places big bet on bricks and mortar, *Financial Times*, retrieved from http://www.ft.com/intl/cms/s/0/c305c71a-4010-11e5-9abe-5b335da3a90e.html

FIGURE 5.15. The business model canvas
Created by Business Model Alchemist, http://www.businessmodelalchemist.com

more than 50 fulfillment centers and warehouses located around the United States to ensure its ability
to rapidly deliver goods to customers.

Manifestations of eCommerce and eBusiness

The dot-com era was intriguing for many reasons, not least of which was the breathtaking pace of innovation that took place over less than a decade. Beyond technology innovation, much of the creativity
pertained to the use of the Internet as a business platform—the notion of business model innovation.
With a lesser dose of "irrational exuberance," Internet-inspired innovation continued to pervade the
latter part of the first decade of the new millennium.

Business Models: Definition

A business model captures the firm's concept and value proposition while also conveying what market
opportunity the company is pursuing, what product or service it offers, and what strategy it will follow
to seek a dominant position. The business model may also identify what organizational capabilities the
firm plans to leverage to turn the concept into reality. In short, the business model tells us what the firm
does for its customers, how it does it, and how it is going to be compensated for what it does. There
are a number of tools that can help entrepreneurs and managers alike to think through their business
model in a disciplined fashion. The business model canvas is a template used to document and develop
the business model (Figure 5.15).

The term *business model* acquired prominence with the emergence of electronic commerce, because
up until the commercialization of the Internet, with few exceptions, it was clear what a firm did and
what its value proposition was (i.e., its business model) once we knew its industry. The statement "I
produce beer," or "I sell groceries," or "I am a real estate agent" clearly conveyed what the firm did,
what its cost structure was likely to be, and most important, how the firm would create and sustain a
revenue stream. In other words, the underlying business model was implicit.

However, the emergence of the network economy created a seemingly unending stream of new business models and new ways to leverage the Internet infrastructure for business opportunities. Consider
Priceline.com, for example. The Priceline name-your-own-price business model is predicated on the

notion that real-time B2C communication made available by the Internet would enable customers to trade convenience for discounts. In other words, a traveler with more time than money—perhaps a student—can communicate to Priceline how much he or she is willing to pay for a ticket between two city pairs. Priceline then shops for the customer's price at top airlines to see if anyone is interested in selling a ticket with such characteristics (e.g., city pairs, dates, price). If any provider accepts the price, the customer's credit card is billed, the flight is ticketed, and Priceline collects a commission. Today, with its "negotiator" app—now available even on smartwatches—that leverages GPS functionality, Priceline allows travelers to name their own price for hotels in the vicinity of their current position (Figure 5.16).

Revenue Models   An important consideration for organizations doing business online, particularly pure plays, is the revenue model they adopt. A firm's revenue model specifies how the firm intends to draw proceeds from its value proposition—in short, how it plans to make money. The dominant revenue models include the following.

FIGURE 5.16. The Priceline negotiator iPhone app

Pay for Service   The pay-for-service model is the most straightforward revenue model. The firm offers a product (e.g., books) or a service (e.g., insurance) for sale, and it is compensated much like a traditional store or service provider.

Subscription   The subscription revenue model is similar in nature to the pay-for-service model in that customers pay for the service they receive, which in this case is content (e.g., news, sports highlights). Unlike pay for service, though, subscription models are typically based on access rather than usage. In other words, customers pay for the right to access the content and then are able to use as much of the service (i.e., content) as they need.

Advertisement Support   Perhaps the most used (and abused) revenue model of the network economy is the advertisement-supported model. The firm's content or services are made available for free in an effort to attract a large audience. The firm then "sells access to its audience" to interested advertisers, much like radio stations do. A critical difference between the traditional and online ad-supported models is that traffic to and behavior on a website can be tracked very precisely at the individual level—something that print media, television, and radio advertisements could never offer. Google, for example, provides a complete suite of tools for advertisers to maximize results from their online advertising efforts (Figure 5.17).

The unprecedented level of accountability offered by online advertising, however, proved to be a mixed blessing. On the one hand, advertisers value the ability to monitor who is consuming their message as well as when, how, and what they are doing afterward. Specifically, sites that require a log-in ID (e.g., *New York Times*) can collect precise demographics and serve up targeted ads. On the other hand, precise data quickly demonstrated that most sites did not get the significant traffic (i.e., hits) they expected. More important, exact click-through data (the percentage of people who take action spurred by web-based advertisements) show that very few of the people visiting a website respond to the ads online by clicking through.

This ability to collect precise data about customers viewing the ads and their behavior spurred a number of innovations. Advertising syndicates, such as Google's DoubleClick and Criteo, are able to offer targeted ads that leverage previous customer behavior—a practice called retargeting. Say you have been looking to take a vacation using Booking.com, the travel intermediary. One property you looked at is the beautiful Geovillage Resort near the town of Olbia in the pristine island of Sardinia. After shopping, however, you left the site. Two days later, while viewing a YouTube video, you notice a banner ad from Booking.com featuring the Geovillage . . . and the hotel is directly bookable by clicking directly on the ad (Figure 5.18) . . . that's retargeting! The aim is to increase customer conversions by leveraging all possible available customer behavioral information. On the balance, however, online

FIGURE 5.17. Google AdSense

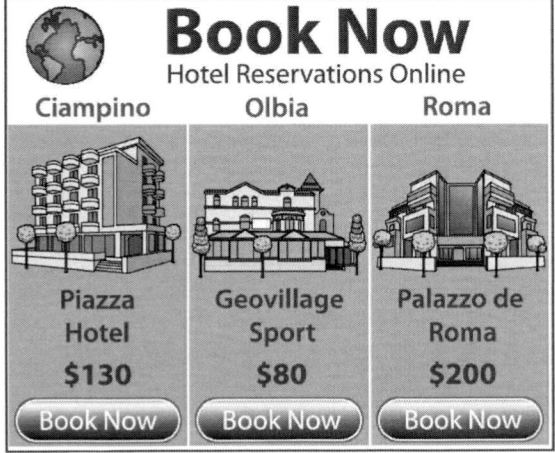

FIGURE 5.18. A highly targeted and actionable advertising banner

[In millions of dollars (177,500.3 represents $177,500,300,000). See source for definitions of types of advertising]

Media supplier	2000	2001	2002	2003	2004	2005	2006	2007	2008	2009	2010
Total Supplier Ad Revenue	177 500,3	168 485,3	172 285,6	176 852,1	188 942,1	196 668,2	204 888,7	205 847,2	194 328,2	163 183,6	170 456,1
Total \1	175 535,2	168 295,7	170 683,9	176 509,4	186 978,7	196 398,4	202 701,1	205 523,3	191 951,4	162 744,4	167 935,8
Direct	31 108,2	32 667,6	33 658,4	36 292,8	39 688,4	42 476,8	45 881,7	48 680,2	48 189,5	42 443,6	42 484,1
Direct mail	18 249,8	19 733,7	20 231,4	21 210,0	22 559,3	23 084,9	24 477,8	24 890,1	23 458,8	19 853,2	20 603,8
Direct online \2	559,7	559,8	1 161,5	2 894,1	4 439,9	6 370,5	8 784,5	11 354,7	13 553,6	13 656,5	15 022,4
Directories \3	12 298,7	12 374,1	12 265,5	12 188,7	12 689,3	13 021,4	12 619,4	12 435,3	11 177,1	8 934,0	6 857,9
National	53 493,7	50 784,0	50 560,6	52 018,4	55 699,3	59 200,4	61 858,4	64 498,0	63 131,7	56 797,1	61 009,1
National television \3, \4	25 574,0	25 458,3	27 143,1	29 048,8	31 452,3	33 230,9	33 712,4	34 819,7	35 141,3	33 722,6	36 209,6
Magazines \3	19 024,6	17 789,1	17 211,9	17 112,4	17 961,4	19 350,8	20 373,4	20 975,2	19 533,3	15 553,5	15 623,3
National digital/online \5	5 665,0	4 953,3	3 651,8	3 244,3	3 541,1	3 930,6	5 066,8	6 098,0	6 056,9	5 548,6	7 144,1
Network and satellite radio	1 065,1	971,1	1 080,4	1 117,6	1 174,6	1 161,2	1 178,3	1 226,3	1 219,9	1 099,8	1 145,4
National newspapers \3	2 165,1	1 612,3	1 473,5	1 495,2	1 569,9	1 526,9	1 527,5	1 378,7	1 180,3	872,6	886,7
Local	90 933,3	84 844,1	86 464,9	88 198,3	91 591,1	94 721,1	94 961,0	92 345,2	80 630,1	63 503,7	64 442,6
Local newspapers \3	46 506,1	42 692,3	42 628,7	43 444,0	45 132,7	45 879,8	45 073,9	40 830,4	33 559,2	23 948,6	21 908,5
Local TV \3, \6	18 530,4	17 887,7	18 999,4	19 551,5	20 046,8	21 281,2	21 023,1	22 000,8	19 706,1	16 995,5	18 670,1
Local radio \3	18 819,0	17 450,0	18 409,0	18 570,0	18 932,0	19 018,0	19 031,0	18 476,0	16 536,0	13 203,0	13 846,6
Emerging Outdoor	195,5	196,0	190,8	280,5	377,5	424,8	544,9	741,0	914,4	920,5	1 146,0
Other Outdoor	5 039,5	4 997,1	5 041,3	5 223,7	5 457,0	5 876,4	6 260,4	6 541,8	6 077,0	4 980,3	4 996,8
Local digital/online \5	1 842,8	1 621,0	1 195,7	1 128,6	1 645,1	2 240,9	3 027,7	3 755,2	3 837,4	3 455,9	3 874,5
Political \7	1 180,2	189,6	995,7	342,7	1 259,1	269,9	1 537,6	323,9	1 776,8	439,2	2 032,8
Olympics \8	785,0	0,0	606,1	0,0	704,3	0,0	650,0	0,0	600,0	0,0	487,5

FOOTNOTES:
\1 Excludes political and olympic revenue.
\2 Includes paid search, lead generation and internet yellow pages.
\3 Excludes internet-based advertising revenues.
\4 Includes English and Spanish-language network TV, national cable and national syndication. Excludes incremental olympic revenues.
\5 Includes rich/online video, internet classifieds, e-mail, digital display and mobile.
\6 Includes local broadcast and local cable TV. Excludes local political advertising revenues.
\7 Total political advertising revenue on local broadcast and local cable TV.
\8 Incremental advertising revenue from olympics on network TV.

FIGURE 5.19. Advertising revenue by category, 2000–2010

Source: U.S. Census Bureau (2011), Accommodation, food services, and other services, *Statistical Abstract of the United States,* retrieved from https://www.census.gov/prod/2011pubs/11statab/services.pdf

advertisements have been garnering increasing attention, also thanks to the introduction of local and mobile targeting. (See Figure 5.19 for advertising priority trends over the last decade.) PwC estimates that worldwide Internet advertising revenue will surpass $239 billion in 2019 and overtake total TV advertising revenues by 2016.[12]

Affiliate   In similar fashion to the advertising model, the affiliate model, pioneered by Amazon.com, seeks to generate revenue from a third party based on customer traffic to the firm's website. In this case, the referring site receives a commission once a customer who originated from the site makes a purchase on another site. This model is enabled by the ability to link pages directly to products (Figure 5.20).

Freemium   The term *freemium* is the contraction of the phrase "free premium." In this model, the firm gives away its product or service for free and attempts to build a large customer base by reducing the obstacle created by the payment. Once the firm has gained traction and enlisted a large customer base, it offers premium services or enhanced versions of the product for a fee (Figure 5.21). While the freemium model should be more associated with the software industry than the Internet, the term was coined during the rise to prominence of the Web 2.0 phenomenon, and it is therefore associated with Internet-based ventures. Interestingly, the success of mobile platforms (see Chapter 12) evolved the freemium model to include microtransactions. Microtransactions consist in purchasing virtual goods or additional services within an app. This model has become dominant in the gaming industry, propelled by the success of the free-to-play (often referred as F2P) model, where players access a substantial part of a game but portions of it or virtual items require microtransactions to be unlocked. The idea is that the app or the game is free to download and play, and revenues are generated through microtransactions or in-app purchases (when applied to game apps) consisting of micropayments for additional features and virtual consumable or nonconsumable items, such as extra life boosts or pieces of equipment to enhance the player's gaming experience.

---

12. PwC (2015), *Outlook insights: An analysis of the global entertainment and media outlook 2015–2019,* retrieved from https://www.pwc.com/gx/en/global-entertainment-media-outlook/segment-insights/assets/PDF/tv-advertising-by-growth-and-scale.pdf

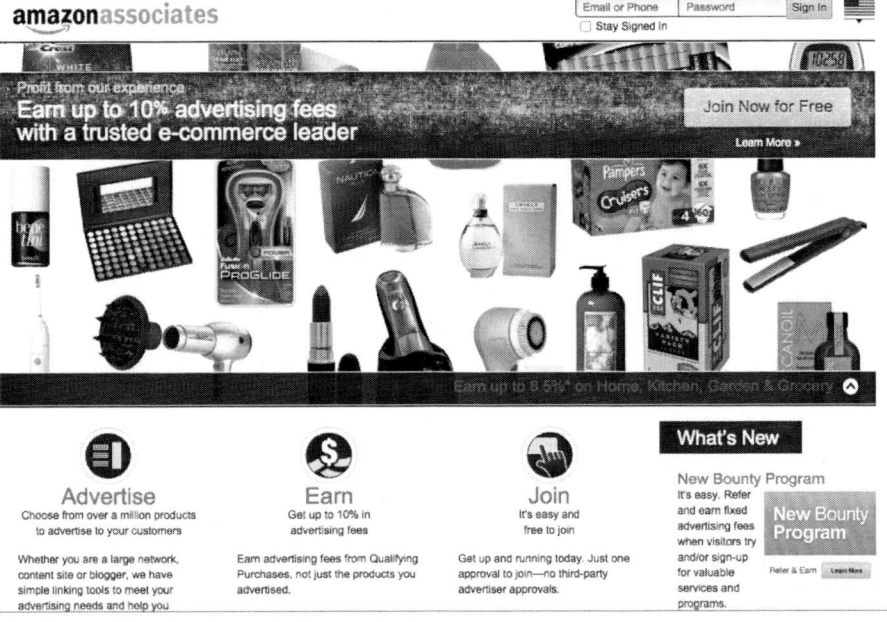

FIGURE 5.20. Amazon's affiliate program

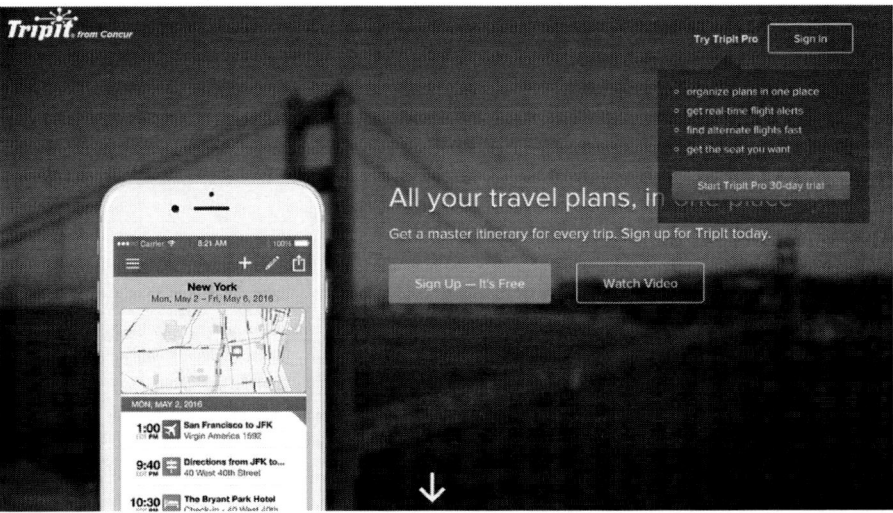

FIGURE 5.21. TripIt Pro: Premium service of the free utility TripIt

Dominant Business Models

As the Internet and the web emerged as stable platforms for commerce, a number of business models were proposed by entrepreneurs and organizations seeking to profit in the "network economy." The sense of possibility offered by the new technology (and plentiful cash from venture capitalists!) and the limited knowledge of the new landscape created the precondition for significant business model experimentation. Some of these business models spawned successful and profitable companies, while others proved to be flawed. We address the most relevant of these models below. Note, however, that just like industrial-age conglomerates, modern firms might have portfolios of business models, and you may not be able to categorize them neatly into one type or another.

Online Retailing   The poster child of eCommerce business models, due in large part to the attention garnered by Amazon.com, is online retailing. Examples abound with both pure play, such as Buy.com, and bricks-and-clicks organizations, like Staples.com or BestBuy.com. The defining characteristic of online retailers is the fact that they take control of inventory that they then resell at a profit. Fulfillment is a critical capability for these organizations. The revenue model is pay for service.

Infomediaries   Information intermediaries, or infomediaries, are organizations that use the Internet to provide specialized information on behalf of product or service providers. The value proposition of the infomediary consists in gathering product and service specifications and reviews and creating a system to quickly search and organize the data. Unlike online retailers, though, infomediaries do not sell the goods and services that they review or take ownership of inventory. Rather, they link to online retailers and receive compensation for referrals as well as advertisement. Infomediaries are typically segment or product focused so as to offer domain-specific expertise. Examples of infomediaries abound, from retail products (e.g., PriceGrabber.com) to travel (Skyscanner.com) to automobiles (e.g., Edmunds.com).

Content Providers   Content providers are organizations that develop and publish content. The content offered ranges from news (e.g., Reuters.com), to gossip (e.g., Eonline.com), to historical and reference information (e.g., Britannica.com), to travel information and tips (e.g., TripAdvisor.com). Traditionally, content providers relied on largely owned content generated by the organization's staff, but there is now a consolidated trend toward user-generated content (e.g., Yelp.com; Figure 5.22). User-generated content offers two advantages. First, it is considered more honest and less prone to marketing influence or manipulation. Second, it has a limited cost of production, since the community typically volunteers its input.

The technologies used by content providers are increasingly converging, with most providers employing a mix of text, images, animations, streaming audio, and video. Because the product being offered by these organizations is information (i.e., classic information goods), fulfillment is not a major concern. The revenue model for content providers can be advertisement supported, subscription, or pay per download.

Online Communities   An online community is a group of people brought together by a common interest (e.g., windsurfing) or goal (e.g., to initiate a class action lawsuit). The community is virtual in

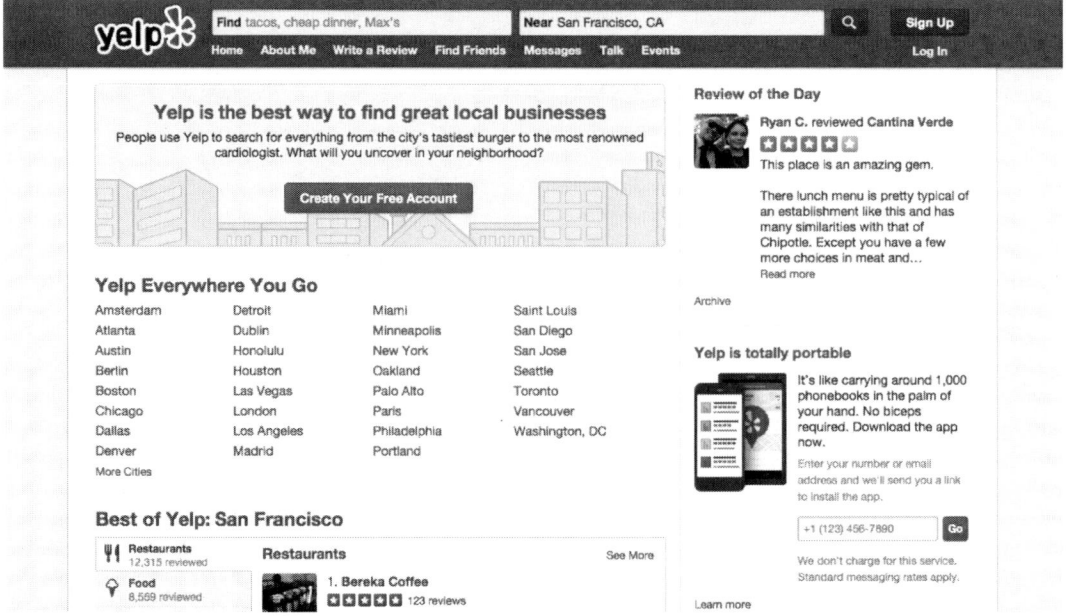

FIGURE 5.22. User-generated content in the form of reviews

that its members primarily interact using information technology and are brought together through a network. Virtual communities work because they alleviate one of the constraints of the physical world: physical distance. Imagine three cities—say, Milan, Italy; Durham, North Carolina; and Sacramento, California—and three individuals who share a passion for windsurfing (e.g., Gabe, Fernando, and Anthony). Before the advent of the Internet, these three individuals would have likely never met each other. However, by virtue of being members of the same online community, they can trade tips, pick each other's brains about equipment and repairs, and even coordinate trips together to meet (physically) at world-class windsurfing destinations.

Before the advent of the Internet, these individuals might have been isolated in their respective cities, unable to find a critical mass of like-minded persons who shared the same interest (Figure 5.23). Today, however, you can find thriving online communities devoted to almost any interest—from tall people on Facebook to timbale collectors on Yahoo! Groups.

Virtual communities are particularly valuable for niche interests, where a critical mass of community members can only be found in large cities. In many cases, they offer business opportunities, but perhaps more important, they have created unprecedented opportunities for nonmainstream interests to thrive because those who share them can now easily find each other.

Business models crafted around online communities became extremely popular once the business community realized their potential to harness network effects (see Chapter 4). A great example of an online community is offered by Yahoo! Answers. The site allows anyone with a Yahoo! account to post questions that are immediately read by other members of the community. The wealth of content on Yahoo! Answers, ranging from where to find historical weather data to how to best exact revenge on an enemy, is generated by the community at no cost to Yahoo!, the sponsor of the network. A similar example is offered by Quora (Figure 5.24), which differentiates itself from Yahoo! Answers by requiring users to register with their real identities. This increases the credibility of answers, and in many cases, those who answer are authorities in their respective fields. Even President Obama uses the site to answer questions from members.

Exchanges   Exchanges are organizations that create a marketplace for buyers and sellers to come together and transact. Thus an exchange does not take control of inventory or worry about fulfillment. Rather, the exchange provides a "market-making" service and is compensated with fees, commission on sales, or consulting fees on more complex business-to-business transactions. The prototypical example of an exchange is eBay. Others include Alibaba.com and Ariba.com (Figure 5.25)—both mainly targeting the business-to-business domain.

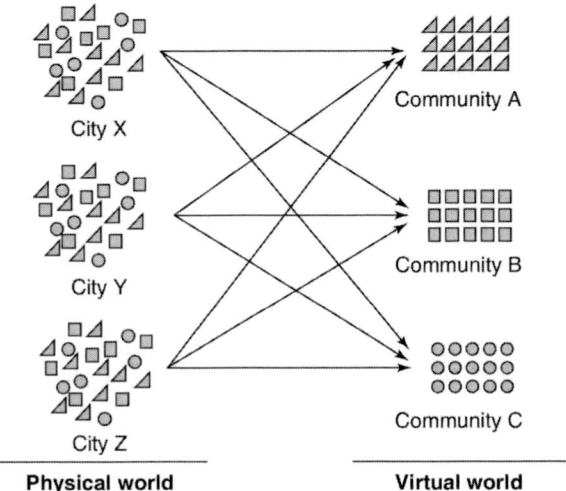

FIGURE 5.23. Virtual communities of interest

The Implications of eCommerce

As we discussed in the introductory chapters, the emergence of new technologies often has dramatic impacts on organizations. The rapid adoption of the Internet and the emergence of the network economy proved to be no exception. General and functional managers must proactively manage these effects. In order to do so, you should be familiar with some of the main effects caused by the evolving use of Internet technology in business.

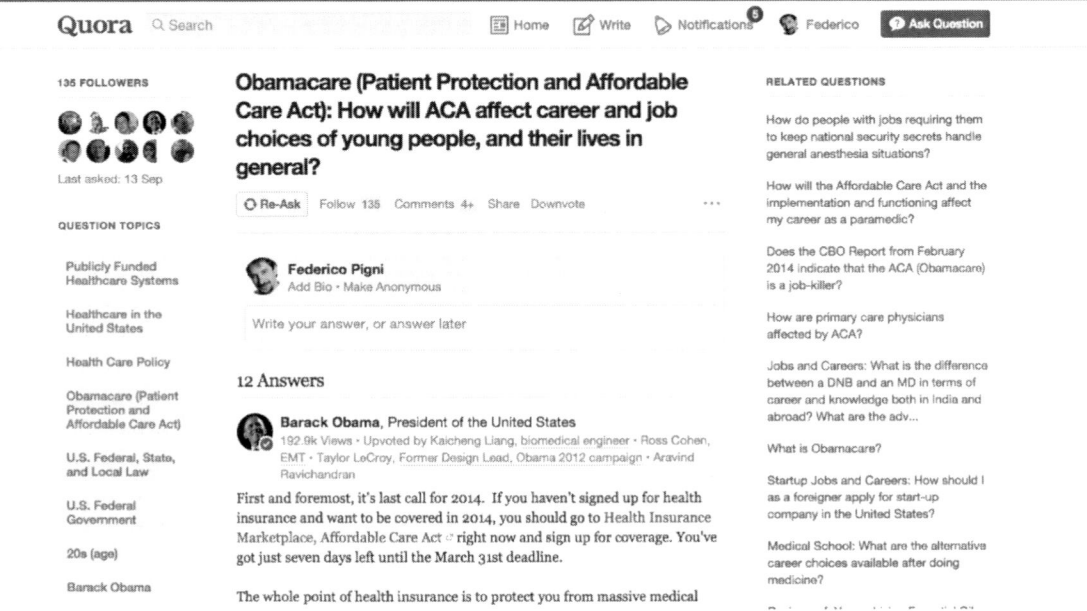

FIGURE 5.24. Have a question? Ask the community!

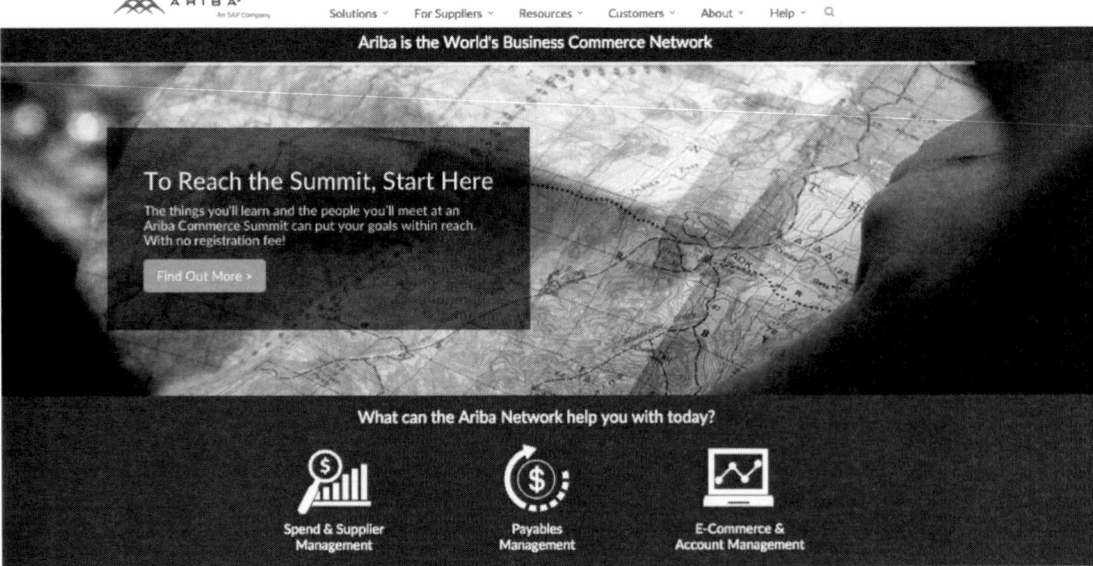

FIGURE 5.25. Ariba.com

Disintermediation

The hallmark of the Internet is connectivity. As such, its emergence and widespread adoption by consumers enabled any organization that so chose to establish (at least technically) a direct relationship with its customers. All of a sudden, it was practical for companies as diverse as hotels and computer manufacturers, automakers and insurance companies, to reach customers directly rather than through one or more middlemen.

The term *disintermediation* refers to the process by which a firm's distribution chain is shortened through the elimination of one or more intermediaries. Disintermediation has a direct impact on those organizations that find themselves being . . . well, disintermediated—such as travel agents and car dealers. Those organizations that were caught in the middle had to recast their value proposition in order to survive. For example, many travel agents have found it difficult to stay in business after airlines, and increasingly hotels, have eliminated commissions. Many others, though, have been able to leverage their superior knowledge about travel products and rules and are now prospering using a consulting, rather than commission, model (i.e., they receive fees from travelers who value their service and knowledge). In the worst-case scenario, a firm facing disintermediation may be forced to harvest and close the business.

Disintermediation has less direct impacts on organizations that, while unable to dismantle their distribution chain, can circumvent some parts of it (e.g., by improving after-the-sale service).

Reintermediation

As managers and observers tried to make sense of the Internet as a business opportunity, many thought that disintermediation would lead to the demise of distribution channels in most industries. While disintermediation failed to eliminate traditional intermediaries, the Internet created opportunities for new intermediaries to exist alongside their brick-and-mortar counterparts—a process known as *reintermediation*. Consider the insurance industry, for instance. Today, insurance companies reach consumers directly (e.g., Progressive.com), through traditional insurance brokers, and through independent online insurance brokers (e.g., Insure.com).

Another example is offered by many of the infomediaries discussed above. While it is true that traditional travel agents have been forced to reinvent their value proposition, a number of Internet travel agents (e.g., Booking.com, Expedia, Opodo) have emerged and are thriving due to their ability to help travelers gather information and uncover low prices. Similar dynamics have occurred in traditional retail and in many other industries.

Market Efficiency

Since its advent, information technology has contributed to reduced search costs and improved efficiency of markets. The Internet and its related technologies continued and perhaps accelerated this process, empowering customers with the instruments and technologies they need to sift through large amounts of product and service data.

Prior to the arrival of the Internet, customers faced significant costs when searching for products and services. They would have to either visit physical stores or call multiple outlets to describe what they were looking for and inquire about availability and price. In either case, the process would be fairly time consuming and therefore costly. The outcome of this process has been heightened competition and an increasing difficulty in profiting from strategies rooted in asymmetry of information or high search costs. Perhaps the best illustration of market efficiency is provided by travel metasearch infomediaries such as Skyscanner (Figure 5.26).

Channel Conflict

The emergence of the online channel created a conundrum for many organizations that had an established distribution chain. Should they disintermediate, following the promise of reduced distribution costs and a direct relationship with customers, or should they work with the channel in an effort to identify mutually beneficial Internet-enabled initiatives? At the heart of this dilemma is the inherent

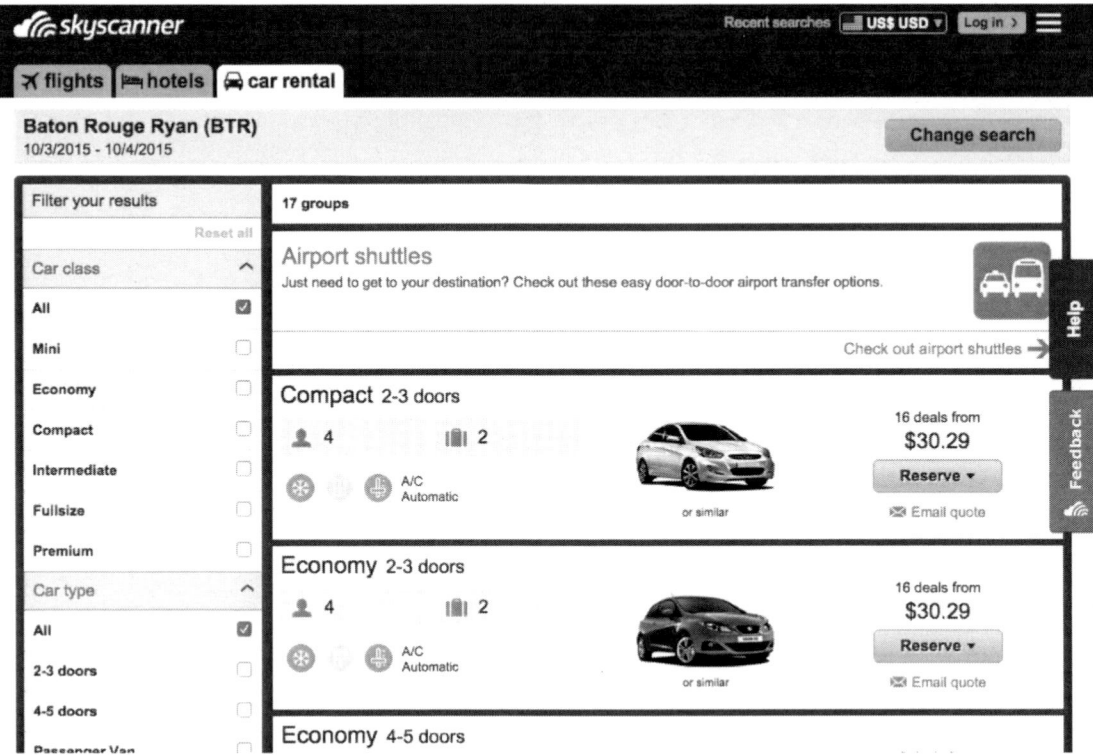

FIGURE 5.26. Subset of results from metasearch infomediary Skyscanner

difficulty of moving distribution from the traditional channel (the one currently producing the revenue stream the organization needs to survive) to the online direct channel (the one that promises the highest profitability in the long run). The term *channel conflict* captures this dilemma.

Two examples highlight the difficulty faced by organizations confronting channel conflict. When Dell began selling computers through its website, it faced no objections from distributors because it had no distributors. When Compaq, Dell's principal competitor at the time, sought to respond by creating its own direct-sale website, it faced significant resistance from electronics store chains carrying its devices (e.g., Circuit City).

Renaissance Cruises had an even more traumatic encounter with the channel conflict dilemma. Taking a page out of the airline and lodging industries, the company decided to embrace the Internet channel in the late 1990s and drastically reduce travel agent commissions. In retaliation, the travel agent community boycotted the Renaissance product, and the firm quickly encountered financial difficulties. A public apology in the pages of the *Wall Street Journal* notwithstanding, these difficulties culminated in bankruptcy once the events of September 11, 2001, severely hampered the travel industry.

Customer and Employee Self-Service

Another important implication of the widespread adoption of electronic commerce and electronic business has been the emergence of customer and employee self-service. Aided by easy-to-use websites and the increasing degree of comfort that the general public has developed with information technology of all kinds, IT-enabled self-service is a growing trend requiring managerial attention (Figure 5.27).

Examples of this trend abound, from kiosks at airline counters, at post offices, in hotel lobbies, and in fast-food restaurants, to self-checkout counters at grocery stores, to web-based software that allows you to compute fairly complex tax returns without ever speaking to a professional. While kiosks have indeed made great strides, it appears that the new frontier of self-service is the mobile platform (see Chapter 12).

eCommerce: From Novelty to the Mainstream

In the little over 10 years since the Internet opened for business, electronic commerce and electronic business became mainstream—searching for information and transacting via the web became the norm for many individuals. As a consequence, the volume of business transacted through the web increased to over $1 trillion worldwide: $426.3 billion in China (10.1% of total retail sales), $305.7 billion in North America (7% of total retail sales), and $419 billion in Western Europe (7.3% of total retail sales).[13] No modern organization would ignore the impact of the Internet and the technologies that leverage it. However, innovation did not stop at what many are now calling Web 1.0, and both technological advances and business innovations continue to emerge at a rapid pace. Below we discuss some of the most recent trends.

FIGURE 5.27. Self-service kiosks
Photo by Gallowolf / CC BY SA 3.0

The Web 2.0 Phenomenon

With the success and widespread adoption of the Internet and the technologies associated with it has come the need to categorize and conceptualize its evolution. The underlying infrastructure and its defining characteristics (see Chapter 4) did not change dramatically since its inception. Moreover, many of the technologies at its core (e.g., the TCP/IP protocol, HTML, JavaScript) are still the bedrock of Internet operations and the pillars upon which innovation happens. However, we have witnessed a significant evolution of the front end and the way in which the Internet is utilized by both organizations and individuals. The term *Web 2.0* was coined to label the second wave of innovation and evolution occurring on the Internet after the shakeout following the original thrust of mainstream Internet innovation during the dot-com era (1993–2001).

While skeptics consider Web 2.0 a hollow marketing term, proponents of the label draw a distinction between the first incarnation of the World Wide Web (Web 1.0) as made of web pages populated with text and static images (Figure 5.28) and the dynamic nature of Web 2.0 sites (Figure 5.29). They consider Web 2.0 a useful umbrella term for categorizing both emerging technologies and business innovations that represent a significant departure from the paradigm of Web 1.0. More specifically, the proponents of Web 2.0 identify a number of defining features that differentiate it from its predecessor.

Two-Way Conversations   The metaphor for the web, when it first became widely utilized in the early 1990s, was the printed publication. The web was made of pages (not a coincidence in terminology!) filled with text, and later images. One key difference between traditional printed publications and web publishing, however, was presented by the information navigation possibilities offered by links in hypertext documents. Despite its navigational interactivity, however, in the early days, the web was a one-way broadcasting medium. Organizations and individuals would *create* web pages, and an audience of visitors would *visit* those pages. Today, the metaphor for individual and organizational web presence is a two-way conversation. Blogs, a prototypical example of Web 2.0 technology, are a vehicle for individuals to communicate with the (potentially) huge audience of web surfers. However, a staple of all major blogs is the possibility for that "audience" to comment and respond to the original blog post. Those responses are themselves public, searchable, and linkable—making them an intrinsic and valuable component of the blog itself. The bloggers themselves can in turn comment on the

13. All statistics taken from eMarketeer, 2014.

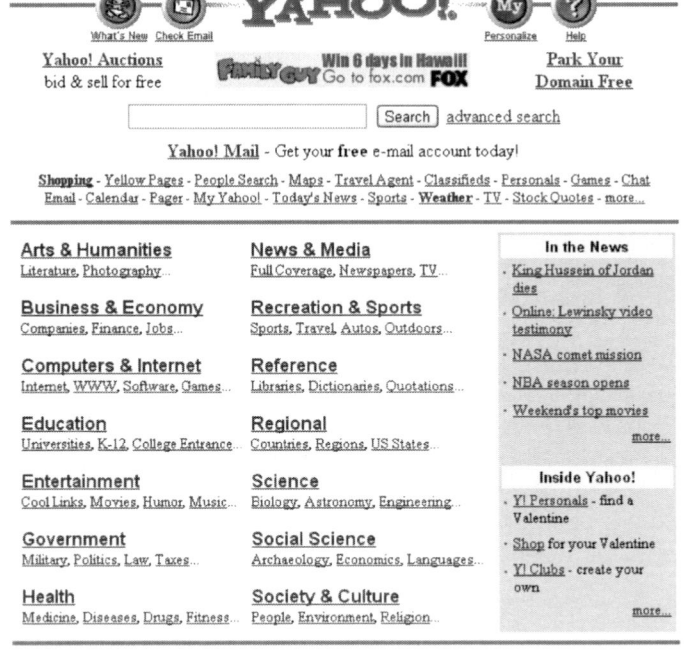

FIGURE 5.28. Yahoo.com website (1999)

comments of the "audience," thus turning the blog into a full-fledged asynchronous conversation. The power of blog-enabled conversations is exemplified by a story reported by CNN online.[14] A JetBlue customer, outraged at having to pay $50 for a regular-size box just because it contained a foldable bicycle, blogged about it. As others responded, the story was picked up from blog to blog, receiving increasing attention. As the story picked up steam, JetBlue refunded the passenger's money and proceeded to change the rule "discriminating" against bicycles.

Some blogs have even turned into profitable business ventures through affiliate marketing and the

FIGURE 5.29. YouTube
Photo by Esther Vargas / CC BY SA 2.0

increased visibility of the blogger. Consider the case of Chiara Ferragni. She started her fashion blog The Blonde Salad in 2009: "Three months after I started the website I started getting first invitations to shows at Milan Fashion Week, some of them for the front row so I was like, 'wow!' I had never been to a show before, and I didn't know the way the fashion world worked, it was totally new to me." Thanks to her blog, she has become an icon in fashion, gracing the covers of magazines like *Vogue* or *Marie Claire*. Ms. Ferragni now leads a team of 13 people, and her venture now generates more than $7 million a year, mainly from her line of shoes as well as ads, commissions, and brand consultancy.[15]

14. Elliott, C. (2009), Pushy bloggers to travel industry: Be nice, *CNN.com/Travel*, retrieved May 29, 2009, from http://www.cnn.com/2009/TRAVEL/traveltips/03/23/blogging.travel.complaints/index.html

15. Veselinovic, M. (2014, October 5), Cash a la mode: How style bloggers are turning social savvy into six-figure salaries, *CNN*, retrieved from http://edition.cnn.com/2014/10/01/world/europe/bloggers-six-figure-salaries/

While blogs present an apt example, two-way inter-activity is a staple of all technologies associated with Web 2.0 (see below). For example, YouTube enables its user base to comment on posted videos with text com-ments and—as you would expect from a video-sharing community—even with video responses!

FIGURE 5.30. Gmail logo
Source: Wikimedia.org

Interactive User Experience If the metaphor for the early web was the printed page, relatively static and unchanging over time, Web 2.0 sites are designed to be more akin to desktop applications than documents. Using a set of programming technologies centered on the Ajax framework (see below), Web 2.0 sites dynamically respond to user behavior and to other events. Such applications are generally referred to as Rich Internet Applications (RIA). Consider, for example, the popular Google e-mail client Gmail (Figure 5.30). Unlike previous web-based e-mail clients, where the inbox was a static page of text and images, the Gmail inbox behaves like a local e-mail client (i.e., a software program that resides on the user's own computer). If a new e-mail arrives, the page is automatically updated with the new infor-mation without any user intervention (i.e., you don't need to refresh the page).

User-Generated Content If the "surfers" of the early web were consumers of content, the modern web surfer could be better labeled a "prosumer."[16] This evolution is in large part due to Web 2.0 tech-nologies that dramatically lower the barriers to the production of content by the general population of web users. One example of user-generated content is blog comments, discussed earlier. But examples of user-generated content abound today on the web, from videos on YouTube, to images on Flickr, to descriptions of locations in Foursquare—the list is seemingly endless and growing daily. However, more subtly, user-generated content also encompasses comments on the content uploaded by other users in any of the above services, reviews produced by travelers on intermediary sites such as Expedia or TripAdvisor, ratings of products on Amazon or eBay, and so on. Perhaps the starkest example of user-generated content is offered by Wikipedia, a complete encyclopedia entirely coauthored by its readers through their voluntary contributions, editing, fact checking, and quality assurance. As a testament to the power of user-generated content and the crowds of users contributing it, *TIME* magazine rec-ognized the generic "you" (i.e., the mass of individuals cooperating and communicating through the web) as the "person of the year." In the explanation, *TIME*'s editors wrote:

> Who are these people? Seriously, who actually sits down after a long day at work and says, I'm not going to watch *Lost* tonight. I'm going to turn on my computer and make a movie starring my pet iguana? I'm going to mash up 50 Cent's vocals with Queen's instrumentals? I'm going to blog about my state of mind or the state of the nation or the steak-frites at the new bistro down the street? Who has that time and that energy and that passion? The answer is, you do. And for seizing the reins of the global media, for founding and framing the new digital democracy, for working for nothing and beating the pros at their own game, *TIME*'s Person of the Year for 2006 is you.[17]

Emergent Structure The publishing metaphor of the early web, along with the technical restrictions imposed by the technology of the time, made it so that content on the web had to be structured by a designer and that users would accept it and work within its limits. However, as technology progressed, making it easier for users to interact with and customize online applications to suit their needs, it became possible to allow structure to take form dynamically. The best example of this principle is the notion of

---

16. *Prosumer* is a term that represents the combination of *producer* and *consumer*—thus indicating that individuals both create and utilize content and resources available on the web.

17. Grossman, L. (2006, December 13), Time's person of the year: You, *TIME* magazine.

a "folksonomy," as opposed to a taxonomy.[18] While a taxonomy implies a preordained categorization mechanism developed by some expert, a "folk[19] taxonomy" (indeed, a folksonomy!) emerges by aggregating and compiling the individual categories created by users. The best example of this principle is a tag cloud—used, for example, to organize pictures in online sharing services such as Flickr (see below).

There is no clear date marking the transition from Web 1.0 to Web 2.0. There is no clear test to establish if a firm should be considered to have a "Web 2.0 presence." However, the value of discussing Web 2.0 for general and functional managers is not in being able to precisely mark the transition to Web 2.0 (assuming such a transition has even happened), but it is in developing an appreciation for how Internet technology has evolved and for the implications that this evolution has had, and continues to have, for organizations and businesses.

Web 2.0 Technologies

While the term *Web 2.0* is relatively general and not precisely defined, it has the value of enabling us to group a wave of technologies and IT innovations that helped move the web from a static platform made of flat pages to a dynamic place in terms of both user experience and content. This technological innovation has resulted in services that are free and easy to use, less structured, and more interactive than traditional Internet services. Interestingly, these services do not lack structure but, in true Web 2.0 form, allow for structure to emerge based on the interests and objectives of their community of users. The following are some examples of these services.

Wiki A wiki is a technology, introduced in 1994, that enables simple coauthoring and editing of web content. Wikis are extremely conducive to online collaboration, can be set up as private or public, and can require authentication or enable anyone to write and make changes to the shared documents. The primary example of a wiki is Wikipedia (Figure 5.31): a global, free, community-written encyclopedia. Wikipedia is literally a phenomenon, having started with little funding in 2001. Wikipedia does not commission any articles; the writing, editing, and quality assurance are all done by the global virtual community of Wikipedia contributors.

In late 2015, Wikipedia counted encyclopedias in 291 languages, with more than 1,200,000 individual encyclopedia entries in each of the 10 most popular languages and nearly five million entries in

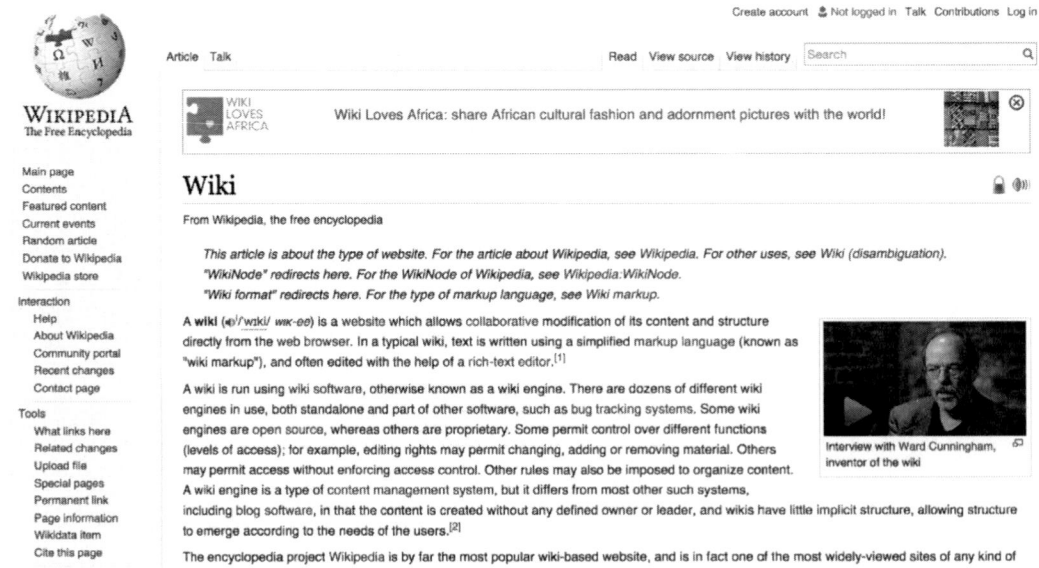

FIGURE 5.31. Wikipedia entry for *wiki*

---

18. A taxonomy, or taxonomy scheme, is a classification of the elements of a given universe (e.g., animals) in a hierarchical form.

19. *Folk* is an English term that represents a group of people.

the English-language encyclopedia alone. As a community-supported repository of knowledge, with a staff of fewer than 10 people and no professional or editorial personnel, it is legitimate to wonder about the quality of the entries in Wikipedia. An article in the journal *Nature* asked that very question and concluded, based on a peer-review test, that Wikipedia is of equivalent quality to the Encyclopedia Britannica Online, a repository of knowledge with a decidedly more august pedigree.[20] Further studies from different disciplines obtained similar results.[21] The test by *Nature*, while certainly not definitive, suggests that harnessing the knowledge and efforts of a huge community may lead not to anarchy but instead to robust content of a quality comparable to that produced by experts—an argument used by the proponents of Open Source software as well (see Chapter 12).

Users' Comments   In September 2009, search giant Google formally launched SideWiki with the lofty goal of allowing people to help one another by adding useful information to any website. Based on the concept of a wiki (an open, community-edited document), SideWiki enabled visitors who installed the Google toolbar and activated the SideWiki to see a sidebar with comments from other visitors—all outside the control of the website owner! While at the time of its launch there were a number of obstacles (e.g., the need to install dedicated software to access the service), SideWiki showed how simple it would be to democratize brand communication and how difficult it could be for brand managers to influence perceptions in a Web 2.0 environment. Interestingly, SideWiki raised the concerns of website owners afraid the system would take comments—an essential part of the content—away from the websites at the benefit of Google. This ignited a controversy that lead to SideWiki being discontinued in December 2011. No real alternatives have been proposed based on the same concept of a global comment system integrating functionalities found on platforms like Reddit or Digg.

Blogs   Blogs, a shorthand for weblogs, emerged along with the public Internet. Despite the techie-sounding term, a blog is nothing but an online journal that an individual keeps and publishes on the World Wide Web for the whole world to enjoy. While the early blogs were just static web pages laboriously updated by their authors, today a blog can be set up in a matter of minutes using tools such as WordPress or Blogger. Launched in 2005, one of the most renowned blogs, the *Huffington Post*, was sold to AOL in 2011 for $315 million (Figure 5.32), and in 2012 it even won the prestigious Pulitzer Prize.

FIGURE 5.32. *The Huffington Post* website

20. Giles, J. (2005), Internet encyclopedias go head to head, *Nature*, *439*, 900–901.

21. Reliability of Wikipedia (n.d.), in *Wikipedia*, retrieved from https://en.wikipedia.org/wiki/Reliability_of_Wikipedia

SIDEBAR 5.1. BEHIND THE SCENES AT TRIPIT.COM

Running a Web 2.0 site (or any eCommerce site for that matter) is no easy feat. Behind the glitter and flash of the front end—the website or mobile app— there is an infrastructure that is both technically and managerially complex. The diagram below takes us behind the scenes at TripIt.com, a high-profile Web 2.0 firm. TripIt provides a free utility, running on the web and as a smartphone app (Figure 5.33), that simplifies travel for its users. TripIt creates a digital itinerary for travelers by combining all components of a trip—airline tickets, hotel room confirmations, rental car agreement, restaurant reservations, and even theater tickets. TripIt creates the itinerary by parsing (i.e., reading) e-mail confirmations that the suppliers send to customers. Its proprietary software, aptly named *The Itinerator*, does this process automatically, adding contextual data (e.g., the location of a given airport, nearby points of interest) and other valuable information (e.g., maps, weather forecasts). Once compiled, these master itineraries are available to the traveler, who can share them with friends, families, coworkers, and any other of his TripIt's connections.

To the typical user of TripIt, the provision of this valuable service seems simple enough. However, delivering the TripIt value proposition requires the reliable operation of a complex infrastructure, the bulk of which is hidden—a technology iceberg of sort (Figure 5.34). The development of TripIt on stealth mode, prior to its public beta launch, took 10 months, but its service is in a constant state of development, and software engineers represent the bulk of the firm's staff.

Figure 5.34 shows the logical design of TripIt's infrastructure. As with any organizational software architecture, you recognize three major layers: the interface, the logic, and data management. The interface layer is concerned with external communication, whether with users or other services. The logic layer is *The Itinerator* itself, the software that extracts relevant data from the confirmation e-mails and combines

them into the master itinerary. The data management layer is concerned with access to the database and storage of new data that is acquired when travelers send their confirmation e-mails.

Wrapped around the proprietary set of applications and systems that make up the TripIt infrastructure are layers of what is called middleware. *Middleware* is a general term that encompasses all those technologies, software programs, and services that are necessary to integrate the components of TripIt's infrastructure as well as connect it to the outside world. In general, the middleware of a modern eCommerce organization includes the following:

- Access gateways that provide authentication for users and services
- Database interfaces that provide access to local and remote data repositories
- Network and communication interfaces that provide the rules of interoperability for applications and software services
- Directory services that provide a way to identify and reach resources on the network

Finally, for TripIt to operate effectively and reliably, a number programming environments and languages have to be mastered by its IT professionals. At TripIt, the following feature prominently:

- Ruby, a programming language well suited for dynamic website development
- Ruby on Rails, a web application framework for the Ruby programming language
- XML, the eXtensible Mark-up Language used to transfer data
- SQL, a querying language for databases

While this sidebar is not intended to be a comprehensive list or an analysis of the technologies that enable the proper functioning of enterprise-class eCommerce applications, it should help you appreciate how complex these operations are.

As a Web 2.0 technology, blogs enable their authors to modify their structure by including other media types beyond text—such as video and images. More important, blogs enable hyperlinking and discussion, thus making them not just a one-way communication medium but one able to support interactive "conversations."

RSS RSS, which stands for Real Simple Syndication, is a syndication technique enabling an organization to create web feeds—short summaries of content with a link to the full-fledged version—that are broadcast to everyone who subscribes to the feed once a trigger event occurs. For example, as a blogger, you may want to use RSS to inform your faithful readers every time the blog is updated.

FIGURE 5.33. Itinerary in TripIt's iPhone app

FIGURE 5.34. Logical design of the TripIt software infrastructure

FIGURE 5.35. Reuters' use of RSS

Reuters, the notorious news agency, uses RSS to distribute its headlines to users and blogs to lead traffic back to its website. RSS represent a convenient tool for generating additional web traffic (Figure 5.35).

In many ways, RSS is a new twist on an early Internet idea: push technology. Push technology emerged in reaction to the explosion of web content and the increasing difficulty of searching for relevant content. It enabled users to specify what content they were interested in, and such content would be delivered to them.

Tags   Tags, short descriptors associated with an object, are not a new technology by any means. However, tags are now widely used on the Internet to give structure to and to categorize the increasing amount of available content. One of the pioneers in the use of tags was Flickr, the online photo management and sharing application. Instead of providing users with a fixed set of predefined categories to use to index the photos they upload, Flickr allows individual users to create their own tags. Subsequently, Flickr uses custom software to identify the emergent structure of the aggregate image database by identifying sets of tags that correlate highly. This approach creates an intriguing emergent structure.

Ajax   Ajax (Asynchronous JavaScript and XML) represents a group of web programming technologies designed to enable the development of interactive client-side applications running on the web. In other words, when using the Ajax technologies, a web designer can mimic the behavior of traditional desktop software applications by enabling the website that the user interacts with (i.e., the client side) to interact, in the background, with a remote server-side application. The Gmail application is a classic example of Ajax use.

Microblogs   Microblogs, brought to fame by the explosion of Twitter into the mainstream, represent the vehicle for unidirectional, short bursts of communication to a self-selected audience of followers. In and of themselves, microblogs are not interactive. However, users quickly figured out how to expand the application's capabilities by enabling retweeting (i.e., forwarding of tweets), link embedding, and threading through hashtags. The rapid evolution of Twitter and its functionalities demonstrates once again the flexibility and malleability of information technology innovations, which can quickly morph and adjust to user interests and needs. Twitter's cofounder and CEO, Evan Williams, captured this concept: "The fundamental idea is that Twitter lets people share moments of their lives, whenever they want, be they momentous occasions or mundane ones. [. . .] What we didn't anticipate was the many,

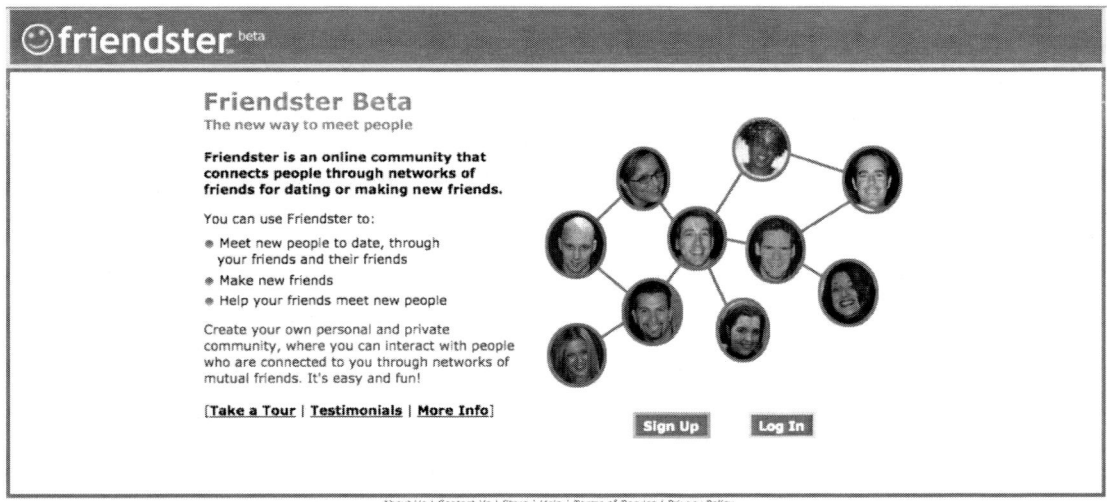

FIGURE 5.36. Friendster.com website in 2003
Source: Internet Archive

many other uses that would evolve from this very simple system."[22] Microblogs are the gasoline on the word-of-mouth fire, enabling immediate communication and rebroadcasting with unprecedented ease. They also offer organizations a tool for real-time communication with interested customers. Leveraging this feature of the technology, for example, is the low-cost airline JetBlue, with nearly two million followers.

Web 2.0 and Business Innovation

Web 2.0 technologies continue to spur business innovation driven by firms seeking to create value in the evolving environment. The following is a description of some of the principal business innovations that have paralleled the evolution of the Web 2.0 phenomenon.

Social Networking   Social networking is perhaps the most visible manifestation of the Web 2.0 phenomenon and in many respects its poster child. This is somewhat ironic, as the essence of social networking has pervaded the Internet since its inception. As early as 1968, when JCR Licklider[23] published a paper titled "The Computer as a Communication Device," the notion of computer-mediated social interactions had been clearly conceptualized. However, the current form of social networking applications, with member's individual profiles, private connections between friends, and easy communication and sharing within a social network, did not emerge until the 2003 public launch of Friendster.com (Figure 5.36). Following the launch of Friendster, a number of other social networking sites emerged, including familiar names such as MySpace, LinkedIn, and Facebook. By some accounts, in 2011 there were almost 200 separate active social networks, including highly targeted communities such as Livemocha.com (online language learning community), Geni.com (online family tree), and VampireFreaks.com (focused on the Gothic-industrial subcultures). Today, Internet users registered over 2 billion active social media accounts—in other words, 29% of world population is participating in social media.[24]

---

22. Williams, E. (2009), The voice of Twitter users, *TED Talk*, retrieved from https://www.ted.com/talks/evan_williams_on_listening_to_twitter_users/transcript

23. J. C. R. Licklider was a computer scientist widely regarded as the driving force behind ARPAnet, the predecessor of the Internet we know today.

24. Kemp, S. (2015), Digital, social & mobile worldwide 2015, WeAreSocial.com, retrieved from http://wearesocial.net/blog/2015/01/digital-social-mobile-worldwide-2015/

Mashups   Mashups represent a tangible and visible example of combinatorial innovation, whereby component parts (e.g., integrated circuits) are combined into novel creations (e.g., personal computers, laptops, digital cameras). In a mashup, the component parts are software artifacts available on the Internet, such as programming standards, communication protocols, databases, and other resources. When a programmer creates a mashup, she will use those components to string together available digital resources into a novel web application that delivers new functionalities. For example, the earth album (http://www.earthalbum.com) is a mashup that combines Google Maps with Flickr's public photos, offering a crowd-sourced album of images from all over the world.

Long-Tail Strategies   In statistics, the notion of a long tail represents a power law relationship between two quantities. A power law between two quantities occurs when the frequency of an object occurs as a power function of certain characteristics of that object (Figure 5.37). The best-known example of this phenomenon in economics is the so-called Pareto principle, or the 80–20 rule (e.g., 80% of your sales will come from 20% of your product catalog). More generally, the long tail represents a phenomenon by which the frequency of an event is related to some characteristic of that same event. For example, Chris Anderson in his 2004 *Wired* magazine article[25] on the subject noted that, according to the Recording Industry Association of America, only the top 10 major label music CDs were actually profitable.

However, Anderson observed that online stores could capture sales from nonhits as well. More specifically, he documented that the online retailer Amazon.com carried, at the time, 2.3 million books and could fill orders of magnitude greater than the total inventory of a typical physical bookstore (about 130,000). Importantly, he also documented that the total sales of books at Amazon.com from the 130,000 books one would also find in traditional stores (i.e., the high-volume "hits") accounted for fewer than 50% of total sales. In other words, the long tail of "not-so-popular" products delivered a greater share of sales than the *fat head* of popular items. While one could argue that this is partly due to the fact that Amazon faced significantly higher competition for the popular items, the findings suggest that customer interests are highly varied and that there is some demand for niche products. When this is the case, a firm has the opportunity to craft a strategy that leverages the dis-homogeneity in customers' demands. Such strategy should focus on minimizing inventory holding and distribution costs—easiest to do with information goods such as digital songs or e-books (see Chapter 4)—as well as enabling customers to search for the more obscure items and even be alerted about previously unknown

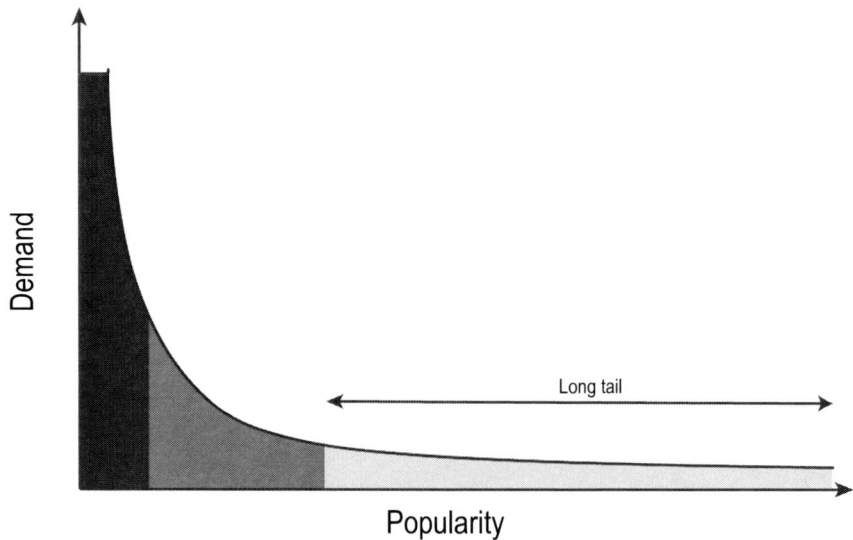

FIGURE 5.37. The long-tail distribution

***

25. Anderson, C. (2004), The long tail, *Wired*, *12*(10), retrieved from http://www.wired.com/2004/10/tail/

items that would be of interest to them based on previous purchases through collaborative filtering[26] or similar technologies.

Interestingly, crowdsourcing is based on the same long-tail concept. Crowdsourcing is an online activity in which an individual or an organization proposes via an open call to a heterogeneous "crowd" of individuals the voluntary undertaking of a task. In this case, the tail is made up of a large number of individuals offering their work, money, knowledge, and experience to business looking for outsourcing activities.[27] Crowdsourcing predates the Internet by centuries. In the late 19th century, Professor James Murray appealed to the "English-speaking and English-reading public" for updating existing dictionaries. Volunteers were asked to read specific books and extract quotations illustrating the words and meanings of words not included in the dictionary they considered worth noting.

Eight hundred volunteers participated in the creation of the first fascicles of the Oxford English Dictionary. This reading program lasted for 70 years and generated more than six million submissions.

FIGURE 5.38. The public appeal of April 1879 to contribute to the Oxford English Dictionary
Source: Oxford English Dictionary (2013), April 1879 appeal, retrieved from http://public.oed.com/history-of-the-oed/archived-documents/april-1879-appeal/april-1879-appeal/

26. Collaborative filtering is the technique of alerting customers about products of potential interest to them based on an analysis of their pattern of behavior relative to people who exhibit similar tastes. A famous example of the use of collaborative filtering is Amazon.com's purchase recommendations.

27. Estellés-Arolas, E., & González-Ladrón-de-Guevara, F. (2012), Towards an integrated crowdsourcing definition. *Journal of Information science, 38*(2), 189–200.

This example may have reminded you of Wikipedia. The difference is that thanks to the extend reach of Internet, "appeals" like the Oxford English Dictionary's can mobilize a larger proportion of the tail. As we reminded earlier, Wikipedia is contributed to by 128,000 individuals who work on 35,000,000 articles written in 290 languages.[28]

Crowdsourcing approaches can be broadly categorized on the basis of the class of problems they address:[29]

- *Knowledge discovery and management.* This is used to solve information gathering, organization, and reporting problems, such as the creation of collective resources. The basic idea is that the necessary knowledge is already available and that the crowd can be leveraged to discover and organize it. The typical example is Wikipedia, where articles are the result of the collaborative writing and research efforts of multiple contributors.
- *Distributed human intelligence tasking.* This approach is used for tasks where human intelligence is required to process data or information instead of computers. Generally consisting in simple repetitive tasks, it is ideal for processing large batches of data that only humans can handle (i.e., tag images, filter image content, verify catalogs, fill surveys, edit transcripts, write reviews). At Amazon's Mechanical Turk, requesting firms submit a project (called HITs—human intelligence tasks) that workers can choose from and be compensated for upon completion.
- *Broadcast search.* This focuses on finding a single specialist, generally outside the field of expertise of the organization. The broadcast-search approach is appropriate for problems where the "right" answer exists but is not yet known by the organization. Innocentive.com is an example of this category. The company seeks innovation solutions from talented individuals who compete to provide ideas and solutions to the submitted business, social, policy, scientific, and technical challenges.
- *Peer-vetted creative production.* This is adapted for ideation problems where an organization resorts to the crowd for supporting the creative phase and receives multiple design proposals. This approach is ideal for design, aesthetics, or policy problems where contributors have direct interests or are potential customers. Threadless.com, for example, acts as a platform where users can both propose and vote on T-shirt designs that are then made available for purchase on the website.

Summary

The years between 1993 and 2000 saw the dawn of the network economy, a landscape of economic activity characterized by pervasive information networks. While the frenzied pace of experimentation has slowed since 2000, electronic commerce and electronic business trends and innovations spurred by the widespread adoption of the Internet have become mainstream.

In this chapter, we sought to provide you with the tools to make sense of past developments and to understand future trends.

- The Internet, traditionally thought of as a network of computer networks, is evolving into a global information grid enabling ever-changing devices, and the people who use them, to easily connect and disconnect from it. The rapid pace of evolution and innovation on the Internet is enabled by its characteristics: distributed governance and the reliance on publicly available open standards supporting a multiplicity of compatible devices and offering a number of services.
- While today the two terms are used largely as synonyms, we defined *electronic commerce* as an online exchange of value and *electronic business* as the digital enablement of internal

---

28. Statistics taken from https://en.wikipedia.org/wiki/Special:Statistics and https://en.wikipedia.org/wiki/List_of_Wikipedias
29. Brabham, D. C. (2013), *Crowdsourcing*, Boston, MA: MIT Press, 44–50.

organizational business processes. Electronic commerce and electronic business find their roots in the development of information technology and networking over the last 40 years. But the recent acceleration of innovation in this area has been enabled by affordable computing equipment, widespread access to the Internet, the increasing ease of use of information technology, and the availability of open standards.

- We have categorized electronic commerce phenomena on two dimensions. By looking at the type of transaction taking place, we classified electronic commerce as business-to-consumer (B2C), business-to-business (B2B), consumer-to-consumer (C2C), consumer-to-business (C2B), and eGovernment. Focusing on the company structure of the organizations involved, we classified concerns involved in electronic commerce such as brick and mortar, bricks and clicks, and pure play.

- We defined a business model as the document that captures the firm's concept and value proposition while also conveying what market opportunity the company is pursuing, what product or service it offers, and what strategy the firm will follow to capture a dominant position. The dominant business models that have emerged in the network economy are online retailing, infomediaries, content providers, online communities, exchanges, and infrastructure providers.

- A key feature of a business model is the revenue model—the firm's plan for building a revenue stream. The dominant revenue models that have emerged are pay for service, subscription, advertisement support, and affiliate.

- The rapid adoption of the Internet and the emergence of the network economy have had some significant implications for both established organizations and upstarts. Disintermediation (the process by which a firm's distribution chain is shortened through the elimination of one or more intermediaries), reintermediation (the process by which new online intermediaries carve a niche for themselves alongside their brick-and-mortar counterparts), channel conflict (the dilemma faced by organizations deciding whether to disintermediate their legacy distribution channels), and the emergence of widespread IT-enabled self-service are the most relevant.

- While the dot-com boom may have slowed down, technology and business innovation is alive and well in the network economy. New technologies such as wikis and Real Simple Syndication (RSS) continue to redefine business models and determine how organizations can create value in the network economy.

- The extended reach of the Internet has eased the access to the long tail, making viable new business models focused on the retail of nonmainstream products. In parallel, crowdsourcing has emerged as an innovative approach to activities outsourcing.

Study Questions

1. What is the difference between the terms *electronic commerce* and *electronic business*? Why has the distinction largely faded in recent years?
2. What are the principal enablers of the continued importance of electronic commerce trends?
3. Define each of the following terms and provide examples: business-to-consumer (B2C), business-to-business (B2B), consumer-to-consumer (C2C), consumer-to-business (C2B), and eGovernment.
4. Define each of the following terms and provide examples: brick and mortar, bricks and clicks, and pure play.
5. Explain what we mean by the terms *business model* and *revenue model*. How do the two differ? What are the principal business models and revenue models adopted by modern organizations?
6. What are the principal impacts of the network economy for both established organizations and upstarts? Define each and provide examples.
7. Identify and provide examples of the most important recent technology and business innovations in the network economy.

Further Readings

1. Anderson, C. (2006). *The long tail: Why the future of business is selling less of more.* New York, NY: Hyperion.

2. Doan, A., Ramakrishnan, R., and Halevy, A. Y. (2011). Crowdsourcing systems on the World-Wide Web. *Communications of the ACM, 54*(4), 86–96.

3. McAfee, A. (2006, Spring). Enterprise 2.0: The dawn of emergent collaboration. *Sloan Management Review,* 20–28.

4. Osterwalder, A., & Pigneur, Y. (2010). *Business model generation: A handbook for visionaries,* game changers, and challengers. Hoboken, NJ: Wiley.

5. Piccoli, G., and Ott, M. (2014). Impact of mobility and timing on user-generated content. *MIS Quarterly Executive, 13*(3), 147–157.

6. Rayport, J. F., & Jaworski, B. J. (2004, December). Best face forward. *Harvard Business Review,* 47–58.

7. Zott, C., and Amit, R. (2013). The business model: A theoretically anchored robust construct for strategic analysis. *Strategic Organization, 11*(4), 403–411.

Glossary

- **Brick and mortar:** A term used to refer to "traditional" organizations, those firms that have physical operations and don't provide their services through the Internet.
- **Bricks and clicks:** Organizations that have hybrid operations involving both physical and online operations.
- **Business model:** A business model captures the firm's concept and value proposition while also conveying what market opportunity the company is pursuing, what product or service it offers, and what strategy the firm will follow to capture a dominant position.
- **Business-to-business (B2B):** A form of electronic commerce involving two for-profit organizations in the transaction.
- **Business-to-consumer (B2C):** A form of electronic commerce involving a for-profit organization on one side and the end consumer on the other side of the transaction.
- **Channel conflict:** A term that captures the dilemma faced by organizations deciding whether to disintermediate their legacy distribution channels.
- **Consumer-to-business (C2B):** A form of electronic commerce enabling individuals to transact with business organizations not as buyers of goods and services but as suppliers.
- **Consumer-to-consumer (C2C):** A form of electronic commerce enabling individual consumers to interact and transact directly.
- **Crowdsourcing:** An online activity in which an individual or an organization proposes to a heterogeneous "crowd" of individuals via an open call the voluntary undertaking of a task. In this case, the tail is made of a large number of individuals offering their work, money, knowledge, and experience to business looking for outsourcing activities.
- **Disintermediation:** The process by which a firm's distribution chain is shortened through the elimination of one or more intermediaries.
- **eGovernment:** A form of electronic commerce involving legislative and administrative institutions in the transaction.
- **Electronic business:** The digital enablement of internal organizational business processes.
- **Electronic commerce:** An online exchange of value.
- **Pure play:** Organizations that have no physical stores and provide their services exclusively through the Internet.
- **Reintermediation:** The process by which new online intermediaries carve a niche for themselves alongside their brick-and-mortar counterparts.
- **Revenue model:** Specifies how the firm intends to draw proceeds from its value proposition—in short, how it plans to make money.
- **Web 2.0:** A term that identifies a collection of trends and technologies that mark the shift from a static, mostly broadcast, paradigm for the World Wide Web to a dynamic paradigm centered around user participation and involvement.

THE STRATEGIC USE OF INFORMATION SYSTEMS

The potential for the strategic use of information technology (IT)-enabled information systems (IS) has been a source of debate since it became clear that information technology had important business applications. The love-hate relationship between business and information systems continues to this day, with stark examples of companies that have successfully harnessed the potential of ever-more-powerful information technology grabbing headlines, market share, and profits, and others who have famously squandered large sums of money with little visible benefit. For example, eBay Inc., the multinational company managing online marketplaces in 27 countries around the globe, has built an empire around the novel and clever use of information systems to enable the connection of far-flung buyers and sellers.

The ability of megastore operator Walmart Inc. to manage information for competitive advantage is the stuff of legends. The firm built its own satellite-based telecommunication network in the 1970s to support real-time communication with its stores located in rural areas of the United States. As a testament to his faith in the potential of information systems pervading the company, founder Sam Walton declared in 1992, "We've spent almost $700 million building up the current computer and satellite systems we have. . . . What I like about it is the kind of information you can pull out of it on moment's notice—all those numbers."[1] Even today, technology is a major concern for the company. As David Cheesewright, president and chief executive officer (CEO) of Walmart International, recently commented, "Wherever we operate, everything starts with the customer, and I see customers' shopping habits changing more rapidly than I can remember. Customers are shopping more online, with mobile devices, and they really like convenience. If our customer changes fast, we have to change even faster

---

1. Walton, S., with Huey, J. (1992), *Sam Walton: Made in America*, New York, NY: Bantam, p. 271.

if we want to continue to exceed her expectations."[2] Walmart's traditional competitor, K-Mart, never reached the same level of proficiency with information systems and IT use. Its resulting inability to compete in the battle for low prices took it perilously close to bankruptcy more than once.

So why are some firms able to exploit information systems for sustained competitive advantage while others cannot? Perhaps the most enduring research result that can help in answering this question is offered by executives' surveys, which show remarkable consistency with the finding that the average non-IT senior manager feels that technology and IS decisions are well outside his or her comfort zone. To this day, many general and functional managers are uncomfortable with planning for the use and management of information systems. This state of affairs is best captured by the following quote from a beleaguered business executive: "What can I do? I don't understand IT well enough to manage it in detail. And my IT people—although they work very hard—don't seem to understand the very real business problems I face."[3]

Compounding the above problem is the fact that the information systems function has traditionally been led by technologists. Because of the vastly different background and knowledge base of business executives and technology executives, the result has often been failed communication and a delegation of "all IT issues" to technologists. More recently, however, we have witnessed a trend reversal, with the IS function being led by many "new school" chief information officers (CIOs), who are well versed in the inner workings of the business. While this is a step in the right direction, it is hardly enough because, as talented as today's CIOs are, they are not spending their time addressing operations problems the way chief operating officers (COOs) do, marketing problems the way chief marketing officers (CMOs) do, or financial problems the way chief financial officers (CFOs) do.

The above call to action is particularly important when it comes to using information and information technology to underpin value-adding strategic initiatives. General and functional managers must feel comfortable with planning and setting direction for the use of information systems resources, with identifying opportunities to use technology to create and appropriate economic value, and with deciding under what circumstances these initiatives can be protected against competitive retaliation.

Part III speaks to general and functional managers and covers the key information systems decisions that all modern managers must be comfortable with making.

- *Chapter 6: Strategic Information Systems Planning.* This chapter provides an overview of the strategic information systems planning process, from the definition of an overall information vision to the identification of strategic initiatives.
- *Chapter 7: Value Creation and Strategic Information Systems.* This chapter sets the background for analyzing the use of information systems and technology to create and appropriate value. We define key terms and explain the framework used to analyze value creation and appropriation potential of specific strategic initiatives.
- *Chapter 8: Value Creation with Information Systems.* This chapter discusses a number of frameworks and analytical models that have been advanced over the years to help managers envision how to use information systems and technology to create and appropriate economic value.
- *Chapter 9: Appropriating IT-Enabled Value over Time.* This chapter completes the puzzle by focusing on sustainability. Once a firm has successfully created value with information systems and technology, it must be able to defend its position of advantage and appropriate the value created over time.

---

2. Walmart (2014), *Walmart CEO outlines company's future: Being customer-driven, investing in its people, leading at the forefront of innovation and technology*, retrieved from http://news.walmart.com/news-archive/2014/06/06/walmart-ceo-outlines-companys-future-being-customer-driven-investing-in-its-people-leading-at-the-forefront-of-innovation-and-technology

3. Nolan, R., & McFarlan, F. W. (2005, October), Information technology and the board of directors, *Harvard Business Review, 83*(10), 96–106.

CHAPTER 6

Strategic Information Systems Planning

What You Will Learn in This Chapter

This chapter focuses on the strategic information systems (IS) planning process and the role that general and functional managers need to play in it. Strategic information systems planning is a fundamental aspect of information systems management because it ensures that information systems and technology decisions are not made in a haphazard fashion. Rather, decisions are made with a clear understanding of business strategy and an overall sense of direction with respect to what the firm is trying to achieve with its use of information systems resources.

Specifically, this chapter will

1. Explain why general and functional managers must be involved in information systems planning decisions despite their lack of technical expertise.
2. Discuss the purpose that strategic information systems planning serves in modern organizations.
3. Identify the key components of the strategic information systems planning process, including information systems assessment, information systems vision, and information systems guidelines.
4. Explain how to perform an information systems assessment.
5. Explain how to decide what role information systems resources should play in your firm using available analytical tools to develop an information systems vision.
6. Explain what role information systems guidelines play in the planning process and how to develop them upon having established an information systems vision.
7. Help you evaluate how well positioned your organization is to achieve its information vision following the guidelines and to develop consistent strategic initiatives.

MINICASE: Strategic Information Systems Planning at CFCU

As you return to your hotel room in Athens, Georgia, tired from your first day at the new client site, you start thinking about the challenge ahead. Your consulting firm was called in by a regional bank—Campus Federal Credit Union (CFCU). The small regional bank has long tradition in the community, having started in 1967 to serve the retail banking needs of local residents through 21 branches, a capillary network of ATMs and, since 2001, online banking facilities.

CFCU's operation centered on personal banking with a wealth of products, ranging from standard checking accounts, to certificates of deposit, to mortgages. While CFCU was a conservative player, offering the pledge of being a safe place for its customer's money, the recent evolution in banking both afforded the opportunity and created pressure to innovate and reach new customers. As you suspected and your meeting today confirmed, however, the bank's main market were local residents with stable financial needs who would benefit from new services—such as online bill pay or flexible personal loans.

Your consulting firm had been engaged by the client to "develop a strategic information systems plan." Yet the series of meetings you had today left you with the distinct impression that the client had already formulated some ideas. In a meeting with you, the senior vice president of marketing said, "We're missing the boat. Large national banks like HSBC target our customers with precise marketing offers. We must invest in business intelligence (BI) and customer relationship management (CRM) tools or we will not survive." From the director of technology services, you heard mostly frustration: "They want me to deliver a world-class infrastructure on a shoestring. The chief financial officer (CFO), to whom I report, makes me justify every information technology (IT) investment. Return on investment (ROI) and net present value calculations are all he cares about! Yet two-thirds of my budget goes to keeping the lights on, and the remainder is spent on various pet projects for one or the other

of the executives. How am I going to modernize our archaic infrastructure under these conditions?"

The chief executive officer (CEO) seemed to recognize some of these issues and thought your help would be instrumental in changing things for the better. In the opening meeting, he said, "Your firm is the best at this and you know our industry well. We need you to assess our current operations and draft a strategic plan; we will follow it at once!" As you organize your notes, a nagging feeling overcomes you—the firm does not seem to have great unity of purpose at the moment, so how does it expect you to be able get all members of the firm on the same page? Plans are vacuous without the commitment of those who have to follow them.

"Well," you tell yourself, "one step at a time." You have certainly been in more difficult situations.

Discussion Questions

1. What do you see as the major pitfalls of the current manner in which the information systems budgeting and prioritization process is run?
2. What do you believe are going to be the major challenges you will encounter on this assignment?
3. What should be your next step as you get to work tomorrow morning?

Introduction

With information technology (IT) increasingly embedded in all aspects of business operations, the most successful organizations are those that are able to establish a productive partnership between IT executives and their functional counterparts. Results of the recurring CIO.com's "State of the CIO" survey indicate that in 64% of the firms in the study, the chief information officer (CIO) had a seat on the primary management committee (e.g., executive committee). However, only 44% of CIOs report directly to the chief executive officer (CEO; see Figure 6.1).[1]

Being able to establish a productive partnership between your organization's technology professionals and the executive team is predicated on recruiting the right people and devoting significant attention to the development of the relationship. However, whether or not you are able (and lucky enough) to establish a productive partnership with the information systems (IS) professionals in your organization, you must be involved in the strategic planning and management of information systems in your firm. Failing to do so, and leaving all information systems decisions to your IT counterparts, will simply result in your joining the ranks of unsatisfied and disappointed general and functional managers scattered throughout the world.

A Word about Strategic and Operational Planning

The realm of strategy pertains to the decisions that an organization makes with respect to how it will develop and deploy its resources over time in an effort to achieve its long-range objectives. Consider for a moment the Roman proconsul Julius Caesar. When he set forth to conquer Gaul (Figure 6.2), he

---

1. Adapted from the authors on the basis of *Computerworld*'s 2015 CIO Survey: Muse, D. (2015, January 26), State of the CIO 2015, *CIO*, retrieved from http://www.cio.com/article/2877303/cio-role/state-of-the-cio-2015.html

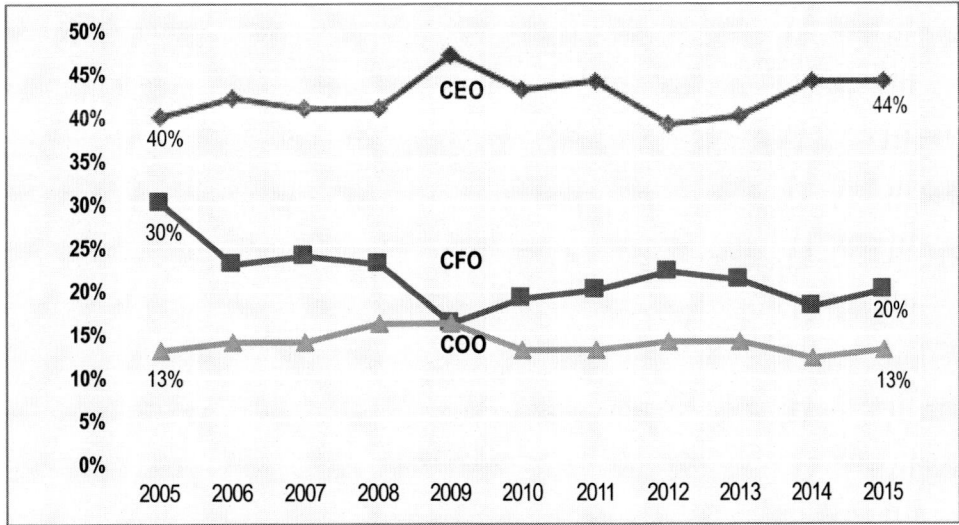

FIGURE 6.1. To whom do CIOs report?

had to decide how to best create and deploy Roman military resources in order to succeed in the conquest—in essence, he had to devise a strategy for the conquest of Gaul. Caesar and his generals had to decide how many legions to raise, how to equip them, how to train them, where to locate camps, and how to organize the logistics of supplies and provisions to sustain the campaign.

As we see here, the realm of strategic thinking, and as a consequence, the realm of strategic planning, is concerned with long-range decisions about resource development and deployment. Conversely, operational decision making is concerned with local decisions in the present. For example, as the famed tenth legion took camp at *Bribacte* (near modern day Autun in Bourgogne), the camp had to operate with day-to-day routines for mounting guard, for cleaning, for provisioning, and so on.

As this simple example from a historic military campaign clarifies, there is a clear difference between strategic and operational decision making. While both strategic planning and operational effectiveness are critical to the success of a venture—whether military or organizational—the remainder of the chapter focuses on strategic IS planning. Thus we are concerned here with how the firm will build and deploy its IS resources in an effort to achieve its long-range objectives.

Strategic Alignment

A firm that has been able to achieve a high degree of fit and consonance between the priorities and activities of the IS function and the strategic direction of the firm has achieved strategic alignment. Research in this area has consistently shown that alignment has a direct impact on firm performance, and alignment is perennially on the top-10 list of CIO priorities. Yet strategic alignment is very difficult to achieve and maintain, particularly in those highly competitive environments where opportunities arise and fade quickly, and strategic priorities change constantly. Thus ensuring a high degree of strategic IS alignment requires as much improvisation as careful planning. Data from McKinsey provides some comfort, suggesting that IT executives have become adept at aligning IT strategy with the needs of the organization[2] and that high-performing IT organizations present an active CIO involvement in the business.[3] However, the IS function still struggles to systematically propose new ways of creating

2. Craig, D., Kanakamedala, K., & Tinaikar, R. (2007, Spring), The next frontier in IT strategy: A McKinsey survey, *McKinsey on IT*, retrieved from http://www.mckinsey.com/clientservice/bto/pointofview/pdf/MoIT11_Survey_F.pdf

3. Arandjelovic, P., Libby, B., & Naufal, K. (2015, February), Why CIOs should be business-strategy partners, *McKinsey & Company*, retrieved from http://www.mckinsey.com/insights/business_technology/why_cios_should_be_business-strategy_partners

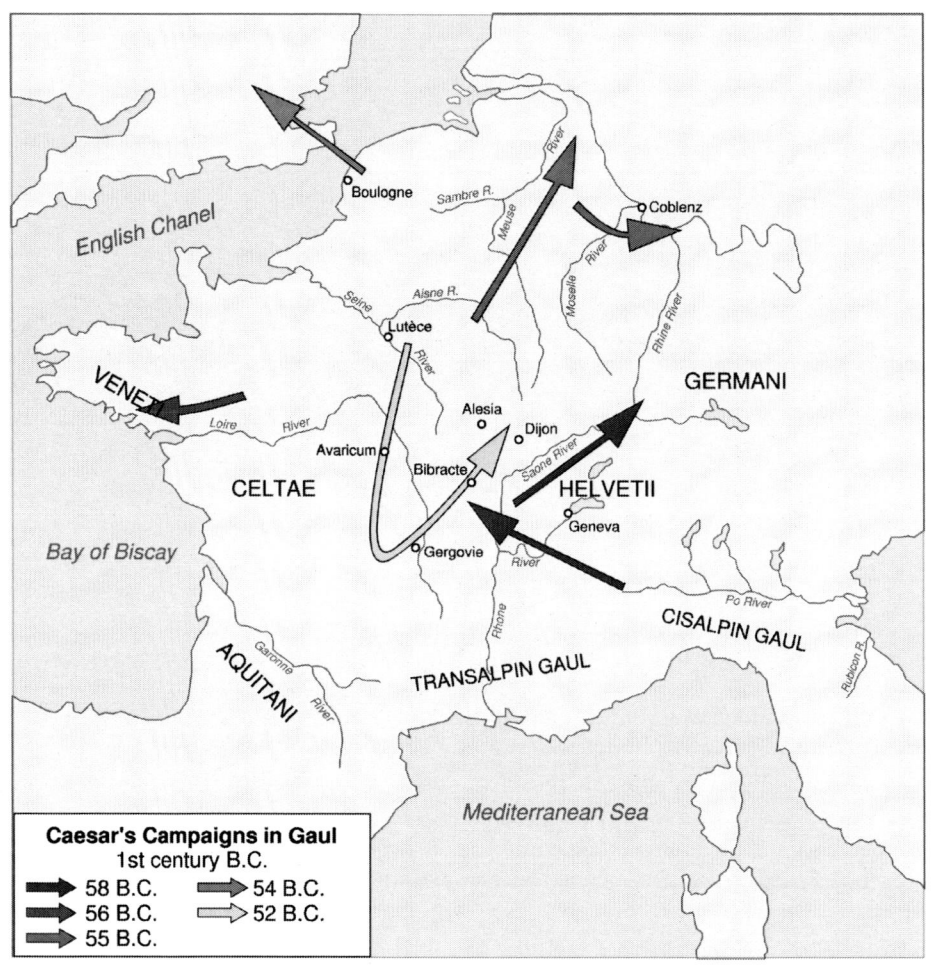

FIGURE 6.2. The Roman Gaelic campaign
Photo by Sémur / CC BY SA 2.5

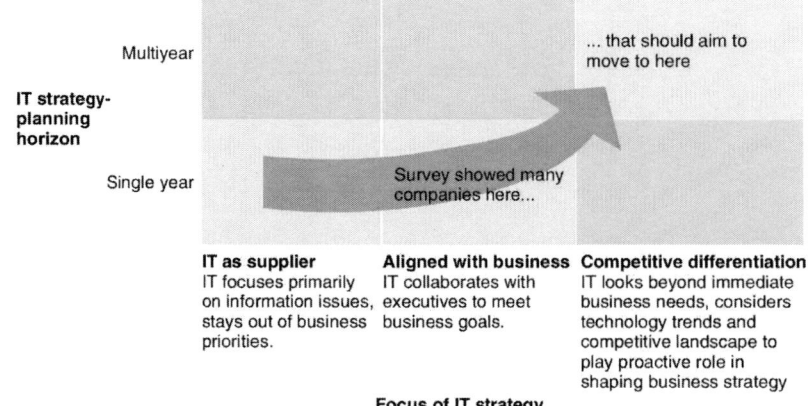

FIGURE 6.3. McKinsey IT strategy maturity matrix
Source: McKinsey (2007)

value using technology resources (Figure 6.3), and executives' current perceptions of IT performance are still negative.[4]

Six Decisions Requiring Managerial Involvement

Jeanne Ross and Peter Weill, of MIT's Center for Information Systems Research (CISR), suggest that senior management get involved in IS management by taking the leadership role on six key information systems decisions (Table 6.1):[5]

1. *How much should we spend on IT?* This is perhaps the most critical question that you, as a general manager or as a member of the executive committee, will be called on to ask because the answer informs all subsequent IT-related decision making.

   As we saw in Chapter 2, organizations are widely different with respect to their strategy and objectives, their culture, their history, their current infrastructure, and so on. It follows that even two head-to-head competitors may need very different investments in IT—different in terms of both quantity (i.e., how much to spend) and quality (i.e., what initiatives should be the recipient of the IT budget).

   This question is designed to force senior executives to discuss and decide on the role of information systems and technology in the organization—something that most executive committees don't do. Failing to ask and answer this question puts the firm's IT department in a reactive mode, having to decide on individual projects with little guidance as to the overall picture.

2. *Which business processes should receive the IT dollars?* This question requires executives to decide which business processes are most important to the firm at a given point—clearly a business decision—and as a consequence should attract IT funding. In other words, it is within the purview of business managers to decide on the allocation of resources among the many possible projects the firm can pursue—information systems and technology projects included!

3. *Which IT capabilities need to be company-wide?* Large organizations constantly battle the trade-off between standardization and flexibility. Increasing standardization enables the firm to manage operations efficiently, while flexibility enables the firm to react more quickly and more effectively to local needs. Because information systems often enable the standardization or flexibility of operations, IS professionals are often left with the responsibility to make this decision. Yet this is a business decision that general and functional managers should not hand over. After all, the executive committee is in the best position to weigh the cost/benefits of standardization and flexibility.

4. *How good do our IT services really need to be?* The quality of service provided by an organization's information systems department is measured by the reliability and up-time of the IT infrastructure, data accessibility and flexibility, responsiveness to user needs, and the like. This question forces executives to make conscious decisions about the degree of service the firm needs and what they are willing to pay for.

5. *What security and privacy risks will we accept?* Remember the old adage "You get what you pay for"? When it comes to computer security and privacy risks, this proverb is more accurate than ever. Security and privacy decisions are about managing, not eliminating, risk (see Chapter 13). Different organizations face different threats and have different degrees of risk

---

4. Arandjelovic, P., Libby, B., & Naufal, K. (2015, February), Why CIOs should be business-strategy partners, *McKinsey & Company*, retrieved from http://www.mckinsey.com/insights/business_technology/why_cios_should_be_business-strategy_partners

5. Ross, J. W., & Weill, P. (2002, November), Six IT decisions your IT people shouldn't make, *Harvard Business Review*, 84–92.

aversion. For example, while a hospital cannot afford to skimp on redundancy and up-time of life support systems, a restaurant may not need to worry about (and pay for) more than basic security and backup procedures. The critical point is that security and risk management decisions are not information systems decisions. Rather, they are business decisions that can have a dramatic impact on the future viability of the business and, as such, need the full attention of the executive team.

6. *Whom do we blame if an IT initiative fails?* This question draws attention to the need to identify business sponsors for most information systems projects. Any project that involves users and organizational departments beyond the information systems group should have a clearly identified business sponsor who is responsible for its successful implementation. It is the job of senior executives to allocate resources (e.g., create time for business managers to be involved with relevant information systems projects) and assign responsibility.

Note that these are wide-ranging business decisions, necessitating senior executives' input, but they require technical understanding of the various alternatives, costs, and implications. Thus they need to be made in partnership with the information systems professionals and the IS function. The planning process helps structure this partnership.

The Purpose of Strategic Information Systems Planning

The six decisions mentioned above are based on the premise that general and functional managers need to be involved in the decision making that affects their organization's investment in, and use of, information systems and information technology resources. In order to be an asset on the planning team, you must understand the planning process, its purpose, and the type of decisions to be made as it unfolds.

As we have established in this book, information systems are complex organizational systems that exist at the intersection of business and technology. For this reason, setting direction for their use and management requires a blend of skills, technical and organizational, that are rarely housed in one organizational function or department. The planning process must occur as a partnership among those with technical skills, the information systems group, and general and functional managers.

The planning process has a number of objectives, chief among them that of clarifying how the firm plans to use and manage information systems resources to fulfill its strategic objectives. Note that we used the term *planning process*, not *planning document*. As most executives will attest, the *process of planning* is as important as, if not more important than, the final documents that represent its output.

Table 6.1. Six key information systems decisions managers must be involved with

How much should we spend on IT?	This question is designed to force senior executives to discuss and decide on what the role of information systems and technology should be in the organization.
Which business processes should receive the IT dollars?	This question requires executives to decide what business processes are most important to the firm at a given point.
Which IT capabilities need to be company-wide?	This question requires executives to weigh the cost/benefits of standardization and flexibility.
How good do our IT services really need to be?	This question forces executives to make conscious decisions about the degree of service the firm needs and that they are willing to pay for.
What security and privacy risks will we accept?	This question forces executives to make conscious decisions about privacy and security risk management.
Whom do we blame if an IT initiative fails?	This question forces executives to clearly identify and assign responsibility for information systems projects.

The planning process requires discussion, clarification, negotiation, and the achievement of a mutual understanding. While these documents can serve to bring new hires, consultants, and vendors up to speed on what the company is looking to achieve with its adoption and use of IS resources, the time spent discussing and writing the documents is what cements mutual understanding for the individuals involved. The planning process offers a number of advantages, discussed next.

Plans Enable Communication

Perhaps the most important outcome of the information systems planning process is that it enables and supports intraorganizational communication. As the planning team members, composed of IS professionals as well as general and functional managers, assess current IS resources and set guidelines for their future use and management, a shared mental image of the role of each member of the team emerges. This communication is critical since individuals typically have different expectations, speak different languages, and often have different objectives and priorities.

Consultants are sometimes brought into the planning team because they bring significant experience and knowledge of the planning process and they can serve as catalysts for discussion and facilitators of the communication process. Yet their firm-specific knowledge is limited, and it will be easy for the organization to dismiss a plan that is formulated by a consulting firm. Thus it is critical that consultants serve as members of the planning team rather than as delegates of the firm.

Plans Enable Unity of Purpose

Organizations achieve their best results when a clear strategy and clear goals have been identified and lead to concerted efforts from the organizational units and employees. The information systems plan serves as a contract of sort, wherein the objectives of information systems deployment are specified and clear responsibilities are agreed upon. When this happens, coordinating action and achieving unity of purpose become simpler.

Plans Simplify Decision Making over Time

When a firm has not developed an IS plan, it has failed to create a context for decision making. Under these circumstances (all too common, unfortunately), the firm will find itself selecting projects to fund as part of the yearly budgeting process, with little sense of overall direction and purpose. As a consequence, projects will be funded year to year in a haphazard fashion, resulting in an uncoordinated infrastructure and redundancy of systems and efforts and leading to a heightened risk of missing opportunities and wasting resources.

The Strategic Information Systems Planning Process

While strategic information systems planning can be a lengthy and complex process, particularly for large organizations, its basic structure is fairly straightforward. It consists of gathering information about the current availability and performance of IS resources. It also involves a series of decisions, increasingly specific, designed to provide a roadmap for decision making about information systems. The strategic IS planning process typically evolves in five phases:

1. *Strategic business planning.* A strategic business plan consists of an organization's mission and future direction, performance targets, and strategy. Strategic plans are a prerequisite to information systems planning. Note, however, that strategic planning is itself informed by available IT and current IS trends. As discussed in Chapter 2, IT is a critical enabler for modern firms, often determining the strategic opportunities available to them.
2. *Information systems assessment.* An information systems assessment consists of the process of taking stock of the firm's current IS resources and evaluating how well they are fulfilling the needs of the organization.
3. *Information systems vision.* An information systems vision consists of a concise statement that captures what the planning team believes should be the role of IS resources in the firm. It

provides an articulation of the ideal state the firm should strive for in its use and management of its resources.

4. *Information systems guidelines*. Information systems guidelines represent a set of statements, or maxims, specifying how the firm should use its technical and organizational IS resources.

5. *Strategic initiatives*. Strategic initiatives are long-term (three- to five-year) proposals that identify new systems and new projects or new directions for the IS organization.

Note that while we are presenting the strategic planning process in a sequential manner, this is a simplification of reality, and the process is really an iterative one (Figure 6.4). In other words, downstream analyses may lead to a reevaluation and change in decisions made earlier. We now will discuss each step in greater detail.

Know Who You Are: Strategic Business Planning

Information systems are enablers of business strategy and operations. They allow a firm to achieve its stated goals while also creating opportunities for new strategic directions and initiatives that new technologies make possible. Thus effective information systems planning can only occur in concert with business planning. In other words, unless the planning team has developed a clear understanding of the firm and what makes it successful, as well as a deep understanding of the business strategy and its future goals and objectives, planning for the use and management of information systems resources is an exercise in futility.

Imagine trying to decide what car you should rent for your upcoming vacation before you have decided where you will go, with how many friends, and at what time of the year. A sporty two-seater may do wonders for you and your better half on a weekend trip to the south of France, but it won't help much if you and your four ice-fishing buddies planned a two-week outing roughing it in Norway.

Know Where You Start: Information Systems Assessment

Once the planning team has a clear grasp on the strategic direction the firm intends to pursue, more research is needed. The team needs to perform an information systems resource assessment that includes taking an inventory of the IS resources the firm is currently using and critically evaluating them in terms of how well they are meeting the business needs of the organization. The planning team should assess the firm's current use of, and satisfaction with, these resources. The objective is to understand what resources are available and whether they are currently satisfying organizational objectives. Note that we refer here to an information systems assessment, not an information technology assessment, as including technical resources, data and information resources, and human resources:

- *Technical resources* are composed of hardware, software, and networking components that make up the firm's IT infrastructure. Inventorying of these resources can be done by examining documents such as IT schematics and speaking with selected IS professionals. (See Sidebar 6.1 for some suggested questions to ask at this stage.)
- *Data and information resources* are composed of databases and other information repositories. An assessment of these resources can be done by

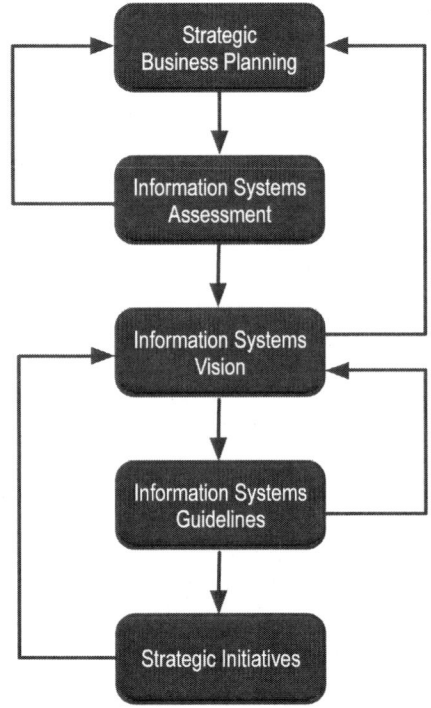

FIGURE 6.4. The iterative strategic IS planning process

examining documents, such as database structure and data schemas, and by speaking with informants, including technical personnel and the customers of the data resource. (See Sidebar 6.2 for some suggested questions to ask at this stage.)

- *Human resources* are composed of IS professionals (those individuals who are responsible for creating and managing the IT resources) and the user community (including general and functional managers as well as end users). An assessment of these resources requires an examination of individuals and their skills, attitudes, and preconceptions, as well as an examination of reporting structures and incentive systems. This can be done by examining documents, such as the firm's organization chart, and speaking with informants from the various hierarchical levels of the IS function and the business. (See Sidebar 6.3 for some suggested questions to ask at this stage.)

During the assessment stage, the planning team reviews company documents and public literature and interviews key informants. The documents analyzed and individuals interviewed depend on the size and structure of the organization. Note that obtaining the needed information requires skilled questioning. Often it is not enough to ask informants a direct question (e.g., how is the IS function performing?); they may not be willing to share the information or, more likely, they may be unable to answer a question posed in this way. But skilled questioning and probing from a number of different angles usually will uncover the needed information (e.g., what IS services do you need that are lacking today?).

The output of the assessment stage should be a snapshot, using both text and graphics, of the current "state of IS resources" in the organization. A well-developed assessment document should clearly convey to the reader what IS resources are currently available and how well they are serving the needs of the organization. It should also inherently suggest potential areas of concern.

SIDEBAR 6.1. TECHNICAL RESOURCES

- What hardware comprises the organization's IT infrastructure?
- What platforms are currently in use?
- What is the current application portfolio?
- Are there any redundant systems?
- What networking infrastructure is currently in place?
- Does the IS organization provide any shared services to the business?
- Is the IT infrastructure centralized or decentralized?
- What systems are on-site, and what systems are off-site?

- Are any components of the IT infrastructure outsourced?
- How do the existing applications relate to one another as a system?
- What is the age of the current application portfolio?
- How are applications normally obtained (in-house development, acquisition)?
- Who owns the IT infrastructure?
- What rules are followed to determine ownership and responsibilities?

SIDEBAR 6.2. DATA AND INFORMATION RESOURCES

- What data are currently collected?
- Where and how are the data collected?
- Where are the data stored? In what format?
- Are data shared across applications? How?
- What applications access the data?
- Who owns the data (e.g., the IS organizations, local departments)?

- Who is in charge of maintaining the accuracy of the data?
- Who is in charge of ensuring the security and backup of the data?
- What rules are followed to determine data ownership and responsibilities?

SIDEBAR 6.3. HUMAN RESOURCES	
• How many full-time IS professionals are currently employed by the organization? • How is the IS function organized? • Who does the head of the IS organization report to? • In what role has the IS organization been explicitly assigned in its mission statement? • What is the current skill set of the in-house IS professionals? • What is the IS sophistication level of the end users and user-managers? • What are the industry performance benchmarks?	• How does the organization compare against industry benchmarks? • Who are the leading competitors? • What performance levels have leading competitors attained? • What are the user-managers' opinions of the current IT infrastructure and application portfolio (e.g., alignment with business objectives, accessibility of accurate and comprehensive information)? • What are the users' perceptions of the current IT infrastructure and applications (e.g., usability, reliability, information accuracy)?

Know Where You Want to Go: Information Systems Vision

With a clear understanding of the organization's business strategy, an inventory of the current resources available, and a solid assessment of their present performance, the planning team begins its real work—looking forward. The first step at this point is to spell out the role that information systems should play in the organization. In some organizations, information systems operations and technology resources are critical to the firm's survival, let alone its success. For other firms, information systems operations are not so critical to their survival and continued success.

Consider the case of eBay Inc. In June 1999, a 22-hour outage at eBay's popular auction website cost the firm between $3 and $5 million in revenue and a 26% drop in stock price, resulting in a $4 billion decline in capitalization. Obviously, flawless IT operations at eBay are a must, at least according to the stock market! Contrast the above case with that of Morton's Restaurant Group Inc., the world's largest owner and operator of company-owned upscale steakhouse restaurants, with upscale steakhouses in the North American, Singapore, and Hong Kong markets. The company has several applications, ranging from unit-level point-of-sale to corporate procurement and financial systems. Disruptions to the performance of these applications, even if protracted, do not endanger the viability of the organization. Imagine, for example, a 22-hour outage of the network or of the point-of-sale systems. Morton units can revert to a manual system and continue with operations. While this is certainly not a scenario that Morton's executives would like to experience, the impacts are much less severe than those that eBay experienced. To get a rough estimate of IT downtime costs, a recent survey reported that, on average, a network outage costs $5,600 per minute, or roughly $300,000 per hour.[6]

With more and more organizations relying on computer-based information systems and cloud applications, protracted disruptions to the firm's IT infrastructure are going to create problems. However, the impact of these disruptions can vary dramatically from organization to organization.

Aside from the impact on day-to-day operations, information systems play a more strategic role in some firms and a tactical one in others. Some organizations' success in the marketplace depends heavily on their ability to introduce IT innovations and manage information systems strategically. Google and Apple Inc. come easily to mind, as do United Parcel Service of America (UPS) and Federal Express.

For these firms, information systems must play a strategic role, and the organization must constantly look for applications of IS that enable it to be more competitive. For others, typically those organizations in more mature and less IT-intensive industries, being cutting edge is less important. In fact, in

---

6. Lerner, A. (2014, July 16), The cost of network downtime, *Gartner*, retrieved from http://blogs.gartner.com/andrew-lerner/2014/07/16/the-cost-of-downtime/

SIDEBAR 6.4. INFORMATION SYSTEMS VISION OF THE LARGE CRUISE LINE

Sidebars 6.4 to 6.7 refer to the same company, a large cruise line operator with multinational operations. The examples are adapted from the actual firm's 2000 information systems planning document. We refer to this company as "The Large Cruise Line."

The IS function will assume more of a leadership role within the corporation. While the IS function will continue to service the organization by providing a solid IT infrastructure, supporting and maintaining existing systems, the IS function will no longer be considered exclusively a support arm to the rest of the organization.

In order to maintain our leadership position, we must use information to do the following:

- Set the customer service standard in the industry for consumers and business partners by using customized and personalized information, beginning with the first contact and continuing throughout the relationship.
- Enable the company to be the employer of choice in our industry by empowering a workforce with accurate, timely information and thus to accelerate change and innovative decision making.
- Assume a leadership role as innovators in the use of the Internet as an enabling technology that drives business growth, internal and external communications, operating efficiencies, and new sources of revenue.

some firms, information systems are nothing more than a "necessary evil"—a resource the company needs to have and use, but not one that will provide a leg up on the competition.

Information Systems Vision   Whether information systems are crucial to the firm's success or merely useful, whether they are strategic or a necessary evil, it is important that the planning team is able to clearly articulate what the role of IS *should be* for the firm. We refer to this statement as the information systems vision (see Sidebar 6.4).

The IS vision is a concise statement that captures what the planning team believes should be the role of information systems resources in the organization. It provides an articulation of the ideal state the firm should strive for in its use and management of IS resources.

The information systems vision must be aligned with and reflect the firm's business strategy and, as a consequence, will be unique and highly specific to your company. While the industry your firm competes in, the product or service it offers, and the competitive environment will have some influence on the role that information systems should play in your organization, the position and role of the IS function should ultimately depend on a conscious decision by senior management and the planning team. Thus companies that compete in the same industry, even head-to-head competitors, will have different information systems vision that reflect their strategic posture.

For example, while the Ritz-Carlton and W Hotels compete in the luxury segment of the lodging industry, the former positions itself to offer traditional luxury while the latter has a much more edgy image catering to a younger and more tech-savvy customer base. We can therefore expect the two hotel chains to have developed very different IS visions.

Deciding what the role of information systems in your organization should be, and developing a concise IS vision that encapsulates it, pose a difficult task. Two analytical tools that have been developed to help managers involved in this process are the critical success factors (CSF) methodology[7] and the strategic impact grid.[8]

---

7. Rockart J. (1979, March–April), Chief executives define their own data needs, *Harvard Business Review, 57,* 81–93.

8. Nolan, R., & McFarlan, F. W. (2005, October), Information technology and the board of directors, *Harvard Business Review, 83*(10), 96–106.

Critical Success Factors   A technique that has been used over the years to help focus managers' attention to the firm's information needs is the critical success factors (CSF) methodology. Critical success factors are defined as the limited number of areas, typically three to six, that executives must effectively manage to ensure that the firm will survive and thrive. CSFs represent those fundamental things that "must go right" for the business to flourish. At the risk of oversimplifying things, the CSF methodology has the merit of focusing attention on fundamental issues and of helping ensure that the planning team is able to prioritize. Note that the CSF methodology asks that managers focus not on information systems but on business objectives—that is, the CSF methodology asks that you identify what the firm must do right (not what the IS department must do right) to ensure the ongoing success of the organization. With the CSFs identified, it becomes easier to think about the role of IS in achieving them.

Let's return to the eBay example. Given that eBay's revenue stream is highly dependent on its website being operational, and given the significant disruptions (and stock market reaction) that follows protracted downtime, one of eBay's CSFs in 1999 was likely to ensure the optimal performance (i.e., reliability and speed) of online store operations. Other CSFs we could imagine for eBay at the time are as follows:

- Continue to grow the size of the marketplace in terms of buyers and sellers.
- Increase online buyer and seller confidence and trust in the marketplace by ensuring the security of transactions, reliable payments, and high levels of customer service.

The Strategic Impact Grid   Another tool that helps in defining the role of information systems in a specific company is the strategic impact grid. The main advantage offered by the strategic impact grid is its ability to enable simultaneous evaluation of the firm's current and future information systems needs. This is achieved by plotting the firm on the following two dimensions: the current need for reliable information systems and the future need for new information system functionalities.

Current Need for Reliable Information Systems   This dimension focuses on current day-to-day operations and the functionalities of the existing systems. Not all organizations, even fierce head-to-head competitors, need the same information systems and the same degree of reliability of their technology infrastructure. The planning team should achieve some consensus about where the firm falls on this dimension by determining the following:

- Is there a risk of a tangible loss of business if one or more systems fail for a minute or more?
- Are there serious negative consequences associated with even small degrading response time of one or more systems?
- Are most core business activities online and do they require real-time or near-real-time information processing?
- Will even repeated service interruptions of up to 12 hours, while troublesome, cause no serious consequences for the viability of the business?
- Can the company quickly revert to manual operations for the majority of transaction types when systems failure occurs? While unwelcome, do such disruptions not endanger the business as a viable concern?

Future Needs for New Information System Functionalities   This dimension is forward looking and is concerned with the strategic role that new IT capabilities play for the organization. While the industry the firm competes in has some bearing on this question, different organizations pursuing different strategies will fall on different locations of the spectrum. The planning team should achieve some consensus about where the firm falls on this dimension by determining the following:

- Do new systems and new functionalities of existing systems promise major process and service improvements?
- Do new systems or new functionalities of existing systems promise major cost reductions and efficiency improvements?

- Do new systems or new functionalities of existing systems promise to close (or create!) major gaps in service, cost, or process performance with competitors?
- Is systems work mostly maintenance of current state-of-the-art functionalities? Does the firm foresee no major new systems that are crucial to business success within the current planning horizon?
- Do new systems promise little strategic differentiation, and do customers not expect any major new functionalities or services?

At the intersection of these two dimensions, we find four possible roles that information systems can play in the organization (Figure 6.5). A common error is to use the strategic impact grid to separately map the firm's current and future position (i.e., where the firm is today and where it should be). The strategic impact grid simultaneously captures current operations and future impact. Therefore, if used correctly, it will show where the planning team thinks the firm falls and, as a consequence, what the use of information systems resources should be going forward.

Support Quadrant   The organization falls in the support quadrant when information systems are not mission critical for current operations, and this state of affairs is not likely to change in the foreseeable future. A mining company may be an example of a firm that falls in this quadrant, as is the Morton's Restaurant Group Inc., discussed above.

When a firm finds itself in the support quadrant, it should view information systems as a tool to support and enable operations, but one that offers little potential to significantly harm or benefit the organization. As a consequence, firms in this quadrant are typically cost conscious and conservative in their IS investments decision making, with the head of the IS function typically reporting to the chief financial officer.

Factory Quadrant   The organization falls in the factory quadrant when it currently has a technology infrastructure that enables the business to operate with the needed degree of efficiency and effectiveness. Disruptions to this infrastructure, even small ones, can endanger the firm's well-being and future viability. Yet within the planning horizon under consideration, the firm appears to be in a stable state and the planning team foresees a limited potential for new systems and functionalities to make a substantial contribution. Like a factory working steadily, if the current state of information systems affairs is maintained, the firm will be in good shape. NASDAQ, the company that runs the largest U.S. electronic stock market, is an example of a firm that must ensure flawless operation of its current systems. Airlines and large chemical plant operators represent other examples.

When a firm finds itself in the factory quadrant, it must closely monitor its current systems and must be willing to fund their maintenance and upgrade. Yet because of the minor future potential for impact of new systems, the organization may take a conservative stance toward future investments.

Turnaround Quadrant   The organization falls in the turnaround quadrant when information systems are not considered mission critical for current operations. Yet unlike firms in the support quadrant, the planning team believes that the current state of affairs is due for a change in the near future, and new information systems or new functionalities of existing systems will be

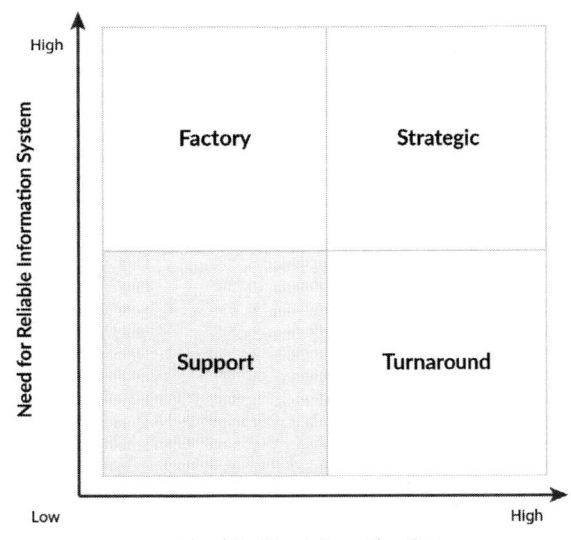

FIGURE 6.5. The strategic impact grid

critical for the business's future viability and continued (or expected) success. As the term *turnaround* suggests, the firm is (or should be) readying to change its information systems posture. Consider, for example, Caesars Entertainment, the Las Vegas–based casino operator, in the late 1990s. A firm historically in the support quadrant, Caesars (at the time still called Harrah's) foresaw the opportunities afforded by emerging business intelligence techniques and spent more than $100 million to secure a leadership position in guest data analysis. When a firm finds itself in the turnaround quadrant, it typically needs to engage in some reorganization (e.g., by reevaluating its organizational structure and creating a CIO position with a seat on the executive team). In the case of Caesars, the $100 million investment was associated with a major internal reorganization that closely aligned the information systems and marketing functions. Finally, when in the turnaround quadrant, the firm will also need to take an aggressive stance with respect to IT investments and the acquisition of necessary skills.

Strategic Quadrant   The organization falls in the strategic quadrant when information systems are critical to the firm's current operations and the planning team foresees new information systems or new functionalities of existing systems to be critical for the future viability and prosperity of the business. In other words, outstanding IS operations and a relentless attention to information systems innovation are a must for companies in this quadrant. Amazon.com and eBay are two examples of organizations whose survival depends on flawless IS operations and who must constantly be on the lookout for new systems. Large banks find themselves perennially on this list as well.

When a firm is in the strategic quadrant, it must be extremely proactive with respect to information systems and IT investments. This is typically done by having a CIO with a strong voice on the executive team. For these organizations, information systems are part of the firm's DNA. For example, Amazon defines itself as a technology company that happens to be in the retail business, rather than a retail company that uses technology. Walmart (definitely not an eCommerce pure play!) also defines itself as a technology company.

Know How You Are Going to Get There: Information Systems Guidelines

While the information systems vision articulates the destination—the ideal state the firm should strive for when it comes to using and managing information systems resources—it provides little guidance as to how the firm should deploy its resources to achieve this goal. Thus the next stage in the information systems planning process consists of identifying a parsimonious set of guidelines that, if followed, will enable the firm to achieve its information vision. This set of guidelines, sometimes referred to as the information systems architecture, is prescriptive in nature—identifying the guiding principles that the firm will follow when using and managing information systems resources.

Why Develop Information Systems Guidelines?   The building of a custom home offers a good metaphor for understanding the role of information systems guidelines. While you have a vision for what you'd like your dream home to be like—including location, style, size, number, and types of rooms—you probably know very little about construction codes, materials, and the like. Thus you engage an architect to whom you describe your vision and rely on her to formalize it in the form of blueprints and schematics (Figure 6.6).

When the architect delivers the drawings and the floor plans, you will be able to see if she captured your vision and to suggest any changes. A good architect will also make suggestions about what changes will make the house better, reduce cost, speed up construction, and so on. Once you sign off on the blueprints, they become binding—a sort of contract. Armed with them, you or your architect on your behalf will engage a builder who will actually create the house.

The blueprints enable the contractor to develop the house according to your vision, without having to interact much with you—or even knowing what your overall vision was. Contractors will know where they should locate the rooms, their size, and where to install plumbing, windows, doorframes, and electrical outlets. They will also know what materials they should use. If you change your mind during construction and request changes, you will be responsible for the cost. On the other hand, if the builder makes a mistake and forgets to create a window opening in the master bedroom, he or she will

FIGURE 6.6. The blueprint of the floor plan of a custom house
Photo by The Man in Question / CC BY SA 3.0

be responsible for the cost of the modifications. The blueprint serves as the guideline for what should happen and for dispute resolution.

The process and purpose of creating information systems guidelines are very similar to those described above in the context of custom home building. The firm executives have a vision for what they want the business to achieve and how they want it to operate. Working in partnership with information systems professionals, as part of the planning team, they will refine their vision and establish a blueprint that will enable communication, establish responsibility, and guide future decision making.

Communication   The primary objective of the information systems guidelines is to simplify tactical and operational decision making and to ensure that future decisions are aligned with the information systems vision. By establishing a coherent set of rules stemming from the information systems vision, these guidelines ensure that future information systems and technology decisions are made in accordance with the overall objectives of information systems use and management in the firm, rather than haphazardly and in an uncoordinated manner.

Imagine, for example, an organization that opts for a strictly supporting role of information systems. Such a company will likely strive to buy low-cost IT products (e.g., buying refurbished or older hardware) and will be conservative when it comes to IT innovation (e.g., waiting to buy applications until they have become a competitive necessity). Conversely, an organization in the strategic quadrant of the strategic impact grid that has identified flawless personalization of the customer experience as a critical success factor may decide to move to a centralized architecture with centralized servers that gather all customer data in one location for easy retrieval and analysis.

Identify Responsibilities   The information systems guidelines also set expectations for behavior, serving a similar binding purpose as policy rules or the custom blueprints and schematics described above. Decisions that are made in accordance with the information systems guidelines are in line with expectations and will typically be deemed appropriate. Decisions that are made outside of the guidelines are treated as exceptions and will typically need substantial justification. If the firm finds itself regularly making exceptions, it will need to reevaluate the quality and accuracy of the information systems guidelines.

Long-Range Decision Support   Because the firm will not engage in the IS planning process every year, the information systems guidelines must be general enough to provide direction over a number of years.

Yet it is crucial that they be actionable. Thus they need to be specific enough to clearly spell out what the firm should do and, as a consequence, what it should not do when it comes to the deployment of information systems resources.

Imagine that you just got an internship with the Large Cruise Line (discussed previously). You are eager to make a contribution and, after reading the company's information systems vision (see Sidebar 6.4), you remember your long-lost cousin Vinnie, who just launched a start-up. The brochure of his flagship product reads, "Our personalization software solution enables your company to track customer preferences and offer outstanding service." A light bulb goes off, and you run to your CIO and suggest, "We should buy and implement this software; it is perfectly aligned with our vision!" She ponders your suggestion for all of five seconds and then denies your request, adding, "I'm glad you read the planning document, but you seem to have stopped reading too early. The second technical guideline (see Sidebar 6.5) rules out relationships with new and not established vendors for core systems like those housing our customer data."

Technical and Organizational Guidelines   Information systems guidelines address every aspect of information systems decision making, both technical and organizational. While technical guidelines and organizational guidelines are deeply intertwined, it helps to separate them out during the planning process and in the planning documents.

Technical Information Systems Guidelines   The information systems guidelines that focus on the technical components of the firm's information systems must address future decisions pertaining to the hardware and software infrastructure, networking services, and the storage and protection of organizational data and information. (See Sidebar 6.5 for an example.)

Technical guidelines will not typically specify the vendors to be used or particular platforms or applications. Instead they are broad enunciations of direction for the technical components of the infrastructure. As the example in Sidebar 6.5 shows, the statements produced by the planning team of the cruise line are aligned with the firm's information systems vision (see Sidebar 6.4) and are both general, thus making them relevant and useful for years to come, and precise, thus specifying what decisions are legitimate and what decisions should not be made.

Organizational Information Systems Guidelines   The information systems guidelines that focus on the organizational components of the firm's information systems must address those decisions that pertain to human resources, the organization of the information systems function, reporting and hierarchical structures, and the like. (See Sidebar 6.6 for an example.)

SIDEBAR 6.5. TECHNICAL INFORMATION SYSTEMS GUIDELINES OF THE LARGE CRUISE LINE

1. The movement toward standardization will evolve over time, and we will remain flexible in our approach. However, our major objective is to achieve centralized and standardized products that are more easily managed and controlled, especially across multiple continents with limited staff to maintain them.

2. We will follow the trends of dominant vendors and be guided by these leaders rather than the niche market players for both hardware and software core systems.

3. We will buy software packages (rather than develop custom code) that provide generic solutions for business functions that are not part of our core competency and not part of what constitutes our competitive advantage.

4. We will not obtain monolithic packages that drive significant duplicate code and data.

5. We will store data centrally for all mission-critical applications.

6. Mission-critical systems will have complete fallback solutions to redundant systems to minimize the impact of any disaster.

These statements focus on IT governance issues (e.g., the relationship between the IS function and the other departments in the organization, who is responsible for proposing and sponsoring application development, how maintenance and new purchases should be evaluated), on outsourcing and vendor relationships, on human resources decisions (e.g., what type of individuals the IS function is looking to hire, the type of IS skills that the firm deems necessary), and the like.

Know How Well Equipped You Are to Get There: Information Systems SWOT

Having defined the information systems vision and the broad maxims to achieve it—the information systems guidelines—the planning team must now review how well equipped the firm is to achieve their vision in accordance with the stated guidelines. This step is the last piece of analysis before the team develops an action plan and proposes tangible initiatives. It consists of a strengths, weaknesses,

---

SIDEBAR 6.6. ORGANIZATIONAL INFORMATION SYSTEMS GUIDELINES OF THE LARGE CRUISE LINE

- We will focus our expenditures on projects of strategic value and long-term importance over short-term fixes that deviate from our overall strategy.
- Outsourcing will be considered for IS operations and legacy applications where possible and feasible.
- Business-supported projects will be governed by the business case and will be evaluated by the full project costs and values in terms of people, process, and technology.
- Business-supported projects will require the participation of the business throughout the engagement.

- While the IS function will be developing systems, at all times our mind-set will be that of a business professional first and will always consider the business opportunity and/or impact of systems that we develop or purchase.
- The IS function will create a mixed environment of both seasoned professionals and new, eager, recent graduates. The persona of our IS function will be that of a level-headed, technologically excited individual.
- We will strive to avoid silos of data and silos of skill sets within our company and thus enable our staff to grow and to minimize disruption when specialized staff are moved to other assignments and/or leave the company.

SIDEBAR 6.7. INFORMATION SYSTEMS SWOT AT THE LARGE CRUISE LINE

Strengths:
- The IS staff is competent in the implementation and maintenance of new technology.
- User-managers, on average, understand information systems concepts and have a good relationship with the IS function.

Weaknesses:
- There are currently four nonintegrated systems housing customer data.
- The current IT infrastructure supports a silo, function-centric approach and does not support flexible timely response to customer needs.

Opportunities:
- New technology, such as the XML standard and data warehousing applications, is now robust enough to warrant migration to integrated data repositories.
- No competitor is currently offering IS-enabled integrated customer solutions.

Threats:
- Our competitor is moving swiftly to establish itself as the customer service leader in our industry through the deployment of integrated, channel-independent customer service systems.
- Our preferred suppliers have developed the capability for electronic data communication, but we are currently unable to connect to their systems. This inability to communicate hampers our efficiency and may drive suppliers to the competition.

opportunities, and threats (SWOT) analysis focused on the firm's current information systems resources and capabilities.

The iterative nature of the planning process becomes clear at this stage. As the planning team members evaluate how well positioned the firm is to attain the information systems vision, they may realize that they are attempting to do too much and the vision, as stated, is not achievable given the current set of strengths and weaknesses and the landscape of opportunities and threats. In this case, the information systems vision should be revised to be more realistic. Failing to do so will create an unattainable, not actionable, vision that will make people cynical and defeat the purpose of the planning process.

As shown in the example (see Sidebar 6.7), this stage of the analysis is designed to reveal the internal factors that can be exploited to achieve the vision as well as highlight the internal weaknesses that must be carefully managed. It also enables an externally focused analysis that seeks to uncover new technologies and trends that generate opportunities for the firm, as well as threats that may undermine the ability of the firm to achieve its information systems vision.

In a well-developed plan, this section of the analysis is consistent with the previous ones and forms the basis for the next section. In other words, having read the SWOT analysis and given the proposed vision and the guidelines, it should become clear what the firm needs to do during the current planning cycle.

From Planning to Action: Proposed Strategic Initiatives

After so much discussion and analysis, it is time to move to action. The last component of the strategic information systems plan is the identification of strategic initiatives. Strategic initiatives are long-term (three- to five-year) proposals that identify new systems and new projects (e.g., supply chain management) or new directions for the IS organization (e.g., create a CIO position reporting directly to the CEO). These initiatives need not be precisely articulated, but they do need to identify a set of future avenues for exploitation of the IS resources. They also must be tightly aligned with the information systems vision and the proposed role of IS in the organization. For example, it would not be appropriate for the planning team to propose a change to the organizational structure, seeking to establish a new CIO position who reports to the CEO, after having decided that information systems play a support role in the organization and having crafted a defensive information system vision.

A number of frameworks and techniques have been developed to support the identification and analysis of strategic initiatives, and they will be discussed in the remaining chapters of Part III.

Summary

This chapter provides the basis for the ensuing chapters and describes the strategic information systems planning process. Specifically, in this chapter we discussed the goals of the strategic information system planning process and its components, with a focus on the role played by general and functional managers.

- Strategic information systems planning is the process by which the firm, by way of the planning team, develops a shared understanding of the role of information systems resources use in the organization.
- General and functional managers play a crucial role on the planning team, despite the fact that they typically lack technical knowledge. Their role is to help identify the firm's strategy and, in light of that business strategy, to help decide how information systems resources should be used to achieve it.
- General and functional managers should also take the lead in answering questions, such as how much money should be spent on IT, to what business processes these funds should be directed, what IT capabilities should pervade the organization, what levels of IT service should be achieved, what degree of IT risk the firm will accept, and who is responsible for IT initiatives.

- As critical members of the planning team, general and functional managers will help in crafting the firm's information systems vision and guidelines. The information systems vision provides an articulation of the ideal state of information systems resource use, while the guidelines offer a context for decision making.
- With the basic planning mechanisms in place, the firm moves to action and identifies strategic initiatives to be implemented in order to achieve the stated information systems vision. These strategic initiatives often stem from what the organization believes are available opportunities, as well as weaknesses that must be managed.

Study Questions

1. Why should general and functional managers be involved in information systems planning decisions despite their lack of technical expertise?
2. Jeanne Ross and Peter Weill of MIT's Center for Information Systems Research (CISR) suggest that senior managers be involved in six information systems management decisions. What are these decisions? What is the guiding principle behind this need for senior executives' involvement?
3. What is the purpose of strategic information systems planning? Who needs to be involved in this process? Why?
4. What are the key components of the strategic information systems planning process? Can you define and describe each one?
5. What purpose do the critical success factors methodology and the strategic impact grid play in the planning process? Can you provide examples of firms in each of the four quadrants of the strategic impact grid?
6. What is the purpose of the information systems vision? Can you provide an example?
7. What is the purpose of the information systems guidelines? Given the information systems vision you have proposed in response to Question 6, can you provide an example of guidelines that are aligned with it?

Further Readings

1. Chan, Y. E. (2002). Why haven't we mastered alignment? The importance of the informal organization structure. *MIS Quarterly Executive, 1*(2), 97–113.
2. Drucker, P. (1954). *The practice of management.* New York, NY: Harper and Row.
3. Freedman, T. (2005). *The world is flat: A brief history of the twenty-first century.* New York, NY: Farrar, Straus and Giroux.
4. Nolan, R., & McFarlan, F. W. (2005, October). Information technology and the board of directors. *Harvard Business Review, 83*(10), 96–106.
5. Ross, J. W., & Weill, P. (2002, November). Six IT decisions your IT people shouldn't make. *Harvard Business Review*, 84–92.

Glossary

- **Information systems assessment:** The process of taking stock of the firm's current information systems resources and evaluating how well they are fulfilling the needs of the organization.
- **Information systems guidelines:** A set of statements, or maxims, specifying how the firm should use its technical and organizational information systems resources.
- **Information systems vision:** A concise statement that captures what the planning team believes should be the role of information systems resources in the firm. It provides an articulation of the ideal state the firm should strive for in its use and management of information systems resources.

- **Planning team:** The set of individuals, company employees, and hired consultants who work together to develop the firm's strategic information systems plan.
- **Strategic alignment:** The degree of fit between the priorities and activities of the IS function and those of general and functional managers involved in the day-to-day operations of the business.
- **Strategic information systems planning process:** The process by which the planning team develops the planning documents.

- **Strategic initiative:** A long-term (three- to five-year) proposal that identifies new systems and new projects or new directions for the IS organization.
- **Strategic plan:** An organization's mission and future direction, performance targets, and strategy. Strategic plans are a prerequisite to information systems planning.

Value Creation and Strategic Information Systems

What You Will Learn in This Chapter

This chapter focuses on the strategic role of information systems and the information technology (IT) that enables them. The definitions, analytical frameworks, examples, and exercises in this chapter will help you develop a knowledge base that allows you to confidently identify and evaluate the added value creation potential of IT-dependent strategic initiatives.

In this chapter, you will become well versed in the language of the added value analysis and strategic information systems. Specifically, this chapter will

1. Define key terminology, including the concepts of total value created, customer willingness to pay, supplier opportunity cost, and added value.
2. Explain how to compute total value created and added value.
3. Explain how to estimate the portion of the total value created that will be appropriated by each of the entities who contributed to its creation.
4. Explain how to differentiate between strategic information systems and tactical information systems.
5. Define and explain how to utilize the concept of IT-dependent strategic initiatives.

MINICASE: Consulting for the Royal Hotel

The Royal Hotel in New York City is a luxury all-suite hotel primarily serving an executive clientele who are visiting Manhattan on business. Typically, these business guests stay for three to six days, during which time they use their hotel suite as a temporary office. Thus Royal Hotel's management has positioned the property to cater to the many needs of this busy and demanding audience. Amenities include in-suite printer and copier, three two-line telephones with voicemail and remote message alert, 24-hour business center, wired and wireless Internet access in rooms and public areas, fitness center, in-suite dining, laundry service, complimentary shoe shine, complete Bluetooth audio system, dedicated high-speed elevators, and more.

Hotel management is proud of their capacity to always meet—and sometimes anticipate—the evolving business guests' needs. Back in the 1990s, they were one of the first properties to offer wired Internet connection in every room. Today, guests can control room facilities through their smartphones, select TV and radio channels, and stream content from their devices to the large-screen wall-mounted television. However, as the old saying goes, "the cobbler's children go unshod." The hotel was still using an aging server lying on a rack in a small equipped room converted from a manager's office. The system is critical for hotel's operations taking care of bookings, accounts receivable, accounting, materials, payroll, and maintenance. The server is a tier-1 "enterprise class" hardware with associated storage and backup units. It is running 24/7 with the exception of scheduled downtimes for maintenance and upgrades. The server costs the Royal Hotel $25,000 and has operating costs (e.g., electricity, software licenses and maintenance) of about $2,100 a year. It has a usable life of five years.

WizTech, a California-based high-tech firm specializing in cloud solutions, has recently contacted the Royal Hotel. This contact is very timely, as the Royal Hotel was about to replace the aging server and assume the costs discussed above. WizTech is beginning to commercialize a cloud solution of the same system the hotel uses that enables any computer connected to the Internet access the property management system (PMS). Thus the cloud solution is a *perfect substitute* for the server. Moreover, to ensure a degree of business continuity, WizTech offers, free of charge, a "work offline service" that enables temporary operations in case of unavailable Internet access; this service is secure and managed seamlessly by WizTech until the connection is back in operation. WizTech's premium solution costs $500 per month. Each customer's cloud solution costs WizTech $1,500 to setup.

Discussion Questions

1. What should the Royal Hotel's IT department do?
2. Does WizTech enjoy a competitive advantage (or disadvantage) in this market?
3. Can you quantify such advantage (or disadvantage)?

Introduction

Perhaps the primary role of functional and general managers in business organizations is to contribute to the *creation* and *appropriation* of economic value by their firm. Consider, for example, the following episode as recounted by Jack Shewmaker, former president and chief operating officer (COO) of Walmart Stores Inc.: "Glen Habern was our data processing manager, and he and I had this dream of an interactive [satellite-based] communication system on which you could communicate back and forth between all the stores and the distribution centers and the general office. Glenn came up with the idea and I said: 'Let's pursue it without asking anybody.'"[1] This quote speaks to the importance of a strong partnership among a firm executive, the COO, and an information technology (IT) professional, who together envisioned a better way to manage information and to create economic value in their organization—in the case of Walmart, this satellite network became the backbone of many of the firm's future strategic initiatives and competitive advantage.

But what does it mean to create value? Why would an organization want to engage in value creation? And perhaps most importantly, how can you ensure that your organization benefits from its value creation strategies and initiatives?

The Analysis of Added Value

Added value is one of those terms that we all too often hear being used in presentations and press releases to convey the idea that a firm is doing something worthy of attention. Consider the following:

- From the website of a state information technology agency: "We will work hard to make sure that everything we do is 'value added' for our customers and achieves [the agency's] vision."
- From Bill Gates: "Analytical software enables you to shift human resources from rote data collection to value-added customer service and support where the human touch makes a profound difference."
- From the title of an article published by the *Washington Times*: "Wi-Fi Going from an Added Value to an Expected Amenity."

---

1. Walton, S., with Huey, J. (1992), *Sam Walton: Made in America*, New York, NY: Bantam, p. 271.

The Benefits of Disciplined Analysis

What does it really mean to create value or to have added value? Can you carry out a disciplined analysis or compute a number for the value added by an initiative you have envisioned? What would this number mean? What decisions could you make based on this analysis?

The analysis of added value is a formal mechanism that managers and analysts use to answer these questions and to evaluate how much of the value created the firm can appropriate in the form of profits. While the analysis of added value can be applied to any firm's initiative, we will constrain our focus to those projects that leverage IT at their core. This analysis is an essential step in the decision of whether or not you should go ahead with the initiative. It stands to reason that if the proposed initiative creates no tangible value, you should shelve it. More insidiously, if the initiative does contribute to the creation of value but your firm will be unable to appropriate such value created, then you should also not go on with it, in most cases.

This type of analysis is useful not only when you are innovating—in other words, when you are endeavoring to create value in novel ways and offering things that no competitor is currently offering— but also when you are evaluating how to respond to a competitor who took the leadership position. The analysis of added value can help you measure how much benefit your competitor is drawing from the innovation and what benefits are likely to accrue to you if you choose to replicate the initiative. While in many cases you will only have limited information and you will not be able to create precise estimations for value created and added value, a disciplined analysis will nonetheless help you carefully analyze the potential of the initiative.

The Definition of Value

Economic value is generated when *worthwhile things* that did not exist before are created. Thus value is generated not when something novel is done but only when this "something novel" is deemed worthwhile by someone else. As entrepreneurship scholars have long recognized, this is the crucial difference between inventors and entrepreneurs. Inventors are those individuals who create new products and new technologies—in short, new things. These new technologies or products can be amazing, technically flawless, and beautifully engineered, but they will not create value until they solve a problem in some market. Entrepreneurs know this full well and focus on *market opportunities* and the development of *solutions* to meet these opportunities—that is, entrepreneurs look for new ways to create value rather than new technologies or new products. Often the novel solution being marketed relies on a new technology, but it is the invention that serves the market opportunity, not the other way around. While the solution offered may not be technically superior or beautifully engineered, it will be commercially appealing precisely because it does contribute to the creation of economic value.

The Firm's Transformation Process Economic value is created through a transformation process when some input resources that have a value of x in their next best utilization are transformed into outputs for which customers are willing to pay $x + v. When such a transformation process takes place, it can be said that value, in the amount of v, has been created. In other words, this new value was not there before and would not come to be unless the transformation process did occur, since the input resources would remain untransformed and simply maintain their original worth of x. Enacting the transformation process is typically a firm that engages in it while seeking to monetize (at least) some of this value created in the form of profits.

Input resources are represented by any factor of production, such as raw materials, labor, equity and debt capital, managerial talent, support services like transportation and storage, and so on. In other words, anything that is used to generate the product or service and then market it, sell it, and support it is to be considered an input resource.

The output of the transformation process is the product and/or service that the firm engaging in the transformation process is seeking to sell and that a customer is interested in acquiring.

Let's return to the example of a large retailer (e.g., Walmart, Carrefour, Tesco). As a retailer, Tesco (Figure 7.1) uses input resources such as labor, physical stores, warehousing facilities, trucks and transportation equipment, energy sources (e.g., diesel fuel for the trucks, electricity for the stores), equity and debt capital, and so on. By employing these resources in its transformation process, which consists of acquiring products in bulk, warehousing them, and then distributing them to conveniently located stores, the firm is able to offer something that its customers are willing to pay for: convenient access to a large selection of mainstream products.

Defining the Components of Value Created

A formal analysis of added value requires some key definitions:

- *Supplier opportunity cost (SOC).* Supplier opportunity cost is the minimum amount of money suppliers are willing to accept to provide the firm with the needed resources.
- *Firm cost (FC).* Firm cost is the actual amount of money the firm disbursed to acquire the resources needed to create its product or service.
- *Customer willingness to pay (CWP).* Customer willingness to pay is the maximum amount of money the firm's customers are ready to spend in order to obtain the firm's product.
- *Total value created (TVC).* The total value created in the transaction is computed as the difference between customer willingness to pay and supplier opportunity cost ($TVC = CWP - SOC$).

FIGURE 7.1. Entrance of a Tesco store in 1949
Photo by Peter McGowan / CC BY 2.0

Supplier Opportunity Cost Supplier opportunity cost, the lower bound of value creation, is an important figure, as it represents the value that the needed resources would have in their next best use. For this reason, it is defined as an opportunity cost. A rational supplier will only provide the firm with its services (e.g., labor, managerial talent, raw materials) if it receives at least the same sum of money it would have received from any other buyer (i.e., another firm seeking to use the resource the supplier offers).

Note, however, that suppliers will typically not be paid an amount equal to their supplier opportunity cost. This is because the firm acquiring the resources will not be able to precisely estimate this number—in fact, in most cases the suppliers themselves may not have a precise estimate available—and the suppliers will happily accept any offer exceeding their opportunity cost.

For an example, think back to the latest job offer that you received and accepted. During the interview, you, the supplier of labor to the hiring firm, formulated some idea regarding your willingness to work for the company and how much you'd want to get paid. When the offer came through, it most likely exceeded this minimum requirement you had established, and you took the job . . . without returning the "excess salary" you received.

The simple example above addresses a very important issue. Supplier opportunity cost is a theoretical minimum; the actual amount of money the firm will disburse to acquire the needed resources (i.e., the firm cost) is the outcome of a negotiation effort in the presence of an asymmetry of information between the negotiating parties. We will see that this important point resurfaces later when we discuss price considerations.

Customer Willingness to Pay The other end on the value continuum is represented by the customer willingness to pay. As we noted above, an inventor is someone who generates a new idea and creates a new product or technology. An entrepreneur is someone who matches a novel product or service to a market opportunity. This difference should be clear now with the terminology of value creation. Unless some customer is willing to part ways with his money to acquire whatever the inventor has created and this amount is larger than the supplier opportunity cost, no value has been generated and no economically viable venture has been created. In other words, value is in the eyes of the customer. The most elegantly engineered and technically beautiful product is valueless unless a customer is willing to pay for it.

The history of information technology products and services is littered with examples of innovations that, while perhaps technically amazing, met with cool customer response and dwindled into market oblivion as a consequence: Do you remember the picture phone (Figure 7.2), the Apple Newton, Audrey (3Com's Internet appliance; Figure 7.3), the Sony Glasstron (head-mounted displays for virtual reality), WebTV, and Webvan's online grocery service? Unless you are a historian of sorts, the answer is most likely no.

FIGURE 7.2. The PicturePhone: An innovation introduced 35 years before its time
Photo by LabguysWorld.com / CC BY 3.0

Computing the Total Value Created

Simply defined, value is the difference between customer willingness to pay and supplier opportunity cost—that is, value is created when resources that in their next best use would be worth a given amount are transformed into something that a customer is willing to pay more for.

Consider a simple fictitious example.[2] Your grandmother was famous for baking a great-tasting cake. In her will, she entrusts the secret recipe to you, so you decide to become an entrepreneur and start baking the specialty cake. You can bake a single cake using amounts of eggs, flour, sugar, and the secret grandma ingredients worth about $4.00 together. An hour of your time invested in making the cake is valued at $9.25, under the assumption that you only qualify for minimum-wage jobs (i.e., if you used the same amount of time to work for the best other job you qualify for, you would earn $9.25). Finally, you

FIGURE 7.3. 3Com's Audrey, the Internet appliance
Source: Wikimedia

use electricity to bake the cake, and some gas and wear and tear on your car to deliver it, in the amount of $3.75. The local gourmet coffee shop, whose owner knew your grandma personally and who had tasted the cake, is willing to pay you as much as $25.00 for each one of your homemade cakes. This is because she thinks that she can get 12 slices out of every cake and sell each one for $3.00, thereby making a nice $11.00 profit.

This information allows us to precisely compute the total value created (TVC) in this *cake-making and -selling* transaction. TVC = CWP − SOC (see Figure 7.4)—that is, TVC = $25.00 − ($4.00 + $9.25 + $3.75) = $8.00. Or, more formally, taking resources valued at $17.00 in their next best use and producing a good valued at $25.00 by a customer, you have contributed to creating a value of $8.00 through a "cake-making transformation process."

Appropriating the Value Created

Up to this point we have discussed the process of value creation—a process in which suppliers, the focal firm (i.e., you), and the customer partake. However, total value creation only tells us if there is *an opportunity* to make a profit. That is, if the total value created is greater than zero, someone will benefit, but we still don't know who.

---

2. While this example could be considered trivial, we encourage you to pay close attention, since it elucidates every aspect of the analysis of added value. The example is clearly fictitious in that it assumes perfect information by all parties involved.

FIGURE 7.4. Total value created

FIGURE 7.5. Value appropriation

Value appropriation is the process by which the total value created in the transaction is split among all the entities who contributed to creating it (i.e., suppliers, the firm, and the customer). It is typically the outcome of a negotiation process between the firm and the suppliers to determine the firm cost and between the firm and the customer to establish product prices (see Figure 7.5). When a firm appropriates value, it does so in the form of higher profits. When customers appropriate value, they do so in the form of savings (i.e., paying less than what they would have been willing to pay).[3]

Let's return to the example of your grandma-recipe cake-making venture. Note that at this point we have said nothing about either your actual cost of making the cake (i.e., the firm cost) or the price you and the coffee shop have agreed upon for each cake you will deliver. In other words, at this point, we know how much total value has been created (a theoretical amount), but we know nothing about how this value is going to be realized and who is going to appropriate it.

Let's assume that while the store that provides you with the ingredients for your cake may be willing to drop the price to about $4.00 per cake because of your bulk buying, you are unaware of the store's supplier opportunity cost and do not negotiate hard. You simply pay the published price of $5.00 per cake in ingredients. Thus your firm cost[4] equals ($5.00 + $9.25 + $3.75) = $18.00.

Now, since you do not know that the coffee house's actual customer willingness to pay is $25.00 (they certainly are not going to tell you!), you accept the coffee house's first offer and do not negotiate hard . . . should you consider a negotiation class at this point?! The price you agree on is $22.00 (Figure 7.5).

We now have all the information we need to compute value appropriation and to determine how much of the total value created each of the entities involved will retain. Here is how the total value created, $8.00, would break down in this case:

---

3. As customers, we have all come across a "good deal" a few times in our lives. A good deal is nothing but a situation where the price we are asked to pay is lower than our customer willingness to pay.

4. Note that in this simplistic example, you are playing two roles. On the one hand, you are a supplier of the labor resource. At the same time, you are the entrepreneur, the firm, who will retain any profits the business is able to generate.

- The suppliers appropriate $1.00 in excess profits—that is, one dollar more than the minimum amount of money they would have been willing to accept to provide you with the needed resources (i.e., supplier opportunity cost).
- You appropriate $4.00 in excess profits—that is, four dollars more than the minimum amount of money for which you would have been willing to stay in this venture (i.e., your firm cost).
- The customer, the gourmet coffee shop, appropriates $3.00 in savings—that is, three dollars less than the maximum amount of money it would have been willing to disburse to acquire your specialty cake (i.e., their customer willingness to pay).

The Definition of Added Value

With the terminology of value creation and value appropriation now in place, we are ready to discuss added value. A firm's added value is defined as *that portion of the total value created that would be lost if the firm did not take part in the exchange.* That is, the firm's added value is measured as that portion of the value created in the transaction involving the firm minus the total value that could be created if the firm did not exist. A firm's added value is therefore the unique portion of the total value created that is contributed by the firm itself. Added value depends on the effects of existing competition.

Recall the example of your cake-making venture. In that example, your firm was the only one in the market that could take the ingredients that were valued at $17.00 and, using grandma's secret recipe, transform them into a final product—this one-of-a-kind cake that customers would be willing to pay a maximum of $25.00 for. We established that the total value created in the transaction was $8.00.

What was your firm's added value then? It was the full $8.00. If you decide not to bake the cake, as the only person who has knowledge of the secret recipe (i.e., the unique transformation process), none of the potential value would be realized. That is, all $8.00 of the new value would be lost as we would be left with the raw resources worth the original $17.00.

Added Value in a Competitive Market

Let's now assume that you were not the only one who had been given the secret recipe in your grandma's will. Much to your surprise, your estranged cousin Bettie also received the secret recipe, and you just found out that she is entering the cake-baking business in your area! In fact, she just contacted the gourmet coffee shop you have been in talks with and is attempting to undercut you. She has the exact same cost structure as you do and produces a cake that is no different in any respect than yours. In other words, you and Bettie produce two products that are perfect substitutes for one another.

Mapping this scenario to the added value model demonstrates that the total value created has not changed (see Figure 7.6), since both you and Bettie encounter the same supplier opportunity cost[5] and produce a cake that the coffee shop owner would pay the same amount of money for.

What has changed in this scenario is your firm's added value. In the first scenario you were the only one who could create the cake. Now if your firm were to leave the exchange, Bettie's firm could step right in and, using the exact same resource, produce the exact same cake. You do *nothing unique* and, as a consequence, your added value is now $0.00.

Pricing Considerations

Again, while we don't need to know price to compute added value (a theoretical value), price becomes important to gauge what portion of the value created each entity partaking to the transaction can appropriate. In our first scenario, when you were the only person who knew the secret recipe for the cake, we assumed you'd agree to the first price the coffee shop owner proposed (Figure 7.5)—$22.00. It should be clear, though, that you were in a position of bargaining power and could have pushed the envelope. In fact, since we know the coffee shop owner's customer willingness to pay, we can assert that you could have charged as much as $25.00.

Once your cousin Bettie enters the market and begins to offer her cake, a perfect substitute of yours, you are no longer in a position of bargaining power. We can therefore expect a price war to cause prices

---

5. This assumes that Bettie also has a minimum-wage job as the next best use of her time.

FIGURE 7.6. Total value created

to drop as low as your firm cost since neither of you offers anything unique (your added value is zero). Under this circumstance, any price you quote that exceeds your firm cost would provide an incentive to the coffee shop and cousin Bettie's firm to strike a deal to cut you out. Cousin Bettie would quote a price lower than yours to get the business, and a lower price would be a better deal for the coffee shop. This would force you to underbid Bettie, and the process would only end when one of you is willing to quote a price equal to the firm cost. In this case, neither competitor will make any extra profit, while the customer, the coffee shop, will reap big savings.

The lesson is clear: no matter how much value your firm contributes to creating, unless you can be (at least in part) unique in your value creation, you will quickly compete this value away to customers. This is, of course, the essence of competition and a force that in your capacity as a manager you need to learn to manage.

The Relationship between Added Value and Competitive Advantage

The insight about pricing discussed above is critical, and it should clarify that a firm should focus on creating value, through innovation and the use of IT, not just for the sake of doing so, but in order to be able to appropriate at least a portion of the total value created. In theory, the maximum amount of value that a firm can appropriate equals its added value. Thus the imperative when engaging in new strategic initiatives is for a firm to create *added value*. The firm's added value is also a measure of its competitive advantage because it measures the extent to which the firm is able to do something unique and valuable.

How Is Added Value Created?

Now imagine one last twist in the story of your cake-making venture. Imagine that, since you have some artistic talents, you are able to garnish the cake with some icing that makes it unique. The coffee shop owner thinks that she can sell each slice of your "personalized" cake at a premium, say $4.00, claiming that the cake is a "coffee shop exclusive."

Personalizing the cake takes you 12 minutes of extra labor ($1.85), and the value of the extra ingredients needed is 15 cents. In this case, your supplier opportunity cost has risen by $2.00. But the extra investment of resources leads to an increase in customer willingness to pay to $4.00. Cousin Bettie has no artistic talents and is unable to personalize her cakes. Your firm's added value is now positive (Figure 7.7).

Perhaps a simpler way of analyzing this is to focus on the value of the different characteristics of your product. That is, with an incremental investment of $2.00, you create an increment in customer

FIGURE 7.7. Added value under competition

willingness to pay of $4.00, over what the competition can do, thus generating added value in the amount of $2.00. Note that price will be once again determined as a consequence of a negotiation process, but you certainly now have a competitive advantage over Cousin Bettie's firm, and you can expect to appropriate as much as two dollars (e.g., charging the coffee shop no more than $20.00).

Two Ways to Create New Value

More important than the calculations produced above is the meaning of this analysis and the considerations that follow from it.

Increasing Customer Willingness to Pay   Added value is created by doing something of value for customers, thereby increasing customer willingness to pay through an investment of resources that does not exceed customer willingness to pay—otherwise we would be simply destroying value and wasting resources. Apple Inc.—the consumer electronics firm originally led by Steve Jobs—is a great example of value creation through increased willingness to pay. Steve Jobs, speaking at D,[6] articulated his firm's great success in digital media as focusing on making great products, pricing them aggressively, and going for volume. Translated into the terminology of this chapter, this approach reads, "Our strategy is to drive customer willingness to pay as high as we possibly can (i.e., great products), and then try to price low enough so that people perceive that they are appropriating significant value when they buy our products, and therefore buy them in large volumes."

The most visible competitive battles take place on this end of the value continuum. The firms that have innovated use marketing to educate customers about their new products and services and to drive up customer willingness to pay (Figure 7.8). However, this focus on customer facing initiatives can be misleading.

Decreasing Supplier Opportunity Cost   By definition, value can be created by increasing customer willingness to pay over supplier opportunity cost but also by reducing supplier opportunity cost without a comparable reduction in customer willingness to pay. In other words, there is great potential to

---

6. The All Things Digital conference—or D for short—is the annual event for the executives of the computer and software industries hosted by the *Wall Street Journal*.

FIGURE 7.8. How value is created

create value by working with the firm's suppliers and creating incentives for them to supply you with needed resources for less money (Figure 7.8).

The prototypical example of this strategy is offered by Walmart Inc., a firm that has made "everyday low prices" its slogan and the key driver behind most of its decisions. In the late 1980s, Walmart worked with one of its largest suppliers, Procter & Gamble, to find creative ways to lower its cost structure. Walmart pioneered a technique now called "continuous replenishment."

Continuous replenishment is based on the idea of "pulled logistics," whereby a supplier (e.g., P&G), not a customer (e.g., Walmart), is in charge of managing the customer's inventory. In the specific case of the Walmart/P&G partnership, leveraging its data network (remember the opening quote?), Walmart provided P&G with real-time purchase data from each of its stores. That is, any time a box of Pampers or a carton of Tide detergent are sold at any Walmart store, P&G receives an electronic notification. This near-real-time knowledge of actual consumer demand enabled P&G to optimize its production schedules and its supply chain operations. As a consequence, P&G's own costs decreased and P&G became willing to supply Walmart for less money than it charged other customers who could not engage in continuous replenishment. In other words, P&G's supplier opportunity cost for dealing with Walmart, and only Walmart, decreased thanks to this data-sharing initiative. On the other end of the value continuum, where Walmart serves the end consumer, no change occurred, as customers didn't need to know about continuous replenishment or see any changes in what Walmart offered, and Walmart still commanded the same customer willingness to pay for its service.

Similarly, CareFusion, a global medical technology firm now part of Becton Dickinson, lowered supply chain partners costs deploying a SaaS platform to foster collaboration. Thus they were able to gain greater supply chain efficiency with limited partners' specific investment. Lower supply chain costs emerged form better supply chain visibility and operations. For example, thanks to this platform, CareFusion partners' could print product labels directly from the system. As all firms in the transaction use the same data and the same codes CareFusion can process inbound deliveries of materials more efficiently. This simple shrewdness brought process time down to one hour a day from the six it usually required. As CareFusion's vice president of operation commented, "What suppliers get—and what we get—is complete transparency. Suppliers have the same information and data about our relationship as I have. They can see my inventory levels. They can see if I'm overstocked or about to run out. They can see their performance level against the delivery targets we set for them."[7]

Some Considerations about the Analysis of Added Value
The above discussion of the analysis of added value and the above examples suggest a few important concluding remarks.

Value Is in the Eye of the Customer   We define customer willingness to pay as the maximum amount of money that a customer is willing to give the firm to acquire its products or services. Unless there is a market for the innovation, no value has been generated.

Customer Willingness to Pay Is Not the Same as Price   Price is a consequence of a negotiation between the firm and the customer, depending on the available information and the degree of competition in the market. Note, however, that a firm that is able to create higher customer willingness to pay does not need to charge higher prices to benefit. Imagine two firms vying for customer business and charging the same price. If one is able to command a slightly higher customer willingness to pay—for example, by having a stronger brand—it will get the customer's business.[8]

---

7. Twentyman, J. (2015), Cloud is new platform for supply chain partners to get together, *Financial Times*, retrieved May 1, 2015, from http://www.ft.com/intl/cms/s/0/c4c07ef8-f316-11e3-a3f8-00144feabdc0.html?siteedition=uk

8. Note that in some industries where the cost structure involves significant fixed costs and small variable costs (e.g., the lodging or airline industries), attracting more customers, even if at the same price as the competition, can result in significant profitability gains. This is because any revenue from incremental business will mostly flow through to the bottom line.

Value Can Be Tangible or Intangible   Our cake-making example suggests that the coffee shop is willing to buy your cake because they can resell it and turn a profit. We buy clothes because of the tangible outcomes they provide (e.g., warmth). However, we also buy them for looks, style, fashion, for the way they make us feel, to fit within a certain group, to support a particular manufacturer, and so on. All these "intangible" drivers of value are as important as the tangible ones. As much as possible, goodwill, brand effects, loyalty, and all other intangible drivers of value should be estimated and measured. Techniques such as focus groups and market research are typically used to do this.

Creation of Value Is Not Appropriation   Beyond increasing customer willingness to pay, there is much opportunity to create added value by focusing on suppliers' opportunity cost and by providing advantages to suppliers to work with the firm. Yet, as a firm, it is crucial only to create value that you can appropriate (i.e., added value). Creating value can be done even in circumstances when this value can be appropriated by others (often customers). You must have added value (which is unique to your firm) to be sure to appropriate it.

Competitive Advantage and Added Value Are Closely Related   While the framework for the analysis of added value is a simplification of reality as it assumes perfect information of all entities involved and the absence of switching costs, it highlights what a firm must do to gain a competitive advantage. True competitive advantage is a function of added value (see Sidebar 7.1). Note, however, that the analysis of added value is focused on the short term and tells us nothing about the long-term resilience (e.g., resistance to erosion) of the firm's competitive advantage. An analysis of sustainability, the focus of Chapter 9, is the analytical tool needed to evaluate if any added value we create can be appropriated

SIDEBAR 7.1. HOW TO PERFORM ADDED VALUE ANALYSIS

Depending on the specific characteristics of the initiative under investigation, the analysis of added value can be more or less straightforward. You should try the following:

Clearly Define the Initiative and Understand What It Entails

The first step in the analysis requires that we are very clear about what the firm will do for customers or suppliers and what resources are necessary to create the product or perform the service being sold by identifying the intended value proposition.

Identify the Comparison

Because added value is defined in comparative terms, it is critical to identify a baseline comparison. This baseline can be the competitor's initiative or the firm's own offers—when the firm is innovating with products or services that improve on the current state of the art in the industry.

Estimate Customer Willingness to Pay

Estimating customer willingness to pay can be a very complex process requiring substantial approximation and research. In order to simplify and focus this process,

it helps to start by listing all the positive customer willingness to pay drivers—defined as what the firm does as part of its offer to increase customer willingness to pay. Note that any initiative has both positive and negative effects. That is, any initiative entails trade-offs; as the firm does some things of value for its customers, it also forgoes doing other things. It is therefore critical to also surface these negative customer willingness to pay drivers and discount their effect.

Estimate Supplier Opportunity Cost

This analysis is similar to the one above and includes both positive and negative change. When the initiative's main contribution to value creation is on the supplier opportunity cost side, supplier opportunity cost must be used. When the main effect of the initiative is on customer willingness to pay, then a simplifying assumption using firm cost as a proxy for supplier opportunity cost is acceptable.

Estimate Added Value

With the above information in hand, you can measure added value and begin to draw value appropriation considerations.

over time. As we learned in this chapter, it is not enough to be able to create value; we must be able to appropriate it. To do so we must protect any added value we create from erosion by competitors.

Strategic Information Systems

Without a doubt, information systems and technology engender a plentitude of confusing lingo, technical terms, and acronyms—a problem compounded by the crowds of half-prepared, fast-talking individuals using terminology incorrectly. In Chapter 2, we were very careful in defining what IS is and in differentiating it from IT. We defined an information system as a sociotechnical system that includes IT, processes, people, and organizational structure.

The distinction between IT and IS is a critical prerequisite to understanding the strategic potential of information systems and the role that information technology plays in the creation and appropriation of added value. This distinction also shows why the firm that focuses solely on IT investments to become competitive (i.e., blindly purchasing computer systems) is wasting its money. IT investments are only appropriate within a larger IS design and only as components of information systems.

Definition: Strategic Information Systems

As you may intuitively expect, not all information systems that an organization seeks to design, develop, and use may be strategic. The foremost objective of strategy in for-profit business ventures is to achieve and sustain superior financial performance. To do so, the firm uses its resources to create value by either reducing supplier opportunity cost or increasing the customers' willingness to pay for its product and services, or both. A firm achieves competitive advantage when it is able to generate added value by creating a unique and positive difference between customers' willingness to pay and supplier opportunity costs. At that point, the firm is in a position to appropriate, in the form of profits, the added value it has created. In short, competitive strategy can be defined as the art and science of *being unique*.

We define *strategic information systems* as those information systems used to support or shape the competitive strategy of an organization. More succinctly, with the terminology discussed in this chapter, we can define *strategic information systems* as those that enable the creation and appropriation of value.

Strategic or Not? Depends on the Purpose   Strategic information systems are not defined by their functionality or the organizational function they support (as categorized in Chapter 3) but are instead defined in terms of their objectives and the purpose they serve (e.g., improving the firm's competitive standing). Consider two examples from American Airlines:

- *The SABRE reservation system*, typically considered to be the foremost example of a strategic information system, was originally created as an airline seats inventory system (i.e., a transaction processing system).
- *The SMARTS system*, also considered a tool that enabled American Airlines to gain a competitive advantage, was expressly designed to enable AA regional sales representatives to craft highly tailored incentive schemes for travel agents. SMARTS was an analytical tool (i.e., a decision support system).

No Need for Proprietary IT   Contrary to conventional wisdom, strategic information systems do not have to rely on proprietary technology. eBay Inc. has provided the starkest example of this rule (Figure 7.9). eBay has dominated the online auction market since its inception using commonly available technology—namely, Internet technologies and the web.

A simple look at a competitor's auction site (Figure 7.10) shows remarkable similarities and comparable functionalities. eBay deploys little in the way of proprietary IT, and its technology has been duplicated by competitors. However, such replication of the technology is not enough, as it is the whole of eBay's initiative, and its information system, that underpins the firm's value-creating strategy and

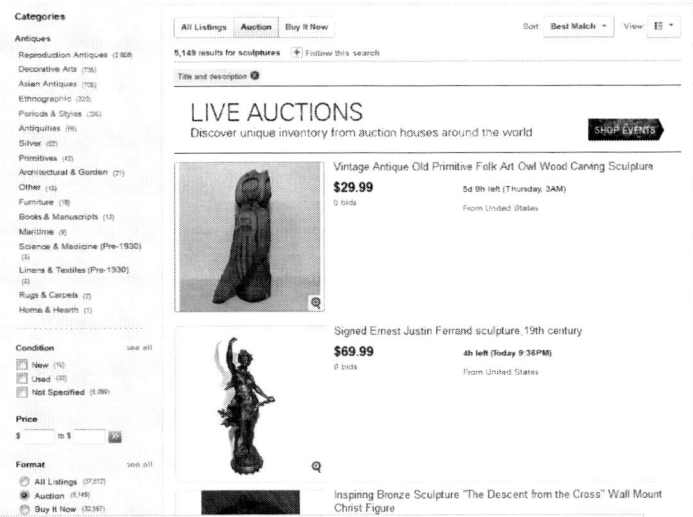

FIGURE 7.9. eBay's auction site

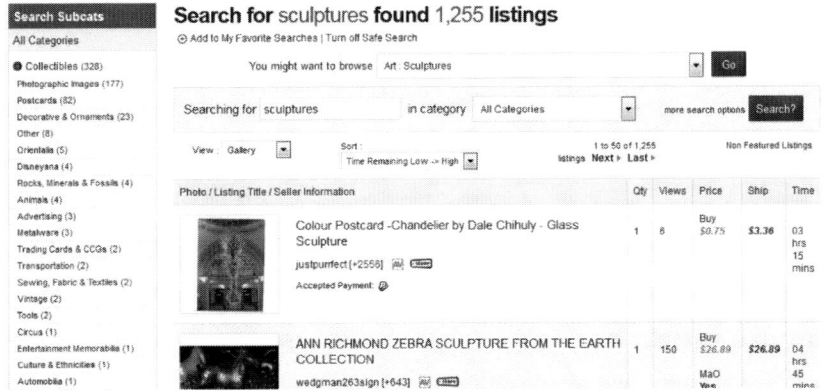

FIGURE 7.10. eBid's auction site

determines its added value. As we discuss more fully in Chapter 9, replicating the IT at the core of defendable strategic information systems is often a useless move.

Strategic versus Tactical Information Systems The definition of strategic information systems that we use is helpful in discriminating and identifying the many systems that are not strategic. These are systems that do not position the firm to create added value, even though they are important (often crucial) for the business's operations. We refer to these as *tactical* information systems. Consider the following examples:

- All organizations that have salaried or hourly employees must pay them and maintain a complex set of records to compute tax withdrawals, accrued vacation time, sick leave, and so on. These software applications, typically called human resource management systems, are critical for the smooth operation of organizations. Can you imagine working for a company that consistently sent you a paycheck with errors? You'd be looking for another job fast! Human resource management systems are critical. Yet they are not strategic. They typically do not enable the creation of added value—rare is the firm that offers a unique value proposition based on its ability to correctly cut paychecks!

- A restaurant's primary information system, anchored by its point-of-sale (POS) software, is used to manage reservations, seating, order taking and delivery, and billing. Clearly, most modern restaurants could not operate as effectively without such a system. Yet POSs are generally tactical in nature, not strategic, because they rarely allow the restaurant to create unique value.
- Similarly, no matter how well it is run, an e-mail system is unlikely to be the foundation of a strategic information system, and the same argument can be made for productivity software such as Microsoft Word and Excel, no matter how advanced their features may be.

No modern organization could run without e-mail and productivity software such as Microsoft Excel. Yet it is important to recognize that, as vital as they are, these systems are not strategic, and implementing or upgrading tactical systems will not create competitive advantage.

IT-Dependent Strategic Initiatives

As a general or functional manager, you may often propose new initiatives that need information systems and IT to be enacted. You will also be called upon to help in the analysis, design, and development of strategic information systems early in your career. As a graduate of a management program, you will be paid for your analytical and decision-making abilities. This will likely include being involved with strategic information systems decisions.

In this capacity, you will be focusing on specific projects and initiatives. We use the notion of *IT-dependent strategic initiatives* in this book to refer to identifiable competitive moves and projects that enable the creation of added value and that rely heavily on the use of IT to be successfully implemented. IT-dependent strategic initiatives have three defining characteristics.

Initiative   IT-dependent strategic initiatives consist of specific projects with clear boundaries that define what the initiative is designed to achieve as well as what it is and is not designed to do. For example, a freight shipper's package tracking initiative has very clear boundaries. It is designed to allow customers to gain visibility with respect to the current location of their parcels by logging onto a website. Tracking tools for online transactions are now available in lots of industries—you can even track your pizza as it is being made and delivered (Figure 7.11)!

Strategic   The firm introduces IT-dependent strategic initiatives with the definite objective of producing new value that the IT can appropriate. In other words, the firm seeks to create competitive advantage through the initiative. The freight shipper's package-tracking initiative, originally pioneered by FedEx in the mid-1990s, was primarily designed to improve customer service (and therefore customer willingness to pay). Note, however, that as it happened, this initiative also had the potential to shift

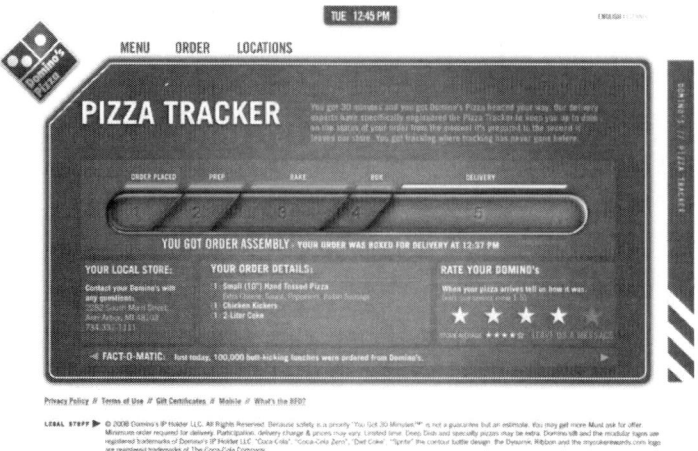

FIGURE 7.11. Domino's Pizza tracking website

much of the current volume of tracking inquiries away from call-center operators and onto the web, thereby reducing firm cost as well.

IT Dependent   IT-dependent strategic initiatives cannot be feasibly created and executed without the use of information technology at their core. Note that this IT core need not use cutting-edge or new breakthrough technologies, as was the case at FedEx, where the technology core of the initiative was certainly not of the bleeding-edge sort. While the Internet and the web were relatively new to the shipping public in the mid-1990s, the technology at their core had been around for more than 20 years. FedEx's package-tracking initiative is clearly IT dependent, as it would not be feasible for the freight shipper to heavily promote a call-center-based package-tracking system due to the high costs of call-center operations versus online automated tracking systems.

Examples of IT-dependent strategic initiatives abound in modern businesses and include some of the most important and recent trends: cloud integration, supply chain management, big data and analytics, 3D printing, and Internet of things (IoT) initiatives. However, as we see in the FedEx example above, IT-dependent strategic initiatives can also have a much more limited scope, including projects such as introducing Internet cafés on cruise ships, insurance companies monitoring drivers' behaviors (e.g., AXA or Progressive; see Sidebar 7.2), or start-ups leveraging smartphones to promote a platform for health management (e.g., Propeller Health; see Sidebar 7.3).

SIDEBAR 7.2. AXA'S INSURANCE DRIVESAVE

Initiative

DriveSave allows AXA customers to receive discounts on their car insurance premiums. The application (Figure 7.12) monitors and informs users on driving characteristics, including acceleration, speed, distance, turning, and stopping force. An overall driving behavior score ranging between 1 and 100 is then calculated. Scores greater than 70 allow customers to benefit from additional discounts. The initiative targets price-savvy, technologically prone, safe young drivers.

Strategic

The initiative has the objective to increase AXA ability to correctly assess customers' profiles and associated risks. By increasing the visibility of customers' driving behavior, insurers can reduce their costs and transform these savings in competitive prices.

IT Dependent

Customer side, the core technological components are embedded in smartphones. The initiative relies on AXA IT capabilities for the development, management, maintenance, and integration of the new system.

SIDEBAR 7.3. THE PROPELLER

Initiative

The Propeller is a sensor for inhalers capable of recording use time, frequency, and location (Figure 7.13). The collected data can be used to better understand the severity and the triggers of asthma and chronic obstructive pulmonary disease (COPD). The target customers are people affected by these pathologies desiring to keep a complete record of their respiratory health for improving their well-being.

Strategic

For patients, value is created in the form of a convenient, unobtrusive, precise, and complete record of Propeller uses. Additional value is created through personalized feedback, information, and medication reminders.

IT Dependent

The initiative is based on Bluetooth communication between the inhaler sensor and patient's smartphone. The development of the application requires particular attention to interface design and data visualization to foster patients' access and understanding of information.

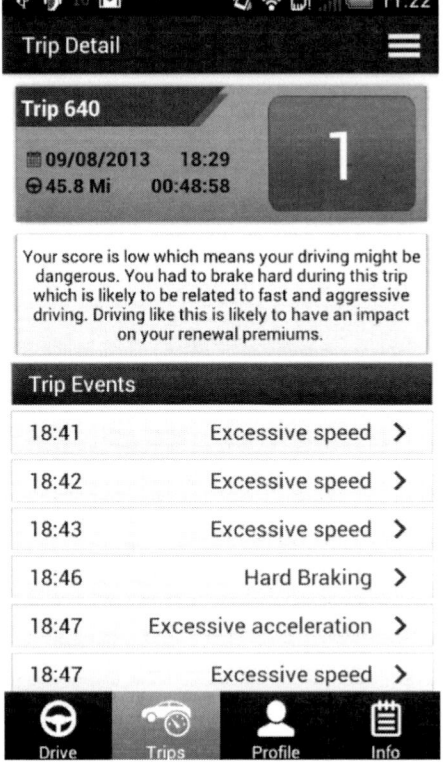

FIGURE 7.12. AXA's DriveSave Android application

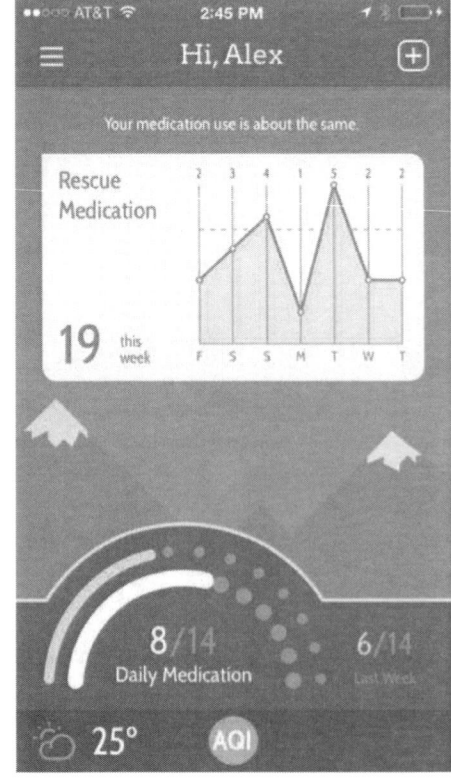

FIGURE 7.13. Propeller Health iPhone application

IT-Dependent Strategic Initiatives, not IT Investments   The notion of the IT-dependent strategic initiative is a critical one to plan for the use and management of strategic information systems. Using this definition forces us to shift attention away from investments in technology and to recognize that IT investments can only pay off if they are part of a larger and cohesive information system design. It is the ability of the IT-dependent strategic initiative to create added value that we must focus on, not the uniqueness or innovativeness of the technology at its core. Thus IT-dependent strategic initiatives do not simply consist of the building of a computer system or application that allegedly generates competitive advantage until it is successfully replicated; rather, they consist of the configuration of an activity system, dependent on IT at its core, that fosters the creation and appropriation of economic value.

Summary

This chapter provides the background for understanding strategic information systems decisions by discussing fundamental concepts and analytical frameworks. Specifically, in this chapter we introduced the notion of value creation and appropriation.

- Economic value is created when some input resources that have a value of $x in their next best utilization are transformed into outputs for which customers are willing to pay $x + $v.
- The value thus created is partitioned among those entities involved in its creation: a firm, its suppliers, and its customers—a process known as *value appropriation*.
- A firm is able to appropriate that portion of the total value created that would be lost if the firm did not partake in the exchange—a figure we termed *added value*.
- Strategic information systems are those that are designed and developed to create and appropriate value. They differ from tactical information systems, which are those systems that, while often critical for the firm's operations, do not enable the creation of distinctive value.
- Information technology (IT)-dependent strategic initiatives consist of identifiable competitive moves and projects that enable the creation of added value and that rely heavily on the use of IT to be successfully implemented. They should be the focus of the search for new value creation.
- General and functional managers, because of their understanding of the firm's processes and customer needs, take center stage in the identification and analysis of opportunities to create value with information systems. When doing so, they should focus on IT-dependent strategic initiatives rather than taking a narrow focus on IT investments.

This chapter laid the foundation for the analysis of value creation and appropriation of IT-dependent strategic initiatives. In the next chapter we examine frameworks and analytical tools designed to help you envision and take advantage of opportunities to deploy IT-dependent strategic initiatives.

Study Questions

1. Explain the value creation process. How does a firm contribute to the creation of economic value?
2. Provide two examples of firms that you think have been able to create value using information systems. The first one should be a firm that has done so mainly by focusing on customer willingness to pay. The second one should be a firm that has done so mainly by focusing on supplier opportunity cost.
3. Think about the last time you bought something that you felt was "a great deal." Why did you think the product or service was such a great deal? Do you believe that the transaction was considered "great" by the firm from which you acquired the product or service? Why or why not? Explain using the framework of value creation and appropriation.
4. What is the difference between value creation and value appropriation? Why is this difference important?

5. Provide an example of a well-known firm that you think currently has added value. Explain your example using added value analysis.
6. Define the concept of strategic information systems and provide an example.
7. Define the concept of tactical information systems and provide an example.
8. Define the concept of IT-dependent strategic initiative and provide an example.

Further Readings

1. Brandenburger, A. M., & Nalebuff, B. J. (1997). *Coopetition: A revolution mind-set that combines competition and cooperation.* New York, NY: Currency.
2. Brandenburger, A. M., & Stuart, H. W. (1996). Value-based business strategy. *Journal of Economics and Management Strategy, 5*(1), 5–24.
3. Cabiddu, F., Lui, T. W., and Piccoli, G. (2013). Managing value co-creation in the tourism industry. *Annals of Tourism Research, 42,* 86–107.
4. Gottfredson, M., and Aspinall, K. (2005). Innovation versus complexity: What is too much of a good thing? *Harvard Business Review, 83*(11), 62–71.
5. Porter, M. E. (1996, November–December). What is strategy? *Harvard Business Review.*

Glossary

- **Added value:** That portion of the total value created that would be lost if the firm did not partake in the exchange.
- **Competitive advantage:** The condition where a firm engages in a unique transformation process and has been able to distinguish its offerings from those of competitors. When a firm has achieved a position of competitive advantage, it is able to make above average profits.
- **Customer willingness to pay:** The maximum amount of money the firm's customers are willing to spend in order to obtain the firm's product.
- **Firm cost:** The actual amount of money the firm disbursed to acquire the resources needed to create its product or service.
- **IT-dependent strategic initiatives:** Identifiable competitive moves and projects that enable the creation of added value and that rely heavily on the use of information technology to be successfully implemented (i.e., they cannot feasibly be enacted without investments in IT).
- **Strategic information systems:** Information systems that are designed to support or shape the competitive strategy of an organization.

Those information systems that enable the creation and appropriation of value.
- **Supplier opportunity cost:** The minimum amount of money suppliers are willing to accept to provide the firm with the needed resources.
- **Tactical information systems:** Systems that do not position the firm to create added value. In other words, they do not enable distinctive initiatives that allow the firm to create unique economic value.
- **Total value created:** The difference between customer willingness to pay and supplier opportunity cost.
- **Transformation process:** The set of activities the company engages in to convert inputs purchased from suppliers into outputs to be sold to customers.
- **Value appropriation:** The process by which the total value created in the transaction is split among all the entities who contributed to creating it (i.e., suppliers, the firm, and the customer).
- **Value creation:** The process by which new economic value is generated through a transformation process.

Value Creation with Information Systems

What You Will Learn in This Chapter

In the previous chapter, we laid the foundations for our discussion of strategic information systems (IS) and information technology (IT)-dependent strategic initiatives. In this chapter, we continue the discussion by focusing on theoretical and analytical models that have been developed over the years to identify opportunities to create value with IT and to design and develop value-adding IT-dependent strategic initiatives.

Specifically, this chapter will

1. Teach you how to think in a disciplined fashion about the question of value creation with information systems resources.
2. Explain how to use traditional models of value creation with information systems and information technology to identify and craft IT-dependent strategic initiatives, including industry analysis, value chain analysis, and the customer service life cycle framework.
3. Explain how to incorporate information resources in your search for opportunities for value creation using emerging frameworks, including the virtual value chain and the customer data strategies framework.
4. Explain how to devise and select initiatives that create value using organizational data.

MINICASE: Smartwatch Ordering at Domino's

On Thursday, April 23, 2015, Mike Lawton, chief financial officer (CFO) of Domino's, the international pizza-delivery chain, was announcing another positive quarter and "fantastic same store sales in both our domestic and international businesses."[1] The tone was enthusiastic. Domino's was outperforming competitors and growing its market share. There were many reasons for this success, but Patrick Doyle, chief executive officer (CEO), president, and director of Domino's Pizza Inc. was absolutely clear. The "catalysts" of their continued positive performance were their business strength and brand equity. He firmly believed that Domino's technology and innovation leaderships were central in evolving the brand through a revolutionary customer experience. The results seemed to prove him right: 50% of domestic U.S. sales were generated via digital ordering channels.

The role of online ordering and innovation has always been central to Domino's strategy. Doyle already said that he believed digital ordering offered

---

1. Domino's Pizza's (DPZ) Patrick Doyle on Q1 2015 results—earnings call transcript (2015, April 23), *Seeking Alpha*, retrieved June 15, 2015, from http://seekingalpha.com/article/3096826-dominos-pizzas-dpz-patrick-doyle-on-q1-2015-results-earnings-call-transcript/

by major pizza chains would help take away business from independent and smaller regional players, fostering growth. Domino's stuck to its words. The company was first in introducing their iPhone app for the U.K. market in September 2010.

The iPhone app automatically detected the Domino's location closest to the customer (Figure 8.1). Once logged into the application, they could either select from the standard menu or from an available list of specials from the chosen location. They could also request a custom order by selecting pie size, crust type, toppings (Figure 8.2), and any other possible personalization (e.g., extra sauce). One of the advantages of the iPhone ordering application is that it did not require the customer to talk to a restaurant employee on duty. As a consequence the app enabled customers to place orders, even during store closing times, and schedule delivery for a specific date/time.

Upon completing their order, customers would pay and then could track the progress of their pizza up to the delivery stage, through the preparation, baking, and quality assurance steps (Figure 8.3).

The app was later improved and made seamlessly available on Android platform. In October 2014, Domino's included an additional voice ordering feature. Similar to Apple's Siri, Microsoft's Cortana, or Google Now, "Dom" takes orders, suggests additions, and guides customers through the purchasing process (Figure 8.4). As Dennis Maloney, head of multimedia marketing, said, "He's fun, but very focused on the pizza ordering experience."[2]

In 2015, Domino's extended its mobile application to support Peeble and Android Wear smartwatches to make the ordering process even easier and monitor its progress. Their strategy was clear: the company aimed at providing an ubiquitous access to their customers. According to Kevin Vasconi, Domino's Pizza chief information officer (CIO), "We are constantly looking for ways to use technology to enhance our customers' experience and provide them with more convenience."

Discussion Questions

1. Do you believe that Domino's smartwatch ordering is an example of an IT-dependent strategic initiative? Explain.

2. Do you believe that this initiative has the potential to create added value? Substantiate your answer.

3. Do you believe that the Domino's smartwatch ordering initiative improves customer service? How?

4. What would you do next if you were put in charge of the initiative?

FIGURE 8.1. Domino's iPhone app welcome screen

Introduction

We concluded Chapter 6 by showing how the strategic information systems (IS) planning process is designed to create an overall context for information systems decision making. The planning documents conclude with the identification of strategic initiatives. In Chapter 7 we laid the foundation for our discussion of strategic information systems and information technology (IT)-dependent strategic initiatives by explaining how you can analyze the impact of such initiatives. In this chapter, we get to the heart of the matter and introduce the frameworks and analytical models that information systems professionals, as well as general and functional managers, use to identify opportunities and to design and evaluate IT-dependent strategic initiatives.

Traditional Models of Value Creation with IT

The strategic potential of information technology attracted considerable attention in the mid-1980s. It was at this time that,

2. Waters, R. (2015), Artificial intelligence: A virtual assistant for life, *Financial Times*, retrieved April 30, 2015, from http://www.ft.com/intl/cms/s/0/4f2f97ea-b8ec-11e4-b8e6-00144feab7de.html

FIGURE 8.2. Customers have playful ways to choose their toppings

FIGURE 8.3. Domino's order tracking feature

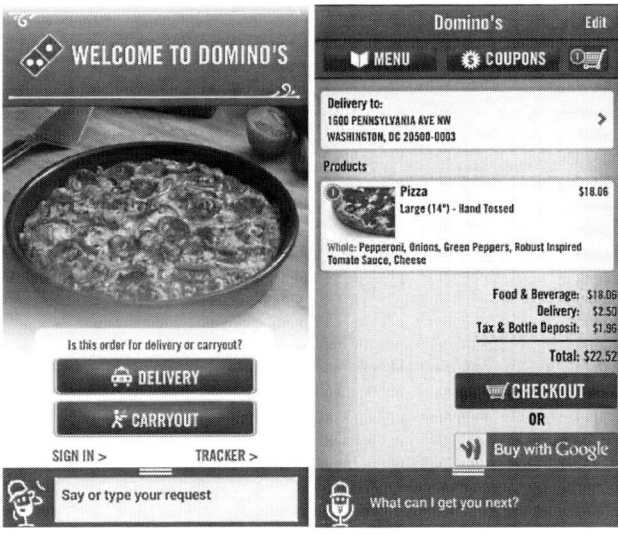

FIGURE 8.4. Domino's new interface and "Dom" integration
Source: Image courtesy of Domino's

prompted by a critical mass of success stories and case studies, academic researchers and consulting firms began to systematically explore and document the role of information systems and IT beyond the automation of work and creation of efficiencies. The use of IT as a "competitive weapon" became fertile ground for research and practice alike.

The emergence of influential strategic models focusing on competitive positioning and competitive advantage helped shine a light on the value creation potential of IT. Three analytical tools were introduced or adapted to the search for strategic information systems opportunities at this time:

- Industry analysis
- Value chain analysis
- Customer service life cycle analysis

Industry Analysis

The industry analysis framework is grounded in the basic notion that different industries offer different potential for profitability.[3] A simple analysis lends support to this assumption (see Figure 8.5). Based on this idea, the industry analysis framework suggests that industry differences can be analyzed a priori

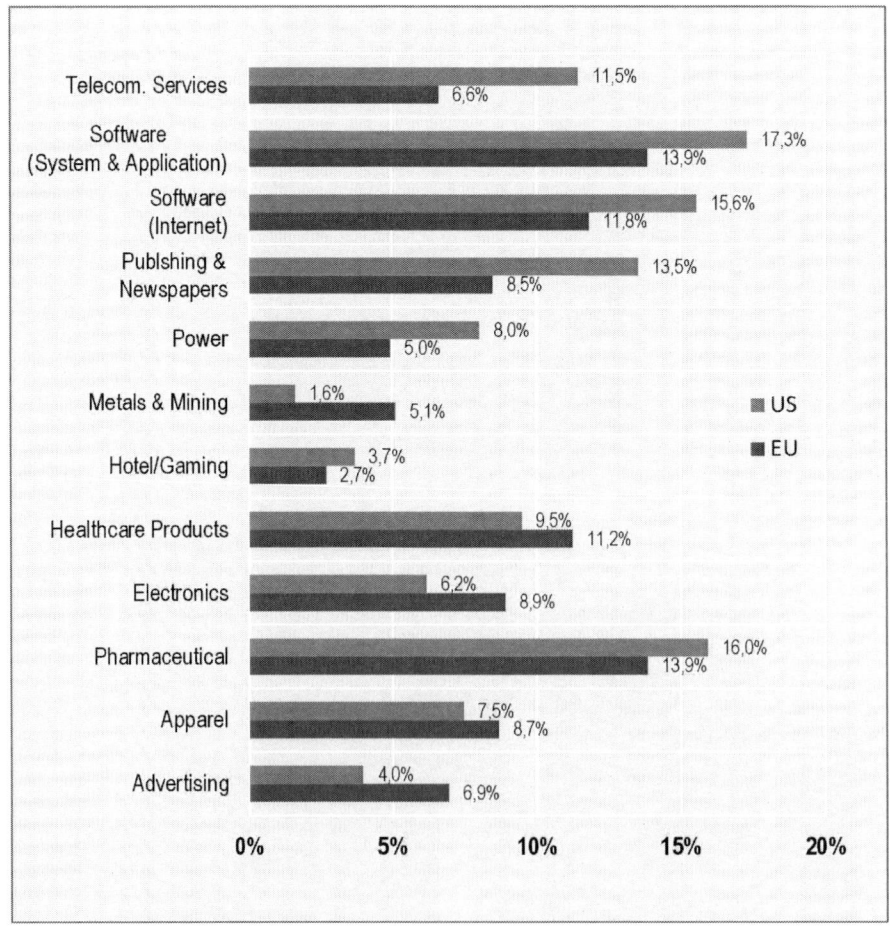

FIGURE 8.5. Industry differences in average profitability (cumulated values of net income on cumulated sales for the sector)
Source: Aswath Damodaran, http://www.damodaran.com, January 2015

---

3. Porter, M. E. (1980), *Competitive strategy: Techniques for analyzing industries and competitors*, New York, NY: Free Press.

by managers using an analytical framework now known as the five forces framework (see Figure 8.6). Armed with the results of this analysis, executives can decide whether to enter an industry or forgo investment.

More important, for an organization that is already a player in a given industry, such analysis can offer guidance as to what to do to increase the appeal (i.e., average profit potential) of the industry. Thus from a simply analytical framework, the industry analysis model becomes a prescriptive one. It is in this capacity that it can be used to surface opportunities to introduce IT-dependent strategic initiatives.

Five Competitive Forces   The industry analysis framework identifies five structural determinants of the potential for profitability of the average firm in a given industry. Each is discussed next.

The Threat of New Entrants   This force represents the extent to which the industry is open to entry by new competitors or whether significant barriers to entry make it so that the existing firms need not worry about competition from outside.

Consider car manufacturing, for example. Car manufacturing is characterized by a substantial need for capital investments in research and development as well as a need for significant production capacity. Moreover, the automotive industry is characterized by strong economies of scale, such that it is important to produce a large number of vehicles to stay competitive. For these reasons, the auto industry is characterized by a low threat of new competitors due to strong barriers to entry.

The Threat of Substitute Products or Services   This force represents the extent to which the products or services marketed by the firm in the industry of interest are subject to potential substitution by different products or services that fulfill the same customer needs.

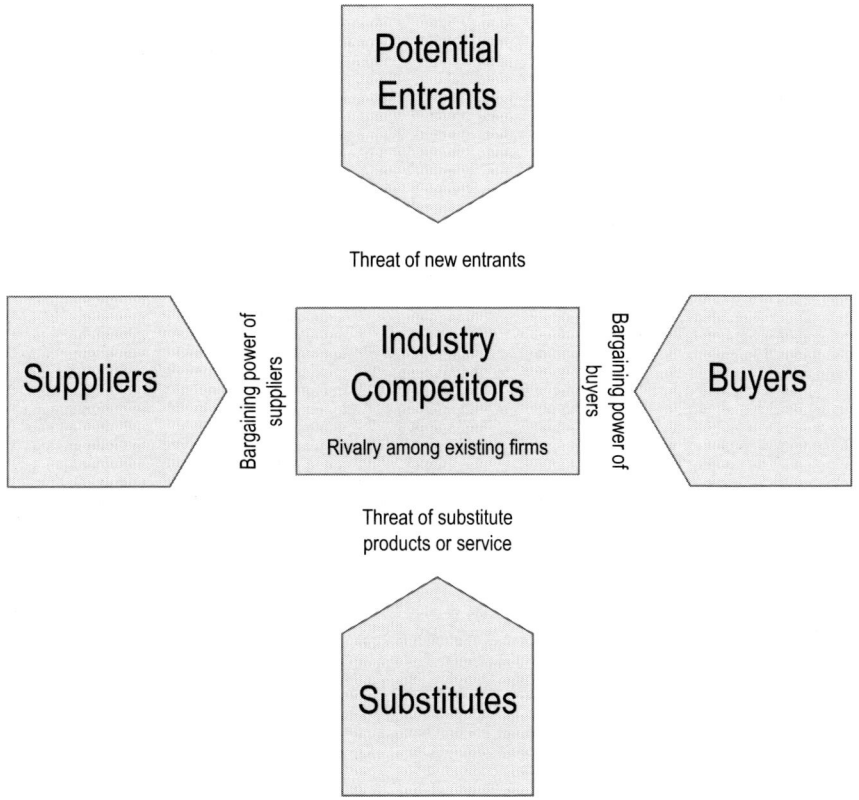

FIGURE 8.6. Industry analysis

For example, products such as the iPod and digital music files, introduced by firms traditionally in the computer industry, have rapidly substituted CD players and other devices traditionally offered by consumer electronics firms. In a clear sign of the times, Sony announced in October 2010 that it would stop manufacturing the iconic Walkman cassette player. Music cassette players have now been fully substituted by MP3s and streaming services!

The Bargaining Power of Buyers   This force represents the extent to which customers of those organizations in the industry have the ability to put downward pressure on prices. Highly concentrated buyers and low switching costs (see Chapter 9) typically conspire to increase the bargaining power of buyers.

Consider, for example, a company like Walmart, which because of huge sales in its more than 9,000 stores worldwide can purchase the bulk of a manufacturer's production capacity. With its size and focus on low prices, Walmart is famous for influencing prices set by its suppliers—some would even say dictating prices to them!

The Bargaining Power of Suppliers   This force represents the extent to which those individuals and firms who sell production inputs to the organizations in the industry have the ability to maintain high prices. This force is the same as the previous one, where the firms in the industry of interest have taken the role of the buyer rather than the seller.

As a future supplier of labor resources, you should pay significant attention to this force. If you can put yourself in a position of bargaining power toward the industry of your interest (e.g., by choosing to concentrate in a field of study that is highly sought after but in short supply), you stand to reap significant benefits in terms of salary.

The Rivalry among Existing Competitors   This force represents the extent to which fierce battling for position and aggressive competition occur in the industry. The degree of competition in an industry can vary dramatically. The term *hypercompetition* refers to industries characterized by fierce rivalry among existing firms and a very rapid rate of innovation leading to fast obsolescence of any competitive advantage and a consequent need for a fast cycle of innovation. The search engine industry may be an example, as is the consumer electronics industry (Figure 8.7).

Industry Analysis and the Role of Information Systems   Researchers and consultants who have adapted industry analysis to the search for opportunities to introduce IT-dependent strategic initiatives suggest looking for ways to use information systems to affect one or more of the industry forces, thereby

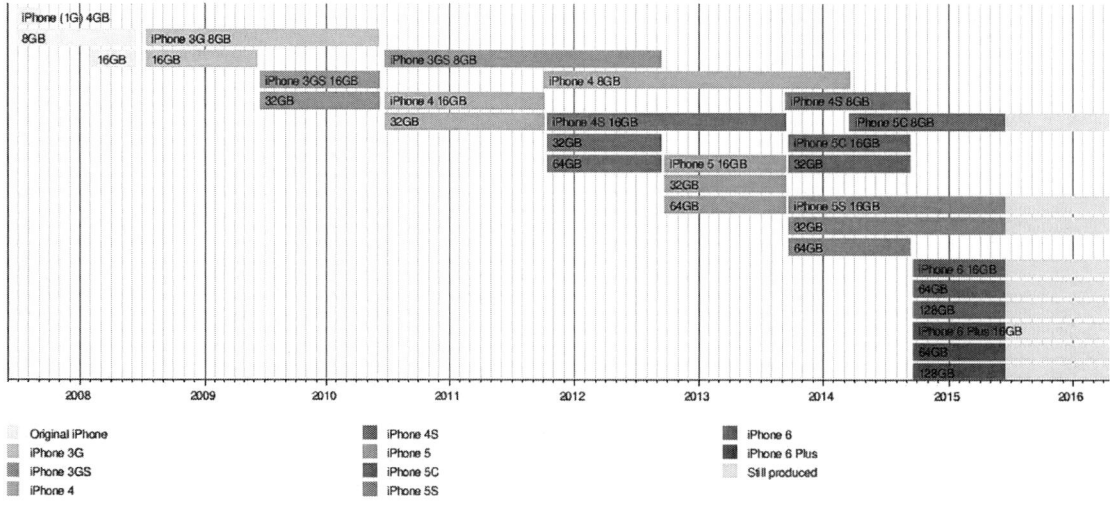

FIGURE 8.7. Consumer electronics: A hypercompetitive industry

tipping things to the firm's advantage. While the five forces framework has a *time-honored* tradition, it is still relevant, and its proponent, Professor Michael Porter, has justified its value in response to major technology evolutions like the Internet[4] and, more recently, the so-called Internet of things[5] (see Chapter 12). The following are some of the questions that are typically asked:

Can the Use of IT Raise or Increase Barriers to Entry in the Industry?   Investments in information systems may be such that they reduce the threat of new entrants. Consider, for example, the need for an ATM network in the banking industry. Entry into the banking industry nowadays requires access to a network of ATMs and, increasingly, online banking facilities. Likewise, access to the lodging industry requires access to a computerized central reservation system (CRS) and a substantial number of interfaces to the plethora of traditional and emerging distribution channels. Again, entry into the gaming industry depends on the possibility to establish a platform popular enough (e.g., PlayStation, Xbox, Wii) to attract developers producing games and ultimately users.

Can the Use of IT Decrease Suppliers' Bargaining Power?   With the emergence of the Internet and its related technologies as viable business tools, examples abound of information systems that have contributed to shift power away from suppliers and toward buyers. Consider, for example, Alibaba (http://www.alibaba.com), the sourcing, procurement, and expertise provider that enables companies to easily access global suppliers. Alibaba enables organizations to dramatically increase their bargaining power with suppliers by reducing the search costs for identifying qualified suppliers.

Can the Use of IT Decrease Buyers' Bargaining Power?   As much as the Internet has helped firms strengthen their bargaining position toward suppliers, it has also reduced their bargaining power toward customers. Just as companies can rapidly shop for alternatives when looking for production inputs, so can their customers. Yet some opportunities to strengthen relationships with customers, thus reducing their incentive to shop around, still exist.

Consider travel intermediaries like Orbitz.com. While competitors are literally one click away, by storing personal preferences (e.g., preferred airlines), personal data (e.g., frequent flier miles), and billing information, travel intermediaries can levy switching costs and reduce their customers' bargaining power. This approach was made popular by Amazon's one-click buying, an innovation for which the firm even received a process patent in 1999 and the "1-Click" trademark.

Can the Use of IT Change the Basis of Industry Competition?   The introduction of a new information system by a firm, whether an incumbent or a new entrant, sometimes spurs a revolution that forces competitors to take notice and react. A stark example of this dynamic was presented by the advent of online retailing in the mid-1990s.

When Amazon.com burst onto the scene, with its ability to offer huge selection and high levels of customer service without a single store, shock waves reverberated in the retail sector. Firms such as Amazon that seized the opportunity presented by the Internet to sell directly to consumers trained consumers to self-serve in ways unheard of before and changed forever the notion of what it means to be a retailer. Today it would be a grave mistake for any large retailer to neglect the online channel of distribution. We can find similar examples in online banking and throughout the travel and tourism sector.

Value Chain

While useful in identifying potential opportunities to improve the profitability of the industry and suggesting ways in which managers can deploy information systems to neutralize or minimize the unattractive features of an industry, much of the potential for the employment of strategic information systems concerns intraindustry competition. In other words, much of the time that you, as general or

---

4. Porter, M. E. (2001, March), Strategy and the Internet, *Harvard Business Review, 79*, 62–78.

5. Porter, M. E., & Heppelmann, J. E. (2014, November), How smart, connected products are transforming competition, *Harvard Business Review, 92*, 11–64.

functional managers, will be spending analyzing opportunities to deploy strategic information systems will be with respect to the ability to create added value. Thus you will not worry so much about average industry performance; rather, given the industry that you are competing in, you will seek to outperform your competitors by using information systems to create added value and competitive advantages.

In Chapter 7, we stated that value is created when a firm employs its transformation process to use resources that have a value of x in their next best use and to generate a product or service that customers are willing to pay $x + v$ for. If what the firm does is unique, such that no competitor is able to offer comparable value, the firm creates added value and has achieved a position of competitive advantage. But what does the firm's "transformation process" look like? How do these input resources become the final product or service that customers pay for?

Primary and Support Activities   The classic framework that has been used to logically represent a firm's transformation process is the value chain (Figure 8.8).[6] The value chain model maps the set of economic activities that a firm engages in and groups them into two sets: primary activities and support activities.

Primary Activities   Primary activities represent the firm's actions that are directly related to value creation. These are the activities that define the firm's unique transformation process such that they are typically performed by all firms engaged in the same or similar line of business. The classic value chain identifies five primary activities: inbound logistics, operations, outbound logistics, marketing and sales, and service. It is the execution of these activities that enables the transformation of the input resources in final products or services—and, as a consequence, the creation of value.

Let's return to the automotive industry. We can think of the car manufacturing transformation process in terms of these five primary activities. A car manufacturer needs to procure and receive component parts (i.e., inbound logistics), have assembly lines that take these components and put them together in the various car models (i.e., operations), deliver the vehicles to the distribution channel and its dealership network (i.e., outbound logistics), create a demand for its make and models (i.e., marketing and sales), and ensure that any problems with its products can be addressed by a network of repair shops (i.e., service).

Support Activities   Support activities represent the firm's actions that, while not directly related to the transformation process, are nevertheless necessary to enable it. These activities do not define the organization's unique transformation process, which is to say that they are typically performed by a wide

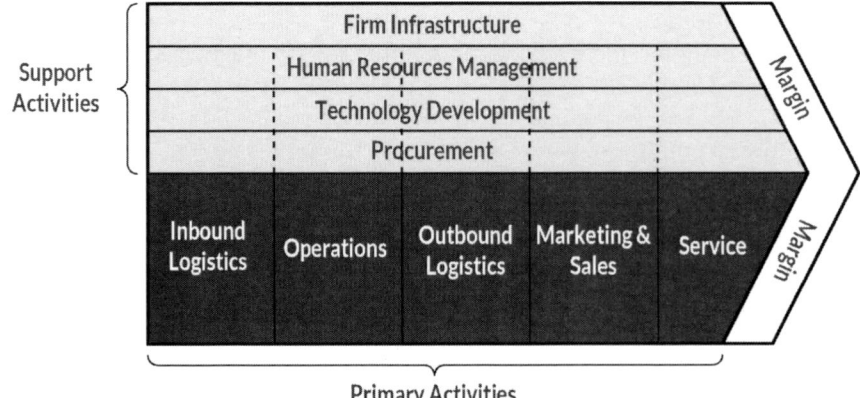

FIGURE 8.8. Value chain framework

---

6. Porter, M. E. (1985), *Competitive advantage: Creating and sustaining superior performance*, New York, NY: Free Press.

range of firms offering diverse products and services. The classic value chain identifies four support activities: firm infrastructure, HR management, technology development, and procurement.

Take HR management, for example. Any firm that relies on labor resources, from car manufacturers to hospitals, must be able to recruit, train, evaluate, pay, promote, fire, and generally manage the labor force. Yes, these activities do not directly impact the product (e.g., the car traveling down the assembly line). However, no firm without an HR function would be in business for long!

As we discussed in Chapter 7, competitive advantage stems from the ability of the firm to transform input resources into a product or service that is both valuable and unique—thereby having created added value. Thus in order to have a competitive advantage, the firm must perform a different set of activities than competitors, or it must perform the same set of activities but in a different (and value-adding) manner. Information systems and IT have a long tradition of enabling such unique transformation processes.

Value Chain Analysis and the Role of Information Systems   Using the value chain to identify opportunities to deploy IT-dependent strategic initiatives requires managers to identify, understand, and analyze the activities the firm performs so that they can be enhanced or transformed using IS resources. This approach is grounded in the assumption that a firm's value chain has both physical and information processing components and that information is a critical enabler of the firm's activities. Thus the search for the strategic deployment of IT should focus on the role that information technology can play in evolving and enhancing current activities.

An example is offered by an IBM commercial. A malicious-looking character is seen walking the aisles of a supermarket stuffing various goods into the pockets of his trench coat under the suspicious eye of a security guard. As he walks out of the store, apparently without paying, he is called to by the guard, who, after some suspense-inducing delay, says, "Sir! You forgot your receipt."

This is an example of how the grocery store checkout process may change in the future using radio frequency identification (RFID) chips embedded in everyday goods. If this vision comes to bear, grocery stores will no longer have checkout lines. Instead we will simply walk out the door after making our selections and our bank account or credit card will be charged with the full amount of our purchases. In this case, the checkout process is radically transformed, leading to substantial efficiency improvements and creating the potential for new initiatives (e.g., tracking household purchases over time).

The Value Network   Another insight that emerged from the introduction of value chain analysis is that a firm has relationships both upstream and downstream. In other words, the firm's own value chain exists in a larger value network that comprises the firm's suppliers upstream and the firm's customers downstream (Figure 8.9). The points of contact between these separate value chains are called linkages, and they offer significant opportunities for the deployment of IT-dependent strategic initiatives.

For example, the inbound logistics activities of your firm can be thought of as an extension of the outbound logistics activities of your suppliers. Recognizing these linkages enables firms to create partnerships and develop interorganizational systems that may benefit all parties involved. Continuous replenishments, the initiative pioneered by Walmart and Procter & Gamble and described in Chapter 7, is a classic example.

The notion of value network has evolved significantly since its introduction. In fact, since the advent of the Internet, a lot of research has explored the role of IT-enabled partnerships and ecosystems. While we could think of the value network as a set of bilateral technology-enabled relationships between industrial firms, an ecosystem is a web, an integrated network of interacting organizations,

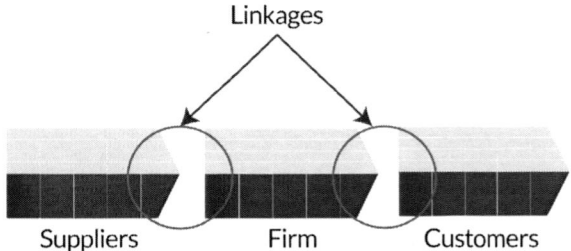

FIGURE 8.9. Linkages in the value network

products, services, and individuals. Internet-enabled ecosystems and the redefinition of industry boundaries are described in Chapter 5.

A Word of Caution   Managerial frameworks are designed to map and simplify the complexity of real organizations in order to enable a disciplined analysis of complicated phenomena. In the case of the value chain model, the objective is to help you as a manager identify opportunities to change the transformation process your organization engages in and thus uncover ways to create new value. It is therefore critical to recognize that a general framework, like the value chain, often needs to be adapted to the specific realities of your firm.

For example, the original model portrayed in Figure 8.8 is clearly best suited to represent the realities of manufacturing companies where raw materials and component parts are transformed into final products that need to be marketed, sold, and later serviced. Service businesses (e.g., consulting and law firms, banks, entertainment venues, laundry services, restaurants) work very differently, and while they also have to complete primary and secondary activities, the activities they perform and the sequence of events can be very different. Figure 8.10, for example, portrays the value chain model mapping the sequence of primary activities as they occur in a hotel or resort.

It is imperative that when using the value chain, or any other managerial framework, you do not simply apply it "as is" but, using your in-depth knowledge of the specific firm you are analyzing, adapt the model to your needs. After all, as supplier of managerial talent, this is what you are paid to do!

Customer Service Life Cycle[7]

The customer service life cycle (CSLC) was originally introduced as a tool to spur managerial thinking about the potential of advanced information technology under the label of customer resource life cycle.[8] While the CSLC framework has a time-honored tradition, its fundamental premise that a firm can use information systems to create value by offering superior customer service has received new impetus with the commercialization of the Internet and the introduction of the web as a viable business tool. As more and more organizations have been able to establish direct relationships with customers (see Chapter 5), the potential for new value creation through superior customer service has increased.

The CSLC breaks down the firm-customer relationship into 13 stages, grouped into four primary phases; for each one, it shows how you can craft IT-dependent strategic initiatives to respond to customers' needs and create economic value.

FIGURE 8.10. Sample value chain of a lodging outfit

7. Portions of this section are adapted from Piccoli, G., Spalding, B. R., & Ives, B. (2001), The customer service life cycle: A framework for Internet use in support of customer service, *Cornell Hotel and Restaurant Administration Quarterly, 42*(3), 38–45.

8. Ives, B., & Learmonth, G. P. (1984, December), The information system as a competitive weapon, *Communications of the ACM, 27*(12), 1193–1201.

Four Phases The CSLC framework suggests that managers step into their customers' shoes and think about the needs and problems that customers experience at each of four major phases in their relationship with the firm: requirements, acquisition, ownership, and retirement (Figure 8.11).

During the requirements phase, the customer realizes the need for a specific product or service and begins to focus on its attributes. During the acquisition phase, the customer orders, pays for, and takes possession of the product or service. The next major phase is ownership; here the customer has the product or is receiving the service and must deal with issues regarding its efficient and effective use. The final phase is retirement, in which the customer may begin to think about repurchasing, trading in, or dismissing old products.

FIGURE 8.11. The customer service life cycle (CSLC)

Thirteen Stages Each of the four main phases is then further broken out into subphases, or stages (Table 8.1). These 13 stages represent typical needs that customers encounter when obtaining, using, and retiring a firm's product or service. The primary objective of the CSLC is to help management identify stages where their organization's customers are frustrated or underserved and where the interaction can be improved through the use of the Internet or the deployment of IT-dependent strategic initiatives. As a creative planning framework, the CSLC is designed to stretch your thinking and help you view your business with a fresh perspective.

Table 8.1. Customer service life cycle (CSLC) stages

Requirements	
Establish requirements	Establish a need for the product or service.
Specify	Determine the product or service attributes.

Acquisition	
Select source	Determine where to obtain the product or service.
Order	Order the product or service from a supplier.
Authorize and pay for	Transfer funds or extend credit.
Acquire	Take possession of the product or receive service.
Evaluate and accept	Ensure that the product or service meets specifications.

Ownership	
Integrate	Add to an existing inventory or integrate with existing internal business processes.
Monitor	Control access and use of the product or service.
Upgrade	Upgrade the product or service if conditions change.
Maintain	Repair the product as necessary.

Retirement	
Transfer or dispose	Move, return, or dispose of product or service.
Account for	Monitor expenses related to the product or service.

Note that the life cycle model covers the entire range of activities a customer goes through in identifying, acquiring, using, and owning a product or service. However, it is typically a subset of these 13 stages that present particular challenges for the firm's customers—and therefore particular opportunity. Moreover, the stages that have the potential to yield the highest payoff will vary by customer segment, product, and over time.

Consider a firm that has recently developed an innovative new product. In this case, the very first stage, establish requirements, may be ripe for innovation. When Priceline.com introduced its innovative bidding model for purchasing airline tickets, hotel rooms, and other products, it encountered problems in educating both consumers and operators about its benefits. McDonald's faced a similar hurdle when they introduced their touchscreen ordering kiosks. Extra employees were hired to educate guests showing them how the kiosk operated. On the other hand, for a mature product competing in a fiercely competitive industry, the real potential may lie in managers' ability to differentiate their product and services by identifying unresolved customer problems—such as the need to effectively account for the total cost of ownership or use of the product or service.

Stage 1: Requirement   In the first stage of the CSLC, the customer identifies a need for the firm's product or service. In many cases, at this point in the life cycle the customer may not even be aware of the emerging desire or may have a limited idea about what possible products or services he or she needs. The ability to reach and communicate with a customer at this stage may enable the firm to gain his patronage.

Home pages for eCommerce websites are designed to support customers' requirements definition. Content, layout, graphics are all conceived to help customers identify the product or service. For example, Netflix homepage[9] is designed to help users find and discover content they would enjoy watching. By using recommendation algorithms, Netflix personalizes the ranking of the entire catalog based on users' unique set of interests, and then adjusts the page layout based on navigation patterns and current devices, placing and selecting relevant content in positions that are most likely to be seen.

Stage 2: Specify   Once customers have established the need for a new product or service, they must specify the characteristics of that product or service in order to know which particular one to acquire. In the specification stage, customers select the product features that best suit their needs.

A nice example is offered by Nike, the sports apparel manufacturer, which allows prospective customers to customize many of the features of its sneakers through the NIKEiD initiative. Using the Internet to interact with customers in the specification stage is, of course, something that is now fairly common. Today consumers can purchase made-to-order personal computers, consumer electronics, and even clothes online.

Another example of providing superior service in the specify stage is offered by Homewood Suites, the extended stay brand of the Hilton Hotels family. Homewood Suites pioneered a program that enabled customers who booked online to see a complete floor plan of the hotel in order to allow them to choose the specific room they wanted: near or far from elevators or vending machines, facing east (so as to be awoken with the rising sun) or west (to sip a drink while watching the sunset). These features later became integral parts of HHonors members' smartphone app, which enabled guests to select and customize rooms, use their smartphones as a room key, and both check in and check out.

Stage 3: Select a Source   The Internet provides a new source for finding desired products, which can significantly reduce vendors' distribution costs. The emergence of the Internet and mobile commerce has created significant opportunity for new intermediaries in a wide range of industries to create value by focusing on this stage. Consider RedLaser, which evolved from a bar code scanner app into a features rich comparison engine. Users can scan items and retrieve information and tips about buying products

---

9. Alvino, C., & Basilico, J. (2015, April 9). Learning a Personalized Homepage. Retrieved from http://techblog.netflix.com/2015/04/learning-personalized-homepage.html

and then enable customers to rapidly compare local and online retailers. Through the app, users could conveniently retrieve product reviews, information on deals, and discount codes of the chosen product.

Stage 4: Ordering   After selecting a source for their product or service, customers must order it. As with all other stages of the CSLC, the primary objective of the firm is to make it as easy as possible for clients to do business with it. This is often easy to do for returning customers, as certain elements of their second and subsequent orders typically are repeated from the first.

Wyndham Hotels and Resorts uses a dedicated application and the Internet to allow customers enrolled in its frequent guest program, Wyndham ByRequest, to configure rooms to their liking. Guests can select whether they want upper or lower floors, whether they want to be near or far from the elevator, and even what kind of pillows they would like and what drinks or snacks they prefer to receive as welcome tokens. This customer service design has a number of potential far-reaching advantages and risks, yet it also helps ensure that Wyndham differentiates itself at the ordering stage of the CSLC. If Wyndham can deliver the room as configured by customers, they are more likely to be satisfied.

Stage 5: Authorize and Pay For   Once customers have placed an order, they need to authorize and issue payment. Convenience and security are the determinants of customer service and satisfaction at this stage. Most firms that accept online orders enable clients to store payment method, shipping location, and preferences details for quick and easy future reordering. With the emergence of the mobile platform as a viable business instrument, many organizations are enabling payment through cell phone to simplify their customers' lives.

Stage 6: Acquire   At this stage, the customer takes possession of the product or begins to use the service. Some perishable or sensitive products may not be able to be shipped, while some information-based products or services may be delivered online directly. Information-based products are far more widespread than most of us realize. They include financial, medical, legal, and accounting services as well as airline tickets, reservations, music, education, books, software, magazines, games, films, and so on—a very sizable, and growing, percentage of the economy.

One of the most familiar products that have dramatically changed the traditional acquisition stage is the digital song. Consider Napster, for example. After its early days as an outlaw, Napster now offers a legal service enabling subscribers to gain access to its catalogue of digital songs. The "song acquisition process," once confined to complete albums on physical CDs available for purchase in stores, is now available in streaming, for both individual tunes or full albums on a subscription basis from the comfort of your home.

Stage 7: Evaluate and Accept   After customers have acquired their new product or service, they may test it out to verify that it works as expected. This is particularly true for businesses purchasing equipment, but it is also the case for consumers purchasing big ticket items, such as cars. When a very innovative product or service is introduced, customers need to be extensively educated about its features and how to maximize the benefits of its use. This is particularly important for products and services that require the customer to undergo a certain degree of process change.

Although the evaluate-and-accept process historically has taken place after purchase, we increasingly see firms in service- and information-based industries letting customers "try out" products prior to purchase. Examples include virtual tours, sample consulting reports, and demo software.

Stage 8: Integrate   Once the product or service is acquired and accepted for use, the customer must add it to his or her existing inventory of resources. Often customers must also adjust their internal business processes to take full advantage of the new product or service.

FedEx offers Ship Manager, a web-based tool for the creation and editing of FedEx labels. Using Ship Manager, customers can develop an address book of frequent shipment receivers, seamlessly create and print package labels, and automatically price the shipment. Through Ship Manager, FedEx devised an IT-based solution to the challenge that customers face when they integrate the FedEx service with their existing operations.

Stage 9: Monitor Use and Behavior   Customers must ensure that resources remain in an acceptable state of operation while they are in use or during the time they receive service. Using the Internet, suppliers can provide customers with the facilities to simplify this monitoring stage. By reducing clients' effort in monitoring usage of the product or service, the provider may be able to command a higher price or simply create a tight bond that customers may find difficult or costly to forego.

Otis Elevators mastered this stage long ago. During the 1980s, Otis introduced self-monitoring equipment that reduced unavailability, service calls, and overall maintenance costs. The new version of this service, called eService, is now web based and allows customers to monitor their elevator system through a web browser and place service calls as needed, 24 hours a day. Another example is offered by Facebook, as it is used by businesses when creating their pages on the dominant social network. Facebook page users have access to Page Insights, a monitoring tool that enables them to assess how well they are engaging their customers and fans online (Figure 8.12).

Stage 10: Upgrade   When customers are using the product or service, it may become necessary to modify or improve it so that it will better fit their unique needs. As competition has heated up in the airline industry under continued pressure from low-cost carriers, the legacy airlines have attempted to differentiate service for their best customers. Many of them now offer preferential seating (e.g., in exit rows) and automatic upgrades to their best customers, who can request upgrades and receive confirmation online (Figure 8.13).

Stage 11: Maintain   Helping the customer analyze, diagnose, and repair the product or service, or suggesting solutions to problems as they occur, affords the firm many opportunities to take what would be a source of dissatisfaction and offer outstanding service.

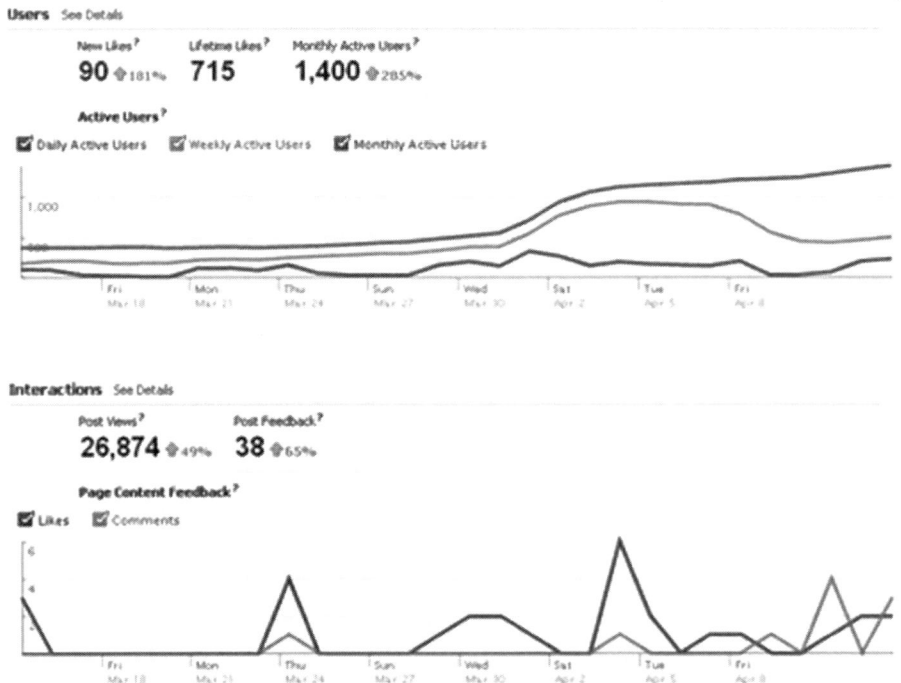

FIGURE 8.12. Facebook Page Insights

The software industry has led the way in this area. Nowadays, upgrading apps is a seamless process, as our iPhones and iPads simply tell us that there is a new version available and we tap the screen to get it. But this process has a time-honored tradition. Like most other programs, Microsoft Windows, the software program we all love to hate and the favorite target of hackers and virus authors, has a facility that will automatically identify, download, and install security patches and bug fixes (Figure 8.14).

Stage 12: Transfer or Dispose   Customers will eventually transfer, resell, return, or dispose of the product or service. As this sometimes happens after a considerable amount of time, the original supplier may not be involved. In some instances, this step may be complicated by regulation and restrictions (e.g., with regard to disposal of old computer equipment).

Some organizations have made support of this process a staple of their offering, recognizing that a customer problem, the need to dispose of an item no longer needed, may be the start of another customer service life cycle. Dell is a firm that realized this very early on with its business clients. With its

FIGURE 8.13. Seat selection online

FIGURE 8.14. Patch management dialog box

Dell asset recovery service, the company will pick up, within two days and at the client's site, any end-of-life machine, format its hard disk to eliminate all the customer's data, and dispose of it according to current legal requirements. At the end of the process, Dell sends a statement to the client detailing what was done and certifying that the equipment was disposed of correctly. Another great example of this strategy is offered by manufacturers of networked printers and copiers that can automatically reorder toner and ink cartridges when they are running out. Customers don't have to worry about the reordering process, while manufacturers ensure themselves a steady stream of consumable sales.

Stage 13: Account For   The final stage of the life cycle focuses on evaluation and accounting of the experience. This stage is particularly important, for example, for large corporations that are constantly attempting to better measure, manage, and control their travel and entertainment (T&E) budgets. Given the complexity and magnitude of this process, an organization may willingly limit its portfolio of T&E suppliers in exchange for the ability to precisely monitor and control total spending while enforcing company policies.

Large travel agents, such as American Express, have long recognized this fact, and have developed web-based products designed to offer tools for accounting and control of travel expenses to their large customers. Armed with these tools, the organization achieves better control of its travel budget while being able to use a larger pool of providers.

Organizations achieve competitive advantage through their ability to envision and implement value-adding strategic initiatives. The most innovative ideas are often not the most costly or resource intensive but simply those based on the best understanding of how customer needs can effectively be satisfied. The CSLC provides you with a basis for evaluating a firm's relationship with customers, benchmarking against competitors, and uncovering opportunities to use the Internet and advanced IT to improve customer willingness to pay through outstanding customer service.

Traditional Models, Not "Old" Models

The analytical frameworks discussed above have been in use for many years and have helped spawn numerous business innovation and IT-dependent strategic initiatives. They continue to accurately represent the way in which many companies organize their work and therefore offer significant insight to those seeking to apply increasingly powerful and evolving IT in the never-ending quest for competitive advantage. Note that the value chain and CSLC are somewhat complementary. The value chain mostly focuses internally while the CSLC draws attention to the relationship between the firm and its customers.

Emerging Frameworks

The strategic role that information systems and IT can play in the modern organization was acknowledged more than 30 years ago. However, recent trends have provided new impetus for the search for IT-dependent strategic initiatives. Perhaps the most important event was the commercialization of the Internet in 1993, an event that took the global network of computers from an unknown tool used by scientists and the military to business organizations. The Internet took the world by storm, and today most of us, both consumers and businesses, could not imagine working (and living?) without it.

Parallel to this upsurge of global networking was the continuance of trends we discussed in Chapter 1—the declining cost/performance ratio of computing equipment, the declining cost of storage, and the consequent widespread adoption of computing in consumer and business life. More recently, in the Web 2.0 phenomenon (Chapter 5), mobile platforms (Chapter 12) have continued to rejuvenate and strengthen the potential of information systems to contribute to business success.

Zara, the world largest fashion retailer, is one of the recent most successful users of IT for strategic advantage. The firm outpaced competitors by quickly adapting to changing demand conditions. The firm designed a flexible production and logistic system heavily reliant on IT. The firm is capable of adapting their collections in real time based on information about customers' tastes gathered from their 6,000 stores located in 88 countries. In recent past, Zara has introduced RFID technology to streamline logistic and point-of-sale operations, directly tackling stock visibility and replenishment. As Pablo Isla, chairman and chief executive officer (CEO) of Inditex SA, said, "It gives us great visibility, knowing exactly where each garment is located. [. . .] It really changes how we operate our stores."[10] Inventory of parts in a manufacturing company are typically held to reduce uncertainty of demand and inbound logistics. Clearly this insurance against uncertainty comes at a cost—the cost of capital tied up, as well as the cost of write-offs for obsolete inventory. A firm that is able to gather and use superior information, and thereby reduce uncertainty, can limit its inventory stocks and run a leaner operation. This is all the more important in computer manufacturing, where technological innovation is rapid and the value of inventoried parts drops significantly when a new, more powerful component is developed (e.g., new generation microchips). Dell significantly reduced uncertainty by turning the production process on its head and gathering demand before building, rather than manufacturing computers that it then sold through a distribution channel.

Affordable, powerful, interconnected computers and cheap storage have created the backdrop for a number of new ways to create economic value with information systems. Traditional models were characterized by a view of information as a support resource to the production and transformation processes that the firm engages in. Thus the search for value creation with IT-dependent strategic initiatives focused on using IT to affect physical activities. Recently developed frameworks, however, recognize that the data that modern organizations generate through their day-to-day operations may have significant value in their own right. These frameworks therefore are designed to help managers identify opportunities to harness information for value creation.

Virtual Value Chain

The virtual value chain (VVC) model[11] maps out the set of sequential activities that enable a firm to transform data in input into some output information that, once distributed to the appropriate user, has higher value than the original data (Figure 8.13). The virtual value chain builds on the generally understood value chain model. In a value chain, through a series of logically sequential activities, raw materials are transformed into products or services that the firm then distributes to customers (Figure 8.15). The process is a value-adding one, such that the products or services being distributed have a higher value (and command higher customer willingness to pay) than the inbound materials and services.

The critical insight underpinning the VVC is that information is no longer just a support resource for physical activities, those described by the physical value chain model,[12] but can itself be treated as an input of a productive transformation process. In the physical value chain, information is treated as a support element, designed to enable the physical activities of the value chain. The virtual value chain model uses the same logic but recognizes information as the entity being transformed (the value of which is being enhanced) through the chain of activities. When fed through the activities of the

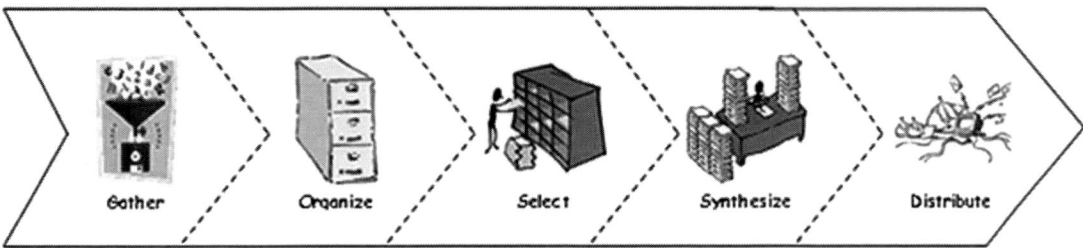

FIGURE 8.15. Virtual value chain framework

---

10. Bjork, C. (2015), Zara parent lifted by weak euro, *Wall Street Journal*, retrieved June 16, 2015, from http://www.wsj.com/articles/zara-parent-lifted-by-weak-euro-1433914365

11. Rayport, J., & Sviokla, J. (1995, November–December), Exploiting the virtual value chain, *Harvard Business Review, 73*, 75–85.

12. In this section, to avoid confusion, we use the term *physical value chain* to refer to the traditional value chain model.

virtual value chain, organizational data can be transformed into valuable insights, new processes, or new products or services.

Five Activities   The proponents of the virtual value chain identify five sequential activities that must be complete in order to harness its power:

1. *Gather*. In the first activity, the firm collects information from transaction processing systems and any other sources—both internal to the organization (e.g., orders received) and external (e.g., census data).
2. *Organize*. In the second activity, the firm stores the gathered data in a way that makes later retrieval and analysis simple and effective.
3. *Select*. In the third activity, users identify and extract the needed data from the data repository created in the previous step.
4. *Synthesize*. In the fourth activity, the firm packages the selected information so that it can be readily used by the intended consumer for the specific purpose to which it is directed (i.e., decision making, sales).
5. *Distribute*. In the fifth activity, the firm transfers the packaged information to its intended user or customer.

Three Classes of Strategic Initiatives   The proponents of the virtual value chain offer three classes of strategic initiatives that firms typically create once they adopt virtual value chain thinking: visibility, mirroring capabilities, and new customer relationships. These three classes of activities are in increasing order of complexity and uncertainty of results, with visibility being the most intuitively appealing and easy to justify financially and new customer relationships being the toughest to sell to senior management. Note that the five value-adding activities of the virtual value chain are performed with each one. What changes is the level of complexity and departure from the traditional way of doing business of the organization.

Visibility   The first application of the virtual value chain is termed *visibility*. In this case, the firm uses the sequential activities in the virtual value chain to "see through" organizational processes that it was previously treating as a black box.

An enduring example of visibility is offered by online retailers. Because their customers' behavior is computer mediated as the consumers shop and purchase online, online retailers collect significant amounts of individual and aggregate data. These data include what web pages a customer views, which web pages seem to go unused, what path through the site customers are taking as they shop, whether and where they abandon the transaction, how customers react to advertising and banners, and so on. In other words, customers' shopping and purchasing processes are significantly visible to online retailers, a degree of accuracy and detail that was unprecedented in brick-and-mortar stores. A similar example is offered by the not-for-profit educational site Khanacademy.org. Through Khan Academy, students of all ages and classes can watch more than 6,000 explanatory videos on a wide range of academic subjects. They can then practice the skills they have learned using engaging online test banks. As students practice and progress in their understanding, the computer records their behaviors. All kinds of metrics, from what exercises they complete and how fast, to what questions they have difficulty with and what topics they master, are recorded. The results are available to teachers (or coaches, as they are called in Khan Academy) to review (Figure 8.16). Armed with this superior visibility in their pupil's learning progression, coaches can take precise corrective action to help their students master the material.

The power of visibility strategies is not only available to pure-play eCommerce firms and web-based not-for-profits. It is available to any organization that digitizes some aspect of its operations. For example, using microcameras embedded in store mannequins and shop windows, physical retailers in the fashion industry are today attempting to replicate the level of visibility available online by tracking the flow of customers coming into the store and relating their purchases to various metrics such as the time spent in front of a display or a window.

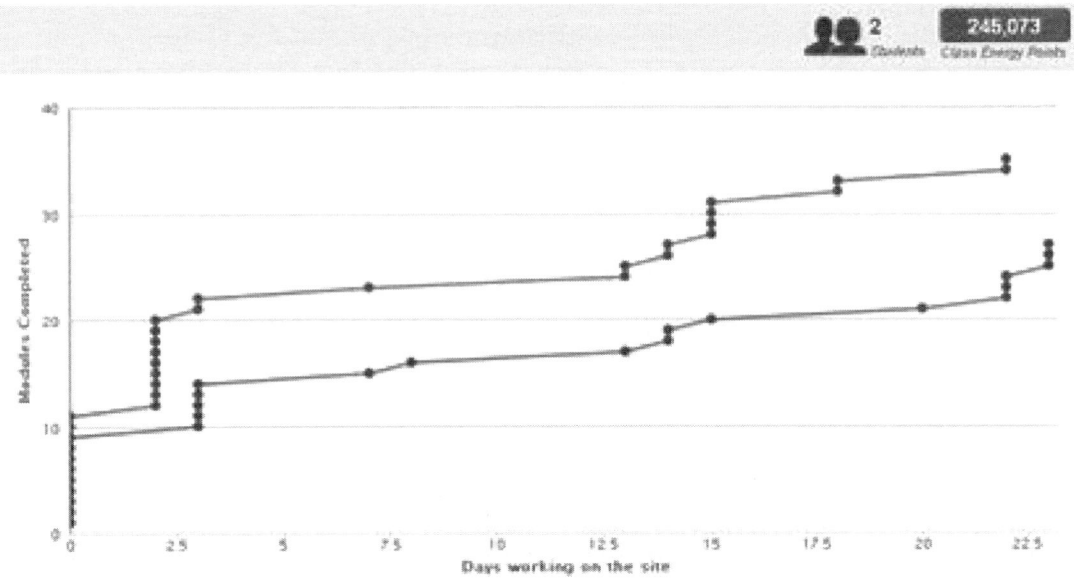

FIGURE 8.16. Sample progression through mathematics modules in Khan Academy

As more and more devices become "intelligent" via embedded microchips and software, the firms that use them have more opportunities to harness the power of visibility. Imagine a firm that manages vending machines, which are increasingly computerized and network connected. What decisions could you make if the vending machines where able to maintain real-time communication with a central server about sales and inventory level? How much more efficient could your firm be with this information? What new strategic initiatives would you implement with this infrastructure in place? In one example of innovative thinking, Coca-Cola rolled out the Freestyle drink dispenser, an RFID-enabled vending machine that draws ingredients from 30 flavor cartridges and is able to mix over 100 different drinks (Figure 8.17). While we may debate whether any of these drinks are actually worth drinking, here lies Coca-Cola's strategy. The Freestyle machine is connected to central servers through the cellular phone network. By letting people mix and match their drinks and keeping track of which drinks are being consumed and when, the firm is betting on being able to perform extremely precise taste tests that will aid new product development and real-time business analytics. Moreover, Coca-Cola leases the machines to fast food outlets, enabling them to access real-time drink consumption data in their outlets, all the while providing greater variety to those soft-drink-crazed individuals who have to have 100 different flavors!

Mirroring Capabilities   A further application of the virtual value chain, termed *mirroring capabilities*, consists of shifting some of the economic activities previously completed in the physical value chain to the information-defined world of the virtual value chain. That is, some of the activities that were previously physical in nature (i.e., completed by employees) become completely information based.

FIGURE 8.17. Coca-Cola's Freestyle drink dispenser
Source: Coca-Cola press kit

Examples of mirroring capability are pervasive in firms that need to perform much testing and simulation. For example, a recent trend among drug manufacturers is to test the effect of new drugs using computer models rather than real patients, thereby drastically speeding up trials and reducing the cost of new drug development. Another example that may be particularly dear to your heart, as busy students, is offered by electronic library reserves. In the old days, your instructor would place some materials on reserve in the library so that you could check them out for a short period of time and study them. Due to copyright restrictions, only a few copies of the material could be placed on reserve. As you painfully know, the day before the exam, the early bird gets the worm, and if you were late, you would be unable to consult the readings. Electronic reserves solve this problem (Figure 8.18). Because material that is digitally uploaded is not tied up when checked out (information goods are not consumed by use; see Chapter 4), all those who want to consult it can and can do so any time they like, day or night, from the comfort of their own room.

Another great example of mirroring capabilities is offered by training in *Second Life*, a virtual reality massive multiplayer computer game. Many organizations, from hospitals, to police departments, to the military, are creating virtual learning environments in *Second Life* where they can leverage the immersive reality characteristics of *Second Life* and create situations that would be extremely expensive and time consuming to design in real life (Figure 8.19). Imagine staging a terrorist attack or a blackout in the emergency room to train crisis response skills! In fact, the traditional approach to this type of training is classroom cases—a technique that pales in comparison to the virtual world in terms of realism and skill acquisition potential.

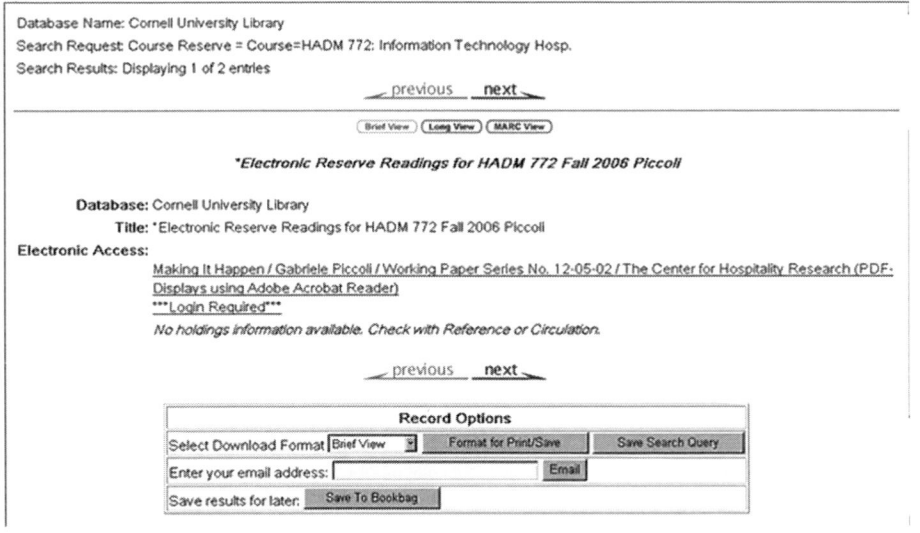

FIGURE 8.18. A library's eReserve application

FIGURE 8.19. A simulated emergency room in *Second Life*

Note that mirroring capabilities are beneficial when transferring the activity to an information-based platform if they enable the firm to perform the activity more efficiently and effectively. They are also beneficial when the activity can be transformed with significant performance improvements. For this reason, a mirroring capability approach is different from a mere automation of the existing activity using computers. To fully grasp this concept, think about the Ergo Bike Premium 8i from Germany's Daum Electronics. The Premium 8i looks like a regular, albeit high-tech, stationary bicycle. However, it allows you to race other bicycle enthusiasts across the world in some of the greatest bicycle race segments on the globe (e.g., Hawaii's Ironman Triathlon). The bike simulates the terrain, giving you the sensory feeling of being there. It allows you to monitor your heart rate and other statistics as well, while talking to your racing partners over headsets. Imagine climbing the Alp d'Huez along with your friends, following in the footsteps (or bike tracks) of the great racers in the history of the Tour de France—Gino Bartali, Fausto Coppi, Eddy Merckx, Greg LeMond, Miguel Indurain. Perhaps then, a better term for this strategy would be digitizing capabilities rather than mirroring capabilities.[13]

New Digital Value   The above two types of strategies, visibility and mirroring capabilities, are mainly concerned with internal operations and the creation of value within the confines of the organization. The third stage, new digital value, is instead concerned with the organization's relationship with the customer and the firm's ability to increase customers' willingness to pay, using the information generated through the virtual value chain to create new value in the form of new information-enabled products or services.

Consider a classic example of this strategy: personalization through suggestive selling initiatives. Using your individual purchase history, as well as a technique known as *collaborative filtering* that compares your purchases to those of others with similar interests, online retailers are able to propose items that may be of interest to you in an effort to increase their sales. This approach, pioneered in retail, is now common in many industries. Current examples come from the music service Spotify and the video streaming service Netflix, which developed a proprietary recommendation engine based on customers' visual preferences further refined through the shopping behavior.

Value Matrix   When introduced to the virtual value chain and the potential for value creation through the use of organizational data, it is natural to gravitate to this way of thinking. However, it is important to remember that most organizations today need to pay significant attention to the traditional environment and their established operations. For as relevant as the potential to create value through information is, much of the opportunity for value creation remains in the firm's physical transformation processes. Thus combining the traditional (physical) value chain and the virtual value chain offers a cohesive framework, termed the *value matrix*, that general and functional managers can use to seek and exploit opportunities for the deployment of IT-dependent strategic initiatives in their organizations (Figure 8.20).

By being mindful of the five steps of the virtual value chain as they apply to data generated throughout the physical value chain, managers can uncover opportunities for new value creation and appropriation. The caveat expressed before about analytical frameworks holds here as well, and you need to map the value matrix that most accurately represents your firm's individual context (see, for example, Figure 8.21).

Value Creation with Customer Data

A class of initiatives for value creation that the proponents of the virtual value chain model have identified is new digital value. The objective of these types of initiatives is to use customer data and information to do something of value for them—thereby increasing their customer willingness to pay. To do so requires significant analysis and an understanding of the firm's characteristics and value proposition.

---

13. We do maintain the original terminology in the framework to keep consistency with the original authors.

FIGURE 8.20. Value matrix

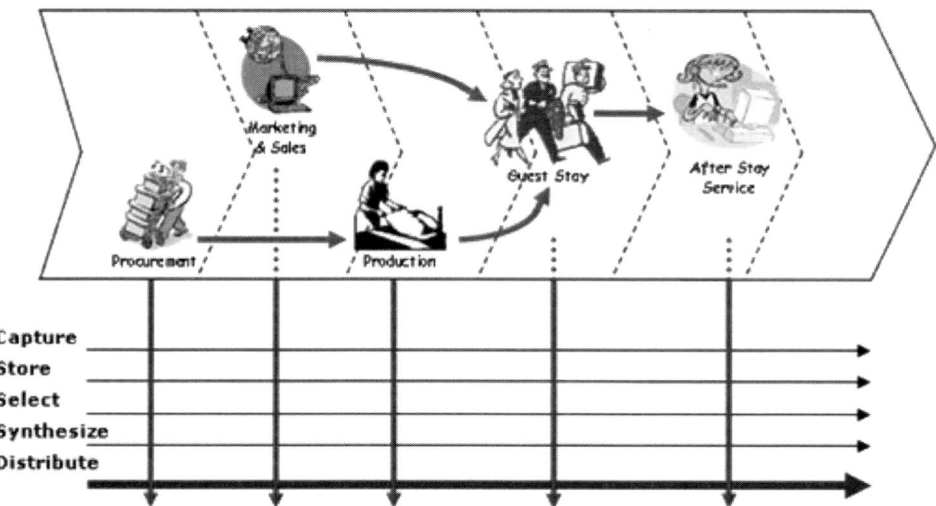

FIGURE 8.21. Sample value matrix for lodging

Analysis of the Value Proposition   Business firms specialize in the production and sale of a specific set of goods and services—the firm's value proposition. The characteristics of these products and services are, barring changes in product mix or significant innovation, fixed. For example, large resorts such as the Hilton Waikoloa Village on the Big Island of Hawaii, or the Atlantis Paradise Island in the Bahamas, offer customers a vacation experience characterized by length of time, amenities offered in the resort, and excursions; a car manufacturer offers customers personal transportation vehicles with different characteristics of size, performance, safety rating, and so on. As you join a specific firm, in a specific industry, it is within the constraints of its unique value proposition that you may be called on to craft a customer data strategy.

Imagine, for example, that you join the workforce at one of these large resorts. As you do, you hear from the large consulting firms that personalization and customization are all the rage and that "customers are demanding it"—you must "go personal!" Their argument is that, since you can collect so much data about your customers' habits and preferences, you can create extensive profiles of your returning customers.[14] Once you know that Joe Resort likes Corona beer, you can have a few chilled

---

14. Resorts use room key cards (Figure 8.31) to (obviously) let customers into their respective rooms, but most importantly, they are used like a debit card to pay for any one of the hundreds of on-premise services. Since the introduction of these cards, resorts have had the ability to unobtrusively collect large amounts of individual-level behavioral and preference data.

bottles waiting for him in his room. He had a long trip all the way to Hawaii, it's hot outside, and he is tired, but as soon as he checks in, he can unwind with his favorite drink. He'd love you for that surprise and wonder how you did it. He will never want to spend his vacation in another resort! This is at least what you are told. Is it true? How do you know if a personalization strategy is the best way to use customer data?

Repurchase and Customizability: The Dimensions of Decision Making   An analysis of your firm's value proposition and characteristics of customer behavior in your industry helps identify initiatives that fit within the context and those that don't. Specifically valuable is information about the theoretical repurchase frequency in the industry and the degree of customizability of the product or service being offered.

Theoretical Repurchase Frequency   The dimension of theoretical repurchase frequency represents the regularity with which the average customer acquires goods and services offered by the firms in the industry or segment of interest (e.g., how often people visit the Hilton Waikoloa Village in their lifetime). Note that this measure is concerned with the potential for high repurchase frequency, not with the actual repurchase rates any one individual firm is experiencing—hence the use of the term *theoretical repurchase frequency*. A firm that has very few returning customers in an industry characterized by high theoretical repurchase frequency is either doing a poor job or missing an opportunity.

Imagine going to a McDonald's in your neighborhood and finding it dirty and painfully slow in service. If this state of affairs is not quickly rectified, you most likely will not return to the same store. However, you will not stop patronizing fast food restaurants—you'll just shift your demand to a store that does an acceptable job. The key point here is that theoretical repurchase frequency is a function of the industry the firm is in and the characteristics of the value proposition it offers. It is not a characteristic of any one individual firm's current performance.

Car manufacturing and real estate are typical examples of industries characterized by relatively low theoretical repurchase frequency. Perhaps the ultimate low repurchase frequency is the "master of business administration (MBA) product"—once you have obtained one MBA, no matter how satisfied you were with the experience, you have no need for another. Coffee shops and grocery stores are at the other side of the spectrum and enjoy high theoretical repurchase frequency.

Degree of Customizability   The degree of customizability represents the extent to which the product or service your firm offers can be tailored to the specific needs and requirements of individual customers or a segment of the customer base. This dimension is a function of the complexity of the product or service itself.

Gasoline, as with most commodities, is an example of a product with a very low degree of customizability. Airline service and vending machine operations also belong in this category. At the other end of the degree of customizability spectrum are large resorts and destination spas. The Grand Wailea Resort Hotel and Spa, on the Hawaiian island of Maui, is a perfect example: along with top-notch accommodations in paradise, the Grand Wailea offers high-end shopping at the Grand Wailea Shops, seven dining options, a world-class spa with hundreds of services, a golf course, a tennis club and fitness center, a number of pools, beach services, excursions, and events, all immersed in a setting characterized by beautiful scenery and art work.

Cruise lines, meeting and conference planning, and home building represent other examples of industries selling products and services characterized by a relatively high degree of customizability.

General Customer Data Strategies   Based on the specific theoretical repurchase frequency of an organization and the degree of customizability of the product and services it offers, we can identify four general customer data strategies (Figure 8.22). Note, however, that these strategies are not a prescription or

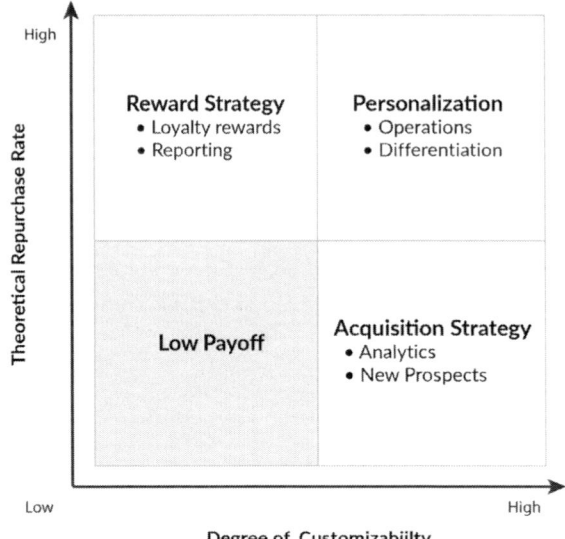

FIGURE 8.22. Customer data strategies

a silver bullet solution. Like any analytical framework, the matrix presented is a thinking tool designed to help you analyze the potential offered by an organization's operations.

The matrix does offer insight as to what strategies are likely to fit best with the characteristics of a given industry and a firm's value proposition. This does not mean that other strategies will not work but simply that they will encounter obstacles and may be difficult to implement—something that as a general or functional manager responsible for their success you'd rather know up front.

While the firm you are analyzing may or may not fit neatly in one quadrant, the matrix will help you evaluate the advantages and disadvantages of each general strategy and, more important, the natural fit of each of the four approaches to your firm's characteristics and value proposition.

Personalization Strategy   A typical service personalization or product customization strategy is most appropriate for firms competing in industries characterized by both a high theoretical repurchase frequency and a high degree of customizability. Under these conditions, the potential is there to collect significant individual-level data because of the repeated interactions the firm has with its returning customers. Moreover, the high degree of customization affords management many opportunities to use this information to tailor the product or service to the specific needs—learned or inferred—of the returning customers. Thus the firm can use the information to modify its operations and differentiate its product or services.

Event planning may be a good example of an industry that fits in this quadrant—particularly those firms that work closely with customers who need the organization of many recurrent events (e.g., large investment banks). Another example may be large IT vendors (e.g., Apple, Intel, or Oracle corporation) catering to business customers with complex business and IT requirements.

Rewards Strategy   A rewards strategy is predicated on the notion that the firm's product and service will be purchased frequently. Yet these same products are fairly standardized, and it is difficult for the organization's managers to tailor them to specific customer requests. Under these circumstances, the firm can use customer data to evaluate the profitability of each customer—actual and potential—and use this information to reward behavior in an effort to increase customer loyalty or boost share-of-wallet (i.e., make sure that customers consolidate their purchase behavior in the industry by sourcing from the firm rather than its competitors).

The firm can also use the individual level data collected to generate accurate reports and improve its operations (e.g., grocery stores performing basket analyses). Note that this means understanding customer profitability as well as customers' propensity to repurchase without incentive—a strategy much more complex and sophisticated than the "buy nine coffee cups and receive the tenth one free" that many firms seem to settle for. The airline industry represents a classic example for this quadrant.

Acquisition Strategy   Even in the face of low theoretical repurchase frequency, a firm in an industry with a high degree of customization may benefit from an acquisition strategy. Following this approach, the firm collects exhaustive data about its current customers in an effort to profile them and develop predictive models to identify and attract new profitable customers while avoiding unprofitable or marginal ones.

A good example of an industry that falls in this quadrant is the wedding reception business—an industry offering highly customizable products but typically enjoying low repurchase frequency.

Another example may be the Grand Wailea Resort Hotel and Spa profiled earlier. Given the significant cost of a vacation in Hawaii, and even more so in a luxury resort such as the Grand Wailea, theoretical repurchase frequency for such a product may be very low. Yet given the complexity of the product and the high degree of customizability it offers to talented managers, an acquisition strategy may work well in this case.

No Potential   When a firm is in an industry characterized by low theoretical repurchase frequency and relatively low degree of customizability, there seems to be little potential for crafting a strategy around customer data. This is because very little data will likely be generated and managers' hands are tied with respect to what they can do with it. A chain of budget or limited service tourist hotels in an exclusive fly-in destination (e.g., Hawaii, Fiji) offers an apt example. Midscale hotels in these locations, such as the Ohana brand of Outrigger Hotels and Resorts (Chapter 6) are generally a "window on an experience" rather than the experience itself, and their value proposition is to offer guests an affordable opportunity to experience a great location. Because of the time commitment and cost of reaching these destinations, repurchase is relatively infrequent. Thus there is little opportunity to enact any of the three strategies discussed above. Under these conditions, the firm may be better off focusing on efficiency and low prices and avoiding the cost of collection, management, and analysis of customer data.

Applying the Model   Let's return to the scenario we used earlier: your job at the Hilton Waikoloa Village. When analyzed through the lens of the general customer data strategies matrix, it becomes clear that a personalization strategy, while intuitively appealing, is probably not optimal. A product like the Hilton Waikoloa Village is characterized by relatively low repurchase frequency—for as affordable and mainstream as travel has become, a week in a large resort remains a fairly expensive vacation option, and the cycle of repurchase is relatively long (e.g., a honeymoon in Hawaii followed by a 5- or 10-year anniversary trip).

How likely is your company to be able to profit from the (considerable) investment in a full-blown personalization strategy? Would it not be better to focus on an acquisition strategy designed to attract profitable first-time resort-goers based on what the firm learns from analyzing and clustering the profiles of its past guests?

Acquiring the Needed Data: The Third Dimension   The strategic initiatives described above are predicated on the firm's ability to capture the needed customer data in a format and a manner that make them amenable to the needed analysis. As with theoretical repurchase frequency and degree of customizability, the immediacy with which customer data can be captured and used varies by industry and context.

The expanded model acknowledges that different industries, because of the general norms about how business is conducted within them, offer a different potential for data capture. In other words, the degree to which data collection can be done easily can vary dramatically by industry and is an important early consideration. Let's examine a simple example. When purchasing hospital services (something that we typically prefer not to do!), we don't think twice about providing our social security number and intimate details about our personal life. In fact, if the doctor came in, looked at us, and said, "Take these pills twice a day; they'll fix you up," we would be outraged. Given the nature of hospital services, it is part of the natural course of good business to be asked many (personal) questions about our medical history, our family history, allergies, and symptoms before receiving a diagnosis.

Compare the hospital experience with the pop-ups asking for user feedback, the "get paid for your opinions!" e-mails that clog our inboxes, the guest satisfaction surveys we rarely fill out in hotels, or the dreaded 20-minute dinnertime phone call on behalf of a company we recently transacted with asking us to rate their service. We largely consider them all to be a disruption and a waste of our time. Of course, the firm would be quite happy to gather the information in a different manner, but for many of these companies, it is just not natural for customers to provide lots of information during the interaction. There is an emerging model to measure customer satisfaction that could save us from this annoyance. Firms like Sprinklr capture and aggregate online mentions and reviews to construct a comprehensive picture of customer satisfaction based on comments of actual customers. But as the ringing phone at dinner reminds us every so often, this new, less intrusive approach has yet to become mainstream.

In summary, it is customer expectations as to what the encounter with the firm should be like—the norms within the industry—that determine what options the firm has when collecting data. While it is acceptable and accepted for a hospital to ask us for our social security number, as it is for a bank or an insurance company, we would be startled if the coffee shop, restaurant, or grocery store in our neighborhood did so.

These simple examples show that some firms are highly constrained when it comes to gathering customer data and may have no better way to obtain it than to pay a representative sample of customers to take the time to respond to surveys. Others have more data than they can ever hope to use. We refer to this as the degree of unobtrusive data capture. Despite being a mouthful, this is a largely intuitive concept that indicates the extent to which, in the normal course of business, customer data are collected and stored in a readily usable format (see Figure 8.23).

An early analysis of practices in your industry can be illuminating. Imagine, for example, a fine dining restaurant. Fine dining is an industry with relatively high repurchase frequency and a relatively high degree of customizability of the experience. A personalization strategy is highly suitable for such

FIGURE 8.23. Data capture constraints

an establishment, yet much of the data needed to carry it out are generated in fleeting customer-server exchanges that are difficult to capture and codify for easy storage and retrieval. Add to this mix the high employee turnover typical of the food service industry, and it becomes clear why, for as much patronage as we give to our favorite restaurants, we generally don't receive a commensurate degree of personal service.

Compare the difficulty a restaurant has with collecting and storing its customer data in a readily usable format to the relative simplicity of the same task at an online retailer. Granted, the potential depth of the relationship is lower, but the ease with which online shops can collect, store, and process the data you provide is much greater—enabling them to provide a more personalized experience than your favorite restaurant!

The degree of unobtrusive data capture for a firm is largely given at any point in time. However, technology improvements and innovation may pay off here if you are willing to shoulder the cost of changing people's habits. For example, while much of the information about customers' gambling behavior in casinos was traditionally left to busy and fallible casino hosts and pit bosses, the advent of electronic slot machines ushered in a new era. Casino executives realized that a modern slot machine is in essence a digital computer and that a computer records all the transactions it performs with great speed and accuracy. Tying these transactions to individual customers once they were convinced to use magnetic strip cards was a relatively small step. Today the natural course of business in the casino industry is such that a company can have an accurate, real-time picture of each of its customers' slot-playing behavior. With the declining price point of RFID tags, this same level of precision and are increasingly integrated to table playing as well, not just slots.

Crafting Data-Driven Strategic Initiatives

Given the wealth of information available to the modern business, it can be extremely confusing to decide where to start looking for opportunities. The amount of data and information generated by the IT infrastructure of modern organizations often overwhelms those who look for opportunities. As a result, general and functional managers often face frustration when they attempt to extract value out of the business data locked into their computer systems. "All this software comes with great reporting capabilities, but who has time to look at them?" they often lament.

In this section, we present a methodology that can be used to identify opportunities to create value with organizational data and then select the ones that hold the greatest potential for value creation and appropriation:

1. Identify relevant transaction processing systems (TPSs).
2. Inventory data currently available in these systems.
3. Conceptualize initiatives that use the available data.
4. Prioritize among the selected initiatives.

Identify Relevant TPS This first step is designed to allow you to narrow the scope of the analysis and focus on the systems that are most likely to hold relevant data—given your functional area and scope of responsibility. For example, a hotel revenue manager is mainly focused on decisions pertaining to room pricing and stay restrictions. While this narrowing of the scope may not be necessary in smaller operations, like a small independent retail store, it is crucial in larger outfits where functional areas must be clearly defined. At this stage, the primary objective is to focus attention on the computer systems that hold data relevant to the area you are focusing on—typically a relatively small set of software programs.

Inventory the Data Currently Available Once the relevant TPS have been identified and listed, you can inventory the data that are currently readily available in them. A first step in this phase may be to gain access to the system and explore its reporting functionalities. The key here is to focus not so much on the analyses that the reports yield but instead to identify the underlying data that are tracked by the application in the natural course of business.

When you are not very familiar with the application, this step may be best accomplished by meeting with power users—those individuals who have intimate familiarity with the software, its capabilities, and the data it stores. This is often the best alternative because power users in your area will speak the same language and will be intimately familiar with the opportunities and challenges that you are likely to focus on. Alternatively, particularly in larger organizations, a meeting with the IT professionals who support the software may be necessary. The outcome of this phase should be a comprehensive list of data items that are reliably tracked within each TPS.

Conceptualize Initiatives   Having laid out all the available data currently being tracked by your TPS, you can simply ask yourself, "Given what I have, what would I like to know?" For this phase, very little formal guidance can be offered; there is no substitute here for creativity and insight.

As you examine the data you have inventoried, some ideas and potentially beneficial analyses will emerge. This is a crucial part of the brainstorming stage, and you should focus at this point on generating ideas without worrying much about their feasibility or financial viability.

Prioritize Initiatives   Once you have articulated a number of potential initiatives, it's time to evaluate their actual feasibility. At this stage, you should make a series of pragmatic decisions regarding the order in which the suggested initiatives should be implemented. This is because justifying data-driven initiatives to acquire the necessary funding is a very difficult task. Financial justification measures, typically requested by executives, are ill suited to the task. Initiatives that are based on data analysis are qualitatively different from automation initiatives, where return on investment (ROI) is much easier to compute. As a consequence, the reputation of the initiative's champion, and the trust executives put in his or her judgment, is of paramount importance. How do you establish such a reputation in the domain of business data initiatives?

The prioritization matrix described in Figure 8.24 may help. It is based on the evaluation of two dimensions: upside potential and data availability.

Upside Potential   The first dimension provides an assessment of the financial benefits associated with the initiative in terms of revenue lift or cost reduction. The extent to which data analysis initiatives have upside potential typically depends on the following:

FIGURE 8.24. Initiative prioritization matrix

- *Time sensitivity.* The degree to which the impact of the decisions that the analysis of the data allows depends on how closely to the time of data collection the analysis is made.
- *Impact immediacy.* This is the degree to which the information is directly usable after it is generated, as opposed to needing aggregation or manipulation.
- *Aggregation requirements.* This is the extent to which the benefits of the analysis are dependent on substantial aggregation of multiple data sources.
- *Trending requirements.* This is the extent to which the benefits of the analysis are dependent on substantial trending of data over time.

Data Availability   The second dimension provides an assessment of the immediacy with which the initiative can be implemented and a measure of the costs associated with it—the higher the availability of the needed data, the cheaper and more immediate the initiative's successful implementation. The following are critical dimensions of data availability:

- *Accuracy.* This is the extent to which the available information is reliable, without duplication, inaccuracies, or outdated elements.
- *Comprehensiveness.* This is the extent to which the data needed to carry out the initiative are complete and free of missing elements and/or values.

Note that this dimension becomes crucial when resources are limited and/or executives are not easily sold on the potential of data as a strategic resource. Developing initiatives around high-availability data enables the firm to establish a track record of project success.

When the initiatives identified earlier are mapped to each of the four quadrants, it becomes apparent which ones can be quickly implemented, maybe as proof of concept or to gain support from other executives. It will also become clear what initiatives are resource intensive and require a much higher level of organizational commitment.

Imperatives   In this quadrant, classified as imperatives, fall projects that have significant upside potential and rely on readily available information. These initiatives can be implemented quickly and with limited investment of resources beyond sunk costs. Consider, for example, a grocery store that has been using checkout scanners for quite some time. With a relatively small investment, the store could compile checkout data and, after comparing it to current inventory levels, provide the store manager with an exception report flagging items that are running dangerously low. While the incremental investment is minimal, the potential upside of this initiative, reducing costly stockouts, can be significant.

Quick Wins   In this quadrant fall projects that, while not having much upside potential, can be readily implemented based on immediately available information. These initiatives are labeled quick wins because they do not require significant resources and a demanding approval cycle. In the absence of clear imperatives, these initiatives can often be used as proof of concept to gain momentum and to establish a track record of successful implementation designed to build credibility with other executives. The credit so built can then be put to use when making the case for harder-to-sell trade-off initiatives. Consider a firm running an online store that uses banner ads on referring sites. Further, imagine that your firm receives a limited amount of traffic and business from these referrals. Using currently available data and log analyzer software, the various referral sites can be evaluated, enabling a ranking with respect to the volume of traffic and business each one provides. If customers referred by one website consistently leave the online store after a few seconds, there is a mismatch between your offer and the referring website's audience. This type of analysis can be very valuable in contract negotiations, even though, given the limited amount of traffic coming from referrals in this example, upside potential is limited.

Trade-offs   In this quadrant fall projects that have significant upside potential but rely on information that is not readily available and consequently tends to be quite costly. This may be because the information is not easy to capture, it is not in a readily usable format, or the initiative requires the pooling of substantial information from multiple sources and substantial data integration. These initiatives are called trade-offs, as they require substantial cost benefit analysis and a rigorous approval cycle before the allocation of the needed resources can be justified. Consider, for example, customer preferences elicited through the waiter-guest interaction at a restaurant. While such data can be very valuable for improving customer service and eliciting loyalty, the data are hard to capture and stored in a manner that makes them easily usable for analysis.

Losing Causes   In this quadrant fall projects that are deemed to have little upside potential and that rely on information that is not readily available. Initiatives that fall into this category should not be implemented unless the cost associated with making the needed data available can be justified and assigned to other projects with positive ROI. In other words, these initiatives should be shelved until a change in circumstances moves them to another, more attractive quadrant.

Conclusions

In this chapter, we continued our discussion of strategic information systems, initiated in Chapter 7 with foundation concepts. Crafting successful IT-dependent strategic initiatives is part art, requiring creativity and insight, and part science, requiring disciplined analysis and attention to detail. The primary goal of this chapter was to support both the creative and analytical aspects of this process by introducing you to traditional and recent frameworks for value creation with information systems and IT. Each of them offers a different focus and a different perspective, which, collectively, should provide you with a comprehensive toolset. Using these frameworks requires an analytical mind-set, lots of discipline, and a good dose of creativity. There is no substitute for experience and practice here. For this reason, this chapter is full of short cases and examples that we hope will help you put the analytical models into a practical context.

Summary

In this chapter, we focused on information technology (IT)-dependent strategic initiatives, discussing the frameworks and analytical models that have been proposed over the years to help you identify opportunities to create value with IT and to design and develop value-adding IT-dependent strategic initiatives.

Specifically, we introduced the following frameworks:

- Industry analysis, focusing on the characteristics of the industry your firm competes in, seeks to help you identify opportunities to deploy information systems to improve the profitability of the industry.
- Value chain analysis focuses on the firm's own unique transformation process. It seeks to spur your thinking about how information systems and technology can be used to introduce new activities and/or change the way the firm's activities are currently performed.
- The customer service life cycle (CSLC) suggests that there is ample opportunity to create value by using information systems and technology to enhance the relationship with customers and enable superior customer service. The CSLC identifies four major phases and 13 stages in which the relationship between the firm and its customer can be mapped. Each one offers opportunities for value creation.
- The virtual value chain recognizes the importance of the wealth of information available to today's organizations in the search for value creation. It identifies five sequential activities that a firm can use to transform raw data input into information outputs that have more value than

the inputs. Using this approach, a firm can develop one of three classes of strategic initiatives: visibility, mirroring capability, and new digital value.

- Customer data can also offer the potential to create value with different strategies best fitting different organizations depending on two dimensions: the theoretical repurchase frequency of the firm's product or service and its degree of customizability. Depending on where the firm finds its offer falling on these two dimensions, it will find a personalization, rewards, or attraction strategy to fit best. The viability of the chosen strategy depends also on the degree of difficulty the firm encounters in collecting and using the needed customer data.

- Once the firm identifies a potentially value-adding strategy, it must ensure that it can appropriate the value created over time. In other words, the firm that has created competitive advantage by way of an IT-dependent strategic initiative must ensure that the advantage is sustainable; this is the topic of the next chapter.

Study Questions

1. Describe the focus and principal objectives of industry analysis applied to information systems. Select one of the five competitive forces, and offer an example of a firm that you believe has been able to influence it by way of an IT-dependent strategic initiative.
2. Describe the focus and principal objectives of value chain analysis applied to information systems. Why is it important to contextualize the value chain? Provide an example of a firm you think has been able to create competitive advantage using information systems. Identify the primary activities most impacted by information systems in this firm.
3. Describe the customer service life cycle (CSLC) and its primary objectives. Provide an example of a firm that, in your opinion, has created competitive advantage using information systems to enable superior customer service. What stages of the CSLC are mostly impacted by the firm's IT-dependent strategic initiative?
4. Describe the basic tenets of the virtual value chain. How does it differ from the physical value chain? Can you identify an example for each of the three applications of the virtual value chain?
5. Think about your last job, or the job you'd like to have once you graduate. Where would you place this firm's product or service on the dimensions of theoretical repurchase frequency and degree of customizability? How difficult is it for the firm to collect and use customer data? Is the firm engaging in a customer data strategy? If not, is it missing the boat?

Further Readings

1. Ives, B., & Learmonth, G. P. (1984). The information system as a competitive weapon. *Communications of the ACM, 27*(12), 1193–1201.
2. Piccoli, G. (2005). The business value of customer data: Prioritizing decisions. *Cutter Benchmark Review, 5*(10), 5–16.
3. Piccoli, G., Spalding, B. R., & Ives, B. (2001). The customer service life cycle: A framework for Internet use in support of customer service. *Cornell Hotel and Restaurant Administration Quarterly, 42*(3), 38–45.
4. Porter, M. E. (1980). *Competitive strategy: Techniques for analyzing industries and competitors.* New York, NY: Free Press.
5. Porter, M. E. (1985). *Competitive advantage: Creating and sustaining superior performance.* New York, NY: Free Press.
6. Porter, M. E. (2001, March). Strategy and the Internet. *Harvard Business Review, 79*, 62–78
7. Porter, M. E., and Heppelmann, J. E. (2014, November). How smart, connected products are transforming competition. *Harvard Business Review, 92*, 11–64.
8. Porter, M. E., and Millar, V. E. (1985, July–August). How information gives you competitive advantage. *Harvard Business Review, 63*(4), 149–158.
9. Rayport, J., & Sviokla, J. (1995, November–December). Exploiting the virtual value chain. *Harvard Business Review, 73*, 75–85.

Glossary

- **Acquisition strategy:** A customer data strategy most appropriate for firms competing in industries characterized by a low theoretical repurchase frequency and a high degree of customizability.

- **Customer service life cycle:** A framework designed to draw managers' attention to the potential for value creation offered by the relationship between the firm and its customers.

- **Degree of customizability:** The extent to which the product or service offered by a firm can be tailored to the specific needs and requirements of individual customers or a segment of the customer base.

- **Degree of unobtrusive data capture:** The extent to which, in the normal course of business, customer data can be collected and stored in a readily usable format by a firm.

- **Industry analysis:** A framework that identifies the five forces shaping the profitability potential of an industry.

- **IT-dependent strategic initiatives:** Identifiable competitive moves and projects that enable the creation of added value and that rely heavily on the use of information technology to be successfully implemented (i.e., they cannot feasibly be enacted without investments in IT).

- **Linkages:** The points of contact between the separate value chains of the firms in a value network.

- **Mirroring capabilities:** An application of the virtual value chain that enables the firm to perform some economic activities previously completed in the physical value chain in the information-defined world.

- **New digital value:** An application of the virtual value chain that enables the firm to increase customers' willingness to pay for new information-enabled products or services.

- **Personalization strategy:** A customer data strategy most appropriate for firms competing in industries characterized by both a high theoretical repurchase frequency and a high degree of customizability.

- **Reward strategy:** A customer data strategy most appropriate for firms competing in industries characterized by a high theoretical repurchase frequency and a low degree of customizability.

- **Theoretical repurchase frequency:** The regularity with which the average customer acquires goods and services offered by the firms within the industry or segment of interest.

- **Value chain:** A framework that maps a firm's transformation process as a set of sequential value-adding activities.

- **Value matrix:** A framework combining the physical value chain and virtual value chain models.

- **Virtual value chain:** A framework that uses the basic value chain structure to draw attention to data as a valuable input resource in the transformation process.

- **Visibility:** An application of the virtual value chain that enables the firm to "see through" organizational processes that it was previously treating as a black box.

CHAPTER 9

Appropriating IT-Enabled Value over Time

What You Will Learn in This Chapter

General and functional managers have historically had a love-hate relationship with information technology (IT). They recognize its potential to help the firm compete, but they often lack the tools to make sound decisions about its use. The plethora of pundits who comment on the strategic potential, or lack thereof, of information systems and IT only add to the confusion. In this chapter, we provide a set of concepts and an analytical framework that will help you establish whether a given IT-dependent strategic initiative can be defended against competitors' retaliation. In other words, we will explore under what circumstances a competitive advantage rooted in an IT-dependent strategic initiative is sustainable.

Specifically, this chapter will

1. Analyze the potential of IT-dependent strategic initiatives to ensure value appropriation over time.
2. Help you recognize the flaws in the arguments of those who suggest that information technology has lost its potential to enable sustained competitive advantage.
3. Teach you to recognize the four barriers to erosion that protect IT-dependent competitive advantage and to estimate their size.
4. Identify the response lag drivers associated with each of the four barriers to erosion and to provide examples of each.
5. Explain how each of the four barriers can be strengthened over time in order to protract the useful life of an IT-dependent strategic initiative.
6. Show you how to use the concepts and frameworks described in this chapter in the context of future IT-dependent strategic initiatives when your firm takes a leadership position.
7. Teach you how to use the concepts and frameworks described in this chapter in situations where your firm may be evaluating whether to retaliate against a competitor who pioneered an IT-dependent strategic initiative.
8. Identify the possible courses of action a firm should take based on analysis and allow you to recommend when the firm should or should not pursue a given IT-dependent strategic initiative.

MINICASE: Smartwatch Ordering at Domino's: Should You Follow Suit?

In early 2015, five years after graduating, your information systems consulting business is thriving. At 6:45 a.m., when you power up your computer to check e-mail and start the day, you see a late-night message from Gregg Yves, the vice president of marketing and customer service initiatives at Regional Chain of Pizza Shops (RCPS), headquartered in Bristol, England. He is an old friend you met through your university alumni network when you were in school and with whom you have kept in touch. Why would he be e-mailing so late? As you read his message, it becomes clear:

> Do you remember when we discussed the Domino's smartwatch ordering initiative?[1] At the time, we were focused on rolling out in-store ordering kiosks in our restaurants and did not pay much attention. It took us some time, but we later caught up. Now they pushed it further

again. Domino's just introduced a new smartwatch app.

I've been thinking about this all night. Should we follow suit as well? Do we need to move rapidly? I'd rather take a wait-and-see approach here, but I'm afraid that if we miss the boat on this initiative, the repercussions could be significant.

You're an expert on this strategic information systems stuff; can you give me your insight and direct my thinking a bit?

Discussion Questions

1. Do you believe that the Domino's smartwatch ordering initiative is sustainable?
2. What are the pros and cons of the wait-and-see approach that Gregg prefers?
3. What is your recommendation? What should RCPS do next?

Introduction

As we discussed in Chapter 7, when it comes to using information systems (IS) and information technology (IT), the primary objective of the modern general and functional manager is to use them to create added value. However, creating added value is just one facet of the job; the firm must be able to appropriate the value created over time to truly benefit. In other words, any *competitive advantage* the firm has created with the implementation of its IT-dependent strategic initiative must be defended over time to ensure that the firm will be able to reap the benefits of its innovation. Failing to do so will quickly lead to a situation where competitors match the leader and customers rather than the innovator end up appropriating the value created.

Can a firm really protect an advantage based on the innovative use of information systems and IT? Can IT-dependent strategic initiatives deliver *sustained* competitive advantage? These seemingly simple questions engender much debate and continue to stir up controversy—they have for over two decades now! On the one side are the skeptics who claim that as the very success of IT continues (i.e., technology becomes cheaper, easier to use, and more pervasive than ever before), its strategic value declines.

Most information systems researchers and professionals, who are on the other side of the debate, disagree. Such disagreement is based on the findings of more than 40 years of information systems research, which has demonstrated that not all information technology is created equal or behaves the same—particularly when used strategically.

Not All IT Is Created Equal

The examples described below show how two different IT-dependent strategic initiatives, based on two different technologies at their core, can produce opposite results when it comes to creating and appropriating economic value.

---

1. See the minicase in Chapter 8 for a description of the Domino's Smartwatch ordering initiative.

High-Speed Internet Access in Hotel Rooms

During the dot-com days of the late 1990s, as the number of Internet users was increasing at a staggering rate, a host of organizations—ranging from airport operators, to coffee shops, to malls—began offering high-speed Internet access (HSIA) and wireless connectivity to their customers. Lodging operators also followed this trend, offering in-room HSIA capabilities in their hotels. Soon HSIA became one of the hottest technologies to come to the lodging industry in a while. Companies offered HSIA as a paid amenity, with $9.95 for unlimited daily use being the most popular pricing option.

While take rates (i.e., guests' actual usage) were much lower than expected, HSIA quickly became a "must-offer" amenity, based on the assumption that business travelers, who were used to high-speed connections at home and in the office, would snub hotels that could not have them surfing in the fast lane.

The inevitable result was an increasing number of properties that offered HSIA, and quickly the amenity became free of charge. For example, in February 2001 the Sheraton Vancouver Wall Centre announced that it was offering HSIA free of charge to all guests. In the press release introducing the initiative, the HSIA vendor declared, "Offering this service as an amenity with no charge to the guest will certainly differentiate the Sheraton Vancouver Wall Centre from its competitors."[2] Any hoped-for differentiation did not last long, however, as more operators had to join the "HSIA as a free amenity" trend. Soon free HSIA moved from a property-level amenity to a brand-level, free amenity. Omni Hotels began offering HSIA system-wide to all guests starting in February 2003, and Best Western and Holiday Inn quickly followed suit, as did many other major chains (Figure 9.1).

Following the trend of countless amenities before it, HSIA was rapidly becoming just another cost of doing business in the lodging industry and a competitive necessity. HSIA is valuable indeed, and more bandwidth is always better. However, because it could not be protected from rapid imitation, all the value it created flowed to hotel guests rather than the hotel companies that introduced it.

The same dynamic played out in restaurants and coffee shops, as the experience of McDonald's and Starbucks demonstrates. McDonald's started its HSIA initiative in 2003, initially charging $4.95 for two hours. It then went to $2.95 for two hours, before finally offering unlimited free Wi-Fi in its stores starting in December 2009. Starbucks went to free Wi-Fi in September 2009 in the United Kingdom and then in all its U.S. stores starting July 1, 2010.

History is replete with examples of technology innovations whose value was "competed away" to customers. But this is not always true, as the next section demonstrates.

FIGURE 9.1. Free Wi-Fi is a standard in three-star hotels

Photo by Wesley Fryer / CC BY 2.0

Business Intelligence at Caesars Entertainment

Caesars Entertainment (Figure 9.2) has been widely celebrated for its innovative use of information systems and IT in support of its efforts to better understand its customers—a type of initiative known as business intelligence (BI) and considered a precursor of big data analytics (Chapter 3). To do so, Caesars (which at the time was known as Harrah's Entertainment)[3] had to invest heavily in IT—an investment estimated to exceed $100 million in the year 2000.

FIGURE 9.2. Harrah's Casino in Atlantic City

---

2. "Industry News," retrieved from http://www.hospitalitynet.org/news/4007069.html

3. In this chapter, we refer to Caesars Entertainment as Harrah's to preserve reference to the historical name the firm had at the time. It is interesting to note that Harrah's success enabled it to acquire Caesars Entertainment, but the firm decided to retain the latter's name after the merger.

While the expenditure may seem significant, the firm made a conscious decision to invest the money in technology rather than follow the industry trend of creating elaborate resorts that would "wow" visitors with their size and design (e.g., MGM Mirage, The Bellagio, The Venetian). Harrah's used a fraction of the money necessary for these developments, often exceeding the $1 billion mark, to create a sound technological and organizational infrastructure brand-wide.

Technology is only the beginning of this story, however. Harrah's did not simply buy a bunch of computer systems, flip on the switch, and watch the dollars roll in. Instead, the firm embarked on a large-scale reorganization, centralizing and focusing operations around the brand and away from individual property interests. As part of the reorganization, Harrah's hired a new breed of analysts, known as decision scientists. These individuals had the mind-set and the skills to gather and analyze data about gamblers' characteristics and activities. By carrying out scientific experiments, Harrah's was able to become both more efficient (i.e., spend less) and more effective (i.e., spend better) in its use of funds to attract and retain gamblers while also increasing share-of-wallet (i.e., the percentage of the gambling budget a gambler would spend with Harrah's rather than its competitors) and customer satisfaction.

The returns on Harrah's use of technology have been considerable, even in the face of a slowing economy. At the same time, the centralized IT infrastructure and the processes it has developed enable Harrah's to expand its distribution with relative ease and control. The expansion strategy that followed produced impressive results, making Harrah's the world's largest provider of casino entertainment following the acquisition in 2004 of Caesars Entertainment for $5.2 billion. Clearly, Harrah's has been able to reap significant long-term results from its IT-dependent strategic initiative. Its revenues and operating income grew to $10.8 billion and $1.7 billion, respectively, in 2007, from $3.4 billion and $283 million, respectively, in 2000.

In 2006, as a maneuver to increase shareholders' value, Harrah's underwent a buyout deal worth $30 billion. However, such acquisition put an additional $24 billion debt on the company. The economic downturn and the fierce competition coming from online and other gambling activities then took their toll. Once the 2008 slowdown hit, the company was overextended. Even though their loyalty program was still producing a higher fair share[4] of customers and spending, their superiority in analytics was not enough to save them from this big hole. Or, as Caesars' chief executive officer (CEO) Gary Loveman said, "So a guy who had $20,000 on a hand at blackjack was still there on $10,000 a hand, but that's half the revenue for me."[5]

After 15 years of proved sustained competitive advantage, the firm's attempt at financial engineering sent Caesars toward bankruptcy. On January 15, 2015, the firm's largest business unit filed for Chapter 11, sinking under the weight of its buyout debt. Interestingly, the most valuable and sought after individual asset of the company remained the collected customers' loyalty program data estimated at a $1 billion.[6]

Big Data for Orange Juice

A company you would not expect to leverage big data and analytics for their products is one that makes orange juice. Contrary to common wisdom, mass producing juices is more than just purchasing batches of fruits and building a way to squeeze them. The Coca-Cola Company developed an IT dependent strategic initiative to standardize the flavor of Minute Maid orange juice because of the several variables impacting their flavor and possibly their sales.[7]

---

4. Caesars Entertainment Corporation (2014, April 10), *SEC Filing Form 8-K*, retrieved from http://investor.caesars.com/secfiling.cfm?filingID=1193125-14-138035&CIK=858339

5. Cohan, W. D. (2015, June 5), A private equity gamble in Vegas gone wrong, *Fortune*, retrieved from http://fortune.com/2015/06/05/caesars-losing-las-vegas/

6. O'Keeffe, K. (2015, March 19), Real prize in Caesars fight: Data on players; customer loyalty program is valued at $1 billion by creditors, *Wall Street Journal Online*.

7. See Stanford, D. (2013, January 31), Coke engineers its orange juice—with an algorithm, *Bloomberg Business*, retrieved from http://www.bloomberg.com/bw/articles/2013-01-31/coke-engineers-its-orange-juice-with-an-algorithm

At the core lies the "Black Book," a model that considers the taste of the source oranges and consumer preferences and matches them with the attributes of each batch of raw juice. Several external data streams ranging from satellite imagery to regional consumer preferences are combined for advanced supply planning and for measuring the more than 600 variables employed to assess taste. The effort to standardize taste stems from consumers' preference for unprocessed—not made from concentrate—juice. As not all oranges are made equal, this IT-based strategic initiative enabled Coca-Cola to adjust mother nature's flavor caprices to a desirable market-driven taste, exactly as they do for soda drinks. Additionally, the processing of information on crop yields, weather, and cost patterns enable the company to plan ahead and instantly adapt supply chain operations and production schedules to maximize yields and optimize costs without impacting perceived taste or quality. This clear advantage is well represented by Doug Bippert, Coca-Cola's vice president of business acceleration: "If we have a hurricane or a freeze, we can quickly re-plan the business in 5 or 10 minutes just because we've mathematically modeled it."[8]

The success of the product was later confirmed. Funded in 2001 by Minute Maid, Simply Orange realized 7% volume growth in the Simply brand in fiscal 2014, far outpacing the industry's volume growth of 4%, and generated more than $1 billion in sales, becoming the number-one orange juice brand in the United States.[9]

The Need for A Priori Analysis

If nothing else, the above examples raise the question of whether managers should approach distinct IT-dependent strategic initiatives differently. Put another way, is there a way, a priori, to reduce uncertainty about whether an IT-dependent strategic initiative can lead to a sustainable advantage? In the remainder of this chapter, we introduce a framework designed to support this analysis.

Appropriating Value over Time: Sustainability Framework

The major criticism levied by skeptics against the potential for sustained competitive advantage associated with IT innovation is that technology is easily replicated by competitors, who can quickly offer the same functionalities. Put in the framework of value creation, the accusation is that IT helps companies create value that they cannot appropriate over time because competitors can easily imitate any IT innovation.

By now, however, it should be clear to the attentive reader of this book that this argument simply misses the point. Because information systems are not IT, as we established in Chapter 2, creating and appropriating value hinges on successfully deploying a defendable IT-dependent strategic initiative. It follows that the focus on the analysis of sustainability should be the IT-dependent strategic initiative, in all its facets, not just the IT core. In other words, even if the IT components used by the firm are (at least in theory) replicable by competitors, it does not follow that the firm's IT-dependent strategic initiative built on that (replicable) technology will be easily copied as well.

Sustainable Competitive Advantage

The ability of a firm to protect its competitive advantage, known as sustainability[10] of the advantage, is often thought of as a binary condition—it is either possible or impossible for competitors to erode the leader's advantage by matching the added value it creates. However, this can be a misleading approach. After all, short of very few resources, such as patents or exclusive access to raw materials, almost any-

8. Coca-Cola's juicy approach to big data (2013, July 23), *Business Intelligence*, retrieved from http://businessintelligence.com/bi-insights/coca-colas-juicy-approach-to-big-data/

9. Bouckley, B. (2014, April 16), Coke's Simply Orange escapes US orange juice squeeze, *Beverage Daily*, retrieved from http://www.beveragedaily.com/Manufacturers/Coke-s-Simply-Orange-escapes-US-orange-juice-squeeze

10. The term *sustainability* is used here in its business strategy connotation. The term has gained much currency lately to refer to environmental sustainability and "green" behaviors. The role of information systems for environmental sustainability will be discussed in Chapter 12.

thing is replicable—in theory! Thus it isn't whether the advantage is theoretically replicable that matters in practice but the difficulty that competitors face in matching the leader's offer.

Consider the example of Amazon.com, a firm that is famous for its relentless pursuit of customer service and customer satisfaction. In an effort to improve these important metrics of success, by the year 2000, Amazon had deployed nine highly automated distribution centers that were strategically located throughout the United States and a number more throughout the world. While it is true that competitors (for instance, the now defunct Buy.com) could theoretically replicate Amazon's distribution, it would be very difficult, time consuming, and expensive for them to do so.

Resource-Based View

In the last couple of decades, much of the thinking in strategic management has coalesced around the resource-based view (RBV) of the firm. Within this approach, a firm is modeled as a bundle of resources. A key contention of the RBV is that a firm's competitive advantage depends on the characteristics of the resources at its disposal, and when the firm controls resources that are valuable, rare, inimitable, and nonsubstitutable, the advantage will be difficult for competitors to overcome.

- *Valuable*. A resource is valuable when it underpins a value-adding strategy (Chapter 7). In other words, valuable resources enable the firm to offer a value proposition that either is superior to competitors' or, while equivalent, can be offered at a lower cost. For example, when Uber leverages its large network of 160,000 active drivers to perform its services, the IT-enabled "drivers" resource is valuable.
- *Rare*. A resource is rare when it is idiosyncratically distributed. In other words, it is scarce and not readily available for acquisition by competitors. Consider a firm that has developed a deep understanding of consumer electronics experience design, such as Apple Inc. While there is a vibrant market for design talent, there is no market to which competitors can go to acquire a "design capability." The same argument could not be made for office space, a resource for which (generally) there is a market with adequate supply.
- *Inimitable*. A resource is inimitable when competitors find it impossible, or difficult, to duplicate it. Returning to the example of Apple's seemingly magic touch in designing consumer electronics that have immediate appeal with a loyal customer base, competitors who seek to imitate such capability find that it is rooted in more than just the hiring and "aggregation" of talent. The difficulty of articulating how this capability comes to be and how it works in practice—a notion known as causal ambiguity in the literature—makes it difficult to replicate.
- *Nonsubstitutable*. A resource is nonsubstitutable when competitors are unable to replicate the firm's overall value proposition (e.g., an IT-dependent strategic initiative) using surrogate resources for the ones that are rare, valuable, and inimitable. In other words, if competitors can achieve the same results as the innovator using different resources, the advantage of the leader will be eroded and the inimitability of some of its resources will be rendered irrelevant. Consider the case of Wikipedia. The organization was able to produce an equivalent product to an encyclopedia by using crowd-sourced authors instead of distinguished expert in their field as one of the key resources. Experts are therefore successfully substituted by collective intelligence in this case.[11]

Response Lag

A practical way to implement the ideas of the RBV framework in the technology arena is to think about sustainability not as a binary condition but rather in terms of how much time and money it would take competitors to erode the advantage that the leading firm has been able to create with its IT-dependent

---

11. For more information, see Blanding, M. (2015, January 20), Wikipedia or Encyclopædia Britannica: Which has more bias?, *Forbes*, retrieved from http://www.forbes.com/sites/hbsworkingknowledge/2015/01/20/wikipedia-or-encyclopaedia-britannica-which-has-more-bias/

strategic initiative. The higher the "time and money" obstacles—termed here *barriers to erosion*—the more resilient the firm's advantage.

Competitive retaliation occurs in stages. Once a firm's rivals find themselves at a disadvantage, they search for the sources of the firm's competitive advantage. If they are successful in identifying those sources, the competitors must decide whether they are able and willing to respond and, if they are, what approach they should take. *Response lag*, the time it takes competitors to respond aggressively enough to erode a firm's competitive advantage, is a measure of the delay in competitive response.

The longer the time and the higher the cost of replication, the more resilient is the firm's advantage. Thus *response-lag drivers* are defined here as the characteristics of the technology, the firm, its competitors, and the value system in which the firm is embedded that combine to make replication of the IT-dependent strategic initiative difficult and costly. Response-lag drivers combine their effects to levy barriers to erosion.

Four Barriers to Erosion

Response-lag drivers can be grouped into one of the following four barriers to erosion of IT-dependent competitive advantage: (1) IT-resources barrier, (2) complementary resources barrier, (3) IT-project barrier, and (4) preemption barrier. The magnitude of each barrier to erosion is determined by the number and strength of its response-lag drivers (Figure 9.3). We briefly describe the barrier to erosion below and detail each of the response-lag drivers associated with them in the sidebars.

Barrier 1: IT Resources IT-dependent strategic initiatives rely on access to the assets and capabilities necessary to produce and use the technology at their core. Two classes of response-lag drivers contribute to the height of the IT-resources barrier; these are IT resources and IT capabilities (Figure 9.4). As an initiative becomes more reliant on preexisting IT resources and capabilities, it becomes increasingly difficult to copy. (Sidebar 9.1 lists and explains in detail all the response-lag drivers associated with this barrier.)

Consider, for example, a firm that controls some highly specific and difficult to imitate IT resources, such as Walmart Stores Inc. In earlier chapters, we described the notion of continuous replenishment, an IT-dependent strategic initiative pioneered by Walmart in conjunction with Procter & Gamble. Continuous replenishment relies on real-time or near-real-time scanner data transfer between a retailer (e.g., Walmart) and a supplier (e.g., P&G). Walmart, having access to the satellite-based network infrastructure among its stores, found this initiative easier and less costly to implement than any of its competitors. In other words, it should not surprise us that continuous replenishment was pioneered by Walmart, as it already had the network infrastructure to do so. Competitors who wanted to replicate this initiative had to first deploy the same (or a comparable) infrastructure.

Using the terminology of the sustainability framework, we can assert that the difficulty Walmart's competitors found in quickly and successfully imitating Walmart's continuous replenishment strategy was in part due to the need to first acquire a prerequisite IT asset—the

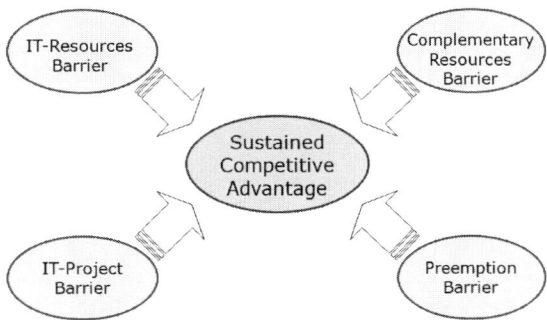

FIGURE 9.3. Four barriers to erosion of advantage

FIGURE 9.4. IT resources barrier

SIDEBAR 9.1. IT RESOURCES BARRIER

IT Assets

IT assets are technology resources available to the organization, including hardware components and platforms (e.g., a private network connecting globally distributed locations), software applications and environments (e.g., a proprietary software using custom-developed analytical models), and data repositories. These resources contribute to building response lag directly by simplifying and speeding up the development and introduction of the initiative's IT core or indirectly by making it difficult for competitors who have no ready access to the needed IT resources to replicate the leader's initiative.

IT Infrastructure

An IT infrastructure is a set of IT components that are interconnected and managed by IT specialists with the objective of providing a set of standard services to the organization. Thus the IT infrastructure provides the foundation for the delivery of business applications. With IT infrastructure-development times generally estimated to exceed five years, the response lag and ensuing barrier to imitation is likely to be substantial.

Information Repositories

Information is now widely recognized as a fundamental organizational resource, and firms are investing significantly to improve their ability to collect, store, manage, and distribute it. Information repositories are often large data stores containing extensive information about customers, suppliers, products, or operations, organized in a structured form that is accessible and useable for decision-making purposes. A firm's information repositories can contribute to the development of substantial response lag by supporting strategic initiatives. Competitors attempting to replicate the leader's strategic initiative must not only duplicate the IT at its core but must also accumulate a comparable information resource—a feat that often takes substantial time.

IT Capabilities

IT capabilities are derived from the skills and abilities of the firm's workforce. These capabilities directly influence the response lag associated with the introduction of IT at the core of IT-dependent strategic initiatives because they facilitate the technology's design and development. These capabilities also play a fundamental role in enabling effective and timely implementation, maintenance, and use of the technology.

IT Technical Skills and Business Understanding

IT technical skills relate to the ability to design and develop effective computer applications. They include proficiency in system analysis and design, software design, and programming. Another element is the depth of business understanding of IT specialists. Business understanding enables the IT specialists charged with developing the technology supporting IT-dependent strategic initiatives to envision creative and feasible technical solutions to business problems. A high level of business understanding also contributes to the creation of response lag by mitigating the risks associated with the introduction of the strategic initiative and the relative investments in technology.

IT-Management Skills

IT-management skills refer to the firm's ability to provide leadership for the IS function, manage IT projects, integrate different technical skills, evaluate technology options, select appropriate technology sources, and manage change ensuing from the introduction of IT. IT-management skills, because of their idiosyncratic and socially complex nature and the learning curve associated with their development, are a source of sustainable competitive advantage. Managerial IT skills can contribute to creating substantial response lag when techniques and routines developed over time can substantially reduce development costs and development lead times. Competitors who attempt to replicate the initiative but lack the same high level of managerial IT skills as the innovator face substantial obstacles to imitation.

Relationship Asset

The relationship asset is accumulated over time and finds its roots in a mutual respect and trusting rapport between the IS function and business managers. When a firm has developed a substantial relationship asset, IS specialists and business managers are able to work together effectively by coordinating and communicating extensively. Having developed the relationship, they share a vision for the role of IT within the business. Business partners share the risk and accept the responsibility for IT projects, and IS specialists are able to anticipate a business's IT needs and devise solutions that support these needs.

networking infrastructure enabling real-time scanner data transfer from stores. Walmart's ownership of this unique asset translated into a response-lag driver (IT infrastructure) that contributed to significantly increasing the magnitude of the IT resources barrier to erosion.

Barrier 2: Complementary Resources

While IT is by definition a fundamental component of any IT-dependent strategic initiative, successful implementation of such an initiative requires that complementary organizational resources be mobilized as well (Figure 9.5). Thus to implement an IT-dependent strategic

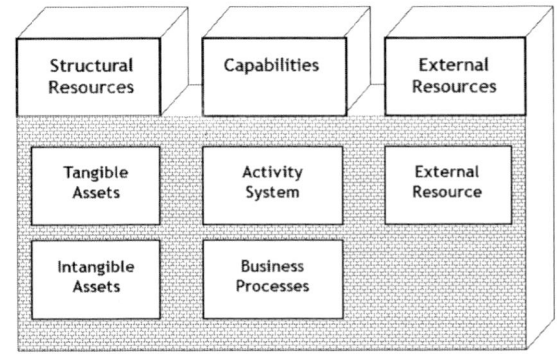

FIGURE 9.5. Complementary resources barrier

initiative, the firm must develop or acquire the necessary complementary resources (e.g., physical assets such as warehouses and distribution centers, intangible assets such as a brand).

As an initiative becomes more reliant on distinctive complementary resources, the complementary resource barrier to imitation strengthens, and replication of the strategy becomes slower, costlier, and more difficult. In this situation, competitors will have to acquire or develop not only the IT at the core of the strategy but also the complementary resources that underpin the initiative. (Sidebar 9.2 lists and explains in detail all the response-lag drivers associated with this barrier.)

Consider again the example of Harrah's Entertainment and its business intelligence initiative. While the firm spent a significant amount of money to acquire IT resources, it also engaged in a radical reorganization when launching the initiative in the late 1990s. This reorganization challenged decades of casino management practice, where each casino within a chain operated in a highly independent fashion. Through its reorganization, Harrah's asked the general managers of each property to report to divisional presidents, who in turn reported up to Harrah's chief operating officer. The firm also created transfer mechanisms and incentives to support cross-property traffic and a general sense that customers "belonged" to Harrah's corporate office, not to each individual casino that signed them up to the program. This change in organizational structure enabled the success of Harrah's brand-wide initiative.

Fast forward now to the year 2001, when Harrah's was receiving substantial praise and attention for its use of guest data and putting pressure on competitors to imitate. How well positioned were its competitors to replicate Harrah's highly centralized customer data strategy? Not very, since the typical competitor still treated each property as unique and independent, with a unique brand and little incentive to share customers and customer data with the other casinos in the chain.

Using the terminology of the sustainability framework, we can assert that Harrah's competitors are likely to find it costly and time consuming to successfully imitate Harrah's business intelligence initiative. This is because, at least in part, their organizational structure is not conducive to the strategy, and a change would be very risky, costly, and time consuming. In other words, Harrah's has access to a unique complementary resource—namely, its idiosyncratic organizational structure, which creates substantial response lag and contributes to heighten the complementary resource barrier. By 2015, this strategic initiative collected information on more than 45 million customers and was considered the most valued single asset of the company, worth $1 billion.

The analysis of complementary resources is important because during the design of the initiative, it is often possible to use IT to leverage the impact of some idiosyncratic complementary resources. Imagine managing

FIGURE 9.6. A popular conveyor belt sushi bar
Image created by Chenyun at the Wikipedia project website

an upscale conveyor-belt sushi restaurant (Figure 9.6). Your store prides itself (and justifies its premium prices) on the superior quality and freshness of its sushi.

Using radio frequency identification (RFID) tags, you can keep constant track of the amount of time each dish has been out on the conveyor belt and thereby ensure that dishes that have been rotating for more than 25 minutes are removed to maintain freshness. With this infrastructure in place, you decide

SIDEBAR 9.2. COMPLEMENTARY RESOURCES BARRIER

Structural Resources

Structural resources comprise non-IT-related tangible and intangible internal assets used by the firm in the enactment of its IT-dependent strategic initiatives.

Tangible Assets

In theory, any tangible resource available to the firm can underpin an IT-dependent strategic initiative. Among these are competitive scope, physical assets, scale of operations and market share, organizational structure, governance, and slack resources.

Intangible Assets

As in the case of tangible resources, nearly any of a firm's intangible resources can support an IT-dependent strategic initiative. Examples of commonly cited intangible resources that can be so applied include corporate culture, top management commitment, and the ability to manage risk. As with tangible IT resources, complementary intangible resources create response lag by making a strategic initiative difficult, costly, and time consuming to imitate.

Capabilities

A firm's capabilities define how the firm carries out its productive activities. These resources specify what activities are performed and what steps or business processes make up those activities. The activities that the firm performs and the manner in which it performs them contribute to response lag and help sustain the competitive advantage created by the initiative.

Activity System

A performance-maximizing activity system relies on a set of economic activities that are both interlocking and mutually reinforcing, expressly showing internal consistency (internal fit) and appropriately configured, given the firm's external environment (external fit). Although IT is one of the fundamental components of the strategy, it still must fit within the entire activity system. When a firm has implemented a given configuration of activities and has developed the IT core supporting the linked activities, replication of the technology alone is insufficient for successful imitation. Indeed, narrowly replicating just the IT core leads to further decline of the imitator's position by wasting time, money, and management attention without eroding the leader's competitive advantage. A classic example of a firm that has an idiosyncratic activity system is Southwest Airlines. Because Southwest does not cater flights, does not offer seat assignments, has a standardized fleet of aircrafts, uses less-crowded airports, and focuses on point-to-point travel for price-sensitive customers, it is relatively resistant to competitive imitation. Merely imitating one aspect of Southwest's activity system will not suffice, but attempting to duplicate the entire package generates considerable response lag.

Business Processes

We defined a business process as the series of steps that a firm performs in order to complete an economic activity. The notion of business process is related to, but distinct from, that of the economic activities discussed above. Economic activities describe the set of undertakings that the firm performs, while business processes describe the way in which the firm performs them. The contribution that business processes make to response lag and to the height of barriers to imitation depends on their distinctiveness and strategic value. When a firm is able to introduce an IT-dependent strategic initiative built around a business process with characteristics of uniqueness and differentiation, it creates a significant barrier to erosion.

External Resources

External resources are assets (such as brand, reputation, and interorganizational relationship assets) that do not reside internally with the firm but accumulate with other firms and with consumers. Generally intangible, external resources are usually developed over time.

When a firm's IT-dependent strategic initiative can make use of or contribute to the development of these external resources, response lag increases considerably and barriers to imitation are augmented. Thus the firm forces competitors to develop a comparable level of external resources before producing an effective response.

to add a display to each dish in order to show the time each dish has been rotating around. This seems like a simple addition, and technologically it is not overly complex. However, it is not simple for your lower rate competitors to replicate, as they would in fact be advertising that their sushi is not nearly as fresh as yours. The lesson is simple. By using technology to leverage an idiosyncratic complementary resource, you have made replication of your strategy much more difficult for competitors.

Barrier 3: IT Project   IT-dependent strategic initiatives rely on an essential enabling IT core. Thus they cannot be implemented until the necessary technology has been successfully introduced. The response-lag drivers of the IT project barrier are driven by the characteristics of the technology and the implementation process (Figure 9.7).

Types of information technology are not homogeneous, undifferentiated entities. To the contrary, they differ substantially with respect to their intrinsic characteristics, their ability to complement other organizational resources, the context in which they are introduced and used, and the degree of organizational change that needs to occur during the implementation process. (Sidebar 9.3 lists and explains in detail all the response-lag drivers associated with this barrier.)

Consider, for example, a website. No matter how complex they are, websites are typically relatively quickly designed and deployed, particularly compared with large infrastructure projects (e.g., data warehouses) that are complex, lengthy, and prone to failure.

Barrier 4: Preemption   You may now be wondering why we term the four forces ensuring sustainability as "barriers to erosion" rather than "barriers to imitation." We do so because in some cases, even if a competitor is able to replicate an IT-dependent strategic initiative, the response may bear no fruit for the laggard. A discussion of the preemption barrier will clarify this point (Figure 9.8).

In some cases, the IT-dependent strategic initiative pioneered by the first mover creates a preferential relationship with customers or other members of the value system and introduces substantial switching costs. Under these circumstances, it is not enough for competitors merely to imitate the leader's strategy; they need to either compensate the customer for the cost of switching or provide enough additional value to justify the customer's decision to incur the switching costs. That is, imitators must be "that much better," where "that much" is an amount greater than the current value of all co-specialized investments[12] that the customer has made. (Sidebar 9.4 lists and explains in detail all the response-lag drivers associated with this barrier.)

eBay Inc., the dominant online auction site, provides a perfect example. Aware of its success, two formidable competitors—namely,

FIGURE 9.7. IT project barrier

FIGURE 9.8. Preemption barrier

---

12. The term *co-specialized investment* simply refers to investments made in conjunction with a specific IT-dependent strategic initiative. Because these investments are specific to the initiative, they will lose part or all of their value if those who made the investment switch to a competitor (see Sidebar 9.4).

SIDEBAR 9.3. IT PROJECT BARRIER

IT Characteristics

Types of information technology differ with respect to their complexity, distinctiveness, and visibility to competitors.

IT Complexity

Different IT applications have different degrees of complexity. The complexity of the technology is a function of the bundle of skills and knowledge necessary to effectively design, develop, implement, and use it. Technology complexity raises the IT project barrier by increasing development lead times for a competitive response.

IT Uniqueness

On the low end of the IT uniqueness continuum are self-contained, off-the-shelf IT products that need little integration or customization (e.g., an electronic mail system). At the high end are custom-developed applications or infrastructure subsystems that are unavailable in the open market. When the IT underlying the innovator's strategy is not distinctive, competitors can engage consultants or service firms to aid them in reducing knowledge barriers, thereby reducing the imitation response lag. Unique IT makes this process much more difficult.

Visibility

Visibility is the extent to which competitors can observe the enabling technology. The visibility dimension can be conceptualized as a continuum spanning from custom developed internal systems, which are virtually invisible to competitors, to immediately visible interorganizational or customer-facing systems that require extensive education and selling to external users or customers (e.g., an online purchasing system). IT that is highly visible and is readily available for inspection by competitors limits the strength of the IT project barrier.

Implementation Process

Since different kinds of information technology are inherently dissimilar, the processes by which they are implemented and become available to the organization also differ. Depending on the implementation characteristics of the IT core of the strategic initiative in question, the strength of the barriers to imitation changes considerably.

Implementation-Process Complexity

Implementation-process complexity is a function of the size and scope of the project, the number of functional units involved, the complexity of user requirements, and possible political issues, among other things. IT infrastructure projects represent a powerful example of complex systems that have a substantial lead time. While the components may be commodity-like (e.g., personal computers, server, telecommunication equipment), it is difficult to integrate them in an effective system.

Degree of Process Change

Business processes often need to change to fit a new system—particularly in the case of large, highly integrated enterprise systems. The challenges escalate when several organizations or operations use the technology involved in the strategic initiative. The more departments that are involved and the more organizational boundaries that are crossed, the harder and riskier the change becomes. Yet as complexity increases, so do the difficulties encountered by competitors in imitating the strategy.

Amazon.com and Yahoo!—launched their own online auction sites. Despite having an eCommerce pedigree, brand recognition, and technical capabilities just as good as eBay's, both firms achieved lackluster results when imitating eBay's IT-dependent strategic initiative. Interestingly, a brief look at both competitors' websites would show that they were remarkably similar to eBay's own. Clearly an imitation strategy didn't pay, but why? Their results were so lackluster, in fact, that both had to close their respective auction sites, unable to viably compete with eBay (at least in the North American market).

The reason for eBay's dominance can be found in its ability to harness a dynamic that occurs in its industry—strong network effects. As you recall from Chapter 4, when strong network effects are present, the dominant player will be the one that first reaches critical mass (in this case eBay, at least in North America). At that point, both buyers and sellers face daunting switching costs, and only "wholesale

SIDEBAR 9.4. PREEMPTION BARRIER

Switching Costs

Switching costs represent the total costs borne by the parties of an exchange when one of them leaves the exchange. They include not only economic costs but also psychological and physical costs: "Switching costs are the norm, not the exception, in the information economy."[13] IT-dependent strategic initiatives, which rely heavily on the collection, storage, manipulation, and distribution of information, are particularly suited to the creation and exploitation of switching costs.

Co-specialized Tangible Investments

When an IT-dependent strategic initiative is deployed, it may require that the firm's customers acquire the physical assets necessary to participate in the initiative. The total capital outlay necessary to obtain these assets is termed *co-specialized tangible investments*. These range from computer hardware and telecommunication equipment to software applications and interfaces between the existing customers' systems and the firm's IT. For example, hotel franchisees buy costly interfaces for the franchising brands' reservation system. These interfaces become valueless if the property is rebranded. The extent to which the IT-dependent strategic initiative requires co-specialized tangible investments determines the potential for strong barriers to imitation associated with the initiative.

Co-specialized Intangible Investments

As is true of tangible investments, the deployment of an IT-dependent strategic initiative often necessitates a firm's customers or channel partners to invest time and money to take part in the initiative. An investment of this kind is known as a co-specialized intangible investment. For instance, to benefit from customer relationship management (CRM) initiatives, customers often need to take the time to complete a profile. Co-specialized intangible investments might include "setup" costs as well as ongoing costs (e.g., retraining new travel associates using a reservation system).

Data and information repositories represent perhaps the most important class of co-specialized intangible investments in the information age. Considerable switching costs can be built on information accumulated over time. An interesting example is offered by information that is valuable only as long as the customer is using the firm's products or services (e.g., revenue-management models and historical records that are brand specific and become valueless if the hotel is rebranded).[14]

The same situation occurs even when switching costs are not readily apparent. Facebook takes advantage of the privileged and long relationship with customers to reach a position of "central" platform. Switching from Facebook to any other social platform would probably signify losing contacts' information, pictures, videos, or comments. Each user invested its time and effort in Facebook uploading content, publishing and sharing status updates. Facebook profiles are the result of the continuous interaction of users on the platform. For Facebook, these data are a valuable asset for profiling users and understanding users' behaviors. For most users, the same data represent their social digital identity.

Value System's Structure

A firm does not engage in economic activity in isolation but as a link in a larger value chain or system that includes upstream and downstream members. The structure of this value system can provide opportunities for preemptive strategies and for the exploitation of the response-lag drivers discussed here. The structure of the value system does not directly affect the strength of the preemption barrier to imitation but instead magnifies or diminishes the preemptive effects of switching costs.

Relationship Exclusivity

An exclusive relationship exists when participants in the value system elect to do business with only one

---

13. Shapiro, C., & Varian, H. (1998), *Information rules: A strategic guide to the network economy*, Boston, MA: Harvard Business School Press, p. 111. Also see this book for an excellent treatment of switching costs in the information age.

14. The software here is neither proprietary nor brand specific, and the data are not acquired over a network or hosted by the brand. Yet the historic data and the models the hotel has developed assume that the hotel has a given brand (e.g., Four Seasons). If the hotel is rebranded, while the software, the data, and the models are retained, its value is much lower because the data and models are specific to the original brand and assume that the hotel sports the related flag (e.g., has access to Four Seasons' brand equity, reservation systems, and loyal customer base).

firm that provides a particular set of products or services. The firm's counterpart (i.e., customer or supplier) places a premium on dealing with either the firm or one of its competitors, but not both. Relationship exclusivity is the norm with IT-dependent initiatives that provide integration services and that benefit from the accumulation of historical information. When first introduced, the American Airlines Sabre terminal for travel agents created strong incentives for relationship exclusivity, as travel agents did not want to waste valuable office space for competitors' proprietary terminals (e.g., United's Apollo), which were considered essentially duplicates of the Sabre terminal.

When a business relationship benefits from exclusivity, the customer faces penalties for hedging behavior and for sourcing the needed product or service from multiple firms, and when competitors introduce competing offers, customers are already invested in their relationship with the incumbent.

Concentrated Value-System Link

At each of the various stages or links in the value system, the degree of concentration in the link is inversely proportional to the number of suitable business entities populating that link—where suitability depends on whether the firm would find the products or services offered by the vendors populating the link acceptable. A highly concentrated link is one where there are relatively few organizations or consumers available for the firm to use or serve. In the case of airline reservation systems, for instance, the total number of travel agents serving the market targeted by the airline sponsoring the system represents the concentrated link.

A market of given size will support only a finite number of competitors, and achieving a substantial penetration in the concentrated value-system link—by definition, a small market—is necessary to successfully preempt imitation. As the degree of concentration increases, the time necessary to secure a relationship with a substantial proportion of the link decreases—all else being equal. Consequently, the leader has a better chance of capturing a substantial proportion of relationships and being able to use switching costs to "lock out" competitors and maximize its barriers to imitation. Conversely, when a link in the value system comprises a large number of business entities, a firm is unlikely to effectively reach a critical mass of entities and raise substantial barriers to imitation in the same amount of time.

defection" of a large portion of the customer base will enable competitors to catch up to the leader—an extremely unlikely event. Being second in the online auction market is not a good place to be![15]

With the language of the sustainability framework, we can assert that eBay, by virtue of being the first company to reach a critical mass of buyers and sellers in a market with strong network effects, was able to erect an insurmountable preemption barrier to erosion.

The Holistic Approach

While the framework for evaluating the sustainability of IT-dependent strategic initiatives breaks the analysis into its component parts—barriers to erosion and response lag drivers—you should always be mindful of the fact that appropriation of value is dependent on these components working together. In other words, when thinking about value creation appropriation, you must think holistically. Attentive readers of this chapter will undoubtedly note that those who suggest that IT does not have the characteristics of rarity and inimitability—and as a consequence cannot be considered a strategic resource—have failed to think holistically.

Recent information systems research[16] corroborates this holistic approach by showing how the combination of information technology and organizational resources—termed *IT-enabled organizational resources*—displays both emergent properties and sustainability potential. In other words, the combination of IT and organizational resources creates a system that often has properties of neither

---

15. Interestingly, the eBay example shows that using proprietary IT is not a necessary condition for superior long-term performance.

16. Nevo, S., & Wade, M. R. (2010), The formation and value of IT-enabled resources: Antecedents and consequences, *MIS Quarterly, 34*(1), 163–183.

IT alone nor the organizational resources individually, but rather the system emerges from the combination (i.e., they are emergent properties). Consider the example of telemedicine. Remote surgery is the notion that a doctor can operate on a patient at a distance with the aid of local staff and robotic equipment that she controls remotely via a computer (Figure 9.9). More common today, a remote surgery system is a sociotechnical system that displays emergent properties. For it to work, you need remotely located doctors with the competencies to perform the surgery and skills in operating the telemedicine equipment. You also need local medical staff to prepare both

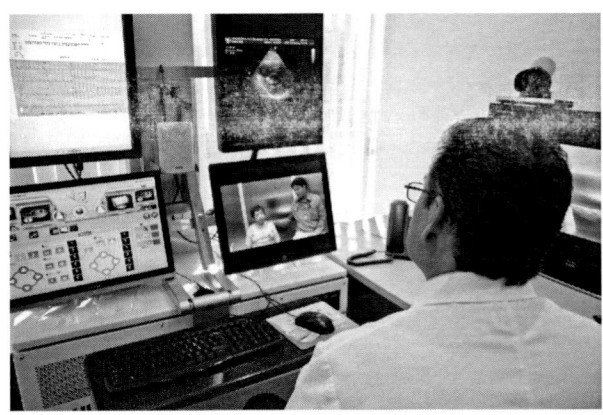

FIGURE 9.9. Telemedicine equipment
Photo by IntelFreePress / CC BY SA 2.0

the patient and the telemedicine robotic equipment. The emergent property is the ability to perform remote heart or cancer surgery,[17] a resource that neither the remote doctors nor the local equipment have independently. Only when the local technology and staff work in combination with the remote heart surgeons can the surgery successfully happen.

The telemedicine example clearly shows the value of holistic thinking. IT-enabled organizational resources have properties that neither IT nor the organization alone possess. However, you will quickly note that these IT-enabled organizational resources do have the potential to be valuable, rare, inimitable, and nonsubstitutable. In other words, they have the potential to provide for creation and appropriation of value to the organization that controls them—demonstrating the short-sightedness of those who suggest that IT cannot be instrumental to sustained competitive advantage because it is easily imitable. The sustainability framework places IT-enabled organizational resources in the context of specific initiatives the firm may introduce. By doing so, it is a valuable analytical tool that helps you as a manager make decisions.

The Dynamics of Sustainability

As high as the barriers to erosion may be, when launching IT-dependent strategic initiatives, a firm has an advantage but still shouldn't "fall asleep at the wheel." Rather, general and functional managers proposing IT-dependent strategic initiatives should have a plan for continuously remaining ahead of the competition. This means looking for opportunities to reinvigorate and reinforce the barriers to erosion described above. Consider the example of Dell Inc., a firm that maintained its leadership position in personal computer manufacturing for more than a decade. At the heart of Dell's strategy was its high-velocity, built-to-order production model for direct sales. The firm continually improved the performance of its production system, as well as introduced further initiatives that leverage its core advantage. For example, in the mid-1990s, Dell took its direct sales model to the Internet and began to sell to individual consumers. Later the firm extended its high-velocity production model to other products, such as high-end servers and consumer electronics—albeit with less positive results. Dell was able to sustain its advantage for nearly two decades, but in order to reinvigorate its competitiveness, the firm was taken private in 2013. As Michael Dell put it, "We're the largest company in terms of revenue to go from public to private. In another week or two we'll be the world's largest start-up."[18]

A current example is offered by Zara, the Spanish garment maker and retailer. Zara was able to first outpace competitors thanks to its vertically integrated IT supported supply chain. Their flexible

---

17. Eveleth, R. (2014, May 16), The surgeon who operates 400km away, *BBC*, retrieved from http://www.bbc.com/future/story/20140516-i-operate-on-people-400km-away

18. Guglielmo, C. (2013), Dell officially goes private: Inside the nastiest tech buyout ever, *Forbes*, retrieved from http://www.forbes.com/sites/connieguglielmo/2013/10/30/you-wont-have-michael-dell-to-kick-around-anymore/

logistic and production systems concretized "fast fashion" by adapting products in real time based on customers' tastes. By 2015, Zara bettered their logistics, introducing RFID technologies at its point-of-sale. This choice additionally streamlined logistics and operations, enhancing stock visibility and replenishment. Zara further improved the performance of its vertical integrated supply chain, introducing new strategic initiatives for leveraging its core advantage.

There are two main dynamics for rejuvenation and strengthening of barriers to erosion over time: capability development and asset-stock accumulation. There is a mutually reinforcing dynamic between barriers to erosion and a firm's IT-dependent strategic initiative. Available response-lag drivers offer the firm a "head start" on the competition. The enactment of the strategy allows the leader to engage in the capability development and asset-stock accumulation processes described below, in turn leading to further development of the response-lag drivers and the preservation of barriers to erosion. (See Table 9.1 for a list of response-lag drivers affected by each dynamic.)

Capability Development   Capability development refers to the process by which an organization improves its performance over time by developing its ability to use available resources for maximum effectiveness. When it comes to IT-dependent strategic initiatives, capability development consists of the ability to engage in "learning by using," defined as the process by which a firm becomes more effective over time in utilizing and managing an information system and the technology at its core. Note that capability development processes can only be set in motion once the IT-dependent strategic initiative is

Table 9.1. Barriers to erosion response-lag drivers

Barriers to erosion	Response-lag drivers
IT resources barrier	IT assets
	• IT infrastructure*
	• Information repositories*
	IT capabilities
	• Technical skills†
	• IT-management skills†
	• Relationship assets*
Complementary resources barrier	Complementary resources*†
IT project barrier	Technology characteristics
	• Visibility
	• Uniqueness
	• Complexity
	Implementation process
	• Complexity
	• Process change
Preemption barrier	Switching costs
	• Tangible co-specialized investments*
	• Intangible co-specialized investments*
	• Collective switching costs*
	Value-system structural characteristics
	• Relationship exclusivity
	• Concentrated links

* Response-lag drivers subject to asset-stock accumulation processes.

† Response-lag drivers subject to capability development processes.

introduced. In the case of Dell Inc., repeated practice with its high-velocity, built-to-order production model enabled the computer manufacturer to consistently increase inventory turns—thereby strengthening its direct sales initiative over time—and subsequently to leverage its advantage to reach previously unserved consumers and small accounts through the Internet.

Asset-Stock Accumulation Critics of the sustainability potential of information systems and IT contend that information technologies today are easily imitable and readily acquirable in the open market. However, many of the assets underpinning an IT-dependent strategic initiative cannot be readily acquired, particularly when they are internally developed. For example, specialized databases and ad hoc forecasting models need to be custom developed; the same goes for an IT infrastructure (e.g., Walmart). This also holds true for many complementary resources as well.

Asset-stock accumulation represents the process by which a firm accrues or builds up a resource over time. Assets of this kind must be built up and developed as a result of a consistent process of accumulation. Google search engine data are an example of this accumulation process. To provide search results, Google needs to first crawl the web and index the content of each page. By 2015, Google was indexing more than 46 billion web pages, whereas its main competitor Bing was indexing 14 billion.[19] The larger data asset, coupled with efficient algorithms, provides Google an advantage, increasing the likelihood to provide users relevant results. The Caesars initiative discussed throughout this chapter is another example. At the core of the initiative there is a comprehensive centralized repository of personal and behavioral data about each gambler and a set of predictive models that forecast a player's projected worth. A firm's ability to collect data and develop the predictive models depends on having information systems for data collection, storage, analysis, and distribution. These only became available when Caesars launched its BI strategic initiative. The process of data accumulation required time to complete. Consider a destination customer who visits a Las Vegas property once per quarter to play blackjack—collecting six data points about her (i.e., information on six visits) requires one and a half years. Even after Caesars' casino operating unit filed for bankruptcy on January 2015, their accumulated customer data were still estimated at $1 billion.

For these reasons, sustainability often does not stem from visionary one-time initiatives, but rather from evolutionary initiatives predicated on a commitment to capability building and asset-stock accumulation. On this basis, the firm can develop the strategic initiative, offering a moving target to its competitors by reinforcing its barriers to imitation over time.

Applying the Framework

When looking to be innovative with information systems and IT, you can easily get wrapped up in wishful thinking about the potential of new ideas and new technologies. Importantly, the sustainability framework is as useful in helping you decide when *not* to pursue an IT-dependent strategic initiative as it is in suggesting when to do it. You can use the framework when evaluating IT-dependent strategic initiatives either as the innovator looking to protect an existing advantage or as the laggard looking for ways to respond. This is done by asking a series of increasingly specific questions.[20]

Prerequisite Questions

Since the focus of the analysis here is on sustainability (i.e., appropriation of value over time), you must assume that the IT-dependent strategic initiative under investigation does indeed create value and is consistent with the firm's priorities. The set of prerequisite questions discussed next can be used as a check.

---

19. The size of the World Wide Web (the Internet) (2015), *World Wide Web Size*, retrieved January 7, 2015, from http://www.worldwidewebsize.com

20. We frame the analysis here by referring to a proposed initiative. Thus we take the perspective of the innovator evaluating a new initiative. The same script can be used, with minor adjustments, by followers as well.

Is the Proposed Initiative Aligned with the Firm's Strategy? This crucial question often goes unasked until late in the analysis. (Sometimes it never gets asked!) This question is important because it is necessary for the proponents of the initiative to be able to formulate how the initiative advances the firm's positioning and strategy. If the firm has developed a strategic information systems plan (Chapter 6), this question is relatively easy to answer by ensuring that the proposed initiative follows the information system's guidelines.

Is the Proposed Initiative Focused on Reducing the Firm's Cost or Increasing Customers' Willingness to Pay? Rare but particularly coveted initiatives have the potential to accomplish both—decreasing the firm's cost while increasing customers' willingness to pay. As we discussed in Chapter 7, the value of this question is in requiring managers to clearly define the value proposition of the planned initiative.

What Is the IS Design Underpinning the Proposed Initiative? This question is designed to further formalize the analysis begun with the second question. At this stage in the analysis, one needs to achieve clarity with respect to the information processing functionalities of the information system supporting the proposed initiative. Each of the four components—IT, people, processes, and organizational structures—also needs to be discussed to evaluate what changes to the current information systems will have to be made and what new resources may be needed. This question is also crucial because it is the first step in evaluating the chances of implementation success of the needed information system (Chapter 2).

Sustainability Questions

While it is impossible to estimate perfectly the magnitude of any particular barrier to erosion, the purpose of this analysis is to refine the design of the IT-dependent strategic initiative, identify areas of potential weakness, and identify areas where changes to the initiative—often small ones at this stage—can substantially strengthen it. Perhaps the most important aspect of this analysis is to identify initiatives that are not sustainable. Because it is important to understand when to avoid investing in expensive projects, the following questions can raise red flags before substantial resources are committed to the initiative.

What Competitors Are Appropriately Positioned to Replicate the Initiative? Based on a clear understanding of the characteristics of the proposed IT-dependent strategic initiative, the objective of this competitor analysis is to evaluate the strength of the IT-resource and complementary resource barriers to erosion. Competitor analysis allows the innovator to identify sources of asymmetry that can be exploited and amplified through the deployment of the proposed initiative. The objective is to design the initiative so that it takes advantage of the existing sources of asymmetry and provides a basis to reinforce them over time through capability development and asset-stock accumulation.

A powerful opportunity here is to take advantage of competitors' rigidities, which are resources that hamper competitors' ability to replicate an innovation. A classic example is provided by firms with strong distribution ties (e.g., Compaq computers, Levi's), which could not easily replicate direct sellers' use of the Internet (e.g., Dell, Lands' End) because of channel conflict. While Compaq, for example, may have had the ability to sell directly from its website, as Dell does, it wasted precious time early on because it could not risk upsetting its dealers, who were responsible for the bulk of its distribution. As a consequence, it experienced a substantial delay in responding to Dell's move online.

This dynamic is playing out as we speak in the car manufacturing industry, where Tesla has decided to retain control of sales and service instead of creating a network of dealers. While its small size may be a driver of this decision, having direct relationships with customers enables Tesla to retain flexibility in the design and implementation of future IT-dependent strategic initiatives.

The result of this analysis is a clearer understanding of which competitors are in a position to respond quickly to the IT-dependent strategic initiative and which ones will instead need to first acquire necessary resources or capabilities. This analysis may also provide guidance as to how hard it would be for competitors to acquire these prerequisite resources. It is clear that when fundamental resources are heterogeneously distributed, substantial response lag can be created. Developing initiatives that amplify and leverage this heterogeneity is a critical step in your analysis.

How Long before Competitors Can Offer the Same Value Proposition?
This question is primarily concerned with the response lag associated with the creation, rollout, and infusion of the information systems at the heart of the IT-dependent strategic initiative. This analysis yields an assessment of the strength of the IT project barrier.

After a visioning stage, where the main characteristics of the initiative are envisioned by managers, the information system at the core needs to be developed and implemented. This process follows a sequential set of stages from inception to full functionality (see Chapter 11). It generally includes the following sequential stages: system definition, system build, and system implementation. Upon completion of the process, the cycle often restarts with maintenance and enhancements to the system.[21]

Competitors looking to have the same information processing functionality in place, and thus be able to offer the same value proposition, need to enter a similar development and implementation cycle. The only difference is that a follower will start the process with an awakening phase rather than a visioning phase.

The awakening stage occurs when the competitor realizes that the innovator has an advantage. The timing of the awakening depends on the characteristics of the initiative and can occur when the competitor begins to witness losses (e.g., market share, revenue), when the innovation is first introduced (typically for customer-facing systems), or even before the innovator has launched the initiative. Knowledge of behavior patterns exhibited by competitors may help in gauging the timing of the awakening and of the subsequent stages.

For example, Burger King has traditionally shown a propensity to quickly enter geographical markets pioneered by McDonald's. While not technology related, this type of knowledge of the competition is what allows the innovator to more precisely estimate lead time. In some rare cases, some competitors will find imitation so daunting that they will elect not to follow. The SABRE reservation system, pioneered by American Airlines, and the Apollo reservation system, built by United Airlines, emerged as the dominant airline reservation systems because other airlines elected early on not to follow the lead of these two carriers. The decision not to engage in the design and development of their own reservation systems was based on a consideration of the expense and risk associated with such projects.

Will Replication Do Competitors Any Good?
Armed with an understanding of which competitors will be in a position to respond to the innovator's IT-dependent strategic initiative and a general idea of how long it may take them to have the same functionality in place, the innovating firm must estimate the magnitude of the preemption barrier to erosion. The fact is that being second sometimes means being left behind (remember the eBay example?). Exploiting the characteristics of the innovation and the industry in which they compete, innovators can sometimes preempt any meaningful response by competitors.

Even when outright preemption is not possible, the attentive innovator often has the ability to create substantial obstacles for any prospective imitator by levying switching costs. Preemption is strongest when the firm can identify a link in the value system where few customers or partners (e.g., suppliers) exist and the partners that do exist place a premium on having an exclusive relationship with only one firm. In this scenario, they may eventually sever their relationship with the firm and do business with a competitor, but they won't trade with both at the same time.

Consider, for example, the case of "Buddy" Valastro Carlo's bakery.[22] Following the success of his reality series *Cake Boss* (Figure 9.10), orders skyrocketed. His business went from the single shop in

21. Thoughtful readers will note that the rationale offered by those who suggest that IT is not strategic because it is easily imitable is that the technology can easily be replicated. In other words, this rationale addresses only the build and implementation phases of the IT development cycle. The attentive readers of this book know that there is much more to IT-dependent strategic initiatives than simply technology development!

22. See *Cake Boss* (n.d.), in *Wikipedia*, retrieved from https://en.wikipedia.org/wiki/Cake_Boss

Hoboken, New Jersey, to nine retail stores, a mail order shop, a cooking school, and a new line of business-to-business sales. To maintain the same high level of customer experience, it was mandatory for Buddy that all stores and the "headquarters" shared information on sales, waiting times, customer details, forecasts, and analysis, such as those offered by CRM solutions like Salesforce. In this case, for the solution to be useful, all of Buddy's business locations must use it. From Salesforce's standpoint, customers (in this case, the bakeshop chain) place a premium on an exclusive relationship. Buddy's business will either use Salesforce for all shops, or it will switch

FIGURE 9.10. "Buddy" Valastro on the set of *Cake Boss*
Photo by Jen Knoedl / CC BY 2.0

them all to a competitor's solution. In either case, it will not work with two vendors at the same time, as that would defeat the original purpose of sharing customer and sales information.

When such conditions are present or can be created, switching costs have the most power in raising the preemption barrier. When switching costs are high, competitors must indemnify any newly won customers for the cost of switching. As we stated previously, competitors must be that much better than the leader, where "that much" is determined by the magnitude of the switching costs.

The set of three questions offered above should provide the innovator, or any follower who is using this analysis as a diagnostic tool, to study the leader's IT-dependent strategic initiative with an idea of how defendable the initiative is and the what options are available to improve its barriers to erosion. No initiative is static, though, and barriers to erosion decay over time as competition runs its course. As a consequence, you should ask one more question to complete the analysis.

What Evolutionary Paths Does the Innovation Create?
Sheltered by its lead time, the innovator can and should seek ways to reinforce its barriers to erosion. Based on their understanding of the capability development and asset-stock-accumulation processes described previously, the leading firm's managers can chart an evolutionary path for the initiative. While the evolutionary paths thus identified must be revised as the situation changes, the analysis to this point can highlight important response-lag drivers that can be strengthened over time. Performing this analysis will also ensure that the evolution of the initiative is intentional rather than haphazard and minimizes the likelihood that opportunities will be missed.

Consider, for example, the case of modern hotels. Because of the nature of the lodging service, where guests often volunteer preference and personal information, many hotels have assembled vast databases of guest needs and likes. Yet until recently the value of guest data for analyses (e.g., customer lifetime-value analysis) was not recognized by managers. (Cynics may suggest that it still largely isn't.) A careful analysis of guest-reward initiatives may have shown that the substantial information repositories that accumulated as a by-product of the initiative are subject to asset-stock accumulation.

More recently, telecom operators have assembled large databases collecting geolocation information from mobile phones connecting to their networks. Companies like Inrix recognized the value of this location data to predict traffic flows and create innovative navigation services challenging incumbents. The value of devices location information manifested only after a certain accumulated "mass." The massive diffusion of mobile phones made the location data collected by telecom companies a foresight asset for creating navigation services. Interestingly, IT giants like Apple and Google had for the same reasons increasing access to location data, potentially disrupting real-time traffic information space.

Similarly, sensor data from smartphones and from the Internet of things have been limitedly exploited since only recently.

Making Decisions

On the basis of the analysis discussed above, you are in a position to decide whether to go forward with a proposed initiative or shelve it for future reevaluation. The following are three possible broad outcomes from the analysis.

Develop the IT-Dependent Strategic Initiative Independently

Independent development is warranted if the analysis suggests that strong barriers to erosion exist and the firm foresees the ability to appropriate the value created by the initiative over the long term (i.e., sustainable advantage can be attained). Independent development is also warranted if the leader can reap an acceptable return on its innovation, even though the analysis shows that competitors will eventually be able to overcome the barriers to erosion.

Note once again that focus should be on the IT-dependent strategic initiative as a whole. The determination of whether the technology at the core of the initiative should be developed in a proprietary manner will depend on the role that the response lags associated with it play in the sustainability of the advantage (i.e., the IT project barrier).

Develop the IT-Dependent Strategic Initiative as Part of a Consortium

When the initiative is unlikely to yield sustainable competitive advantage for the innovator but, even after replication by competitors, will improve the overall profitability of the industry, the firm should attempt to create a joint venture with competitors or engage them in a consortium. In this scenario, the leader should strive to minimize costs and risks associated with the initiative and seek to share them with competitors since all will benefit in the long term.

Shelve the IT-Dependent Strategic Initiative

When the analysis suggests that the initiative will not offer strong barriers to erosion, and retaliation by competitors will degrade the average profitability of the industry (e.g., any value created is driven to customers by competition), the firm should shelve the proposed initiative. If the firm does go ahead with the initiative, the likely outcome is competitors' imitation and the creation of value that will be competed away and appropriated by customers. For these types of initiatives, the firm should refrain from being the innovator and instead plan to follow only when strictly necessary. Because of the fast-declining costs of IT and IT implementations, being a follower with nonsustainable innovations enables the firm at least to replicate the leader's initiative at a much lower cost.

Summary

In this chapter, we demonstrated that quibbling about the strategic potential offered by information technology (IT) is not a productive use of management time and efforts. A large number of cases, including eBay Inc., Dell Inc., Harrah's Entertainment, and Walmart, provide evidence that IT-dependent strategic initiatives, with technology at their core, can be a source of sustained advantage for the modern firm.

More important, though, this chapter armed you with the tools to make recommendations about whether a specific firm should pursue a specific IT-dependent strategic initiative or if it is better served by forgoing the financial investment and implementation effort. Specifically, we learned the following:

- When analyzing the potential to defend a competitive advantage created by an IT-dependent strategic initiative, you must estimate the magnitude of the following four barriers to erosion: IT resources barrier, complementary resources barrier, IT project barrier, and preemption barrier. The extent to which an IT-dependent strategic initiative can be protected from competitors' retaliation is a function of the presence and significance of the response lag drivers that underpin it.

- An IT-dependent strategic initiative is defendable when the magnitude, in terms of time and money, of one or more of the barriers to erosion is such to discourage imitation or to render it impossible or impractical.
- IT can be critical to the sustainability of competitive advantage. However, aside from rare occasions, it is not IT itself that ensures sustainability but rather the characteristics of the IT-dependent strategic initiative that technology enables.
- The useful life of an IT-dependent strategic initiative (i.e., the span of time while the firm is able to protect the added value it created) can be extended by rejuvenating the barriers to erosion. Two processes, capability development and asset-stock accumulation, enable the firm to maintain its leadership position.
- The outcome of the analysis is one of three recommendations: (1) pursue the IT-dependent strategic initiative independently when the firm can protect it or reap an acceptable return on investment before competitors can successfully retaliate, (2) pursue the IT-dependent strategic initiative as part of a consortium when the firm cannot protect it but all the firms in the industry will be better off once replication has occurred, or (3) do not pursue the IT-dependent strategic initiative when the firm cannot protect it and industry profitability degrades once replication has occurred.

Study Questions

1. The chief executive officer (CEO) of your company, where you serve as the chief information officer (CIO), recently read the article title "IT Doesn't Matter" (see Further Readings list). He calls you into his office to "pick your brain" and asks, "Why do we invest money in IT when every one of our competitors can buy the same technology?"
2. Why is the difference between information systems and information technology so important to the analysis of sustainability?
3. Describe each of the four barriers to erosion.
4. For each barrier to erosion, provide an example of an IT-dependent strategic initiative that, in your opinion, leverages the barrier. Can you identify which response-lag drivers underpin the barriers to erosion in your examples?
5. Review your answers to the questions at the end of the opening minicase. Have they changed? Why or why not?
6. Identify some businesses that currently appear to have a sustainable advantage. How do information systems (IS) contribute to this sustainability? Highlight any cases where this sustainability appears to have a non-IS foundation or where there is no complementary IS to support the firm's value proposition.
7. Identify some businesses that currently appear to have no sustainable advantage and as a result are losing market share, are in (or close to) Chapter 11, or have gone out of business in the last year. Did a competitor's IS contribute to this decline, or was there some other fundamental problem?
8. Can IS create a sustainable competitive advantage, or only support a firm in achieving a sustainable competitive advantage based on a compelling value proposition? Use evidence to support your argument.

Further Readings

1. Carr, N. G. (2003, May). IT doesn't matter. *Harvard Business Review, 81*, 5–12.
2. Cohan, W. D. (2015, June 5). A private equity gamble in Vegas gone wrong. *Fortune*. Retrieved from http://fortune.com/2015/06/05/caesars-losing-las-vegas/
3. Nevo, S., and Wade, M. R. (2010). The formation and value of IT-enabled resources: Antecedents and consequences. *MIS Quarterly, 34*(1), 163–183.
4. Piccoli, G., & Ives, B. (2005). IT-dependent strategic initiatives and sustained competitive advantage: A review and synthesis of the literature. *MIS Quarterly, 29*(4), 747–776.
5. Porter, M. E. (2001, March). Strategy and the Internet. *Harvard Business Review, 79*, 63–78.
6. Porter, M. E., and Heppelmann, J. E. (2014, November). How smart, connected products are transforming competition. *Harvard Business Review, 92*, 11–64.
7. Tapscott, D. (2001, July 1). Rethinking strategy in a networked world. *Strategy and Competition*, third quarter, 1–8.

Glossary

- **Asset-stock accumulation:** The process by which a firm accrues or builds up a resource over time.
- **Barriers to erosion:** The difficulty, expressed in time and money, that competitors must overcome to match the value proposition offered by the leading firm.
- **Capability development:** The process by which an organization is able to improve its performance over time by developing its ability to use available resources for maximum effectiveness.
- **Competitive advantage:** The condition where a firm engages in a unique transformation process and has been able to distinguish its offerings from those of competitors. When a firm has achieved a position of competitive advantage, it is able to make above-average profits.
- **IT-dependent strategic initiatives:** Identifiable competitive moves and projects that enable the creation of added value and that rely heavily on the use of information technology to be successfully implemented (i.e., they cannot feasibly be enacted without investments in IT).
- **Resources:** Assets (i.e., things the firm has) and capabilities (i.e., things the firm can do) that the firm can deploy and leverage as part of its IT-dependent strategic initiatives.
- **Response lag:** The time it takes competitors to respond aggressively enough to erode a firm's competitive advantage; the delay in competitive response.
- **Response-lag drivers:** The characteristics of the technology, the firm, its competitors, or the value system in which the firm is embedded that combine to make replication of the IT-dependent strategic initiative difficult and costly. Response-lag drivers combine their effect to levy barriers to erosion.
- **Sustained competitive advantage:** The condition where a firm is able to protect a competitive advantage from competitors' retaliation.

PART IV

GETTING IT DONE

The last part of this book is dedicated to the many issues that surround the management of information systems and technology in modern organizations—from budgeting and operational planning, to design and development, to ongoing operations. Keeping with the focus of the text, this section is not overly technical. Rather, it concentrates on what general and functional managers need to know to be actively involved in the management of their firm's or function's information systems resources.

Your involvement with the decisions discussed in this section is essential. While you can typically avoid worrying about hardware decision making, the same cannot be said of software applications and the issues that surround them. Software applications enable and constrain how work is done and have a direct impact on organizational operations and climate. Thus, as the organizational expert and the person responsible for the success of your business function, you must have a say in the funding and prioritization of projects, you must be intimately involved in the design or selection of new systems, and you must be cognizant of the organizational risks associated with security and privacy failures.

In order to be an asset to the team making the aforementioned decisions, you must understand the processes that surround them, remain up to date on the information systems trends that concern these decisions, and be well versed in the vocabulary and issues pertaining to the management of information systems resources. Part IV of this book is devoted to these topics:

- *Chapter 10: Funding Information Systems.* This chapter focuses on the decisions and techniques pertaining to the funding and the governance of information systems. It also discusses outsourcing decisions and the outsourcing decision-making process.
- *Chapter 11: Creating Information Systems.* This chapter describes the process by which IT-enabled information systems come to be. It discusses the three main avenues for new systems creation: systems design and development, systems selection and acquisition, and end-user development.
- *Chapter 12: Information System Trends.* This chapter introduces the enduring and emerging information systems trends that concern general and functional managers. It then describes and discusses the characteristics and implications of each one.
- *Chapter 13: Security, Privacy, and Ethics.* This chapter makes the case for why general and functional managers need to be intimately involved in information security, privacy, and ethics decisions. It then provides the background to partake in the organizational debate of these issues.

CHAPTER 10

Funding Information Systems

What You Will Learn in This Chapter

We begin Part IV by discussing how modern organizations support, fund, and manage their information systems (IS) efforts.

Specifically, this chapter will

1. Explain the relationship between strategic information systems planning and the yearly budgeting and prioritization process.
2. Articulate the role that general and functional managers play in the yearly budgeting and prioritization process.
3. Allow you to define, comprehend, and use the appropriate vocabulary, including concepts such as total cost of ownership (TCO), business case, and steering committee.
4. Evaluate the three main funding methods used by modern organizations: chargeback, allocation, and overhead. You will also learn their respective advantages and disadvantages.
5. Explain the yearly budgeting and prioritization project and help you to evaluate individual and portfolio risks of information systems projects.
6. Define the terms *outsourcing* and *offshoring* and identify the primary drivers of this enduring trend. You will also be able to articulate the principal risks of outsourcing and offer some general guidelines with respect to the outsourcing decision.

MINICASE: Budgeting at Performance Boards Inc.

As the chief information officer (CIO) at Performance Boards Inc., you chair the information technology (IT) steering committee. Performance Boards has recently been acquired by Big Sporting Manufacturer Inc. and is currently operating independently as a wholly owned subsidiary. During the yearly IT budgeting process, or the "ultimate fighting championship," as you call it, you are the unwilling center of attention—the arbiter of all disputes. It's that time of year again, as shown by the calls you are receiving from other managers you hardly hear from all year.

Every July the budgeting process starts with a call for projects. Every functional area responds with a rank-ordered list of initiatives that need funding and their supporting business cases. Once the steering committee reviews the preliminary proposals, each executive sponsor presents the case for his or her proposed projects. Armed with this information, the steering committee deliberates and chooses the projects to be presented to the executive team for inclusion in the overall budget. Typically, whatever the steering committee proposes, the executive team approves. The executive team's main concern is overall IT spending. Bjorn Dunkerbeck, the founder and chief executive officer (CEO) of Performance Boards, is adamant that the firm should be in line with the manufacturing industry benchmark of 3.3% of revenue as a yearly IT budget.

This year, the third year of declining revenues for the firm, the ultimate fighting championship is shaping up as an all-time great—not a good thing for you! You had set aside 64% of the budget for the information systems function to control, in accord with industry allocation benchmarks. Your group needs the money for security, disaster recovery, general maintenance, infrastructure management, and administrative expenses. Yet, because of the tightening budgets, for the first time in your tenure as CIO, you are being questioned and required to justify the allocation to the IS function.

At this point the human resource project and the inventory management projects seem most likely to get green-lighted. The vice president of human resources has been asking for an upgrade to the benefits package management application for three years now. His business case shows both productivity improvements and higher retention of employees. The chief operating officer presented the business case for the manufacturing group. He has shown a substantial return on investment (ROI) associated with the proposed supply chain and just-in-time inventory management initiatives.

The VP of accounting and the new director of sales, Robby Naish, are exerting lots of pressure to obtain funding for their projects as well: an upgrade to the accounting management system and a sales force automation (SFA) application, respectively. Naish has just finished reiterating his case to you on the phone. Being new to the firm, he is becoming quite frustrated with Performance Boards' approach to budgeting: "How am I supposed to compete with a project that increases productivity and one that improves efficiencies through automation? They can easily compute an ROI, but my project is not suited to that type of analysis. I can surely come up with some fictitious ROI number. I can pull them out of the thin air if this is how you guys do business!"

As you review the current informal ranking of projects, you can't help but think that you need to find a way not to alienate the functional managers and project sponsors. The last thing you need is for the IS function to be perceived as a roadblock to the success of the other functional areas and ultimately of Performance Boards Inc. as a whole.

Discussion Questions

1. What should you do next? What are some of the options at your disposal to ensure that you do not alienate your colleagues?
2. Are there any structural problems with the budgeting process at Performance Boards Inc.? What improvements would you suggest for next year—if any?

Introduction

In Chapter 6, we discussed the information systems (IS) strategic planning process. Strategic information systems planning involves identifying the long-term direction of information systems use and management within the organization. It provides a framework for decision making and project selection. Within this framework, the firm develops yearly operational plans and budgets in order to prioritize information systems spending.

As a general or functional manager, you need to understand how the budgeting and prioritization processes work so that you can make the most of them. All too often we see organizations funding information systems using simple metrics, like percentage of revenue or fixed increments over the previous year's budget. While these metrics have a place in the budgeting process, the yearly budget is an opportunity to formally evaluate competing projects and make the (sometimes tough) comprehensive prioritization decisions necessary to align information systems with the firm's strategy. The firm that fails to do so misses the opportunity to offer guidance and a clear mandate to the IS function. The consequence is that a lack of direction and cohesive effort will degrade service (in many cases leading to outright failure) and demoralize the firm's IS professionals.

Note that this prioritization role should not be delegated to the information systems group but should be made in concert with business managers (i.e., those who need the information systems) and IS professionals (i.e., those who make and manage the information systems). An information technology (IT) group that does not deliver consistently is often the product of an executive team that fails to provide clear priorities. Note that this occurrence is not at all uncommon. A recent PwC survey highlighted that only a minority of business leaders is directly addressing in their strategies the challenges emerging from digital transformation—a paradoxical result given the effectively perceived importance that information systems resources have today for the success of most enterprises.[1]

Information Systems Governance

Information systems governance is generally defined as the set of decisions rights and the guiding accountability framework designed to ensure that IT resources are employed appropriately in the organization.[2] IT governance in the modern firm has two principal aspects: the management of downside risk and the fostering of upside potential. The first facet, IT risk governance, is concerned with decisions for minimizing threats (e.g., security risks) and failures (e.g., unsuccessful project implementations). The second facet, IT value governance, is concerned with maximizing the value of IT investments and the firm's ability to leverage its information systems resources.

While to any casual observer it would appear obvious that the board of directors within an organization needs to pay close attention to information systems and IT decisions, one of the most enduring research findings is that most boards of directors abdicate this duty. For example, the consultancy company PwC reported that the influence of emerging digital technologies and cybersecurity are two major concerns among the surveyed 863 directors, recognizing the critical role IT plays in their firm's success. However, only 49% of the respondents reported being even moderately involved in setting IT strategy[3]—and often executives can't quite articulate who should and why.

As we stressed in Chapter 6, while firm executives need not evaluate every project, they do need to set up the framework for decision making about information systems resources within their organization.[4] There are a number of models and approaches that guide the design of an IT governance framework for an organization. The specifics of these models are beyond the scope of this book. However, research has highlighted five key areas of concern that boards of directors must proactively address (see Table 10.1). In order for a board of directors to take a proactive stance to IS governance, these five areas of potential risk must be monitored and cyclically evaluated.

Beyond the management of the principal risks associated with information systems use in organizations, the governance framework an organization puts in place must also ensure that the use of IT resources is aligned with organizational strategy and priorities.

Steering Committee

Larger organizations often formalize management involvement in information systems decision making by forming a steering committee. The steering committee brings together representatives from the various functional areas, the CEO (or other general management staff), and key IS professionals (e.g., the CIO) who convene regularly to provide guidance to the IS function and share the responsibility for aligning its efforts with the larger business strategy. The steering committee is typically the venue where business cases are presented for approval or as a filter before the budgeting process. It's the steering committee that makes decisions on the investment approach, portfolio, and risk. Furthermore, it is generally responsible for the prioritization of the investments. The steering committee is also the main recipient and evaluator of progress during system development and implementation efforts.

1. PwC (2014), *6th Annual Digital IQ Survey*, retrieved from http://www.pwc.com/us/en/advisory/digital-iq-survey/assets/6th-annual-digital-iq.pdf

2. Weill, P., & Ross, J. (2004), *IT governance*, Cambridge, MA: Harvard Business School Press.

3. PwC (2014), *What matters in the boardroom—director and investor views on trends shaping governance and the board of the future*, retrieved from http://www.pwc.com/en_US/us/corporate-governance/publications/assets/pwc-what-matters-in-the-boardroom-director-investor-views.pdf

4. Weill, P., & Ross, J. (2011, April 25), Four questions every CEO should ask about IT, *Wall Street Journal*.

Table 10.1. Five categories of risk the board of directors must address

IT competence risk	This risk factor captures the degree of IT related knowledge of the board of directors. While boards of directors need not all be as knowledgeable as CIOs or IT professionals, it is critical that they have the ability to follow IT discussions and ask relevant questions. Moreover, there should be a leading IT director who maintains an up-to-date competence on IT matters.
Infrastructure risk	A firm's IT infrastructure represents the set of IT components that are interconnected and managed by IT specialists with the objective of providing a set of standard services to the organization. It provides the foundation for the delivery of business applications. The board of directors must be keenly aware of the weaknesses and risks associated with the firm's IT infrastructure.
IT project risk	In Chapter 3, we provide a sample of high-profile IT project failures. IT projects are generally complex and expensive undertakings that, if not properly managed, can put the organization in peril. The board of directors must ensure that the appropriate guiding framework for IT projects is in place. In large organizations, this may require a project office, a certification process for project managers, and a portfolio approach to IT project management (see below).
Business continuity risk	Business continuity refers to the activities a firm performs to ensure that critical business functions remain operational in a crisis and that the organization can withstand unforeseen disasters (see Chapter 13). The board of directors must ensure the existence of a business continuity plan and that such a plan is periodically tested and revised.
Information risk	Information risk pertains to the many hazards associated with the collection and use of organizational, partner, and customer data (see Chapter 13). The board of directors must craft a governance system that ensures that an officer of the organization has clear responsibility for signing off on and ensuring compliance with established privacy and security policies.

Source: Parent, M., & Reich, B. H. (2009), Governing information technology risk, *California Management Review, 51*(2), 134–152.

Funding Information Systems

As with any other organizational asset, the firm must account for and fund information systems assets and expenses. Information systems are typically designed, built, implemented, and managed to achieve some business goal (e.g., improve factory floor efficiencies, increase sales effectiveness and customer repurchase). The exception is provided by shared services (e.g., security, planning and administration, business continuity initiatives) and infrastructure investments. There are three main methods used by modern organizations to fund information systems: *chargeback*, *allocation*, and *overhead*. Each one offers advantages and disadvantages.

Chargeback

The chargeback approach calls for direct billing of information systems resources and services to the organizational function or department that uses them. It is grounded in the pay-per-use principle. For example, a department may be charged for networking expenses based on the volume of traffic it initiates and for personal productivity software based on the number of concurrent software application licenses it runs.

The main advantage of chargeback mechanisms is their perceived fairness and the accountability they create for both users and the IS function. Another advantage of such systems is the degree of control they afford to general and functional managers, who can proactively control their function's information systems expenses. However, maintaining such detailed costing mechanisms can generate substantial direct and indirect expenses, including the cost of tracking and those for auditing and dispute resolution of charges.

Chargeback systems typically treat the IS function as a cost center. That is, the units are billed on the basis of actual costs. In some instances, particularly when the IS function has some unique skills, it may become a profit center and compete for service provision with external vendors. In rare cases, it may also sell its services to other firms, not only to internal users, and return the profits to the organization.

Allocation

The allocation approach calls for direct billing of information systems resources and services to the organizational function or department that uses them. However, rather than a pay-per-use metric, it computes allocations based on more stable indicators such as size, revenues, and number of users. For example, a hotel chain may charge individual hotels in the chain on the basis of the number of rooms. A chain of retail outlets may charge each unit a fixed percentage of revenue or square footage.

The allocation method seeks to strike a balance between the pay-per-use fairness and the high cost of the chargeback method. Since rates are typically set once a year, the expenses each unit can expect are also more predictable. Some functional managers prefer the predictability of fixed allocations, while others prefer the higher degree of control offered by the chargeback mechanism.

Overhead

The overhead approach treats information systems as a shared expense to be drawn from the organization's overall budget rather than to be paid for by each unit. This is the simplest approach to funding information systems, since decisions are made once a year during the budget approval process. It also provides the most control to the IS function over spending decisions. As a consequence, the IS function is more likely to experiment with and evaluate new technologies.

The main drawback of the overhead approach is a lack of accountability for both the functional areas and the IS department. On the one hand, since users are not billed directly, they are less likely to proactively manage their usage and filter their requests for service and new projects. Moreover, they remain largely unaware of their impact on the overall IS budget, which often leads to misconceptions about the cost of IT resources and the reasonable expectations for service. On the other hand, since the IS function has little accountability to the individual functional areas, it is more likely to be less responsive and to offer poorer service.

Recognizing their complementarities, some organizations adopt a blend of funding approaches for IS function. For example, while infrastructure services and maintenance may be billed based on the overhead method, new projects and new systems may be billed based on an allocation approach.

The Budgeting and Project Prioritization Process

The yearly budgeting process is a tool organizations use to communicate plans and enforce control systems. As a planning tool, the budget provides an assessment of what the firm believes future financial flows will be. As a control mechanism, the budget helps encourage and enforce specific behaviors. More subtly, the budget can be used to allocate decision rights and power. In 2014, IT advisory firm Gartner found in its IT Key Metrics Data report that IT spending ranged from 1% to 6.7% of revenue in the industries surveyed (Figure 10.1).

For example, in an organization where the information systems function controls the bulk of the IT budget, decisions regarding the use of the IT resource will be highly centralized. In this case, the information systems group will be able to identify and create efficiencies, but users will enjoy limited flexibility. Conversely, if much of the IT budget is controlled by individual units, they will be able to fund tailored initiatives, but integration and firm-wide efficiencies are left without a strong sponsor.

Typically, control over the IT budget is split, with a portion allocated to the information systems function for infrastructural expenses and projects that enable the business to operate in a reliable and secure manner (e.g., disaster recovery planning, business continuity initiatives, information systems

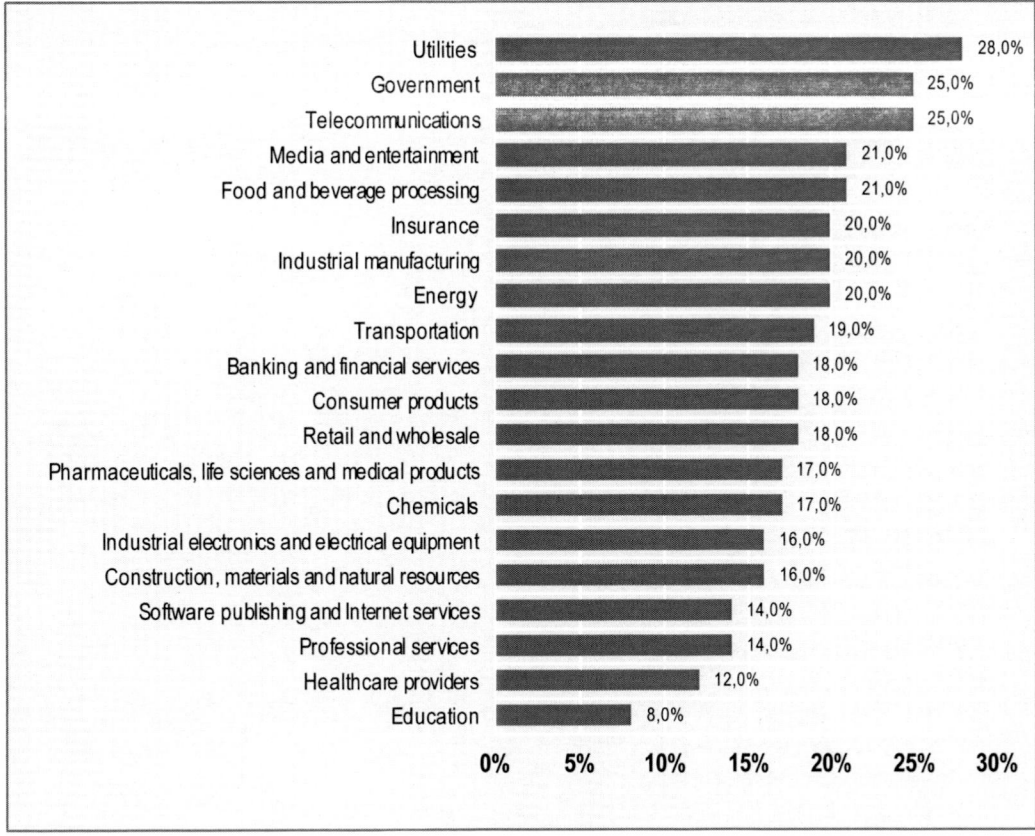

FIGURE 10.1. IT spending as a percentage of revenue

Source: Gartner Inc. (2014), *IT key metrics data*, retrieved from https://www.gartner.com/doc/2635815/it-key-metrics-data

security management). The remainder is controlled by the individual units, for funding operations of existing systems and for funding new projects (Sidebar 10.1).

Making the Budget

The budgeting process requires trade-offs between diverging interests and the prioritization of projects under resource constraint. This can make a very stressful process within which executives must argue and rally support for their initiatives, all the while attempting to ensure that information systems resources are deployed to meet the strategic demands of the business.

The budgeting process varies by organization, but there are typically two decisions to be made: determining the appropriate budget for ongoing operational expenses (e.g., maintenance) and evaluating large capital expenditures (e.g., new systems). Published industry benchmarks can be instrumental in offering some guidance, but it is essential to stress that your firm's budget is dictated by its vision and architectural guidelines (Chapter 6) and the unique contingencies it faces. For instance, a firm that has been very successful in rationalizing and consolidating its infrastructure can be expected to have below-average ongoing IT expenses. Conversely, if a firm ran a number of legacy applications in need of substantial upkeep, it would be spending above average.

A sound appreciation for the role of information systems in the firm (i.e., the information systems vision) is even more important when evaluating capital expenditure and new information systems projects. This is critical, not so much for the evaluation of individual initiatives, but for the evaluation of the aggregate degree of information systems risk the firm is willing to accept.

SIDEBAR 10.1. SAMPLE OPERATIONAL IT BUDGET		

This sample operational IT budget is loosely based on that of a major hotel chain.

Expenses	Amount (U.S. dollars)	Percentage
Payroll	3,140,000	31.4
Travel and entertainment	270,000	2.7
Depreciation[1]	450,000	4.5
Amortization[2]	1,080,000	10.8
Training	30,000	0.3
Equipment/hardware/software purchases[3]	90,000	0.9
Maintenance	680,000	6.8
Telecommunications expense	520,000	5.2
Disaster recovery	10,000	0.1
Miscellaneous other operating expenses	180,000	1.8
Corporate IT allocation[4]	3,530,000	35.3

[1] Capitalized equipment is subject to depreciation.

[2] Capitalized software is subject to amortization.

[3] Equipment below the capitalization threshold.

[4] IT allocation from the parent company. For firms without a parent company, this line would spread over the other items in roughly the same percentages.

Funding Information Systems Projects: Making the Business Case

The business case is a formal document prepared and presented by the general or functional manager sponsoring the project. It provides the rationale for pursuing the opportunity. Its primary objective is to explain and provide evidence to convince the executive team, typically during the budgeting process, that the initiative will pay off and its funding is warranted. Note that not only will a firm require a business case to be developed for new systems, but often the business case will be used to evaluate ongoing spending decisions and to evaluate existing systems as well.

Traditionally business cases required fact-based investment analyses grounded in financial indicators such as internal rate of return (IRR), return on investment (ROI), net present value (NPV), return on assets (ROA), or payback period. They required an analysis of the timeline of the project and its future cash flow stream and supporting evidence for project benefits and cost estimates. However, in order to provide these analyses, project proponents all too often had to make assumptions and arbitrary judgments.

The business case approach is a standard in modern organizations.[5] However, despite their popularity, business cases have encountered significant criticism.

Limitations of the Business Case

The traditional business case technique is increasingly receiving criticism. The skeptics suggest that business cases strictly based on fact will often require so many assumptions and speculations that they will become based on fiction. This problem is less likely with "automation" initiatives (i.e., first-order change as defined in Chapter 2), but it is particularly evident for projects that rely on business or

___

5. Ward, J., Daniel, E., & Peppard, J. (2008), Building better business cases for IT investments, *MIS Quarterly Executive*, 7(1), 1–15.

technical innovation and, as a consequence, are characterized by significant uncertainty as to the final outcome. Financial projections are also difficult to make for projects that have mostly "soft" benefits. Consider as an example a firm that decides to invest significantly in social media, as the global pizza-delivery chain Domino's has done recently. Today Domino's Pizza has more than 10 million fans on its Facebook page. These fans participate in the chain's social media initiatives (e.g., contests, polls, specials)—a recent contest asked Instagram users to post photos of restaurants that are still using an outdated Domino's logo and hashtag them with #logoinformants and #sweeps. The initiative was a winner, with more than 4,500 submitted photos. It is quite clear that Domino's has an established presence in social media and has gained significant traction with this initiative. However, what is the value of such customer engagement? How much more revenue would an initiative like this generate? These remain very difficult questions to answer.

The limitations of a traditional business case approach are clearly exemplified by the president of a large hotel chain explaining how his firm justified a recent customer relationship management project: "You can't justify such a project with traditional methods. There is too much uncertainty beforehand. You know this is the right project because it fits with your strategic positioning and brand. This is how we are going to differentiate our product in the marketplace."[6]

Overcoming the Limitations of the Business Case

In order to overcome the limitations of a traditional business case, some observers point to the value of heuristics. A heuristic is a simple rule that is good enough to make decisions, recognizing that adjustments along the way will be necessary. This approach offers another advantage: it systematizes the reevaluation of both the costs and benefits of projects during their development. Another valuable approach consists of relaxing the focus on fact-based business cases and allowing proponents of a project to ground their request on faith (i.e., project rationale based on beliefs about market trends, customer expectations, competition, strategy, etc.) and fear (i.e., need to engage in projects to keep from falling behind the competition or to avert a likely negative outcome). Typically, a well-crafted business case will include all of the above: fact, faith, and fear-based arguments.

Recent literature has advanced a more formal approach to modern business cases, one that develops in six sequential steps:[7]

1. *Define business drivers and investment objectives.* Business case writers should begin by establishing the business drivers underlying the need for the project and by clearly spelling out the investment objectives and their relationship with the business drivers. If the firm has engaged in the strategic IS planning process (Chapter 6), much of the work underlying this first stage has already been completed.

2. *Identify benefits, measures, and owners.* Business case writers should then identify all the potential benefits accruing to all stakeholders if the project is successfully implemented. Note that benefits could extend beyond the investment objectives or even be unintended. Once all benefits are identified, the business case writer should explain how benefits will be measured and who will own them (i.e., who will be representing the stakeholder group that the benefit will accrue to).

3. *Structure the benefits.* The value, and the challenge, of business cases revolves around the ability to accurately assess the actual realizable benefits of the project. Structuring the expected benefits using the grid below (Figure 10.2) can foster deep, focused discussions that can significantly increase the precision of benefits evaluations.

4. *Identify organizational changes enabling benefits.* Heading each column in Figure 10.2, benefits are categorized as the ones that accrue from doing new things (e.g., creating Facebook-only pizza specials, thus being able to track demographics of interested customers), doing

---

6. Personal communication with authors.

7. Ward, J., Daniel, E., & Peppard, J. (2008), Building better business cases for IT investments, *MIS Quarterly Executive*, 7(1), 1–15.

		Type of Business Change		
		Do New Things	Do Things Better	Stop Doing Things
High ↑	Financial Benefits			
Degree of Explicitness	Quantifiable Benefits			
	Measurable Benefits			
↓ Low	Observable Benefits			

FIGURE 10.2. Benefits evaluation grid for business cases

things better (e.g., improving call center operations by centralizing customer information for easy access by representatives during a call), and ceasing to do things (e.g., stopping the printing and shipping of paper procedure manuals by transferring them online). While this may appear to be a simplistic categorization, it helps to list the type of change explicitly.

5. *Determine the explicit value of each benefit.* Heading each row in Figure 10.3, benefits are categorized by the extent to which they can be made explicit. It is important to specify, during the writing of the business case, the extent to which a benefit is measurable in order to ensure the maximum degree of precision in their estimation. Benefits can be classified as follows:

   a. *Financial benefits.* Computed by applying cost/price metrics or other recognized financial formula to measure the benefit.

   b. *Quantifiable benefits.* Computed by gathering metrics, expressed in number form, that provide evidence of change univocally attributable to the project.

   c. *Measurable benefits.* A measure is available to monitor a given benefit, but changes in such metrics cannot be univocally tied to the project.

   d. *Observable benefits.* There exist agreed-upon criteria, albeit not quantifiable, to evaluate the impact of the project on this class of benefits. Failing to structure this evaluation often results in the business case writer overlooking potential benefits or stopping at a level of precision in their evaluation that is unnecessarily coarse.

6. *Identify costs and risks.* A complete business case concludes with an estimation of the costs the firm will incur to see the project through to completion, as well as the degree of uncertainty and risk surrounding successful completion. Project costs will include all technology development expenses, licensing fees, training, and change management initiatives. Beyond the development costs, the firm should include the total cost of ownership (TCO). TCO is a financial estimate designed to explicitly recognize the full life cycle costs of IT assets. The costs of information systems and technology typically far exceed the costs of acquisition (e.g., selection, licensing, implementation) and include expenses that occur after the system is up and running but are necessary to maintain it in operation over its life-span. These include ongoing training of users and support personnel, maintenance, upgrades, security, and business continuity investments. Even the end-of-life costs associated with retiring the asset should be included in TCO calculations. TCO is an imprecise measure that depends on substantial estimation and assumptions about feasible configurations and future events. Nonetheless, it is essential to estimate TCO as comprehensively as possible when developing the business case. Today there is commercial software that can be used to aid in TCO computations (Figure 10.3), and major vendors offer TCO tools online. Specifically, cloud vendors are providing free TCO calculators in an effort to support business case development for their solutions.

When discussed in the abstract, the business case development process can sound highly theoretical. Conversely, the technique discussed here is very practical and pragmatic. Sidebar 10.2 illustrates it in action.

FIGURE 10.3. TCO computation for operating systems migration project

SIDEBAR 10.2. WRITING THE BUSINESS CASE[8]

The Business Objective

This company is a major global provider of mobile telephone services to both consumers and businesses. Following an internal restructuring of its service and territorial divisions, the U.K. consumer division wished to improve the service provided to customers and its ability to promote new network services and features to existing customers. The company believed that excellent customer service was one of the few ways it could differentiate itself from competitors in a very competitive market. It had also invested considerable amounts of money in new network facilities and needed to increase sales of its higher end services to recoup this investment.

The company identified that service improvement and the promotion of its newer services could be achieved by upgrading its call center systems. Most service requests from customers came into the call center. If the request was dealt with promptly, the company believed the call center agent could then discuss newer service offerings with the customer.

In addition to dealing with incoming service requests, agents would also make outbound marketing and promotional calls to customers. A new customer-profiling system would be deployed so that the service being promoted, and the script used, could be tailored to the perceived customer needs. Agents would also collect data from customers during service and promotional calls and record it in the profiling system. This data would be used both to improve future targeting and to develop new service offerings.

Business Drivers

In terms of external drivers, the company perceived competing mobile telephone services as being indistinguishable, so it was difficult to differentiate its

---

8. The case presented in this sidebar is minimally modified from Ward, J., Daniel, E., & Peppard, J. (2008), Building better business cases for IT investments, *MIS Quarterly Executive*, 7(1), 1–15.

offerings on brand alone. In the past, it had tried to compete on price but had found it difficult to sustain this. Hence it saw service as a differentiator.

In terms of internal drivers, the company needed to recoup the high investment it had made in network access and infrastructure by increasing customer take-up of its higher-end services.

Investment Objectives

The company identified two objectives for the investment in upgraded call center systems:

- Significantly improve the service provided by the call center and reduce service failures.
- Increase the take-up of newer services and collect customer profiling information to better target new services.

Benefits

The main benefits that would be realized by achieving the two objectives are shown in Figure 10.5. The total expected financial benefits amount to £1,805,000 ($3,587,400) per annum.

The benefits framework shown in Table 10.2 is typical of many IT investments. It includes a full range of benefit types, from observable to financial. While the senior managers involved were keen to show that the financial benefits provided an acceptable return to the organization, they recognized that the observable benefits were of most interest to the hundreds of call center agents who were required to use the new systems and adopt new ways of working. The agents' buy-in to the new system was key to making the investment a success.

The benefits in this example also cover the full range of business changes, from discontinuing things the company wished to avoid, such as call-backs to customers due to service call failures, to doing new things, such as promoting new higher-value services during service calls. The example also demonstrates that it is easier to put a financial value on things the company is already doing and wishes to either stop or do better. It is, however, harder to determine a robust quantity or financial value for benefits resulting from innovation.

Investment Costs and Risks

In this section are detailed investment costs that the mobile phone company incurred in implementing its new call center systems (Table 10.3) and the risks involved (Table 10.4).

Individual Project Risk

An important aspect of business case writing is the estimation of project risk. This is an important assessment, both when evaluating the risk of individual initiatives and also particularly when measuring the overall risk of all projects under development in the organization at a given point in time. Information systems projects are renowned for their high degree of risk and incidence of failure. However, the risks associated with any one particular initiative can vary widely based on the following:

- *Project size.* Project size, expressed as the estimated monetary investment, is a proxy for project complexity and the potential consequences of failure. Note that you should focus less on the absolute size of the project (e.g., $12 million) than on its size relative to the typical kind of project the information systems group in your firm undertakes. In other words, a $12 million initiative carries different risk for a firm that typically handles $20 million projects than one that is mostly familiar with $150,000 efforts.
- *Experience with technology.* The degree of experience a firm has with the technologies (e.g., hardware, software development, environment) at the heart of the project is a primary determinant of risk. Working with new and unproven technologies carries more risk than using mature ones. However, the relative novelty of the technology to the firm is also an important source of risk.
- *Organizational change.* The degree of organizational change that the project requires is another important determinant of risk. As we discussed in Chapter 2, third-order change is much more difficult (and risky) to implement than second- and first-order change.

With respect to the cost/benefits that a system is expected to deliver, different initiatives vary significantly with respect to the size of the investment they call for and the expected useful life over which

Table 10.2. Benefits evaluation grid

Objective type	Doing new things	Doing things better	Stop doing things
Financial		*Benefit:* Increased customer retention due to improved service provision *Measure:* Reduction in customer defections; Avoided defections due to service failure = 1,750 per annum; Cost per defection = £500—saving of £875,000 per annum *Benefit owner:* Customer accounts manager *Benefit:* 20% reduction in call servicing costs *Measure:* Cost per service call; Number of calls per annum = 5.6 million; Total servicing costs = £1.2 million—savings of £240,000 per annum *Benefit owner:* Telechannel sales manager	*Benefit:* Stop callbacks to customers after failed service calls *Measure:* Number of callbacks; Number in previous years = 1.5 million; Cost per callback = £0.46—savings of £690,000 per annum *Benefit owner:* Call center operations manager
Quantifiable			*Benefit:* Eliminate call waiting times more than 2 minutes for customers *Measure:* Number of calls currently waiting more than 2 minutes = 1.1 million *Benefit owner:* Call center operations manager
Measurable	*Benefit:* Call center staff able to undertake sales calls/promote new services *Measure:* Number of sales calls per staff member or sales per staff member; Current value = 0 (call center currently purely inbound) *Benefit owner:* Telechannel sales manager	*Benefit:* Customers not switching to competitors' products and services *Measure:* Number of defections to competitors; Current number of customers switching = 5,500 per annum *Benefit owner:* Customer accounts manager	
Observable	*Benefit:* Call center staff motivated by being trained about newer services *Measure:* Increased call center motivation *Benefit owner:* Call center staff manager	*Benefit:* Ability to develop future services based on customer data *Measure:* Quantity and quality of customer profile data *Benefit owner:* New service development manager	*Benefit:* Stop customers becoming frustrated/rude because of service failure *Measure:* Call center staff opinion *Benefit owner:* Call center staff manager

Table 10.3. Investment costs

Investment costs	
Purchase of new call center hardware and software	£250,000
Cost of implementation technical consultants	£120,000
Internal systems development costs (for configuration)	£150,000
Infrastructure upgrade costs	£75,000
Business change costs	£270,000
Training costs	£80,000
Total	£945,000
Net increase in annual systems support and license costs	£80,000

Table 10.4. Risks of the project

Risk analysis	
Technical risks	Complexity of the systems functionality
	Number of system interfaces and systems being replaced
Financial risks	Confidence in some investment costs—especially business change
	Confidence in the evidence for some of the benefits
	Business criticality of areas affected by the system
Organizational risks	The extent of changes to call center processes and practice
	Limited existing change management capability
	Call center staff capability to promote more technical services
	Customer willingness to share information for profiling purposes

they will deliver the benefits. A large enterprise system will require a significant up-front investment but will deliver its benefits over decades. Conversely, a redesign of the company website will typically require a fraction of the investment but will also obsolesce much more quickly.

A portfolio approach can be used to optimize the blend of projects under development and ensure a balance of the overall risk, as well as proactively manage the cost/benefits of the applications under development.

Portfolio Management

After evaluating the risk of each proposed project, management should take a portfolio approach to information systems risk management. The set of ongoing information systems projects a firm has under way can be categorized in to subclasses based on the objectives of the initiative: Strategic projects seek new value creation and appropriation. Informational projects seek increased control and better information management. Transactional projects seek efficiency and cost cutting. Infrastructural projects seek integration and streamlining of the firm's IT infrastructure (Figure 10.4).

During the budgeting process, when the firm evaluates the collection of initiatives for the coming year, it should determine the appropriate level of aggregate risks it is willing to accept. The risk profile will change depending on the blend of strategic, informational, transactional, and infrastructure projects the firm chooses to engage in (Figure 10.5). Note that this evaluation is a managerial decision, not an IT decision. While information systems professionals must help in evaluating project risk, it is the responsibility of the steering committee or the board of directors to decide what overall degree of risk the firm should accept given its overall strategic information systems plan.

A portfolio approach to managing information systems risk ensures that the funded initiatives fit the risk profile that the firm has deemed appropriate. For instance, firms in the strategic quadrant (Chapter 6) typically need to take on much higher aggregate risk than those in the support quadrant. The blend

FIGURE 10.4. IT project portfolio components
Adapted from Weill, P., & Broadbent, M. (1998), *Leveraging the new infrastructure—how market leaders capitalize on information technology*, Boston, MA: Harvard Business School Press

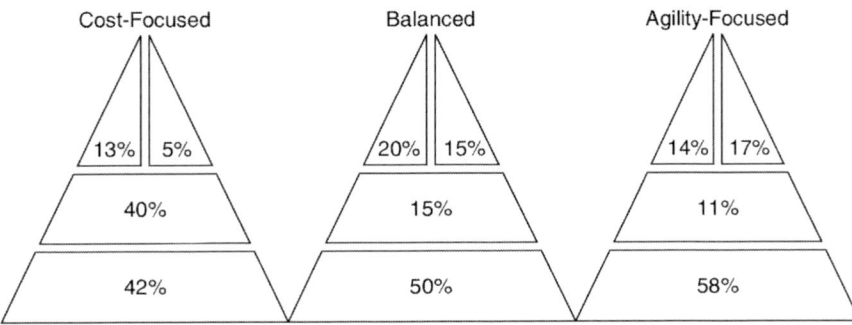

FIGURE 10.5. IT project portfolio profiles
Adapted from Weill, P., and Broadbent, M. (1998), *Leveraging the new infrastructure—how market leaders capitalize on information technology*, Boston, MA: Harvard Business School Press

of projects they engage is also different. This is due to the fact that in the first case information systems assets and initiatives are instrumental to the success and growth of the firm. The same cannot be said for those organizations that choose a very defensive approach to information systems use and management (e.g., support quadrant). In such a case, a high degree of aggregate portfolio risk is a signal that the firm is not managing information systems in accord with its strategic information systems plan. It may be that the organization needs to reevaluate and update its information systems vision, perhaps moving into the turnaround quadrant. Conversely, it could be that the firm is failing to take advantage of the budgeting and prioritization process to enforce the existing (and appropriate) plan.

Outsourcing

Information systems outsourcing is often used as a means of funding information systems operations by engaging outside providers. Outsourcing is the process of acquiring products or services that used to be created internally by the organization, from an outside provider. Information systems outsourcing is the process of contracting with an outside firm to obtain information systems services. Such services can range from automation of specific processes (e.g., payroll), to management of specific assets (e.g., data center), to development of new applications, to outright management of the IS function as a whole (i.e., full outsourcing). Outsourcing of information systems services is now estimated to be a \$300 billion industry, as measured by worldwide spending, and interests all sectors of the economy (Figure 10.6) The growth of cloud services and the digitization of business is impacting the IS outsourcing market changing its composition. "The IS outsourcing services market, also many times referred to as 'traditional' datacenter outsourcing, continues to be impacted by the fundamental transition in procuring outsourced services using traditional methods (e.g., more labor oriented) to using more automated methods in the form of cloud-based outsourced services," said David Tapper, vice president of outsourcing, managed, and offshore services at IDC.[9]

Drivers of Outsourcing

When outsourcing information systems and IT to a specialist, the outsourcing firm is typically driven by one or more of the following considerations:

Reduced Cost   Perhaps the primary driver for the outsourcing decision is the intention to capitalize on the provider's ability to create economies of scale in the production of IT services. Large providers of information systems services can consolidate their infrastructure (e.g., data centers) and enjoy superior bargaining power when dealing with technology vendors (e.g., hardware and software firms). Additionally, IT outsourcing decisions significantly impact non-IT operating costs, such as sales, general, and administrative costs.[10] This is an important aspect to consider when building the business case for outsourcing as operating costs are much larger than IT costs. Narrowing the focus of IT outsourcing as a substitute for internal IT investments may hide many potential costs and benefits.

Access to Superior Talent   Many organizations find it difficult to attract top IT talent. The reason is simple: Top IT graduates want to be challenged and want to remain on the cutting edge of technological development. But many organizations cannot (and should not!) make this objective a priority. Conversely, IT service providers are in the business of continually seeking to improve their information systems operations, evaluate new technologies, and attract the best talent.

Because of these structural differences, outsourcing contracts offer the opportunity for organizations to access top IT talent and receive an infusion of technology and information systems management expertise.

Improved Control   In many organizations that resort to outsourcing, particularly full outsourcing, the driving force for the decision was an attempt to reclaim control over the IT function when it was perceived to be inefficient and unable to provide the appropriate level of service to the organization. By engaging in a contractual arrangement with an outside provider, the theory goes, the firm can surface costs, making them explicit, and hold the provider to its service level agreements.

Improved Strategic Focus   For many organizations, information systems operations are considered (rightly or wrongly) a nuisance rather than a core strength of the firm. For these organizations, outsourcing has considerable appeal because it enables the firm to focus on what it considers its strengths and eliminate what is often a little understood function that generates significant frustration for senior management.

Financial Appeal   Outsourcing arrangements where the service provider acquires the infrastructure and IT professionals of the outsourcing organization liquidate some of the tangible and intangible assets tied up in the IT infrastructure. As such, these deals can strengthen the balance sheet and have considerable financial appeal.

---

9. Tapper, D. (2015, April), Worldwide and U.S. IS outsourcing services 2015–2019 forecast, *IDC Market Analysis*.

10. Han, K., & Mithas, S. (2013), Information technology outsourcing and non-IT operating costs: An empirical investigation, *MIS Quarterly, 37*(1), 315–331.

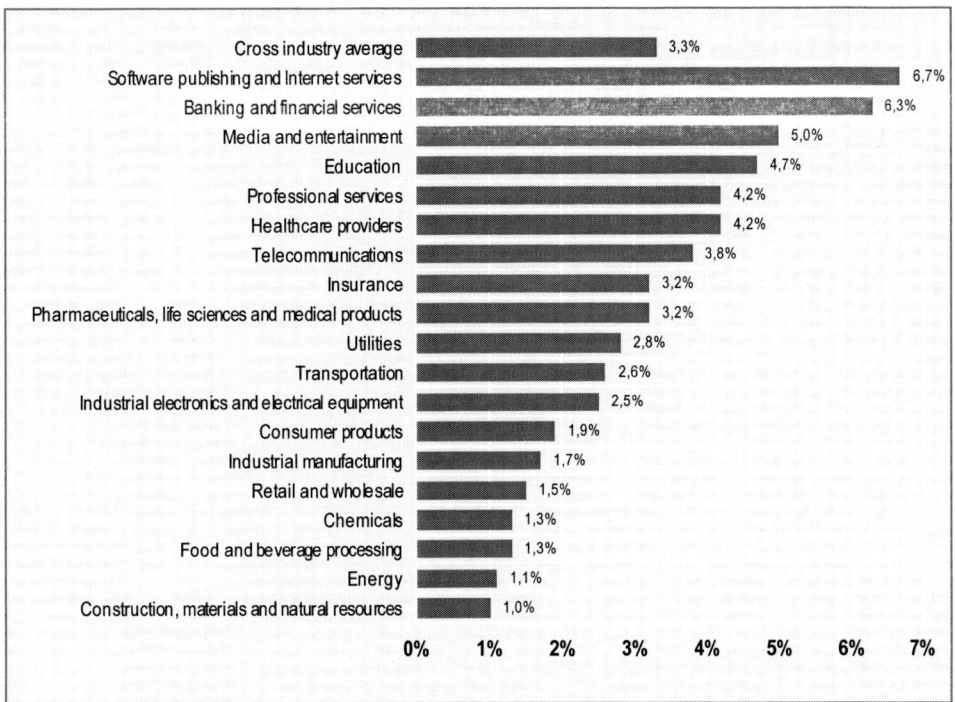

FIGURE 10.6. IT spending in outsourcing as a percentage of total IT spending by industry
Source: Gartner Inc. (2014), IT Spending Key Metrics Data

The Risks of Outsourcing

While the drivers of outsourcing described above provide a strong case for the decision, the outsourcing literature and history have provided many examples of outsourcing deals gone bad. The following are the major potential drawbacks that must be carefully evaluated before taking the plunge.

The Outsourcing Paradox   Organizations that resort to information systems outsourcing often do so out of frustration with their current IT operations. Yet if you have little faith in your ability to manage information systems internally, how can you expect to be able to make sound outsourcing decisions (i.e., draft advantageous contracts) and monitor the performance of the service provider? How can you determine the appropriate amount to pay for the services and the service levels you should expect? How do you know that you are getting what you paid for?

The Dark Side of Partnerships   The word *partnership*, when used in a business context in particular, can be very misleading. While the outsourcing firm and the service provider are "partners," as they work together to ensure the success of the operation, each has a responsibility to shareholders to maximize its own performance. This conflict of interest sometimes leads to friction and court battles. Imagine, for example, a service provider that is under pressure to cut costs and increase profitably. This result can be achieved by reducing customer service, particularly in areas where service levels are difficult to measure, hard to monitor, have no penalties attached, or have not been clearly specified in the contract.

Changing Requirements   One of the primary dangers in an outsourcing relationship is given by the length of the contracts in relation to the speed of technological and business needs evolution. For example, a 10-year contract will see significant change in organizational requirements before it is up for renewal. Yet outsourcing contracts are often very lengthy and specific in order to limit the possibility of self-interested behavior (e.g., service degradation).

Hidden Coordination Costs   One of the biggest surprises awaiting organizations that outsource information systems is the extent of coordination efforts needed to work with the provider. Coordination efforts include communicating requirements, monitoring and measuring the provider's activities and services, handling dispute resolution, and the like. These coordination efforts come at a cost of course, a cost that must be estimated beforehand and used in the decision-making phase.

The Deceptive Role of Information Systems   While many organizations outsource on the contention that they are not in the "IT business" or that "IT is not a core competency" for the firm, a lot of organizations underestimate the critical role that information systems play as enablers of business success.

Offshoring

Outsourcing has received substantial recent attention in the United States because of the prominence of the debate over loss of jobs to foreign countries allegedly brought about by one of its variants: offshoring. *Offshoring*, short for offshore outsourcing, is the process of engaging a foreign provider to supply the products or services the firm no longer intends to produce internally.

Offshoring has received much impetus since the commercialization of the Internet, which significantly lessened the impact of geographical and time differences on the transaction of information-based services (e.g., software design and development). Offshoring growth has been fueled by many of the same drivers of outsourcing, particularly cost and quality, with much of the business moving to India and China—countries that enjoy a significantly lower cost of living than the United States or Europe and offer a seemingly endless pool of highly qualified IT talent.

Making Optimal Outsourcing Decisions

As with any other complex and far-reaching managerial decision, there are no silver bullet solutions when it comes to outsourcing. The outsourcing decision requires a clear understanding of the characteristics of the organization and of the relationship with the service provider—a debate that general and functional managers must be involved in.

The strategic grid (Chapter 6) can provide helpful guidance by mapping the current and future role that information systems are expected to play in the firm. Typically, firms that find themselves in the support and factory quadrant may find it easier to outsource, given the standardized and well-understood role played by information systems resources. More difficult is the decision for firms in the turnaround and strategic quadrants. Here, due to the critical role that information system assets must play in enabling the firm's strategy, outsourcing may be both challenging and risky. In this case, particularly for firms with limited access to new technologies or superior IT talent, outsourcing may be the only viable solution. However, these firms will typically provide critical information systems services in house.

In most cases a firm should not resort to full outsourcing, locking itself into one provider, but should instead rely on selective outsourcing arrangements. Selective outsourcing arrangements are those where the firm relies on multiple providers offering different services. In such arrangements, the firm often retains an internal information systems group that enables it to compete for the contract against outside service firms.

Perhaps the clearest advice that can be offered to firms considering outsourcing is to maintain a core group of information systems specialists and a strong CIO function: First, having the in-house expertise to match the organization's business needs to the appropriate information systems services—whether these services are provided in-house or not—is fundamental. Second, it is critical to have a group of internal employees with an allegiance to your firm who understand what the service firms are providing and how best to manage the relationship. Third, it is critical for the in-house information systems group to be skilled at negotiation, contract writing, and the ongoing monitoring of service level agreements.

Summary

This chapter begins our discussion of the techniques and methodologies that modern organizations use to introduce and manage information systems (IS) within the framework provided by the strategic information systems plan. As a general or functional manager, you must understand this process in order to fund initiatives of interest to your area and to partake in the overall budgeting and prioritization process in partnership with other executives and information systems professionals.

Specifically, in this chapter we learned that

- Total cost of ownership (TCO) is a financial estimate designed to explicitly recognize the life cycle cost of information technology (IT) assets. The costs of information systems and technology typically far exceed the cost of acquisition (e.g., selection, licensing, implementation) and include expenses that occur after the system is up and running but are necessary to maintain it in operation over its life-span.

- Project sponsors use TCO in the formulation of the business case. The business case is the formal documentation used to garner support and win funding for the initiative. The project sponsor presents the business case to the executive committee or, in larger organizations, to the steering committee. The steering committee, composed of representatives from the various functional areas and IS professionals, provides guidance for the use of information systems assets and shares the responsibility for aligning IS efforts with business strategy.

- Modern organizations use one of three approaches to the funding of information systems operations and projects: chargeback, allocation, and overhead. The chargeback method, requiring direct billing based on actual usage, gives the most control to users but has the highest administrative costs. The allocation method, requiring direct billing based on measures such as size or revenue, seeks to strike a balance between fair billing and administrative overhead. Finally, the overhead method, drawing funding directly from the overall organization's budget, is the simplest to administer but reduces accountability of both the IS function and units using the services.

- The yearly budgeting process is the tool organizations use to assess future information systems requirements and prioritize funding. The budgeting process enables the firm to encourage and enforce specific behaviors and to allocate information systems decision rights and control. It can be a fairly stressful and emotionally charged process in which managers compete for funding of their projects.

- During the budgeting process, the firm has an opportunity to evaluate the risk of proposed projects, both individually and as a portfolio. The firm must take this opportunity to evaluate whether the degree of risk associated with its current portfolio of projects matches the risk profile the firm deemed appropriate during strategic information systems planning.

- Information systems outsourcing is the process of contracting with an outside firm to obtain information systems services. Modern organizations outsource their complete IS function (i.e., full outsourcing) or some of their IS assets and services (i.e., selective outsourcing), seeking one or more of the following benefits: reduced costs, access to superior information systems talent, improved control over IS resources, a freeing up of resources to focus on core competencies, and liquidated IT assets. When evaluating outsourcing of information systems services, you need to consider the following risks: a firm with admittedly poor IS management will have difficulties evaluating providers and negotiating good contracts; outsourcing partners seek to maximize their own performance, which often creates friction; IS requirements evolve rapidly; and information systems operations are often more strategic than executives realize.

Study Questions

1. Describe the relationship between strategic information systems planning and the yearly budgeting and prioritization processes. What is the objective of each?
2. Why should general and functional managers be involved in decisions about the funding of information systems assets and services?
3. What is a business case? What is its purpose? Who should be developing and presenting the business case for a new information system?
4. Define the following terms: *total cost of ownership (TCO)* and *steering committee*.
5. Describe each of the three main information systems funding methods and discuss the advantages and disadvantages of each.
6. What are the key drivers of new information systems project risk? Why should a firm evaluate the aggregate risk of its portfolio of projects? What should the organization do if the current level of portfolio risk is not aligned with the degree of risk deemed appropriate according to the strategic information systems plan?
7. Define and differentiate the following terms: *outsourcing, information systems outsourcing, offshoring, full outsourcing,* and *selective outsourcing*. What are the principal drivers and risks associated with information systems outsourcing?

Further Readings

1. Han, K., and Mithas, S. (2013). Information technology outsourcing and non-IT operating costs: An empirical investigation. *MIS Quarterly, 37*(1), 315–331.
2. Huff, S. L., Maher, P. M., & Munro, M. C. (2006). Information technology and the board of directors: Is there an IT attention deficit? *MIS Quarterly Executive, 5*(2), 1–14.
3. Lacity, M., Willcocks, L., & Feeny, D. (1995, May–June). Information technology outsourcing: Maximizing flexibility and control. *Harvard Business Review, 65,* 84–93.
4. Lacity, M., Willcocks, L., & Feeny, D. (1996, Spring). The value of selective IT sourcing. *Sloan Management Review, 37*(3), 13–25.
5. McFarlan, F. W. (1981). Portfolio approach to information systems. *Harvard Business Review, 51,* 142–150.
6. McFarlan, F. W., & Nolan, R. L. (1995, Winter). How to manage an IT outsourcing alliance. *Sloan Management Review, 36*(2), 9–24.
7. Nolan, R., & McFarlan, F. W. (2005, October). Information technology and the board of directors. *Harvard Business Review, 83*(10), 96–106.
8. Parent, M., & Reich, B. H. (2009). Governing information technology risk. *California Management Review, 51*(2), 134–152.
9. Ross, J. W., & Weill, P. (2002, November). Six IT decisions your IT people shouldn't make. *Harvard Business Review,* 84–92.
10. Rottman, J., & Lacity, M. (2004). Twenty practices for offshore sourcing. *MIS Quarterly Executive, 3*(3), 117–130.
11. Ward, J., & Daniel, E. (2006). *Benefits management: Delivering value from IS and IT investments.* Hoboken, NJ: Wiley.

Glossary

- **Allocation:** A method of funding information systems where the cost of services is billed to the organizational function that uses them based on some stable metric (e.g., size, revenues, number of users).
- **Business case:** A formal document prepared and presented by the general or functional manager sponsoring the project. It provides the rationale for pursuing the opportunity.
- **Chargeback:** A method of funding information systems where the cost of services is billed to the organizational function that uses them based on actual usage.
- **Chief information officer (CIO):** The individual in charge of the information systems function.
- **Governance:** In general terms, the set of processes, policies, and practices for administering and controlling an entity.

- **Information systems outsourcing:** The process of contracting with an outside firm to obtain information systems services.
- **Information systems governance:** The set of decisions rights and the guiding accountability framework designed to ensure that IT resources are employed appropriately in the organization.
- **Offshoring:** The process of engaging a foreign provider to supply the products or services the firm no longer intends to produce internally. Short for *offshore outsourcing*.
- **Overhead:** A method of funding information systems where the cost of services is not billed to the organizational function that uses them. Rather, information systems assets and services are funded directly from the organization's overall budget.
- **Steering committee:** A committee, composed of representatives from the various functional areas and IS professionals, that provides guidance for the use of information systems assets and shares the responsibility for aligning IS efforts with business strategy.
- **Total cost of ownership (TCO):** A financial estimate designed to explicitly recognize the life cycle cost of IT assets.

CHAPTER 11

Creating Information Systems

What You Will Learn in This Chapter

This chapter covers a very important subject: the process by which organizational information systems come to be. While as a general or functional manager you may not concern yourself with hardware decisions, you must partake in the software design, acquisition, and implementation processes. Your involvement is essential because technology professionals rarely can evaluate the cost/benefit trade-off and impact of new information systems on the organization and its business success drivers.

Specifically, this chapter will

1. Help you appreciate how complex it is to design and implement information systems (IS) and the stable, robust, secure technology at their core.
2. Articulate the advantages and disadvantages of custom software design and development versus acquisition of an off-the-shelf product.
3. Describe and teach you to use the main methodologies for custom software design and development. Specifically, you will be able to identify the major phases of the system development life cycle (SDLC) and discuss its advantages and disadvantages. You will also become familiar with the prototyping approach and will be able to identify its principal advantages and disadvantages.
4. Identify the systems selection methodology so you can choose a prepackaged software program for a specific organization.
5. Describe the reasons for the increasing prominence of end-user development in modern organizations and articulate the benefits and risks of this approach to software development.

MINICASE: Project Management Blues

"What am I going to do now?" you find yourself asking out loud while staring at the ceiling in your office. "Should I de-escalate this project or press on?" It felt like you were in one of those management case studies—except that it was real and it was you!

You replayed the events leading up to this dilemma. It all started when you were appointed the lead of the HRBPS team—the project team in charge of creating the new human resources benefits package management system. You had made a very successful business case presentation and received public praise from the executive team. "Finally! Someone who does

not speak techno-mumbo-jumbo but can present an IT project in business terms!" L. J. Lalli, the chief executive officer (CEO), had exclaimed. It had been your ability to interface with both the developers and the business stakeholders that had landed you the project manager position. You were the first project manager in your firm to come from a functional area (human resources) instead of the information systems function.

The project had proceeded very well, with great support from the user community—your former colleagues, of course. This was due in large part to your knowledge of HR and your stakeholder-friendly approach. You had made a conscious choice to seek user feedback and to honor as many requests for enhancements as possible. "You have to freeze the requirements," Erik Khan, the lead system analyst, had objected. "Otherwise it's going to be anarchy." But you had dismissed his complaints as "development team grumblings." Those guys were never happy with a little uncertainty anyway. Having been on "the other side" as a stakeholder in a number of system development projects, you knew full well that unhappy users were the fastest route to system failure.

Now you were beginning to second guess your decision. The original schedule called for releasing the beta version of the application for user testing later this week. Instead you had only 40% of the approved functionality coded. Moreover, your team was looking at a list of 22 enhancements, 2 of which would require a change in the database structure. Projected completion, without the proposed enhancements, entailed seven more months (a 45% increase on the original).

It was now apparent that the original project had also been underfunded. The current estimate for finishing the project with the approved set of requirements called for a 62% budget increase (over the original). It was unclear how much more it would cost to exceed the requirements since the 22 proposed enhancements had yet to be evaluated by the system architect.

You were due to present a progress report to Ms. Lalli tomorrow afternoon, but you were still unsure about what course to take. The only certainty at this point was that you had to make your pitch for a project extension and ask for further funding at the meeting. Your plan was to report on the current state of affairs, paint a picture of the final product, and seek support. But what was the final product going to be?

Discussion Questions

1. What should your agenda for tomorrow's meeting be? Should you press on with your strategy, or is a change of course in order?
2. What would you do differently, if anything, given the chance to start this project all over again?

Introduction

Once a firm has developed a strategic plan for the use of information systems (IS) resources (Chapter 6) and has gone through the budgeting and prioritization processes (Chapter 10) to identify what specific information systems it needs, it is ready to act. Whether the information systems rely on custom-developed technology or off-the-shelf software, it is critical that you as a general or functional manager understand how information systems come to be. Armed with this knowledge, you can proactively participate in the process.

While general and functional managers need not be concerned with hardware decisions, they must take part in the software design, acquisition, and implementation processes. Aside from the significant portion of your budget devoted to information systems management and development, general and functional managers' involvement in information systems funding and design is essential because never before has a firm's success depended so much on the use of the right software applications. Deciding what the characteristics of the "right" applications are is a business decision. It is a decision based more on the business case and the understanding of the business processes the software will enable (or constrain!) than on any technical consideration.

How Hard Can IT Be?

Consider the following three recent examples, each playing out in the last few years. On a separate sheet, answer the question before reading on to find out what really happened:

- The U.S. subsidiary of one of the major food producers in the world inked a deal to implement SAP (the leading enterprise system application) in an effort to centralize and rationalize operations across its nine divisions. The project required streamlining processes, standardizing software applications, and implementing the same organizational structure across the units. How much time and how much money would you budget for this project?
- A large hospitality company with more than 2,000 branded hotels developed a customer information system to enable its customer relationship management (CRM) strategy. The

custom-developed functionalities of the software application at the heart of the information system included a property-management system, the loyalty and CRM applications, and the reporting modules. How much time and how much money would you budget for this project?

- A major telecommunication carrier scheduled an upgrade of its customer service systems from version 6 to version 7 of a leading off-the-shelf application. The newer, more powerful version, exchanging information with 15 other systems (e.g., billing), would simplify customer service representatives' access to customer data and would increase the amount of customer information available for sales and service transactions. How much time and how much money would you budget for this project?

There are few technologies and products that have evolved as far and as fast as information technology (IT) has. However, the astounding successes of IT can be misleading, tricking you into severely underestimating what it takes to build and implement a stable, robust, secure system that will work under a wide array of organizational conditions.

Should you check your answers one last time before reading on? OK, here's what happened:

- The implementation of SAP by the major food service company took more than six years and more than $200 million. It was mired by setbacks and dead ends, with high-profile casualties, including the project leader, who was reassigned midway through the implementation.
- The large hospitality firm invested more than $50 million in the design and development of the application and in integrating it with the other applications in the firm's infrastructure. The project took about two years and by its conclusion it had cost about $120 million. The resulting system, the firm's largest investment in recent history, was considered a success.
- The upgrade at the telecommunication company was a complete failure. The new system was unstable, crashing for days at a time, and the old system was no longer usable. The customer service difficulties translated into an estimated $100 million in lost revenue during the three months it took to complete the upgrade. A rival acquired the firm, which was mired in difficulties, for half its original valuation.

The critical insight to be gained from this simple exercise is that organizational information systems usher in a wealth of complexities that go far beyond those associated with the personal computing environment that is most familiar to the typical end user (i.e., purchasing and installing Microsoft Office; Figure 11.1). Unfortunately, managers are surrounded by the misleading rhetoric of statements like "IT is easy; the hard part is people," or "Today, firms can easily develop or purchase technology to obtain the capabilities to rapidly match their competitors," or "IT is a commodity."

These views are gross oversimplifications of reality. When they are held by those who have never been involved in large-scale information systems development efforts, they dangerously hide the truth: organizational information systems' development efforts are very complex and risky endeavors. A McKinsey study performed on more than 5,400 IT projects showed that, on average, they run 45% over budget, 7% over time, while delivering 56% less value than expected, and that 17% of them produce negative consequences to threaten "the very existence of the company."[1] IT projects are complex and risky precisely because they involve both technical and social challenges—and the intersection of the two.

Rob Austin, a professor at the Copenhagen Business School and author, captured this notion best when explaining why information systems projects will likely never be as disciplined and predictable as other engineering processes (e.g., the building of a factory). He stated the following:

In classic IT terms, important "requirements" are often not discernible in advance. If this statement sounds wrong to you, try on the alternative—that it's always possible to discern all the important requirements in advance, regardless of the size and complexity of the system and

1. Bloch, M., Blumberg, S., & Laartz, J. (2012, October), Delivering large-scale IT projects on time, on budget, and on value, *McKinsey Quarterly*.

FIGURE 11.1. The potential and risk of IS projects
Source: Baseline Magazine, http://www.baselinemag.com

the rate of technological and business change. [. . .] Indeed, what makes a system great in the end, usually, is not just that it satisfies requirements that were known in advance. The difference between a great, value-adding IT system and a clunky dog that everyone hates is often in the details that are discovered along the way, as the system is implemented and users begin to have a more tangible sense of how it will work.[2]

The interplay of many different actors (often with divergent agendas), the sheer size of many organizational systems, the myriad of expected and unforeseen organizational conditions the system must support, and the constantly evolving nature of the modern firm make these projects extremely challenging. These projects require technical expertise. They also call for a big dose of managerial skill and informed involvement by general and functional managers.

Fulfilling Information Processing Needs

In Chapter 2, we stated that the primary reason modern organizations introduce information systems is to fulfill their information processing needs. Information systems leverage IT at their core to optimize the manner in which the firm captures, processes, stores, and distributes information.

How does the firm go about introducing the information processing functionalities needed to fulfill its information processing needs? How do information systems come to be in modern organizations? At the most general level of analysis, this process has two main components—technology development and information system deployment:

- *Technology development.* Modern information systems are built on an IT core. Whether the technology is acquired and integrated into the existing firm's infrastructure or is custom built by (or for) the organization, generating the IT core is a prerequisite to delivering the needed information processing functionalities.
- *Information system development.* Creating the needed IT core is not sufficient to fulfill the information processing needs of the firm (see Chapter 2). The firm must successfully integrate the technology with the other components of the organization (i.e., people, processes, structure) to develop a working information system. This is the implementation process.

---

2. Austin, R. (2005, July 1), No crystal ball for IT, *CIO Magazine*, retrieved from http://www.cio.com/article/2448685/project-management/no-crystal-ball-for-i-t-.html

The technology development and implementation processes are intertwined, not sequential. Because of systemic effects (Chapter 2), the components of an information system must interact with one another without friction. Thus the design of a new software program (i.e., technology development) must take into account how the technology will be employed (i.e., processes), by whom (i.e., people), and with what purpose (i.e., structure). That is, technology development must take into account future implementation as it is being designed.

Three Approaches

There are three general approaches to the acquisition of information processing functionalities and the introduction of IT-based information systems. Note that each of these approaches encompasses both the technology development and implementation processes. However, the critical differences among them pertain to how the technology components—and more specifically, the software that defines the capabilities of the system—are designed and developed:

1. *Custom design and development.* With this approach the organization implements a software application that is expressly made, whether internally or through outsourcing, for the unique needs of the firm.
2. *System selection and acquisition.* With this approach the organization implements an off-the-shelf software application that is mass-produced by a vendor.
3. *End-user development.* With this approach the organization uses a software application created by its end users, rather than the firm's information systems professionals.

We describe below the advantages and risks associated with each approach. We also introduce the most prevalent methodologies used to articulate the information systems design and development process in each case. Our objective here is not for you to become an expert in systems design and development. Rather, it is to help you nurture an understanding of the process so that you can successfully take part in it.

Make versus Buy

In some cases, custom developing the software at the heart of a new information system is not an option for your firm; it is a necessity. This is the case when the system must enable a new initiative and no market for such a product already exists. For example, when Amazon first introduced its personal recommendation system, electronic commerce was largely uncharted territory and the firm was indeed shaping the online retailing industry. Waiting for an off-the-shelf product to be developed was not an option.

Typically, though, the firm will have to weigh the choice between custom development and purchase of the needed technology. Each approach offers some advantages and disadvantages and increasingly firms decide to reverse course—a process known as insourcing. In 2013, General Motors' chief information officer (CIO) Randy Mott ended a $3 billion a year outsourcing contract, deciding instead to up the number of GM software engineers from 1,400 to 8,000. He summarized the rationale for the decision: "Because we brought the [information technology] work back in-house, we can take the lid off of what is possible."[3]

Advantages of Custom Development   While prepackaged software is available in the marketplace, in many cases the firm will still engage in custom design and development to capitalize on the advantages of this process. Such advantages include the following.

Unique Tailoring   The defining characteristic of custom-developed software applications is that they are molded to fit the unique features of the firm that commissions them. A quote by Bill Bass, former

---

3. Beent, J. (2015, February 17), Why GM hired 8,000 programmers, *Wall Street Journal*, retrieved from http://www.wsj.com/articles/gm-built-internal-skills-to-manage-internet-sales-push-1424200731

senior vice president for eCommerce at Lands' End, provides an apt metaphor: "Fitting 100 some million women in the U.S. in 8 or 10 basic sizes as well as they would like is really impossible."[4] When we purchase clothes in standard sizes, they often fit well in one area and less well in another. Typically we accept this substandard fit. Yet those who find it hard to locate fitting clothes (and can afford it) can purchase tailor-made garments—perhaps using the Lands' End custom website.

The human body is unique and no two people are alike. The same holds true for modern organizations. Thus off-the-shelf software will "fit" well in some areas of the firm but may create problems in others and require some adjustment from the organization.[5] Conversely, custom-made software, like a tailor-made suit, can be designed to fit perfectly with the organization's characteristics and needs.

Note that while every organization is unique, not all its processes are. For example, while Lands' End and Eddie Bauer are two different organizations, they both provide e-mail for their employees and do so in a very similar fashion. Standard mail server software will likely serve the needs of both firms quite well. Conversely, if the business processes that the software is designed to enable are unique and value adding (i.e., a source of competitive advantage), commercial off-the-shelf software may undermine their uniqueness and be detrimental to the firm.

Flexibility and Control Custom-developed software applications offer the highest degree of flexibility and control to the organization. Because the project team builds the system from scratch, the software can be molded into any form the stakeholders (e.g., management, end users) would like it to take, and the firm owes no licensing fees to software vendors. Moreover, since the firm retains control over the code, the system can be evolved, at any time, in any direction the firm would like.

This level of control is not achievable with software purchased from vendors, since software houses need to develop applications that serve the needs of a large number of buyers. Moreover, the software house has to prioritize the features that will be coded into the upgrades. Typically they are the ones that have the broadest appeal, rather than niche requests from individual clients.

Advantages of Purchasing As the software industry has evolved and grown dramatically over the last 30 years, the off-the-shelf offer has become comprehensive. Purchasing software from a vendor yields a number of advantages to the organization.

Faster Roll-Out An organization that purchases new software is typically interested in the information processing functionalities it enables, not in IT itself. Thus how quickly the firm can be "up and running" with the new information system is an important concern. Purchased software dramatically reduces the time it takes to obtain the software and begin the implementation process. Rather than engaging in the lengthy custom development process, the firm researches and evaluates existing packages before selecting one. Upon purchasing the selected application, the implementation phase is ready to start.

Knowledge Infusion Another advantage offered by off-the-shelf applications is access to the expertise coded in the software. Because software programs can enable and constrain the manner in which users complete a task or execute a business process (Chapter 2), an organization that purchases prepackaged software also acquires a "way of doing business." Consider the example of a call center operator who takes orders from catalog shoppers. The design of the application will determine the order in which the interaction takes place (e.g., greeting, items to be shipped, verification of address, payment) and what data are necessary to complete the transaction (e.g., no order can be completed without a valid phone number).

This notion of knowledge infusion is now an important design and marketing tool for software vendors who proactively seek out best practices in order to code them into their applications. Returning

---

4. Ives, B., & Piccoli, G. (2003), Custom made apparel and individualized service at Lands' End, *Communications of the AIS, 11*(3), 79–93.

5. As we will see, this adjustment of the organization typically takes place during implementation, when, taking the software as given, a working information system is developed.

to the call center example, an often mentioned best practice in call center operations is to enable personalized interactions with each customer. Thus a call center software vendor may code a feature in its application that automatically brings up the customer's order history so that the representative may engage in informed conversation with the customer.

Economically Attractive   While it is always difficult to generalize when it comes to system design and development costs, purchasing off-the-shelf applications typically allows the firm to capitalize on the economies of scale achieved by the vendor. As with the example of mass-produced and tailor-made clothing, when a vendor can produce many units of the same software application, it enjoys declining fixed costs that, in turn, lower the unit cost. This is particularly true with software, a classic information good (see Chapter 4) characterized by very high costs of producing the first copy and negligible reproduction costs.

High Quality   A great deal of debate surrounds the issue of software quality, with the skeptics pointing to the many examples of prepackaged applications that have significant bugs. Yet large software houses with mature products will point to their sizable testing budgets and large installed base of users as evidence that their applications have been put through the paces and thus all major problems have surfaced.

Buy and Make

The make versus buy decision is typically treated as a dichotomous one (i.e., the firm must choose one or the other approach).[6] Yet modern firms are increasingly adopting blended approaches, first acquiring systems and then modifying them extensively.

A Cutter Consortium survey found that, when asked about the degree of customization required by large off-the-shelf applications the firm purchased, less than 12% of respondents said they modified the software slightly or not at all. A quarter of them reported modifying the application "a great deal." Furthermore, half the respondents reported that the degree of package customization they engaged in exceeded their preimplementation expectations.[7]

Keeping with the current integration trends (Chapter 3), off-the-shelf applications are becoming larger and more complex and are increasingly crossing departmental boundaries. Under these circumstances, we can expect the need for extensive customization of prepackaged products only to increase—a fact lost on unsophisticated general and functional managers who expect the application to work immediately after installation, the way simple personal productivity software does.

Build Your Own: Systems Design and Development

Until the rise to prominence of the software industry, the acquisition of prepackaged software was the exception, rather than the norm, for most organizations. Its long tradition notwithstanding, designing and developing organizational software applications and information systems has always been a complex, failure-prone undertaking. Viewed by many as more akin to alchemy than to a reliable science, systems design and development continues to frighten non-IT managers, who perceive it as a minefield of technical, behavioral, and managerial challenges (Figure 11.2).

In order to manage the risk and complexity associated with custom development, information systems specialists, academics, and consultants have contributed to the creation of a number of systems design and development methodologies.

Systems Development Life Cycle

The two dominant systems development methodologies today are the system development life cycle (SDLC) and prototyping. The SDLC approach is predicated on the notion that detailed justification

---

6. To simplify the discussion, we discuss each approach separately as well.

7. Ulrich, W. (2006), Application package survey: The promise versus reality, *Cutter Benchmark Review,* 6(9), 13–20.

| How the customer explained it | How the project leader understood it | How the analyst designed it | How the programmer wrote it | How the business consultant described it |

| How the project was documented | What operations installed | How the customer was billed | How it was supported | What the customer really needed |

FIGURE 11.2. The system development life cycle (SDLC) as perceived by many managers
Source: ProjectCartoon.com

and planning is the vehicle to reduce risk and uncertainty in systems design and development efforts. Thus spending considerable time up front, the project team improves the chances of solving the right business problem with the right information system design. For this reason the SDLC is a highly structured methodology where the outputs of one stage become the inputs of the next and where the project team strives to keep changes after the project has started to a minimum.[8]

The SDLC methodology is articulated in three phases—definition, build, and implementation—each one further divided into three steps (Table 11.1).

Definition   The definition phase of the SDLC is concerned with clearly identifying the features of the proposed information system. The critical actors in this phase are the prospective end users and the general or functional managers who represent the main stakeholders.

From the information systems staff, systems and business analysts get involved. Systems analysts are highly skilled information systems professionals who are well versed in both technology issues and communication. Their role is to help users identify and articulate the system requirements and serve as a liaison with the technical staff (i.e., developers). Business analysts are individuals with expertise in business process redesign as well as technology. They help ensure that the business processes and software programs at the heart of an information system are jointly optimized and work smoothly together.

Investigation   During investigation, proponents of the new system must identify what business issues the system will pertain to. Managers who envision new ways of operating are the driving force at this

---

8. The SDLC is often called the waterfall model because, as water flowing down a waterfall never flows upward, there should be no going back once a stage has been completed.

Table 11.1. Principal phases of the SDLC

Definition
Investigation
Feasibility analysis
System analysis

Build
System design
Programming
Testing

Implementation
Installation
Operations
Maintenance

stage, as they formulate the main goals, scope, and value proposition of the new system. This stage is typically very informal. The next stage brings a greater discipline to the analysis.

Feasibility Analysis   In order to ensure that scarce organizational resources are put to best use, the project team must heavily scrutinize the proposed project prior to giving the formal go-ahead. Specifically, the team must evaluate the technical, operational, and economic feasibility of the project.[9]

Technical feasibility is the evaluation of whether the proposed system is viable from an IT standpoint. The team must ask whether the state of the art in hardware, software, and telecommunication equipment is such that the proposed system will work as intended (e.g., it will have enough storage capacity and an acceptable response time). The history of new systems development abounds, with examples of technology implementations that predated their time, thus undermining system success.

Operational feasibility, sometimes called behavioral feasibility, is the evaluation of whether the information system as a whole, not just the technology component, is viable. This analysis requires an evaluation of the other three components to make sure that employees have the skills necessary to utilize the new technology and that they will accept (or can be given incentives to accept) the new work system. During this phase, the project team must envision how business processes will be redesigned and must foresee possible drivers of user resistance and rejection.

Economic feasibility is the evaluation of the financial viability of the proposed system. A number of techniques have been developed over time to justify the proposed investment, including return on investment (ROI), payback, and net present value computations. Ultimately, evaluating financial feasibility consists of performing a cost/benefit analysis in order to ensure that the money to be spent on the system design and development project meets the firm's financial hurdles for investment. The business case provides the basis for this analysis (see Chapter 10).

The outcome of the feasibility analysis is a document culminating in a "go" or "no-go" recommendation. At this point the firm has invested a small amount of resources, relative to the full project cost; thus if the project is to be called off, this is an appropriate time to do so.

System Analysis   Once a decision has been made that the system is worth pursuing, the project team needs to identify and articulate the system requirements. Systems analysts and the stakeholders (i.e.,

---

9. Note that the feasibility analysis for a new system is informed by its business case (Chapter 10), but there are differences. The business case mainly focuses on justifying the pursuit of the project (i.e., cost/benefit analysis), while the feasibility analysis looks comprehensively at all the factors that can hamper system success—technical, operational, and economic.

Reservation functions	❖ Clear all fields by clicking a Reset button ❖ Retrieve guest profile info for the selected main guest ❖ Modify guest profile info for selected main guest ❖ Retrieve previous reservations for modification ❖ Select a main guest by typing his/her name in full ❖ Select a main guest by typing the first few letters, then selecting from a suggested list of 5 names ❖ Add multiple rooms or a single room for multiple days to a reservation ❖ View the calculated tax for a reservation ❖ View the calculated total cost (before and after tax) ❖ Modify rates for individual room-nights on-the-fly ❖ Record pre-paid amount and method of payment ❖ Add notes specific to a reservation

FIGURE 11.3. User requirements

end users, management) take center stage at this point. If the system is not simply automating existing tasks but is instead enabling redesigned business processes, business analysts will join the team.

In large systems implementations, it is impossible to involve all users at this stage; rather a subset of the user population joins the team, sometimes full time. Note that it is critical to choose users who are representative of the broader population—that is, the team should include not only the users who are highest performing or most well versed with technology (so-called superusers) but also underperforming and, most importantly, dissenting users (those individuals who may indeed resist rather than support the new system).

Another important aspect of user involvement is that it should not be "window dressing" or "impression management." Systems analysts must genuinely seek out and value stakeholders' input in the process. The system analyst is the specialist in this phase, not the user. It is therefore the system analyst's job to ensure a productive and comprehensive surfacing of requirements.

As the outcome of this stage, the project team produces the systems requirements document (Figure 11.3). This document details what inputs the system will accept, what outputs it will produce, what users will have access to what information, and so on. The document typically includes mock-up screens and scenarios (Figure 11.4) and is sent to the stakeholders for review and approval.

In a strict application of the SDLC methodology, once the stakeholders approve the document, the systems requirements are "frozen" and the cost of future changes, if any are requested, becomes the responsibility of the stakeholders. This step is necessary to minimize the impact of scope creep—the phenomenon by which stakeholders add or change requirements during the build phase of the SDLC, thus significantly increasing cost and considerably delaying development.

Build   The build phase of the SDLC is the most technical, and the one that most people picture when they imagine how software is designed and developed. This phase is the primary domain of developers: systems architects and programmers. The objective is to take the system requirements document and produce a robust, secure, and efficient application.

System Design   The build phase begins with the system design stage. Taking the results of the definition phase (i.e., what the applications should do), architects create the structure of the system (i.e., how the application will perform its tasks). At this stage, the team identifies what hardware will be used, what languages will be adopted, what data structures are needed, and so on. The output of this stage is a precise set of documents that programmers use to write code.

Programming   This is the process of translating the abstract software design into a set of commands or instructions that can be executed by the hardware. If the application requires the creation of new databases, their structure is also developed at this stage (Figure 11.5).

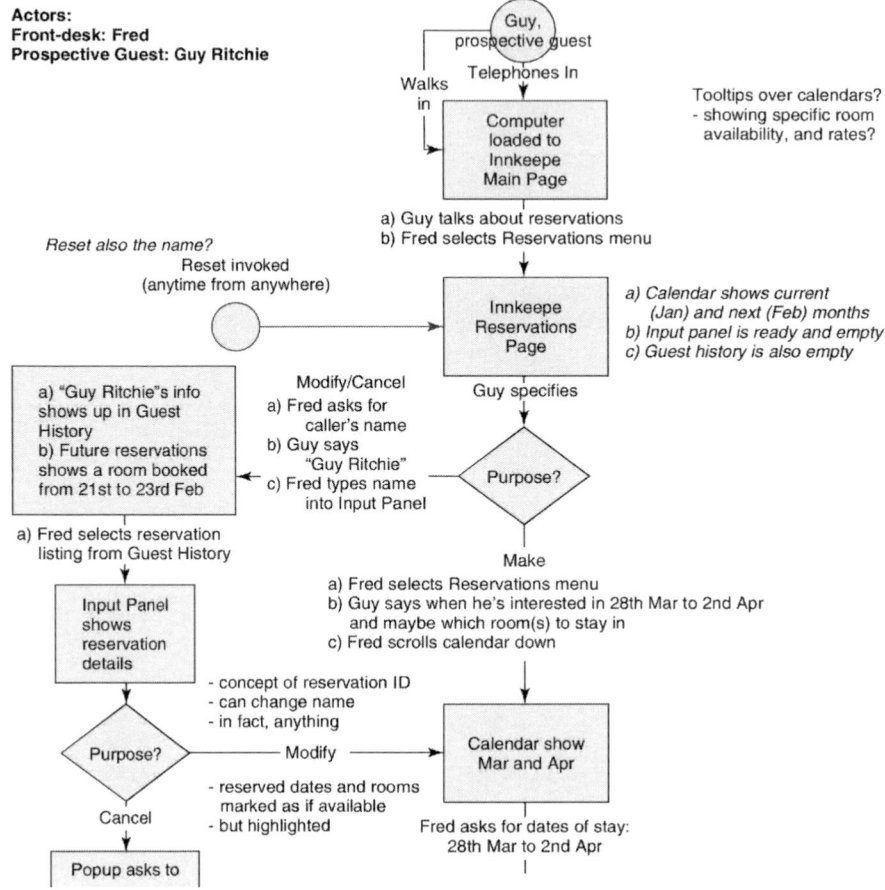

FIGURE 11.4. Sample scenario for hotel reservation process

An important element of the programming stage, but one that developers often detest, is the documentation. Thorough and clear documentation is essential in organizational software programs because they are large, complex, and expected to last for a number of years. Without adequate documentation such systems become impossible to support and maintain, let alone upgrade and evolve over time.

Testing   While system testing is a process that programmers are constantly engaged in as they develop, formalized assessment of components and subsequently of the complete applications is an essential stage in the SDLC. While most non-IT personnel rarely think about testing, this stage can take as much time and resources as the programming stage. The testing phase is articulated in alpha testing, carried out by developers themselves, and beta testing, carried out by releasing the beta version to a limited set of actual users who use it and report any problems they identify.

Note that the objective of the testing stage is not to identify and correct all the possible bugs plaguing the system, as this is uneconomical and rarely needed. Rather, the testing phase is designed to stress the system, to make sure that it can perform under production circumstances, and to correct the most important errors. The objective is to release the application when it is good enough, not when it is flawless.

Implementation   Once the software has been developed and tested, the project team needs to ensure that it is properly integrated with the other components of the information system. This is the implementation phase, an extremely delicate time when project management skills and executives' involvement are essential.

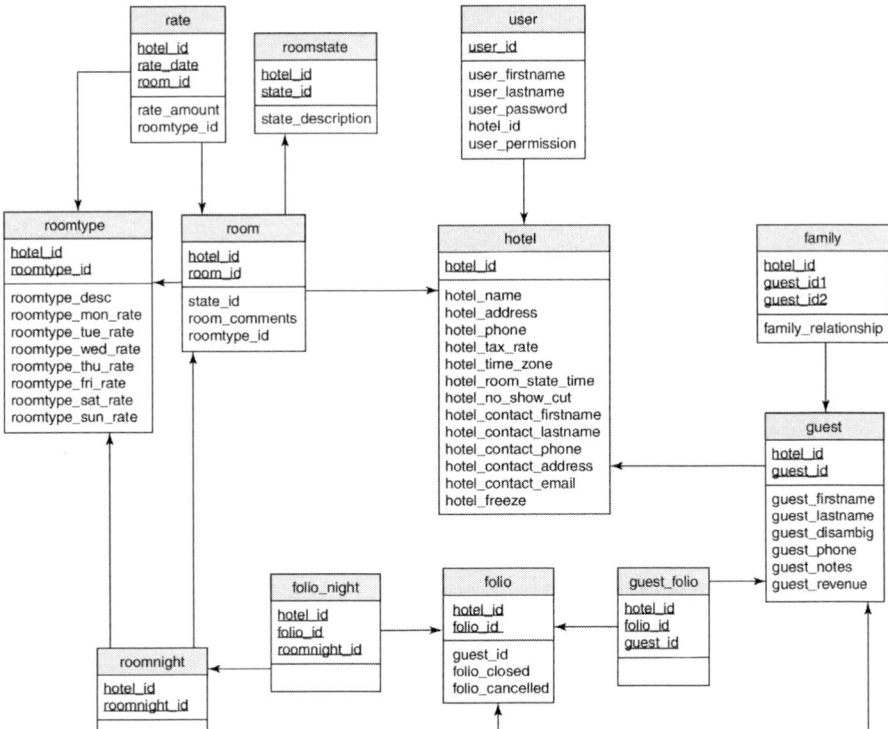

FIGURE 11.5. Database design underlying hotel property management system

Installation   During the installation stage, the system is loaded on the production hardware and the databases are populated. Installation typically takes place during slow periods for the organization and, if at all possible, while the system is not needed (e.g., over a weekend, at night). If an existing system is being replaced, the firm migrates from the old one to the new one following one of four approaches (Figure 11.6):

- *Parallel*. The old and new systems are run for a time together. This approach is the most conservative, as it offers insurance against failure of the new application. It is also the most costly as it requires significant redundancy of efforts. In some cases this approach is the only option (e.g., systems that must operate 24/7/365).
- *Direct*. The old system is suddenly discontinued and the firm cuts over to the new one. This is the most radical approach but one that sometimes cannot be avoided (e.g., the old system stops functioning).
- *Phased*. The new system progressively replaces the functionalities of the old one. This approach is best suited to modular or componentized applications that can be rolled out in stages.
- *Pilot*. Well suited for multiunit operations (e.g., hotels, chain retailers), this approach allows the firm to run the new system in one business unit or in one of the firm's departments before rolling it out completely.

Beyond the technical aspects of the installation phase, there are two critical processes that take place at this time: end-user training and change management. End-user training typically occurs in formal settings, such as classrooms or makeshift computer labs. Change management is the process of smoothing the transition from the way the various stakeholders interacted with the previous system and carried out their work to the new work practices. User resistance and inertia are the biggest dangers at

FIGURE 11.6. Migration approaches

this point. To the extent that stakeholders had been actively involved in the early stages of the SDLC and the design of the system, this phase will be less traumatic, thus minimizing risks of rejection.

Operations   At this stage, the system is up and running, and the organization begins to use it. The project team is disbanded and the new system becomes a permanent asset of the firm to be maintained and managed.

Maintenance   Once the system is in place and is up and running, both errors that had escaped the testing phase and enhancements that had escaped the requirements definition phase begin to emerge. Maintenance is the process of compiling this information, prioritizing requests, and implementing both fixes and improvements. Note that as comprehensive and well designed as a new system may be, the organization is in continuous evolution. As a consequence, over time it is normal for a gap to emerge between the current system's functionalities and the firm's needs. (Remember this the next time you are tempted to ask, "What were they thinking when they designed this system?!")

The functionality gap is closed on an ongoing basis by way of upgrades and additions until such ongoing maintenance becomes economically unfeasible and management makes the case for the development of a new information system. For this reason, some authors have begun to suggest that the traditional sequential SDLC approach needs to be reevaluated.[10]

Advantages of the SDLC Approach   The SDLC is a highly structured methodology that provides a systematic approach to reducing the uncertainty and risk associated with systems design and development projects. It clearly identifies roles and expectations for the members of the project team, and it offers a blueprint for how these individuals should interact. By demanding a thorough justification and requirements definition, it is particularly well suited for large-scale projects where changes that occur during development or implementation can be very costly.

The SDLC also offers a vehicle for communication and negotiation between the project team and the many project stakeholders. It does so by requiring evaluation and approval of deliverables for every phase, thereby stimulating discussion, facilitating the identification of priorities, and surfacing hidden trade-offs.

Limitations   While the SDLC methodology has evolved from the traditional waterfall approach into a more iterative process (e.g., spiral model) in which designers and developers are allowed some reevaluation of previous stages, the SDLC remains a highly structured approach. Thus its critics point out

---

that it creates substantial overhead in terms of time and cost, and does not enable the project team to properly address the inevitable changes that occur during the life of complex projects.

Prototyping

Recognizing the limitations inherent in the SDLC methodology, the prototyping approach is rooted in the notion that it is impossible to clearly estimate and plan in detail such complex endeavors as information systems design and development projects. Instead the team is better served by staying nimble and iterating quickly through multiple designs to zero in on the optimal one.

The growing acceptance of prototyping methodologies was enabled by tools that speed up the development process, such as nonprocedural programming languages. These tools allow developers to rapidly create working (or partially working) models of the proposed system and garner stakeholders' feedback about the system's design, functionalities, user interface, and so on.

Prototyping Life Cycle   One of the applications of the prototyping methodology is within the confines of the SDLC, as a way to elicit user requirements and seek input into the design of the user interface. The value of this approach stems from the fact that it is simpler for users to react to a prototype than it is for them to envision and articulate requirements in the abstract. Moreover, by involving users in the development of the front end of the application, the design team can foster their support and increase the chances of acceptance of the final system.

However, prototyping can be used as an alternative to the SDLC to develop a complete system according to the following steps:

Requirements Definitions   At this stage the development team seeks basic requirements. The degree of precision needed is much less than that needed in the SDLC because requirements are not frozen at this point. Rather, the understanding is that future feedback and modification will heavily shape the system.

Initial Prototype   Armed with the basic requirements, the team develops a first iteration of the system. The system could be only a shell (i.e., nonfunctional user interface), a partially functional application, or a "first-of-a-series" fully functional prototype.

Evaluation   At this time the stakeholders review the prototype and provide feedback on the current design as well as requests for enhancements and new functionality.

Revision   Based on the feedback generated during the evaluation stage, the development team designs and codes the requested changes. This phase leads to a new prototype to be submitted to the stakeholders for evaluation. Note that at any time during these iterations the team and the stakeholders may conclude that no further investment in the project is warranted. In this case the firm stops the development effort.

Completion   Once the stakeholders and the development team are satisfied with the functionalities of the system, the iterative evaluation/revision process stops and the development team finalizes the system. At this stage the developers code important features that users typically do not request (e.g., security, administration). Documentation and testing follow, prior to the formal release of the system.

Advantages of the Prototyping Approach   Given the characteristics of the prototyping approach, systems developed this way tend to be more quickly delivered and closer to the users' expectations, since the stakeholders are more involved throughout the development effort. Thus prototyping is best suited to smaller-scale projects and those that radically change the manner in which work is done. The prototyping approach also enables the firm to experiment with new technologies and new system functionalities because it requires a smaller investment of resources than the SDLC before the product can be evaluated—thus limiting the risk and sunk costs.

Limitations   The premium that the prototyping approach puts on speed and functionality development may cause the team to release a system that is lacking from a security, robustness, and reliability standpoint. Systems built using the prototyping approach are typically less thoroughly tested and documented than those using a more structured approach. Moreover, the rapid pace of iteration and release of new prototypes can mislead stakeholders who underestimate the complexity of software development. The consequence is rampant scope creep.[11] These limitations make the prototyping approach ill suited for large-scale and complex systems development efforts.

Agile Development

A new breed of software development approaches has taken hold recently, in part due to the increasing popularity of prototyping. The software development approaches are collectively labeled as agile software development methodologies and are today widely adopted by organizations.[12] Although recent research found that development projects still follow the established waterfall (50%) and iterative models (25%) and that only one-fourth was using agile methodologies, the same report suggests that by 2018 the majority of software projects will be agile.[13]

The philosophy of agile software development has been captured in a document called *the agile manifesto*. The opening statement in that document reads as follows:[14]

> We are uncovering better ways of developing software by doing it and helping others do it. Through this work we have come to value:
> * *Individuals and interactions* over processes and tools
> * *Working software* over comprehensive documentation
> * *Customer collaboration* over contract negotiation
> * *Responding to change* over following a plan
>
> That is, while there is value in the items on the right, we value the items on the left more.

The agile manifesto clearly identifies the priorities and key characteristics of agile methodologies. First and foremost it is adaptability and speed. Agile methods do not call for the substantial amount of planning that characterizes traditional methodologies. Agile proponents believe that planning for all requirements and contingencies in all but trivial system developments is impossible. Significant planning will in fact backfire and limit the ability of the development team to adjust to inevitable new information. Agile developers therefore focus on developing applications with speed and releasing the system often—typically in less than a month. It is this rapid iteration of development and release that will surface accurate requirements and rapidly enable the development team to converge to a system that meets customers' expectations.

A second defining characteristic of agile development methodologies is teamwork in open space offices that facilitate communication. Agile proponents advocate the use of small cross-functional teams with a customer representative and daily face-to-face meetings. In order to organize the work and maintain the aggressive schedules that characterize agile projects, developers "chunk" the work into manageable yet self-standing components. The team then iterates through all the phases of development—from requirements elicitation through testing and customer acceptance.

Scrum, started by Jeff Sutherland in 1993, is the most used among agile methodologies due to its ability to deal with rapidly changing user requirements. Scrum software development progresses via a series of iterations called sprints, lasting usually two to four weeks. Sprints generally begin with a brief planning phase and for the length of the sprint the team meets every day—the daily Scrum—and

---

11. *Scope creep* is a term that refers to uncontrolled changes in the magnitude of the project.

12. VersionOne (2015), *9th annual state of agility survey*, retrieved from http://www.versionone.com/pdf/state-of-agile-development-survey-ninth.pdf

13. Gartner Inc. (2014, November 19), Predicts 2015: Application development, retrieved from https://www.gartner.com/doc/2916817/predicts--application-development

14. "Manifesto for agile software development," retrieved from http://www.agilemanifesto.org

end with a review and retrospective. The principle behind the sprint is that at the end of each sprint, the software should be ready for delivery to a client—at least in principle. While agile development methodologies are still relatively new and in flux, they have gained acceptance within the software development community and are now applied in projects of varying complexity. As such you may find yourself partaking in agile development, as a customer representative on a cross-functional agile team.

Outsourced Development

Custom-designed software programs are increasingly developed by software houses that "fill in" for the firm's information systems professionals. These arrangements, typically called *software development outsourcing*, vary greatly, with some firms only outsourcing the programming and testing stages, while others resort to an external provider to see them through the entire system development life cycle.

The outsourcing of software development projects has increased dramatically in popularity following the widespread adoption of the Internet. Software programs, as a classic information good (Chapter 4), can be designed and developed anywhere in the world. As a consequence, an increasing proportion of U.S. firms' custom software development is now done overseas. Consider virtual teams of developers as an example. Software projects are increasingly completed by development teams that work together but are not physically located in the same office. While cost considerations may come to mind as the principal reason to establish virtual teams, research by Cutter Consortium shows that more than 85% of respondents saw the ability to pool the most qualified talent on the project as the principal driver for their adoption.[15]

With the widespread adoption and internationalization of custom software development, a set of tools to evaluate the quality of providers has emerged. The most popular, the Capability Maturity Model (CMM), ranks software development organizations according to their ability to produce quality software on a scale of 1 to 5 by evaluating a set of standard processes thought to determine software quality. Work on the CMM started at the Software Engineering Institute (SEI) at Carnegie Mellon University (CMU) in the early 1990s as a project funded by the United States Department of Defense (DoD). The DoD was looking to better understand how it could systematize software development processes so as to ensure reliable development and avoid both the failures and unpredictability that characterized it. A natural extension of this effort was to employ the CMM to evaluate vendors and software contractors. The CMM is based on the core notion that reliable and consistent implementation of a specific set of processes represents a higher level of software development maturity and, as a consequence, ensures higher quality software products (Figure 11.7).

The original CMM has evolved significantly over the years and, as a testament to its success, it is now used to evaluate and improve the quality of many other organizational processes (e.g., customer service, acquisition). Today software houses, particularly those engaged in outsourced customer development, seek Capability Maturity Model Integration (CMMI) certification[16] and you, as a buyer of their services, should ask for such information. The CMMI Institute at Carnegie Mellon is in charge of the certification process and periodically releases aggregate statistics (Figure 11.8).

One of the principal value propositions of custom software development outsourcing is in its superior cost/quality ratio. Firms in countries with high costs of living, like North America or Western Europe, can outsource development to countries such as India, Ireland, or China, with a large pool of highly skilled software engineers and programmers and a lower cost of living (i.e., lower wages). Outsourcing developments to these regions of the world enables the firm to receive superior-quality products at a fraction of the cost of internal development (Figure 11.9).

Buying Off-the-Shelf Applications

The SDLC provides the basis for the system selection and purchasing process that organizations use to design and develop information systems based on off-the-shelf software programs (Table 11.2). The

---

15. Piccoli, G. (2006), Virtual teams: No longer an "emerging" organizational form, *Cutter Benchmark Review,* 6(7), 95–96.

16. CMMI stands for Capability Maturity Model Integration and represents the current version of the CMM.

FIGURE 11.7. The five levels of software process maturity
Based on CMMI Product Team (2010), CMMI for Development, Version 1.3, Technical Report (Carnegie Mellon University/Software Engineering Institute), CMU/SEI-2010-TR-033

systems selection process often starts when managers learn about the capabilities of a new application that is being advertised, described in the press, or promoted by consulting firms. Following the systems selection process is important because it enables a systematic investigation of these applications as well as competing products—thus ensuring that all issues are considered and that the firm choose the best solution for its current needs.

Definition

Both the investigation and feasibility analysis stages are qualitatively similar to those in the SDLC. At this time, the proponents of the system articulate a vision for the proposed information system and evaluate its technical, operational, and economic viability. It is in the remaining stages of the definition phase that the major idiosyncrasies of the systems selection process occur.

System Analysis During the system analysis stage, the selection committee focuses on eliciting the specific functionalities required of the proposed system. As with the SDLC, this phase entails the interplay of system analysts and stakeholders. However, the degree of precision and detail sought by the selection committee is less than that needed for custom development. The objective here is to have enough of an understanding of the systems requirements to formulate evaluation criteria.

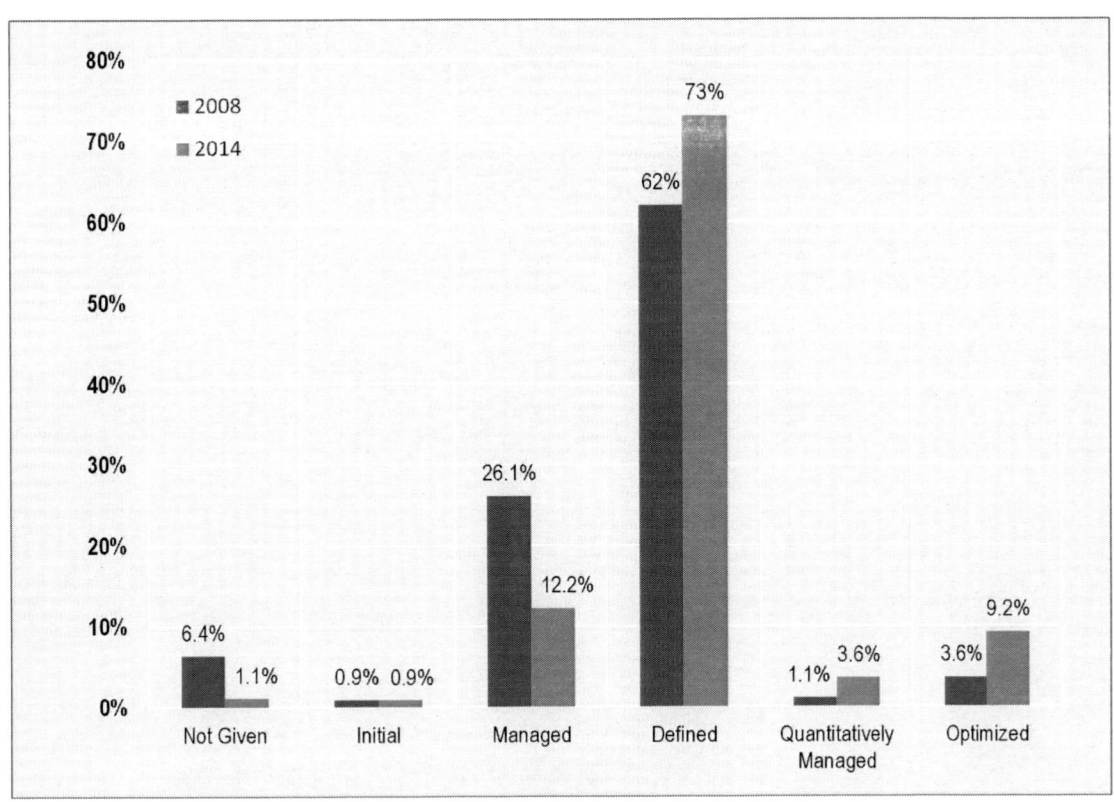

FIGURE 11.8. Process maturity level of appraised organizations trends
Adapted from Maturity Profile Report (2014), CMMI Institute

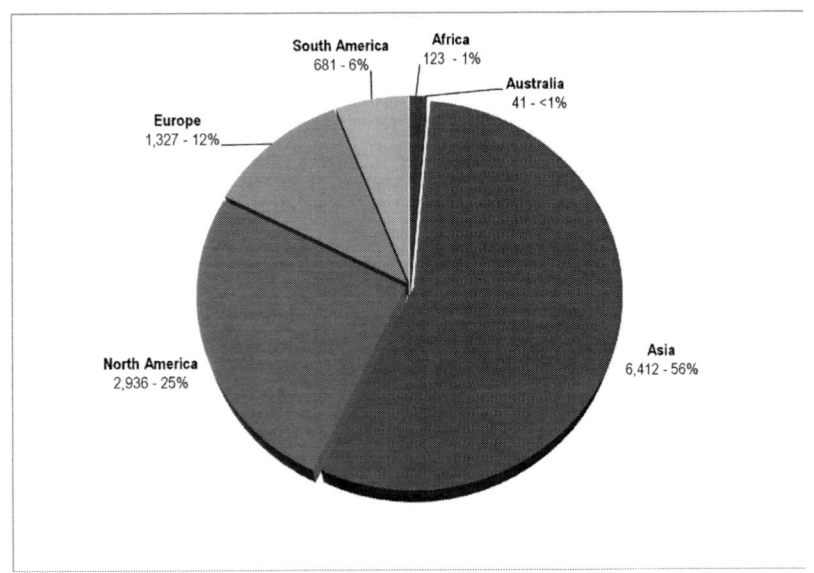

FIGURE 11.9. Distribution of CMMI-rated firms in the world
Adapted from Maturity Profile Report (2014), CMMI Institute

Table 11.2. Phases of the systems selection processes

Definition
Investigation
Feasibility analysis
System analysis
Formulate evaluation criteria
Compile short list of vendors
Compile and distribute request for proposal (RFP)
Evaluate alternatives
Negotiate contract

Build
System design (customizations)
Programming (customizations)
Testing

Implementation
Installation
Operations
Maintenance

Formulate Evaluation Criteria   Systems selection is the structured attempt to evaluate all commercially available software solutions that can enable the proposed information system. In order to do so, it is necessary to develop a set of metrics that can be uniformly applied to all packages under investigation. The criteria must also be amenable to communication to software vendors by way of the request for proposal (RFP) process.

A common approach is to use the system requirements document to identify the features that appropriate applications should have and group them into three categories:

- *Essential features.* Those capabilities that the system must have. Systems that miss any one of these features are automatically discarded.
- *Value-adding features.* Those capabilities that, while not essential, offer significant advantages for which the firm would be willing to pay a premium.
- *Nonessential features.* Those capabilities that are "nice to have" but produce small tangible advantages for which the firm is not willing to pay a premium.

Compile Short List of Vendors   Armed with the evaluation criteria, the selection committee seeks information about existing solutions. Websites, trade press, vendor brochures, and trade expos are all viable sources of information. The information gathered is used to identify a preliminary short list of vendors.

This stage is important for two reasons. First, creating targeted RFPs that yield high-quality responses, and then evaluating those responses, is time consuming. Second, products that fail to meet necessary requirements can be identified fairly quickly, and vendors will appreciate not being asked to respond to RFPs that they have no chance of fulfilling.

Compile and Distribute the RFP   The RFP is the formal communication document used to elicit substantial, detailed information from the short-listed vendors. Most organizations have a template for such documents. The RFP should explain what the selection committee has identified as the critical system requirements, the environment in which the system will be used, and any required performance metrics and expectations.

Upon its distribution to the short-listed vendors, those interested will respond to the RFP. The selection team should ask vendors to adhere to a template, making cross-comparisons of the applications simple, and should ask for pricing information. Vendors should also provide such pricing information according to the firm's template, ensuring that the pricing mechanisms for the applications, any customization, and ongoing maintenance and upgrades are clear and comparable across vendors. Finally, the selection committee should specify a deadline by which vendors must respond in order to be considered.

Evaluate Alternatives   Once all interested vendors have responded to the RFP, the competing solutions are evaluated using the criteria developed earlier. The selection committee compiles the list of top vendors and seeks any further information needed to make a final decision. This includes on-site demonstrations, evaluation of reference sites, and the like. The outcome of this stage in the selection process is a rank-ordered list of the acceptable candidates.

Negotiate Contract   Negotiations can be relatively quick and simple, or they can be a very involved process requiring input from professionals and legal counsel. The objective of the selection committee is to draft and sign a contract that provides the firm with the needed solution and insulates it from future risks. Common elements of negotiation are the components and magnitude of costs (e.g., installation, training, customization, maintenance, upgrades), the eventual liabilities and service-level agreements, control over the intellectual property, and the extent to which modifications are allowed.

Build

The build phase in the system selection process mirrors that of the SDLC but is much narrower in scope. When the software program is to be installed without configuration or customization, as is the case with simple applications, the firm can move directly to formal testing and implementation. However, as we mentioned above, it is becoming increasingly common for organizations that purchase off-the-shelf applications to configure and customize them extensively.[17]

To the extent that customization is necessary, the firm will engage in system design and programming of the required enhancements. This is where a tightly written contract becomes important, as the customization process can add significant time and cost to the project. The contract should specify who is responsible for customizing the application—the vendor, the firm, or a third party (e.g., independent consulting firm, integrator)—and the conditions of the customization effort (e.g., schedule).

Whether customized or not, the firm should test the system. In the case of off-the-shelf applications, the testing stage is mostly concerned with system performance rather than with the identification and correction of bugs.

Implementation

The implementation phase is also quite similar to the one described earlier regarding the SDLC. Installation is performed following one of the approaches described earlier. Interestingly, even within the same class of software applications (e.g., enterprise resource planning [ERP]), a firm may choose different approaches to move from the old to the new system. Note as well that the degree of process change and training required to get buy-in from users is typically greater when implementing off-the-shelf applications. This is because a prepackaged program is not designed with the idiosyncrasies of your organization in mind. Rather the software house builds the program to appeal to the broadest market possible.

---

17. *Configuration* is the process of tailoring a software program using built-in parameters. *Customization* is the process of changing the functionality of the software program beyond available options. Customization requires that the new functionalities be coded using a programming language.

Asking for stakeholders' input during the selection and evaluation of competing solutions is one way to enroll them in the process and reduce rejection risks. However, you should still plan to invest considerable resources during the implementation phase to set up the application, train employees, and engage in change management—particularly when the application is larger in scope and forces a change in traditional work practices.

End-User Development

As we discussed in Chapter 1, the ease of use of information technology has steadily increased, while its cost has declined dramatically over the years. These two forces have conspired to bring the power of software development to the masses in the form of end-user development. *End-user development* is an umbrella term capturing the many ways in which knowledge workers, not IT professionals, create software.

End-user-developed systems range from spreadsheet models (e.g., an ROI calculator written in Microsoft Excel), to personal or departmental databases, to full-fledged software programs built with user-friendly computer languages (e.g., Visual Basic for Applications) or development tools such as fourth-generation languages. These "shadow systems" are now prevalent in modern organizations.[18]

The Benefits of End-User Development

The chief benefits of end-user development stem from user empowerment and the fact that some of the burden on typically overworked information systems departments is lifted. The benefits include the following:

- *Increased speed of development.* The user community typically must direct requests for new systems, and improvements to current ones, to the IS function. In turn, the IS function must prioritize the deployment of its scarce resources. As a consequence, those projects that end users can complete independently will be completed faster by virtue of not entering the queue.
- *End-user satisfaction.* One of the main problems with new systems is users' dissatisfaction or outright rejection. When users create their own applications, they are more likely to be satisfied with the result; they either have created the functionalities they wanted or have themselves decided what features to forgo.
- *Reduced pressure on the IS function.* End-user development can limit the number of requests the IS function receives, enabling them to be more focused on the projects that, because of their scope and complexity, really require their attention.

The Risks of End-User Development

Unfortunately, end-user development presents a number of difficult-to-manage risks that limit its value to the organization:

- *Unreliable quality standards.* There is a reason why software development is a lengthy process. Quality software requires a number of activities that may not be readily apparent but are necessary—such as testing, documentation, security, integration, and the like. Because of the limited skill set and knowledge of most end users, the quality of their work varies dramatically.
- *High incidence of errors.* Audits of spreadsheets used in organizations show that a sizable percentage, between 20% and 40% (sometimes 90%), contain errors. The focus on outcomes (i.e., what the program does) and rapid development typically conspire to increase the likelihood of errors in end-user-developed applications.
- *Continuity risks.* Because end-user development often does not comply with traditional system development methodologies, it may be difficult for anyone but the individual who wrote the program to understand it, enhance it, and support it. Lack of documentation compounds this

---

18. Ulrich, W. (2006), Application package survey: The promise versus reality, *Cutter Benchmark Review,* 6(9), 13–20.

problem. A common scenario involves people like you, who develop great applications during internships only to see them fade into company oblivion once they leave the firm.

- *Increased pressure on the IS function.* While end-user development can relieve some of the development demands on the IS function, it often creates more requests for assistance during the development process and, over time, more requests for help managing the applications after release.

Summary

This chapter continued our discussion of the techniques and methodologies modern organizations use to introduce and manage information systems (IS) within the framework provided by the strategic information systems plan.

Specifically, in this chapter we focused on the three approaches used to introduce new organizational information systems: custom design and development, system selection and acquisition, and end-user development. We learned that

- The astounding progress that has characterized information technology (IT) over the last 40 years often misleads general and functional managers. Being mostly familiar with personal computing, they underestimate how much time and how much money it takes to build a stable, robust, and secure system that will work under a wide array of organizational conditions. In order to avoid these misconceptions, managers must become familiar with the process by which IT-based information systems come to be in modern organizations.

- Introducing an organizational information system is a two-step process requiring technology development and the implementation process. These two processes, while often described separately, are complementary and intertwined.

- Modern firms introduce new information systems using one of the following approaches: custom design and development, system selection and acquisition, or end-user development. The critical difference among them is the manner in which the software applications at the core of the information system are developed. In the first approach, IT professionals within the organization or those who are contracted develop uniquely tailored software for the firm's needs. In the second approach, the selection committee chooses an off-the-shelf application. In the third approach, it is the firm's end users, rather than the IT professionals, who create the software.

- The main methodology for custom system development is the system development life cycle (SDLC). The SDLC, predicated on the notion that detailed up-front planning is the vehicle to reduce risk and uncertainty in systems design and development efforts, is best suited for the development of large, complex software applications. The SDLC is articulated over three main phases—definition, build, and implementation—and nine stages. The primary limitation of the SDLC is the creation of substantial overhead and rigidity that limit the project team's ability to address the inevitable changes.

- The prototyping methodology has emerged as a viable alternative to the SDLC. Prototyping is rooted in the notion that it is impossible to clearly estimate and plan in detail such complex endeavors as information systems design and development projects. Instead the team is better served by staying nimble and iterating quickly through multiple designs to zero in on the optimal one. Prototyping's advantages include user satisfaction (particularly for small-scale applications or those that dramatically change work practices), rapid development, and experimentation. The drawbacks include the risk of lower-quality systems than those developed using a more structured methodology and scope creep.

- Agile methods place emphasis on the development team and user involvement. Each iteration introduces features or changes into the product, and these are reviewed by the development team and the users. Agile methodologies provide the ability to change development direction later in the development.

- With the advent of the Internet and the growth of the software industry in countries with access to a large pool of talent and a low cost of living, it is increasingly viable to outsource development of custom applications.
- The software industry has grown to a point where almost any application a firm needs is available off the shelf. When building information systems around prepackaged software applications, the firm must engage in a formal systems selection and acquisition process. Doing so ensures that the selection team evaluates all possible solutions and acquires the one that is best suited to the firm's needs. The selection and acquisition process mirrors the SDLC, with some important variations during the definition and build phases.
- The advent of powerful and easy-to-use computer languages and software development tools has enabled an unprecedented degree of software development by end users (i.e., non-IT professionals). The benefits of end-user development include increased speed, end-user satisfaction, and a reduced pressure on the IS function to develop new applications. The risks of end-user development include unreliable quality standards, high incidence of errors in the applications, continuity risks, and increased pressure on the IS function to support development and management of end-user applications.

Study Questions

1. Describe the reasons general and functional managers often fail to understand the complexities of organizational information systems development. Can you provide an example from your experience?
2. What is the difference between technology development and information systems development? What is the relationship between these two processes?
3. How do the three information systems development approaches in use today in modern organizations differ? Can you provide an example of each?
4. Provide arguments in support of both the make and buy approaches. What are the principal advantages of each decision? Increasingly firms approach information systems development as a "buy and make" process. What do we mean by "buy and make"? Why is this approach gaining increasing popularity today?
5. Describe the systems development life cycle (SDLC) methodology in the context of a "real" example. In other words, think about (or imagine) a situation where you proposed the need for a new information system. For this system development effort, describe what happened (or should happen) during the definition, build, and implementation phases.
6. Repeat question 5, this time using the prototyping methodology.
7. Repeat question 5, this time using the systems selection and acquisition methodology.
8. Articulate the advantages and disadvantages of end-user development.

Further Readings

1. Bloch, M., Blumberg, S., & Laartz, J. (2012, October). Delivering large-scale IT projects on time, on budget, and on value. *McKinsey Quarterly*.
2. Paulk, M. C., Weber, C. V., Curtis, B., and Chrissis, M. B. (1995). *The Capability Maturity Model: Guidelines for improving the software process*. Boston, MA: Addison-Wesley.
3. Pink, D. H. (2004, February). The new face of the silicon age: How India became the capital of the computing revolution. *Wired*.
4. Sutherland, J. (2014). *Scrum: The art of doing twice the work in half the time*. New York, NY: Crown Business.
5. Wade, M., & Büchler, B. (2013, January 22). Anchored agility: How to effectively manage the balance between local flexibility and global efficiency. *APC Sim's Report*.
6. Wagner, E., & Piccoli, G. (2007). A call to engagement: Moving beyond user involvement in order to achieve successful information systems design. *Communications of the ACM, 50*(12), 51–55.

Glossary

- **Agile:** A group of software development approaches methods aimed at reducing the substantial formalization that characterizes traditional methodologies.
- **Build:** The build phase of the SDLC is concerned with taking the system requirements document and producing a robust, secure, and efficient software application.
- **Business analyst:** Individuals with expertise in business process redesign as well as technology. They help ensure that the business processes and software programs at the heart of an information system are jointly optimized and work smoothly together.
- **Custom-designed software:** A software program that is created in single copy to address the specific needs and design requirements of an organization.
- **Custom software development:** The process by which an organization, or a contracted software house, creates a tailored software application to address the organization's specific information processing needs.
- **Definition:** The phase of the SDLC concerned with clearly identifying the features of the proposed information system.
- **End-user development:** The process by which an organization's non-IT specialists create software applications.
- **Implementation:** The phase of the SDLC concerned with taking the technology component and integrating it with the other elements (people, process, structure) to achieve a working information system.
- **Off-the-shelf application:** A software program that is mass-produced and commercialized by a software vendor.
- **Programmer:** A highly skilled IT professional who translates a software design into a set of instructions that can be executed by a digital computer.
- **Prototyping:** A systems development approach predicated on the notion that it is impossible to clearly estimate and plan in detail such complex endeavors as information systems design and development projects.
- **Scrum:** The most used agile software development methodology that progresses via a series of iterations called sprints, lasting usually two to four weeks.
- **Software application:** A software program or, more commonly, a collection of software programs, designed to perform tasks of interest to an end user (e.g., write a memo, create and send invoices).
- **Software development outsourcing:** An arrangement where an external provider (i.e., a software house) custom develops an application for an organization.
- **System analyst:** A highly skilled IS professional whose role is to help users identify and articulate the system requirements.
- **System architect:** A highly skilled IT professional who takes the system requirements document (i.e., what the applications should do) and designs the structure of the system (i.e., how the application will perform its tasks).
- **System development life cycle (SDLC):** A software development approach predicated on the notion that detailed justification and planning is the vehicle to reduce risk and uncertainty in systems design and development efforts.
- **System selection and acquisition:** The process by which an organization identifies and purchases an off-the-shelf software application to address its information processing needs.

CHAPTER 12

Information System Trends

What You Will Learn in This Chapter

In this chapter, we introduce some emerging and some enduring trends in information systems (IS) and technology management. Understanding these trends and technologies, the associated vocabulary, and the benefits and risks they engender for modern organizations is critical for you as a general or functional manager. You will hear much of this vocabulary from consultants, at conferences, and in the media, and you must learn to navigate it successfully. More important, as a manager you will be (or should be!) called on to participate in the debate about whether your firm should embark in the type of initiatives described in this chapter. Understanding these trends is therefore a prerequisite to being an asset in the discussion.

Specifically, this chapter will

1. Define the term *mobile platform* and its relevance in today's consumer and technology environments. Describe some of the emerging trends in the mobile space, as well as the key trends surrounding it.
2. Describe the importance of Green IS and energy informatics, the reasons for their emergence, and their potential impacts.
3. Define the notion of digital data genesis, digital data streams, and advanced analytics; the reasons for their emergence; and their potential impacts.
4. Define the concept of *Internet of things* and discuss the implications of its diffusion.
5. Define the term *digital manufacturing* and understand both its strengths and current weaknesses.
6. Describe advanced analytics and how they differ from business intelligence.
7. Define the notion of customer-managed interactions, the reasons for its emergence, and its potential impacts.
8. Define the term *open source software* and be able to identify the primary commercial models crafted around the open source movement. You will also be able to articulate the principal advantages and risks associated with the implementation of open source solutions in modern organizations.

MINICASE: Improving Environmental Sustainability through Service

Sitting at your desk in front of a blank document, you recalled how you got here. Yesterday was a fantastic spring day in Milan and you felt like a caged tiger in that boardroom overlooking Piazza del Duomo. The temperature outside was 22 degrees Celsius (71 degrees Fahrenheit) and a cool breeze was clearing the crisp air. You had enjoyed bicycling to work that morning; it reminded you of biking to high school from your hometown. One of the few kids in your circle of friends without a moped or a scooter, you used to trek the eight kilometers (five miles) from your house to the school every day, rain or shine, warm or cold. Northern Italy had the kind of weather that made bicycling enjoyable for eight months out of the year, and Milan is in the flatlands of the Po River valley, so bicycling was easy.

Coming out of your daydreaming, you glance back to the room. The topic at hand is an old problem for the administration of the city of Milan: pollution. The city has tried all kinds of options to reduce emissions, from limiting traffic in certain areas, to alternating the use of cars between those with even- and odd-numbered license plates, to downright shutting down traffic in the city when the pollution numbers become too high. Your consulting firm has been involved in many of these changes, the latest being a voucher allowing one to drive within the downtown area of the city called *Ecopass*—an idea borrowed from the city of London. The plan did not work as hoped, with residents complaining and some members of the board calling for the creation of classes (or levels) so that drivers would pay proportionally to how much their car pollutes. With all these exceptions, Ecopass soon became a logistical nightmare and its potential effect was drastically reduced—hence today's meeting.

One of the options being discussed was to improve the bus system by increasing the number of busses on the road and the frequency of their stops. This proposal was based on the well-known relationship between convenience and public transportation usage. The more stops and the higher the frequency of stops, the higher the number of people who would choose to take the bus rather than use their car. However, buses were also polluting vehicles; they are expensive to purchase and to operate. This option sounded to you like the usual incremental thinking. Solving the problem was not a matter of little tweaks and fixes; this city needed a radical shift.

While you were the youngest person in the room, still half in your spring-day-inspired daydreaming, you blurted out, "Why not use bicycles?" The room went quiet and everyone was staring in your direction. The first to speak was the mayor herself. She said, "What do you mean?" Her voice was a combination

of annoyance and intrigued curiosity. A bit tentatively, you said, "Well . . . I mean . . . bicycles, you know? Like they have in Paris and Copenhagen." Now fully focused, you were picking up steam, the power of your idea becoming clearer as you spoke: "We would need rental stations where people could pick up and drop off bicycles whenever they needed them, day or night. If we make this convenient enough, I'm sure residents of Milan would be quite happy to contribute to reduce pollution in their city."

There was silence in the room. The first to break it was the mayor again. She had looked at you and said, "Good idea. I want a feasibility study ready on my desk in one month." With that, she shook your hand and left.

As you looked at your computer, you recalled some of the considerations underpinning your intuition the day before. The initiative of the city was one focused on reducing pollution and improving environmental sustainability. Your job was to create a system that would encourage people to use bicycles instead of their cars or even public transportation. Some things worked in your favor. Italians in general were indeed environmentally conscious. They were also conscious about appearances, and while jumping on a bike might wrinkle their designer clothes, they would gladly do it if it could show others that they cared about their city. However, Milan was the bustling economic center of Italy, and people did not have time to waste. It was also the most technologically advanced city and Italy, for example, was projected to maintain a very high penetration of smartphones (Figure 12.1).

You were convinced. The right design of the initiative would make it a success. Information technology would have to feature prominently in your design, no question. How? Well, that was the heart of the matter.

Discussion Questions

1. What do you believe is the optimal design for your proposed bicycle rental system?

2. What is the role of information systems, if any, in enabling the design?

3. What are the main challenges you believe you will have to overcome in order to achieve widespread adoption?

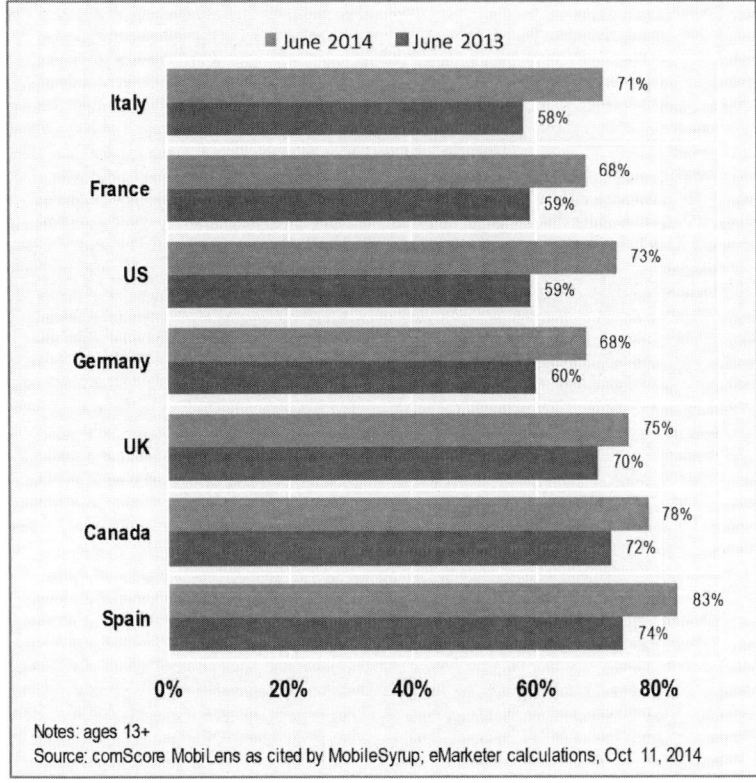

FIGURE 12.1. Smartphone penetration as a percentage of total handsets
Adapted from eMarketer, no. 180786

Introduction

In this chapter, we discuss the most relevant and influential trends in information systems (IS) and technology management. We focus on those emerging and enduring trends that are capturing media attention and that consulting companies are promoting today. These are the trends that you will need to confront as you join the workforce in the immediate future.

This chapter is particularly important, as the ability to identify new trends is critical for successful managers. But the task of navigating the many emerging trends and identifying which technologies will succeed is no easy task. Even Bob Metcalfe, a pioneer in networking technology who coinvented Ethernet and founded 3Com Corporation, missed the mark completely when in 1995 he proclaimed, "Almost all of the many predictions now being made hinge on the Internet's continuing exponential growth. But, I predict the Internet will soon go spectacularly supernova and in 1996 catastrophically collapse."[1] A good sport, Metcalfe admitted he was wrong and "ate his words" when he publically put the article in a blender and literally drank it after delivering the keynote speech at the Sixth International WWW Conference in December 1997.

We organize this chapter around the technologies at the core of each trend. This is a conscious approach that mirrors how decisions are made in modern organizations. Typically, an organization will become aware of an emerging information systems trend through publications, consulting companies, or conferences and events. The trend is defined by the functionalities of the technology at the core or the features and characteristics of a new class of software applications—from which the trend typically takes its name and its impetus. It is critical for you to realize that, no matter how sophisticated a technology may be, in order for it to have a positive impact on the organization, you must be able to design

---

1. Metcalfe, R. (1995, December), Column: From the ether, *InfoWorld*.

an information system around it (see Chapter 2). Thus, for each of the trends discussed in this chapter, we analyze the technological capabilities as a departure point to understand the organizational impacts that they engender.

The Mobile Platform

Perhaps the most visible trend in computing today is the widespread adoption of the mobile platform. As of January 2014, American adults reported using smartphone and mobile apps more than PCs to access the Internet, and in May 2014, mobile apps accounted for more than half of all time spent online.[2] Smartphones or tablets have the ability to run an operating system and therefore software applications—just like any other digital computer. The commercial products we all know are the devices running the Google Android operating systems, the iOS from Apple, and Windows Mobile from Microsoft. But smartphones trace their roots to the efforts started in the early 1990s by the likes of IBM and Nokia to pack functionality into the portable phone—thus rendering it a multipurpose device rather than just a telephone. The history of the smartphone intersects with the rise, during the same years, of palmtop devices. These were handheld computers known as personal digital assistants (PDAs), like those produced by Palm Inc. (Figure 12.2) and later Handspring (Figure 12.3). Those devices were conceived as computers with an operating system and, as a consequence, software developers recognized opportunities to build applications for the mobile platform.

FIGURE 12.2. The Palm Vx

FIGURE 12.3. The Handspring Visor
Photo by Waldohreule / CC BY SA 3.0

As people were carrying around cell phones and PDAs and hardware kept increasing in power, combining the two devices was a natural extension (and a very good example of the polymediation trend introduced in Chapter 1). While it is not our intent here to produce an exhaustive history of the smartphone, this brief discussion of its genesis helps you appreciate the context in which we have seen the rise of portable computers that look like cell phones and application stores where you can easily download software for your portable device. As with any platform, and more specifically with computing platforms, a heated competitive battle rages to establish a dominant operating system; there's no doubt that today the market is totally dominated by only two major players (Figure 12.4).

Similarly, the success of tablets has affected both the existing market of notebooks and portable computers. While tablets also trace their roots to earlier computing innovations, it was the launch of the Apple iPad in 2010 that established the category as it is defined today—a category created with unprecedented speed (Figure 12.5).

Many other manufacturers quickly followed suit, most notably Google Android. The last technological cornerstone of both smartphones and tablets is the ability to connect to both WiFi networks and cell phone data networks (e.g., the 3G and 4G networks). Thanks to its technological characteristics—portability and connectivity—the mobile platform gives users the opportunity for constant access to computing power and access to online services (Chapter 1).

Characteristics of the Mobile Platform

While mobile devices are digital computers, just like your desktop and laptop personal computers of old, vendors are trying hard to pass on the message that they are a new breed of devices. Leading this

2. Lipsam, A. (2014), Major mobile milestones in May: Apps now drive half of all time spent on digital, *comScore*, retrieved July 31, 2015, from http://www.comscore.com/Insights/Blog/Major-Mobile-Milestones-in-May-Apps-Now -Drive-Half-of-All-Time-Spent-on-Digital

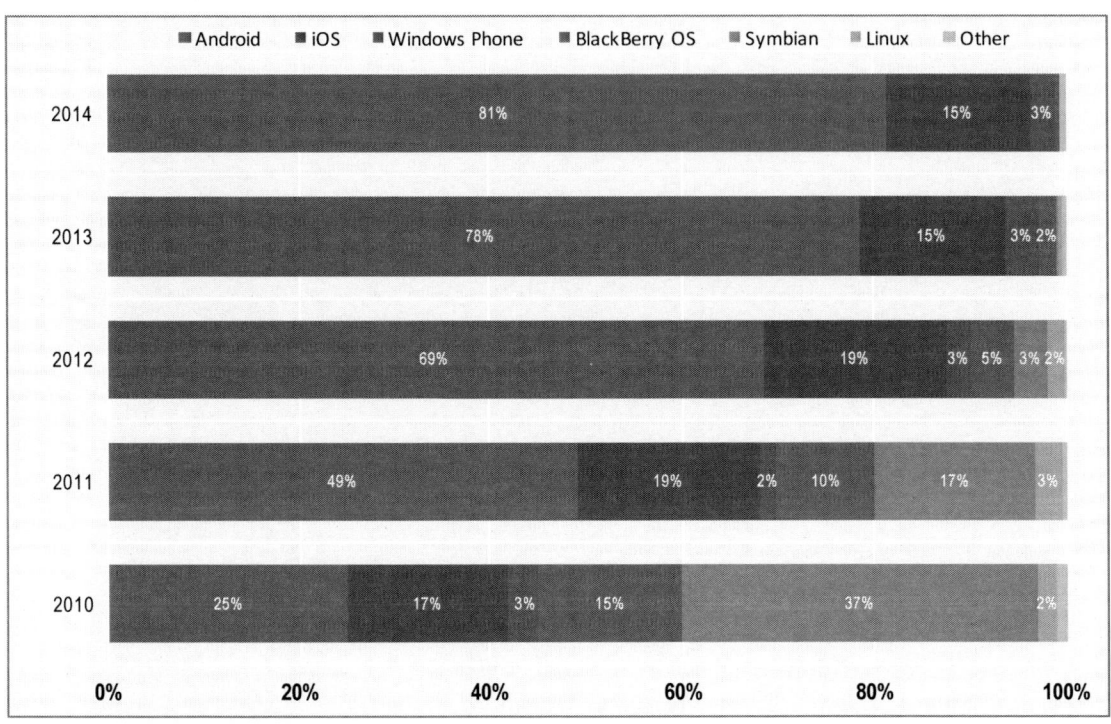

FIGURE 12.4. Market share of smartphone operating systems, 2010–2014
Created from IDC data as reported on Wikipedia (https://en.wikipedia.org/wiki/Mobile_operating_system)

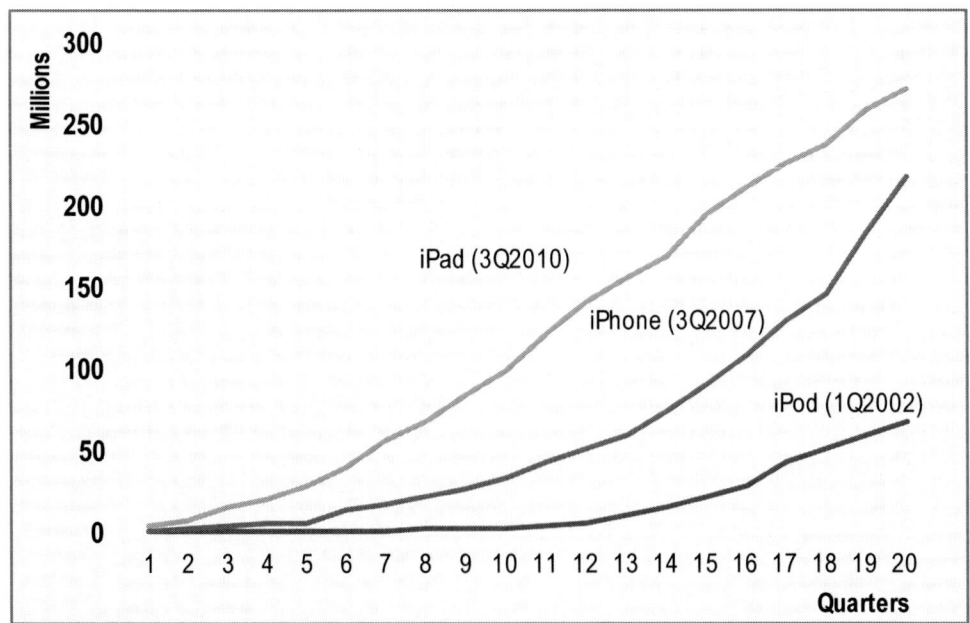

FIGURE 12.5. Cumulative units shipped by quarters since launch (with launch quarter appearing in parentheses)
Source: Data from AAPLinvestors.net (2015), "iPad versus iPhone versus iPod," retrieved from http://aaplinvestors
.net/stats/iphonevsipod/

trend is Apple, who has been increasingly talking about the "post-PC era"—ushered in by the iPod, the first post-PC device, and subsequently by the iPhone and the iPad. While mobile devices are architecturally like any other digital computer, they do have some peculiar characteristics that make them particularly appealing for organizations and end users. Particularly relevant are the characteristics that we could term ubiquity, identifiability, and context awareness.

Ubiquity   Ubiquity represents the idea that users of the device can access needed resources from (in theory) anywhere.[3] Mobile devices offer the highest level of potential ubiquity among commercially available information technology (IT) because they marry portability with connectivity. Consider the travel industry as an example. As a travel industry executive envisioning opportunities to connect to and provide service to your customers, you would quickly realize that smartphones (and perhaps tablets) are the only devices that travelers are all but guaranteed to be carrying during a trip. Those are the devices that enable the user to access informational resources anywhere they can find coverage for their data plans. Imagine being without a hotel room as you land at the airport. No problem—simply geolocate your business meeting by typing in your address, search for hotels within a five minutes' walk radius from that address, evaluate rates, and book. Now you have a room!

Identifiability   Identifiability represents the idea that mobile devices uniquely identify their user. In order to access the data grid, both smartphones and tablets utilize the cellular network and use a subscriber identification module (SIM card). Each SIM card has a unique identifier, and since telephones are usually personal devices, each user can be uniquely identified to the network. This feature of the technology enables a wide array of strategies. Consider the example of a pizza chain such as Pizza Hut. Using your smartphone app, you can create and order your pizza. You don't have to specify the address and payment information because you are automatically identified. In fact, you could even save your favorite custom pizza orders and simply reorder them as desired.

Context Awareness   Context awareness is enabled by the fact that mobile devices can be geolocated. In other words, modern smartphones that incorporate a GPS receiver can communicate their position to any software application running on them. Such applications can then make use of the location of the person carrying the device and infer the context in which the user is embedded at the time or the vicinity to other geolocated entities (i.e., a restaurant, a friend). You can quickly imagine many possibilities to craft business initiatives around the availability of this information. You can also quickly imagine many privacy violations and other abuses that these capabilities of mobile devices engender!

Mobile Commerce

With the increasing miniaturization of devices, digitization of content, and emergence of wide area wireless and cellular networks, organizations sought to extend their reach and use mobile devices for enabling transactions with customers. The term *mobile commerce* (or M-Commerce, mCommerce) refers to the ability to complete commercial transactions using mobile devices, such as smartphones and tablets. mCommerce has existed conceptually since the advent of electronic commerce, but it has recently received significant impetus as consumers have shown an increasing interest in electronic commerce and self-service through digital mobile devices. mCommerce transactions are mainly generated by smartphones and now account for more than one-third of the worldwide eCommerce market. Japan and Korea lead this trend and mCommerce transactions represent more than 50% of the total eCommerce market (see Figure 12.6).[4]

---

3. We specify "in theory" because, despite technical feasibility, many users are constrained in their access to resources by their data plans.

4. Criteo (2015), *State of mobile commerce 2015Q1*, retrieved from http://www.criteo.com/media/1894/criteo-state-of-mobile-commerce-q1-2015-ppt.pdf

FIGURE 12.6. Smartphone retail mCommerce sales in the United States, 2013–2018
Source: Adapted from eMarketer (2015), *Mobile commerce roundup*, retrieved from
https://www.emarketer.com/public_media/docs/eMarketer_Mobile_Commerce_Roundup.pdf

Consider the following example. You booked your flight with Air France and forwarded your reservation to TripIt, the online itinerary management company. Before leaving for the airport for your 4:00 p.m. flight, you receive an alert from TripIt informing you that your flight is delayed by 72 minutes due to some mechanical problem to your aircraft inbound from another airport. As a consequence, you decide to delay your departure from home to say good-bye to your kids coming home from school. After departure, your flight accumulates more delays and you realize that you will miss your connection. On the plane, which is equipped with WiFi connectivity from GoGo Inflight, you check the TripIt App and see a list of alternate flights to your destination, which was automatically calculated by TripIt based on your itinerary and the delay information published by the airlines. The list shows you departure times, gates, flight status, and open seats. As you land, you dash out of the gate like an Olympic sprinter to quickly reach the gate of the next best available flight (instead of lining up at the transfer desk with non-mCommerce-enabled passengers!), and you are on your way to your destination with minimal disruption to your schedule. This scenario would appear quite futuristic just some years ago, but it is a reality today.

Another example is offered by local eCommerce players like Groupon or LivingSocial. LivingSocial and Groupon, the leaders in this market as of 2015, enable their members to see negotiated discounts (i.e., coupons) that only activate if enough people sign up (i.e., a large enough group). The discount and size of the group to activate the Groupon are set by those partner merchants. The idea of group buying has been around for a long time and early eCommerce players attempted to craft business models around it. The best example was Mercata,[5] a venture backed by Paul Allen of Microsoft fame launched in May 1998. However, Mercata did not succeed and, after burning through more than $100 million in venture capital investment, eventually had to close its doors in 2001. The success of this next wave of players is not guaranteed, but Google offered $6 billion for Groupon in 2010 (Groupon rejected the offer!) as a testament to the sentiment that this time around, IT-enabled group buying represents a significant business opportunity. What had changed? The widespread use of social networking

---

5. Check the Internet Archive for a snapshot of Mercata back in 2000! http://web.archive.org/web/*/http://www.mercata.com

applications such as Facebook and Twitter, as well as the comfort that a large segment of the population has with IT-enabled self-service, both play an important role. Most notably, however, Mercata was an eCommerce venture, while Groupon and LivingSocial are mCommerce players. It is the prevalence of smartphones and the ability to leverage ubiquity, identifiability, and context sensitivity that seems to have drastically lowered the barriers to adoption of group buying solutions.

Location-Based Social Networking

Social networking is now a staple of all aspects of life for Internet citizens (see Chapter 5). The rise to prominence of the mobile platform has enabled social networking firms to allow users to reach (some would say annoy!) their contacts more often and in a more timely manner using mobile versions of their service. Location-based social networking is an extension of mobile social networking, whereby the geographical location of the user becomes an integral component of the service, enabling efficient access to context-dependent services. Pioneers of this space, such as Foursquare (Figure 12.7) and the now defunct Gowalla, enabled individuals to tap into their social networks while on the move. As such, location-based social networks represent an extension to the social context of the pervasive computing trend toward the widespread adoption of embedded sensors. They enable social network users to bridge the gap from access to their friends' ratings and reviews (what friends say) to their actual behavior (what friends do)—the ultimate high-tech version of "voting with your feet!" Imagine this scenario: You are visiting a new city and you're hungry, but you are not sure what restaurant to take a chance on. Using location-based social networking, you can see what outlets are in the vicinity and read what your friends, or the extended Foursquare community members, indicate as the best spots.

Augmented Reality

Augmented reality is a field of computing that has received increased attention thanks to the launch of a few augmented reality applications for smartphones, such as Wikitude, Layar, Google Translate, and the public trial of devices like Google Glass. Augmented reality has been around in some form or another since the early 1990s but gained traction in the consumer market because of the rapid diffusion of the mobile platform.

In its simplest form, augmented reality consists of superimposing an information layer on top of a real image. Current applications use the camera, GPS receiver, compass, and accelerometer of modern smartphones to identify a scene or objects and then, using a database of entries downloaded to the device, superimpose contextual information on recognized objects. There is no consensus about the

FIGURE 12.7. Foursquare

FIGURE 12.8. Voyager Xdrive in action

kind of applications that will benefit from augmented reality, and applications are still experimenting with the market leveraging novelty as core value proposition. An intriguing example is offered by Italian gaming company Illusion Networks. The firm created in 2010 an impressive augmented reality application for the iPhone 3Gs called Voyager Xdrive (Figure 12.8). It allows travelers who are walking about in the Roman Forum to see a three-dimensional reconstruction of the Forum the way it was during Constantine's rule (320 AD) and, for the buildings and monuments currently in view, to see and hear a description of them.

Interactive content and content enhancement are value drivers IKEA experimented with their 2014 catalog app that allowed customers to experience digital furniture over real space, taking pictures of the augmented environment. To use the application, it was sufficient to point the smartphone on selected catalog pages and then place the catalog where the furniture is supposed to be placed to see it virtually appear.

On the business side, in 2014, SAP introduced two new augmented reality applications supporting warehouse picking and field technicians, aiming at improving hands free operation, work efficiency, and productivity.[6] These two applications represent the potential impacts augmented reality applications could have on internal business process and operations.

Augmented reality is not confined to the mobile platform. Car manufacturers, for example, are planning to use the windshield of a car as the surface on which to superimpose information layers. But on the mobile platform, augmented reality may be extremely disruptive, mainly because it will further reduce information barriers and information asymmetry and will do so "on the go" rather than forcing users to be sitting at a computer. Like the commercial Internet two decades ago, augmented reality has the potential to arm users with an unprecedented quantity of easily accessible and usable information. The difference is that such information will be available to them anytime and anywhere. Reconsider the example of the restaurant. As you are deciding where you want to go tonight for drinks to relax from a tough day on the road during your business trip to Chicago, in the lobby of your hotel—The Ole Fogey—you activate the Layar browser on your Android phone and scan the environment around you. You immediately see that two blocks over, at The Edgy Hotel, the bar is happening with a cool event—DJ MasterFun is in town. Ultimately, the night is a success, you unwind from your working day, and you promise yourself that on your next trip to Chicago you will book a room at The Edgy, not the

---

6. For SAP concept videos, see SAPEnterpriseMobile (2013, May 12), SAP & Vuzix bring you augmented reality solutions for the enterprise, *YouTube*, retrieved from https://youtu.be/9Wv9k_ssLcI; and SAP (2014, February 24), SAP and Vuzix bring you the future of field service, *YouTube*, retrieved from https://youtu.be/UlpGDrSmg38

old and stodgy Ole Fogey. This example provides a glimpse into the power of augmented reality. This type of contextualized, real-time information access would not have occurred unless you had a portable instrument that worked seamlessly and easily at the moment you needed it (i.e., in the lobby of the hotel as you were making a decision). It is unlikely that you would have searched for the information about local venues on a laptop in your room and even less likely that you would have done that from home prior to your trip. Yet this information, and the ensuing experience, had a powerful effect on your travel experience (not to mention on brand perceptions and the brand development of the hotels involved!).

As John Doerr, partner at venture firm Kleiner Perkins Caufield and Byers, put it, "We're at the beginning of a new era for social Internet innovators who are re-imagining and reinventing a Web of people and places, looking beyond documents and websites."[7] While the mobile platform is advancing rapidly and provides a wealth of opportunities, it is still unclear how organizations will be able to take full advantage of it. As with any technology, it needs to be evaluated in the context of its potential for value creation (Chapter 8) and appropriation (Chapter 9).

Green IS[8]

Environmental sustainability, the notion that it is imperative for the human species to take the lead in the conservation of the natural environment and the sustainable management of its resources, is now one of the critical items on the world's agenda. The impetus toward environmental sustainability has become a focus of the business and information systems community as well. In 2008, for example, technology advisory firm Gartner singled out "Green IT" as a primary strategic imperative for CIOs.[9] Today, IT sustainability practices have become more common and are still a priority for more than 50% of CIOs in Europe and Asia Pacific regions.[10] This is due to the fact that producers and users of IT negatively influence environmental sustainability because of environmental impacts related to the purchase, use, and disposal of IT (e-waste) and emissions from data centers using significant amounts of electricity. Thus green IT initiatives are focused on minimizing the direct impact of IT production and use on the environment.

However, the exclusive focus on information technology typical of the green IT movement is too narrow and should be extended to information systems, defined as those sociotechnical organizational systems designed to collect, process, store, and distribute information (see Chapter 2). Shifting the focus from Green IT to Green IS enables a broadening of the role of IT in not only minimizing adverse impacts on environmental sustainability but also proactively generating and implementing solutions. Consider the example of United Parcel Service (UPS), the global package delivery and logistic firm. UPS developed proprietary software to collect and record the state of its vehicles from a wide variety of data points produced in real time by the electronic components found in its vehicles. As a result, UPS was able to access more than 200 items of vehicle-related data, such as RPMs, oil pressure, seatbelt use, the number of times the truck is placed in reverse, and the amount of time spent idling. UPS captures these time-stamped data constantly throughout the day, augmenting them with location data (from GPS readings). The data collected provide 2,000 to 5,000 readings every day for each truck. Similar information is tracked for each package delivered, and the two sources of information are transmitted to a central repository where they are consolidated for analysis. With this information, UPS can answer very specific questions of operational importance (e.g., What route did the driver take between the delivery at 125 Lenox Rd. and 15 Avalon St.?) and use the answers to work with drivers to reduce the distances they

---

7. Kleiner Perkins unveils new fund to invest in social web entrepreneurs (2010, October 22), *Tech Journal South*.

8. Significant portions of this section are drawn and adapted from Boudreau, M.-C., Watson, R. T., & Chen, A. (2008), From green IT to green IS, *Cutter Benchmark Review, 8*(5); and Watson, R. T., Boudreau, M.-C., & Chen, A. J. W. (2010), Information systems and environmentally sustainable development: Energy informatics and new directions for the IS community, *MIS Quarterly, 34*(1).

9. Thibodeau, P. (2007, October 9), Gartner's top 10 strategic technologies for 2008, *Computerworld*.

10. Computer Science Corporation (2014), *CSC Global CIO Survey: 2014–2015* (p. 25), retrieved from http://assets1.csc.com/cio_survey_2014_2015/downloads/CIO_Survey_Disruptive_innovation.pdf

drive and the fuel they consume. These data are also used to improve safety by ensuring compliance with UPS and community safety standards (e.g., When did the driver fail to buckle up after a delivery?).

The UPS example shows the power of information systems that are targeted to the challenge of reducing energy consumption and emissions. More broadly, it makes the case that information systems expressly designed to tackle the environmental sustainability challenge can help a firm limit its impact on natural resources while improving, rather than hampering, the firm's quest for profits and growth. Recognizing this central role of information systems in the quest to foster sustainability, some scientists have advanced an even broader notion: energy informatics, which is concerned with analyzing, designing, and implementing systems to increase the efficiency of energy demand and supply systems. Its core idea is as follows:

$$\text{Energy} + \text{Information} < \text{Energy}$$

In other words, when augmented with information, energy systems will consume less energy.

Digital Data Genesis and Streaming

The attentive reader will notice that the central role that sensors play in the energy informatics paradigm is not constrained to energy efficiency and environmental sustainability problems. Rather, we are rapidly moving toward a world where events, transactions, and processes are all digitized in real time as they occur. When a process (e.g., purchasing a book) is digitized, it is carried out through a digital computer (e.g., purchasing a book online). When an entity is digitized (e.g., a radio frequency identification [RFID]-enabled gaming chip), we have the ability to access an informational representation of that entity (e.g., the position of the chip on the gaming table) and thus generate relevant data (e.g., how many times the chip has been played) from it. Interestingly, such data are natively generated in digital form. To understand this concept, consider the multibillion-dollar Wynn Las Vegas casino. Historically, casinos have not placed significant value on customer data. Until the publicity given to customer relationship management (CRM) and business intelligence (BI) practices (see Chapter 3), a large casino's standard operating procedure was to value customers on the basis of judgments made by hosts and pit bosses. This approach tended to give undue weight to the contribution of a few big gamblers—the so-called whales—while undervaluing the multitude of smaller but often more valuable players. With the advent of state-of-the-art digital slot machines, it became feasible and cost effective to build comprehensive profiles of avid players, without disrupting their experience, in order to craft a targeted rewards strategy.

Casinos are now expanding their use of technology to capture valuable customer data by embedding radio RFID transceivers in the chips used at table games. Embedding RFID transceivers in chips means that table games' data are generated in real time and with the utmost precision. Then they are recorded in an easily storable and retrievable format without interfering with the customer's enjoyment. Today, as gaming chips become digitized, monitoring, guessing, and data entry are unnecessary behaviors because data are "born digital" and can be automatically collected and stored in a computer.

We call this trend digital data genesis (DDG), as it neatly captures the notion of creating data in digital form at their inception. However you want to refer to this trend, it is evident that the pace of digital data generation and streaming is accelerating rapidly as the number of connected physical devices increases (Figure 12.9). It follows that great opportunity exists for value creation fueled by this trend.

Beyond casinos, examples of digital data genesis are all around us (Figure 12.10). When we type search terms in Google, we are generating data in digital form (i.e., data about what is interesting to us); when we place a call with our mobile phone, we are generating data in digital form (i.e., data about our location, the person called, and the like); and when a smart electrical outlet is recording power flow, it is generating data in digital form (i.e., data about the electricity usage profile of the device that's plugged in).

In order to take advantage of the opportunities afforded by digital data genesis (DDG), a firm must develop a digital data genesis capability. Such capability consists of a threefold process:

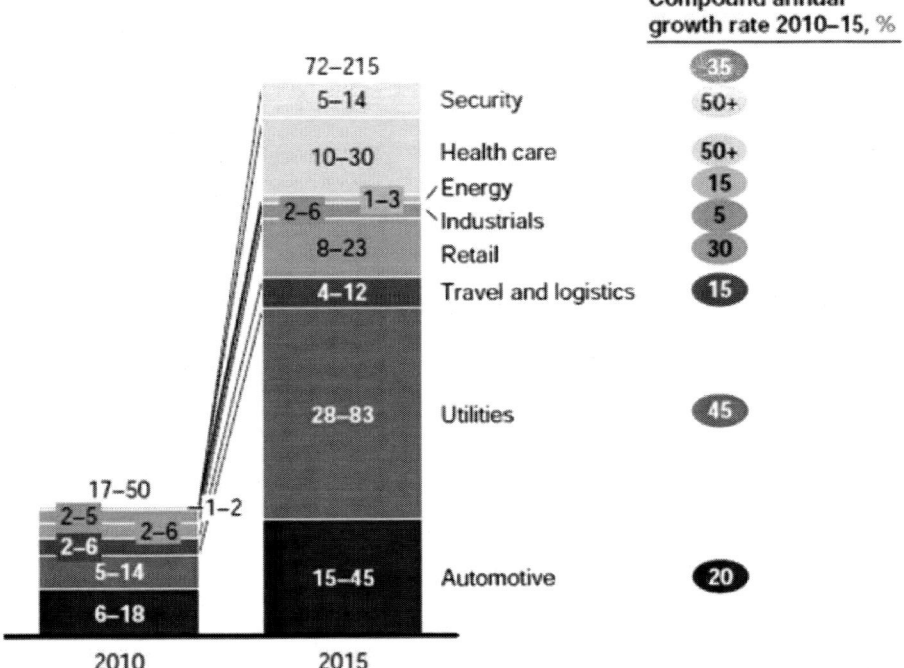

FIGURE 12.9. Estimated connected devices worldwide (in millions)
Adapted from McKinsey Report (2011), *Big data: The next frontier for innovation, competition, and productivity,* retrieved from http://www.mckinsey.com/insights/business_technology/big_data_the_next_frontier_for_innovation

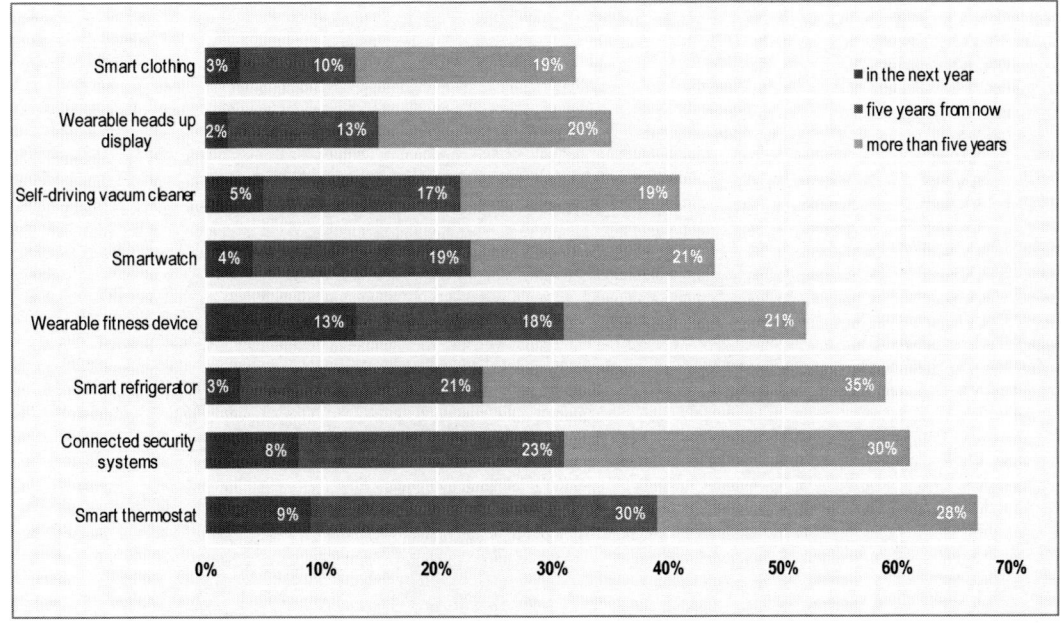

FIGURE 12.10. Projected adoption of connected technologies by consumers
Source: Accenture (2014), *The Internet of things: The future of consumer adoption,* retrieved from https://www.accenture.com/us-en/insight-Internet-things-future-consumer-adoption.aspx

1. Choosing IT to generate and capture data in native digital form
2. Integrating IT in the business processes that generate the data of interest
3. Managing the digital data produced

Note that the DDG capability is concerned with the generation and management of the data, not with the data's actual use—for example, through analytical processes. In other words, DDG is a prerequisite to being able to compete on analytics, and the outcome should be measured by a consistent ability to generate data in digital form. There are countless examples of DDG. Consider, for example, Google's use of Gmail. Whenever you write an e-mail using Gmail, you are generating many forms of digital data. An interesting one is misspelling information. By monitoring common spelling errors, how they are corrected, and where in a sentence they appear, Google has been able to generate so much insight about the spelling process that in its (now defunct) communication product—Google Wave (Figure 12.11)—the spellchecker was able to confidently correct a large proportion of spelling errors automatically, without asking for user input.

A digital data genesis strategy requires a disciplined approach to digital data generation, capture, and streaming predicated on the recognition of the value of data and the consequent need to architect systems that originate it in a digital format. Take customer service interactions, for example. Customer service is increasingly computer mediated, both online (e.g., eCommerce transactions) and offline. Every computer-mediated customer service transaction where digital identification of the customer occurs (e.g., a log-in, a swipe card, a customer number) provides an opportunity to capture data. The trend toward computer-mediated customer service is likely to accelerate with the increasing use of mobile technology and the high degree of accessibility and proximity it provides.

Digital data genesis is a manifestation of the ongoing progression in IT adoption and use in organizations, rather than a revolution. However, digital data genesis suggests that there is value in proactively thinking about how to generate data from everyday transactions. This is a shift from the mind-set of traditional business intelligence approaches focusing on mining and extracting value from already available data that were generated as a byproduct of organizational transactions.

Analyzing Digital Data Genesis Opportunities

The proliferation of sensors and sensor data that produce usable information with unprecedented speed and granularity provides the opportunity to design information systems to expressly take advantage of this environmental change. At its most fundamental level, digital data genesis offers the opportunity to bridge the gap between the digital and physical world. In other words, as more and more physical activities come with an automatically generated information representation of the activity, it is increasingly possible to extract value from the symbiotic relationship of physical and digital systems. Consider the

FIGURE 12.11. Google Wave

example described in the opening minicase, where a layer of information could significantly improve the performance of a physical transportation system.

One approach to analyzing this symbiotic relationship between physical activities and information is through the lens of ubiquity, uniqueness, unison, and universality.

Ubiquity   Information access that is unconstrained by time and space ranks high on the ubiquity scale. Data that are generated natively in digital form are theoretically available in real time. Ubiquitous information provides opportunities for rationalizing the use of resources. Consider the example of a bus that automatically alerts you when it is five minutes away from your stop. Access to such information would allow you to leave the house at the optimal time, thus decreasing time spent in the cold and making the bus service more convenient for you—a result that, before the advent of ubiquitous information, could be achieved only by moving the stop closer to your house.

Uniqueness   Information access that is personalized and individually tailored to the needs of a person or other entity ranks high in uniqueness. In the age of customer relationship management and collaborative filtering (Chapter 3), we have become accustomed to receiving personalized service. Digital data genesis enabled unprecedented levels of uniqueness. Consider the music service Spotify, which can make music suggestions tailored to your individual needs because it has a complete informational representation of your music listening behavior.

Unison   Information that is consistent and devoid of redundancies ranks high in unison. At a procedural level, unison translates into the standardization of the activities necessary to perform an activity. For example, a city transit system would be characterized by high degree of unison when it maintains one account per customer. This account presents all information relative to the person's interaction with the various transportation services (i.e., subway, bus, bicycles), using a consistent user interface on the many devices one can use to transact with the city transit (e.g., kiosks, websites, mobile apps).

Universality   Information that is standardized and easily shareable across platforms ranks high in universality. A firm like TripIt leveraged digital data genesis to achieve high universality when it devised a system to read travel confirmation e-mails from any travel provider and create a master itinerary for the traveler. At a procedural level, universality describes the ease with which separate processes can interlock and coordinate. For example, the ability to pay a bill with a credit card when travelling abroad and have that charge translated into our currency automatically is an example of high universality.

As you become sensitive to the digital data genesis phenomenon and you begin to see opportunities to harness data that are natively digital, you can focus on the dimensions of ubiquity, uniqueness, unison, and universality to maximize their potential for value creation.

Digital Data Streams: Value Comes in Little Streams

With DDG, we refer to the paradigm shift in data generation. Data are "born digital," and thus they can be automatically collected and stored in a computer. Digital data streams (DDSs), instead, are composed by the flow of data originating from DDG activities and can be intercepted and used by organizations or individuals. A DDS is a continuous digital encoding and transmission of data describing a related class of events.[11] The transmission or flow of these digital representations of events is a DDS, which may be human generated (e.g., a tweet, an instagram) or machine generated (e.g., a CO_2 reading, a GPS location).

The emergence of DDS is creating strategic opportunities for existing firms and enabling the formation of new enterprises. The catalyst for this seismic change is DDG, the massive generation of real-time structured and unstructured data, and the availability of these events in data streams that organizations can leverage for decision making and operational change. For example, Uber is the world's largest

11. Piccoli, G., Rodriguez, J., & Watson, R. T. (2015), *Leveraging digital data streams: The development and validation of a business confidence index*, paper presented at HICSS, Kauai, HI.

"taxi" company—speculatively valued at $50 billion[12]—but it owns no vehicles! It harnesses real-time digital data streams of its drivers' cars and matches them with real-time demand for rides. Existing organizations are also successfully leveraging the real-time flow of "big data" for new value creation.

Anatomy of a DDS

At the highest level of abstraction and generality, a DDS can capture and thus represent up to six basic elements describing an event (Table 12.1). These elements are "primitives," meaning that they cannot be described in terms of other elements, or inferred from them. These primitives derive from what are commonly known as the 5W+H of narrative (who, what, when, where, why, and how). Discovered and rediscovered several times throughout history,[13] they originate in rhetoric and the second century BCE work of Hermagoras of Temnos, Gorgias of Leontini, Cicero, and Quintilian.[14] In rhetoric, 5W+H are the *circumstances*, the elements (*moria peristaseos*—particulars of circumstance) of an event, and in narrative, they represent the basic grammar of a story. Computer scientists attempting to extract events from multimedia DDSs have revitalized the 5W+H model.[15] While the model can readily handle structured (e.g., a single numeric) or ill-structured (e.g., a text string) data, extracting value from ill-structured data is challenging and has galvanized considerable text mining research.

We now turn our attention to the DDS's "life cycle" and its two main aspects: DDS creation and DDS exploitation (Figure 12.12).

DDS became available to organization through three consecutive stages:

Table 12.1. Elements of a digital data stream segment

Element	Description	Example
When	The time when the data segment was created	A time stamp with date, time, and time zone
Where	The location of the entity when the segment was created	Latitude, longitude, elevation
Who	The unique identifier of the entity that caused the data segment to be created	Person's customer number, RFID of a pallet, URL of a website
What	The activity that caused the segment to be created	The identifier of an item in a sales transaction, the arrival of a ship in a port
How	The means by which the event was initiated, authorized, or completed	Credit card number for payment, status of arriving flight (e.g., safe landing)
Why	Motivation for the action related to data segment creation	Birthday gift, planned destination

12. Myers, C. (2015, May 13), Decoding Uber's proposed $50B valuation (and what it means for you), *Forbes*, retrieved July 15, 2015, from http://www.forbes.com/sites/chrismyers/2015/05/13/decoding-ubers-50-billion-valuation-and-what-it-means-for-you/

13. Franzosi, R. (2012), On quantitative narrative analysis, in *Varieties of Narrative Analysis*, ed. J. A. Holstein and J. F. Gubrium, Los Angeles, CA: Sage, 75–96.

14. Franzosi, R. (2012), On quantitative narrative analysis, in *Varieties of Narrative Analysis*, ed. J. A. Holstein and J. F. Gubrium, Los Angeles, CA: Sage, 75–96.

15. Xie, L., Sundaram, H., & Campbell, M. (2008, April), Event mining in multimedia streams, *Proceedings of the IEEE*, 96(4), 623–647, doi:10.1109/JPROC.2008.916362

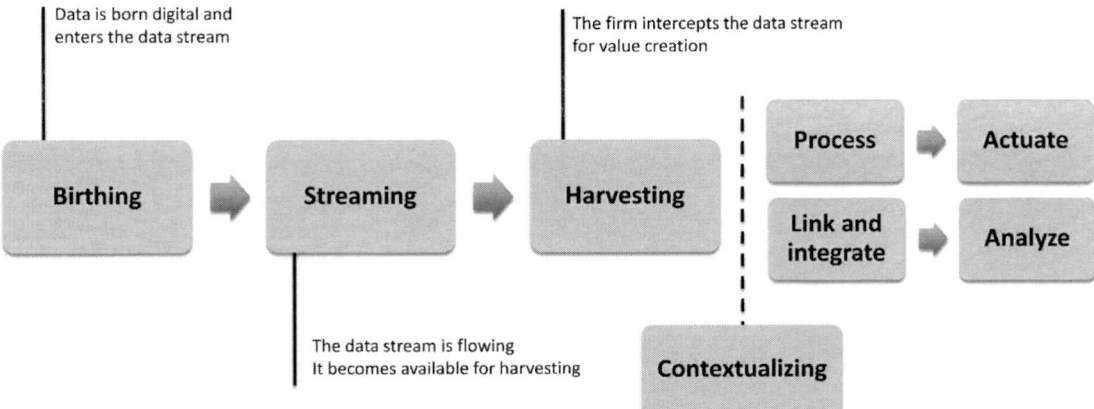

FIGURE 12.12. The main stages of DDS creation and exploitation

- *Generate.* This is the stage at which DDG happens and the digital information of the event occurs (i.e., a tweet, a Google search, the GPS position of an object). When such a DDG event is not isolated but rather is part of a series (or a stream) of DDG events, there is an opportunity for DDS generation. For example, a single click on a hyperlink is the digital representation of a person's decision (a DDG event). Activity on a website is a stream of personal decisions and is aptly called the clickstream, which is a well-known example of a DDS. Sensor readings, smart metering, or a person's activity on Pinterest, Twitter, or Uber are all activities that lead to DDS generation.
- *Stream.* When data are available, channeled, and transmitted as a continuous flow, we refer to them as a DDS. The streaming phase concerns the manner and format in which the data becomes available. The stream is characterized by (1) the type of technologies used to create the channel (e.g., application program interfaces [APIs]), (2) the nature of the content (e.g., video, blog post, review, sensor reading, including considerations of accuracy), (3) the source (e.g., public, business, individual, or community), and (4) the legal status of the data contained in the stream or derived from it (e.g., rights reserved and sensitivity).
- *Harvest.* At this stage, an organization taps into the DDS and extracts some or all the data being streamed. The harvest stage is described in terms of the technologies adopted to perform the data harvesting. The technology used are complementary to those used for streaming. So, for example, if the stream is accessible through an API that returns a JSON formatted response, a proper method to post the request and JSON parsers should be used.

Upon successfully harvesting the DDS, an organization can put it to use. While consideration about value creation and appropriation are discussed in Chapter 7, it is important at this point to discuss the mechanics of DDS utilization. Organizations exploit DDS via two general class of activities: process-to-actuate and assimilate-to-analyze (Figure 12.12).

- *Process-to-actuate* occurs when a firm takes action based on real-time DDS processing. An insurance company monitoring a weather forecast data stream and sending text messages to its customers in the area where hail is expected in the next 30 minutes illustrates the immediacy of process-to-actuate. The firm combines events that are currently streaming in a DDS (i.e., real-time, location-specific, short-term weather forecasts) and the results of a static database query and other contextual data in order to alert its potentially affected customers in a timely manner. The result is superior customer service and fewer insurance claims because customers have been able to garage their vehicles at the right time.

- *Assimilate-to-analyze* occurs when a firm merges multiple data streams and static databases in an effort to analyze the data. The focus is on extraction of insights rather than immediate action—as in the process-to-actuate approach. To avoid the financial risks associated with planning errors, some firms have integrated external DDSs in their demand forecasting system. For instance, Tesco and other retailers merge and analyze data from multiple digital data streams to generate forecasts to estimate demand. Predictions are based on information generated from store location, product characteristics, recent weather history, and weather forecasts. Note how the result of the analysis is not immediate automatic action, as in process-to-actuate, but rather the presentation of superior insight that enables better decision making.

Naturally, firms can combine these two approaches so that a prescribed action is the result of the analysis of multiple data streams and database records. In some cases, the process-to-actuate approach requires the combination of multiple DDS.

While managers intuitively appreciate that new DDSs enable the creation of new value, the challenge is to reconcile these opportunities with managerial and business ecosystem needs. More specifically, organizations are often overwhelmed by the potential of new data sources, to the point that they are unable to decide what to pursue.[16] Moreover, there are yet many events of interest that may not be appropriately captured in a DDS. Thus tactical decisions about what initiatives to pursue depend on the potential that different events produce for value creation and the ready availability of events in a DDS. We formally discussed these opportunities in Chapter 7.

The Internet of Things

There is an emerging buzzword that has been gathering steam in the press and business literature as of late: the *Internet of things* (IoT). The label attempts to capture the convergence of a few trends: the ubiquity of the Internet and Internet access and the increasing "computerization" of everyday devices and objects. These "intelligent"[17] or "smart" objects utilize the TCP/IP protocol and are able to communicate using the existing Internet infrastructure. Having been trained as academics, we are not very fond of buzzwords, but we must recognize that the IoT is a reality, suffice to say that today more data are being generated by machines than human activities and there are many more devices connected to the Internet infrastructure than there are individuals. The Internet itself had to accommodate a larger addressable space for opening to the projected 30 billion "things" connected by 2020. The move from IPV4 to IPV6, for example, was a necessary precondition to accommodate all the new connected devices, as the Internet is already experiencing a shortage of available addresses.[18]

Smart objects bridge the physical world with cloud services offering new product functionalities and determining new opportunities for value creation. It is their numbers and the need to make sense of the data they produce that makes the IoT trend relevant to our interest in advanced analytics. Consider the example of the Google's Nest thermostat. When introduced, it was a pioneering instrument that offered Internet connectivity for remote heating/cooling systems management and programming. A major feature of the product was its ability to learn automatically from user behaviors, user interaction, and motion sensors. If you ever had to deal with a traditional programmable thermostat, you know the frustration users endure to set a program they are happy with. This same thought spurred Tony Fadell,

---

16. Heudecker, N., Randall, L., Edjlali, R., Buytendijk, F., Laney, D., Casonato, R . . . Adrian, M. (2014, November 28), *Predicts 2015: Big data challenges move from technology to the organization*, retrieved from https://www.gartner.com/doc/2928217/predicts--big-data-challenges

17. Most discussions of the IoT use the term *intelligent* or *smart* very loosely to refer to any device that is able to perform computations. IoT devices incorporate a digital computer and are therefore able to process and execute instructions coded into software.

18. McMilian, R. (2015, May 13), Coming this summer: U.S. will run out of Internet addresses, *Wall Street Journal*, retrieved from http://www.wsj.com/articles/coming-this-summer-u-s-will-run-out-of-internet-addresses-1431479401

founder of Nest, to find a solution in 2009.[19] Formerly at the head of Apple's iPod and iPhone divisions, Fadell was concerned by the high levels of carbon dioxide that were pumped in the atmosphere because of the lack of an easy and automatic way to control heating and cooling systems in homes and offices. The Nest thermostat had to have an intuitive interface, a color display, and a set of convenient features, setting the product apart from its legacy counterpart. But above all, the thermostat had to automatically learn from users' preferences and habits to efficiently manage the temperature, also allowing remote user control through the Internet.

Today, Nest sells a suite of products for homes. When other Nest products such as the smoke detector or the surveillance camera are in range, the devices can exchange data through a local wireless network and coordinate their operations. For example, the camera can start recording when smoke is detected or when the thermostat determines that you are not home.

This case well exemplifies the general architecture behind the IoT. Smart devices are digital computers in the shape of everyday objects that are capable of interconnecting to exchange data. They can process instructions, but they often have sophisticated software that enables them to perform substantial analysis and modify their operation over time. Furthermore, interconnectivity allows the devices to coordinate to create novel applications that each of them individually could not perform—for example, increase security and safety by providing a video feed during a fire to potentially improve the effectiveness of rescue operations. Generally IoT devices pack limited computational power and storage capacity but rely on cloud services as the backbone of their computational power. Consider the example of Amazon's voice-operated home assistant—the Amazon Echo (Figure 12.13). The device has a microphone that is constantly listening to (but not recording) conversations. When a user utters the appropriate keyword (Amazon, or Alexa), it awakens and begins to interact with the person, using natural speech. The speech processing does not happen on site—the sound is transferred to a cloud service managed by Amazon, it is processed (i.e., understood), and a response is generated. Interestingly, Amazon provides an API to this cloud service—called the Alexa Skills Kit (ASK)—that enables independent providers to build applications for the Echo without having to know any speech processing. All speech processing is handled by Amazon in the cloud.

It should be clear now that the complexity behind the IoT is centralized in cloud-based powerful systems that providers make accessible to their devices (Figure 12.14). Consider the example of Nest. Camera features, like facial detection or advanced motion analysis, are too computationally taxing to be embedded in devices and are therefore cloud based. As with any cloud service, they have the added advantage of being highly scalable, always up to date, and accessible through a multiplicity of devices (e.g., smartphones with the appropriate apps).

FIGURE 12.13. Amazon voice-activated assistant—the Echo
Photo by Frmorrison / CC BY SA 3.0

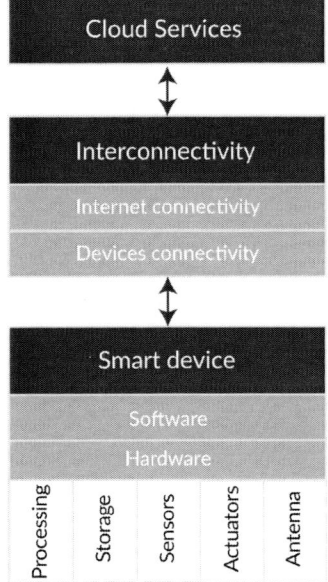

FIGURE 12.14. IoT layered architecture
Adapted from Porter and Heppelmann (2014)

19. Levy, S. (2011, October 25), Brave new thermostat: How the iPod's creator is making home heating sexy, *Wired*, retrieved August 26, 2015, from http://www.wired.com/2011/10/nest_thermostat/

Smart device capabilities can be grouped in four main areas:[20]

- *Monitoring* is the ability of smart objects to detect and sense the physical world. They can measure data about themselves (e.g., state of operation) and the surrounding environment. Our running example, the Nest family of products, demonstrates this concept. The thermostat, camera, and smoke detector all capture environmental information. The Nest thermostat, for example, can monitor temperature, humidity, near and far field activity with a 150 degree of view angle, and ambient light.
- *Control* refers to the possibility to set product functions and personalize user experience either directly from the device interface or remotely through the Internet. The Nest thermostat, for example, provides a convenient interface for setting user preferences (i.e., the temperature) and an extended set of features accessible via a web browser or through the mobile app.
- *Optimization* monitoring and control enable functionalities to optimize product operations to enhance performance and to enable predictive diagnostic, service, and repairs. In this sense, Nest suggests that the use of their learning thermostat saved U.S. customers about 10% to 12% on their heating bills and about 15% on their cooling bills.[21]
- *Autonomy* the combination of previous capabilities allows for autonomous product operations, enhancement and personalization, self-coordination of operation with other devices, as well as self-diagnostics. The case where the camera turns on when smoke is detected is an example of the planned coordination of objects.

As future managers, it is important to comprehend the value opportunity, the risks, and the challenges of IoT. More specifically, you should do the following:[22,23]

- *Focus on value.* IoT projects are IT strategic dependent initiatives. Everything you learned about value still applies. You should then avoid adding "smart" functionalities that your customers do not perceive as valuable.
- *Consider networks and ecosystems.* IoT interconnectivity requires thinking in terms of the network and the ecosystem in which the smart devices will be deployed. Creating a new ecosystem is like mastering the network effect with the added difficulty of having to deal with multiple stakeholders. Importantly, once the market tips in favor of a system, it will be extremely difficult to compete and the only options will be to become compatible with the dominant solution or differentiate by leveraging a potential niche.
- *Manage and analyze data.* The quantity of data in a DDS is potentially infinite and the IoT is already generating massive amount of data that need to be filtered and processed. This will challenge current data management practices and governances in most IT departments.
- *Watch out for privacy and security.* IoT could provide sensitive information about users and their behaviors. Location, health, or purchasing patterns are all events that can be captured by smart devices and susceptible to user concerns about privacy and ownership rights. Additionally, IoT layered architecture exposes organizational systems to possible security risks. The 2015 hack into the Jeep Cherokee connected car exemplifies the struggle of the automotive

---

20. For a more in-depth analysis of them, see Porter, M. E., & Heppelmann, J. E. (2014), How smart, connected products are transforming competition, *Harvard Business Review*, 92, 11–64.

21. Nest Whitepaper (2015), *Energy savings from the Nest Learning Thermostat: Energy bill analysis results*, retrieved August 2015 from https://nest.com/downloads/press/documents/energy-savings-white-paper.pdf

22. For a more in-depth analysis of them, see Porter, M. E., & Heppelmann, J. E. (2014), How smart, connected products are transforming competition, *Harvard Business Review*, 92, 11–64.

23. Lee, I., & Lee, K. (2015), The Internet of things (IoT): Applications, investments, and challenges for enterprises, *Business Horizons*, 58(4), 431–440, doi:10.1016/j.bushor.2015.03.008

industry to design IT secure applications.[24] The set of competences required to compete in the IoT space may favor IT companies, used in the development of these systems.

• *Prepare for the unexpected*. The possible complexity of IoT systems requires managers to be prepared for systemic effects generated by the interaction of systems and systems' components that are either positive or negative. While business and organizations are obvious players in the IoT market, makers can now use low-cost, low-power, and marketed components to create new offerings. This could give life to a variety of niche applications and possible competing solutions. Leveraging the network of makers related to your products and monitoring crowd-sourcing platforms are additional strategies to consider in this still undefined market.

IoT implications for business are disruptive. The IoT paradigm radically changes how value is created for customers and competition among firms and its boundaries. In this sense, new business ecosystems will arise, compete, and eventually coexist. Having been through the eCommerce and eBusiness revolution, we see many parallels. IoT is a natural extension of the Internet, linking together the physical and digital worlds. The opportunities and impacts we are experiencing are just the beginning, but they allow us to grasp the future exactly as it was for the early Internet applications back in the 1990s.

Wearable Devices

In the IoT paradigm, devices or objects in physical space have computational power thanks to embedded IT and can therefore exhibit programmable behavior due to their ability to execute instructions. The very same technology trends that have enabled the IoT are underpinning the emergence of another class of smart objects: wearable devices. Wearable devices, or wearables, are smart clothing items or accessories worn by individuals. The concept of wearable devices has been around since the early days of the Internet. However, it is the widespread use of mobile devices in the last decade that may have set the stage for the success of wearable devices.

Just like IoT objects, wearables look and behave just like their "dumb" counterparts. However, thanks to embedded IT, they provide functionality designed to facilitate or support their owners' activities. Wearables are a diversified category of devices ranging from bulky head-mounted displays or backpack systems to rings or futuristic subcutaneous devices (see Table 12.2).

Wearables represent an important subset of IoT, but their peculiarity is that they are physically worn by the user. As such, they provide for a more intimate interaction with their users. If you own a smartwatch (Figure 12.15) or a fitness band (Figure 12.16), you are already experiencing early examples of the new user interaction and engagement opportunities offered by wearables.[25] You are probably now aware of the calories you burn per day, the kilometers and steps you take, your heartbeat, or the hours you slept last night.

Wearables are still in their infancy, even though the concept has been around for almost two decades now. Early examples of nonobtrusive interaction are those garments

FIGURE 12.15. An example of smartwatch
Photo by LG Electronics / CC BY 3.0

FIGURE 12.16. An example of fitness band
Photo by LG Electronics / CC BY 3.0

24. Greenberg, A. (2015, July 21), Hackers remotely kill a Jeep on the highway—with me in it, *Wired*, retrieved August 12, 2015, from http://www.wired.com/2015/07/hackers-remotely-kill-jeep-highway/

25. Jones, N. (2015, July 15), Wearables: New interactions and new opportunities, *Gartner*, no. G00279085.

Table 12.2. Wearables applications and product categories

Application	Product category
Health care and medical	Blood pressure monitors
	Continuous glucose monitoring
	Defibrillators
	Drug delivery product
	ECG that monitors pulse
	Insulin pumps
	Medical alert
	Oximetry
	Patches
	Smart glasses
Fitness and well-being	Activity monitors
	Emotional measurement fitness and heart rate monitors
	Footpads and pedometers
	Sleep sensors
	Smart glasses
	Smart clothing
	Smartwatches
	Audio earbuds
	Heads-up displays
Entertainment	Bluetooth headsets
	Heads-up displays
	Imaging products
	Smart glasses
	Smartwatches
Industrial	Hand-worn terminals
	Heads-up displays
	Smart clothing
	Smart glasses
Military	Hand-worn terminals
	Heads-up displays
	Smart clothing

Source: Walker, S. (2013), Wearable technology—market assessment, *IHS Electronics & Media*, retrieved from http://cdn2.hubspot.net/hub/396065/file-2568104498-pdf/Blog_Resources/IHS-Wearable -Technology.pdf?t=1427903372862

capable of automatically sensing wearer parameters and eventually adjusting their behavior, like the notorious *Back to the Future*'s Marty McFly self-adjusting shoes (we are really dating ourselves now!).[26] The much-hyped Google Glass and the more recently unveiled Microsoft HoloLens served as a proof of concept for understanding the emerging behaviors augmented reality would generate in the consumer space. We just got used to people fiddling with a smartphone when walking, and now we should be ready to consider it normal when people stare at us vacuously—since they are really not looking at us but reading overlaid augmented reality data.

---

26. Gaddis, R. (2014, July 5), What is the future of fabric? These smart textiles will blow your mind, *Forbes*, retrieved August 14, 2015, from http://www.forbes.com/sites/forbesstylefile/2014/05/07/what-is-the-future-of-fabric-these-smart-textiles-will-blow-your-mind/

In the corporate space, wearables are used for hands-free operations, maintenance, tracking productivity, accessing customer data in real time, receiving alerts, and training. Corporations are still trying to cope with the "bring your own device" (BYOD) trend,[27] but scenarios of "bring your own wearable" (BYOW) are not so farfetched.[28] Wearables have potential applications to increase customer engagement through loyalty and reward programs, point-of-sale, and integrated shopping experiences. For example, Macy's strategy for engaging millennials shoppers make use of customers' location DDSs generated by Apple's iBeacon technology to deliver personalized content directly on customers' smartphones. The aim is to directly influence in-store retail sales.[29] For consumer-facing applications, like Macy's, smartwatches enable information services that are both unobtrusive and easy to operate.

As with any early technology trend, the market is still fragmented and it is unclear what applications, if any, will be successful. Both established and new players are shaping the market, and a war of platforms is raging, with Android OS, Apple WatchOS, Microsoft Windows, and Tizen as the main contenders. As Brian Krzanich, CEO of Intel, put it during the 2015 Consumer Electronic Show's keynote speech, "The rise of new personal computing experiences, intelligent and connected devices, and the wearable revolution are redefining the relationship between consumers and technology."[30] Only time will tell if he was correct.

Digital Manufacturing

"These are the days of miracles and wonders," Paul Simon sang back in 1986, and the digital revolution is wondrously bridging the world of ideas and information with the tangible reality of things. Augmented reality is an example: information coming from the digital world enhances what our senses can perceive of the physical one. The development of 3D printing is taking this a step further. Digital objects can materialize in physical world. Interestingly, the process is exactly the opposite of traditional manufacturing techniques like lathing or milling. 3D printing is an additive process where layers of material are laid down following a fully digital project.

In a few years, the range of applications of 3D printing expanded enormously from prototyping to the manufacture of fully functional components. The rapid technological developments made 3D printers cheaper while increasing their precision, resolution, speed, and printable materials, making them viable alternatives to current manufacturing processes.

From a managerial perspective, the core aspect to balance is the trade-off of flexibility and unitary cost. While 3D printing can't match traditional production methods' economies of scale, it provides unmatched levels of flexibility. 3D printing can provide an endless set of shapes, colors, sizes, and other customizations, limitedly adding to the manufacturing cost. This is the result of a reduced need for assembling product components, as the whole product can be printed from the inside. For example, GE aviation moved to 3D printing for a series of fuel nozzles for their engines that otherwise needed assembly for their components. Even on a volume of 45,000 units per year, they were able to cut costs by 75%.[31]

---

27. BYOD is the acronym for Bring Your Own Device and refers to the policy of allowing employees to use their own smartphones or wearables at work to access company IT services and applications. Studies show that BYOD policies may positively impact productivity, employees' satisfaction, and costs. However, opening corporate networks to consumer-grade devices raises security concerns and several critiques to BYOD policies.

28. Salesforce Research (2015), *Putting wearables to work*, retrieved from https://www.salesforce.com/form/conf/thank-you-wearables-report.jsp

29. Halzach, S. (2014, September 25), Is the new technology at Macy's our first glimpse of the future of retail?, *Washington Post*, retrieved from http://www.washingtonpost.com/news/business/wp/2014/09/25/is-the-new-technology-at-macys-our-first-glimpse-of-the-future-of-retail/

30. Business Wire (2015), Intel CEO outlines the future of computing, retrieved from http://www.businesswire.com/news/home/20150106006877/en/Intel-CEO-Outlines-Future-Computing

31. D'Aveni, R. (2015, May), The 3-D printing revolution, *Harvard Business Review*, 40–48.

Managers should understand and anticipate the transformations brought about by the digitization of manufacturing:[32,33]

- *Offering*. Accelerated product development cycles are the renewed benefits of 3D printing. Prototypes can be built and delivered to customers as soon as their digital design is available. The diffusion of 3D printers could deeply impact the product offering. You may consider just selling or "loaning" the digital design, allowing the customers self-manufacture the product. However, once the digital design is available, protecting it from copying or redistribution will require special attention, as with all information goods. If the competitive advantage is not found in the manufacturing process anymore, the design and engineering skills become the resources on which your competitive advantage is built.
- *Operations*. As more products are manufactured through 3D printing, operations and supply chain management will need to change radically. Operational efficiency will emerge directly from the reconfiguration of the phases of manufacturing and delivery of products. As Maurice Conti, director of strategic innovation at Autodesk, which worked with Nike on innovative 3D manufacturing processes, said, "It's a hugely significant advance, not the least because once you start doing things this way, it obviously takes a lot of the labor cost out of the equation."[34] A scenario where your Amazon order is not only shipped but manufactured and shipped in 24 hours is no more farfetched. These are the promises of "instantaneous inventory management," where stock will no longer exist.
- *Capabilities*. Transitioning from the physical world to the digital world and back again is the challenge organizations face with 3D printing. Organizations will need to refocus their skills to differentiate through their own design and product customizations in a fiercely competitive IT enabled digital space. At the operational level, organizations have traditionally designed for manufacturing, but designing for printing requires a different set of skills.
- *New competitors and ecosystems*. Initially systems with lower entry barriers will see the birth of new business for quickly manufacturing niche products and customer designs. The impacts of the digitization of manufacturing may involve increased competition from new intermediaries. Paralleling the experience of the music industry, specialized intermediaries could emerge as platforms for the distribution of the digital designs. Makers, too, could challenge with improved designs your products, released under creative commons licensing and put in the public domain. As we will see in the next sections, open source designs may emerge from the collaboration of makers and users, competing directly with commercial products.

Digital manufacturing appears as the next stop in the journey from the digital to the physical world and "has the potential to revolutionize the way we make just about everything,"[35] to echo President Obama. IT is the enabler of this manufacturing revolution that is giving birth to a total new class of digital products. The challenge for managers will be to organize for this change and prepare for a new wave of business opportunities.

Advanced Analytics

In Chapter 3, we introduced and discussed the concepts of business intelligence and big data. You now have a better understanding of the fact that modern organizations have to contend with an unprecedented volume of data. Research firm IDC started its 2014 Digital Universe Study by stating, "This is

32. D'Aveni, R. (2015, May), The 3-D printing revolution, *Harvard Business Review*, 40–48.

33. Cohen, D. (2014, January), 3-D printing takes shape, *McKinsey Quarterly*, p. 6.

34. Koten, J. (2013, June 10), A revolution in the making, *Wall Street Journal*, retrieved from http://www.wsj.com/articles/SB10001424127887324063304578522812684722382

35. Gross, D. (February 2013), Obama's speech highlights rise of 3-D printing, CNN, retrieved from http://edition.cnn.com/2013/02/13/tech/innovation/obama-3d-printing/

the digital universe. It is growing 40% a year into the next decade, expanding to include not only the increasing number of people and enterprises doing everything online, but also all the 'things'—smart devices—connected to the Internet, unleashing a new wave of opportunities for businesses and people around the world."[36] The firm estimated the size of this "digital universe" at 4.4 zettabytes (trillion gigabytes). Furthermore, organizations today increasingly contend with continuous flow DDSs, along with more traditional static data sets. Importantly, these data are often unstructured. Structured data are configured within an overarching organization—as, for example, data that are configured within the structure of a relational database schema. The notion of unstructured data is often misused. For example, we often hear people refer to Tweets or other text documents as "unstructured data." But text *does* have structure, we object. The confusion stems from the fact that it is not the type (e.g., free form text, images, video) that determines whether the data are structured or unstructured but rather its metadata.[37]

The defining feature of the current big data and analytics trend is the number of sources of new data, born in digital form and often available in real time. They enable the extraction of an unprecedented amount and variety of insight. Dan Porter, the director of statistical modeling for the Obama's U.S. presidential campaign, neatly captured the importance of this trend: "While refining algorithms and statistical models provides incremental improvements, the real boost in predictive and explanatory power comes from adding new data sources."[38]

While succeeding without a data analytics strategy may have been possible in the past, the ability to capture, manage, and extract insight from a large and varied set of sources of data is increasingly a strategic imperative—table stakes for modern business organizations.

We can think of business analysis as the examination of the structure of business data in an effort to reveal useful insights that enable superior decision making. The continuing effects of the information revolution and the changing nature of business data have created unprecedented opportunity to (creatively) extract value from data. As a consequence, the analytics element of BI, or advanced analytics, as some call it, rose to prominence. While analysis is conceptually part of business intelligence, today advanced analytics, and the associated techniques, are outside the scope of the traditional BI infrastructure. Traditional BI analysis focuses on structured, mostly internal, data and is performed with "enterprise IT tools" in integrated suites (e.g., Oracle Business Intelligence Enterprise Edition 11g).

Advanced analytics refers to analysis of business data that is less structured than BI analysis. The tools are generally evolving instruments that require greater skills to be used (e.g., R, Python, Octave). Much of the data used in advanced analytics is not neatly structured in carefully designed data warehouses and is instead collected ad hoc, requiring substantial preprocessing and cleaning.

Machine learning makes algorithms identify occurrences and unknown patterns in data and can be trained to look for the same occurrences in new data sets. It's like having an analyst capable of looking for trends within massive amounts of data (beyond human capacity). This opens to a new category of applications that from data can derive reliable predictions. Instead of causality, machine learning derives empirical models fitting the available data.

NoSQL databases are the data infrastructure of the massive data set used in advanced analytics and are different from traditional relational database management systems (RDBMS), as they provide both a flexible structure to better support the exploration of data and heterogeneous format and sources and a greater scalability that enables the system to distribute the access and analysis of massive datasets by dividing and distributing the work on commodity servers.

---

36. IDC, The Digital Universe of Opportunities: Rich Data and the Increasing Value of the Internet of Things April 2014.

37. The prefix *meta* roughly translates from Greek as "about." Thus metadata is data used to describe other data—that is, data about data. Database schemas or JSON key–value pairs represent examples of common metadata.

38. Speaking at the LSU Analytics Speakers Series on January 21, 2015.

While BI vendors rapidly incorporate new techniques in their BI suites and the boundary between the two is somewhat artificial, advanced analytics is today much more akin to academic research than corporate work.[39]

The Advent of Supercrunchers

Nobel Prize winner Herbert Simon once stated, "In an information-rich world, the wealth of information means a dearth of something else: a scarcity of whatever it is that information consumes. What information consumes is rather obvious: it consumes the attention of its recipients. Hence a wealth of information creates a poverty of attention and a need to allocate that attention efficiently among the overabundance of information sources that might consume it."[40] In his 2007 book, Ian Ayres argued that the future belongs to individuals who are both creative and quantitatively oriented—the so-called supercrunchers.[41] It is these individuals, the theory goes, who will be able to exploit the availability of data to their advantage and the advantage of their organizations by quickly and effortlessly testing their hunches and intuitions with data. Along the same lines, economics professor Hal Varian put it this way when he was serving as visiting scientist at Google: "The sexy job in the next ten years will be statistician. . . . People think I'm joking, but who would have guessed that computer engineer would have been the sexy job of the 1990s!"[42] Indeed these authors anticipated that data would become free and ubiquitous—as suggested by the digital data genesis paradigm—and the natural consequence that the ability to take advantage of such data becomes the valuable complementary scarce resource.[43]

While Varian used the term *statistician*, he was arguably referring to a wider skill set. If you are accustomed to reading the technology and business press, you know that the more general and more popular term most commentators have settled on is *data scientist* (Figure 12.17).

Providing a precise definition of this term is deceptively difficult—after all, aren't all scientists concerned with data?! While many abhor the term data scientist, suggesting it is a marketing laden way of saying *analyst*, most observers agree that "data science" encompasses more than statistics. It also includes the ability to identify useful data sources and generate new data streams. It encompasses the ability to organize and manage large amounts of diverse data. Finally, it comprises communication and

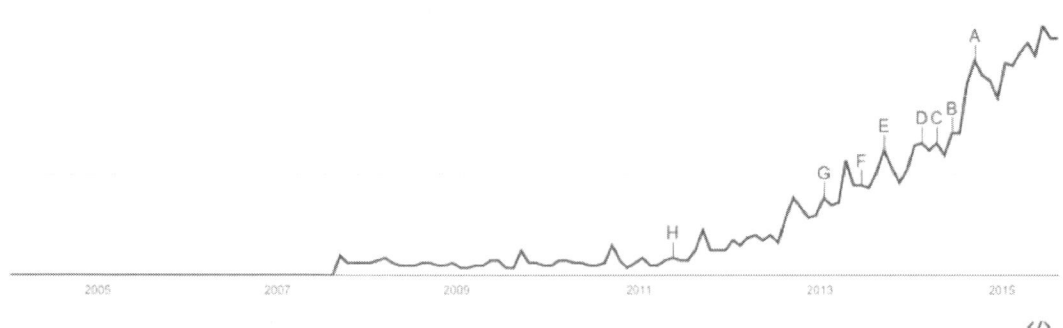

FIGURE 12.17. Google Trend results for the search term *data scientist*

39. Dwoskin, E. (2014, August 9), Big data's high-priests of algorithms, *Wall Street Journal*, retrieved from http://www.wsj.com/articles/academic-researchers-find-lucrative-work-as-big-data-scientists-1407543088

40. Simon, H. A. (1971), Designing organizations for an information-rich world, in *Computers, Communication, and the Public Interest*, ed. M. Greenberger, Baltimore, MD: Johns Hopkins Press.

41. Ayers, I. (2007), *Super crunchers: Why thinking-by-numbers is the new way to be smart*, New York, NY: Bantam.

42. McKinsey (2009, January), Hal Varian on how the Web challenges managers, retrieved from http://www.mckinsey.com/insights/innovation/hal_varian_on_how_the_web_challenges_managers

43. Davenport, T. H., & Patil, D. J. (2012), Data scientist: The sexiest job of the 21st century, *Harvard Business Review, 90*(10), 70–76.

persuasion competences to ensure that results of all the "data science" are actionable and implemented in the organization.[44]

Software and service provider IBM describes data scientists as "an evolution from the business or data analyst role. The formal training is similar, with a solid foundation typically in computer science and applications, modeling, statistics, analytics and math. What sets the data scientist apart is *strong business acumen*, coupled with the *ability to communicate* findings to both business and IT leaders in a way that can *influence* how an organization approaches a business challenge. Good data scientists will not just address business problems, they will pick the right problems that have the most value to the organization."[45] In other words, good data scientists must have the technical skills and instruments to extract insight from data, but they must also have the skills and instruments to decide what insight is worth extracting. This book is devoted to helping you develop those skills, which here we call value creation and appropriation competencies.[46]

Customer Managed Interactions

In Chapter 3, we discussed customer relationship management (CRM). CRM has been, and continues to be, a major focus for organizations, particularly business organizations, but its limitations are now apparent. CRM is firm centric, only relying on transactional and behavioral customer data pertaining to the interactions of the customer with the firm engaging in it. CRM promises the ability to get to know customers intimately and be able to anticipate their needs. However, a firm engaging in CRM has a limited view of customers' actions and behaviors. Moreover, many events are unforeseeable or, when planned, only the customer knows about them. In response, the concept of customer managed interactions (CMI) is emerging, promising to solve some of the limitations of CRM described above. CMI is predicated on a shift in the collection and control of the data. In the CMI approach, customer data are stored and managed by the customer—or on his or her behalf by an infomediary (see Chapter 5)—rather than by the firms who originally handled the transaction. Thus customers maintain control over the decision to interact, the timing of the interaction, the channel to be used, and the data generated.

This approach solves the fundamental limitation of CRM initiatives because the customer's personal data warehouse holds a complete record of all relevant transactions, simplifies the data integrity and redundancy challenge, and since the transaction is initiated by the customer, it reflects any unforeseeable or life-changing events that may be relevant.

When a customer is ready to transact with your organization, he or she will share the relevant data and his or her requirements with you and, perhaps, some of your competitors. Each of the interested organizations can elect to respond with an offer that the customer evaluates prior to making a selection (Figure 12.18). This scenario may appear overly futuristic, and in fact it certainly is at this point for most goods. However, the process described above is no different from one that we are all very familiar with—the request for proposals (RFP) process.

Today the RFP process is relegated to big ticket items because the economics of the process are such that it is not feasible for most consumer goods. Yet as the price-per-performance of computing equipment continues to fall and IT becomes more and more pervasive, both in business and homes, we can envision a time when the RFP process becomes feasible for the majority of consumer goods: airline tickets, CDs, books, home appliances, and the like.

Note that the CMI approach is not necessarily about the lowest prices. Conversely, for most industries and most organizations, CMI success will likely stem from the quality of the recommendation and

44. Davenport, T. (2015, June 17), Clear storytelling boosts value of analytics, *Wall Street Journal: The CIO Report*, retrieved from http://blogs.wsj.com/cio/2015/06/17/better-analytical-storytelling-by-people-and-machines/

45. IBM (n.d.), *What is a data scientist?*, retrieved from http://www-01.ibm.com/software/data/infosphere/data-scientist/

46. We personally believe that there is an emerging role in organizations that we would call *analytics strategist*. Data strategists share many similarities with data scientists but, because of their training and experiences, are more focused on the business application of the analyses rather than their mechanics.

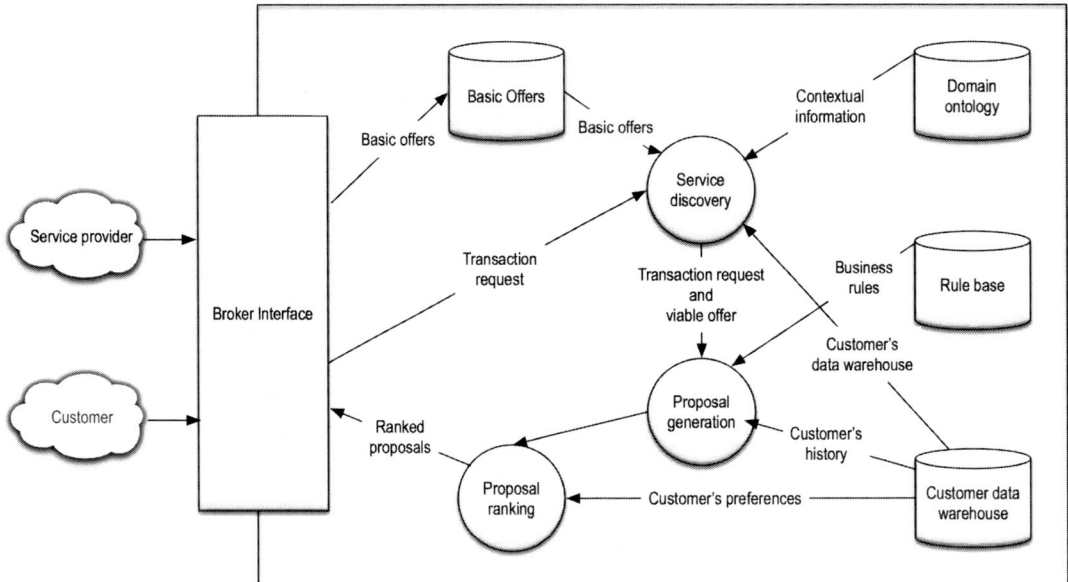

FIGURE 12.18. Customer interactions in the CMI paradigm

the fit of the solution to the customer need. As the firm has access to much better customer data, it is reasonable for customers to expect much better-fitting solutions. The technology is now in place to support the move of CMI to the mainstream. The Internet has created the infrastructure for data transfer, the falling cost of storage justifies the development of comprehensive personal data repositories, and standards like XML provide the infrastructure for formatting messages among loosely coupled agents.

Consider, for instance, Quicken, the personal financial management software. While Quicken is typically focused on the financial side of the transaction, if you use credit cards as the exclusive form of payment and diligently download your statements to Quicken, you can develop a pretty comprehensive personal data repository. The leap to a situation where every transaction comes with an associated XML message describing it isn't big. For simple goods, such as airline tickets, this is already possible, as the reservation fully defines the relevant characteristics of the product.

Open Source

Open source software no longer qualifies as an emerging trend. Gartner estimates that by 2016 open source code will be present in the portfolio of mission-critical software (not just any application!) of at least 95% of mainstream IT organizations.[47] Indicating the consolidation of the trend toward open source software use, as in 2010 only 75% of organizations relied on this class of software for mission-critical functionality.

The trend toward open source software use gained significant momentum with the emergence of the Internet, but it remains today an important and evolving IT opportunity for modern organizations. For example, Linux represents the most famous example of open source software, but a number of other initiatives are today references in their class. Today, projects like the Apache Web Server, Apache Hadoop, the JBoss Application Server, MySQL RDBMS, Eclipse IDE, MongoDB, and many more are among industry leading products in their respective categories, well illustrating the large impact of open source software on the IT industry.

---

47. Driver, M. (2014, August 13), Widespread use of open-source software demands strong and effective governance, *Gartner Research*, G00267430.

```
dBDate = CDate(BirthDate)
dRelDate = CDate (RelativeTo)
iAns = Year(dRelDate) — Year (dBDate)
if Month(dBDate) <> Month(dRelDate) Then
      bSubtractOne = Month(dBDate) > Month(dRelDate)
Else
      bSubtractOne = Day(dBdate) > Day(dRelDate)
EndIf
```

FIGURE 12.19. Sample source code

The open source movement has coalesced around the Open Source Initiative (OSI), an organization dedicated to promoting open source applications and system code, focusing on its benefits and qualities for the business community. In 2006, the OSI website captured the evolution of the movement: "Open source software is an idea whose time has finally come. For twenty years it has been building momentum in the technical cultures that built the Internet and the World Wide Web. Now it's breaking out into the commercial world, and that's changing all the rules. Are you ready?"[48]

Open Source: Definition

Open source software is often confused with free software—as in free of charge. In fact, licenses for open source software may or may not be offered at no cost (free-of-charge software is called freeware). Rather, the term *open source* is used to differentiate it from closed source, or proprietary, programs that prevent users from accessing and modifying the source code. The mission of the OSI captures this notion: "Open source is a development method for software that harnesses the power of distributed peer review and transparency of process. The promise of open source is better quality, higher reliability, more flexibility, lower cost, and an end to predatory vendor lock-in."[49]

Software programs are created by software engineers, who design the algorithm, and programmers, who code it using a specific programming language. The code generated by the programmers, which can be understood by anyone who is well versed in the programming language used, is called the source code (see Figure 12.19).

In order for the program to work, the source code has to be transformed (i.e., interpreted or compiled) into a format that a computer can execute, called the object code. Typically, when you purchase a software license from a software company (e.g., Microsoft Office, Oracle Database 12c), you are given the object code and the right to run it on your computers, but you are not provided with the source code. In fact, any effort to reverse engineer the object code to gain access to the source code is considered a violation of the intellectual property of the software house and will land you a well-founded lawsuit.

Unlike proprietary software, open source programs are distributed with the express intent of enabling users to gain access to the source code and modify it. An open source license typically exhibits the following characteristics:

- *Free redistribution.* The software can be freely given away or sold.
- *Available source code.* The source code is published and freely obtainable.
- *Derived works.* Licensees can modify the software and redistribute it under the same license terms as the original.
- *No discrimination.* The license is available to any entity, including for-profit organizations and commercial users.
- *Technology neutrality.* The license, and all its provisions, must be free of restrictions tied to the use of any technologies or type of interface.

---

48. Open source initiative, retrieved June 12, 2006, from http://www.opensource.org
49. Open source initiative, retrieved May 5, 2011, from http://www.opensource.org

Open Source Is Open for Business

Analysis of the open source licensing characteristics shows that the open source movement encourages, rather than opposes, commercial applications and commercial redistribution. This friendliness toward business applications has been the catalyst for widespread acceptance and growth of open source software as a viable alternative to proprietary programs.

A number of organizations have emerged in an attempt to capitalize on the open source movement. The following three models are currently being implemented.[50]

Sponsored Open Source A number of not-for-profit foundations provide support and coordination to open source efforts. For example, the Apache Software Foundation coordinates enhancements to the Apache web server, and the Mozilla Foundation supports the development of the Firefox web browser and many other products (Figure 12.20).

Some corporations also sponsor their own open source projects, typically "opening" their own software products by releasing the source code. The first example in this area was offered by Netscape Corp., which released the source code of its web browser in 1998. More recently, Sun Microsystems released the source code of its OpenOffice suite and NetBeans products and in November 2006 even released the source code of its Java programming language.

Open Source Service The open source service model emerged in the late 1990s with increasing attention being garnered by the Linux operating systems. While licenses to Linux had to be free, a number of firms, led by pioneer Red Hat Inc., began charging for installation, support, training, and all the other ancillary services typically associated with software sales. Today a number of upstarts and established firms compete in this market, including big names such as Hewlett-Packard (HP), Unisys, and Novell. They support a whole stable of open source applications such as Linux (operating system), Apache (web server), and MySQL (database management system).

Professional Open Source The latest evolution in the open source model is professional open source. This label refers to organizations that, while being part of the open source movement and subscribing to the open source licensing terms, maintain fairly tight control over the software programs they sell. For example, a professional open source organization will have its own core set of programmers and developers who provide direction for the project. At the same time, though, the group will leverage the greater community of open source programmers, testers, and adopters. These organizations rely on their knowledge and understanding of the core source code to provide better services when a client adopts their software.

Advantages and Disadvantages of Open Source Software

As a general or functional manager, you will without a doubt be part of a system selection committee. Increasingly, such committees have the option of adopting open source software rather than purchasing proprietary programs. While decisions of this kind are very context specific, below we identify the main benefits and drawbacks of open source.

Advantages The principal advantages of open source touted by its proponents are a function of the ability of open source projects to leverage a large community of developers, programmers, testers, and customers. These advantages include the following:

- *Robustness*. Proponents of open source software claim that mature projects (e.g., Linux) are more robust, more reliable, and generally higher quality than comparable proprietary applications (e.g., Microsoft Windows).

---

50. For a more in-depth analysis and treatment of them, see Watson, R., & Boudreau, M. C. (2005), The business of open source: A strategic perspective, *Cutter Benchmark Review*, 5(11), 5–12.

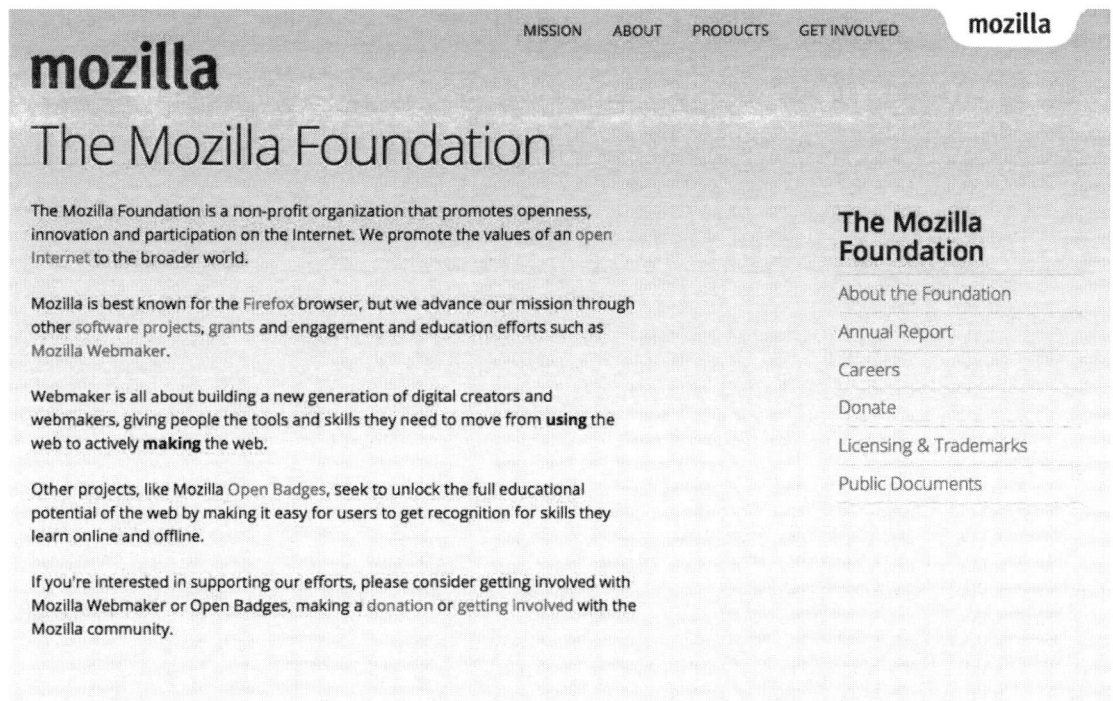

FIGURE 12.20. The Mozilla Foundation website

- *Creativity.* Open source software harnesses the creativity of thousands of developers around the world. As such, it is more likely to generate breakthrough new solutions (e.g., Firefox tabbed browsing, now a standard in this class of applications) than traditional products created by a small community within one software house.
- *Limited lock-in.* Open source software is not without switching costs, but supporters claim that such costs are much lower than those associated with proprietary software. For example, customers of open source software can make their own modifications to the source code rather than having to rely on the software vendor to do so.
- *Simplified licensing.* Because of the structure of an open source license, customers need not worry about complex legal constraints (e.g., number of concurrent users). They simply install as many copies of the program as they need.
- *Free license.* While not regarded as one of the chief benefits of open source by the open source movement, total cost of ownership is still an important factor to those firms that adopt open source applications. Because open source generally can be licensed for free, costs are lower than those associated with proprietary applications.

Disadvantages   Software is by no means simple (or cheap) to install and operate, and open source software is no exception. Thus the skeptics respond by raising the following concerns:

- *Unpredictable costs.* Skeptics like to say that free software is like a free puppy—yes, you get it for nothing, but then you will encounter many (often unplanned) costs along the way. Recent studies suggest that while in 80% of cases open source software is deployed to reduce costs, in only 50% of them, savings can be proved.[51] Thus you need to carefully evaluate an open source installation based on total cost of ownership (see Chapter 10).

---

51. Chandrasekaran, A., & Lerner, A. (2015), Should I use open source in my infrastructure?, *Gartner Research*, G00271630.

- *Support varies widely.* Depending on the product and where your firm acquired it, support can range from high quality to nonexistent, even in relation to the maturity—and widespread adoption—of the software.
- *Security.* Skeptics claim that publishing source code gives an advantage to those who want to break its security. Proponents of open source respond that a large community of developers will identify and close more weaknesses than a small team of company developers.
- *Compatibility.* Standardization of products using one or a few vendors simplifies compatibility and integration. There is no guarantee that open source solutions will be compatible with one another and/or with proprietary software.
- *The legal landscape.* Open source software requires that no portion of the code is protected by copyright. Recent court challenges have raised the specter that there is no way to ensure that copyrighted code will not make it into open source solutions, thus opening customers to liability. In response, some of the firms that support open source software (e.g., JBoss, HP, Red Hat) have adopted indemnification clauses in their licensing agreements.

In summary, the decision of whether to go with open source and with what products depends on the characteristics of the organization and the maturity of the software program. Some products, such as the Linux operating system, are already so robust that in early 2005 the MIT Media Lab felt comfortable advising the Brazilian government to shun Microsoft products for open source software, contending that "free software is far better on the dimensions of cost, power, and quality."[52] Other products require a much stronger commitment in terms of support and investments. It is essential that organizations adopting such products have the expertise and resources to implement and maintain them.

Summary

In this chapter, we introduced some emerging and some enduring trends in information systems (IS) and technology management. Understanding these trends and technologies, the associated vocabulary, and the benefits and risks they engender for modern organizations is critical for you as a general or functional manager, as you will be called upon to participate in the debate about whether your firm should embark in initiatives that leverage the technologies and trends discussed in this chapter.

Specifically, in this chapter we learned the following:

- The mobile platform represents the current frontier of technology adoption. Both individual users and businesses are integrating the mobile platform—in the form of smartphones and tablets—in their technology portfolios. While based on the traditional digital computer architecture, mobile devices offer peculiar characteristics such as ubiquity, identifiability, and context awareness. These characteristics make mobile "post-PC" devices uniquely suited to support emerging applications and uses such as mobile commerce, location-based social networking, and augmented reality—thus ushering in a wealth of opportunities for value creation.
- Information systems can play a crucial role toward advancing the global imperative of environmental sustainability. Broadening our attention from Green information technology (Green IT), and its focus on reducing energy consumption of IT devices and data centers, to Green IS enables a broadening of the role of IT in not only minimizing adverse impacts on environmental sustainability but also playing a proactive role in generating and implementing solutions.
- The widespread adoption of information technology and the increasing computer mediation of organizational and social processes has created the possibility to utilize data that are born digital. The digital data genesis (DDG) trend creates the opportunity. The sensors introduced in objects like the smartphone are an illustrative example of this trend. The continuous digital

---

52. MIT urges Brazil to adopt open-source (2005, March 17), *Reuters*, retrieved February 6, 2011, from http://msnbc.msn.com/id/7220913

encoding and transmission of data related to the captured events generate digital data streams (DDSs).

- The Internet of things (IoT), made of smart objects, is set to bring a totally fresh new breed of DDS. The IoT paradigm radically changes how value is created for customers and competition among firms and its boundaries. In this sense, new business ecosystems will arise, compete, and eventually coexist.

- With digital manufacturing, it is possible to directly print objects from their digital representation and design. The flexibility of the process and 3D printers' increasing capabilities generate the opportunity of a new breed of products and services, disrupting current product manufacturing practices.

- Advanced analytics move the interest of data analysis and gathering to external sources, providing the opportunity for greater insight. The heterogeneity of the data, their massive volume, and greater speed challenge established analysis practices, skills, and technologies.

- In Chapter 3, we discussed customer relationship management (CRM), its advantages, and some of the principal limitations of CRM initiatives: firm centricity and limited predictive ability. In response to these limitations, the customer managed interactions (CMI) trend is emerging. In the CMI approach, customer data are stored and managed by the customer—or on his or her behalf by an infomediary—rather than by the firms who handled the transaction.

- Open source software programs, those programs that enable the adopting firm to receive and modify the source code, are increasingly becoming a viable option for organizations. When weighing the decision to adopt open source instead of a proprietary software program, you need to evaluate the following advantages and disadvantages of open source projects: The pros include robustness, creativity, limited lock-in, simplified licensing, and free licenses. The cons include unpredictable costs, varying degrees of quality support, security concerns, compatibility concerns, and a potentially complex legal landscape.

Study Questions

1. Which of the trends associated with the mobile platform do you believe are most likely to become mainstream in the next three years? Why?
2. Explain the difference between smart devices and wearables, making specific examples.
3. Describe the concept of energy informatics. Describe where you believe energy informatics would have the strongest potential impact on environmental sustainability.
4. Identify two DDSs that you believe are relevant in a sport and suggest an IT dependent strategic initiative based on both of them.
5. How does the CMI trend respond to the limitations of customer relationship management? Who would you think is best positioned to take advantage of the emergence of CMI?
6. What is open source software? What are the main advantages and disadvantages of open source software? When would you consider an open source software implementation in your organization? When would you not?

Further Readings

1. D'Aveni, R. (2015, May). The 3-D printing revolution. *Harvard Business Review*, 40–48.
2. Gubbi, J., Buyya, R., Marusic, S., & Palaniswami, M. (2013). The Internet of things (IoT): A vision, architectural elements, and future directions. *Future Generation Computer Systems, 29*(7), 1645–1660. doi:10.1016/j.future.2013.01.010
3. Lee, I., & Lee, K. (2015). The Internet of things (IoT): Applications, investments, and challenges for enterprises. *Business Horizons, 58*(4), 431–440. doi:10.1016/j.bushor.2015.03.008
4. Porter, M. E., & Heppelmann, J. E. (2014, November). How smart, connected products are transforming competition. *Harvard Business Review, 92*, 11–64.
5. Scoles, S. (2015, August 19). The future of the Internet, according to its father. *Popular Science*. Retrieved from

http://www.popsci.com/vint-cerf-interplanetary-Internet

6. Watson, R. T., & Boudreau, M.-C. (2011). *Energy informatics*. Athens, GA: Watson Press.

7. Watson, R. T., Piccoli, G., Brohman, M. K., & Parasuraman, A. (2004). I am my own database. *Harvard Business Review, 81*(11), 18–19.

8. Watson, R. T., Piccoli, G., Brohman, M. K., & Parasuraman, A. (2005). Customer-managed interactions: A new paradigm for firm-customer relationships. *MIS Quarterly Executive, 4*(3), 319–327.

Glossary

- **Augmented reality:** A field of computing concerned with superimposing an information layer on a real image, thus providing users with a simultaneous view of real objects and contextual information about those objects.

- **Cloud computing:** A general term referring to the ability to obtain and use computing functionality (e.g., storage, software) over the Internet.

- **Customer managed interactions (CMI):** A paradigm where the customer retains control over the decision to interact, the timing of the interaction, the channel to be used in the interaction, and the data generated.

- **Customer relationship management (CRM):** A strategic orientation that calls for iterative processes designed to turn customer data into customer relationships through active use of, and learning from, the information collected.

- **Digital data stream (DDS):** The continuous digital encoding and transmission of data describing a related class of events. The transmission or flow of these digital representations of events makes the DDS, which may be human generated (e.g., a tweet, an Instagram) or machine generated (e.g., a CO_2 reading, a GPS location). DDG is about capturing the event; DDS is about leveraging the potential of the flow of these events for decision making and operational change.

- **Digital manufacturing:** A production process where layers of material are laid down following a fully digital project. Digital manufacturing is an additive process working the opposite of traditional manufacturing techniques like lathing or milling, where material is removed to obtain the desired object.

- **Energy informatics:** An emerging discipline that is concerned with analyzing, designing, and implementing systems to increase the efficiency of energy demand and supply systems.

- **Internet of things (IoT):** Interconnectivity of physical smart objects, sensors, or other devices, bringing the benefits of the Internet into the physical space.

- **Location-based social networking:** An extension of mobile social networking whereby the geographical location of the user becomes an integral component of the service, enabling efficient access to context-dependent services.

- **Mobile platform:** A platform is an underlying computer system on which application programs can run. With the term mobile platform, therefore, we refer to the hardware/operating systems combinations that enable mobile computing (e.g., Apple iPad/Apple iOS or Samsung Galaxy Tab/Google Android).

- **Open source:** A type of software licensing agreement that enables the licensee to obtain and modify the source code of the software program.

- **Wearable devices:** A diversified category ranging from bulky head-mounted displays or backpacked systems to rings or futuristic subcutaneous devices. The interest in wearable technologies lays in the massive personal and behavioral data that they could potentially generate.

CHAPTER 13

Security, Privacy, and Ethics

What You Will Learn in This Chapter

This chapter discusses some important topics of managerial interest that are often delegated to information technology (IT) specialists: security and IT risk management, privacy, and information systems ethics. The first objective of this chapter is to convince you that, as future general and functional managers, you will have to be involved in these decisions. The second objective is to help you gain an understanding of the circumstances in which choices and trade-offs are made so that you can actively participate in decision making. Specifically, in this chapter you will

1. Learn to make the case that information systems security, privacy, and ethics are issues of interest to general and functional managers, and explore why it is a grave mistake to delegate them exclusively to IT professionals.
2. Understand the basic IT risk management processes, including risk assessment, risk analysis, and risk mitigation.
3. Understand the principal security threats, both internal and external, and the principal safeguards that have been developed to mitigate these risks.
4. Be able to identify the nature of privacy concerns that modern organizations face, and be able to articulate how general and functional managers can safeguard the privacy of their customers and employees.
5. Define ethics, apply the concept of ethical behavior to information systems decisions, and be able to articulate how general and functional managers can help ensure that their organization behaves ethically.

MINICASE: Reinventravel.com Comes under Fire

As you watch the sun setting over the San Francisco skyline from your hotel room window, you can't avoid feeling that you really dropped the ball this time. You can still hear Clive Sturling, your chief information officer (CIO), as he tells you, "Don't worry about security. That's techie stuff; I'll take care of it. Just grow the business. That's what you are good at." You had not asked about security again after that conversation, perfectly happy to leave the "techie stuff" to him, and that was before you launched the company over two years ago!

Well, it was him on the phone a minute ago, ruining what had been a perfectly good day. In a daze, you replay the conversation in your mind: "We have been attacked," Clive had said. "It was a distributed denial of service attack, not much we could do with our current security infrastructure. The site was unavailable for about 70 minutes; it wasn't defaced or otherwise ruined, just down. I don't think many people noticed. The attack ended about an hour ago. I didn't want to call you before checking if they had compromised any files. It doesn't look like it."

Not much we could do? Isn't he the one who said not to worry about security? The site was down for "only 70 minutes." Does he know that in that amount of time Reinventravel.com typically processed 19,000 transactions? Granted, evenings were a bit slower, but there must have been at least 4,500 customers who noted the outage. Your emotions kept mixing at a dizzying pace. You were angry at Clive; you trusted him and he let you down. However, you felt sympathetic to his position as well. You had been the one who told him to "run IT on a shoestring," to help you speed the path to profitability as much as possible.

Oddly enough, as you begin to recover from the shock of the news, your college days flash into your mind, bringing a smile to your face. You had started in this field only three and a half years before, when you learned in one of your classes about the opportunity to revolutionize how people seek and purchase travel products. That day in your information systems class seemed like decades ago; now you were the chief executive officer (CEO) of a growing company with 52 employees, over 70,000 active customers and members, and revenues approaching $8 million. Clive had built the search engine in just eight months alone! He was a wizard with that kind of stuff. Half the time, you had no idea what he was doing, but as for the user interface, you certainly appreciated and understood that part of his work; everyone did! It was so far superior to anything that had been seen before . . . it was that fabulous demo that got you your first round of venture capital financing.

Financing . . . that word snapped you back to reality! You had to get ready for dinner. The meeting with your venture capital (VC) was in less than an hour, and you had yet to take a shower. With the first round of financing beginning to run out and minimal profits, a second round was a must. You had hoped to spend the evening discussing your plan for growing the customer base and beginning to monetize your membership, seeking their guidance and help with regard to the three potential partners you were evaluating. "Well, that ain't going to happen," you mumbled.

What should you do? Should you tell your VC about the denial-of-service attack? It may not be your choice; these guys liked to do their homework, and the odds were good that they were poking around the site when the outage happened. No time to call your legal counsel; you had to go it alone on this one.

Clive had been very unclear about whether an intrusion had occurred along with the denial-of-service attack. At this point you had little faith with regard to his staff's ability to find out; it seems that security and monitoring had not been ranking very high on their priority list! Reinventravel.com stored quite a bit of personal information about customers, including identifying information and credit card data. Should you communicate to the customers that an attack had occurred? Should you issue a press release? There was no evidence that security had been compromised and even less that personal data had been stolen. A denial-of-service attack only made a website unavailable for some time, did it not? "No way, Clive and his staff would know if data had been stolen," you told yourself.

This was increasingly looking like a situation you were ill prepared to address. But as your father always said, "You wanted the bicycle? Now you have to pedal." As you began to feel the adrenaline pumping again, you exclaimed, "Here we go!" and jumped up from your chair. You had 55 minutes to develop your plan before dinner.

Discussion Questions

1. Do you agree with the assessment that you had dropped the ball? Or are you being unduly harsh on yourself?

2. Who do you think should be making security calls at Reinventravel.com? Shouldn't this be the CIO's job?

3. What should you do tonight? Should you approach the topic at dinner or wait and see if anyone else raises the issue?

4. What should you do in the next few days? Should you issue a press release? Should you contact your customers directly? Should you focus on overhauling your security safeguards to prevent future similar problems and forget today's incident?

Introduction

This chapter focuses on three topics: information systems security and information technology (IT) risk management, privacy, and information systems ethics. These topics, while distinct, are connected by a common thread. Information systems security, privacy, and ethical concerns were born along with the introduction of computer systems and information technology in organizations. However, the recent widespread adoption of the Internet and the proliferation of information for business use have dramatically amplified these threats. The computer security industry, for example, is estimated to be already in the billion-dollar range, with Gartner research estimating its size at about $75.4 billion in 2015. A ComputerWorld survey found that almost half of the organizations studied expect to increase their IT spending on security, yet at a slower pace than the surge in detected accidents.[1]

Security breaches have significant business impacts. A scientific event study found that public traded companies that experienced security breaches lost an average of 2.1% of their market capitalization (an average loss of over $1.6 billion per incident).[2] PwC reports in turn that 53% of securities exchanges have experienced cyberattacks. The economic and political relevance of IT security is well illustrated by the words of FBI Director James Comey, who declared in an interview, "There are two kinds of big companies in the United States. There are those who've been hacked by the Chinese and those who don't know they've been hacked by the Chinese."

A failure in security, privacy, or ethics can have dramatic repercussions on an organization, both because of its potentially damaging direct effects (e.g., computer outages, disruptions to operations) and its increasingly negative indirect effects (e.g., legal recourse, image damage). Consider the following three recent examples: Ashley Madison is the self-proclaimed "most famous name in infidelity and married dating" website, notorious for its slogan inciting extramarital affairs. In 2014, the adultery business was flourishing and generating over $100 million gross revenues per year. The company faced a major debacle in July 2015 when a group of hackers under the name "The Impact Team" gained access to the firm's servers and downloaded personal information concerning the registered 37 million users and other sensitive company's information. Hackers requested parent company Avid Life Media to take Ashley Madison and its companion site EstablishedMen.com permanently offline or they would release "customers' records, including profiles with all the customers' secret sexual fantasies and matching credit card transactions, real names and addresses, and employee documents and emails."[3] Avid Life Media ignored the threat and hackers kept their word, releasing 9.7 GB of data on the anonymous Tor network (Figure 13.1).

In the following days, at least two people reportedly committed suicide. Avid Life Media was exposed to five class action lawsuits demanding half a billion dollars in repairs and more were coming as the analysis of the data showed that at least 90% of the female profiles were fake and used just to attract subscribers—in other words, the site was allegedly a fraud. What distinguishes the Ashley Madison data breach—as author Lily Burana commented—is the fact that "it's the first major hack in which the reputations and family lives of millions of private citizens could potentially be shattered. Names that have been leaked into the Great Internet Forever may now be forever linked to adultery, wreaking havoc in marriages, social circles, and careers."[4]

---

1. Gartner says worldwide information security spending will grow almost 4.7 percent to reach $75.4 billion in 2015, retrieved from http://www.gartner.com/newsroom/id/3135617, and Forecast 2015: IT spending on an upswing, retrieved from http://www.computerworld.com/article/2840907/forecast-2015-it-spending-on-an-upswing.html

2. Cavusoglu, H., Mishra, B., & Raghunathan, S. (2004, Fall), The effect of Internet security breach announcements on market value: Capital market reactions for breached firms and Internet security developers, *International Journal of Electronic Commerce, 9*(1), 69–104.

3. Zetter, K. (2015, August 18), Hackers finally post stolen Ashley Madison data, *Wired*, retrieved from http://www.wired.com/2015/08/happened-hackers-posted-stolen-ashley-madison-data/

4. Burana, L. (2015, August 26), Ashley Madison aftermath: Breaking down the hack that exposed millions of people's carnal interests, *New York Times*, retrieved from http://nytlive.nytimes.com/womenintheworld/2015/08/26/ashley-madison-aftermath-breaking-down-the-hack-that-exposed-millions-of-peoples-carnal-interests/

Avid Life Media has failed to take down Ashley Madison and Established Men. We have
explained the fraud, deceit, and stupidity of ALM and their members. Now everyone gets to
see their data.

Find someone you know in here? Keep in mind the site is a scam with thousands of fake
female profiles. See ashley madison fake profile lawsuit; 90-95% of actual users are male.
Chances are your man signed up on the world's biggest affair site, but never had one. He
just tried to. If that distinction matters.

Find yourself in here? It was ALM that failed you and lied to you. Prosecute them and claim
damages. Then move on with your life. Learn your lesson and make amends. Embarrassing now,
but you'll get over it.

Any data not signed with key 6E50 3F39 BA6A EAAD D81D ECFF 2437 3CD5 74AB AA38 is fake

FIGURE 13.1. The message hackers included in their release
Source: Piratebay.to

In November 24, 2014, Sony Entertainment Company experienced a massive release of confidential information coming directly from its systems. The hacking group called "The Guardian of Peace" claimed to have stolen allegedly 100 terabytes of sensitive data, including usernames, passwords, and documents containing employees' personal information, including a list of employee salaries and bonuses, Social Security numbers and birth dates, HR employee performance reviews, criminal background checks and termination records, correspondence about employee medical conditions, passport and visa information for Hollywood stars and crew members who worked on Sony films, and internal e-mail spools.[5] The stolen data also includes confidential information on unreleased series and copies of unreleased theatrical movies. The peculiarity of this breach is that supposedly hackers spent a year after compromising the security of a system to gather all the credentials necessary to shut down the entire network, steal data, and permanently delete information on multiple servers (Figure 13.2).

The hack raised concerns and gained political attention because of the alleged responsibility of the North Korean government, blaming Sony for the disrespectful portrait of their leader in *The Interview*. To avoid further retaliation, Sony decided to pull the movie from theaters, an action publicly condemned by President Obama, who considered it a mistake. The movie was finally released in selected—mainly independent—theaters and streaming services. Sony stated the hack cost the company $15 million, covering "investigation and remediation costs," as it did not involve customer data. Clearly this doesn't account for the difficult quantifiable loss of trade secrets, reputation, and diplomatic consequences.

If you believed that at least in your car you would be safe from IT security threats, you should think again. In July 2015, hackers Chris Valesek and Charlie Miler caught the automotive industry by surprise when they wirelessly carjacked a 2014 Jeep Cherokee on the highway from 10 miles away.[6] Serious vulnerabilities in the Uconnect info-entertainment system allowed the hackers to take control of a vehicle in a normal usage situation. The "duo" went a long distance compared to their previous exploits on a Ford Escape and a Toyota Prius that required them to physically connect to cars' onboard diagnostic port. For the first time, carjacking moved from behind the wheel to the hackers' couch! This pressed Chrysler to issue the first "cybersecurity recall" for 1.4 million vehicles, as the vulnerabilities affected several other models, and to issue a software patch (Figure 13.3). It also led Sprint—the provider of cars' connectivity—to block the vulnerable ports. Interestingly, the case showed the complete absence

---

5. Zetter, K. (2014, December 12), Sony got hacked hard: What we know and don't know so far, *Wired*, retrieved October 5, 2015, from http://www.wired.com/2014/12/sony-hack-what-we-know/

6. Greenberg, A. (2015, July 21), Hackers remotely kill a Jeep on the highway—with me in it, *Wired*, retrieved from http://www.wired.com/2015/07/hackers-remotely-kill-jeep-highway/

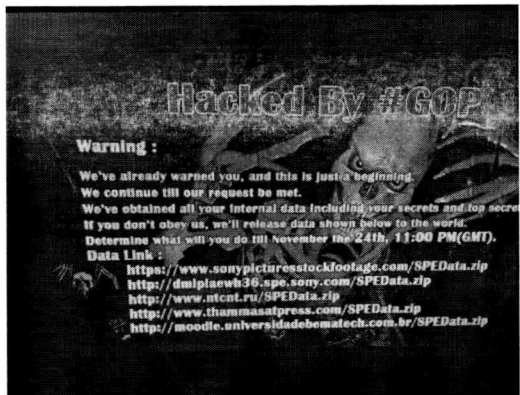

FIGURE 13.2. The screenshot of a compromised system a former Sony employee posted on Reddit.com Reddit.com Hacking (2014, November 24), *I used to work for Sony Pictures. My friend still works there and sent me this. It's on every computer all over Sony Pictures nationwide*, retrieved from https://www.reddit.com/r/hacking/comments/2n9zhv/i_used_to_work_for_sony_pictures_my_friend_still/

FIGURE 13.3. Chris Valask's tweet after the car was patched

of precedents, pushing both the industry and the government to action. Whether through legislation or industry standards and competition, the case pressured carmakers to take IT security seriously.[7]

As we mentioned in Chapter 6, security, privacy, and ethics are areas where, as general and functional managers, you cannot abdicate your responsibility. Yet in order to actively participate in decision making on these three fronts, you must be able to understand under what circumstances choices and trade-offs are made and what the principal threats and responses are.

IT Risk Management and Security

Information systems security refers to the set of defenses an organization puts in place to mitigate threats to its technology infrastructure and data resources. IT risk management is the process by which the firm attempts to identify and measure information systems security risks and to devise the optimal mitigation strategy.

Security is an area that has increased in importance along with the widespread adoption of information technology and even more so with the development and growth of networks. The diffusion of smartphones and the development of mobile ecosystems—either Android or iOS—are bringing new

---

7. Greenberg, A. (2015, July 21), Senate bill seeks standards for cars' defenses from hackers, *Wired*, retrieved from http://www.wired.com/2015/07/senate-bill-seeks-standards-cars-defenses-hackers/

challenges both at the personal level (e.g., personal account hijacking) and organizational level (e.g., hacks of executives' smartphones). More recently, security and IT risk management have come to the forefront of managerial attention because of the increasing threat of cyberterrorism. For instance, President Obama recently stated, "Cyberthreats pose one of the most serious economic and national security challenges to the United States, and my administration is pursuing a comprehensive strategy to confront them," and added, "As we have seen in recent months, these threats can emanate from a range of sources and target our critical infrastructure, our companies, and our citizens."[8] As computer systems are increasingly underpinning the infrastructure of developed economies, they become legitimate targets of terrorism threats.

Why Is Security *Not* an IT Problem?

The pervasiveness and possible cost of security threats should suffice to convince general and functional managers that security is a matter of strategic interest, not something that "the IT people should worry about." Speaking to the prevalence of such threats, a 2015 PwC survey found that security incidents are increasing 66% year after year (Figure 13.4).[9]

However, security should be on managers' radar screens also because of its peculiar characteristics that run the risk of leaving it underfunded unless general and functional managers get directly involved in the threat assessment and mitigation process.

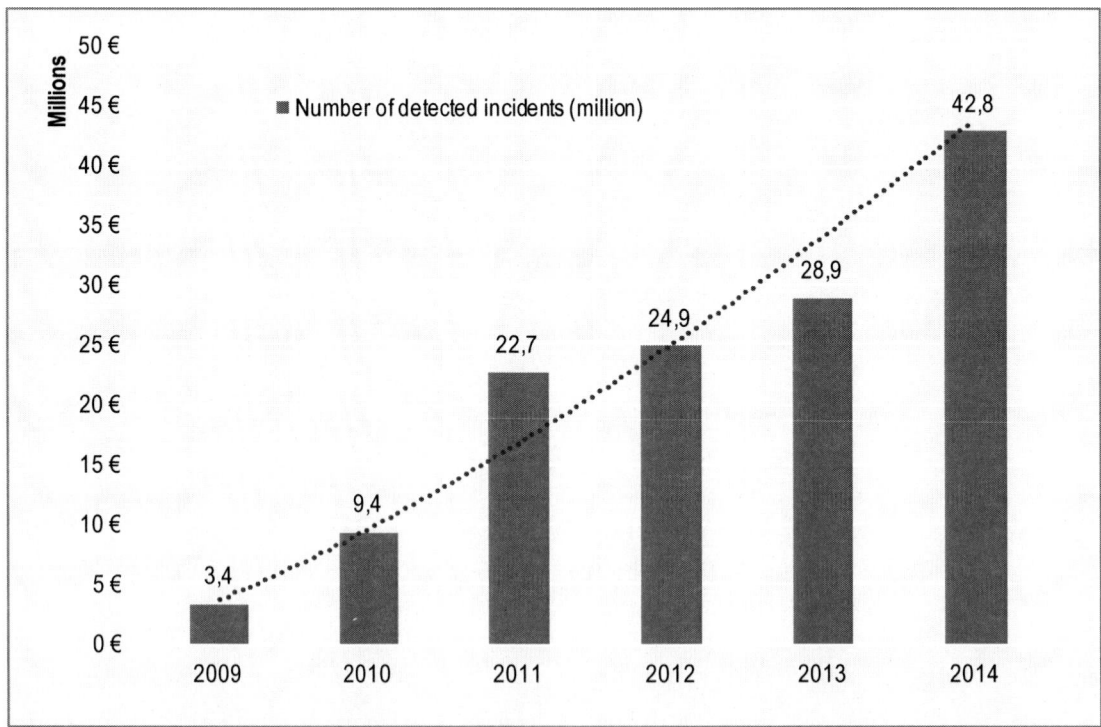

FIGURE 13.4. Five years overview of detected security incidents
Source: PwC (2015), *Global state of information security survey*, retrieved from http://www.pwccn.com/home/eng/rcs_info_security_2015.html

8. Baker, P. (2015, April 1), Obama expands options for retaliating against foreign hackers, *New York Times*, retrieved from http://www.nytimes.com/2015/04/02/us/politics/us-expands-foreign-cyberattack-retaliation-options.html

9. PwC (2015), *Global state of information security survey*, retrieved from http://www.pwc.com/gx/en/issues/cyber-security/information-security-survey.html

The game of chess offers a great metaphor for the information security management and IT risk management processes. In the game of chess, the objective of the players, some more skilled than others, is to circumvent the defenses of the opponent in order to checkmate him. Security is a constantly evolving game of chess—one where current defenses, and their limitations, are the basis for future attacks. A difficult game, indeed. But what do you get if you win the security chess game? Nothing. In fact, the best security is the one that leads to nothing happening. As in the opening minicase, all the "excitement" occurs when your security has been breached.

More specifically, security is a negative deliverable. In other words, all the money spent on managing IT risk and securing the firm's IT infrastructure and the data repositories produces no revenue and creates no efficiencies. It has no return on investment (ROI). Instead, it limits the possibility that future negative fallout will happen. As a consequence, it is difficult to secure funding for security efforts, a tendency nicely captured by Gene Spafford, a professor of computer science and security expert: "People in general are not interested in paying extra for increased safety. At the beginning, seat belts cost $200 and nobody bought them."[10]

Moreover, it is difficult to take credit for doing a great job when all you have to show for your efforts is that nothing bad has happened. This is particularly true when "lucky" firms around you also have not suffered an attack (or have yet to notice that one has taken place!) and skeptics in your organization can point to them as "proof" that you are overinvesting in security.

Consider the hurricanes that hit the coast of Louisiana and Mississippi in the summer of 2005 (Figure 13.5). One of the reasons for the devastation of the city of New Orleans was the underfunding of the levy system protecting the city. However, seeking funding for such a protective system is about asking for money for projects designed to avert a possible negative outcome that may occur sometime at an imprecise moment in the future. This is a difficult task and one that officials who are in power for relatively short periods of time have little incentive to fight for—particularly when many other (more appealing) projects compete for the same funding.

Because security is the type of investment that is difficult to gain funding for, particularly when competing for limited resources with projects that promise big results (efficiency improvements, revenue enhancements, and the like), it is all the more critical that it is not left to the IT group to make the case.

FIGURE 13.5. Satellite image of Hurricane Katrina
Credit Jeff Schmaltz, MODIS Rapid Response Team, NASA/GSFC; NASA Visible Earth (2005, August 29), *Hurricane Katrina (12L) approaching the Gulf Coast*, retrieved from http://visibleearth.nasa.gov/view.php?id=74693

---

10. Sullivan, B. (1999, March 30), Is Microsoft to blame for Melissa?, *ZDNet*, retrieved from http://www.zdnet.com/article/is-microsoft-to-blame-for-melissa/

General and functional managers must get involved in the security discussion, understand the threats, and assess the degree of risk that the firm should be allowed to take.

Forward-looking IT managers have begun to better "sell" security benefits, and the recent high-profile hacks made 61% of the chief executive officers (CEOs) surveyed by PwC in their Annual CEO Survey[11] declare to be worried of cyber threats and lack of data security and 78% of them consider cyber security technologies strategically important for their firms. Yet whether you are blessed with the help of "forward-looking" IT professionals or not, it is your responsibility as a general or functional manager to weigh in on the difficult trade-off decision between purchasing more security and accepting higher risks. If you are to do so, you must understand the basic threats and fundamental trade-offs engendered by computer security. This does not mean that you must develop an extraordinary amount of technical knowledge, as you will not be called on to personally implement the security measures. Instead you must understand the managerial process of IT risk management and information systems security decision making.

Risk Assessment

The risk assessment process consists of auditing the current resources, technological as well as human, in an effort to map the current state of the art of information systems security in the organization. An understanding of the current resources will provide an idea of the current set of vulnerabilities the firm is facing.

For instance, Dell is a firm with a very prominent website. Dell's website is not only the face of the company, but it is also one of its main sources of livelihood. If customers cannot access it, Dell loses revenue by the minute. Thus for Dell the risks associated with a denial-of-service attack that brings the website down is a very tangible one. The same could not be said for the Boat Yard Grill, a restaurant in Ithaca, New York, and its website (http://www.boatyardgrill.com).

The risk audit is useful because it provides the basis for a risk analysis. Risk analysis is the process by which the firm attempts to quantify the risks identified in the audit. We use the word "attempt" to stress that precisely quantifying the monetary consequences of some of these risks is impossible. What do you think is the value of the loss of customer confidence in the Chrysler brands after the hack of their cars? What is the value of the loss of confidence your customers may feel if they log on to your website or Twitter account one morning only to see it defaced with questionable pictures and comments (Figure 13.6)?

The impact of some security risks is harder to measure than others. However, the exercise is useful insomuch as rational decision making suggests that the amount you invest in security safeguards should be proportional to the extent of the threat and its potential negative effects. This is a critical point. Because security risks are really business risks—nobody would argue that loss of customer confidence is "an IT issue"—general and functional managers must be deeply involved in IS security prioritization decisions.

Risk Mitigation

Risk mitigation is the process of matching the appropriate response to the security threats your firm has identified. As Bruce Schneier, the noted computer security and cryptography expert, aptly put it, "There are two types of encryption: one that will prevent your sister from reading your diary and one that will prevent your government."[12]

Risk mitigation allows your organization to devise the optimal strategy given the set of security risks it faces. Such optimal strategy is the one that yields the best trade-off between the degree of security the firm attains and the total investment in countermeasures necessary to achieve it (Figure 13.7). The total cost for security is a combination of anticipation costs, those expenditures designed to anticipate and

---

11. PwC (2015), *18th Annual Global CEO Survey*, retrieved from http://www.pwc.com/gx/en/ceo-survey/2015/assets/pwc-18th-annual-global-ceo-survey-jan-2015.pdf

12. Schneier, B. (1996), *Applied cryptography: Protocols, algorithms, and source code in C*, Somerset, NJ: John Wiley & Sons.

FIGURE 13.6. Tesla Twitter account compromised on April 25, 2015

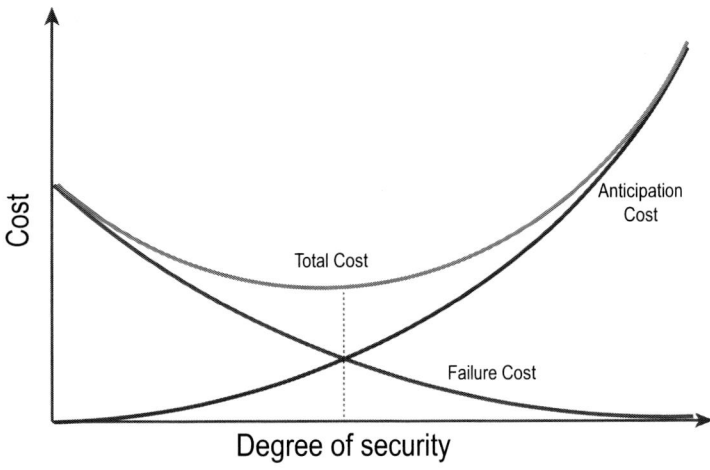

FIGURE 13.7. Cost/security trade-offs

mitigate the threats (e.g., purchasing and installing antivirus software), and failure costs, the negative financial fallout ensuing from a breach of security (e.g., loss of revenue during a website outage).

When faced with a security threat, the firm has three mitigation strategies available. Note than none of the three strategies described below is superior or inferior to the other in the absolute. The typical organization uses, consciously or unconsciously, a blend of all three.

1. *Risk acceptance.* This strategy consists of not investing in countermeasures and not reducing the security risk. The more an organization gravitates toward this strategy, the higher the potential failure cost it faces while minimizing anticipation costs.
2. *Risk reduction.* This strategy consists of actively investing in the safeguards designed to mitigate security threats. The more an organization gravitates toward this strategy, the higher the anticipation cost it faces while actively reducing failure costs.
3. *Risk transference.* This strategy consists of passing a portion (or all) of the risks associated with security to a third party (e.g., by outsourcing security or buying insurance).

As the firm seeks to identify the optimal IT risk management and information systems security strategy, it will endeavor to identify the optimal blend of the three mitigation strategies. The ideal portfolio of security and risk management measures is based on the specific security threats the organization faces, as well as management's willingness to accept these risks. The major threats confronting the modern organization, and the safeguards available to respond to these threats, are discussed below.

The Internal Threat

Internal security threats are those posed by individuals who have direct, on-premises access to the firm's technology infrastructure, or those who have legitimate reasons to be using the firm's assets. Internal security threats are important because the firm that is able to secure its assets against improper internal use has not only mitigated an important risk but is well on its way to mitigating the outside threat (i.e., the external threat can be seen a subset of the internal one). The recent PwC survey found that for 35% of companies, the sources of security incidents were current employees. This is very interesting data if you consider that among outsiders, hackers and competitors are the main sources of incidents and account only for the 24%.[13] When addressing internal security threats, we can separate them into two broad categories: intentional malicious behavior and careless behavior.

Intentional Malicious Behavior   This type of threat is typically associated with disgruntled or ill-willed employees. This is a particularly troublesome threat because it is almost impossible to prepare for. Imagine, for example, that a member of the sales and direct marketing team is selling customer e-mail addresses to spammers. Unless this person makes a careless mistake or discusses his behavior with others, his actions may go undetected for a long time.

Careless Behavior   This type of threat is typically associated with ignorance of, or disinterest in, security policies. Consider the case of the U.S. Department of Veterans Affairs, where a laptop containing personal information on as many as 26.5 million veterans had been stolen from the home of an employee. The data, including names, social security numbers, and dates of birth, were not supposed to be transferred onto an unsecured laptop or taken off of the department's premises. In this case, employee carelessness and lack of attention to existing procedures was the root cause of the failure.

A more recent example is the case of the French television network TV5Monde, the second largest television network in the world, behind MTV. Inadvertently reporter David Delos broadcasted to the network's Twitter, Instagram, and YouTube accounts credentials (Figure 13.8). Other than showing a lack of any security measure concerning passwords safeguarding, the video revealed the habit of network employees to use easy-to-guess—namely, insecure—credentials. The YouTube password appearing in the video, for example, was "lemotdepassedeyoutube" ("the password of YouTube" in English). To some accounts, the network's highest-level network account password was "azerty12345," the French-keyboard equivalent of "qwerty12345."[14] This careless behavior resulted in all the social networks being hacked and 11 stations stopping their broadcasts for 6 hours to an audience of 257 million homes.

Into this category fall a number of other behaviors that are more or less dangerous. For example, failing to modify default passwords, breaking the organization's policy on Internet and web usage, not following guidelines about saving data on personal or portable devices, or failing to destroy sensitive data according to planned schedules.

The External Threat

Before the advent of the Internet and widespread connectivity, the importance of internal security threats far outweighed the danger posed by hackers and other outsiders. Mitigating the outside threat

---

13. PwC (2015), *Global state of information security survey*, retrieved from http://www.pwc.com/gx/en/issues/cyber-security/information-security-survey.html

14. Machkovech, S. (2015, April 10), Hacked French network exposed its own passwords during TV interview, *ArsTechnica.com*, retrieved from http://arstechnica.com/security/2015/04/hacked-french-network-exposed-its-own-passwords-during-tv-interview/

FIGURE 13.8. Social media passwords going live on France 2 national public channel
Source: JT (2015, April 9), *13 hours*, retrieved from http://www.francetvinfo.fr/replay-jt/france-2/13-heures/jt-de-13h-du-jeudi-9-avril-2015_866269.html

prior to pervasive networking simply amounted to physically securing the firm's IT assets. This is not the case anymore.

Today there is an incredible array of ways in which your firm's infrastructure can be attacked and compromised. Viruses, Trojan horses, worms, time bombs, spyware, keystroke tracking tools, spoofing, snooping, sniffers—these are just some of the most popular examples of malicious code and techniques that modern organizations find themselves fighting off. Couple this seemingly unabated tide of new releases and new forms of harmful software with human threats like crackers, thieves, social engineers, and industrial espionage contractors, and you realize why security is continually ranked as one of the top worries for the modern chief information officer (CIO).

Those individuals who attack an organizations' IT infrastructure are typically called hackers. While some consider this a misnomer, contending that the term hacker simply means someone who possesses superior computer skills, the term has come to be associated in the media and general terminology with more or less maliciously intentioned individuals who attempt to subvert computer security defenses.

Below we address some of the external security threats confronting modern organizations.

Intrusion Threat   The intrusion threat is perhaps the most commonly envisioned when thinking about computer security. It consists of any situation where an unauthorized attacker gains access to organizational IT resources. Consider the following example. In the late 1980s, a group of teenage hackers was found guilty of gaining unauthorized access to surveillance satellites and using them for unauthorized purposes. As the story goes, the kids were discovered because the satellites were found marginally out of position at the beginning of every working day and the matter was further investigated. When the intruders' behavior was logged and monitored, it was discovered that upon taking control of the satellites, they were redirecting them on a nudist beach and taking pictures.

While the story screams urban legend, it is a great example of a (harmless) intrusion by individuals who did not attempt to inflict losses on the organization. Yet it is an intrusion nonetheless, as individuals without proper authority gained access to one of the organization's resources and used it for unintended purposes. More common, and less fun, examples include individuals who access private information by stealing or guessing legitimate passwords. This can be done by "sniffing" a network connection with specialized software and intercepting passwords that are not encrypted.

Social Engineering   An even simpler method is what is called "social engineering," which is a fancy name to describe a very simple practice: lying to and deceiving legitimate users. Social engineering is roughly defined as the practice of obtaining restricted or private information by somehow convincing legitimate users, or other people who have the information, to share it. This is typically done over the telephone or other communication media, and its success depends on the skills of the "social engineer," coupled with the gullibility and lack of training of the victim. Once the information has been obtained, say a password, the social engineer perpetrates the intrusion.

Phishing   The process of social engineering can be "automated" using a technique called phishing. Phishing consists of sending official-sounding spam (i.e., unwanted e-mail) from known institutions (e.g., MasterCard). The message indicates that the institution needs the recipient to confirm or provide some data and contains a link to a web page, which is a copy of the original, with fields for providing the "missing" information.

The act of phishing is the act of collecting personal information, and a number of creative methods have been devised to direct traffic to the phony website (e.g., using links or fake promotions) and fool people into complying by crafting official-sounding messages from reputable institutions (Figure 13.9). Once on the target page, the user is asked to input some sensitive information—such as user name and password (Figure 13.10)—with the sole objective of stealing it for later use. While this appears simplistic, phishing has turned out to be a very effective way to obtain personal data—as indicated in a recent study by Google and the University of California,[15] which estimated that most effective phishing websites can fool 45% of visitors.

Note that the low degree of sophistication of the phishing e-mail in Figure 13.9 may lead to warnings from both the e-mail client and the web browser opening the page (Figure 13.11). As in any high-stakes game of chess, the security game is replete with moves and countermoves, but a more sophisticated attack could likely have gone undetected.

From: SalesForce.com [mailto:orders@salesforce.com]
Subject: Payment confirmation for order # 48901801992

Message Body:

Dear user,

Thank you for purchasing Salesforce Performance Plus plan.
This message is a confirmation that your credit card has been charged.

For more information regarding this payment, please download the payment confirmation invoice :
https://na5.salesforce.com/home/payments.jsp?download_invoice=1&payment_id=48901801992</%22glasssplashbacklondon.co.uk/wp-content/plugins/cached_data/sf_payment_invoice_48901801992.zip/%22>

Service : Salesforce Performance Plus
Amount : 1600 USD
Transaction # : 48901801992

For more information regarding this payment, please check the attached merchant receipt.
Note: This payment will appear on your statement as "SalesForce AUTH #48901801992"

Thank you.

FIGURE 13.9. Phishing e-mail message targeting Salesforce.com users and providing a link to a malicious software aimed at compromising user's computer
Source: Salesforce.com

15. Bursztein, E., Benko, B., Margolis, D., Pietraszek, T., Archer, A., Aquino, A., . . . Savage, S. (2014), Handcrafted fraud and extortion: Manual account hijacking in the wild (pp. 347–358), ACM Press, doi:10.1145/2663716.2663749

Backdoors and Security Weaknesses   Another way to gain unauthorized access is to exploit weaknesses in the software infrastructure of the organization under attack. Commercial software typically comes with "backdoors." A backdoor is code built into a software program to allow access to the application by circumventing password protection. Backdoors are built into software in the event that high-level accounts, such as administrative accounts, are for some reason inaccessible (e.g., the password has been lost, or a disgruntled employee is blackmailing the firm and will not unlock the software). While backdoors must be changed during the installation process, sometimes this step is forgotten and the default backdoor is allowed to exist while the program is operational. Hackers can then easily gain access to the application and take control of it, giving themselves high-level access rights.

Beyond default backdoors, software programs have weaknesses (i.e., bugs). Typically these bugs are annoying because they prevent the application from functioning normally. For example, a program

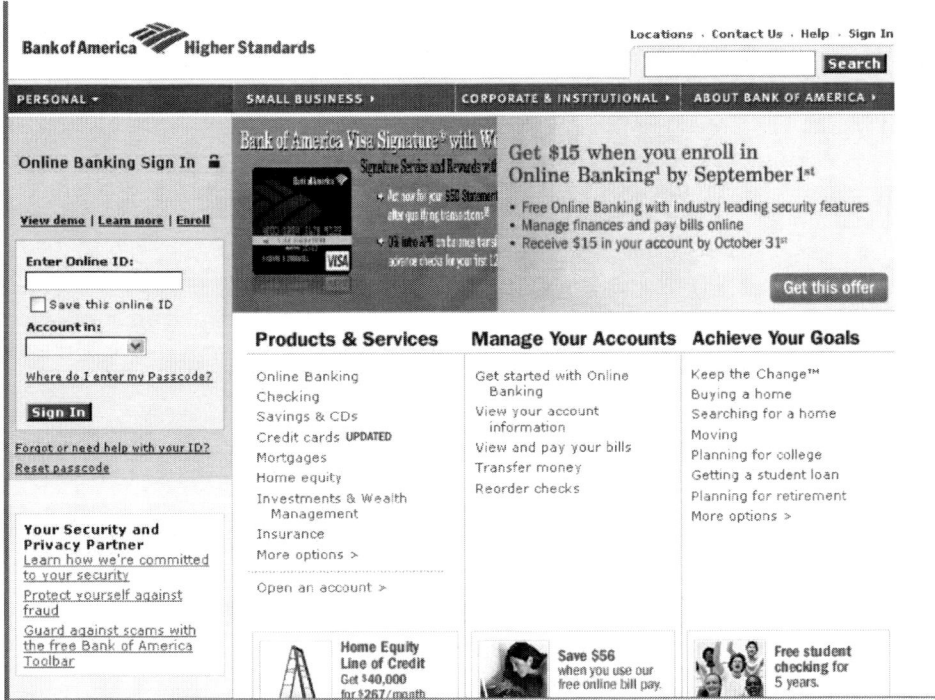

FIGURE 13.10. Capture page posing as a legitimate business

FIGURE 13.11. Warning message from browser

will shut off unexpectedly or freeze. At times, though, they can be extremely dangerous, as they create security holes that an ill-intentioned intruder can exploit.

The intrusion threat is particularly troublesome because it has significant and long-lasting potential impacts. First, it may go undetected for a long period of time, enabling the intruder to perpetrate her crime(s) over time. Second, the intruder may be able to gain access to private information and even steal records. Third, when intrusion is discovered, it will require a thorough investigation in order to identify where the intruder came from, whether she created backdoors that can be exploited in the future, and so on. Fourth, if information about the intrusion becomes public—something that is required by law in many states in cases where individuals' private information has been compromised—the firm will likely suffer significant damage to its reputation.

Going back to the opening example, it is now clear that even when intrusion by pranksters occurs (e.g., kids taking pictures of nude beaches, funny fellows who deface your website, or talented computer users who enjoy the challenge of breaking in solely to obtain bragging rights with their friends), the expense in terms of time, money, and trust recovery effort your organization must engage in can be quite high.

The Threat of Malicious Code Another security threat that modern firms face daily is presented by malicious code—also known as malware. The term *malicious code* refers to software programs that are designed to cause damage to individuals' and/or organizations' IT assets. Below we identify the main categories of malicious code and discuss their characteristics.

Viruses Computer viruses are an increasingly pervasive security threat. By some accounts, there nearly one million new threats are released every day.[16] These viruses are more and more often produced by putting together "component parts"—malicious scripts that can be assembled into complete viruses by relatively unskilled individuals, aptly called script kiddies.

A computer virus is a type of malicious code that spreads by attaching itself to other, legitimate, executable software programs. Once the legitimate software program runs, the virus runs with it, replicating itself and spreading to other programs on the same machine. By doing so, the computer virus, much like a biological virus, is able to prosper. If the infected files are shared and executed by others, their machines will be infected as well.

Following the infection phase, the payload delivery phase occurs. The payload is the typically harmful set of actions that the virus is designed to perform. They may range from simply annoying the user (Figure 13.12; a famous early virus dropped letters from the screen and nothing more) to wreaking havoc and bringing significant damage to the user (a popular one is the wiping out all data on the hard disk, as in the case of the Sony hack). Some viruses deliver their payload immediately after infection, while others, known as time bombs, deliver it at a specific point in time or when a certain action is performed by the user. For instance, the Michelangelo virus discovered in 1991 was designed to deliver its payload on March 6, the birthday of the Italian master.

With the advent of the Internet and the widespread use of electronic mail, virus authors have found a new way to spread their "work." An e-mail virus is malicious code that travels attached to e-mail messages and has the ability to self-replicate, typically by automatically e-mailing itself to multiple recipients.

Trojan Horses A Trojan horse is a computer program that claims to, and sometimes does, deliver some useful functionality. However, like the legendary war machine the Greeks used against the people of Troy (Figure 13.13), the Trojan horse hides a dark side and, like a virus, delivers its malicious payload. Unlike a virus, a Trojan horse does not self-replicate but is passed on by those who share it with others.

---

16. Harrison, V. (2015, April 14), Nearly 1 million new malware threats released every day, *CNN Money*, retrieved October 5, 2015, from http://money.cnn.com/2015/04/14/technology/security/cyber-attack-hacks-security/

Worms A worm is a piece of malicious code that exploits security holes in network software to replicate itself. Strictly speaking, a worm does not deliver a payload, like a virus. A worm simply replicates itself and continues to scan the network for machines to infect. The problem is that, as the worm infects more and more machines on the network, the traffic it generates quickly brings the network down—with substantial damage. The original Internet worm, originating at Cornell University in 1988, was estimated to cost infected sites from $200 to $53,000 for repairs.

Spyware Spyware applications have sprung up with the advent and widespread adoption of the web. The term *spyware* suggests that the software runs without the awareness of the user and collects information. Broadly speaking, spyware is software that, unbeknownst to the owner of the computer, monitors behavior, collects information, and either transfers this information to a third party via the Internet or performs unwanted operations.

Typical examples of spyware include adware, software that collects information in an effort to use it for advertisement purposes by opening pop-ups or changing a user's homepage; keyboard tracking, software that logs keyboard strokes in an effort to steal passwords and other sensitive information; and stealware, software that redirects payments legitimately belonging to an affiliate and sends them to the stealware operator.

While spyware differs from viruses, in that it cannot self-replicate, it can create significant problems for an organization. Beyond the malicious and often fraudulent effects of spyware, these programs divert resources and often slow down the user's legitimate work.

FIGURE 13.12. The DROL virus

FIGURE 13.13. The Trojan horse as represented in the movie Troy
Photo by Ross Burgess / CC BY SA 3.0

Ransomware Generally spread as innocuous attachment to e-mail messages, this malicious code limits the access to user's resources and system, demanding a ransom in exchange. An example of this category is the famous CryptoLocker isolated in 2014. As the name implies, once executed, the payload begins to encrypt users' data files, targeting Office documents, AutoCAD files, and pictures. The payload then displays a warning (Figure 13.14) requesting the payment of a ransom of $300 within 72 hours or else the decryption key will be destroyed.

The success of CryptoLocker, which allegedly extorted over $3 million, fueled the spawn of similar dangerous initiatives.

Denial-of-Service Attack Denial-of-service attacks are particularly powerful today given the predominance of online operations and the number of firms that use websites and other online services for their operations. A denial-of-service attack is a digital assault carried out over a computer network with the objective of overwhelming an online service so as to force it offline.

Consider a website as the service of interest. A website is managed by a web server that receives requests from clients all over the Internet and sends them the pages they request. When a web server receives more requests that it can handle, it will attempt to serve them all but will begin to slow down, like a waiter who has been assigned too many restaurant tables and is scrambling to serve them all. If

FIGURE 13.14. CryptoLocker's ransom request

Source: Federal Bureau of Investigation, Washington Field Office (2013, November 8), CryptoLocker Ransomware top story screenshot, retrieved from https://www.fbi.gov/washingtondc/news-and-outreach/stories/image/cryptolocker-ransomware-top-story-screenshot/view

the number of requests is high enough, the service will likely shut down, thus becoming unavailable to legitimate traffic as well.

Denial-of-service attacks can be extremely dangerous because a skilled intruder will employ a denial-of-service attack to divert attention and then occupy resources of the attacked organization. While the firm is busy averting the denial-of-service attack, the intruder can exploit available security breaches or create backdoors to be exploited later.

Responding to Security Threats

The management of computer security is a continuous effort. The principal objective is to identify the different threats and develop safeguards that match up with them and limit their incidence of success.

Internal Security Threats Prevention of internal threats is no simple feat since security products and technologies can only partially help. Prevention of internal threats requires the development and enforcement of security policies and auditing standards designed to ensure that such policies are understood and respected by those within the organization.

Security Policies The most easily preventable security risks are those caused by ignorance of sound security practice. A security policy spells out what the organization believes are the behaviors that individual employees and groups within the firm should follow in order to minimize security risks. They include what computing services will be made available and what computing services will not be made available within the firm. They specify what password standards the firm should follow (e.g., length, characters to be used, renewal schedules) and what rights different types of users will have. They specify the level of care that employees need to use with their passwords (e.g., do not share password with anyone, do not send passwords over clear channels such as unencrypted mail messages), what computing resources and what data should be accessible within the organization, and what data can be downloaded to personal devices and what needs to remain within the company. The policy should address legitimate uses of portable devices, what data can be downloaded to them, and how such devices should be secured by those who own them. A security policy may even address the level of care that employees should exercise when they leave the premises (e.g., not reviewing sensitive data on laptops while on airplanes).

Beyond having comprehensive security policies in place, the organization must audit them to ensure compliance. For example, accounts of terminated employees need to be swiftly deleted or made unavailable to prevent access from former employees who at best will see material they should not and at worst will be able to damage company resources (e.g., delete data).

External Security Threats   In addition, the prevention of external threats is also no simple feat.

Intrusion   A number of techniques and technologies to prevent intrusion have been developed over the years. The cornerstone of securing against intrusion is the use of passwords. Passwords ensure that resources are only made available to those who have the appropriate authentication levels. Thus a password can be used to block unauthorized external users as well as indicate to whom resources should be available among the legitimate users.

Organizations typically enforce standards to ensure that passwords are reasonably difficult to guess. For example, many security policies require that passwords have a minimum length; they use letters, numbers, and special characters; they don't use dictionary words, and so on. However, there is an inherent trade-off between the complexity of a password and human ability. In other words, if passwords are too difficult to remember, people will write them down, creating a new security risk! For this reason, the computer security industry is hard at work devising more robust identification schemes, such as biometrics—the use of physical traits (e.g., fingerprints, iris scans) as a means to uniquely identify users (Figure 13.15).

A firewall is a software tool designed to screen and manage traffic in and out of a computer network. Thus a firewall is used to secure the perimeter of the organization's computing resources, employing a number of technologies and techniques. Firewalls can also be used to enforce security policies (e.g., blocking traffic from websites deemed risky and blocking the download of some file types).

Firewalls are a very important security tool, but you need to remember that perimeter protection is only as strong as its weakest link—much like the perimeter protection of a castle. For example, no matter how powerful your firewall is, if there are unsecured modems that an attacker can dial into, the network is not secure. Once an attacker gains access to the organization's resources through the unsecured modem, the strongest perimeter security is made useless—the intruder is working on the inside now.

Consider as well that any resource that is brought outside the perimeter is not secured by the firewall—hence the inherent danger associated with the proliferation of mobile devices. For instance, if an employee copies sensitive data to her laptop and then takes the machine on the road, the firm's firewall is useless in protecting such data. With data increasingly prevalent, and portable devices achieving widespread adoption, perimeter security is increasingly insufficient.

Another technique that has been developed to safeguard against the intrusion threat is encryption. Through the encryption process, content is scrambled in such a way that it is rendered unreadable to all recipients, except those who hold the key to decrypt it. Encryption ensures that if the wrong individuals gain access to the data, they will be unable to make out its meaning. Encryption techniques are used to secure transmissions as well as to secure stored data. Consider once again the

FIGURE 13.15. Fingerprint scanner
Source: U.S. Customs and Border Protection

example of the lost laptop discussed above. If the data it contained had been encrypted, the loss to the firm would simply amount to the cost of the asset—less than a thousand dollars in most cases.

Security policy and audits will help a firm ensure that no backdoors are left open after the installation of a new software program. With respect to security holes and weaknesses in software due to bugs, the IT staff in the organization must monitor bug reports and install patches—pieces of add-on code published by the software house that wrote the program designed to eliminate weaknesses that surface after the release of the software program. The problem is that many organizations lack the staff to constantly monitor this information and may fall behind in patch installations, thus opening the firm to unnecessary risks. To obviate this problem, many of the large software houses (e.g., Microsoft) have now developed patch management software that automatically alerts users to the availability of newly released patches—and, if configured to do so, downloads and installs them automatically (Figure 13.16).

Malware Safeguarding against malware requires that the firm's IT professionals install the appropriate detection software (e.g., antivirus, spyware sweepers; Figure 13.17). With the large number of new viruses being released, antivirus and other detection software is only as good as its most recent update. For this reason, organizations that manage their own networks are increasingly attempting to centralize these applications and push updates to individual users so as to ensure that safeguards against malware are up to date.

Training and policies can also be very helpful in mitigating the malware threat. Simple behaviors, such as not opening e-mail attachments from accounts you don't recognize (e.g., intriguing@sexylips .com) or limiting downloads from the Internet to trusted websites, go a long way in preventing infection.

Denial-of-Service Attack Preventing a denial-of-service attack is very difficult. This is because in a well-orchestrated denial-of-service attack, the requests for the service are not issued from the same few locations, which would make it easy to recognize and block. Instead, in what's called a distributed denial-of-service attack, the attacker will hijack or spoof multiple machines and initiate the attack from these multiple locations.

Managing Security: Overall Guidelines

As a general or functional manager, you are not likely to be involved in the technical details of the procedures and safeguards chosen to mitigate the specific security threats identified in risk assessment. However, you should expect to be involved in setting the agenda for how the overall set of risks is to be addressed. In this role it is paramount that you recognize one important characteristic of security investments: security is a negative deliverable, one that produces no upside but helps in limiting damage ensuing from an uncertain negative event. For these types of investments, it is difficult to obtain appropriate funding.

Moreover, when it comes to security, it is impossible to ensure success. In other words, it is impossible to claim that the organization is absolutely "secure." Rather, it is possible to find out that the organization was not secure after a breach had occurred. Amid all these difficulties, general and functional managers play a critical role.

Have a Plan and Specify Responsibilities You would be surprised to find out how many organizations do not devise formal plans to be enacted during an attack or who fail to assign formal responsibility for security design and enforcement. This is particularly true for the design of new applications, as requirements requested by the business sometimes weaken the security of the applications. In this case, the overall responsibility for security choices and trade-offs should reside with a business owner or other appropriate senior person, not with IT. When outside contractors are engaged in the development, security requirements should be spelled out in the contract.

A crisis management plan should specify who needs to be contacted in an emergency and what their roles should be. The plan must address questions such as what the first reaction measures should be: Should the systems under attack be shut down or left operational? When and how should authorities, such as the FBI, be contacted? What will the firm disclose about the attack, if anything, and who should be in charge of press releases or of customer communication? What recovery plans need to be enacted under the various scenarios? In short, the plan should script all those decisions that are difficult to make when the firm is actually under attack.

Revisit Often Security is a constantly evolving area for a number of reasons: first and foremost, the breathtaking pace of technical evolution. Every new technology and software program your firm adopts ushers in a unique set of security and risk management challenges that should be proactively

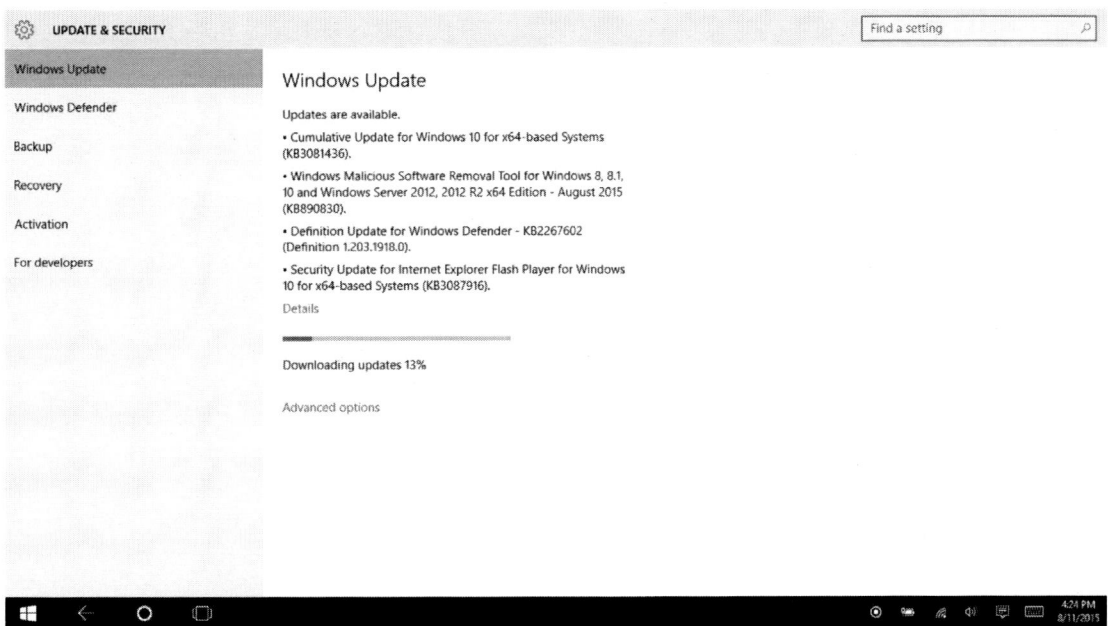

FIGURE 13.16. Automatic patch management software

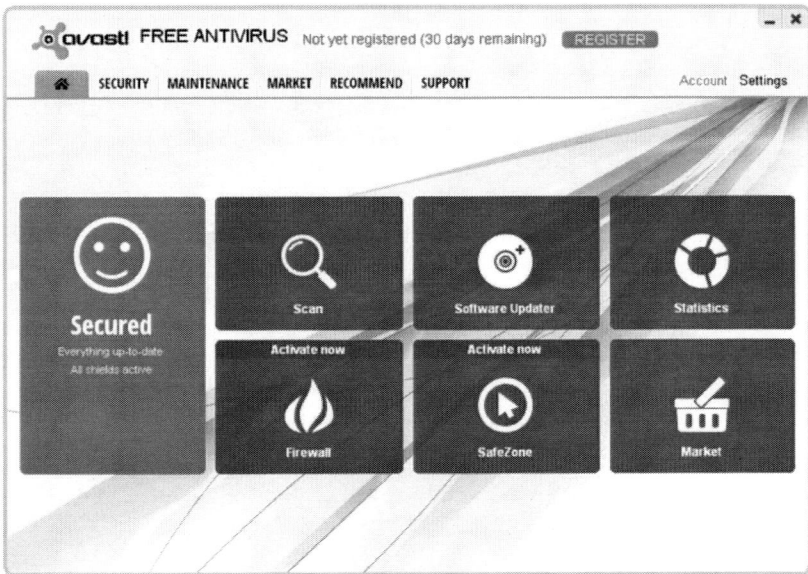

FIGURE 13.17. Antivirus software

addressed—whether that means taking specific steps to manage it or consciously accepting the risk. Thus you must ensure that security audits and reassessment of security plans are done periodically.

Develop a Mitigation Plan   A well-architected security infrastructure and plan can go a long way toward tempering the many security threats modern firms face. But no matter how good your security is, there is always the chance that your firm will be successfully attacked and that your defenses will be breached. What you do in this case can be critical, particularly when you become vulnerable to an intrusion.

The first reaction to an attack is often to shut everything down. This is a mistake, since diagnosing where the attack is coming from, its severity, and its reach is much easier to do if the system is maintained operational and the attacker is kept unaware of the fact that you spotted the security breach.

The first order of business at this point should be to determine how the attack took place in order to eliminate its chance of occurring again. The next step requires an assessment of the damage, particularly as it pertains to the loss of sensitive data. A series of laws have been recently passed across the globe requiring firms to immediately notify those parties whose data may have been compromised. Whether this is a necessity or not in your jurisdiction, it is a wise move to immediately communicate the problem to those affected. As much as you would like to keep the matter private to avoid the negative publicity, people understand that security breaches do sometimes occur, but they will be much less forgiving if they discover an attempt to cover up the problem.

Privacy

Privacy concerns emerge in the relationship between individuals and organizations because, when dealing with business firms or nonprofit and governmental organizations, customers (and employees) often provide personal information under the assumption that the organization will take "good care" of it. We as customers and/or employees provide personal information in order to receive the benefits of the transaction (e.g., employment, value proposition). Yet a prerequisite to the transaction is that we hold some degree of trust in the organization that we are dealing with. We trust that our information is reasonably secure, despite many data breaches over the years (Figure 13.18), and the organization has taken steps to prevent unauthorized use of it by those who have no legitimate reason to access it.

In other words, we must have trust in the firm's information systems security. Even more important, we must trust that the organization will be a steward of our personal information and that it will refrain from employing it in ways that will be harmful to us or our interests. For instance, even if we have great faith in the firm's security, we still must believe that the firm is ethical enough not to collect our data and immediately turn around and sell it to spammers in order to make a "quick buck."

Consider the following incident: "In 2003, the public learned that JetBlue Airways had turned over records on more than a million of its passengers to a government contractor. The contractor sought the information to test a security application designed to identify suspected terrorists. However, the sharing violated JetBlue's privacy policy, which promised that the company would not provide personal information to third parties. The CEO issued a public apology and indicated that he had no knowledge of the data transfer at the time it was made. Nonetheless, JetBlue had to confront a lawsuit from privacy groups and passengers."[17]

What was the problem? After all, JetBlue was only trying to aid in efforts to prevent terrorist attacks and ultimately improve the safety of its own passengers! The problem is that JetBlue had not developed an appropriate process for dealing with privacy concerns in the face of the proliferation of customer data it stewards and the mounting number of potential (perhaps legitimate) uses of those data.

More recently, Tim Cook—with a clear interest in reinforcing the positive perception of Apple's strategy concerning data privacy—stated, "Some of the most prominent and successful companies [in Silicon Valley] have built their businesses by lulling their customers into complacency about their

---

17. Culnan, M. J. (2006), Privacy in search of governance, *Cutter Benchmark Review*, 6(1), 5.

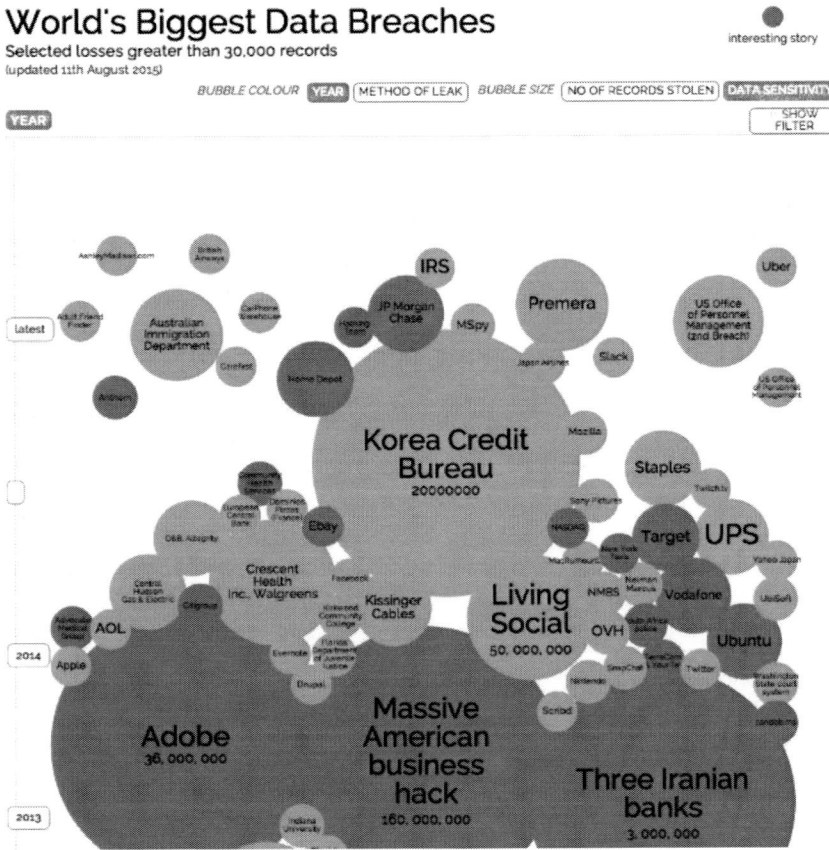

FIGURE 13.18. Greatest data breaches of all time
Source: World's biggest data breaches (2015, October 2), *Information Is Beautiful*, retrieved from http://www
.informationisbeautiful.net/visualizations/worlds-biggest-data-breaches-hacks/

personal information. They're gobbling up everything they can learn about you and trying to monetize it. We think that's wrong. And it's not the kind of company that Apple wants to be."[18]

Cook's words well depict how the offer of personalized services based on technologies such as big data analytics often comes together with unsolved privacy concerns. In fact, big data analytics are presented as the technology that will support the future of the knowledge economy.[19] This technology undeniably bears new promises for product and service development for all sectors of activity. Traditional sectors such as the banking industry as illustrated in the example above could use big data to improve the provision of their services. New sectors such as smart sensing applications in the field of sports and well-being could benefit from big data technologies and provide new services tailored to users' specific needs.

18. Panzarino, M. (2015, June 2), Apple's Tim Cook delivers blistering speech on encryption, privacy, *Tech Crunch*, retrieved from http://techcrunch.com/2015/06/02/apples-tim-cook-delivers-blistering-speech-on-encryption-privacy/

19. See, for example, the EU Council Conclusions of October 25, 2013, on the Digital Single Market and the EU strategy on the data value chain, EUCO 169/13, retrieved from https://www.consilium.europa.eu/uedocs/cms_data/docs/pressdata/en/ec/139197.pdf; OECD (2013, June 18), *Exploring data-driven innovation as a new source of growth: Mapping the policy issues raised by "big data,"* retrieved from http://www.oecd-ilibrary.org/science-and-technology/exploring-data-driven-innovation-as-a-new-source-of-growth_5k47zw3fcp43-en

Privacy Defined

If there could be some doubt regarding whether computer security is an "IT issue" or a "business issue," there is no such doubt regarding privacy. Given the ethical concerns and the potential for liability associated with privacy, general and functional managers should be front and center in identifying and responding to the privacy concerns of the organization. This is not surprising when you consider that, by some estimates, nearly 80% of organizations collect information, and half of them indicate that this information is sensitive in nature.[20] But what is privacy exactly?

First of all, it is important to understand that from a legal perspective, there are two distinct approaches to privacy regulation: an American concept, based on precautionary principle reasoning, and a European concept, based on the idea of private information as a form of intellectual property.

Privacy can be defined as the ability of individuals to control the terms and conditions under which their personal information is collected, managed, and utilized. Private information is the information that can be traced back to the individual—for instance, a person's name, picture, address, social security number, or medical history.

It is evident from the above definition that privacy is not security, even though there is much confusion between the two terms. Privacy subsumes security—that is, a firm that is unable to secure customer or employee data will not be able to ensure privacy. More specifically, privacy is about informed consent and permission to collect and use identifying information, while security is about safekeeping of the collected data.

Privacy concerns are not only tied to perceptions or attitudes at an individual level but connected to organizational and institutional elements like privacy policies and reputation. Indeed, privacy concerns arise because of the existence of a perceived value of privacy by users or "situational cues that enable one person to assess the consequences of information disclosure."[21]

Privacy Risks

Privacy risks are a byproduct of the success that firms have been enjoying with their use of information technology. In a world where competition is global and it is not possible to have a personal relationship with the thousands or millions of customers your firm is trying to reach, IT-enabled information systems have created the ability to "know" individuals we do not interact with directly.

In many cases, these developments have been welcomed by those involved (e.g., customers).[22] Many of us enjoy the personal recommendations produced by online retailers or online services (e.g., Spotify) or the fact that we don't have to repeat our preferences every time we book a reservation with the same hotel chain or airline. But these very advances in technology that allow us to better compete and better suit our customer needs create the potential for highly damaging privacy violations.

Function Creep As we discussed in Chapter 4, information is not consumed by use and can thus be employed multiple times in different applications and for different purposes. For example, information about the number of soda cans sold by a vending machine can be used to compute revenues at one time and forecast future sales at another.

Function creep occurs when data collected for a stated or implied purpose are then reused for other, unrelated, objectives. In the case of the soda vending machine, this is not a problem, but when individuals' personal information is concerned, privacy issues take center stage.

Consider the famous example of Eckerd Corporation, the U.S. drugstore chain. Eckerd settled a lawsuit with the Florida attorney general's office contending that the firm had engaged in deceptive trade practices and breached customers' privacy by sending unsolicited promotions based on the

---

20. Piccoli, G. (2006), Doing privacy right: Using data and preserving trust, *Cutter Benchmark Review*, 6(1), 3–5.

21. Heng Xu et al. (2011), Information privacy concerns: Linking individual perceptions with institutional privacy assurances, *Journal of the Association for Information Systems*, 12(12), 798–824.

22. While the arguments here can be extended to other entities, such as employees or suppliers, we use the example of customers throughout for simplicity.

prescriptions customers had filled in the past. The firm now obtains express permission from customers before sending them marketing material on behalf of pharmaceutical companies. It also endowed a $1 million chair in ethics at Florida A&M School of Pharmacy as part of the settlement.

While the above incident could be ascribed to the heightened sensitivity surrounding medical information, the quick backpedaling reaction and image damage the firm suffered are also significant. At the heart of this is a perceived breach of trust due to the fact that information the customers had provided with one intent was being used for other aims. The intention of the firm may be a good one—to provide valuable personalized information, for instance. However, the customers' perceived loss of control over their personal data opens the door to concerns of abuse and negative reactions.

Proliferating Data Sources Perhaps even more difficult to manage than the potential for function creep is the dizzying proliferation of data sources and technologies that generate customer data. Consider modern cellular phones. Such devices enable a fairly precise estimation of their physical location. This capability can be lifesaving in the case of 911 calls. Yet the potential for privacy invasion is just as significant. Can you imagine walking down a street and being pestered with "eSolicitations" from nearby businesses?

Beyond technology advances and the adoption of devices that surreptitiously generate the data, modern consumers themselves seem to revel in providing more and more information on a voluntary basis. Whether this is plain old self-expression, the need to feel part of a community, or the fact that we are becoming increasingly used to voicing our preferences to get tailored offers, is irrelevant. The amount of personal information individuals are posting to sites like Facebook, YouTube, or Flickr is unprecedented—not to mention the use of geolocation services like Foursquare or Facebook Places. The point about oversharing was made in a very powerful manner by the site PleaseRobMe.com (Figure 13.19), which scraped Twitter feeds that were pushed through Foursquare to show how easy it would be to identify the empty houses of the "oversharers" and potentially go and rob them. Indeed, Twitter limited the access of the geolocation information of tweets following the rising criticism. You can see how navigating this landscape in a legal and ethical manner without missing opportunities for business success is becoming increasingly difficult for organizations.

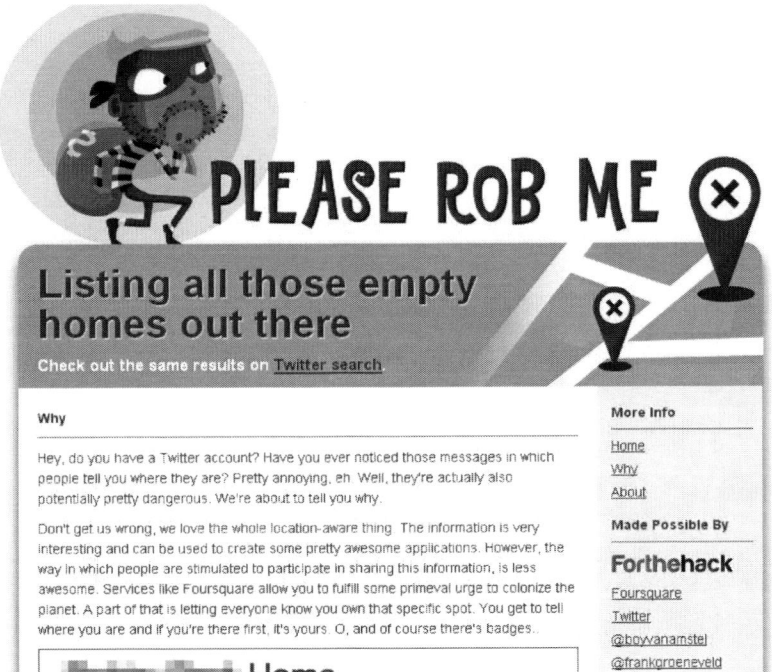

FIGURE 13.19. PleaseRobMe.com

Improving Data Management Technologies   Not only is personal data easier to generate than ever before and proliferating, but it is increasingly simple and cost effective to merge data repositories. Consider one of the most celebrated examples of the successful organizational use of customer data: Harrah's Entertainment Inc. Harrah's collects individual demographic data that its customers provide when signing up to its loyalty program and individual behavioral data when its customers stay at hotels, gamble, and redeem offers. Harrah's also collects nongambling data from external data providers such as Acxiom. It then merges all this information in its data warehouse to develop a complete profile of each customer.

The development of data management technologies enables initiatives of this kind and has created an unprecedented level of opportunity for data-driven strategies. It also creates much pressure for, and risk of, function creep if not managed carefully.

The Legal Landscape   In an environment as difficult to navigate as privacy, it would be quite helpful to have comprehensive legal guidance. Unfortunately, though, with some exceptions, information technology evolution outpaces legal development. To further compound the problem, the Internet has all but destroyed traditional geographical boundaries, making legislation difficult to enforce and easier to circumvent.

It used to be that a community, a state, or an entire nation would be able to easily regulate behavior within its jurisdiction. For example, if a state did not want to allow its residents to gamble, it would simply not issue gaming licenses. Today this level of legislative control is no longer possible, when everyone with a computer can travel to any website in the world with the click of a button.

Big Data and Privacy   Big data analytics rely on the extraction of users' profiles, on behavioral analysis, and ultimately on the processing of large amounts of personal data; as such, this creates new challenges in terms of privacy. Uncovering hidden patterns of behavior brings what belongs to the intimate sphere of the individual to the sphere of commercial relationships. This could easily be felt as a privacy breach, as individuals do not expect public and private organizations to enter their intimate sphere. Furthermore, additional risks arise from the possibility of using wrong predictions (e.g., offering products for pregnant women to a woman who cannot manage to get pregnant), exposing secrets (e.g., sending ads for pregnant women to the home of a minor while her parents do not know she is pregnant), or service providers being victims of external attacks that could publicly expose users' intimate sphere. All these risks of privacy breaches could jeopardize users' trust in online services.

Safeguarding Privacy

Fair information practices have been proposed as a basis for privacy governance. Fair information practices are based on the five principles of notice, choice, access, security, and enforcement.

- *Notice* refers to the right of individuals to be informed when their personal data are being collected and to be informed about how it is or will be used.
- *Choice* calls for the ability of individuals to be informed of, and object to, function creep, whether within one firm or across firms who share information (Figure 13.20).
- *Access* refers to the right of individuals to be able to access their information and correct any errors that may have occurred in their records.
- *Security* calls for organizations that house individuals' private information to ensure its safekeeping and to protect it from unauthorized access.
- *Enforcement* calls for organizations that collect and use private information to develop enforceable procedures to ensure that the above principles are upheld.

Noted privacy expert Mary Culnan offers the following straightforward guidelines for organizations that seek to comply with the above fair information practices: say what you do, do what you say, and be able to prove it.[23]

---

23. Culnan, M. J. (2006), Privacy in search of governance, *Cutter Benchmark Review*, 6(1), 5–13.

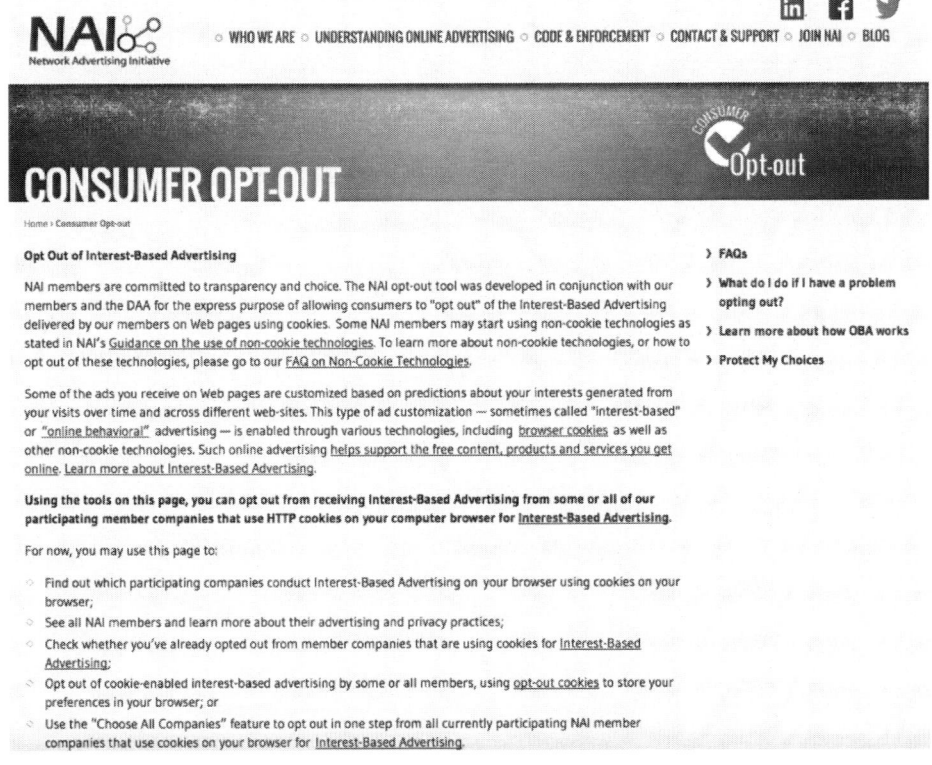

FIGURE 13.20. Privacy control tool for opting out of targeted advertisements based on web browsing behavior

Say What You Do   This first guideline requires that the firm develop a codified set of policies and procedures for safeguarding privacy. It also requires that the firm communicates these policies to affected individuals (e.g., customers, employees). Being able to follow this guideline is predicated on the firm's ability to audit and identify the personal information it collects and stores. It also necessitates a clear understanding of how the information is used today, how it may be used in the future, and whether it is transferred or otherwise shared with partners.

Do What You Say   The second guideline requires that those who represent the firm know, understand, and can enact the policies the firm has developed. Ensuring this level of compliance requires both training, so that the employees are aware of the policies and know how to best enact them, and follow-up, so that procedures are audited and behavior is monitored.

Be Able to Prove It   The third guideline requires that the firm document its policies and the processes it has developed to ensure privacy. This guideline acts as a sort of insurance against possible privacy violations. It enables the firm to demonstrate that it takes privacy concerns seriously and has been diligent in minimizing the possibility of privacy violations.

Ethics

Many of the judgment calls about privacy that were discussed in the previous section are really ethical choices. But what is ethics? What does it mean to be ethical? How do you as a general or functional manager ensure that the people you manage act in an ethical manner when it comes to information systems use?

Ethics: Definition

Webster's Dictionary defines *ethics* as "the discipline dealing with what is good and bad and with moral duty and obligation." Ethics is the branch of philosophy that concerns itself with morality by studying right and wrong and attempting to draw a distinction between good and evil.

Examples of unethical behavior in business abound. The corporate scandals that have led to the demise of one-time stock market darlings like Enron Corp., Global Crossing, Lehman Brother, or Bernie Madoff, or Volkswagen cheating pollution emissions, have clearly shown that we cannot assume that all of today's managers are equipped to make appropriate ethical choices. These corporate scandals have led to legislation, such as the Sarbanes-Oxley Act in 2002, which increases the scope of management and director's responsibilities as well as the reporting requirements that public firms have to comply with. However, unethical behavior in business circles has roots that go beyond a legislative vacuum.

While many react with outrage to unethical behavior, arguing that "everyone knows what's right and what's wrong," this stance oversimplifies reality. Because of the intense technical training that most business and management schools focus on, the fact that managers will make ethical decisions is often mistakenly taken for granted. Most managers are ill equipped to make ethical decisions because they typically lack formal training in the area and because their attention is usually on the objective they are trying to reach. A Former CIO at Metro-Goldwyn-Mayer Studios aptly captured this dilemma: "When your job is building the best-performing database you can, you don't always think about the ethical implications of how that data will be used."[24]

Moreover, aside from those spilling over into illegal behavior, ethical choices are rarely straightforward. In fact, ethical dilemmas are typically rooted in the choice between multiple suboptimal courses of action that force well-intentioned individuals to make difficult trade-offs.

Fortunately, many business and management schools are formally introducing ethics into the curriculum. This education is necessary to enable future business leaders to confront ethical dilemmas and develop a sophisticated understanding of ethics before joining the workforce.

Information Systems Ethics

Information systems and new technologies, with their penchant for enabling new ways of doing business, constantly introduce the potential for ethical dilemmas. Moreover, because of the rapid pace of the evolution of IT and the slow pace at which legislation is passed, formal explicit rules lag behind the possibilities offered by new technologies. Ethical guidelines fill (or should fill) the void, providing direction in the absence of explicit laws. Consider the following scenarios:

- As you are driving home, you hear a song from your youth. You had totally forgotten about that one head-banging band; memories of friends and happy times fill your mind. As you walk into your house, you think about downloading an MP3 version of the song from one of the many file-sharing networks available today on the Internet.

    While you know that downloading the song is "technically" illegal, you are confident that you will not have the time and interest to find and purchase the CD. You just want to listen to the song again and daydream a bit more . . . and what was the name of that other hit the band had . . . ?

- As the IT director for your organization, you have some leeway with the priorities you assign to various projects. You recently reallocated resources and delayed the customer relationship management (CRM) implementation to speed up the enterprise resource planning (ERP) roll-out that is already running considerably behind schedule. You have reason to believe that Jack, one of your project managers, forwarded your e-mail about the shift of resources to the VP of marketing.

    As the IT director, you are well aware that all company e-mails are backed up on the mail server, and you know the backdoor that enables access to every account. As you walk over to

---

24. Wilder, C., & Soat, J. (2001, May 14), The ethics of data, *InformationWeek*, retrieved March 7, 2011, from http://www.informationweek.com/837/dataethics/htm

the mail server late one evening, you tell yourself that it is critical that a general be able to fully trust his troops—you must find out whether you can trust Jack.

- It was your college-days dream: running your own company! Reinventravel.com had been it for the last four and half years. An industry magazine called it "the intermediary that reshaped how people buy travel." But now your dream had turned into a nightmare. After filing for Chapter 11 bankruptcy protection and trying to restructure, it was clear that Reinventravel. com would not make it.

  The decision was tough. You had been offered $7.2 million by your largest competitor—MightyTravel—for the preferences and historical transaction data of your customers. While you never liked the folks over at MightyTravel, they assured you that they would use the data to offer a more targeted and personal travel experience to your former customers. Your privacy policy never explicitly addressed what you would do with customer data, and the $7.2 million will allow you to honor salary and pension commitments to your employees. As you sign the contract, you reassure yourself, thinking that your customers will appreciate receiving more targeted offers from MightyTravel . . . everyone prefers targeted offers . . . right?

What is common to all three scenarios is the fact that each of the ethical dilemmas they capture would not have been possible just a few years ago. New technologies brought them about as a byproduct of their enabling new ways to collect, process, store, and distribute information. More important, all three scenarios paint an accurate picture of typical ethical dilemmas: the appropriate course of action is far from clear and no choice is without a negative impact on other individuals.

Ensuring Ethical Uses of Information Systems

There are no silver bullets to ensure ethical behavior in the context of organizational information systems. Developing a culture of ethical decision making is critical. Such a culture should create the preconditions for and reward behavior that strives for harm minimization, respect, and consistency. Professional communities, such as the Association for Computing Machinery (ACM) or the Association of Information Technology Professionals (AITP), have attempted to create an ethical culture that goes beyond individual organizations by promulgating codes of ethics. For example, the ACM first introduced its code of ethics in 1992 with the following preamble:

Commitment to ethical professional conduct is expected of every member (voting members, associate members, and student members) of the Association for Computing Machinery (ACM).

This Code, consisting of 24 imperatives formulated as statements of personal responsibility, identifies the elements of such a commitment. It contains many, but not all, issues professionals are likely to face. [. . .]

The Code shall be supplemented by a set of Guidelines, which provide explanation to assist members in dealing with the various issues contained in the Code. It is expected that the Guidelines will be changed more frequently than the Code.

The Code and its supplemented Guidelines are intended to serve as a basis for ethical decision making in the conduct of professional work. Secondarily, they may serve as a basis for judging the merit of a formal complaint pertaining to violation of professional ethical standards.[25]

Ethical dilemmas typically pit the interest of one person or group (e.g., shareholders) against that of another (e.g., customers). Applying the principle of harm minimization, one needs to weigh the relative impact that the decision will have on all individuals affected and strive to moderate damage to any one individual or group. The principle of respect requires that information systems decisions be made in an effort to treat each of the affected parties with the utmost consideration. Finally, the principle of

25. ACM (n.d.), *ACM code of ethics and professional conduct*, retrieved May 10, 2015, from http://www.acm.org/about/code-of-ethics/#sect2

consistency provides a test for evaluating decisions. It requires a person confronted with an ethical dilemma to consider whether he would approve if everyone else made the same choice he is considering.

A practical and pragmatic approach to foster a culture of ethical decision making is to establish an information systems ethics code of conduct. A code of conduct, typically used by professional associations, offers two advantages. On the one hand, it communicates to all parties the organization's principles of ethical information systems use. Thus it can be used as an educational mechanism to point employees in the right direction. On the other hand, it identifies the firm's formal stance, thus enabling detection of, and distancing from, unethical choices made by any member of the organization.

Summary

In this chapter, we focused on three topics of interest to general and functional managers: information systems security and information technology (IT) risk management, privacy, and information systems ethics. A failure in security, privacy, or ethics can have dramatic repercussions on the organization, both because of potentially damaging direct effects (e.g., computer outages, disruptions to operations) and increasingly negative indirect effects (e.g., legal recourse, image damage).

In this chapter, we sought to convince you that, as future general and functional managers, you will have to be involved in these decisions. We also helped you gain an understanding of the circumstances in which choices and trade-offs are made so that you can actively participate in decision making:

- Information systems must be secured against both internal and external threats. The internal threat is due to either ill willed or careless members of the organization and is mitigated by way of security policies and training. The external threat comes from skilled individuals, referred to as hackers. The external threat takes the form of malware, intrusion attempts, and denial-of-service attacks. Each of the threats is matched by the appropriate safeguard.
- Information systems security and risk management are not "IT issues." Because of the impact of the security breaches on the current and future viability of the organization, it is critical that general and functional managers take an active role in security decision making. This is done by participating in risk assessment, the process designed to evaluate the potential impact of threats confronting the firm, and risk mitigation, the process of identifying the appropriate response to these security threats. This involvement is necessary in order to make the appropriate trade-off decision among risk acceptance, risk reduction, and risk transference.
- Privacy concerns, like security threats, need general and functional managers' full attention. This is because privacy, like security, is a negative deliverable—that is, investments in privacy help the organization avoid a possible negative occurrence (e.g., lawsuit, loss of customer trust, negative impact on the firm's image) rather than generate benefits, such as improved efficiency or increased revenues.
- In order for the firm to safeguard the privacy of its employees and customers, it must subscribe to fair information practices. Fair information practices are based on the five principles of notice, choice, access, security, and enforcement. Moreover, the firm should produce a codified set of security policies, monitor and enforce compliance with them, and document both the policies and the processes it has developed to ensure privacy.
- The recent flurry of corporate scandals has ignited interest in business ethics. When it comes to information systems, ethics becomes a crucial guiding light for management behavior as legislation often lags behind technology improvements. Thus developing a culture of ethical decision making is essential for modern organizations.

Study Questions

1. Imagine that you have just been hired by a retail financial institution. How would you explain to your CEO that she needs to get involved in information security decisions?

2. What are the three costs associated with information systems security? What is the relationship among them?

3. Define what is meant by internal and external threats. How do the two differ? How are they related?

4. Define and provide an example of each of the different types of intrusion threats. Describe the appropriate countermeasure for each of your examples.

5. Define and provide an example of each of the different types of malicious code threats. Describe the appropriate countermeasure.

6. What is a denial-of-service attack? Why are these attacks particularly dangerous?

7. Imagine that you have just been hired by a retail financial institution. How would you explain to your CEO that she needs to get involved in privacy decisions?

8. How is privacy defined? What are the principal privacy risks? Can you provide examples of each one?

9. What is ethics? What are the principal challenges associated with information systems ethics?

Further Readings

1. Austin, R. D., & Darby, C. A. (2003, June). The myth of secure computing. *Harvard Business Review*, 120–126.

2. Dutta, A., & McChronan, K. (2002). Management's role in information security in a cybereconomy. *California Management Review, 45*(1), 67–87.

3. Pavlou, P. A. (2011). State of the information privacy literature: Where are we now and where should we go. *MIS Quarterly, 35*(4), 977–988.

4. Purcell, R., & Fusaro, R. (2000, November–December). Chief privacy officer. *Harvard Business Review*, 20–22.

5. Smith, H. J., Dinev, T., and Xu, H. (2011). Information privacy research: An interdisciplinary review. *MIS Quarterly, 35*(4), 989–1015.

6. Morey, T., Forbath, T. "Theo," and Schoop, A. (2015, May). Customer Data: Designing for Transparency and Trust, Harvard Business Review. Retrieved from https://hbr.org/2015/05/customer-data-designing-for-transparency-and-trust."

Glossary

- **Backdoor:** Code built into software programs to allow access to an application by circumventing password protection.

- **Biometrics:** In the context of computer security, the term *biometrics* is used to refer to the use of physical traits as a means to uniquely identify users.

- **Denial-of-service attack:** A digital assault carried out over a computer network with the objective to overwhelm an online service so as to force it offline.

- **Encryption:** A technique designed to scramble data so as to ensure that if the wrong individuals gain access to the data, they will be unable to make out its meaning.

- **Firewall:** A hardware or software tool designed to screen and manage traffic in and out of an organization's computer network.

- **Hacker:** The term *hacker* simply means someone who possesses superior computer skills. It has come to be associated in the media and general terminology with more or less maliciously intentioned individuals who attempt to subvert computer security defenses.

- **Information systems security:** The set of defenses an organization puts in place to mitigate threats to its technology infrastructure and data resources.

- **Intrusion:** The intrusion threat consists of any situation where an unauthorized attacker gains access to organizational IT resources.

- **IT risk management:** The process by which the firm attempts to identify and measure information systems security risks and to devise the optimal mitigation strategy.

- **Malware:** The general term malicious code, or malware, refers to software programs that are designed to cause damage to individuals' and/or organizations' IT assets.

- **Phishing:** The process of collecting sensitive information by tricking, in more or less automated ways, those who have it to provide it, who think that they are giving it to a legitimate concern.

- **Privacy:** In the context of information systems, privacy is the ability of individuals to control the terms and conditions under which their personal information is collected, managed, and utilized.
- **Ransomware:** A malware that limits the access to a computer system or users' data and that requires the user to pay a ransom to regain control.
- **Risk analysis:** The process by which the firm attempts to quantify the risks identified in the risk assessment.
- **Risk assessment:** The risk assessment process consist of auditing the current resources, technological as well as human, in an effort to map the current state of the art of information systems security in the organization.
- **Risk mitigation:** The process of matching the appropriate response to the security threats your firm has identified.

- **Social engineering:** The practice of obtaining restricted or private information by somehow convincing legitimate users or people who have it to share it.
- **Spyware:** Software that, unbeknownst to the owner of the computer, monitors behavior, collects information, and either transfers this information to a third party via the Internet or performs unwanted operations.
- **Trojan horse:** A computer program that claims to, and sometimes does, deliver some useful functionality. But the Trojan horse hides a dark side and, like a virus, delivers a malicious payload.
- **Virus:** A type of malicious code that spreads by attaching itself to other, legitimate, executable software programs.
- **Worm:** A piece of malicious code that exploits security holes in network software to replicate itself.

PART V

CASES

TROUBLESHOOTING INFORMATION SYSTEMS AT THE ROYAL HOTEL

Introduction

In early May 2015, after his first year in the master's program at the Very Famous University (VFU), Blake Cantera landed a summer internship with Fancy Consultants & Company (FC). Upon receiving FC's call, Blake was thrilled. FC was a highly regarded local IT consulting firm serving the needs of clients ranging from independent midsized hotels to large multinational grocery chains.

While small and nimble, FC afforded the opportunity to work with large clients on cutting-edge projects. It also offered significant potential for personal growth and, with its flat organizational structure, FC prided itself on picking independent and self-reliant young consultants who'd work immediately on projects rather than toil in the "analyst limbo" for years. This was the most appealing aspect of FC for Blake, who knew that he would be able to do some real work over the summer.

After a brief introduction to FC systems and culture and a two-week orientation discussing the FC approach to consulting, Blake was assigned to his first account. As expected, this was a relatively small account. On the bright side, Blake was sent alone to manage the whole project, from start to finish. He was thrilled; July had not even started and he was already doing some real work!

The Royal Hotel

The Royal Hotel in New York City was a luxury all-suite hotel primarily serving an executive clientele visiting Manhattan on business. Typically, these business guests stayed for three to six days, during which time they used their suite as a temporary office. Thus the Royal Hotel's management had positioned the property to cater to the many needs of this busy and demanding audience. Amenities included in-suite plain paper fax, printer, and copier; three two-line telephones with voice mail and remote message alert; high-speed Internet access; and plasma TVs and entertainment centers in each of the 482 guest suites. The Royal Hotel also provided three restaurants and a coffee shop on the premises, a 24-hour business center, a fitness center, suite dining, laundry service, complimentary shoeshine, and dedicated high-speed elevators. While business fluctuated in relation to the economic cycle, the Royal welcomed over 150,000 guests per year, bringing in total revenues of upward of $30 million.

This made for a fairly complex operation that needed to run smoothly and consistently. Given the high percentage of repeat guests, it was important that guest rooms be spotless and consistently in working order.

The Task

As he arrived at the property for a one-week assignment, all expenses paid, Blake thought to himself with a smile, "I can get used to this . . ." But, with just enough time to take a shower, he had to get ready for a dinner meeting with the general manager (GM).

The Royal Hotel's GM was a no-nonsense, old-school hotelier with a distinctive German accent. He quickly zeroed in on the task, in response to Blake's comment about the "very good" quality of service provided by the Royal Hotel: "Our level of service is unacceptable! We are very good by most hotels' standard, but we are not 'most hotels.' Our guests are extremely discerning; it is completely unacceptable to have a light bulb out in the bathroom when the guest checks in, particularly if she is a returning guest. And that's not as bad as a stain on the carpet or a clogged toilet. I had one of my best customers call down to report a clogged toilet last week; can you imagine? Unacceptable! I need you to make sure this never happens again."

As he sat listening to the GM, Blake briefly questioned the wisdom of taking on so much responsibility so quickly; he had not even finished his master's! But this was a brief moment of doubt, and he remembered one of his father's famous sayings: "Did you want the bicycle? Now you have to pedal!" Blake silently chuckled to himself and tuned back into the GM's tirades with a confident smile. He already had the answer to the problem.

The Solution

After examining the property and interviewing a number of people, including the directors of housekeeping, maintenance, and IT, Blake recommended that the Royal Hotel adopt M-Tech's Cappuccino! Rapid Response Solution (see Appendix 2.1 for a description of the product). In his presentation to the executive team, highlighting the main advantages of the proposed information system, he mentioned the following:

- *Rapid response.* The Cappuccino! application enabled the use of a phone interface, allowing housekeepers to report problems with the room (e.g., light bulb out) as soon as the problem was identified rather than having to wait until the housekeeper ended the shift and verbally communicated the problem to the maintenance department.
- *Quality control.* Since the new information system allowed immediate reporting of problems, it reduced the chance of "slippage through the cracks" occurring when housekeepers at the end of the shift forgot to communicate the problem. It also eliminated the risk that maintenance would forget or claim it did not receive the request.
- *Preventive maintenance.* The maintenance department would be able to identify recurrent problems and stop them before they occurred again.
- *Reporting.* Management would be able to extract a number of extremely valuable reports from the system (see Appendix 2.1 for details). This would allow managers to reward best performers and motivate employees.

Upon receiving the go-ahead from the executive team, Blake negotiated with the vendor for the application license, configuration and start-up costs, support, and a week of on-site training. But as he was preparing for the upcoming rollout and implementation, he was called to a new account. This unexpected call was bittersweet. Yes, he would not be able to see his very first project through, but the partner at FC must have noticed his performance since he was being reassigned to a project with a regional credit union in Cortland, New York. Not quite New York City, but the project was larger and more high profile. This was a good move for a summer intern!

As Blake handed the Royal Hotel project to his replacement and classmate at VFU, Jack Scarso, he was a bit nervous. Having been on a couple of teams with Jack back at school, Blake did not hold him in the highest esteem. Yet, telling himself that Jack deserved a fair shake, Blake turned over all the paperwork and his draft information system design, adding a word of caution:

"Jack, the GM is very impatient about this project. Make sure you don't let his anxiety for an operational system rush you into a half-baked design. This is a complex operation, there is a heck-of-a-lot going on here. Good luck!"

Sic Transit Gloria Mundi[1]

A month and a half had gone by since Blake left the Royal Hotel. While he heard from Jack a couple of times regarding minor questions, he assumed everything had gone well. He felt good about the quality of the material he had left with Jack, as well as the quality of the Cappuccino! application and the contract he had negotiated.

He had missed staying at the Royal Hotel, having traded down to a Ramada Inn across the street from the bank headquarters. But he felt good about the project as he wrapped up the documentation. A full-time offer was a sure bet!

"Here it comes," Blake smiled as he recognized the cell phone ring tone associated with his boss's personal cell phone. As he picked up, Blake quickly realized he was in for a surprise. Blake's boss sounded quite unhappy as he said, "What happened at the Royal Hotel? I just got a call from the GM over there. He said that they did what you and Jack proposed, and they wasted a bunch of money on a system nobody is using! I had my doubts about Jack, but I thought you'd have no problem with this project. You don't start school for another two weeks, right? My assistant just booked you on a flight back to NYC; you should have confirmation in your inbox."

Blake realized that this was not the time to voice his own doubts about Jack. Rather, he simply took ownership of solving the problem and began modifying his plans on the fly. Out were the preclass barbeques and trading summer internship stories with classmates. Two weeks was probably just enough to attempt to straighten out the mess made by Jack. Blake's attempts to get in touch with Jack were futile. Jack's internship had ended and he was backpacking through the woods of Utah to, as he put it, relieve stress and recharge his batteries before school started again.

Upon returning to the Royal Hotel, Blake found that the machine dedicated to Cappuccino! was sitting in a corner collecting dust. It looked like it was abandoned soon after roll-out, a suspicion confirmed by

---

1. A phrase meaning "thus passes away the glory of the world" used to remind us that nothing is permanent and that we must stay humble. As Blake found out, so fleeting can be the fortunes of a summer internship.

the director of IT, who mentioned that the installation and training session had been smooth sailing. Employees had been very eager to learn about the system but seemed to lose that interest rapidly afterward.

The director of housekeeping and the director of maintenance did not have much to add, simply noting that employees found that the old manual system worked much better for their needs. The GM, on the other hand, had much to say, his German accent more pronounced than ever. The words were still ringing in Blake's ears as he left the meeting: "I invested a lot of money in this software. You better deliver all the results you promised in your presentation."

As Blake prepared to troubleshoot this failed information system and to devise a solution to make it work, he remembered the words of his information systems professor at VFU: "Focus on the information system design, not the technology investment!" "Therein lay the solution," Blake thought with a tinge of hope.

Discussion Questions

1. Despite having relatively little specific information about why the system failed, what do you think are the main reasons for such failure?

2. How could you fix these problems?

3. Reflecting on this experience, what do you think were the main mistakes, if any, that Blake made in handling the engagement?

BENEFITS ▼

Cappuccino!
Solve tomorrow's issues today

01 Improve Response Time
Cappuccino!'s unique telephone interface and alphanumeric pagers can log and dispatch work requests in under a minute and without human intervention.

02 Eliminate lost calls
Whether entered over the telephone or at the terminal, Cappuccino! tracks and ages work orders until they are completed.

03 Ensure Proper Follow-up
Real time graphs of work order aging facilitate the follow up process for dispatchers.

04 Expand Reporting Pool
Multilingual prompts and deficiency cards empower non-English speaking personnel to report problems in their native language.

05 Reduce Housekeeping costs
Cappuccino! is the most efficient way to collect inspection data. No more tedious paperwork and timeconsuming data entry. Inspector does it all.

06 Improve Quality
With Cappuccino!, defects in your guest rooms will not go unnoticed for long. Inspector is sure to catch anything that your Rapid Response and PM programs happen to miss.

Cappuccino!

Rapid Response

No matter how comprehensive your preventive maintenance program is, issues like burnt light bulbs, leaks, and guest requests are unavoidable in any hotel. Cappuccino! helps your staff report, respond to, and resolve issues like these faster than ever before!

Reporting

Housekeepers are in the guest rooms everyday and they must be the hotel's eyes and ears. With Cappuccino!, they can report deficiencies directly to the computer.

- No more hard to decipher work order tickets.
- No more busy signals or holding for a dispatcher.
- No more language barriers.

An automated attendant walks them through the reporting process step by step in the language of their choice - English, Spanish, French, and Chinese, to name a few. In a matter of seconds, Cappuccino! automatically generates, prioritizes, and dispatches a work order to any tablet, smartphone, touch tone phone or PDA so they get corrected before a guest is affected.

Response and Resolution

The resulting work order contains all of the information that response personnel need to complete the call. Whether it's a toilet overflowing, or a guest who needs towels, your staff will be able to respond faster than ever before! Response staff can then use the same automated attendant to tell you when they've started and completed the work.

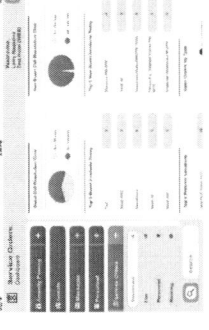

Cappuccino! turns your hotel staff into a proactive team working together to maximize guest satisfaction by solving tomorrow's issues today!

Meanwhile at the Hotline

Instead of spending their time answering employee calls and entering data into a computer, your hotline operators and guest service agents are now free to focus on guest requests and monitor all pending calls at Cappuccino!'s visual Dashboard (shown next).

In the end, the issue is resolved, often before a guest ever even notices, and the detailed work order history is being maintained by the computer automatically.

Inspection

Tracking your team's performance is an important part of maintaining the highest levels of quality. When your team is performing well your property is at its best. Cappuccino! makes it easy for you to measure your team's performance and analyze quality levels on you property.

The Quality Check Challenge

Room inspections have traditionally been nothing more than filing in a paper form by hand and manually calculating a score at the end. Sometimes this raw data is entered into a computer manually in order to create reports which can be used to analyze quality levels and performance. This traditional process is time-consuming, tedious, and costly. Because of these challenges, manual room inspection forms are often never entered into a computer for analysis and are simply kept in an employee file.

Cappuccino! helped me convince my Manager that we were understaffed by comparing our available man hours to the workload in the system.

Cappuccino!

see what you ever wanted to know, but you never dared to ask!

Mobile Capabilities

Cappuccino! provides features that were previously available only on a PC so users can access information via tablets and smartphones. Utilizing a team-based approach, service orders are automatically directed into group "buckets." Staff members can be assigned to single or multiple teams, thereby receiving notice for only those requests that pertain to their skill set. This better utilizes the strengths and abilities of individual employees which reduces costs and increases productivity.

Smart Scheduling

Cappuccino! is designed to handle one of the most common issues guest room attendants encounter: trying to clean a room only to find that a guest is still in it. Cappuccino! provides guest room attendants with a way to set a time to return later and then re-issues the room to the most appropriate guest room attendant when the time has elapsed. This ensures that no room is forgotten and staff members are utilized to maximum effectiveness.

When cleaning a room, guest room attendants are provided with information about the guest and their preferences. In addition to the guest name, special instructions can be provided such as their desire for extra pillows.

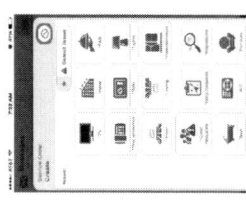

Empower Staff Members

Instead of spending their time answering employee calls and entering data into a computer, your hotline operators and guest service agents are now free to focus on guest requests and monitor all pending calls at Cappuccino's visual Dashboard (shown next). In the end, the issue is resolved, often before a guest ever even notices, and the detailed work order history is being maintained by the computer automatically.

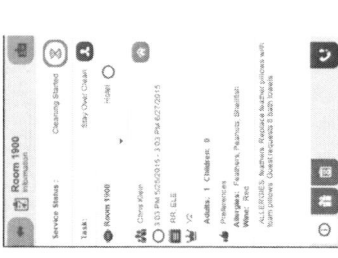

Key Features

- Requests are received and handled by staff members on the field
- Guest related issues include guest name for recognition
- Every step is tracked including start, complete, response time, issue and more
- Guest initiated requests are flagged as incident or request
- Upon completion, issue is flagged for follow-up by guest agent
- Escalation rules ensure prompt attention

Cappuccino! provides a simple but thorough system, and we couldn't be more pleased with the solution...

REPORTS

01 Most frequently occurring recurring issues

Cappuccino! is the most effective way to collect recurring issues data. No more paperwork and timeconsuming data entry

02 Top reporting and/or completing performers

With Cappuccino!, you finally measure your employees easily identifying your best performers!

03 Response time reports

How quickly did you solve customer's issues? With Cappuccino! get perfect visibility on guest request fulfillment and easily track repeat guests and recurring issues.

04 Productivity reports

Productivity will virtually leap out of Cappuccino's report generator to show you how well your team is performing. Once armed with this kind of data, you'll be able to target training programs and increase productivity like never before.

ELOANDOCS: Riding the Tide of Technology without Wiping Out

Introduction[1]

On a warm summer evening in Northeast Ohio, Albert Michaels, the Chief Technology Officer (CTO) of local software company eLoanDocs, was enjoying his evening drive home. Though his eyes were on the road in front of him, his mind was stuck on the topic of the day behind him: the "cloud". How could eLoanDocs take advantage of this emerging and exciting new technology platform? Cloud computing held the promise of greatly reduced costs and nearly unlimited scalability for a company like his and seemed like it might be the wave of the future for hosted software providers. But the barriers to his customers' adopting the cloud were potentially high. And if those barriers were overcome, the competitive landscape in which eLoanDocs operated might shift in unfavorable ways. As a technology professional, adopting the cloud seemed to him to be a forgone conclusion. But his years of experience had shown him that it's rarely easy to be one of the early adopters.

Inefficiencies in the Mortgage Industry

The home mortgage closing process in the early 1990s was slow, paper intensive, and ripe for innovation. Realtors, mortgage lenders, title companies, and borrowers met and collaborated in primarily local marketplaces. The myriad documents required to support the mortgage approval process were exchanged through a combination of fax, mail, courier, and in-person reviews. Realtors, mortgage brokers, and escrow officers worked together to ensure that all of the necessary documents were generated, supporting services such as appraisals were ordered and performed, and required documents

were signed by the borrower. The average time between a consumer application for a mortgage loan and the final closing was about 90 days. Closings were often delayed or rescheduled when late-breaking changes in the loan terms or associated costs required the lender to generate new documents. The majority of documents required for the mortgage closing were generated by the mortgage lender, but these documents were traditionally reviewed and signed by the borrower at the place of settlement (closing), generally at the title company. Mortgage lenders sent documents to the title company and to the borrower through mail, overnight express delivery, or courier. A successful closing required that the mortgage lender generate final documents and send them to the title company at least one day before the scheduled closing.

Technology to the Rescue

In 1994, a Cleveland-based title and settlement services company, Premium Title, was determined to reduce their costs and differentiate their service to the market by adding technology to the mortgage-closing process. Premium Title's owners created a separate company, eLoanDocs, to connect the various parties involved in the process by using technology. eLoanDocs' founders wanted to improve the speed and accuracy of the mortgage-closing process while increasing market share for Premium Title and other connected business partners. The founders believed that they could create a company that would grow quickly and that would generate significant return for their investors.

In industries where larger companies with dedicated IT staff existed, standard protocols had been developed to exchange information electronically. For example, in the automotive industry, Electronic Data Interchange (EDI) had been used for years to exchange purchasing and billing information between manufacturers and

---

1. This case was originally published as: Cain, James; Levorchick, Ma; Matuszak, Alan; Pohlman, Allan; and Havelka, Douglas (2015) "eLoanDocs: Riding the Tide of Technology Without Wiping Out," *Communications of the Association for Information Systems*: Vol. 36, Article 38. Available at: http://aisel.aisnet.org/cais/vol36/iss1/38

their suppliers. [2] There were no standards for electronic communication between business partners in the mortgage industry and, since the Internet was not being used broadly for commercial purposes, intercompany data exchange was dependent on proprietary communication networks.

eLoanDocs launched a proprietary electronic interchange in 1995 that connected Premium Title with several mortgage lenders in the Cleveland area along with a few local service providers such as appraisal vendors and surveyors. Proprietary data formats were defined for title insurance and appraisal orders, and mortgage documents were delivered electronically using the common HP Printer Command Language (PCL) print stream data format. The PCL[3] is a page description language (PDL) that allows a document's appearance to be described at a high level. This allowed Premium Title, using equipment commonly available at the time, to define the documents needed in their industry and share them with the necessary business partners.

eLoanDocs purchased off-the-shelf communications software and customized it to their needs; they also purchased computer servers, network equipment, and modems to run their electronic interchange. The computer equipment and telephone lines were hosted in their modest office space in Cleveland, Ohio. The small network of participating companies each installed modems, standard communication software, and eLoanDocs' proprietary software application to exchange documents that represented orders for services and the delivered real estate products such as appraisals, flood search certificates, and surveys. The electronically delivered documents replaced slower, lower-quality, or less-reliable courier and fax deliveries. eLoanDocs was successful in building a network of local mortgage service providers, but struggled to extend the technology and business model outside of Northeast Ohio.

---

2. Hart, P. J., & Saunders, C. S. (1998). Emerging electronic partnerships: Antecedents and dimensions of EDI use from the supplier's perspective. *Journal of Management Information Systems*, 14(4), 87–111.

Roos, D. (n.d.). The history of e-commerce. HowStuffWorks.com. Retrieved from http://www.howstuffworks.com/history-e-commerce1.htm

3. Hewlett Packard. (1992). PCL 5 printer language technical reference manual. Retrieved from http://www.hp.com/ctg/Manual/bpl13210.pdf

Wikipedia (n.d.). "Printer command language." Retrieved from http://en.wikipedia.org/wiki/Printer_Command_Language#See_also

Right Technology, Right Place, Right Time

In the late 1990s, eLoanDocs realized that the emergence of the Internet as a driver of commerce would present both a threat to their network and an opportunity to extend their mortgage data interchange to more parties across the country at a lower cost. In 2000, eLoanDocs re-launched their mortgage industry electronic collaboration network on the Internet with the debut of their new software product, Document Posting Service (DPS). DPS used standard communication protocols such as HTTPS and SFTP over the Internet, which eliminated the need for modems and proprietary communications software. DPS also featured HTML Web user interfaces for settlement agents to avoid the need for software to be installed at each customer location. DPS was a multi-tenant application (Figure 3.1) that provided software as a service (SaaS) to the mortgage industry.

SaaS allows customers to use software that is owned, delivered, and managed remotely by one (or more) providers. [4] This model allows the provider to maintain one set of code and data for many different customers. In essence, SaaS allows customers to rent software rather than buy it. The advantages of SaaS for customers include cost savings, scalability, accessibility, upgrades without disruption, and resilience. Some disadvantages also exist, the primary one being security. [5]

Market acceptance for DPS was tremendous, with several major mortgage lenders signing contracts to deliver all of their closing documents to settlement agents using eLoanDocs. As a small company facing growth challenges brought on in part by a boom-or-bust mortgage industry, eLoanDocs took a pragmatic approach to new product development. Product development investments were guided by immediate opportunities with existing customers that would lead to short-term revenue and possible broader market appeal. Following this model, eLoanDocs extended their product line beyond closing-document delivery to include borrower-disclosure delivery and electronic-signature capability.

---

4. Singleton, D. (2011). What is SaaS? 10 frequently asked questions about software as a service. Software Advice. Retrieved from http://blog.softwareadvice.com/articles/enterprise/saas-faqs-1072811/

5. McLellan, C. (2013). SaaS: Pros, cons and leading vendors. ZDNet. Retrieved from http://www.zdnet.com/article/saas-pros-cons-and-leading-vendors/

FIGURE 3.1. Multi-tenant Architecture

Supportive Regulatory Changes

Federal and state legislation in 1999 opened the market for electronic signatures in the real estate industry, and eLoanDocs developed services to take advantage of this legislation. The Uniform Electronic Transaction Act (UETA) was first adopted by California and Pennsylvania in 1999.[6] At the time of writing in 2015, 47 of the 50 U.S. states have adopted this act. The remaining three states (New York, Illinois, and Washington) have not adopted the act, but have statutes pertaining to electronic transactions. The UETA's purpose is to bring into line the differing state laws over such areas as retention of paper records and the validity of electronic signatures to support the validity of electronic contracts as a viable medium of agreement. The Electronic Signatures in Global and National Commerce Act (ESIGN) is similar to the UETA with the exception that it pertains to the validity of electronic signatures on the federal level instead of the state level.[7] It also brings validity to signatures for foreign commerce.

The Changing Business Tides

eLoanDocs' business was growing fast, but the computers that hosted eLoanDocs' services were still run out of a small office computer room. On a hot summer day in late July 2000, Cleveland faced scattered power outages due to heavy draw on the power grid for air conditioning. Power was lost in eLoanDocs' office for over eight hours, well beyond the two-hour

battery backup that was in place to support the computer systems. Dave Griffith, data center manager for eLoanDocs, said "we tried to find portable generators for rent but there was nothing available big enough and we couldn't even get the generators close enough to our computer room to run extension cords" (personal communication). eLoanDocs' electronic services were unavailable to customers for most of the day. Customers suffered costly business delays due to this extended system outage on one of the busiest days of the month for mortgage closings.

It was clear that eLoanDocs needed to improve their computer hosting infrastructure in order to maintain a leadership position as a provider of electronic services to the mortgage industry. Up until this time, eLoanDocs did not have the necessary financial strength or the technical management experience to bring their computer infrastructure up to the needed levels of scalability and reliability. With major new customers ready to sign contracts and the memory of the 2000 power outage fresh in their minds, eLoanDocs management raised the needed capital and engaged a technology consulting firm to prepare for the next level of capability. In early 2001, eLoanDocs moved their computer servers to a private cage in a dedicated third party co-location data center in Chicago, Secure Hosting. The Secure Hosting facility in Chicago featured redundant power feeds, on-site generators, multiple Internet providers, and state-of-the-art physical and network security. Secure Hosting quickly became eLoanDocs' most important and most expensive vendor.

Security Considerations

By 2004, eLoanDocs was doing business with seven of the top 10 mortgage lenders in the US, and documents and data for over 50% of the mortgages in the country

6. Whitaker, D. R. (1999). Rules under the uniform electronic transactions act for an electronic equivalent to a negotiable promissory note. *The Business Lawyer*, 55(1) 437–453.

7. Stern, J. E. (2001). The electronic signature in global and national commerce Act. *Berkeley Technology Law Journal*, 16(1) pp. 391–415.

FIGURE 3.2. Existing Infrastructure

flowed through eLoanDocs' systems. eLoanDocs had become a critical part of the mortgage industry, but with fewer than 50 employees and under $15 million in annual revenue, the company was hundreds of times smaller than most of its giant financial institution customers.

Given the sensitive nature of the information that eLoanDocs was handling, the attention given to cybersecurity breaches at well-known companies like Apple, JP Morgan Chase, Target, and The Home Depot, and the consequences of these breaches,[8] many of eLoanDocs' largest customers began to demand that it demonstrate the reliability and security of their computer hosting facility through extensive load testing, system failure testing, and third party security audits. Some customers sent their own security teams to the eLoanDocs office in Cleveland and to the Secure Hosting data center in Chicago to review eLoanDocs' policies, procedures, and capabilities. Paul Hunter, eLoanDocs CEO, was excited to show off Secure Hosting to the top mortgage companies: "The first time the National Mortgage security team visited the Secure Hosting facility they were thrilled to see the biometric security, diesel generators with 3 days of fuel on-site, and our private cage that was secured on all sides. eLoanDocs finally looks like the big player that we are" (personal communication).

By 2007, demands for additional capacity in the network and customer requirements to maintain an active disaster recovery data center drove eLoanDocs to make several significant investments. First, eLoanDocs acquired a competing mortgage technology company based in Seattle, WA, FastForms. eLoanDocs then moved their primary data center from Secure Hosting in Chicago to FastForms's co-location provider in Seattle, SunGuard. Finally, eLoanDocs built an identical redundant hosting facility in Cleveland using another co-location provider. In late 2009, eLoanDocs completed implementing a highly scalable and virtualized computer hosting infrastructure in Seattle with real-time replication of all customer documents and data to the backup site in Cleveland. The Cleveland facility could automatically take over all of eLoanDocs' services in the event of an extended outage in the Seattle data center (Figure 3.2). The time and expense required to build and maintain their services in secure and redundant data centers gave eLoanDocs a significant advantage in the market because few technology providers could make the necessary investments in infrastructure and software required to compete. In addition, eLoansDocs implemented best practices for disaster recovery (DR) planning including risk assessment and business impact analysis and training for and testing of the DR plan.[9]

8. Snyder, B. (2014). 5 huge cybersecurity breaches at companies you know. Fortune. Retrieved from http://fortune.com/2014/10/03/5-huge-cybersecurity-breaches-at-big-companies/

9. ComputerWeekly.com. (2011). IT disaster recovery plan best practices: Fundamentals in DR Planning. Retrieved from http://www.computerweekly.com/report/IT-disaster-recovery-plan-best-practices-Fundamentals-in-DR-planning

McBeth, C. B. (2014). Business continuity and disaster recovery best practices from the availability trenches. Forbes. Retrieved from http://www.forbes.com/sites/sungardas/2014/11/19/business-continuity-and-disaster-recovery-best-practices-from-the-availability-trenches/

FIGURE 3.3. Cloud Infrastructure

With the new infrastructure in place, eLoanDocs met customer service level agreements (SLAs) for 99.9% uptime of services in 2011 and 2012. eLoanDocs had developed a mature set of policies and procedures around information security and had published results of a third party SSAE 16 Type II compliance audit twice a year to customers. The organization had six full-time staff dedicated to data center operations and a full-time information security officer. Their internal staff had accumulated significant expertise in data center operations, but the company experienced, on average, a 20 percent annual turnover rate due to an active job market for their staff members' highly sought-after skills. One eLoanDocs employee was recruited to manage networks for Microsoft's hosting facilities in Washington. Michelle Fletcher, eLoanDocs' Director of Technical Operations, complained "I'm having a hard time keeping my best people working here at eLoanDocs. We just don't have enough scale to keep these people challenged and there is no way that eLoanDocs can match the pay of the big guys." (personal communication).

eLoanDocs' annual vendor expenses for data center hosting, data networks, computer hardware maintenance, and software support subscriptions were nearly US$2 million per year. Employee costs and third party audit expenses brought the overall cost of eLoanDocs' data center hosting, security, and compliance to about US$3.5 million annually.

Clouds Ahead?

Just as the rise of the Internet enabled eLoanDocs' explosive growth in the 2000's, technological changes beginning in 2010 led to new opportunities and competitive challenges for the company. Giant technology vendors such as Amazon began to offer comprehensive computer hosting services with a new model: cloud computing (see Figure 3.3). Amazon, Microsoft, Google, and other companies built data centers at massive scale that were designed to allow them to sell computing capacity to the market at prices significantly below what companies could achieve on their own.[10] Cloud computing vendors offered a model where a company could simply purchase the needed amount of processing power, memory, disk storage, and Internet bandwidth on a monthly subscription model. Customers could increase or decrease their usage on demand. Public cloud providers also offered high availability, multi-site data replication, and full disaster recovery capabilities as optional or standard services.[11]

Using a cloud hosting service such as Amazon Web Services (AWS), a small software vendor could launch a new service with twice the computing capacity of eLoanDocs in a matter of days. Matt Pittman, VP of

10. Cloud Computing tutorials: http://www.tutorialspoint.com/cloud_computing

11. Beal, V. (2015). Cloud computing. Retrieved from http://www.webopedia.com/TERM/C/cloud_computing.html

IBM. (n.d.). What is cloud? Retrieved from http://www.ibm.com/cloud-computing/us/en/what-is-cloud-computing.html

Strickland, J. (n.d.). How cloud computing works. HowStuffWorks.com. Retrieved from http://computer.howstuffworks.com/cloud-computing/cloud-computing.htm

FIGURE 3.4. Hybrid Cloud Infrastructure

Sales for eLoanDocs, said: "I can't compete on price with mortgage technology competitors like EchoSign that launched their products hosted at Amazon. Their costs are so low that they are giving away basic services with a freemium model. I just hope that companies like this don't start cutting into our core client base" (personal communication).

Services like AWS were examples of the "public cloud"—inexpensive computing capacity that can be purchased on demand, with many different customers' workloads and information intermingled on the same computer servers and storage devices. Cost advantages available to customers of public cloud services were enhanced by aggressive competition in the industry, which sparked an ongoing price war between providers. Amazon reduced their prices a total of 41 times between 2008 and late 2013. CFO Marty Buckley had calculated that, by switching to a public cloud provider for all of their data center needs, eLoanDocs' annual technology costs (including expected staff reductions) would be $750,000 less than current spending levels.

Public cloud providers also maintained strict security policies and published third party security audit results, but large financial institutions were not ready to trust their most critical information and systems to the public cloud as of 2013. eLoanDocs' security officer Randy Wallace had his doubts about the viability of cloud hosting for eLoanDocs: "I just finished another grueling vendor audit from a giant mortgage lender's security team. These guys want visibility into all of our processes and they want to make sure that eLoanDocs has control over every aspect of our systems. I just don't know how we could ever convince them that a cloud service is secure" (personal communication).

Concerns regarding the security of data stored in the cloud continue to be an on-going challenge for many IT executives.[12]

Recognizing the need for more-secure and more-flexible cloud computing options, computer hosting vendors such as Rackspace began to offer private cloud solutions to the market. Rackspace provisioned and supported a set of dedicated hardware to any customer that wanted to keep their applications and information segregated from other customers. The private cloud offerings used the same technologies as public cloud providers and still provided cost advantages due to economies of scale. Buckley had calculated a US$350,000 annual savings should eLoanDocs move to a private cloud solution. However, Albert Michaels was concerned about service availability and uptime with a third party private cloud solution: "With our services hosted in our data centers I know 100% for certain that my team can find the source of any problem and fix it within minutes, helping us to meet our customer SLAs. How do I know that a cloud provider will have the same ability and motivation to get things back up and running when there's a problem?" (personal communication).

A third cloud hosting model appeared called hybrid cloud (Figure 3.4). This model allowed customers to take a measured approach to moving some of their computing to outsourced cloud providers. With a hybrid cloud offering such as VMware's vCloud, a software company

12. Corbin, K. (2015). Security concerns cloud federal data center overhaul. CIO. Retrieved from http://www.cio.com/ article/2878657/data-center/security-concerns-cloud-federal -data-center-overhaul.html

could easily host some of their applications and data on their internal servers while moving their development, test, or disaster recovery systems to the cloud. Hybrid cloud solutions offered many of the security benefits of internally hosted systems while also providing scalability on demand. Arlene Christianson, eLoanDocs' VP of Operations, felt that hybrid cloud was not a good fit for eLoanDocs because "if we go with a hybrid cloud solution, we will need two separate security and compliance audits and sets of controls" (personal communication). Buckley estimated that moving to a hybrid cloud solution would reduce eLoanDocs' technology costs by about US$200,000 per year.

A Necessary Decision

By the middle of 2014, the computer systems that eLoanDocs had installed in 2009 were nearing the end of their useful life and had no more capacity for expansion. As eLoanDocs prepares for their next generation of data center hosting architecture for 2015 and beyond, the choices they face are complex and will have significant implications for the future of the company.

- Should eLoanDocs continue with their current model of designing, building, and managing their own computer hosting infrastructure using their co-location partners?
- Would eLoanDocs' financial institution customers accept a move of eLoanDocs' services to a public or private cloud provider?
- How should eLoanDocs go about choosing a cloud hosting provider?

As Albert Michaels considered his options, his mind was roiled by a number of questions:

- Will eLoanDocs' customers—with their focus on data security—accept a cloud-based solution? If so, to what degree? And how many customers would accept some form of cloud-based solution?
- If customers do accept one of the cost-saving cloud services solutions, what barriers exist to prevent new competitors from rapidly entering the market and eroding eLoanDocs' market share?
- What is the value that customers believe they are receiving from eLoanDocs?
- Could it be that customers actually value the secure environment that they can visit and audit in person? If so, might convincing those customers to adopt a cloud-based solution to their document delivery problems actually be a damaging move to eLoanDocs in the long term?

- Speaking of security, which solution actually provides better protection of customers' data? Though ownership of the hosting hardware enables eLoanDocs to literally pull the plug if a breach is detected, how does that compare to the security benefits associated with outsourcing to a cloud provider? Is one solution more likely than the other to be targeted for attack? Is either solution better able to detect and prevent intrusions?
- Assuming that the system will be attacked at some point, what ability will eLoanDocs have to identify the compromised data? How might that ability change if hosting services are outsourced to a cloud provider?
- How robust is the existing disaster recovery strategy? Which solution best fits the redundancy needs of eLoanDocs?
- How might the eLoanDocs employees react to adoption of a cloud-based hosting solution?

As Albert considered these and other questions, the only answer he felt sure about was that it was an exciting time to be alive and working in the technology industry.

Glossary

Cloud computing: Using network resources to perform computations without the need, or often the ability, to determine the exact resources used at any time.

Co-location facility: Physical location that provides reliable power, secure physical facilities, and networking services to clients for a monthly operating fee. Clients provide their own hardware to run in the co-location facility.

Disaster recovery: Alternative to normal system operations intended to be used in case of catastrophic events (e.g., widespread power outages, local natural disasters)

High availability: High rate of system uptime, typically in excess of 99 percent. Also refers to technologies required to achieve a high rate of system uptime, such as redundant hardware components.

Hybrid cloud: System configuration in which some combination of public cloud, private cloud, and dedicated server solutions are mixed and used together to form the complete system.

Infrastructure as a service (IaaS): A type of cloud computing where the cloud provider provisions and maintains the computer hardware, storage, and networking for their clients, while the client is responsible for maintaining the operating systems and software.

Multitenant: Software configuration in which a single instance of the system serves multiple clients. Clients typically have no visibility or awareness of the data (or even the existence) of other clients.

Private cloud: Ownership and management of cloud computing resources win an organization's firewall, or optionally dedicated equipment managed by a cloud hosting provider on behalf of a customer.

Public cloud: Computing resources that are hypothetically available to any user connected to the same cloud service provider.

Recovery point objective (RPO): Amount of time for which data may be lost due to catastrophic events. Recovery time objective (RTO): Amount of time that a system may be unavailable due to unexpected circumstances (e.g. a catastrophic event that prevents the function of the system)

Replication: Act of making exact copies of systems. Disaster recovery plans often use replication in order to minimize the RPO of a running system by using identical hardware located at geographically remote sites and synchronizing the data storage in real time.

Software as a service (SaaS): Licensing software solutions such that the hardware and the software are typically remote to the licensees and administered and maintained by the licensors.

SSAE 16 Type II: Statement on Standards for Attestation Engagements (SSAE) 16 is the professional standard used for issuing reports in accordance with the American Institute of Certified Public Accountants' Service Organization Control (SOC) reporting framework, which consists of SOC 1 (SSAE 16) along with SOC 2 and SOC 3 (AT 101) reporting. Additionally, the SSAE 16 standard effectively replaced the aging and antiquated SAS 70 auditing standard that had been in use for approximately twenty (20) years.

Virtualization: Creating a logical instance of a real system in such a way that it appears to an end user as a real system. A virtual machine—configurations of powerful servers so that multiple operating systems can be run with their own disk storage partitions—is a common example of virtualization.

ONLINE EDUCATION

Thirty years from now the big University campuses will be relicts. Universities won't survive. It is as large a change as when we first got the printed book.
—Peter Drucker[1]

Introduction[2]

As the Internet had become yet another arrow in the quiver of educational institutions and in industries as diverse as elevator manufacturing and financial services, the above quote by Peter Drucker sounded, in January 2015 on the snowy campus of Ivey University, like a warning echoing from the past. Erica Wagner, dean of the School of Information Management, recalled the quote while scanning a recent article in *Mashable*, citing the recent LinkedIn acquisition of online education company Lynda.com for $1.5 billion.

The Internet and the competition of massive open online courses, or MOOCs, are making administrators like Dr. Wagner question themselves about the future of the institution and programs they had been entrusted to lead. Whereas these new online players seemed to have had minimal incremental effect on prestigious research universities such as Ivey, the future appeared far more uncertain for "middle-tier" institutions that may be required to increase the proportion of online learning compared to more traditional classroom teaching in order to lower their costs. Enrollment in undergraduate programs at Ivey was more selective than ever, due to rising demand. Campuses were teeming with construction workers developing new buildings, adding to existing ones, remodeling teaching and office space, equipping ever more sophisticated labs, and, most importantly it seemed, developing more parking space!

While the number of students in executive education programs had been declining steadily over the last decade, forcing the school to shorten some of its programs from five to three days, many blamed the recent recession for these results, others the competition of new players on nondegree executive education.[3] However, as she pondered the future, Dr. Wasgner recalled a passage from an article in *The Economist* that she had seen a few years before. The memory brought back some of her own uneasiness: "The innate conservatism of the academic profession does not help. The modern university was born in a very different world from the current one, a world where only a tiny minority of the population went into higher education, yet many academics have been reluctant to make any allowances for massification."[4]

Was everyone missing the forest for the trees? Was the Internet a disruptive technology in the education industry, simply brewing under the surface to soon blindside slow-to-react incumbents?

Education and Research at Ivey

Like its peers, Ivey University had a complex mission and a large community of stakeholders, ranging from students and faculty to alumni and the local and global community. At the highest level of analysis, Ivey performed two main activities: the creation of new knowledge (i.e., research) and the dissemination of knowledge (i.e., education).

As a prestigious Research I institution, Ivey spent a considerable amount of resources supporting the development of new knowledge by hiring some of the brightest young faculty members and accomplished researchers. Among its faculty it counted twelve Nobel Prize winners and boasted many world-class research centers.

While the research mission was pursued in basement labs and offices throughout campus, the most evident manifestation of Ivey's contribution to society was

---

1. Lenzner, R., & Johnson, S.S. (1997), Seeing things as they really are, *Forbes*, retrieved from http://www.forbes.com/forbes/1997/0310/5905122a_print.html.

2. This is a fictitious case developed with the exclusive intent of supporting class discussion.

3. Bradshaw, Della (2015, May 17), New market entrants create competition for business schools, *The Financial Times*, retrieved from http://on.ft.com/1JrEyeH

4. The digital degree, *The Economist*, June 28, 2014, retrieved from http://www.economist.com/news/briefing/21605899-staid-higher-education-business-about-experience-welcome-earthquake-digital

its teaching mission. A large school like the School of Information Management at Ivey University had truly global reach.

Its largest population was about 2,200 undergraduate students. The school also trained master's students, leaving the workforce for one or two years (a substantial opportunity cost on top of the direct costs of going back to school) to gain an advanced degree and the skills to accelerate their career. Ivey had a medium size but a very selective master's program, with about 300 students enrolled. Finally, the school educated the next generation of faculty and researchers by way of its PhD program.

A very recognized brand in the business world, Ivey also offered a number of executive education and professional education programs. These were typically highly condensed courses, held on Ivey's own campus or satellite locations, designed to serve the needs of corporations seeking to update the skills of their workforce or to offer working students a chance to access the wealth of knowledge that the school's faculty had to offer without having to resign from their job.

Global Expansions

Because of its brand recognition around the world, the School of Information Management and a number of other schools at Ivey had been focused on global expansion through partnerships and the opening of satellite campuses. The school had partners in Asia and Europe and was currently evaluating whether to enter the South American market.

The reason for global expansion was simple: With the skyrocketing demand for high-quality education in emerging markets around the globe, there was great opportunity to extend the Ivey brand. Expansion was not without challenges, with revenue models being at times challenged and a myriad of logistics and quality assurance hurdles to be overcome. However, as with almost every other recognized education brand entering the new markets, a wait-and-see attitude could be extremely risky.

Online Players: A Real Threat or a Nuisance?

Since Peter Drucker's prediction, there had been a significant amount of development in online educational offerings. University of Phoenix, the largest for-profit institution, had about 250,000 students now, but they attained 600,000 enrollments only a few years ago. While quality concerns lingered, not just on prestigious university campuses, online universities seemed to be gaining traction.

Perhaps even more interesting and threatening were open source content creation and delivery entities. The best example was offered by Coursera, the for-profit education platform that was the brainchild of Daphne Koller and Andrew Ng, who were offering their computer science courses online, drawing the attention of over 100,000 students. Coursera, now backed by over $140 million in funding, had come a long way, giving access to 1,472 courses available to interested students from all over the world and a running count of over 16 million learners, 2 million course completions, and 136 university partners. Coursera was focused on academic courses in topics, ranging from math to science to history to the humanities, and it was originally geared to college students. As Dr. Koller put it, "Online education is a more effective way to teach basic facts and skills in part because students can learn at their own pace. Taking classes online gives people the opportunity to pause and reflect and grapple with the material."[5]

Not all online educational offerings were by upstarts. Indeed, traditional universities had their own offerings, and Ivey itself had launched its own online education effort during the late 1990s: iIvey. While the number of courses offered at iIvey had slowly but steadily increased, and some of the school's programs required them as prerequisites, the iIvey effort seemed to have lost steam after the bursting of the dot-com bubble. Yet with about forty courses available, a price tag between $1,000 and $1,500 per course, and a global reach, iIvey still offered quite a bit of potential, if nothing else, for revenue.

The Future

As Dr. Wagner watched the snow drop a fresh dusting of white powder on the roof of the gothic buildings across the quad, she pondered some of the words of the article she read:

> Other industries next in line for disruption like education and health care would be wise to pay attention. Most of what they do depends on the control of information that will soon no longer be scarce. Education reformers have long predicted a world where top professors spread their knowledge across the globe through electronic tools. But the knowledge students need is not only located in those few professors' minds. Once we digitize not just the distribution of

5. Wolfe, A. (2015), Daphne Koller on the future of online education, *Wall Street Journal*, retrieved from http://www.wsj.com/articles/daphne-koller-on-the-future-of-online-education-1433532321

knowledge but the production of it, the existing university system loses its *raison d'etre*. Why would people come to a single physical location at higher and higher costs when the knowledge it houses is no longer scarce?[6]

And the words of Dr. Koller in a recent WSJ article seemed to echo Drucker's words: "School experience will be like turning the tap—and great education comes out for anybody. We'll have data from hundreds of thousands, millions of people at a level that's unprecedented. I think we're at the cusp of a revolution of treating human learning as science."[7]

---

6. McQuivey, J. (2011), Why the end of scarcity will change the economics of everything, retrieved from http://mashable .com/2011/04/28/scarcity-economics/?utm_source=feedburner &utm_medium=feed&utm_campaign=Feed%3A+Mashable +%28Mashable%29&utm_content=Google+Feedfetcher

7. Wolfe, A. (2015), Daphne Koller on the future of online education, *Wall Street Journal*, retrieved from http:// www.wsj.com/articles/daphne-koller-on-the-future-of -online-education-1433532321

Would this really happen? And how would it affect a top university like Ivey? As the dean of the School of Information Management, Dr. Wagner was not only entrusted with the future of the school she led but she also felt a responsibility to help the university community at large thrive in the network economy. Could Ivey miss the wave of the future? "Not on my watch!" Dr. Wagner told herself while getting ready for the first of many of the day's meetings.

Discussion Questions

1. Do you agree with Peter Drucker's opening quote?
2. Is the Internet a disruptive technology in the education industry in general? And for Ivey's School of Information Management in particular?

TRIPIT: The Traveler's Agent

*TripIt is a platform opportunity. If we are
successful, we will be the "home base" for
all of a consumer's travel information.*
— Gregg Brockway, president and cofounder

With the summer travel season underway in July 2008, Gregg Brockway (MBA '95), TripIt's CEO, was introducing the company's 11th employee to the rest of the team at TripIt's headquarters—a small space the firm occupied in San Francisco's Potrero District.[1] Founded in October 2006, TripIt was a free online travel service that aggregated travelers' bookings with many top airlines, cruises, hotels, and travel Web sites into a comprehensive itinerary. Having just secured $5.1 million in financing from O'Reilly AlphaTech Ventures, European Founders Fund, and Sabre Holdings,[2] the company was at a critical point in its evolution. The capital, earmarked primarily for product development and marketing, was a welcome relief to Brockway and his team, but they could not afford to misspend it. The success or failure of the company depended on growing the number of users quickly, partnering with the right online travel firms, and defining a sustainable business model.

Industry Background

The travel industry was composed of a complex network of suppliers—including airlines, car rental agencies, cruise lines, hotels, and more—that provided services to companies and individuals through direct and intermediary channels, which were mainly traditional and online travel agencies. Suppliers and intermediaries served leisure and business customers, the latter of which included two sub-segments: unmanaged business travelers, who booked travel without a company policy limiting type of travel, supplier, or fare;[i] and managed business travelers, whose employers contracted with corporate travel management firms that provided streamlined services, often leveraging scale to negotiate lower prices.

Before the advent of the Internet, traditional travel agencies served as indispensable intermediaries between customers and industry suppliers. Lacking the information and access necessary to coordinate a trip, customers relied on travel agents for help researching and purchasing accommodations, transport, and entertainment. Agents then provided customers with travel itineraries, which detailed the trip's components.

In the mid-1970s, airlines introduced electronic commerce to the travel industry by giving travel agents access to their Computerized Reservation Systems (CRS). These systems, called Global Distribution Systems (GDS), drastically increased efficiencies for travel agencies.[ii] Once the GDS were adapted to the Internet, travel agencies began conducting business online through licensed and customized versions of the reservation technology.[iii] By the mid-1990s, Internet entrepreneurs and software giant Microsoft, along with established players such as Sabre Holdings, had created the first major online travel agencies (OTAs). For example, Microsoft's Expedia and Travelocity, both launched in 1996, allowed travelers to research, arrange and book travel directly, bypassing traditional travel agents.[iv] Expedia, Travelocity and other OTAs differed from suppliers by offering bundled travel packages, which had primarily driven growth in this sector. During a trip's planning and reservation phases, which sometimes began months in advance, a traveler often solicited multiple channels; for example, one might schedule accommodations directly through the hotel, visit an OTA to reserve flights, visit a car rental Web site to reserve a car, and use a traditional travel agency to book entertainment and day excursions.

As the Internet travel industry grew, established OTAs competed with both the suppliers themselves

---

1. This case was originally published as: Applegate, L., Piccoli, G. and Brohman, K. "TripIt: The Traveler's Agent," *Harvard Business School Publishing*, 9–809–059.

2. In 2007, Sabre Holdings, which owned online travel companies such as Travelocity, was the global leader in computerized travel reservations. The company's reservation system technology originated through a collaboration between IBM and American Airlines initiated in 1953. Source: "Sabre Holdings Corporation," via Hoovers, Inc., www.hoovers.com, accessed August 2008.

(airlines, hotels, etc.) and a steady wave of startups touting traveler-empowering innovations such as group planning, information-sharing, and social networking, as well as personalized travel information such as traveler alerts and weather updates (see Exhibit 5.1 for a list of top online travel sites, Exhibit 5.2 for a sample list of entrants to the online travel industry, and Exhibit 5.3 for a sample of popular social networking sites). User-generated content also became an important part of the travel cycle with innovative companies like TripAdvisor leading the way. Indeed, 47% of respondents to a 2007 industry survey asserted that user-generated reviews were "somewhat influential" or "strongly influential" in their travel purchase decisions.[v] To nurture customer loyalty, many established travel sites added such features, often through acquisitions and partnerships.[vi] While price comparisons, reviews and other content lured heavy traffic to OTAs, many site visitors purchased services elsewhere, making it increasingly difficult to "monetize" (charge revenues for) these added services.[vii]

The massive marketing spend by OTAs, suppliers and new entrants made online travel one of the fastest growing online categories, both in terms of total dollars and category penetration. In 2007, U.S. online travel service purchases exceeded offline travel purchases for the first time in history:[viii] Of the U.S. travel industry's estimated $267 billion in gross bookings for leisure and unmanaged business travel, $137 billion came from online channels and $129 billion[3] from offline channels (see Exhibit 5.4).[ix] While the industry continued to be reshaped by OTAs, which claimed $36.3 billion in bookings, direct supplier Web sites claimed the majority of online car rental, flight, and hotel sales, at 69%, 69%, and 59%, respectively, for leisure and unmanaged business customers.[x] Online channels competed for market share with traditional travel agencies and other offline supplier channels (e.g., call centers taking direct reservations from travelers) which, combined, held 49% of the market. While the number of traditional travel agencies dropped 6.2% between 1998 and 2008,[xi] these outlets continued to serve many business travelers and other consumers seeking customized, attentive service.[xii] Given the frequent use of both online and offline travel services, many analysts predicted that the hybridization of the industry, wherein both suppliers and intermediaries would offer online and offline support to customers, was inevitable.[xiii]

Building TripIt

TripIt was a free online travel organizer that aggregated travelers' bookings from many top airlines, cruises, hotels, train providers, and travel Web sites. After forwarding reservation confirmation e-mails to plans@tripit.com, travelers received a chronological master itinerary, supplemented with features such as travel guides, driving directions, and weather reports, which could be viewed and shared online. (See Appendix 5.1 for a sample itinerary.) TripIt users could customize their itineraries by adding meetings and other activities, and they could keep tabs on travel plans of family, friends and colleagues through their shared TripIt itineraries.

TripIt founders Brockway and Scott Hintz first met while working at Hotwire—an online travel intermediary selling surplus[xiv] flights, car rentals, hotel reservations, cruises, and bundled travel packages at a discount—(Brockway cofounded Hotwire in 2000.[xv]) According to Hintz, a self-described travel geek, the inspiration for TripIt came from the founders' belief that although online travel services had been widely used for over a decade most online services were designed from the provider point of view, and opportunities remained to improve the consumer's experience. Hintz, TripIt's vice president of business development, explained: "While I was head of product, business development and supplier relations at Hotwire, I gained a deep understanding of the online travel process. Nevertheless, every time I planned a trip it was always a lot of work! I'd plow through my e-mail inbox trying to find all my confirmations—hotel, air, car—and then I'd print them and put them in a manila folder, which I then had to carry around. There had to be a better way to organize travel."

Brockway left Hotwire after the company's 2003 acquisition by IAC/InterActiveCorp,[xvi] but remained with IAC/InterActive until 2006. Hintz left IAC/InterActive in early 2006. The two reconnected in late 2006 to discuss developing a business that would dramatically simplify the consumer travel experience. The founders believed the consumer's itinerary should be the organizing principle for the service, around which the information and activity flows that occurred throughout the travel life cycle, from pre- to post-trip, should revolve (Exhibit 5.5). Brockway, TripIt's president, recalled, "We kept thinking about how we could solve more than one problem at once, and the more we thought about it, the more we felt it was really about the information and we kept coming back to the itinerary as the centerpiece of the travel experience." Hintz added, "This was around the time that Facebook was becoming superhot.

---

3. The online and offline figures do not total $267 billion due to rounding.

EXHIBIT 5.1. Comparing U.S. Travel Web Sites (%Market Share Based on # of Visits during July 2008)

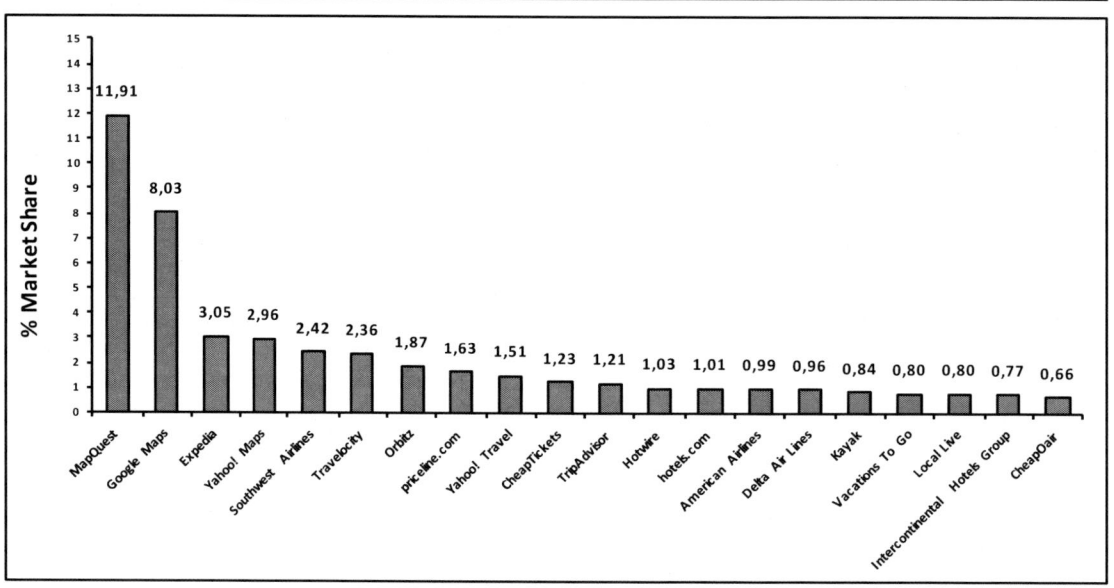

Web Site	Compare Supplier Prices & Services	Read Ratings and Reviews	Purchase Services	Access Maps and Directions
MapQuest				X
Google Maps				X
Expedia	X		X	
Yahoo! Maps				X
Southwest Airlines			X	
Travelocity	X		X	
Orbitz	X		X	
Priceline.com	X		X	
Yahoo! Travel	X	X	X	
CheapTickets	X		X	
TripAdvisor		X		
Hotwire	X		X	
hotels.com	X	X	X	
American Airlines			X	
Delta Airlines			X	
Kayak	X	X	X	
Vacations To Go	X	X	X	
Local Live				X
Intercontinental Hotels Group	X	X	X	
CheapOair	X	X	X	

Note: The table is not an exhaustive list of the Web sites' functionalities, but merely highlights primary features.

Source: Web site list from Jeffrey Grau, "US Online Travel: Planning and Booking," eMarketer, Inc., August 2008, p. 10. All other data compiled by Casewriter.

EXHIBIT 5.2. Sample of Travel Web Sites Offering Networking and Itinerary Sharing

Company	Year Launched	Functionalities
DOPPLR	2008	Itinerary sharing targeted to business travelers
Groople	2004	Group travel planning, booking, itinerary sharing
Gusto!	205	Social networking, trip planning
Home&Abroad	2006	Trip planning, itinerary sharing, user-generated content
Hotel Planner	2003	Group travel planning
Meetup	2006	Online organization of offline gatherings
Nile Guide	2008	Trip planning, itinerary building, user-generated content
RealTravel	2005	Blogs, reviews, travel deals, itinerary building and sharing
Travbuddy	2005	Social networking and reviews
TravelMuse	2008	Group travel planning, booking, itinerary building
TripConnect	2005	Social networking, photo sharing, user-generated content
Triporama	2005	Group travel planning

Note: Itinerary building and sharing mechanisms on these sites did not include TripIt's "Itinerator" functionality, which decoded e-mail confirmation information from various sources automatically to generate an itinerary.

Source: Adapted from Michael Cannizzaro et al., "U.S. Online Travel Overview: Seventh Edition," PhoCus-Wright (November 2007), PhuCusWright, Inc., p. 1.6, 1.7.

So, we also wanted to support the social networking that takes place around travel. Once again, we kept coming back to the itinerary as the organizing framework for the social relationships, too." The vision for TripIt evolved into a product that not only aggregated a traveler's itinerary (see Exhibit 5.6), but also would create a network of friends and provide ratings and recommendations for travel services (see Exhibit 5.7 for TripIt's three-pronged functionality).

Convinced there was a need for such services, Brockway and Hintz turned to Andy Denmark, a highly experienced software developer and the brother of former Hotwire colleague Thor Denmark, to assess the feasibility of their vision. Because of the convergence of technological and business trends in the travel industry, the three quickly agreed that the idea behind TripIt was feasible and the timing was perfect. They believed that the proliferation of disparate online travel services, the increasingly heavy reliance on digital transactions (especially e-mail) in travel planning, and the widespread use of open source software made it possible to combine information from multiple online sources. In October 2006, Brockway and Hintz incorporated

TripIt and the following month Denmark left his post as a software engineer at Opsware to become TripIt's vice president of engineering. (See Exhibit 5.8. for brief background on the cofounders and Exhibit 5.9. for a timeline of key company events.) Shortly thereafter, the three cofounders began building a prototype (the alpha phase), which they self-financed—a process called "bootstrapping." Brockway explained: "When we founded Hotwire, in 1999, we raised $75 million in our first round so we never really controlled the business. In the case of TripIt we decided to delay seeking outside financing so we could control our own destiny. Control is not everything, but keeping the team small and nimble was important to us."

Building the "Itinerator"

The initial challenge for the cofounders was developing the software that would reliably and accurately read, decode, and then recode the information contained in a traveler's e-mail confirmations from suppliers and intermediaries (see Exhibit 5.10 for the architecture of the Itinerator). Hoping that their vision would become a platform for the travel space, like Google and Facebook

EXHIBIT 5.3. Sample of Popular Social Networking Web Sites, 2008			
Web Site	**Year Founded**[a]	**Active Users**	**Details**[a]
MySpace	2003	110 million[b]	MySpace users shared photos, profile information, and messages. The site also allowed classified listings and blogs, and hosted music and video-sharing Web sites.
Facebook	2004	80 million[b]	Facebook was originally geared toward students, but later opened to the general public. Users shared photos, personal profiles, and messages. The site also hosted various third-party applications and games.
Bebo	2005	42 million[c]	Bebo allowed users to share photos and profile information, and customize homepages with videos and animation. The site also broadcasted internet soap operas. AOL acquired Bebo in 2008, and planned to add instant messaging and other capabilities to market the site to business users.
WAYN[d]	2002	13 million	U.K.-based WAYN (Where Are You Now) was geared primarily toward travelers. Users shared profiles, and could keep track on each others' travel histories and schedules.

Sources:

[a] For MySpace, Facebook, and Bebo, compiled via Hoovers, Inc., www.hoovers.com, accessed September 2008.

[b] Kevin Allison, "Facebook Heads MySpace in Unique Visitors," *Financial Times*, June 27, 2008, at http://www.ft.com/cms/s/0/302914bc-40a7-11dd-bd48-0000779fd2ac.html, accessed September 2008.

[c] Joshua Chaffin, "Secret Life of Bebo's Online Drama," *Financial Times*, June 8, 2008, at http://www.ft.com/cms/s/0/bd124bd4-3583-11dd-998d-0000779fd2ac.html, accessed September 2008.

[d] Year founded, number of active users, and details adapted from WAYN, "About Us," at WAYN Web site, www.wayn.com/aboutus, accessed September 2008.

EXHIBIT 5.4. U.S. Travel Market by Channel and Sector, Gross Booking ($ billions)/Market Share (%), 2005–2007						
Leisure and Unmanaged Business		**Corporate**		**Total**		
Online	*Offline*	*Online*	*Offline*	*Online*	*Offline*	*Grand*
$66/28%	$73/31%	$29/13%	$64/28%	$95/41%	$137/59%	$233
$80/32%	$74/29%	$36/14%	$63/25%	$116/46%	$137/54%	$253
$94/35%	$70/26%	$43/16%	$59/22%	$137/51%	$129/49%	$267

Note: Totals may not add to 100 due to rounding. 2007 data is projected.

Source: Adapted from Michael Cannizzaro et al., "U.S. Online Travel Overview: Seventh Edition," PhoCus-Wright (November 2007), PhuCusWright, Inc., p. 2.1, 2.3.

EXHIBIT 5.5. TripIt Travel Lifecycle

Source: Company documents.

EXHIBIT 5.6. TripIt's Itinerary Functionality

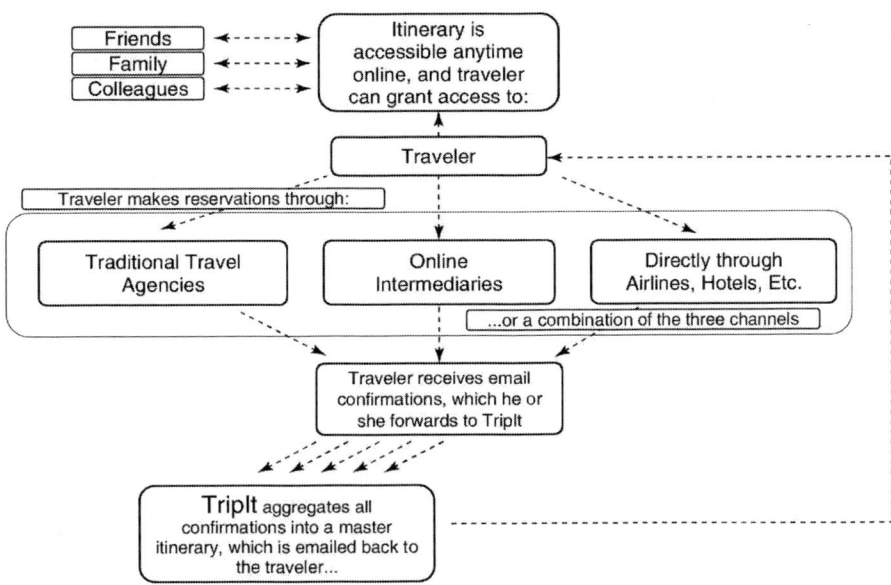

Source: Casewriter.

had done successfully in information search and social networking, the cofounders were very attentive to the effect that technology design choices in the early stages of development would have on the company's future ability to deliver new services—either launched by TripIt or created by others who wished to tie into the TripIt travel community. Denmark felt that the ability to collect and store travel information rather than simply organizing e-mail travel confirmations, while more technologically challenging, would dramatically increase the company's "options value" in the future. He explained:

We looked at open industry standards in travel, but large travel companies prefer to own their portion of the itinerary despite the fact that

EXHIBIT 5.7. Cofounder's Vision

Source: Company documents.

it's clear that people don't book in one place. Online and offline travel companies have not invested a lot of money to make data easily sharable with other travel providers. Yet there is a lot of unstructured data in people's e-mail and it's nasty hard work from a technical point of view to get that information into a structure that a computer can understand so that it can be stored in databases and combined with other data sources to create valuable information that can be customized and then distributed to whatever device people want to use—be it a cell phone, a computer, or even a GPS system. We believe that the technology we have built to take unstructured e-mail messages—no matter what form they are in—and create a structured database is a significant barrier to entry that allows us to jump out front. We call this technology the Itinerator. It's a powerful differentiator but we will need to move fast to stay in front.

Given the need for rapid growth, solving the "semantic" decoding of e-mails and structuring of data to create the Itinerator was just the first technical hurdle that the company faced. The second challenge was to build the technology so that it could scale quickly in terms of the size of the network supported and the functionality and service offerings provided. Finally, the team knew that the offering would need to be very easy

to use and provide tremendous benefits to users. As a result, they knew the technology would also need to go through several iterations of fine tuning to ensure that it worked, that it met a widespread market need, and that travelers would be willing and able to use it. To meet these challenges, the cofounders relied on open systems software to launch the Itinerator. Denmark explained: "The increasing popularity of open source software and open standards made it possible for us to automate the process of building a travel itinerary by decoding information stored on e-mails. This would have been a technologically difficult task just a few years ago. We use technologies that are ubiquitous and widely supported. There isn't one single piece of commercial software at TripIt!"

In March 2007, the company secured its first round of external financing: $1 million from O'Reilly AlphaTech Ventures (OATV). The money was designed to take the firm through public beta release. The team believed that the ability to show rapid user adoption was crucial for investors.

The initial funding was also used to build a team of software developers with strong computer science and engineering backgrounds who could build the beta product and then rapidly build new offerings that leveraged it. While searching for strong technical expertise, the cofounders also wanted employees who had the personality, talents and interests needed to move into managerial roles. "As a small tech start-up," they said,

EXHIBIT 5.8. Brief Backgrounds of Cofounders

Greg Brockway, president

As an online travel industry veteran, former cofounder of discount online travel company Hotwire and former president of Expedia's luxury travel company Classic Vacations, Inc., Brockway knew the ins and outs of booking and planning travel online. Prior to his work in the online travel industry, Brockway was a director at the private equity firm Hellman & Friedman and worked in the merchant banking group at Morgan Stanley & Company. Brockway received his MBA from Harvard Business School and had been a featured speaker at numerous industry conferences, including TravelCom, Internet World, eTravel, and EyeForTravel on the topics of travel, e-commerce, and revenue management.

Scott Hintz, vice president—Business Development

Hintz brought years of travel, product, strategy, and technology experience to the TripIt team. At TripIt, Hintz was tasked with the challenge of making TripIt.com so easy to use that it encouraged travelers to use the service. Prior to TripIt, Hintz was senior vice president of product development for Hotwire and led the product management, business development and travel relationships teams. Prior to Hotwire, Hintz spent five years as a strategy consultant for Accenture advising clients such as Chrysler, Canon USA, United Airlines, Hewlett-Packard, and Visa USA on corporate strategy, process design, and business planning. Hintz received a B.S. from the Wharton School at the University of Pennsylvania and an MBA from the Stanford Graduate School of Business.

Andy Denmark, vice president—Engineering

At TripIt, Denmark's job was to keep the site running as smoothly as a perfect vacation. Denmark came to TripIt with more than 13 years of software development and operations experience. Prior to joining TripIt, Denmark was director of Suites Engineering at Opsware, Inc. (formerly Loudcloud) and was responsible for the engineering strategy for product suite integration. Before Opsware he was the chief technology officer for the real estate portal CityRealty.com and founder and chief engineer for the Internet consulting firm Mediabridge Infosystems. Denmark had a B.S. in Electrical Engineering and an M.S. in Computer Science from Columbia University.

Source: Company documents.

"managers need a strong understanding of the technology and developers need to understand how to build a business."

Launching TripIt

TripIt launched a private alpha site for friends and family in April 2007 and two months later released a password protected beta version to the public with a request to early adopters to help improve the service. By July 2007, TripIt enabled users to build itineraries by e-mailing the confirmations and accessing complementary information from over 140 suppliers (see Exhibit 5.11 for a list of suppliers as of July 2008). For example, in addition to airline, train, hotel and car rental firms,

TripIt's Itinerator software could directly access maps and routing information from Google, tourist information from Wikipedia, and weather information from the National Weather Service. In addition, while TripIt's social networking functionality was in its earliest stages, the service also allowed users to identify a network of travelers and share travel plans with them. TripIt's "My Friends" functionality allowed users to create profile pages that highlighted upcoming trips and enabled users to keep track of the travel plans of people in their traveler network. TripIt's social networking aspect tapped into the travel industry's information-sharing trend, and also served as a marketing tool; TripIt users could send "invites" to join TripIt to friends and

EXHIBIT 5.9. TripIt: Timeline of Key Events

Date	Event	Type of Financing
2006		Bootstrap
Oct.	Brockway and Hintz incorporated TripIt in Delaware	
Nov.	Denmark joined team	
Dec.	Itinerator platform prototyped	
2007		
Jan. to Mar.	Build platform prototype	
Mar.		Series A: $1 million from O'Reilly AlphaTech Ventures
Apr.	Friends and family alpha test	
Jun.	Password protected public beta test	
Jul.	Itinerator's itinerary building functionality largely in place/social network functionality introduced	
Sep.	Official public beta launch. Number of unique visitors to TripIt website = 38,579	
2008		
Jan. to Mar.	Functionality added, including mobile accessibility, cruises and an alert feature for changes to a traveler's itinerary	
Apr.		Series B: $5.1 million from Sabre Travel Network, European Founders Fund, O'Reilly AlphaTech Ventures
May	Social network functionality increased to allow users to create personal profiles. Number of unique visitors to TripIt website = 92,283	
Jun.	Event plans (e.g., shows, sporting events) added to Itinerator. 11th employee hired website	

Source: Casewriter.

colleagues. (Tracking usage of this feature over time, the cofounders discovered that a TripIt user who used the social networking functionality, on average, invited 1.5 people to join TripIt, of which 50% decided to become members.) The third component of the TripIt platform—user ratings and recommendations—would, however, be added later.

By late 2007, the TripIt team felt that the company's position as the nexus between consumer travel and social networking would enable it to become the traveler's indispensable home base. The team identified numerous value-added offerings that could be rolled out on the TripIt service but the limited resources available made prioritizing product development critical.

TripIt's approach to product development was informed by the inherent tradeoff in consumer applications: as the degree of control the application gave to users grew, so too did the complexity of the service. As complexity increased, the offering could become less intuitive and user friendly. TripIt's philosophy was to start with simple specifications and iterate as fast as possible by monitoring both users' feedback and actual usage. While committed to this iterative development strategy, Brockway hinted at the difficulties of fully embracing it on his TripIt's blog: "Release early, release often is a great philosophy and a sound strategy, but in reality it's hard to not have stage fright around a first release."[xvii]

The team also struggled with whether to commit resources towards developing proprietary functionality versus tying into functionality already available from

EXHIBIT 5.10. The Itinerator Architecture

Source: Company documents.

other industry players. This was particularly evident with the ratings and recommendations functionality under development by Tripit and available from several online sites. With so much user-generated content already available, TripIt could minimize the need to re-enter this information by partnering with established sites such as TripAdvisor. However, partnering had its drawbacks. Hintz explained:

On TripAdvisor there are many reviews but they are often contradictory. Users need to be able to calibrate reviews. If someone who always stays at youth hostels is telling you that a specific hotel is a great property, you may not trust that review as much as someone who stays at five star hotels. Given our database of travel activity and our social networking capabilities, TripIt users will be able to calibrate ratings based on the person's travel history. As a result, they can build a network of people they trust whose ratings and recommendations are much more valuable to them. This is the potential value of our early decision

to design the Itinerator so that we can actually capture and store detailed itinerary data. Now we can leverage that platform to build offerings that are unique to TripIt.

User-Driven Product Development

TripIt's leadership team had targeted three main users: road warriors; highly organized travelers; and small groups who frequently traveled together (see Exhibit 5.12). These targeted travelers shared the need to simplify the pre-trip planning process, organize travel information, and share it during the trip (e.g., with other travelers, a spouse, or an administrative assistant). In the first six months of 2008, the company sought to attract these users and rapidly roll out the new features they requested. For example, mobile support (i.e., the ability to access TripIt with mobile devices, such as Blackberries, iPhones, etc.) was rolled out first in January 2008 through an e-mail-based command interface called *TripIt To Me* that allowed travelers to send commands to TripIt servers and receive their itinerary or other information back by e-mail. (A

EXHIBIT 5.11. Sample Travel Booking Sites Compatible with TripIt as of July 2008

Airlines

Aer Lingus	American Airlines	easyJet	Northwest	United Airlines
Air Canada	BMI	ExpressJet Airlines	Midwest Airlines	US Airways
Air France	British Airways	Flybe	Qantas	Virgin America
Air New Zealand	Cape Air	Frontier Airlines	Ryanair	Virgin Atlantic
airTran	Cathay Pacific	Hawaiian Airlines	SAS	Virgin Blue
Alaska Airlines	Continental	JetBlue	Singapore Airlines	WestJet
Aloha Airlines	Delta	KLM	Swiss International	Tiger Airways
ATA Airlines	El Al Airlines	Lufthansa	Thai Airways	

Online Travel Agents: Consumer

Booking.com	Expotel	HotelsMadeSimple.	Opodo (UK)	Snow.com
Cheap Tickets	Hotwire	MakeMyTrip.com	Orbitz	Travelocity
eLong	Hotels.com	NeedaHotel.com	Priceline	TravelNow.com
Expedia	HotelDiscounts.com	OctopusTravel.com	RockResorts.com	Venere.com

Online Travel Agents: Business

Cliqbook	GetThere	Orbitz for Business	Rearden Commerce	Travelport
Expedia	Hotelscene	Passkey	Travelocity	TripSync

Online/Offline Travel Agencies

AAA	American Express	American Express STA Travel	BCD	Carlon Wagonlit

Reservation Systems

Amadeus	iHotelier	ResNet	Worldspan ViewTrip	Defense Travel System
MyTripandMore.com	Sabre Virtually There			

Hotels

Best Western	Doubletree	Hyatt	Marriott	Super 8 Motel
Cambria Suites	Four Points by	Holiday Inn	Omni Hotels	Tablet Hotels
Choice Hotels	Four Seasons	InterContinental	Palms Casino	Travelodge
Clarion	Hampton Inn	Joie de Vivre Hotels	Quality Inn	Westin
Comfort Inn	Homewood Suites	Kimpton Hotels	Radisson Hotels	Vail Resorts
Comfort Suites	Howard Johnson	La Quinta	Sheraton	
Crowne Plaza	Hilton	Luxury Collection	Sleep Inn	

Rental Cars

Ace Rent A Car	Avis/Avis Europe	Dollar	National	U-Save Car & Truck Rental
Advantage Rent-A-Car	Budget	Enterprise	Payless Car Rental	
Alamo	CarRentals.com	Hertz	Thrifty	

Rail Travel

Amtrak	Eurostar	Rail Europe	The Trainline	ViaRail Canada

Cruise

Celebrity Cruises	Royal Caribbean	Norwegian Cruise Lines	Travelocity

Restaurant

OpenTable	Top Table

Source: Company documents.

EXHIBIT 5.12. TripIt's Targeted User Groups

Road Warriors
- Very frequent travelers (10+ times per year)
- Appreciate anything that simplifies or makes travel more efficient
- Maniacal about miles, points, travel frequency

Highly Organized Travelers
- Travel often but, more importantly, they like to be organized with lots of advance planning
- Planning the trip could be more than half the fun
- Want to share experiences with friends
- Often take complex/exotic trips

Small Groups
- Family reunions, sports outings, friend reunions, weddings, associations / community groups, religious groups, corporate meetings
- Wide spectrum of needs but all need help organizing and sharing plans with group members

Source: Company documents.

---

full-fledged mobile interface, called *TripIt Mobile* was launched in April 2008.) Brockway recounted how user feedback—not just market research—informed product development:

> TripIt was founded on the idea that travel is a social thing and sharing would be core to success. But people don't always know what they want in a new service offering. For example, in our early focus groups the need to share trip information was not rated very highly. Instead, people said they wanted low prices, a single itinerary, etc. Despite the feedback, in our initial beta we enabled people to share individual trips. Once they became users and saw the value of sharing, they asked to share with a network, and that became the *MyNetwork* and later *Who's Close* functionality, which alerts our users when people they know are visiting the town or city they live in. Now we have three tiers of sharing and we are rolling out a fourth. User feedback also let us know that many of our targeted users wanted cruise bookings, support for alternative lodging arrangements, such as hostels, and access to train reservation sites.

Hintz added: "We need to keep a close ear to the ground, listen to what our users are asking for and occasionally take a leap of faith. If a new feature is a total thud we'll redirect without having invested too many resources."

Based on user feedback, in March 2008, TripIt rolled out its *TripIt Alerts* feature that showed all the essential happenings in a traveler's account in one simple, easy-to-read list. It included updates about anyone in *MyNetwork* and a summary of changes to trips. By May 2008, TripIt allowed users to create robust user profiles similar to those on social networking sites and display personal information, photos, trips taken, cities visited, etc. One month later TripIt added the ability to plan events to the Itinerator's functionality. Tripit was able to read confirmation e-mails from many of the top event Web sites—e.g., Tickets.com, TicketMaster, TicketWeb, StubHub, Broadway.com, LasVegas.com, Fandango, Eventful and Eventbrite—as travelers booked events such as dinner and a show, sporting events, and movies, in advance. Interestingly, a Travel Industry Association survey concluded that 25% of events were purchased online while people booked travel.[xviii]

TripIt's Revenue Model

In 2008, OTAs such as Expedia and Travelocity made very small margins on airline tickets—typically the first component of travel purchased. Consequently, OTAs sought to cross-sell higher margin products, such as hotels and car rentals, to increase profitability. According to Brockway's estimates, 20% to 40% of consumers who purchased air travel also required lodging and other travel services for the same trip. And while OTAs aggressively cross-sold these complementary services, only 5% of the total revenues resulted from cross-selling. Hintz explained the problem:

Today a lot of the leakage from airlines and OTAs goes to Google, which makes a lot of money when customers ignore e-mail reminders and special offers by Expedia, Orbitz or the airlines themselves, and type something like "Boston hotels" in a Google search box. We believe that in the future we can be extremely helpful to travel suppliers and intermediaries by helping them capture more of that traffic and by providing them useful information to target consumers most likely to use their services. In fact, we consider that our business model will look more like Google and Facebook than it will look like current players in the industry.

While the TripIt team often discussed the possibility of creating paid premium services for travelers in the future, they believed that monetizing TripIt's current offerings and platform would primarily come in the near-term from advertising dollars associated with increased traveler traffic and partnerships with travel suppliers who wanted to access those travelers. Brockway explained:

> We think about monetizing at the trip level. If you send us an air ticket, we will say: "Hey did you think about a hotel? Here is where you have stayed in the past, here is where your network has stayed, here is where the TripIt community has stayed, and here is what they think about this place." We believe travel suppliers will pay us for this type of targeted advertising just like they pay Google today. We want to be positioned to generate revenue each time we make a suggestion and to generate even more revenue if someone "clicks through" and books a reservation.

Given its current revenue model, the company's profit model would be based on the spread between the cost of generating itineraries in TripIt and the revenue that each itinerary would generate in terms of referrals—Cost Per Action (CPA)—and other advertising revenues.

Measuring Progress

Although few formal processes and procedures existed, TripIt's leadership team and board of directors used Quickbooks and free software from Google to follow nine key monthly performance indicators: number of unique visitors to the site, number of trips in the Itinerator, trip yield (i.e., the number of new trips in Itinerator/number of unique visitors to the site), number of active accounts, account yield (i.e., the number of new accounts/number of unique visitors to the site), revenue per trip, marketing cost per trip, earnings before interest taxes depreciation and amortization (EBITDA), and available cash. From the official beta release in September 2007 through May 2008, TripIt's key performance indicators had shown improvement (see Exhibit 5.13 for results). Notably, 30% to 40% of TripIt's traffic was from travelers located outside of the U.S., primarily from English-speaking countries such as Australia, Britain, and Canada. Of the progress, Brockway said: "We are focusing on growth first, engagement second, and monetization third. We are approaching 100,000 unique visitors, which is great; but to attract the kind of advertising dollars we want, we need to reach about 500,000 visitors each month. About half our new accounts come from viral activity. To spur the growth we need we are rolling out more social features and new application program interfaces to connect easily with more partners."

Growing TripIt

The TripIt team did not believe that traditional online advertisements, such as search engine marketing, would generate significant traffic and itinerary generation. With broadcast advertisement largely out of reach in terms of available budget, TripIt needed to creatively build its user base through other means. Through mid-2008, TripIt had grown through word of mouth. Hintz explained:

> A friend of mine told me: "I didn't know how much I needed TripIt until I tried it." Today, because we can parse your e-mail confirmations, we can provide maps, driving directions, local weather, and tourist information automatically linked to your itinerary without you even asking for it. People love this, and once they see how much time we save them and the value of the services we offer, they sign on. In the future, we will be able to provide even more value. For example, we could even link to the GPS in your rental car and provide your itinerary and maps from TripIt. We could even suggest what radio station you might want to listen to in a new city. But the value we provide grows with each user we add and so too does the value to travel suppliers and other partners who might want to join our network.

Given the need to grow its user base quickly, TripIt was actively pursuing partnerships, including OTAs such as Travelocity or Orbitz and other travel content providers. For example, Brockway explained, "OTAs with

EXHIBIT 5.13. Performance Metrics Actual Results (August 2007 to May 2008)

Metric	2007					2008				
	August	September	October	November	December	January	February	March	April	May
Unique visitors										
Actual	2,998	38,579	47,264	50,941	46,171	60,394	83,766	84,203	98,651	92,283
% change		1187%	23%	8%	-9%	31%	39%	1%	17%	-6%
Trips (net new additions)										
Total	1,166	5,836	12,791	18,319	23,946	33,577	51,735	69,892	89,903	107,826
Actual, net	700	4,670	6,955	5,528	5,627	9,631	18,158	18,157	20,011	17,923
Trip "Yield"										
Actual	23.3%	12.1%	14.7%	10.9%	12.2%	15.9%	21.7%	21.6%	20.3%	19.4%
Activated accounts (total)										
Actual	1,522	6,231	12,012	16,279	20,674	27,774	42,876	56,685	70,394	81,892
New, net		4,709	5,781	4,267	4,395	7,100	15,102	13,809	13,709	11,498
Account "Yield"										
Actual	0.0%	12.2%	12.2%	8.4%	9.5%	11.8%	18.0%	16.4%	13.9%	12.5%
Revenue per trip										
Actual	$ -	$ -	$ -	$ -	$ -	$ 0.01	$ 0.004	$ 0.015	$ 0.004	$ 0.019
Mktg cost per trip										
Actual	na	na	na	na	na	$ 1.10	$ 0.66	$ 0.58	$ 0.54	$ 0.74
EBITDA										
Actual						$(119,139)	$(122,485)	$ (137,112)	$ (297,659)	$ (175,000)
Available cash ($000s)										
Actual						$ -	$ -	$5,031,520	$4,509,495	$4,340,000

Source: Company documents.

significant bookings could potentially insert an 'Add to TripIt' button on their confirmation page."

The TripIt team believed that partnerships could represent the next stage of growth and evolution. With limited resources, however, the team was constantly evaluating and prioritizing its investments. For example, an investment in partnerships may not pay off immediately. Yet, delaying the investment in providing tools for partners could limit growth. Brockway captured the trade-off: "We can't provide customized tools for everyone who wants to partner with us. We need to have a robust set of tools that makes it easy for others to tie in and create value-added applications. It is a trade-off, whether we focus our time and investment dollars on making it easy for providers and intermediaries to tie in to TripIt or whether we focus on continuing to deliver user-driven features to drive organic growth. The reality is that we need to do both, but that will take more money and resources than we currently have."

Raising More Money

In April 2008, the company obtained $5.1 million from three investors: its series A investor, OATV; Sabre Holdings—the parent of online consumer travel service, Travelocity, and the legendary Sabre Travel Network (launched by American Airlines in the 1980s); and the European Founders Fund—a German investment group, which invested in some of the most successful Internet startups in Europe, including alando (acquired by ebay) and Jamba! (acquired by VeriSign/Newscorp), as well as in U.S. social networking companies Facebook and LinkedIn. The financing was critical to avoid running out of cash before profitability was achieved (see Exhibit 5.14 for fiscal year 2008 financial projections). But obtaining the financing proved to be more difficult than the cofounders had expected, given the popularity with early users. Brockway explained:

It felt like we had made a critically acclaimed film and we were now struggling to get distribution in major movie markets. OATV wanted to bring in other investors and we did get term sheets from other venture capitalists, but we didn't find the term sheets attractive. They didn't seem to fully understand our value proposition. In addition, the potential Series B VCs all wanted to provide more money then we needed and take a larger percentage of the company. But then we decided to talk with travel industry players and they immediately got it. So too did the European Founders Fund. We now feel that TripIt is well positioned to strengthen our network and establish a global footprint.

EXHIBIT 5.14. Pro Forma Financial Forecasts for 2008 (some data is disguised)

	Q1	Q2	Q3	Q4	2008 Total
Number of itineraries	15,315	17,645	45,000	65,000	142,960
Revenues (total)	$459	$859	$2,700	$71,000	$75,018
Expenses					
Employee salaries and benefits	283,360	337,493	490,211	605,478	1,716,541
Consultants	46,350	39,550	29,050	26,850	141,800
Sales & marketing	32,444	47,037	61,978	64,528	205,986
Other expenses	25,355	88,354	76,638	44,488	234,834
Total expenses	387,509	512,434	657,877	741,344	2,299,161
EBITDA	(387,048)	(511,575)	(655,177)	(670,344)	(2,224,143)
Capital Expenditures	4,410	5,950	12,625	6,250	29,235
Total cash expenditures	(383,146)	(638,644)	(667,802)	(676,594)	(2,366,186)
Cumulative cash expenditures	(1,355,433)	(1,994,077)	(2,661,879)	(3,338,473)	(3,338,473)
Beginning cash	53,500	4,770,354	4,131,710	3,463,908	53,500
Cash from operations	(383,146)	(638,644)	(667,802)	(676,594)	(2,366,186)
Cash from financings	5,100,000	0	0	0	5,100,000
Ending cash	$4,770,354	$4,131,710	$3,463,908	$2,787,314	$2,877,314
Total employees (full time equivalents)	8.0	11.0	18.3	21.3	21.3

Source: Company documents.

With the new capital, the TripIt leadership team needed to decide how to maximize the money and increase the company's value. Denmark elaborated:

> Our core competency is itinerary management. That's what we are good at. We need to be faithful to our core competencies. For example, I am not going to hire twenty people to work on travel expense reporting. TripIt technology is a platform, a conduit. People entrust their data to us because we can combine it with other useful information and develop a personalized itinerary that can be shared with family and friends. If we build the technology in the right way, you can imagine all kinds of applications that could provide value to individuals and their social networks. In time, we can also provide value to other players in the travel industry. We don't have to do everything ourselves—but we do need to maintain our position in the center of the ecosystem.

The cofounders retained equity control of the company after the second round of financing, but management no longer controlled the board of directors. In 2008, TripIt had five directors: Brockway and Hintz, two investors (Mark Jacobsen of OATV and John Samuel of Sabre Holdings), and one independent seat held by John Lilly, CEO of Mozilla Corporation.

Charting the Future

While confident that TripIt was positioned to stake a sustainable, competitive claim in the rapidly-evolving travel industry, Brockway felt growing pressure from investors, who believed the company should soon demonstrate the capacity to generate revenues. In the words of Jacobsen: "Within the next six months we should begin generating revenue and we will need to watch our cash burn very closely." To achieve profitability, TripIt needed to not just grow its user base and generate itineraries, but also to generate advertising revenues from suppliers and intermediaries. While the business model and product offerings of other players overlapped with that of TripIt, the team believed that the Itinerator, and the database it generated, uniquely positioned the company to serve as a traveler-centric "home base" for travelers.

Given the attractiveness of the travel market, the TripIt team worried about the number of travel startups that would look to copy them in the event that their service took off. Travel was a hyper-competitive industry and while they were pioneering new ground, missteps would be very costly. That said, the only company that was publicly positioning itself similarly to TripIt was Rearden Commerce (www.reardencommerce.com). With AMEX as a principal backer, Rearden Commerce had, however, targeted the managed corporate travel market, selling its service to companies that, in turn, made the service available to employees. Brockway articulated another key difference between the two companies:

> Rearden wants to be the site that not only helps you manage your travel needs, but also books all your travel. They just received $100 million in funding, but in my opinion one location for booking all your travel is not where the world is going—especially for the consumer and small business segments. People always want to shop around, and information from multiple sources will always need to be organized. We are building an information asset which reflects the collected travel experience of the TripIt community. If we do a good job, this is something that nobody else will have. We are the *traveler's agent*, not a *travel agent.*

Discussion Questions

1. What is TripIt? How does it create value?
2. Would you have invested in TripIt if given the chance?
3. How would you grow TripIt today?

Endnotes

i   Michael Cannizzaro et al., "U.S. Online Travel Overview: Seventh Edition," PhoCusWright (November 2007), PhuCusWright, Inc., p. 1.9.

ii   "Travel Agencies and Services," via Hoovers, Inc., www.hoovers.com, accessed August 2008.

iii   Ibid.

iv   "Microsoft Journeys Into Travel Service," *St. Petersburg Times,* July 30, 1996, via Factiva, accessed August 2008.

v   Michael Cannizzaro et al., "U.S. Online Travel Overview: Seventh Edition," PhoCusWright (November 2007), PhuCusWright, Inc., p. 2.10.

vi   Ibid, pp. 1.5, 1.8.

vii   Ibid, p. 3.2.

viii   Ibid, p. 1.1.

ix   Ibid, p. 2.1.

x   Jeffrey Grau, "US Online Travel: Planning and Booking," eMarketer, Inc., August 2008, p. 5.

xi   "Tourism Industry Dominated by Handful of Web sites in Online Searches, According to University of north Texas Study," *Targeted News Service*, July 31, 2008, via Factiva, accessed August 2008.

xii   Ibid.

xiii   Michael Cannizzaro et al., "U.S. Online Travel Overview: Seventh Edition," PhoCusWright (November 2007), PhuCusWright, Inc., p. 2.4.

xiv   "Hotwire, Inc.," via Hoovers, Inc., www.hoovers.com, accessed August 2008.

xv   "Finding Great Travel Deals Gets Even Easier as Hotwire Adds TWA and Hawaiian Airlines," *PR Newswire*, November 30, 2000, via Factiva, accessed August 2008.

xvi   "IAC/InterActiveCorp," via Hoovers, Inc., www.hoovers.com, accessed August 2008.

xvii   http://blog.tripit.com/2007/06/index.html.

xviii   TripIt Adds Event Tickets to Travel Itineraries, June 24, 2008 press release, at http://www.tripit.com/press/releases/20080624, accessed September 4, 2008.

APPENDIX 5.1. Example of a TripIt Itinerary

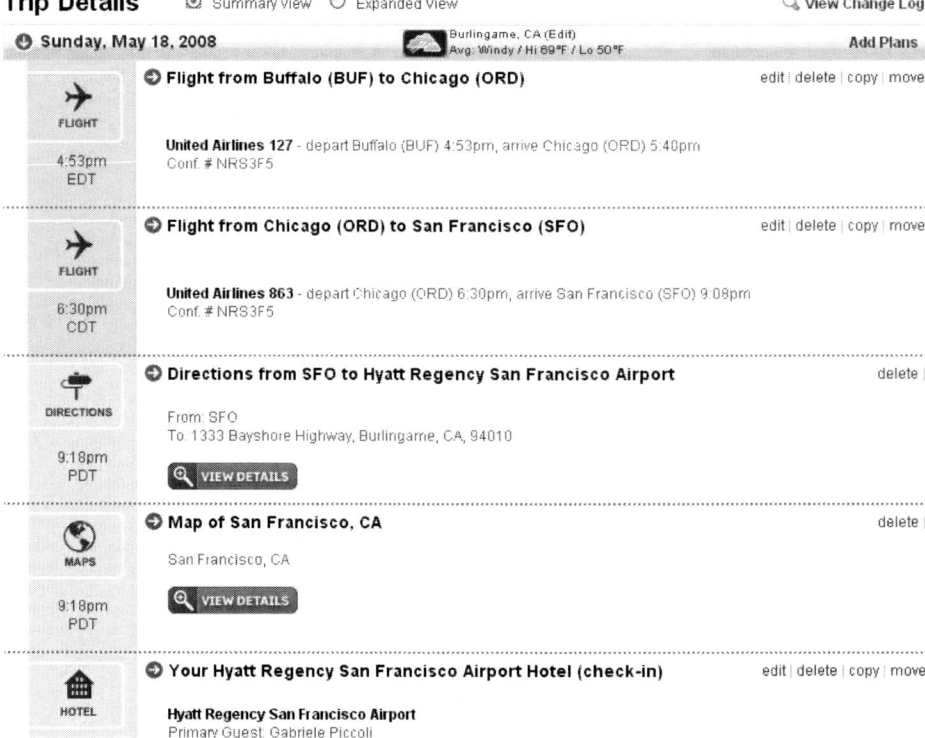

Source: Company documents.

OUTRIGGER HOTELS AND RESORTS

I am involved with every decision that senior management takes. They look to me for an IS slant to it—whether an IT solution can capitalize on opportunities or eliminate threats. They also expect my team to independently develop an IS strategy that will further the business.

—Joe Durocher, SVP & CIO

Every manager must have an IT strategy. You can't delegate to technologists and only worry about your allocated cost or what training your employees need. You must understand how to be master of your own destiny and make IT work best for you. Too many managers still don't get that.

—Rob Solomon, SVP Sales & Marketing

Outrigger History[1]

On Black Friday, September 13, 1929, Roy C. Kelley arrived in Hawaii with his wife Estelle. An architect by training, Mr. Kelley joined the firm of C.W. Dickey and was responsible for designing many of Honolulu's landmark buildings, including the main building of the old Halekulani Hotel and the Waikiki Theater on Kalakaua Avenue.

Nine years later Kelley set out on his own and opened his architecture firm, building numerous homes, apartment buildings, and hotels on the island of Oahu. In 1963, Kelley took over the land occupied by the old Outrigger Canoe Club and Outrigger Hotels became a reality with the mission of bringing the dream of a vacation in Paradise within the reach of the middle-class traveler. Included in the agreement were leases on three Waikiki lots that later became the Outrigger East, Outrigger West, and Coral Reef hotels. The Outrigger Waikiki Hotel was built on the site of the old canoe club, arguably the prime spot on Waikiki beach, in 1967. Throughout the next two decades, Outrigger

Hotels Hawaii, as the company was named, continued its expansion in Waikiki. When in the seventies the zoning authority put a cap on new construction in Waikiki, Outrigger began to expand through acquisition rather than construction, ultimately becoming the largest chain in the State of Hawaii with over 7,000 rooms and a total of 15 properties concentrated in Waikiki (see Exhibit 6.1). Thanks to its clustered configuration, Outrigger Hotels Hawaii was able to maintain a centralized management structure fitting Mr. Kelley's "management by walking around" style.

In 1989, Outrigger Hotels Hawaii, now under the leadership of Roy Kelley's son, Dr. Richard Kelley, took over management of The Royal Waikoloan Hotel on the Big Island of Hawaii. When hurricane Iniki, heading for Waikiki in 1992, barely missed Honolulu and ravaged the island of Kauai, it provided further impetus for Outrigger's geographical diversification strategy to and beyond neighboring islands. The firm, now expanding into management agreements with third-party owners, added properties on Maui and Kauai and ultimately grew to a total of 26 locations in the Hawaiian Islands (see Exhibit 6.2).

In 1996 the firm made its first international foray, opening the Outrigger Marshall Island Resort on Majuro Atoll in the Republic of the Marshall Islands. Through partnerships, joint ventures, acquisitions, and new developments the firm continued to grow internationally, adding properties in Guam, Fiji, Tahiti, Australia, and New Zealand (see Exhibit 6.3).

While growing geographically, Outrigger Hotels Hawaii also began to diversify its product portfolio with the addition of condominium resorts beginning in 1990. Because of its geographical and product diversification, in 1995 Outrigger Hotels Hawaii changed its name to Outrigger Hotels and Resorts, and in 1999 re-branded fifteen of its hotels in Waikiki to launch a new hotel brand called OHANA Hotels of Hawaii. Reflecting on the decision, President and CEO David Carey commented: "We had an identity crisis because the market moved up, we upgraded the on-beach properties where

---

1. This case was originally published as: Piccoli, G. "Outrigger Hotels and Resorts: A Case Study," *Communications of the AIS*, (Vol.15 Article 5), 2005, pp. 102–118.

EXHIBIT 6.1. Outrigger Properties in Waikiki

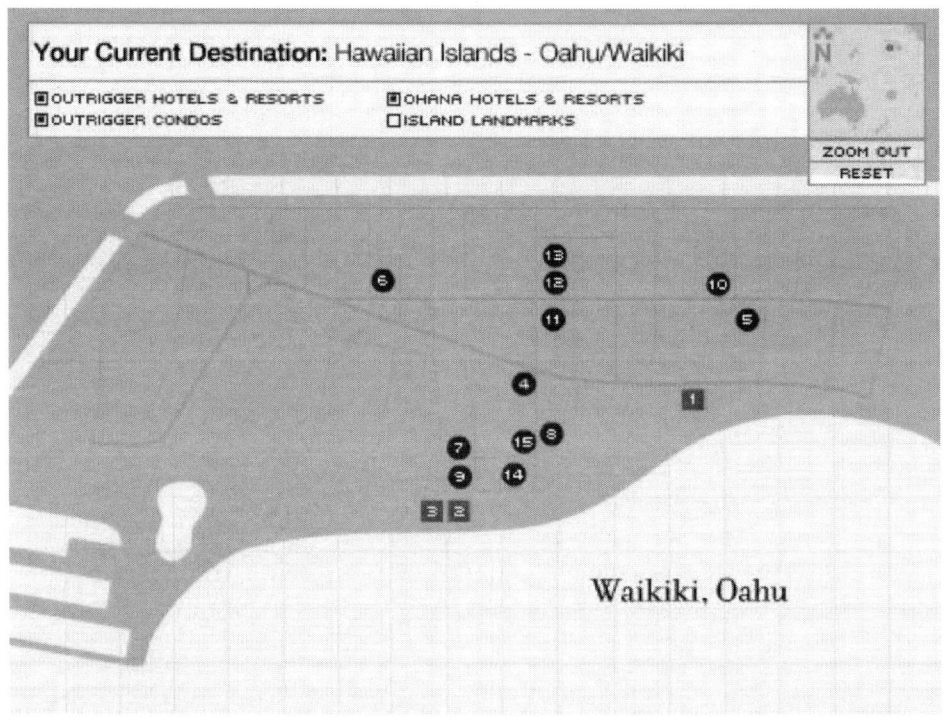

EXHIBIT 6.2. Outrigger Properties in the Hawaiian Islands

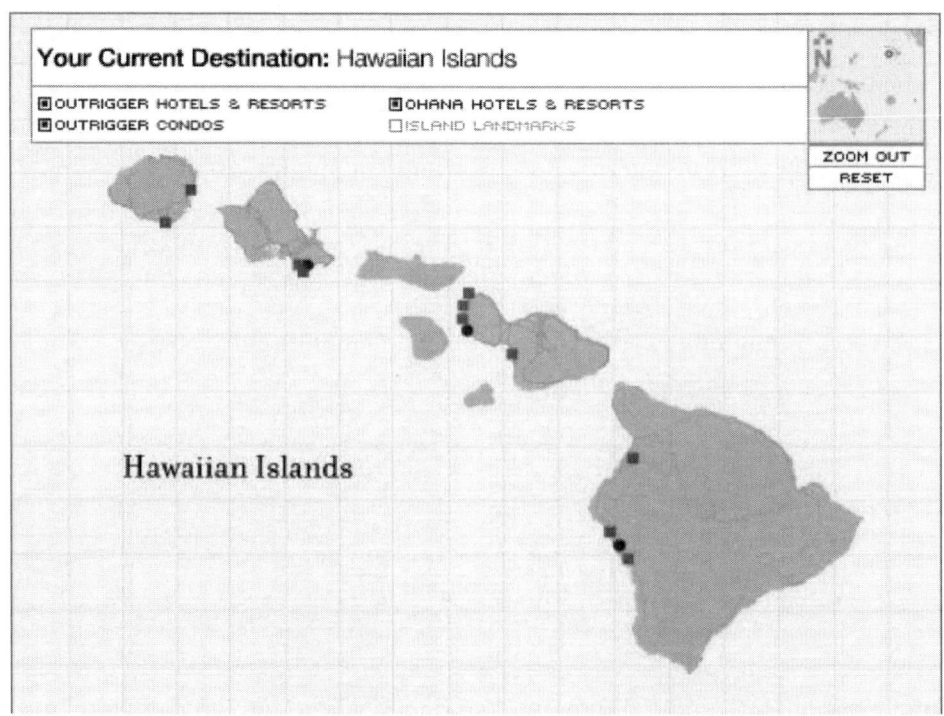

EXHIBIT 6.3. Properties Managed by Outriggers Hotels and Resorts (International)

we had higher demand and bought some nice properties in neighboring islands. But we had huge variation in the portfolio—if you stayed at a budget property vs. a beach front property, you'd be very confused as to what an Outrigger was."

In an effort to bank on the name awareness that the Outrigger brand had developed with consumers, the on-beach properties became upscale full-service hotels under the Outrigger brand. The condos, also typically on-beach upscale locations, maintained the Outrigger brand. Conversely, the OHANA brand was positioned to cater to the budget traveler looking for value on off-beach properties. Perry Sorenson, COO, explained the OHANA value proposition: "OHANA hotels are something between a Holiday Inn and a Hampton Inn. No expectation of restaurants, but expectations that you have a friendly staff, that the room is going to be clean, and you will be taken care of. Not a lot of extras, but good value."

Condominiums represented an increasingly important share of the total portfolio of properties (see Exhibit 6.4), even though the firm had sort of stumbled upon the opportunity condominiums offered. Condominiums appealed to the independent traveler who would do much research and planning on his own.

Condominiums were also very complex, non-standard products that travel agents and wholesalers found hard to sell. As Sorenson explained: "The addition of condominium properties was a customer driven initiative. We kept receiving inquiries about condominium vacations and had to direct customers to competitors who also ran hotels. That did not make any sense."

As the firm learned over time, condominiums were very different than traditional hotel and resort operations. While management agreements with condominiums varied substantially, unit owners typically had the option to join a pool of units that Outrigger was responsible for marketing and managing. Owners typically received 55% of the gross income the units generated and Outrigger funded its operations with the remainder. Beyond labor costs, the primary expenses included the costs of marketing and selling the properties, front desk and housekeeping operations, and in-unit maintenance. Maintenance of the common areas, defined as anything from the unit's inside wall paint outward, was the responsibility of the AOAO (the owners association) and was funded through annual dues. This state of affairs was simpler in the Australian condominiums—referred to as strata title properties. There, the management company had to buy and control the lobby area, and the contracts were generally 25 years in length and required standardization of revenue splits. This approach created simplicity and clarity that made it more efficient for the management company to operate.

Because condos were rarely built as business ventures, but rather were designed as primary or vacation homes for the tenants, they offered little office or staging space for management companies to operate in. They also lacked many of the typical hotel services and departments such as food and beverage, room service, laundry, and daily maid service. Working with a relatively unsophisticated and widespread ownership base, with some condominiums having almost one owner (i.e., one contract) per unit, presented significant challenges. Jim Hill, Regional Director—Maui, summarized the challenge: "The thing that is hardest to do in condos is to change anything. You'll sit in a board meeting with the association and they'll say no, no, no, when the next property over offers a more appealing layout and better amenities. But that same person will ask you in another meeting why isn't the revenue higher?"

These difficulties notwithstanding, Outrigger found the condo business appealing when it made its first foray into it in the early 1990s, because it provided a means for expansion through management contracts without the need to acquire expensive properties. Condo products varied widely, ranging from studios to two bedroom apartments, and did not have all the services typically associated with a hotel, like room service, on-property restaurants, and retail shops.

Outrigger had grown to a sizable firm, encompassing about 3,600 employees (of which about 230 were at corporate), a portfolio of properties exceeding U.S. $1.4 billion,[2] and approximate revenues of US $45 million.

The Hotels and Resorts Industry

As the new millennium dawned, the global lodging industry was estimated to exceed $295 billion in sales, about 11% of the world's economic output, and employed more than 250 million workers (see Table 6.1

Table 6.1. Performance of Global Hotel Industry

Occupancy	63.5%
Avg. Number of rooms	706
ADR	$91.62
RevPAR	$58.18

Table 6.2. Performance of Hawaii Hotel Market

Occupancy	72.1%
Avg. Number of rooms	706
ADR	$198.41
Revenue*	$78,488

* Amounts per available room

for performance indicators).[3] The leisure travel segment accounted for about 45% of total volume.[4]

With respect to the Hawaiian market, which was Outrigger's traditional stronghold, recent figures showed performance levels above the average of the global industry (see Table 6.2). Being quite isolated from any large population pool, Hawaii was a classic destination market with an exclusive fly-in customer base. The major feeders were U.S. westbound traffic and Japanese eastbound traffic. These markets were thought to yield very high return rates—estimated by some to be around 50% westbound and over 65% eastbound. This trend made for a very location-savvy customer base. Peculiar to this market was also the trend of multi-island stays, with guests visiting more than one destination during the same trip.

Because the Hawaii and Pacific Rim markets were exclusive destination markets, the use of packages—including air and accommodations—was pervasive. Historically, packages were assembled and sold by wholesalers and tour operators who purchased both air and hotel rooms in bulk and re-marketed them to the traveling public. With the widespread adoption of the Internet, a new type of package was emerging under the leadership of large online travel agencies: dynamic packages. A dynamic package was one that enabled the guest to choose air, hotel, car rental, and even activities, ticket them independently, and then price them out as

2. "Outrigger's President and CEO David Carey Named Hotel Person of the Year by Travel Agent Magazine." (2003, January). Hotel Online Special Report. Retrieved June 1, 2004 from the World Wide Web: http://www.hotel-online.com/News/PR2003_1st/Jan03_DCarey.html.

3. "Hotels and Other Lodging Places." *Encyclopedia of Global Industries*, 3rd ed., 2003. Business and Company Resource Center. Infotrac. http://infotrac.galegroup.com/itweb/nysl_sc_cornl?db=bcrc

4. Worldwide Hotel Industry Study, 2002, Horwarth International.

EXHIBIT 6.4. Rooms Breakdown in Each of the Three Products

Outrigger Resorts

Outrigger Waikiki On the Beach	Oahu	525 Rooms
Outrigger Reef On the Beach	Oahu	858 Rooms
Outrigger Guam Resort On Tumon Bay	Guam	600 Rooms
Outrigger Reef Fiji	Fiji	207 Rooms and 47 bures
Te Tiare Beach, An Outrigger Resort	Tahiti	41 Bungalows

OHANA Hotels

OHANA East	Oahu	445 Rooms
OHANA Islander Waikiki	Oahu	283 Rooms
OHANA Reef Lanai	Oahu	110 Rooms
OHANA Waikiki Tower	Oahu	439 Rooms
OHANA Waikiki Village	Oahu	442 Rooms
OHANA Waikiki West	Oahu	663 Rooms
OHANA Reef Towers	Oahu	480 Rooms
OHANA Waikiki Malia	Oahu	327 Rooms
OHANA Waikiki Surf East	Oahu	102 Rooms
OHANA Royal Islander	Oahu	101 Rooms
OHANA Waikiki Surf	Oahu	302 Rooms
OHANA Maile Sky Court	Oahu	596 Rooms
Best Western The Plaza Hotel	Oahu	274 Rooms
Honolulu Airport	Oahu	307 Rooms
OHANA Maui Islander	Maui	360 Rooms
OHANA Keauhou Beach Resort	Hawaii (big Island)	309 Rooms
OHANA Oceanview Guam	Guam	191 Rooms
OHANA bayview Guam	Guam	148 Rooms

Outrigger Condominiums

Outrigger Waikiki Shore	Oahu	25 Apartments
Outrigger Luana Waikiki	Oahu	N/A
Outrigger Palms at Wailea	Maui	89 Apartments
Outrigger Maui Eldorado	Maui	100 Apartments
Outrigger Royal Kahana	Maui	191 Apartments
Outrigger Napili Shores	Maui	101 Apartments
Outrigger Kiahuna Plantation	Kauai	190 Apartments
Outrigger at Lae nani	Kauai	60 Apartments
Outrigger Kanaloa at Kona	Hawaii (big Island)	83 Apartments
Outrigger Royal Sea Cliff	Hawaii (big Island)	61 Apartments
Outrigger Fairway Villas	Hawaii (big Island)	78 Apartments
Outrigger at the Beacon, Queenstown	New Zealand	14 Rooms, 23 Apartments
Outrigger at Clearwater Resort	New Zealand	N/A
Outrigger on the Beach at Salt Kingscliff	New South Wales	N/A
Outrigger Ettalong Beach Resort	New South Wales	N/A
Outrigger Heritage Port Douglas	Australia	15 Rooms, 42 Apartments
Outrigger in the Village Port Douglas	Australia	8 Rooms, 13 Apartments
Outrigger on the Inlet Port Douglas	Australia	10 Rooms, 21 Apartments
Outrigger Beach Club & Spa Palm Cove	Australia	104 Rooms, 195 Suites
Cairns Resort by Outrigger	Australia	127 Rooms
Outrigger 1770 at Agnes Water	Australia	N/A
Outrigger Hervey Bay	Australia	27 Rooms, 139 Suites
Outrigger Mooloolaba International Beach Resort	Australia	201 Apartments
Outrigger Sun City Resort	Australia	266 Apartments
Outrigger Coolangatta Beach Resort	Australia	90 Apartments

a bundle. Dynamic packages were appealing to suppliers because the price of each item was not disclosed, making price comparison difficult and alleviating commoditization fears. They were appealing to perspective travelers because they increased choice and fostered flexibility. Finally, they appealed to online travel agents because they built upon their value proposition—customer choice—and had the potential to improve their margins.

As a mature destination, Hawaii had been entered by many of the larger branded hospitality and resort companies. The largest hospitality firms, such as Marriott International, Hilton Hotels and Resorts, and Starwood, had a significant presence with eight, five, and eleven properties respectively. But the largest operators in Hawaii were geographically- and leisure-focused players such as Outrigger, ASTON Hotels & Resorts Hawaii (with twenty-eight properties), and Marc Resorts Hawaii (with eleven properties).

Outriggers Organization

Outrigger Hotels and Resorts was a management company wholly owned by a holding corporation called Outrigger Enterprises. Reflecting its real estate development roots, Outrigger Enterprises also owned a real estate ownership company called Outrigger Properties (Exhibit 6.5).

Outrigger Properties wrote and managed real estate contracts with third-party owners and supervised the owned assets (accounting for about a third of all properties in the Outrigger portfolio), as well as the development of new properties. The firm also monitored the real estate market for optimal times to invest in available properties or sell assets in the portfolio and raise needed capital. Outrigger Properties managed leasing contracts with the many independent retailers occupying food and beverage outlets—rarely run internally by Outrigger—and shops within the hotels and resorts in its portfolio. Sorenson explained the tradeoffs associated with this decision: "We are the third largest retail landlord in Hawaii, with about 300,000 square feet of retail space, so we have access to the best restaurant operators. Leasing restaurants allows us to focus our energies on hospitality and [the] profitability of the rest of the hotel, but of course you lose some control when you outsource. It takes a hotel mentality to do room service very well for example."

Outrigger Hotels and Resorts, the operating arm of Outrigger Enterprises, was responsible for the writing of new management contracts, as well as overseeing property renovations, and operations of the managed hotels, resorts, and condos. Outrigger Properties generally negotiated a base and a percentage of revenue with tenants; revenues from leased space were assigned to the hosting property's own P&L. Room revenue made up the bulk of each property's revenue, with rental income as low as 5% in hotels with little retail space and as high as 20% in some of the most appealing locations. Other more marginal revenue lines were parking, in-room entertainment, telecommunications, and kids' clubs operations.

Outrigger Hotels and Resorts had historically maintained a highly centralized organizational structure. As the firm grew in size and geographical distribution a more traditional structure emerged, but, reflecting its roots, Outrigger Hotels and Resorts remained consolidated where possible. For example, the two beach-front Outrigger Hotels on Waikiki beach were managed as one. As Chuck Shishido, OHANA Hotels VP of operations and a 33-year veteran of the company, explained: "We have centralized services—accounting, IT, finance, engineering, purchasing, and special projects—that support all the properties on Oahu, as well as indirectly the neighboring islands. There is also one executive housekeeper in charge of all properties. We run the OHANA Hotels like a 4,200 room distributed hotel. It is very efficient."

Since each property in the Outrigger family had its own P&L, these shared services were charged back to them based on room count, revenue, or usage, depending on the service. As the firm expanded internationally it became more decentralized, with resorts in the Pacific Rim working much more like independent operations and organized like traditional resorts. Recognizing the significant advantages offered by its centralized structure, Outrigger was looking at the possibility of better integrating its international resorts. However, distance presented new challenges—1,800 miles separated its southernmost Australian property from its northernmost property alone. Sorenson explained: "We need a reservation solution for Australia, a real-time coordination with a central reservation service. They are operated as individual hotels; the central 800 number today is just switched to the correct hotel. A centralized system would offer tremendous value because we get drive-in business and substantial potential cross-property traffic."

The Outrigger Customers and Competition

Outrigger's original mission was to bring the opportunity for a vacation in paradise within the reach of middle-class families. As the firm began to diversify its portfolio, the profile of its customers and the competition changed as well. The typical Outrigger guest

EXHIBIT 6.5. Organization Chart and Bios of Key Personnel

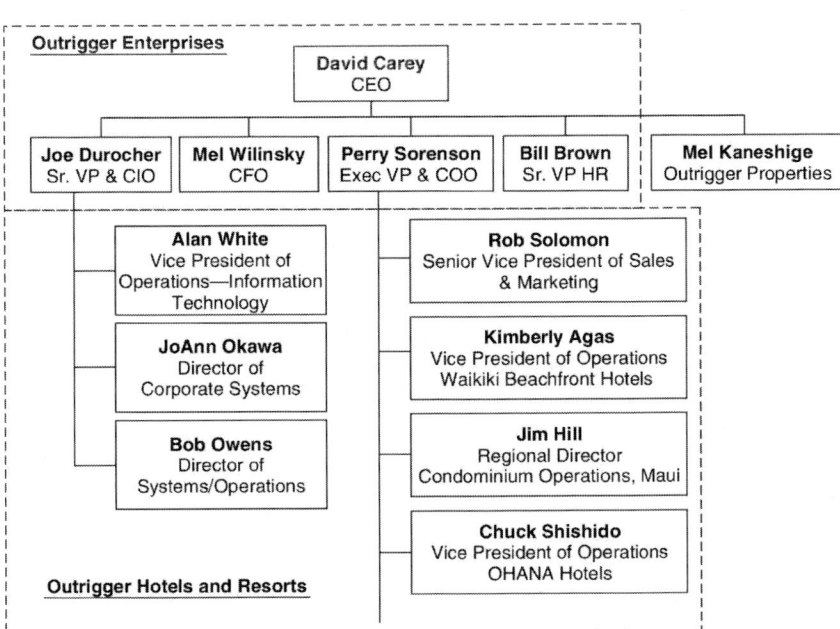

W. David P. Carey III, President and Chief Executive Officer

David Carey joined Outrigger Enterprises, Inc. as executive vice president and general counsel in 1986, and was named president of the company in 1988, and chief executive officer in 1994. After graduation in 1982, Carey moved to Honolulu and was an attorney specializing in corporate and real estate law at Carlsmith Wichman Case Mukai and Ichiki, where Outrigger Hotels was one of his major clients. Carey is a member of numerous business and community organizations, including the Hawaii Tourism Authority, Hawaii Hotel Association, and others. Carey has a B.S. in electrical engineering from Stanford University, a J.D., cum laude, and an M.B.A., with distinction, from the Santa Clara University. He was a member of the Beta Gamma Sigma Honor Society.

Joe Durocher, Senior Vice President and Chief Information Officer

Joe Durocher first joined Outrigger in 1986 as Vice President of Information Systems. During his tenure, he was instrumental in the installation and maintenance of the company's Stellex reservations and front desk computer system. After 10 years with Outrigger, Durocher left the company to join Hilton Hotels Corporation as SVP & CIO, where he was responsible for data processing and related strategies for all of Hilton's non-gaming hotels, amounting to well over 300 properties with over 110,000 rooms worldwide. While with Hilton, Durocher was instrumental in the replacement of Hilton's Hiltron central reservation system with Hilstar, a new state of the art central reservations system. Durocher rejoined Outrigger Enterprises in 2000. Born and raised in Hawaii, Durocher received his B.S. in Electrical Engineering and MBA from the University of Hawaii. He is a Certified Systems Professional (CSP) and Certified Data Processing Professional (CDP). Durocher is also a member of the Beta Gamma Sigma honor society.

Perry Sorenson, Chief Operating Officer

In his position as a chief operating officer Perry Sorenson is responsible for all aspects of hotel operations as well as Outrigger's current expansion across the Pacific. He joined Outrigger as executive vice president in 1991. Sorenson's career spans over 20 years in the hospitality industry. He was previously EVP and COO for Embassy Suites, Inc., the world's largest all-suite hotel chain. Sorenson directed the rapid growth of Embassy Suites operations as it expanded from five to 105 hotels in five years. Prior to joining Embassy Suites, Sorenson was vice president of operations for Holiday Inns Inc., where he was the recipient of the Holiday Inn Corporation Chairman's Award for Service Excellence. He has also held management positions with Radisson Hotel Corp. and Rockresorts, Inc. He is currently a member of the Native Hawaiian Tourism & Hospitality Association and sits on the board of various other community and industry organizations. Sorenson received his BA in psychology and MBA from the University of Utah.

Robert L. Solomon, Senior Vice President, Sales & Marketing

Before joining Outrigger, Solomon spent 15 years with Dollar Rent A Car as senior vice president, with additional responsibilities as vice president, Pacific sales. Solomon's professional career has also included senior management positions in California with various corporations as well as government agencies in California. Solomon is well known within Hawaii's visitor industry, having served on numerous boards and committees, including the research and marketing committees of the Hawaii Visitors & Conventions Bureau and the Oahu Visitors Bureau. He is the immediate past chair of the Marketing Committee for the Oahu Visitors Bureau, and presently chairs the Internet Subcommittee for the Hawaii Visitors and Convention Bureau Advisory Committee. Solomon holds Masters degrees from Princeton and Yale universities in the fields of public and international affairs and Southeast Asia studies.

Alan White, Vice President of Operations-Information Technology

White joined Outrigger Hotels & Resorts in 2001, and is responsible for all data processing for hotel operations. In his time with Outrigger, he has produced numerous new interfaces to the company's proprietary Central Reservations System (CRS) and Property Management System (PMS). White also created electronic interfaces to more than 13 different suppliers, who account for nearly 30 percent of the total reservations for Outrigger and OHANA Hotels.

White has extensive operation experience in hotels ranging from F&B area to the front desk to general management. Prior to joining Outrigger, White worked at Pegasus Solutions, Inc. for over a decade. Born in Paris, France, White was educated at Providence College in Rhode Island, the Universitat Freiburg in Switzerland and George Washington University in Washington, D.C. He did his advanced graduate studies at the Sino-Soviet Institute and the Osteuropa-Institut.

Kimberly Agas, VP Operations, Waikiki Beachfront Division

Agas joined Outrigger in 1984 while attending college and has worked at eight different properties throughout her years with the company. Prior to her tenure at the Outrigger Waikiki, she was hotel manager for the OHANA Village and OHANA Coral Seas hotels. Recently, she was promoted to the newly created position of Vice President-Operations, Waikiki Beachfront Division, and she will assume the duties of general manager of the Outrigger Reef on the Beach.

Agas is a graduate of Liberal Arts program at Leeward Community College and the University of Hawaii at Manoa where she studied Economics. Since joining the company she has been awarded the company's prestigious President's Award six times.

Chuck Shishido, VP Operations, OHANA Hotels & Resorts

Chuck Shishido, CHA joined the company in 1972 as a part-time worker in the housekeeping department of the then Outrigger Reef Towers while pursuing an accounting degree at the University of Hawaii. In 1975, Shishido was promoted to assistant hotel manager at the Outrigger Reef. A year later, he transferred to the Outrigger Reef Towers as hotel manager. For the next thirteen years, Shishido moved between six different Outrigger properties as hotel manager. He was promoted to Group Manager in 1990 and was responsible for four properties in the Lewers Street area. In 1994, he was appointed general manager of the Outrigger Waikiki on the Beach and remained there until he was called upon to assist in the launch of OHANA Hotels & Resorts.

Shishido, holds a Bachelor of Arts degree in accounting from the University of Hawaii and is a member of the Hawaii Hotel & Lodging Association.

Jim Hill, Regional Director, Condominium Operations, Maui.

Jim Hill is responsible for the daily operation of the Outrigger Royal Kahana, in capacity as General Manager, as well as overseeing operations for Outrigger's three other condominium resorts on Maui—the Outrigger Napili Shores, Outrigger Maui Eldorado and the Outrigger Palms at Wailea. Hill, who has been with Outrigger for over 17 years, previously served as General Manager for the Outrigger Kiahuna Plantation located on the island of Kauai.

was often a multigenerational customer with a sense of loyalty to the Outrigger family (about 25% of guests were returning to Outrigger) and an annual income exceeding $75k. Outrigger guests were almost exclusively leisure travelers, with some mixing business and travel (e.g., attending a conference and extending the stay for some leisure time with the family afterwards). This customer base created seasonality, with winter and summer being the high seasons when properties like the Outrigger Waikiki on the Beach reached an ADR of $260 and an overall occupancy around 90%. Group business was limited, with some overflow from the conference center looking for meeting space for break-out events. Solomon profiled Outrigger's customer base: "Our customers are independent-minded and look for an experience that is more regional and attuned to the destination, but still within their comfort zone. They may stay with big brands in their road warrior capacity, but that's not what they are looking for in a tropical destination."

Competing for these customers, Outrigger went head-to-head with such major brands as Marriott International, Hilton Hotels and Resorts, and Starwood Hotels and Resorts—the latter having a big Sheraton presence in Waikiki. These brands enjoyed name recognition, significant brand awareness amongst the traveling public, a flow of customers redeeming points, available capital, and availability of programs for employees such as discounted travel beyond Hawaii and the Pacific region. In response, Outrigger leveraged some of the premier locations in the markets it competed in, like the Outrigger Waikiki on the Beach, strong name recognition and long-term relationships with the travel distribution network, a strategic focus on vacation destinations, a deep local knowledge and community ties, and good employee relations. Kimberly Agas, VP of Operations for Outrigger's Waikiki Beachfront Hotels and a 20-year veteran with the company, explained: "Our employees are trusted to help the guests have a wonderful stay, and have the flexibility to act on their initiative. The teams of employees include our partners in the retail, restaurants and activities. We are concerned with the holistic experience, an all encompassing experience. In much of our unionized competition everyone has a narrow job [description] and outside of that they will refer you to a colleague, out of respect, because of contract restrictions, or because that's how they look at it: 'this is all I have to do.'"

The typical OHANA guest was a value-minded and Hawaii-savvy leisure traveler with income below $100k a year. Typically, OHANA guests had visited Hawaii multiple times, stayed longer than average, and visited more often. Business travel was mainly composed of military and corporations with operations on multiple islands. Groups accounted for less that 10% of OHANA's overall traffic. Shishido explained: "We have about 50% return guests. Your first trip you want a beach front hotel, the atmosphere, the ambiance—you want the full Hawaii experience. When you come more often, you still want the experience, but you look for more value and instead of spending $250-$300 a night for a beachfront you can stay longer off-beach for $70-$80 a night."

With seasonality similar to that of the full service Outrigger Hotels, OHANA Hotels typically achieved an ADR around $66 and approximate occupancy levels of 75% over the year. A number of small regional chains (such as Marc Resorts and Castle Resorts) and many off-beach independent hotels existed in the Waikiki market. But Outrigger's senior management thought that OHANA hotels had no direct competition. Solomon explained: "There is no quality branded competitor for OHANA. Because of the real estate costs and lack of efficiencies, competitors like Holiday Inn, Cendant, and Choice can't build and operate their product at their price point here. There are many independent no-name products."

Pricing for off-beach properties was much harder to manage because of the commodity nature of the hotels not enjoying a premium location, even though wholesalers concerned about their own brand and customer satisfaction were more willing to carry the OHANA brand over independents because Outrigger backed OHANA's quality promise. OHANA was the largest operator in Waikiki and the largest Hawaii owned operator.

Two types of customers were typically staying at the condominiums. On the lower side of the $90k to $160k income brackets were families visiting during school breaks and looking to control expenses and control their vacation experience. They valued the full kitchen—a standard in every unit—and the two bedrooms and two baths. This was substantiated by the fact that condos had four times as many reservations coming from the Internet direct and tended to recover faster after a soft economy. On the upper side of the spectrum were 'newlyweds' and 'nearly dead' couples who liked the privacy and space afforded by a condo. As Hill explained: "On the upper end of the scale people like the convenience to have a full size refrigerator and kitchen amenities but they may never cook. If they want to cook the kitchen is available, but chances are they'll never use it. That's why, against conventional wisdom, the new trend is to put restaurants with more resort services in condominium properties."

While high degrees of variability existed between properties, returning guests to the same property ranged typically between 20% to 40%. With its expanding portfolio, Outrigger believed it enjoyed significant cross-property traffic as well, but it had little hard data on this.

Condominiums enjoyed almost no branded competition. Instead, because of the need to convince individual owners to join the pool of Outrigger managed units, the firm competed with small local management companies and individual owners' beliefs that they could do a better job alone. This idiosyncrasy of condominium operations amounted to having two customers—the unit owners and the guests—who, unaware of the workings of condo operations, were looking for the same level of service they would receive at a resort. On average, a condominium with mostly two bedroom units would achieve ADRs around $175, while properties with mostly studio and one bedroom units would settle around $140.

Outrigger operated a Central Reservation Office (CRO) in Denver, Colorado with anywhere from 40 to 70 reservationists (FTEs), mainly depending on the volume of business. A corporate marketing staff of 12 people, allocated about 6% of revenue, was responsible for managing the brand and for going to market. An additional 2% of revenue was used to fund reservation and other distribution costs. Reservations were centralized for all properties in Hawaii. Outrigger Hotels had a staff of two or three people at each property to follow through (e.g. to reconcile inconsistencies, create rooming lists, and identify VIPs). For the OHANA hotels this was done as a shared service. Beyond Hawaii reservations were only taken at each property.

Outrigger executives believed that distribution was a cornerstone of its success, with about 50% of the business coming from wholesalers (classified as anything that is on a contract basis) who often sold Outrigger products as part of a package. Consumer direct (via voice or the Web), travel agents, government and military, and corporate clients made up the difference. For international properties the source of business percentage from wholesalers was close to 80% and almost all reservations were faxed to the property. But the lines were blurring with the increasing prominence of online travel agents (e.g., Expedia) and the advent of dynamic packages. Solomon explained: "We strive to make distribution as broad as possible, and for each pipeline (voice, Web direct, GDS, fax) we want to make it as efficient and user friendly as possible. The customer is in control; more than half of those who transact in the wholesale channel can pick the hotel."

The firm felt that it had been able to capitalize on the use of technology to increase distribution efficiencies in the face of ever rising labor costs. Conversion rates at the CRO had improved from 20% to 45% to 50% with widespread consumer adoption of the Internet. The firm estimated that as much as 60% of callers had already researched the Outrigger Web site and had made a purchase decision but, as Solomon put it, "had one more question." In an effort to provide support right on the Web site, the firm introduced live chat functionalities and also offered e-mail confirmation for significant savings in labor and postage costs.

Outrigger Strategy

At the heart of Outrigger Hotels and Resorts' strategy was a drive to position its properties in places where people could enjoy a vacation experience leveraging Outriggers' own core competencies. The firm was very careful not to create a cookie cutter approach, but instead to deliver an experience that was respectful of the culture and the special characteristics of the localities in which it operated—a "sense of place" as the firm called it. As Carey put it: "Our business is really about being a 'window' to an experience, not the experience itself. We are the enabler through which people can engage in the leisure experience they desire. We don't try to export Hawaii when we go elsewhere, but we do honor the same values in the places we operate hotels and resorts."

The firm was embarking in a $315M renovation of the heart of Waikiki that required the leveling of five existing OHANA hotels—almost 2,000 rooms—that required significant investment in asset maintenance. In this area the firm planned to create about 500 rooms—a substantial reduction in room count—with a sizeable retail component. The firm's real estate ownership in the area totaled 7.9 contiguous acres and, with its biggest real estate investment being in Waikiki, a renewal of the area had benefits beyond the creation of new hotels and retail space. This bold project limited the firm's ability to expand in the short term, but Outrigger remained committed to growth and expansion once the renovation was completed. Carey explained the rationale for the firm's growth strategy: "Given our key competencies, expanding to Guam, the Pacific, and Australia was a source-customer or distribution-driven growth strategy. It leveraged both markets where the customers knew us because they had experienced our hotels before and [markets] where we had relationships with global distribution channels."

Outrigger's senior management felt that its key competencies resifded in providing hospitality to guests visiting their properties and successfully marketing those properties through leisure distribution channels, which before the widespread adoption of the Internet by consumers had accounted for over 80% of travel to Hawaii and other fly-in leisure destinations. To complement these basic competencies, Outrigger felt it had developed a superior capability to manage in a multicultural environment, including multicultural and multilingual employees and guests.

Outrigger had its roots in the economy segment of the market, but the firm's executives believed that it was not feasible to compete on price alone and had begun to focus on service delivery as well to build customer preference. Aided by a turnover rate in the single digits in the tight Hawaii labor market, and an average of 25 years of employee tenure with the company, it implemented a value-based management system that called for upward evaluation of managers and a focus on helping employees understand the principles behind Outrigger's service delivery strategy. As a testament to the firm's ability to fulfill its employees' needs, Outrigger had managed to be a mostly non-union shop in the heavily unionized Hawaii labor market. Carey summarized the firm's positioning: "We operate properties that have good locations, we have a strong travel distribution network, and our employees really provide hospitality from the heart. That creates a differentiated product making price less important."

Beyond maintenance of the product under capital constraints, at the operational level three dimensions were deemed fundamental for success: providing guests with a rewarding experience and a sense of place, enabling employees to reach their potential and being an integral part of the community. These dimensions were reflected in the firm's Management Incentive Plan (MIP), structured along three dimensions: Operating Cash Flow, guest satisfaction surveys (using reports produced by the independent research firm Leisure Trends), and employee satisfaction.

Beyond these critical success factors within the firm's control, Outrigger was wedded to the success of its destination markets given the proliferation of competing choices for consumers' entertainment budgets. Moreover, the firm was dependent on airlines. As leisure decisions became more and more impulse-driven it became more difficult for travelers to find available seats at suitable times and prices. Carey summarized these challenges: "If Hawaii does well, so do we. I spend a lot of time working with local tourism authorities to improve the appeal of the destinations we operate in.

But airlines can be a bottleneck. We may not have available lift at times when we need it. If the airlines are full or they have decided in their yield model that they are going to only sell their top fares, there is nothing we can do. From purely the hotels' perspective, the best thing for us is an airline price war to Hawaii."

The major carriers, those driving the most traffic into Hawaii and the Pacific region, were under constant financial pressures. The events of September 11th 2001 and the recession that had hit the United States had depressed airline travel and had negatively impacted Outrigger's own financial performance. While the firm had been able to recover from these setbacks and was seeing high occupancies, terrorist threats and alerts remained a significant concern.

Outrigger IT Infrastructure

Joe Durocher, the CIO of Outrigger Enterprises, was hired by David Carey in 1986. Durocher recalled his early days with the firm: "Mr. Roy Kelly was a hands-on manager. He once told me he hated two things: computers and vice presidents. As the VP of IT, I had two strikes against me. Yet, in 1986 I was brought in to overhaul Outrigger's IT infrastructure and we built Stellex—our integrated CRS/PMS. At the time all our properties were in Waikiki, within one square mile of each other."

Stellex, introduced in 1987, was a COBOL application running on a Tandem NonStop platform and a proprietary Enscribe database management system that guaranteed complete redundancy and 24 x 365 uptime. In 1992 Outrigger introduced Stellex 2.0, its first major update to Stellex, which ran on a Sun Microsystems UNIX platform and provided revenue management functionality and reservation center support. Because of its unique need for substantial wholesale interaction, Outrigger engaged Opus to build their revenue management module for Stellex 2.0. Outrigger retained control of the source code and over the years made substantial enhancements, mainly to manage wholesale relationships. The firm felt that its centralized IT infrastructure was a source of competitive advantage. Durocher discussed the trade-offs associated with centralized IT: "Decentralizing IT would decrease our capabilities while increasing overall costs. But centralized IT creates friction at times. When a hotel is sold for example, the IT allocation may increase for other properties."

Stellex provided the anchor to which all other operational systems, including telephone switches, call accounting, and in-room entertainment, connected. All of the properties in the Hawaiian Islands had access to Outrigger's centralized IT systems, served from the

Honolulu-based data center, through the firm's proprietary Wide Area Network (Exhibit 6.6).

Stellex, for example, was accessed using an ASP model by all the properties in the Hawaiian Islands, the firm's Denver-based CRO, and the Portland-based Web servers, greatly simplifying the achievement of single image inventory, disaster recovery, and overall IT management. This enabled the properties to operate with PCs (as few as 12 in a typical 500-room property) and networking equipment. The Point of Sales (POS) systems were not centralized, since Outrigger leased retail and restaurant space. This state of affairs generated some friction at times, as Alan White, VP of Property Technology, explained: "We offer to interface their POS to Stellex and pay for interfaces to automate room charges. But many of those POS are old and can't interface, they must be upgraded first. Restaurants have to write a manual charge voucher and walk it to the front desk for input. It's not a popular or efficient way to do it."

Due to the need for local support, the high telecommunication costs, and the reliability of international networks deemed unacceptable, Outrigger had yet to extend this centralized model to its operations in Australia and the Pacific. The properties in Australia and New Zealand, all condominiums, used a highly specialized PMS particularly well suited for strata title properties and their special tax code requirements. Durocher explained: "None of the properties in Hawaii has a server on property. In the outer regions we have standalone PMS's and on-property reservations. We don't even try to keep Stellex in sync, they just open and close. If a date is getting full, they issue a stop-sell. Reservations that are taken centrally are automatically e-mailed."

Outrigger's IT function comprised a staff of twenty-six full time employees, including four data entry

EXHIBIT 6.6. Property-Level IT Infrastructure (Hawaii Properties)

operators and three developers housed in a separate limited liability company designed to help Outrigger take advantage of tax incentives offered by the state of Hawaii. One corporate IT professional supported the Australian properties' application needs. Hardware support was contracted out to local vendors. The function was organized along user needs rather than traditional departmental lines (e.g., data entry, application development, support). Alan White, VP of Property Technology, led the group in charge of creating and supporting IT solutions for the hotels. JoAnn Okawa, Director of Corporate Systems, led the group in charge of creating and supporting IT solutions for the firm's back-office needs (e.g., general accounting, HR, payroll, purchasing). Bob Owens, Director of System Operations, and his group managed the data center and supported the other two groups. They also performed advisory work for the international properties that had local MIS managers in charge of procuring and managing technology solutions locally. This organization enabled operations personnel to unequivocally ask the Property Technology group for support, while administrative personnel referred to the Corporate Information Service group.

The IT function at Outrigger was designated a cost center. Its operations were funded through allocations to the business units and to each property using four different methods. A charge, based on room count, was assessed for use of property technology. The same mechanism was used to account for use of administrative systems. Group sales software (i.e., Newmarket's Delphi) was charged based on each property's meeting space. Finally, any ad-hoc solution (e.g., the writing of a specialized report) was charged directly to the requesting unit. Traditional metrics to measure success (e.g., on-time and on-budget project delivery) were used, and the IT function had recently introduced service level agreements. Durocher explained the rationale for the decision: "Service level agreements enable the management of expectations, increase accountability, and offer choice to user-managers. If you feel you are paying too much, you can reduce your allocation accepting less service. Or you can request more service and we'll adjust your charge. Of course, we still get some of the 'I want more service but I don't want to pay for it.'"

Beyond maintaining and upgrading Stellex, Outrigger's IT professionals engaged in minimal application development—mainly writing customized reports, and configuring and interfacing off-the-shelf applications. Outrigger had implemented JD Edwards ERP as the cornerstone of its back-office operations in 1990, years before the ERP craze swept the business world.

JD Edwards ran on an IBM AS 400—a very mature and stable platform. The use of outsourcing was limited to the Web site, developed and hosted by a third party in Portland, Oregon. Yet, in order to maintain the integration of direct channels, Stellex served as the Web site's booking engine through an XML interface that Outrigger's IT group used as the proof of concept for the interfaces with wholesalers—a key initiative for Outrigger. Durocher explained: "With many wholesalers we have real-time electronic interfaces—they can check availability and we get their reservations instantaneously. Without the interface, if they create a reservation six or three months out, we don't see it until reporting time, ten days out, when we receive a fax and manually input it. It is virtually impossible to revenue manage like that. Many big brands have great revenue management systems, but don't have real-time wholesaler data. Moreover, we can write wholesale contracts brand-wide."

Outrigger felt that its electronic interfaces afforded it a competitive advantage and preferential treatment from interface-enabled wholesalers, a relationship that proved particularly important during slow periods or a soft economy. Electronic interfaces generated substantial efficiencies, including automatic billing and invoicing without human handling, lowering estimated costs to $0.75 from an estimated $10 for manually handled ones. But not all wholesalers were able or interested in automating reservation processing. This was particularly true for small operations or those for whom Hawaii and the Pacific represented a small percentage of business. Solomon summarized the challenge: "The industry is a mess from a connectivity standpoint. We are fortunate that we have the in-house expertise and the recognition from senior management of how important this is. Even the big companies often don't understand the conditions for success. The dirty little secret of the travel industry is that the fax machine still rules."

White added: "I spend 30–40 hours a week working with wholesalers on interfaces. There are many legacy systems out there; the fax is state of the art. We have made great progress with the more advance wholesalers or those that upgraded recently."

Outrigger found the Open Travel Alliance (OTA) XML standards, specifying common message format and common content, of great help. But being able to pick the right partner, and avoid costly failures, remained the major challenge. While Outrigger felt it had been successful to date, with an estimated 33% of total reservations received electronically through the various channels, it still handled more than half a million faxes a year—about eight hundred a day from its largest wholesaler alone before its recent migration to the electronic interface.

The firm had recently acquired business intelligence software, a data mart, and analytical tools from E.piphany running on a Windows 2000 platform. The data mart held detailed data for three years, enabling analysis down to the individual guest folio. Data were consolidated afterwards, enabling only aggregate analyses. While E.piphany was a recent purchase, Outrigger had been disciplined in collecting data for some time. White explained: "We had 10 years of high quality data from Stellex; we are very rigid about data capture standardization like room category, naming conventions, request codes, [and] what goes where. For example, postal and country codes are mandatory fields. Our employees' long tenure helps, and peer pressure is a great asset—nobody wants to be the one that ruins the value of these reports for all."

The data collected by Stellex, including source of business, stay information, and consumption, were extracted every night by load programs that scrubbed (i.e., cleaned) them, and transferred them to JD Edwards for accounting and E.piphany for analysis. Feeding historical data and forward looking availability and reservation activity, Outrigger had learned to harness the analytical power of E.piphany to do forecasts and generate business intelligence both at the source of business and at guest levels. White elaborated: "We want the marketing data. It is stupid to have a treasure trove like that and not use it. We mine it. We send thank you letters to recurring guests, we can give you history on who visited, how they got here, what in-flight magazine we should hit. We sold a resort once and they figured they would have to hire 3 people to achieve manually what our reports gave them automatically. They even set their rates based on E.piphany forecasts."

The IT group served as custodian of the data, but any user with security clearance had access to E.piphany data though a web interface; the data was used for marketing and operational analysis (e.g., analysis of call patterns to evaluate the appeal of Voice over IP solutions). More challenging was to incorporate the information into daily operations. Outrigger found it hard to justify a frequent guest program—with an average repurchase cycle for returning guests of three years, a once a year purchase was considered very high in resort operations. Speaking about recognition programs, Sorenson explained: "Individual properties have their own customer database and a strong informal recognition system. We haven't been able to justify the investment technologically to do it brand wide. It would

be a natural extension of the recognition we give our return guests, but it must be cost-effective."

Agas added: "If a guest did not tell us he is returning when making the reservation, our current system does not have a database with guest history. Many times we recognize our frequent return guests at the door, or during check in at the front desk, but without any guest history in on current system a new employee may not acknowledge the return guest or their special occasion. We have special programs (e.g., for honeymooners, wedding anniversaries), but we need to know their history to appropriately acknowledge them."

IS Assessment

Outrigger's senior executives found technology to be a great asset to enable communication, as Outrigger's operations spanned 11 time zones, and felt confident that the IT function was enabling the firm to compete effectively. Carey indicated: "We think that our IT capability in the leisure travel space exceeds the major chains and we have an ability to implement things very quickly. [That's] the advantage of being small."

The IT function was thought to be able to operate more efficiently than the competition, often offering the same level of service with one or no property-level IS professionals when the competition needed three to six. Outrigger also felt that its size enabled it to move faster than the competition. Bob Owns, Director of Systems/Operations, explained: "We don't do anything slow here. Major systems in other firms take a year to plan, a year in committees that assign responsibilities, and two or three years to build. A year is a really along time here to develop and implement anything. But we are not a huge company, and capital is a constraint, so we are always challenged to get way ahead of the curve, speculate, and build with a forward thinking mentality. You don't get bored here."

As the firm was expanding aggressively, and had yet to find an integrated solution for its international properties, some questioned the viability of reinvesting in Stellex. Its rapid geographical and product growth notwithstanding, the IS group felt that its legacy technology—specifically its mature ERP, integrated PMS/CRS, and electronic interfaces with distribution partners—was serving the firm well. White explained: "Stellex is 18 years old. So three years ago we developed the business case for PMS and CRS functionalities. We could not find anything better, with one exception—Stellex is a green screen application that needs a windows GUI."

The firm was prompted to re-evaluate the role of Stellex after a failed attempt to migrate to a more modern platform thought to simplify connectivity with the other off-the-shelf computer systems in the portfolio. After testing in two properties over an eight month period the project was aborted, principally blaming the difficulty in effectively managing wholesale relationships and billing manually with the new PMS.

Outrigger engaged in limited formal technology training and relied mainly on on-the-job training when it came to software applications. While this created difficulties for people who were hired from outside the firm, Sorenson explained: "Our people have been working with Stellex so long that they have effective workarounds when necessary, and we have very low employee turnover. If someone new comes in we have many experienced employees to help them; this makes training easier."

As guests became used to ever increasing technology choices and availability both at home and on the road, even resorts focused on the leisure traveler felt the pressure to provide it to guests—whether they used it or not. But for a mid-size company like Outrigger, chasing the technology curve could be dangerous. Agas articulated the challenge: "Our guests say: 'I do wireless at home, why can't I do it here?' As a company we use our buying power to do what's best for the company. But as two beachfront properties with guests paying the highest ADR and expecting more, sometimes we are held back when it gets to technology as we explore what is best for all."

The Future

Outrigger's senior management felt that the firm could leverage its hospitality and marketing expertise, as well as big brand name recognition, by entering into management agreements with third party owners and large brands. While it remained committed to growing and strengthening the Outrigger family of brands, it also had plans to engage in this type of partnership.

Another important trend affecting Outrigger's future strategy was the rapidly changing hospitality distribution landscape and the role of the retail travel agent. Travel agents had historically provided significant amounts of information, counseling, and reassurance to leisure travelers, but more and more consumers were now turning to the Internet for this information. This presented Outrigger with the challenge of populating the new electronic world. The emergence of powerful online agencies (e.g., Expedia, Orbitz) was creating significant opportunities and threats. Carey captured them: "We have grown up with wholesalers; we know how to yield manage the merchant model. The major chains are not yet embracing the capabilities of the internet. They look at Internet bookings through third party providers as a threat. We see it as just another wholesaler; we know how to revenue manage the merchant model. We all must recognize the consumer's desire to shop before they buy. The single web site solution will not work in my opinion."

This was particularly true with wholesalers using electronic interfaces. With these partners, Outrigger was able to open and close rates dynamically. Yet, questions remained as to the long term effects that powerful online intermediaries were having on customer loyalty and brand preference. As some senior managers put it: "Whose customer is it, Expedia's or ours?" For a company with relatively small scale and a niche positioning, the commoditization threat could be quite dangerous. Durocher summarized the challenge: "In the days of Mr. Kelley and Dr. Kelley, Waikiki was running at 98% occupancy annually. Get the reservations in accurately was the main concern. That world has changed, now we compete in mature destinations."

With the increasing competition in its key markets, Outrigger felt that strengthening electronic relationships with distributors, improving its trademark hospitality and customer service, better managing inventory yield, and better integrating its international properties were crucial stepping-stones to the firm's continued success. The right information systems strategy was crucial to enabling these goals.

Discussion Questions

1. What is Outrigger Hotels and Resorts' strategic position? What are its strengths and weaknesses? What are the firm's Critical Success Factors (CSF)?

2. How well are current IS resources serving the needs of Outrigger Hotels and Resorts?

3. What should be, in your opinion, the role of the IS function at Outrigger Hotels and Resorts?

4. Can you articulate both the IS vision and guidelines for the firm?

5. Based on your proposed IS plan for Outrigger Hotels and Resorts, what strategic initiatives would you propose?

UPSCALE MARKETS:
Value Creation in a Mature Industry

As he walked into the office, Blake Ives was already thinking about his next move. As the CEO of Upscale Markets, a seven-store local grocery chain in Dallas, TX, he had been inspired by the recent move by the Korean subsidiary of UK-based grocery giant Tesco, plc. Called Home Plus in Korea, the grocery chain set out to leapfrog the dominant local player, E-mart, to become the largest grocery provider in Korea. However, with a smaller number of stores than its rival, Home Plus had to think creatively. The result was a series of stores located in subways . . . with the peculiarity that the store windows, which looked remarkably similar to the Home Plus store aisles, were in fact virtual (Figure 7.1).[1]

Each virtual item on display had a QR code[2] (Figure 7.2) that, when scanned with a smartphone, would add the item to the individual's shopping basket for delivery at his or her home later that same day. Home Plus claimed that the innovation had been very successful and had allowed the company to become the No. 1 online grocery chain in Korea and to closed the gap with E-mart for No. 1 overall. Reported results were very encouraging with over 10 thousand consumers visiting the virtual stores using their mobile phones.

As he heard the story Ives immediately thought: "The great intuition of Home Plus has been converting idle time (waiting in the subway) to productive time (shopping). Most consumers considered grocery shopping a necessary chore . . . they certainly do not enjoy it. I am sure that Home Plus has created significant value."

Could he pull off a similar feat? Could his grocery chain use online shopping as vehicle to expand without the cost-prohibitive effort of building new stores?

As his mind raced, Ives realized that he needed to walk before he could run. Dallas did not even have a subway system! But it did not have any web-based online grocery store either, "and that's where the opportunity is!" Ives mumbled to himself. Upscale Markets could be the first to offer online grocery shopping and home delivery in its local market, and this move could indeed provide the first mover advantage that Ives was looking for, boosting sales and market share.

Such a bold move had to be thought out thoroughly however. He had to perform a clear analysis of added value to be sure that the initiative would be a success. Luckily, he had a friend in Houston, TX—Larry Cantera—that had enjoyed online grocery shopping for a few years already through a local grocery chain called Rice Epicurean. Ives immediately called him and, after a few minutes catching up, he asked Cantera to describe his experience. Cantera responded:

Since my daughter Julie was born, our lives have become more hectic. With both of us working, grocery shopping became even more of a burden. On most weeks my wife or I were going to the grocery store twice a week. I did one big run on Saturday, when everyone else in the world was in the store. From the time I stepped out the door until I had the groceries home and in the fridge took about two hours. Later in the week we'd be shopping for bread, cold cuts, milk, and whatever we had forgotten.

Last week I spent fifteen minutes completing the on-line order. My wife maybe spends another five minutes going over with me anything special she thinks we need. After six weeks I have pretty much everything we ever order on our master list at Rice Epicurean.

---

1. This case is adapted from: Ives, B. and Piccoli, G. "Rice Epicurean Online Shopping: Decadence or Destiny," *Communications of the AIS* (Volume 9 Article 18), 2002, pp. 314–329.
2. A Quick Response code (abbreviated QR code) is a two-dimensional bar code readable by cameras like those that come standard on smartphones. Reading of a QR code can trigger an action, typically opening of a Web page in the smartphone mobile browser.

BACKGROUND

In South Korea, Tesco Homeplus has a fewer number of stores compared to No.1 company E-mart. Koreans tend to shop in stores near their homes just because it's more convenient and reachable. As a result, No.2 company Tesco Homplus had to overcome the obstacle - a fewer number of stores.

MISSION

Could we become No. 1 without increasing the number of stores?

IDEA

Let the store come to people!

We created virtual stores hoping to blend into people's everyday lives. Our first try was subway stations. Although virtual, the displays were exactly the same as actual stores - from the display to merchandise. Only one thing was different, people use smart phones to shop.

This is how it works.
1. You scan the QR code of product with your phone,
2. The product automatically lands in your online cart.
3. When the online purchase is done,
   it is delivered to your door right after you get home.

RESULT

People can shop at Tesco Homeplus wherever they go, not having to visit the actual store. Moreover, they could change their waiting time to shopping time. After this campaign, online sales increased tremendously. 10,287 consumers visited the online Homeplus mall using smartphones. The number of new registered members rose by 76%, and sales increased 130%. Currently, Homeplus has become No.1 in on-line market and is a very close 2nd offline.

FIGURE 7.1. Home Plus Subway Virtual Stores

FIGURE 7.2. Example of QR Code

This was promising and inspired Ives to continue his research. Understanding the value proposition offered by Rice Epicurean held the key to his own decision making.

Rice Epicurean Background

Rice Epicurean Markets was the self-reported oldest family-owned chain of supermarkets in Houston, Texas. It traced its roots to Rice Boulevard Market, opened in 1937 by William H. Levy, grandfather of the current owners. In 1937, Rice Boulevard was a dirt road in a largely undeveloped future suburb of Houston. Seven decades later, that store, considerably increased in size, sat in the middle of one of the most desirable living areas in Houston. In 1957 a second store was opened. Its first customers included rice farmers living west of Houston; by the time the new millennium rolled around those rice fields had become Houston's prestigious Galleria area. Rice Epicurean's other four stores were located in similarly well-to-do neighborhoods, including one almost across the street from a recently opened giant HEB Central Market. The six stores ranged in size from 20,000 to 42,000 square feet.[3]

Founder William Levy sought to provide quality products and personal service to his customers. With its founding in 1988 the Rice Epicurean chain continued that tradition: "For Rice to now compete with the larger chains, we re-created ourselves in a successful effort to be the best grocery store in town . . . each store operated by Rice Epicurean Markets is still merchandised to be in tune with its particular neighborhood. The charge card system with monthly billing, introduced in 1964, remains in effect. Rice Epicurean Markets prides itself on the growing number of employees who have been

with the chain for 20 years or more and can tell you by name, the customers and their families who have shopped with them for many, many, years."[4]

The stores, while smaller than other Houston chains, sought to maintain a rich inventory of typical grocery store items as well as gourmet products, chef-prepared foods, high-quality bakery products, and, in most stores, full-service meat departments. Home delivery was not new to Rice Epicurean, as Phil Cohen, director of loyalty marketing and customer services, explained: "People don't know this, but we've been delivering groceries for a very long time . . . We have customers who've been faxing in their orders for years. We have our own delivery vans, and we deliver out of each store."[5]

Customers could also join the chain's loyalty card program. The "Experience Card" provided lower prices on promotional items, discounts on products and services from Epicurean's Experience partners around Houston, and, in some instances, rebate coupons for a certain level of purchases.

Online Shopping

In the summer of 2002, Rice Epicurean announced, primarily through in-store promotions, its new Home Runs online shopping program and, Ives explained: "It has continually operated until today the same fashion, even though they have recently changed the name to RiceDelivers."

RiceDelivers had two online shopping options. One, priced at $9.99, was home delivery of orders above $100. This was available from individual stores to customers in designated zip codes. The second option was in-store pick-up. This $5.99 option was available to any customer who could reach the store. Orders could be placed from Rice Epicurean's Web page seven days a week, twenty-four hours a day. They could be picked up or delivered in one-hour time slots as selected by the customer; pickup was available from 9 A.M. until 7 P.M. seven days a week and home delivery from noon until 6 P.M. Monday through Friday.

Customers wishing to try out online shopping were directed by a brochure to go to the Rice Epicurean home page and click on "RiceDelivers.com." A Web page identified the four stores that were participating in the program as well as the zip code areas each store

3. This section draws on material from the History page (http://www.riceepicurean.com/about_rice/about_home.html) of the Rice Epicurean Web site.

4. http://www.riceepicurean.com/about_rice/about_home.html.

5. DeMers, J. (May 20, 2002). "Online Groceries Give It Another Try," *Houston Chronicle*, http://www.mywebgrocer.com/news_05–23–02_HoustonChronicle.htm.

provided home delivery to. Once a store was selected, the customer was automatically redirected to the Rice Epicurean virtual store run for them by a third-party application service provider, MyWebGrocer.[6]

Once at the MyWebGrocer (MWG) site, a new customer first set up an account by providing her e-mail address, a password, and, if she were a member, her Experience Card number. After registering, the customer could begin to shop. Items could be selected from the Groceries, Health & Beauty, and Home Supplies links in an index panel extending down the left quarter of the screen (Figure 7.3). A customer selecting the Grocery option, for instance, would then be shown a list of grocery categories (e.g., baby store, bakery brands, dairy, deli). Clicking on "Produce" would then reveal subcategories for Fresh Fruit, Fresh Vegetables, Organics, and so on. A subsequent click on "Fresh Fruit" would reveal a list of fruit (apples, bananas, berries . . .).

Clicking on one of these then revealed in the middle half of the page an alphabetized list of the products. Each entry included a picture of the product (if one was available), the vendor and name of the product, some descriptive or instructional information, the size or weight of a typical purchase, the unit price, the actual price of the item, the price for non–Experience club members (if applicable), and buttons to add to the shopping cart or to save to a list as well as the possibility to get a richer description of the product. In some cases, a pull-down menu was displayed for specifying the weight of the desired order (e.g., for sliced ham from the deli). The "Details" button revealed the products UPC code and, where available, bigger pictures and further descriptive information.

Having found the product, either by drilling down as described above or by using a search feature, the customer could either add a product to the shopping basket by clicking on the "buy" flag next to a product or instead add it to a shopping list that was then available in the current or subsequent visits. From the master list the customer could add items to the shopping cart, vary the number of items, or remove the item from the master list. Other lists could also be created—for instance, for Thanksgiving dinner or the items necessary for a favorite recipe.

Once the order was completed, the customer would go to checkout, where, if it were her first visit, she would provide billing and delivery information including name, address, phone number, and credit card information. A secure server at MWG then processed this information.

Order Fulfillment

Customer orders were accessible to the store from a password-protected electronic workbench located on a secure MWG server. Once retrieved from the site, the orders, sorted in shelf-sequence order, could either be printed or loaded onto handheld devices.[7] These then guided the pickers in pulling the items from the store shelves. Once picked, the order items would be scanned and the Experience Card and Credit Card info entered. A printed point of sale receipt was then available to accompany the order, as was an exception report providing in preprinted form a six-digit order number, the scheduled time and date of delivery, and the name, address, and phone number of the recipient. There were also blanks for filling in the local details about the order, including the number of bags and their location (e.g., freezer, cooler). Handwritten on this form were any substitutions made by the picker. This latter form was printed from a secure server on the MWG site.

Technology requirements for the store were minimal. In addition to the optional handhelds, stores required an Internet-connected PC for accessing the workbench and for transferring prices, weekly ads, and so on. A small kernel of code was also necessary for interfacing the handhelds to the system.

MyWebGrocer

CEO Rick Tarrant founded MWG in October of 1999. His sister-in-law, a mother with three young children, suggested that if he and his brothers wanted to do something commercial with the Internet, they could build something so that she could shop at her local grocery store without ever having to get out of her SUV.

At the core of Tarrant's business was the information processing engine behind the online shopping experience now available at Rice Epicurean and many other stores throughout the United States. Offering a nonexclusive relationship and operating on a fee per transaction basis, MWG played the role of application service provider for chains that could either not afford or did not wish to develop an online shopping application. A sample store on the MWG site provided prospective retail partners first-hand experience with online shopping. The MWG Web site also explained some of the benefits to prospective shoppers: "The easy-to-use

---

6. http://www.mywebgrocer.com.

---

7. If stores had handheld devices available, these could direct pickers to the appropriate shelf and, by scanning, ensure that the correct product had been picked.

FIGURE 7.3. Aisles in Virtual Store for Rice Epicurean

customer interface will accurately reflect each store's inventory and pricing, including specials and frequent shopper program discounts. The Shopping Solution has been designed to work for multiple stores in different geographic areas, offering different inventory at varying prices. Inventory and price changes are made easier than in traditional brick and mortar stores!"

MWG claimed that the time required to set up a virtual store varied from two weeks to forty-five days.[8] MWG personnel, including an account executive, would "install and setup the Internet Shopping Solution and train store personnel, or fulfillment center management, in the most efficient methods for order fulfillment" (see Sidebar 7.1 for examples of tasks necessary in the implementation). The sheer number of items carried by each store complicated this process.[9]

---

8. Retailers, however, reported that the time required to actually get ready for going online could be considerably longer, particularly for multiple-store operations. Among the issues were working with grocery wholesalers to set up the price list to be transferred to MWG. One retailer estimated it had spent between six months and a year getting the system in place.

9. Typical grocery stores carry anywhere from 35,000 to 50,000 stock keeping units (SKUs), including many such as deli or bakery items or store brands that are store or chain unique. It has been estimated that there may be a total of 700,000 or more unique SKUs across U.S. grocers and that approximately 25 percent are replaced each year. Splinder [2002b] reported that MWG had about 140,000 SKUs in their database thus far.

The Economics of Online Shopping

MWG felt the economics of the scheme were compelling. Among the new costs were labor for picking and delivery, equipment, storage space, and a transaction fee paid to the service supplier. Mike Spindler, former president of MyWebGrocer, had provided an explanation of the breakdown of costs in the early days of online grocery shopping:

> Generally we have found that a picker can pick two, $100 orders each hour from beginning to putting them into the car, if they are picking single orders. If loaded labor costs are $15.60 that means labor runs about $7.80 per order. If they are picking multiple orders simultaneously, then that cost/order decreases significantly.
>
> Most grocers already have ample computing and communication systems in store. Incremental gear would include a handheld picking device, a drive-up call box and when volume warrants a cooler/freezer combination up by the pickup aisle. If delivery is contemplated, a vehicle is necessary.[10]

Upscale Markets could expect to pay a transaction fee of $4.00. The fee was the same for home delivery or in-store pick-up. There was also a small installation fee and whatever money the retailer chose to spend on

---

10. [MyWebGrocer.Com, 2002]

SIDEBAR 7.1. PARTIAL LIST OF STEPS IN GETTING A STORE ONLINE

1. Grocer provides a file of products handled in each store. This includes UPC code, description, size, unit-of-measure, department, and movement over some period of time. MWG matches this against their own library of products, identifies the nonmatches or poor descriptions, ranks them by sales volume, sorts by department, and returns to retailer for better descriptions of the most important items.

2. MWG has a discussion with the grocers IT department about how often prices change, including weekly specials, and arranges to get a feed of information matching what the grocer uses to feed his POS in-store. We begin getting these files, either by e-mail or FTP, as soon as possible. Once set up, this process is automated.

3. In cases where the retailer has a planogram of the store, MWG aligns aisles with products. If they do not have accurate data, MWG asks the store manager to fill out an electronic survey. Pickers can update changes from the handheld.

4. Grocers provide MWG with files of new products and of discontinued products. This too is eventually automated.

5. For new products MWG asks retailers to use a scheme called content exchange to ensure new and revised products descriptions, images, ingredients, sizes are correct and current. Using UPC codes, grocers could check to see if the item was in the MWG database. If not, they, or a third party, could provide a graphic, description, and so on.

6. MWG works with store category managers to make sure descriptions of perishables are kept current.

7. MWG works with operations and merchandising managers to set up rules of engagement for such issues as privacy policy, hours of operation, substitution policy.

8. MWG sets up each store using the above factors and tests it with real orders from employees. Here pickers are taught how to pick efficiently and how to handle customer service issues.

9. MWG provides advice on how the store should market the program.

10. Online shopping at the store is launched.

advertising and promotions.[11] The hand-picking systems cost about $1,250 per machine,[12] and a call box and coolers and freezers at the pickup location could run anywhere from $8,000 to $12,000 per store.

Harvesting the Benefits

According to Spindler, there had historically been compelling benefits to retailers: "The average order is greater than $100 per basket for online shoppers. Even

the top 10% of in-store customers average only about $60 per basket."[13]

Spindler's supposition about increasing market basket size had been reported [MyWebGrocer, 2001] as having been independently verified: "A Bain & Company study looked at very loyal Jewel[14] shoppers who had switched to Peapod (offered, at the time, through Jewel). Those shoppers where spending 45% of their overall replenishment requirements budget at Jewel each week when shopping in store. After the switch to the online purchase/delivery combination offered by Peapod, these same shoppers bought 65% of their weekly requirements through that outlet."

While MyWebGrocer explained the increased per basket revenues by increased purchases of products that

---

11. The installation fee for a single store had historically varied from $2,000 to $2,500 but for chains of forty or more stores the fee could be as little as $250 per store.

12. Handheld-equipped chains, depending on volume, had from one to five handhelds per store, usually with a spare device available at headquarters. The Symbol SPT 1800, a rugged PDA running the Palm operating system, was often used as it was able to sustain up to a four-foot drop to a concrete floor. The devices included bar code scanners and wireless connections that could be configured for local or wide area use.

13. [Spindler, 2002b]

14. Jewel is a grocery chain located in Illinois, Indiana, and Iowa. Peapod was one of the pioneering online grocery shopping enablers.

might previously have been bought elsewhere, Cantera told Ives that he had an alternative explanation.

> We are trying to get by on just one delivery each week. I suppose paying with real money rather than with my time may make us keener to reduce the number of weekly transactions with the store. First, because I didn't want to spend over $1,000 a year on grocery deliveries and second because I wanted to get the maximum benefit out of the $520 that we were proposing to spend. We are also trying to buy things at the grocery store we might have, in the past, bought from the drug or baby store—particularly heavy things like formula or bulky things like diapers.
>
> That means we are freezing more things, looking at alternative storage schemes—say to keep bananas from ripening too fast—and also asking for help from Rice Epicurean. For instance, each week I order a dozen bananas in two bunches. The system allows me to attach a note to any item ordered. In this case I have a standing request to the picker to look for two bunches that are of varying degrees of ripeness.

In addition to greater revenues per existing customer, Spindler felt that retailers would get even greater benefit from new customers attracted by the online option: "Most customers are incremental to the store. In most cases we find that the grocer offering online service will receive the inverse of its normal store market share in incremental customers. In other words if a store has 20% market share in its area, 80% of its online customers have been shopping at other stores. . . . The customer base is small, generally around 1% or less of total store business, but is growing rapidly, as much as doubling every 6–8 months."

This dynamic was probably applicable to Upscale Markets being the pioneering online grocer in the Dallas, TX market. The MWG team had also historically felt that the online format tended to attract shoppers who were "willing to pay a premium for the offered service" and who were "not nearly as likely to switch out items already in their shopping lists for similar items that are 'on deal'."[15] That, as Mike Spindler had explained at the time, translated into higher profits. "Given that 50% of your online customers are new and a labor rate of about $16 per hour (loaded), the average order yields a pre-tax profit of between $8 and $13—better by far than in-store current yield."[16]

Providing exceptional customer service was a major objective for Rice Epicurean and, for Cantera at least, the online shopping appeared to provide a convincing way to deliver on that promise.

> One thing that surprised me was the level of personal service—far more than I ever experienced in any store, including Rice Epicurean. They have called to confirm product switches and I have called them to request changes. For instance, we are on the border, but just outside of the store's delivery area, so I called to ask them to make an exception and deliver to us—which they agreed to do. When the groceries are ordered you get both a Web page and e-mail confirmation of the order and, when they are delivered, are asked to check them off against the receipt.

Some retailers, however, had found this richer interface to offer more problems than opportunities, as John A. Catsimatidis, the chief executive of Red Apple Group, described: "It's a pain in the neck. . . . What is particularly tough . . . is trying to guess a customer's tastes. 'Is it ripe, is it too ripe? What size tomatoes do they want?' I'm not saying that some day online grocery shopping won't become a reality, but not within the next decade" [Pristin, 2002].[17]

MWG's Web site claimed 110 retail grocery chains as partners in North America. The firms also had the opportunity to sell manufacturing programs, including advertising and favored product positioning, on the Web site.

Internet Grocery Shopping had been among the biggest casualties of the dot-com meltdown of 2000–2001. Among the dead and wounded had been Webvan, Kozmos, Streamline, and HomeRuns.Com [Intel, 2002]. Hoovers.Com described the demise of Webvan: "In summer 2001 [Webvan] turned off the lights and quit filling orders. It's reported 2000 sales were about $178 million, but it reported a loss of nearly a half-billion dollars . . . stopped filling orders, shuttered its Web site, and fired its workforce. It later filed for Chapter 11 bankruptcy protection, and in October sold its distribution technology and some warehouse assets" [Hoovers.Com, 2002].

---

15. [MyWebGrocer, 2001]

16. [Spindler, 2002a]

17. Red Apple Group is parent to Gristede's, a New York store using the EasyGrocer.com solution for online shopping [Pristin, 2002].

Another Internet startup, Peapod, was still competing in Chicago, New York, Connecticut, Massachusetts, and Washington, D.C. Founded in 1989, Peapod had initially pulled items from affiliated supermarkets, but the company had more recently turned to centralized distribution from its own warehouses.

Upscale Markets at a Crossroad

Ives asked Cantera if he thought he would still be buying his groceries online in a year or two.

> We have been doing it for almost ten years now and we will likely continue if someone is there to provide the service, though it would be complicated when our nanny is no longer here to receive the delivery. When we buy a house the store pick-up might be attractive if the store is closer or on the way home from work. It's unlikely we will stop because of the expense. Today my wife and I have a fair amount of disposable income, but I wouldn't have been doing this when I was living from paycheck to paycheck.
>
> If someone offered delivery at lower prices, a wider choice of groceries, or some other significant inducement, we might switch. On the other hand, if we find our store carrying products we have a hard time finding, our incentive to stay will increase.

After asking Cantera to kiss his beautiful little girl for him, Ives thanked his friends and set down the receiver and began to formulate his thoughts about online grocery shopping. Would it remain a small niche market for the decadent or would in-store grocery shopping go the way of bank clerks, gas jockeys, and pay telephones, largely pushed aside by more customer convenient or cheaper order fulfillment alternatives? Upscale Markets was very similar to Rice Epicurean in terms of locations, items sold and customer base. Was it the right time for his firm to open an online store? "Time to carry out a formal analysis" Ives told himself as he sat down at his computer.

Discussion Questions

1. What is the value proposition to the customer of Web-based shopping? How does it compare to the other innovations in customer service that Ives mentions at the end of the case?

2. What new capabilities do the following innovations bring to customer service in the grocery industry: Scanner data, Loyalty card data, Web Shopping?

3. What would you do if you were Ives? Should Upscale Markets implement online grocery shopping in the Dallas, TX market? How similar, or different, should it be from the Rice Epicurean initiative in Houston, TX?

4. How sustainable is any competitive advantage for Rice Epicurean? For MyWebGrocer?

References

DeMers, J. (May 20, 2002). "Online Groceries Give It Another Try," Houston Chronicle, http://www.mywebgrocer.com/news_05–23–02_Houston-Chronicle.htm.

Hoovers.Com (September 5, 2002). "Webvan Inc, History," http://www.hoovers.com/premium/profile/boneyard/3/0,5034,59643,00.html (current October 18, 2001).

Rice Epicurean (2002). "Rice Epicurean Markets," http://www.riceepicurean.com (current October 18, 2001).

Intel Corporation (2002). "MyWebGrocer.com: Bagging Customers in a Difficult Sector," Intel Business Computing Case Study, http://www.intel.com/eBusiness/pdf/cs/webgrocer0221.pdf, (current October 18, 2001).

MyWebGrocer (February 2001). "Online Grocery Shopping: Learnings from the Practitioners: Executive Summary," http://www.fmi.org/e_business/webgrocer.html (current October 18, 2001).

MyWebGrocer (June 2002a). "Grocers Find Profitable Growth in the Darndest Places," MyWebGrocer.Com News, http://www.mywebgrocer.com/news_06–14–02_GrocersFindProfitableGrowth.htm (current October 18, 2001).

MyWebGrocer (August 19, 2002b). "Guess What the Fastest Growing Food Channel Is? (Hint: It Isn't Supercenters)," MyWebGrocer News (current October 18, 2001).

Pristin, T. (May 3, 2002). "Ordering Groceries in Aisle 'WWW,'" New York Times.

Spindler, M. (September 10, 2002a). Personal communication.

Spindler, M. (October 18, 2002b). Personal communication.

HGRM: Bringing Back High Touch Hospitality

My father used to say "True hospitality is about knowing how to genuinely welcome your guest, as a guest, not a client." The world has changed, it is more fast-paced and technological, but true hospitality is still about connecting with the guest.

—Paola Fontana

It is normal in our business to invest fifty thousand euros in the renovation of a single room. But most hoteliers don't invest that much in a relationship with thirty thousand guests a year.

—Carlo Fontana

As he was walking into the brainstorming meeting, Carlo Fontana, the General Manager of Hotel Lugano Dante and Hotel Berna, felt that his vision was taking shape. He saw the possibility for using technology in his two hotels to recapture the essence of true hospitality and personal service, in spite of the hypercompetitive nature of the modern hotel industry. He and his team had spent the better part of the last three years perfecting an information system they called Happy Guest Relationship Management (HGRM). The application had become the nervous system of the operation of his two hotels and Fontana believed it could be scaled to serve the needs of other hoteliers. However, many questions remained with respect to the best approach to take his brainchild to market. Was there a need that the application was going to fulfill? Would hoteliers understand how an application like HGRM could help them bring back the true essence of hospitality? Would his team have the resources to deliver on the vision that was beginning to form? The world was in the grip of the most severe economic recession in decades, but Fontana was feeling strangely optimistic about the future.

The Fontanas: A Family of Hoteliers

Carlo Fontana, and his sister Paola who oversaw the financial administration of the two hotels he managed, came from a family of hotel operators. Their father, Roberto, after graduating with a law degree in 1958, put aside his career as a lawyer to take over the family hotel, a 5-room property in Milan, Italy. The decision was precipitated by the untimely death of his own father, who had operated the property during World War II. Once set on a career as a hotelier, he convinced two of his college friends and their families to invest with him and took over the Hotel Berna, at the time a 72 room hotel near the Milan railroad station.

In the 1970s, amidst unrest and turmoil in Italy, Roberto Fontana and his partners decided to diversify abroad. They looked for opportunities to open a hotel in Canada or the United States. When it became apparent that it would be too expensive and difficult to cross the Atlantic they looked to Switzerland. The choice fell on the Lugano Dante, a 35-room three-star hotel built in the eighteen century. They purchased and remodeled the property, re-opening it in 1985 as the only air conditioned four star hotel in Lugano Switzerland. The hotel had 55 rooms but, unheard of at the time, no restaurant. Seeking to attract more business guests and to diversify into the conference and meeting segment, the Fontana's invested in a further expansion in 1996. In 2012 the Hotel Lugano Dante had 87 rooms and a business center able to accommodate over 200 people. The expansion proved a winning one and yearly occupancy percentage climbed to a remarkable 91% in the nineties and over the following decade. While the recent slowdown in the global economy had taken its toll, Fontana believed adding value through service rather than hard discounting and price erosion (see Exhibit 8.1).

Like his father, a lawyer by training, Carlo Fontana accepted the challenge to become a self-taught hotelier at age 23 when his father needed help running the Hotel Lugano Dante. Fontana recalled: "When I got into the industry, in 1990, the business was completely different. Two room types, one rate per room for each of the four seasons, simple breakfasts and no computers. You opened the door and welcomed the guest. It is not so simple anymore."

Under his leadership the two portfolio hotels, both in the four-star segment, had grown in size and

EXHIBIT 8.1. Hotel Lugano Dante and Hotel Berna Historical Performance						
Year	Occupancy Rooms	% Rooms	Bed nights	% Beds	ADR room	RevPAR
2011	24.694	81,51%	36.215	68,43%	CHF 262,29	CHF 232,01
2010	25.259	83,38%	36.644	69,24%	CHF 284,64	CHF 233,40
2009	26.641	87,51%	38.382	75,52%	CHF 279,94	CHF 240,53
2008	27.170	88,93%	39.844	75,08%	CHF 273,52	CHF 238,20
Year	Occupancy Rooms	% Rooms	Bed nights	% Beds	ADR room	RevPAR
2011	38.615	86,72%	63.697	89,49%	128,20 €	111,17 €
2010	34.620	77,75%	55.424	77,87%	123,08 €	95,69 €
2009	35.372	79,43%	56.497	79,38%	120,67 €	95,86 €
2008	38.649	84,91%	60.816	85,45%	124,43 €	105,37 €

Year	TripAdvisor		Booking.com		Expedia	
2011	96.6%	180	93.1%	200	NA	8
2010	96.2%	191	92%	166	NA	10
2009	94.3%	99	NA	21	NA	8
Year	TripAdvisor		Booking.com		Expedia	
2011	90.8%	645	88.4%	1021	89.9%	127
2010	87.9%	311	84.7%	800	91.4%	127
2009	88.5%	166	84%	307	92%	1-3

Source: Company documents.

performance. The Hotel Berna was a 120 room hotel near Milan's Central Railways Station in Italy, and the Hotel Lugano Dante, held the most centrally located 87 rooms in Lugano Switzerland facing Cioccaro Square and historic downtown (see Exhibit 8.2).

By 2012, competition had intensified in both markets. While Lugano had historically been the "Caribbean of Switzerland" as the first sun of the season would come to Lugano, globalization and the entry of low cost airlines made it easy for people to visit the top European destinations thus increasing dramatically Lugano's competition for leisure travelers. Sabrina Dandrea, the Revenue Manager, framed an additional challenge in the home market: "Our competition here in Lugano is mainly five-star hotels. The other four-star properties seem to compete mainly on price, with aggressive last-minute discounting that, we believe, is the antithesis of any sensible revenue management approach. We differentiate through service and our returning customers appreciate that. But it is hard to convey our difference to perspective guests."

The challenges of a changing hotel industry were even more significant for the Hotel Berna given that Milan faced both oversupply and commoditization. The Hotel Berna was strategically located for leisure travelers near the Central Railway Station, which was the

hub for trains and also the underground and the shuttle busses that connected Milan to its three airports. While perfectly located for leisure travelers, the Hotel Berna was surrounded by many similar properties and it drew 92% of its reservations from online channels. Fontana commented: "Berna faces competition from four- and five-star hotels in the railroad station area. There are 13 hotels on our same street, 5 of them are four-star like us. There are another fifty within five hundred meters. They are all different: some are new, some are old, some have great service, some do not. But it is hard to convey how different you are to a transient guest who finds you on Booking.com or Expedia."

The Modern Guest and the Need for Personalization

The hospitality business, as its name implied, had always been about creating a welcoming environment for busy travelers. However, what it meant to provide hospitality had dramatically changed as hotels catered to increasingly tech-savvy, time-starved, impatient, global travelers. These tech-savvy customers had embraced the Internet and were increasingly shopping online. PhocusWright, one of the leading research and advisory firms to the hospitality industry, found that modern travelers shopped on multiple channels prior

EXHIBIT 8.2. Hotel Lugano Dante and Hotel Berna Fact Sheets

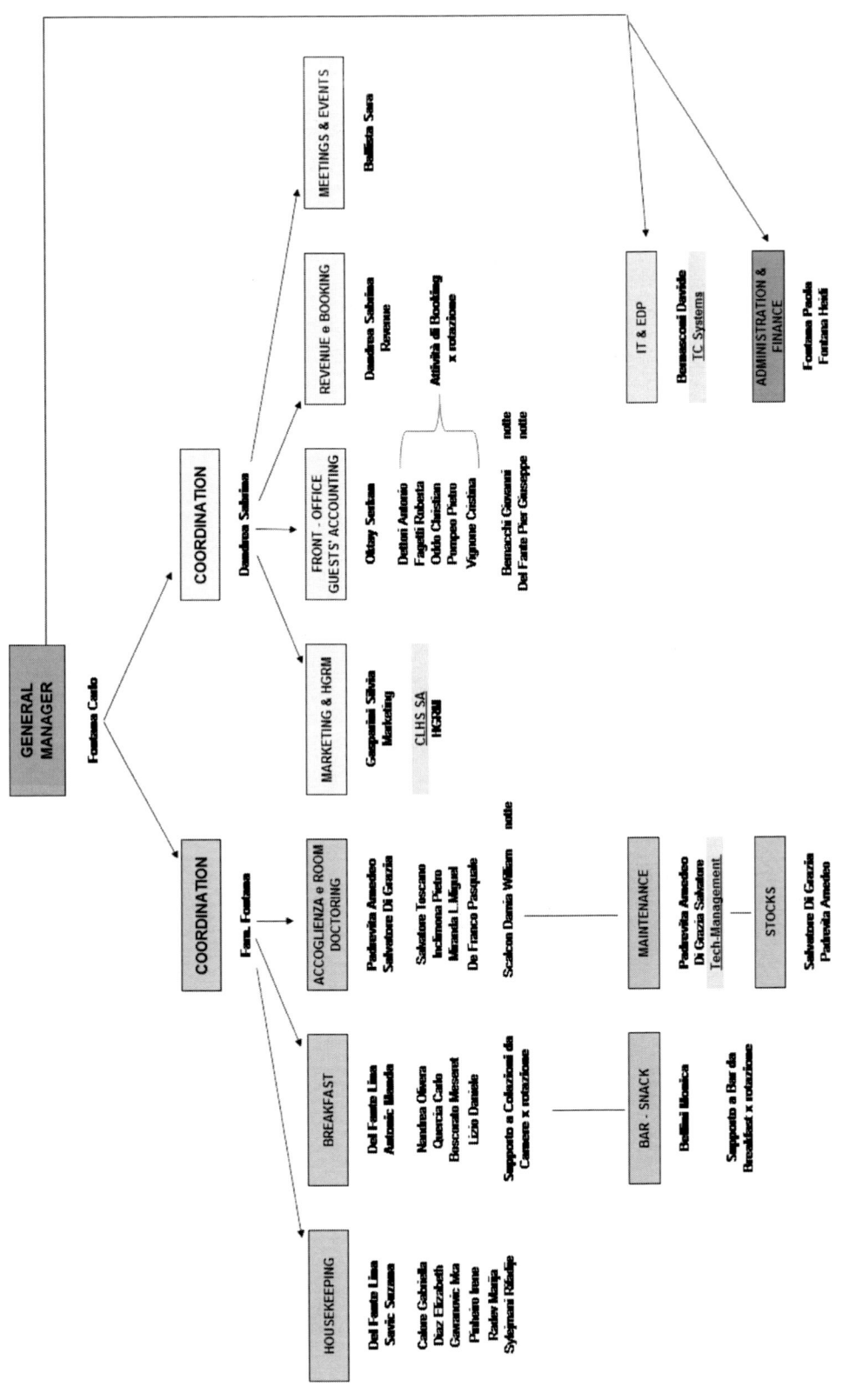

EXHIBIT 8.2. Hotel Lugano Dante and Hotel Berna Fact Sheets (continued)

	Hotel Lugano Dante Center	Hotel Berna
Location	Lugano, Switzerland	Milan, Italy
Rooms	87	122
Stars	4	4 (main building) / 3 (addition)
Facilities	Smoke free facility	Smoke free facility
	Shuttle bus	Shuttle bus
	baby-sitting service	laundry and ironing service
	spa	conference center
	currency exchange	business center
	laundry and ironing service	free Wi-Fi
	conference center	parking garage
	business center	bar
	free Wi-Fi	international newspapers
	parking garage	
	bar	
	international newspapers	
Guest Mix	Business 40%	Business 60%
	Leisure 60%	Leisure 40%
Trip advisor ranking	1st of 63 in Lugano	6th of 441 in Milan
Total Reviews	773	2341
Competitive set	Hotel Villa Sassa Grando Hotel Eden Hotel Splendide Hotel International au Lac Hotel Federale Hotel Lido Seegarten	Starhotels Ritz Starhotels Echo Andreola Central Hotel Michelangelo Hotel Starhotels Anderson

Source: Company documents.

---

to booking, with over seven in ten reporting that they found online reviews from sites such as TripAdvisor useful in deciding where to stay.[18] For the average European hotels this activity amounted to 27% of rooms being sold online.[19] While the Internet had been blamed for the increasing commoditization of the hotel product,[20] many believed that the Internet had merely made information more widely available to all. Greater access to information made it increasingly difficult for

hotels that provided undifferentiated products (i.e., travel commodities), to sustain premium prices. Rather than rely on the advice of traditional travel agents or hotel brochures, the modern traveler was increasingly self-reliant and seeking independent advice. The leading provider of such independent advice, TripAdvisor, received over 69 million unique visitors per month.[21] These trends were accelerating with the widespread adoption of smartphones and tablets. Mobile internet-connected devices enabled information access during the trip—rather than limiting access to before and after the voyage as was typical with traditional computers. PhocusWright reported that American travelers, typically on the forefront of technology use, already engaged in local activity search (62%), travel product research (43%), local activity purchase/reservation

18. PhoCusWright (2011) Consumer Travel Report, Second Edition

19. PhocusWright (2011) European Online Travel Overview, Seventh Edition

20. Commoditization represents the notion that hotels offer undifferentiated products and that the average consumer is unable to discern the difference between properties in the same segment (e.g., all four-star properties in a certain area are equivalent). When commoditization takes place, pressure on margins increases as hotel operators find themselves competing on price.

21. Company data (http://www.tripadvisor.com/pages/about_us.html)

(31%) and travel product purchase/reservation (23%) using mobile devices during a trip.[22]

For hotel operators these trends translated into a shortening of the booking window[23] that made it more difficult to plan operations and manage revenue and price optimization. Customer Relationship Management (CRM) had been proposed as a solution to the increasing commoditization of hotel services since the early 1990s, but it had generally met with uneven results. The main limitation of off-the-shelf CRM solutions was that implementation was complicated in such a people-intensive business as hospitality. The CRM implementation problems were often different in chain versus independent operations. In large chains, where scale and the existence of tightly controlled procedures created an appropriate environment for the successful implementation of software applications, CRM implementation was complicated by the need for significant personalization for each and every guest. Conversely, in boutique hotels where the unique operating environment and the hands on presence of owner/operators enabled personalization, the lack of scale posed a problem. As a consequence CRM packaged software providers found the hospitality industry to be a difficult sales environment despite the recognition by all that the need for customer relationship management solutions was a high priority.

Envisioning the HGRM Systems

The need for an information system that would help the hotels under his management to better structure their relationship with customers became increasingly clear to Carlo Fontana over the years as he tried to counter the increasing commoditization of the hotel product. In Milan, for example, the Berna hotel paid as much commission to Booking.Com as it paid in rent to the building owner. As Fontana put it with a nervous chuckle: "In Milan we have two owners." Constantly reading and seeking ways to improve his firm's operations, Fontana was inspired by the experience of Wyndham ByRequest (HBS Case # 803092). Learning about the initiative confirmed his hunch that a four-star hotel could, with the help of technology, provide a five-star level of attention to its guests. It was at this point that the input from an eclectic mix of friends and co-workers (see Exhibit 8.3) provided the catalyst for a workable design for a

custom-built Hotel and Guest Room Management (HGRM) system. Riccardo Capellini, the architect and developer of HGRM, recalled his first conversation with Fontana: "I was working for the marketing firm in charge of the Lugano Dante website and Carlo came to me. He said he needed to reduce the main direct cost for his hotel staffing, while knowing that staff was the key to crafting great customer experiences. He asked me if information technology could help him create more time for his staff to invest in quality interactions with guests."

Prior to starting to build his own IT application, Carlo Fontana and his friends had evaluated other available options, which spanned from general CRM solutions, such as SugarCRM or RightNow (an Oracle Corp. product), to specialized CRM applications designed for the hospitality industry, such as Amateo or Serenata. The first kind generally focused on large organizations and Fontana believed they represented significant overkill for the relatively small operations at Lugano Dante and Berna Hotels. The latter did not provide a scalable solution that would encompass the vision Fontana and his team were gradually formulating. For example, while the guest history and sales components of the available hospitality applications were fairly well developed, none allowed for building a personalized webpage for each individual guest. After two years of research Fontana decided it would be easier to develop his own CRM system in house. Capellini had since retired and offered to help with the development on a consulting basis. Fontana recalled: "In late 2007 I phoned Riccardo Capellini and asked him how feasible it would be to create a personal web page for every customer to whom we send a confirmation so that the guest could tell us their room preferences. He called me back after 5 minutes and said: 'I think we can do it.'"

Design had formally begun. While Fontana tried to include the hotel employees early on, articulating and conveying the vision proved quite difficult. Reservation and front desk would be the first operations impacted. Serkan Oktay, Front Office Manager, recalled the first meeting about the new HGRM system: "We had a four-hour meeting during which Carlo and Riccardo showed workflow diagrams and flowcharts. There were arrows going in all directions and I got lost almost immediately. I remember walking out thinking—I am not sure what I just saw but, whatever it was, it will never work."

From Technology Design to Happy Guests

The HGRM system went live, in its first iteration, at the Hotel Lugano Dante in November 2009 with the

---

22. PhocusWright (2011) Traveler Technology Survey 2011

23. The booking window represents the amount of days in advance of a trip, that the average customer will place a reservation. Booking windows are generally longer for leisure than business travel and for longer than shorter trips.

EXHIBIT 8.3. HGRM Development Team Bios

Carlo Fontana

Graduate with a law degree at the *Università degli studi* in Milan in 1990. After a brief internship at the Michelangelo Hotel in Milan, in the same year he began his career at the Hotel Lugano Dante Center in Lugano, first working as a reception secretary, then as a Front Office manager and director's assistant, until becoming the general manager.

Since 2003 he has also been general Manager at the Hotel Berna in Milan.

From April 2009 until May 2011 he was the President of Hotelleriesuisse Lugano and since 2003 he has been a member of Hotelleriesuisse Ticino. Finally, he is also member of the Provincial hotel-keepers association board of directors (APAM).

Paola Fontana Benea

Graduated with a degree in Economics at the Bocconi University in Milan in 1989. In the following years she specialized in Finance and Control and went through 8 years of experience in M&A and Administrative reorganization.

She joined the company to oversee the remodeling and expansion of Luganp Dante SA and assumed responsibility for administration, human resources, accounting and finance.

Riccardo Capellini

He has been active in the IT industry since 1980, developing software solutions for yearbooks, automatic layout and data management. More recently he conceived and developed the database of the Canton Ticino tourism board (www.ticino.ch) and the database of the Locarno Film Festival along with many other IT projects destinations and cities in the Ticino region. He was the first IT architect of HGRM with Carlo Fontana.

Davide Bernasconi

Began his career as an accountant at the Villa d'Este Hotel where he rose to the IT Director position at age 28. In this position he managed the hotel infrastructure and became a Fidelio Opera expert. Prior to taking the IT directorship at Hotel Lugano Dante Hotel and Berna Hotel three years ago, he was an independent consultant and at lecturer in the Master's program at the University of Rome.

Silvia Gasparini

She serves as CRM & Marketing Manager at the Hotel Lugano Dante, managing all aspects of brand communication and customer relationships as well as overseeing the use of HGRM with the objective of pursuing excellence through personalized service. She holds a Bachelor of Science in Tourism from the IULM University in Milan and a Master in Science and Economics—International Tourism from the University of Italian Switzerland in Lugano.

Alberto Capellini

Currently serves as the software architect and lead developer on the HGRM project and is responsible for software development, version management and deployment procedures. Over the past 15 years, he has gained experience in all stages of the software development life cycle for small- and medium-size projects. Prior to the HGRM project he worked in the university setting and participated in EU-funded innovation and research projects in the areas of Service Oriented Architectures, Business Process Modeling and semantic technologies. He has a background in Computational Physics (Milan University) and Applied Mathematics (TUE, The Netherlands).

Sabrina Dandrea

She graduated in 2002 with a Diploma of Tourism Specialist from the SSAT School of Tourism in Bellinzona, Switzerland. She joined the Hotel Lugano Dante Center soon after where she is in charge of Revenue Manager. In this position she oversees all aspects of distribution of the hotel inventory, negotiations with and monitoring of partners and channels of distribution, as well as the hotel's own website.

Source: Company documents.

---

reservation confirmation module. Through their personal page prospective guests could immediately see all the details of their reservation, so accuracy of all aspects of the reservation became paramount. Silvia Gasparini, who was hired 19 days before the HGRM launch as CRM & Marketing Manager, recalled those days: "In the typical hotel, customers have very limited visibility to their information. So, if we have the wrong room type, number of guests, rate codes they only find out upon check-in—when it is too late. With HGRM you cannot make mistakes from the very beginning of the relationship, so it forced us to ensure that all information was correct from the moment a reservation was made."

While not a design feature that was planned ahead, Fontana believed that the visibility and openness of the relationship with the customer created positive pressure for employees to be precise and attentive to details. As he put it: "When someone inputs a reservation incorrectly, everyone knows almost immediately." One of the key design principles in HGRM was user friendliness and ease of use for everyone using the system. What that meant for a customer, however, was different from what it meant for a booking agent. The HGRM project team discovered and had to cope early on with the fact that some employees were more ready than others to adapt to this level of quality and standardization. The first module that was implemented affected the reservation department. Employees in the department were well versed with technology. However, the application triggered increased levels of communication and attention immediately shifted to the quality of that communication. This was especially difficult since customers came from all over the world and spoke many different languages. One of the earliest insights during the development project was that HGRM would need to define e-mail templates and then make them available in multiple languages.

A more significant challenge emerged when the second major module of HGRM was introduced: housekeeping. Davide Bernasconi, the IT Director of Hotel Lugano Dante and a member of HGRM's development team, described the decision making process during this phase: "Dr. Fontana was focused on customer centricity. I remember he created this huge flow chart with the guest in the center (see Exhibit 8.4). So, we were promising outstanding customer service and the worst possible scenario would be to not deliver on this promise operationally. So we said, let's extend this platform internally . . . from that point system functionality simply exploded."

Standard practice in the hospitality industry was that housekeepers relied on paper to manage their "rooming lists." Once the Hotel Lugano Dante started prompting guests to select preferences and to customize their rooms, it created a substantial increase in overhead, with reams of paper being generated for housekeeping. This approach was further complicated by the dynamic operations typical in most hotels, where unpredictability is high as people reserve and cancel rooms at the last minute, request late check-outs, changes of room, and so on. It became immediately apparent that HGRM would require redesign of the current housekeeping system. Further, since one of the original principles behind the development of HGRM was a drastic reduction in the use of paper, the redesign would also need to reduce—not add—to the paperwork. The commercial launch of the iPad became the foundation of the redesign and the decision was made to invest in the new technology so that each housekeeper could check out an iPad at the beginning of his or her shift (see Exhibit 8.5). Bernasconi recalled: "We were in a learn-as-you-go mode. Housekeepers were very nervous that the iPad would get stolen or would break. There were countless other challenges we faced and decisions we had to make. For example, we had no place to safeguard the iPads at night and recharge them and there was no store catalog where you could go to buy 'hotel iPad furniture.' So we contacted a local carpenter and asked him to custom build a locker for us."

While the idea behind the housekeeping module was to eliminate paper and to streamline the work by replicating on the iPad the work orders for housekeepers, it soon became apparent that the platform created a number of other options to improve both efficiency and

EXHIBIT 8.4. Original Guest Centric Flow Chart (excerpts)

Hotel Lugano Dante – Client Lifecycle

Author: Andrea Realini
Version: 1.4
Date: 14.12.2007

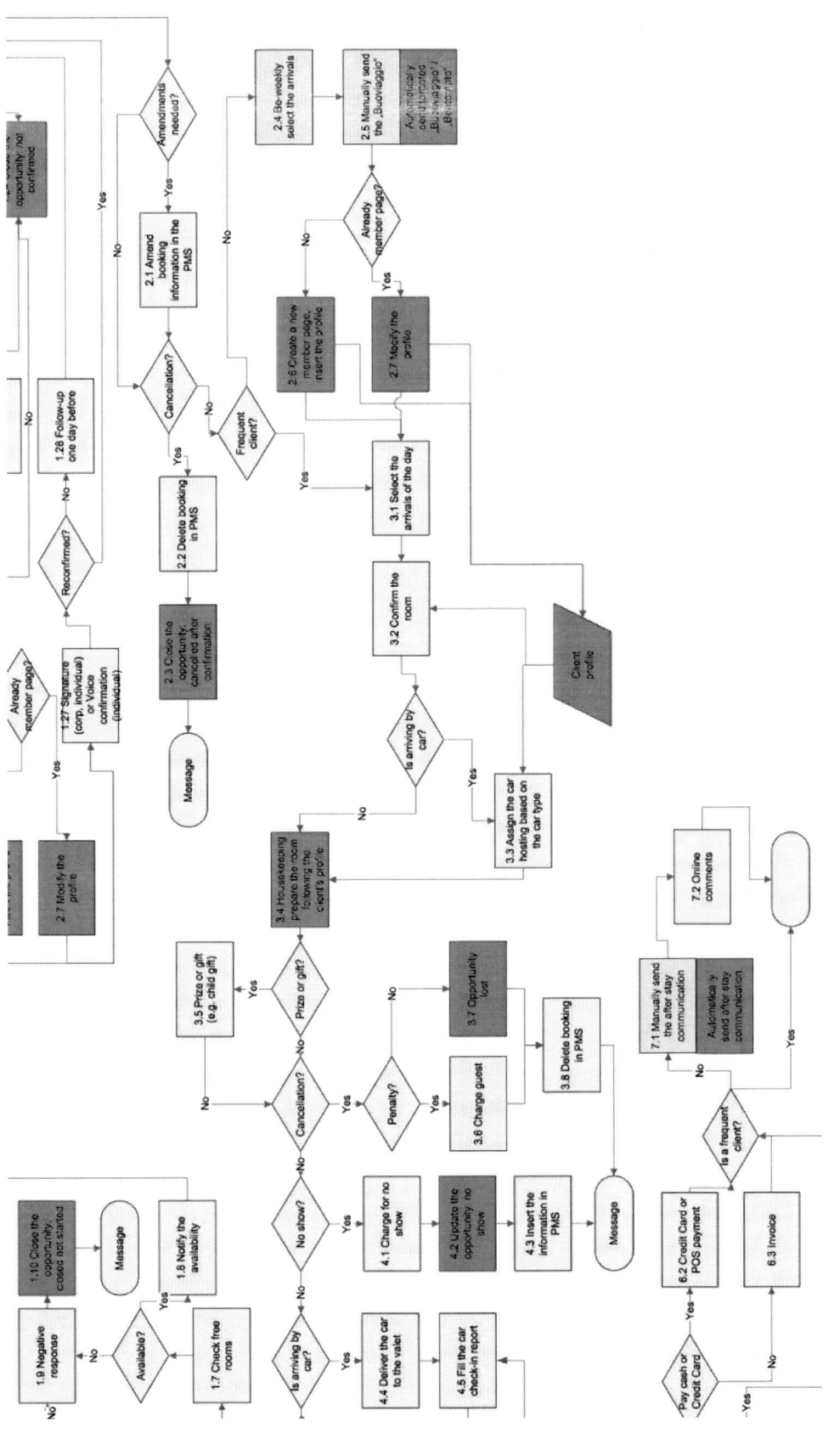

Source: Company documents.

EXHIBIT 8.5. Direct Costs and Development Timeline of the HGRM Project

Planning, design and development (theoretical labor cost)	CHF 396,967
Design and development (external consulting)	CHF 100,383
Graphics and image design	CHF 11,508
Hardware and software purchases	CHF 13,065
Other direct costs	CHF 4,680

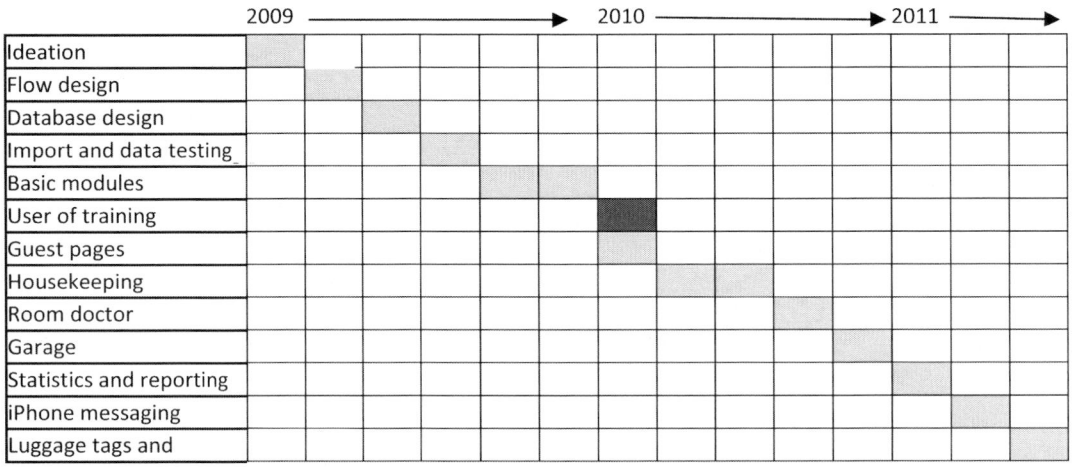

Source: Company data.

service quality. For example, once housekeepers were carrying networked computers (iPad), an internal messaging system would enable communication with the front desk without having to make a call. More mobile staff, like bellmen and maintenance accessed HGRM functionalities through an iPhone. At each step in the implementation, processes needed to be redesigned to fit with the customer-centric vision and the need to streamline work to enable staff to spend more time serving customers better. For example, preventive maintenance no longer required that housekeepers write trouble tickets on a piece of paper, call, or remember to communicate them to maintenance at the end of the shift. Instead, the project team figured out that housekeeping could mark room maintenance requests immediately, through what became known as the "room doctor" module. Once marked in real-time, housekeeping staff could forget about it and maintenance would automatically be alerted on their iPhone and fix the problem immediately without waiting until the end-of-shift. There was initial concern that the use of iPads would slow down housekeepers and they would be unable to complete the assigned 15 rooms per shift. A year after implementation some reported that the system enabled a much more efficient approach to the work, particularly considering the increased personalization of the rooms. Irene Pinheiro, a

housekeeper explained: "I have to add more information when I am in the room. For example, which side of the bed the guest prefers, or other things I notice. But the system saves me time in other areas. When I start the shift I know what I have to put in each room and I prepare ahead of time. If I notice a problem I send a message, and I don't have to remember. Also, we have fewer arguments, like—I told you about that broken lamp, no you didn't—you know."

Perhaps the most revolutionary idea to come from the HGRM initiative was the fact that housekeepers were empowered to be much better customer service agents. While a customer-facing staff position, historically housekeeping suffered from a lack of information, such as which rooms were currently occupied, the name of each guest etc. The project team at the Hotel Lugano Dante sought to change that by providing this information to hotel staff and then required them to greet the guests by name during their many daily chance encounters. This was a radical shift for some employees who were comfortable in the old paradigm. One housekeeper rejected using the iPad system because she did not want to have a relationship with guests and eventually quit. Others had the opposite reaction. Pietro Inclimona, one of the bellhops, stated: "When a guest checks in, either at the garage or in the lobby, the front desk pushes a button. I get a notification on my iPhone, along with the housekeeper on the floor of the guest's assigned room. The message has the name, room number and preferred language of the guest. When I go to park their car I can greet them personally and the housekeepers do the same on the floor. You should see their faces. They are so surprised! But they appreciate it, and we often get better tips."

While lamenting the fact that perhaps some of the human touch was being sacrificed to the efficiency of the electronic messaging system, after one year of using the new system, many staff felt empowered and more competent. They also felt part of the innovation, both as the system grew thanks to their comments and suggestions, as well as through recognition when human resources published e-mails and comments from guests acknowledging their individual efforts. During the implementation process, the project team also realized how a seemingly innocuous system like HGRM, designed to empower and support the staff, could in fact generate substantial stress. Gabriella Calore, one of the housekeepers, recalled learning about the introduction of the housekeeping module: "Dr. Fontana announced we would be getting iPads at the Christmas Party. I told him immediately, tell me how much it cost and I will pay now since I will surely break it because I know nothing about computers. But he told us: 'don't worry; this device will help you save time and give more attention to the guest.'"

Beside the general fear that new technology could produce in the staff, particularly in older employees, HGRM seemingly challenged tradition and threatened people who had become accustomed to a position of power. Bernasconi, who had been in charge of the roll-out and had personally trained each staff member, described the "terror" that some department heads experienced when they learned they would need to use computer to manage their area (e.g, create work shifts, carry out inspections). In addition to concerns about using computers, others were concerned about the shift to a paperless work environment. More subtly, the technology created the perception in people who had come to feel indispensable that if a computer could perform the task and keep track of the information, they would soon become expendable. Patience, empathy and understanding were the tools Bernasconi drew upon to counter these fears. "I was more worried than them," he recalled "but I kept repeating that everything was going to be alight." Reflecting on the two and half year development journey, Carlo Fontana concluded: "If we had thought about the full complexity of the current version of HGRM (see Exhibit 8.6, 7 and 8) at

---

EXHIBIT 8.6. Hotel Lugano Dante IT Infrastructure

Source: Company data.

the beginning, we would never have even started. However, today HGRM has over 190 areas of functionality and it represents the nervous system of our operations. We could not function without it."

The Hotel Lugano Dante served as the beta testing site for the system. Lina Del Fante, the housekeeping manager summed up the experience: "We are constantly improving the system with new functions, as you master a task they roll out the next improvement." With the core set of functionality thoroughly tested, HGRM went live at the Hotel Berna on January 27th 2011, in "big-bang" fashion, with all functionality available at the time of roll-out. Bernasconi led eight hours of formal training, and then camped out at the Berna for a

EXHIBIT 8.7. Architecture and Functionality of HGRM

Source: Company documents.

EXHIBIT 8.8. Sample Functionality and Screen Shots of HGRM Guest Personalized Welcome Booklet

Hotel Lugano Dante

Some useful information to help ensure a pleasant stay with us! For further information contact the Reception Desk.

* WE ARE A 100% SMOKE FREE HOTEL, we offer clean, fresh smelling rooms and public spaces.
* 100% FREE WIFI: excellent WIFI connectivity free of charge for you to use 24 hours a day.
* FREE MINIBAR: the content of your minibar - non alcoholic - is offered to you free of charge.
* BREAKFAST SERVICE: Served every morning from 6:30 am until 11:00 am.
* BAR SERVICE: Bar is open until midnight, every night. Phone 605.
* LAUNDRY & IRONING SERVICE: feel free to ask form more information on washing and/or ironing service and times.
  TURNDOWN SERVICE: service on demand from 6.30p.m. to midnight.
  BABYSITTING SERVICE: conceived for your relax and to offer special moments to your childen. The service is available only on request.
* NETBOOK & PRINTER: on request and upon availability we offer to all our guests a netbook with a modern color printer. To recreate your own office in your room!
* FITNESS CENTER: our more energetic guests can enjoy the admission to our Fitness Center where the best fitness equipment is available for therir use. Also available are aerobics classes, a solarium and Sauna.
* CHECK-OUT: Check- out time is 11 am on the day of departure. We'll be happy to take care of your luggage.
* SHUTTLE BUS SERVICE to Lugano and Malpensa airports (ticket prices vary).

WEATHER FORECAST

Friday 06 April	Saturday 07 April	Sunday 08 April	Monday 09 April	Tuesday 10 April
Min: 9° Max: 16°	Min: 9° Max: 18°	Min: 7° Max: 14°	Min: 8° Max: 13°	Min: 9° Max: 13°

Dear Mr.

Piccoli

At Hotel Lugano Dante, we offer our sincerest welcome and we wish you a pleasant stay with us.

We hope you like your room and that it meets all of your needs.
If there is anything you desire, do not hesitate to ask, we will be happy to assist you immediately.

Thank you for choosing us.

 DOTT. CARLO FONTANA
GENERAL MANAGER

ARRIVAL: **Friday 06 April 2012**
DEPARTURE: **Monday 09 April 2012**
NIGHTS: **1** ADULTS: **2** ROOM NUMBER: **532**

For you: (WiFi) 100% free of charge

Need to use your laptop?
User: **300513** Password: **350**

Need to use one of our Internet workstations in the lobby? Please ask your identity number and PW (valid for 1 hour) at the Reception desk.

Need to print directly from your Apple mobile device or laptop? You may use the printer in the lobby, please ask Reception staff for assistance.

I look after your room with the utmost care an attention.
Please do not hesitate to ask me if there is anything you may need.

Have a pleasant stay!

 Suzana Savic
HOUSEKEEPING

Source: Company documents.

Sample Functionality and Screen Shots of HGRM Room Status Module

Source: Company documents.

Sample Functionality and Screen Shots of HGRM Guest Preferences and Notes Module

Source: Company documents.

week as the new operational system was turned on. The roll-out went surprisingly smooth, as a testament to the staff efforts at the Hotel Lugano Dante in streamlining both the work system and the technology.

Early Results

By 2012, Fontana and his team felt very good about the results obtained to date. They believed that the system had positive effects on both internal operations and on customer relationships. These operating and customer impacts had also begun to influence financial results. Internally there was anecdotal evidence that the system had contributed to staff motivation and attention to details. For example, a number of housekeepers who had never used a compute prior to accessing HGRM with iPads, now carried personal smartphones and owned computers at home. Extrinsic motivation also came from customer attention and curiosity. As Lina Del Fante, the housekeeping manager, put it: "The best thing has been the guests' reaction. They are very impressed when they see us with the iPad." Reservation staff also felt more motivated as they reported that they

were now recognized as the first line of quality assurance, rather than as simple data entry clerks.

With respect to customer encounters, the staff measured success in terms of customer usage (see Exhibit 8.9) and guest commentary (see Exhibit 8.10). They also felt that HGRM supported them in their efforts to provide outstanding service, with anecdotal evidence offered by guest public ratings (see Exhibit 8.11). Monica Bellini, the Lugano Dante's Bartender, stated: "The system extends my own memory. I can see who is staying at the hotel and what they ordered in the past. It makes it easier to prepare for the day." Moreover, by standardizing processes and providing timely information (e.g., automatic message when a guest checked in), many employees felt that HGRM helped them be more professional and provide better service. Fontana summarized HGRM's contribution to financial performance: "We have not yet identified the Key Performance Indicators (KPIs) to measure the impact of the system, however we try to charge a premium price over the competition and we rely on comments from guests, on TripAdvisor or Booking.Com, to support this higher

EXHIBIT 8.9. Historical HGRM Usage Statistics

		Hotel Lugano Dante				Hotel Berna			
Year	Month	Welcome e-mails*	E-mails opened	Quick check-in	Pref.	Welcome e-mails	E-mails opened	Quick check-in	Pref.
2011	April	540	934		82				253
2011	May	652	1097		123				301
2011	June	508	872		126				308
2011	July	538	873		142				288
2011	August	526	955		149				275
2011	September	660	1059		146				236
2011	October	671	1107	134	137	84	107	274	279
2011	November	595	968	123	118	344	380	273	329
2011	December	427	1622	100	98	904	947	251	281
2012	January	481	779	81	90	1323	1354	281	352
2012	February	599	1122	98	124	1316	1399	257	338
2012	March	966	1452	119	147	1428	1531	302	358
2012	April	741	1247	105	116	1371	1479	176	191

*Each welcome e-mail is followed by a reminder three days prior to arrival and a follow-up e-mail after the guest stay

Source: Company data.

price. These comments are impacted by the system and the superior service we can provide . . . we think it's working."

A measure of external validation for the years of hard work came when Fontana and his team had they received 3rd place in the IFIP *Outstanding Industry Contribution Award*. Fontana accepted the award at the ENTER 2012 conference in Helsingborg, Sweden alongside the CEO of KLM, the Dutch national airline. In summer 2012, the Hotel Lugano Dante was also awarded the 2012 Guest Satisfaction Award by its peers, the members of the Swiss Quality Hotels chain with which the Lugano Dante was affiliated. The award was based on an analysis of the online brand reputation of the chain's 82 member hotels and Fontana believed the superior reputation of the Lugano Dante was a direct expression of the level of service that HGRM enabled his staff to provide.

The Future:
Turning an Idea into a Company

Despite the size and reach of the HGRM system, many opportunities for new functionalities existed. For example, from her position as the CRM and Marketing Manager, Gasparini saw the potential for new guest services: "If I know that you will arrive by train, I can alert you about a labor strike. We are also thinking of enabling last minute preferences on the mobile." However, the tension toward new features was balanced by the need to make the system more robust. When the Hotel Berna was scheduled to go online Alberto Capellini had been brought on to help scale the system and to customize it to the needs of the new property. In addition, interest was mounting from other hoteliers. This led the Fontanas to begin to seriously consider the idea of spinning off HGRM as an independent venture. Bernasconi, who would play a key role in the new HGRM business unit described the vision that was forming: "We can provide a solution that is not Microsoft and is not Oracle. It is a work system that was developed by hoteliers for hoteliers. We have experienced the same problems as hoteliers; we lived the same issues they live, every day. We can help you solve them."

At the brainstorming meeting to define what the new venture would look like, the consensus emerged that the work system they had pioneered could be the

EXHIBIT 8.10. Hotel Berna: Historical Monthly Guest Ratings

Month	Service	Cleanliness	Location	Room	Value
Apr-09	94.4	92.1	85.3	82.4	87.3
May-09	95.9	93.4	86.9	81.2	85.6
Jun-09	90.3	94.5	88.9	86.9	89.6
Jul-09	91.2	93.1	91.8	85.4	85.4
Aug-09	95.2	95.2	87.6	85.6	88.3
Sep-09	92.3	94.3	91.2	83.8	88.9
Oct-09	88.3	89.7	87.0	80.2	83.9
Nov-09	91.2	87.8	90.7	82.1	88.2
Dec-09	93.6	92.2	95.9	86.0	91.0
Jan-10	91.0	89.5	93.0	81.6	85.3
Feb-10	91.7	89.8	90.8	80.2	85.2
Mar-10	91.2	93.2	91.2	79.0	83.4
Apr-10	94.6	93.7	93.5	88.1	82.5
May-10	92.9	92.8	88.7	81.0	88.6
Jun-10	94.2	91.4	89.1	84.4	86.3
Jul-10	94.0	91.7	88.7	81.9	87.3
Aug-10	94.2	94.0	88.8	86.6	88.1
Sep-10	92.6	93.0	89.8	83.8	90.0
Oct-10	86.9	89.4	87.3	77.1	83.8
Nov-10	87.0	88.7	89.7	76.5	79.5
Dec-10	94.9	91.2	89.4	80.2	85.8
Jan-11	93.6	94.1	88.1	82.7	89.4
Feb-11	94.5	93.5	90.5	79.3	87.1
Mar-11	94.8	94.4	93.2	82.8	86.3
Apr-11	93.1	93.2	84.6	81.7	85.5
May-11	95.0	94.6	86.0	83.6	90.3
Jun-11	95.0	95.8	90.2	83.7	87.4
Jul-11	95.6	94.0	93.0	87.8	91.3
Aug-11	93.8	93.7	91.5	87.7	91.5
Sep-11	93.4	94.2	91.6	88.5	89.6
Oct-11	96.4	94.4	93.1	88.6	90.3
Nov-11	94.7	93.6	91.8	82.7	88.7
Dec-11	92.0	93.2	91.4	77.4	89.4
Jan-12	93.2	93.2	88.9	85.6	90.0
Feb-12	96.6	92.9	90.7	83.1	92.6
Mar-12	97.1	92.1	90.1	84.3	90.8
Apr-12	94.1	93.7	89.8	83.6	87.2

Ratings are computed from online sources (e.g., TripAdvisor, Booking.com, etc.)

Source: Company data.

EXHIBIT 8.11. Sample of Guest Reviews

Dindi_SE
Basel, Switzerland

Contributor

15 reviews

Reviews in 11 cities

8 helpful votes

"Fantastic, love the details"

 Reviewed 29 April 2012

We were happy with the service of the hotel even before we arrived, as they allow us to choose, through an e-mail sent to us a day before the trip, many elements of our stay, from the kinds of pillows we wanted to what sort of beverages we would appreciate on our minibar. Getting there by car was trickier than what we expected, as our GPS didn't want to collaborate. Thankfully, we contacted them by phone and they directed us perfectly to their garage door. All employers were very friendly and helpful, the sweets at the reception are very appreciated and we also got bags with cookies on check-out, fantastic! The breakfast buffet options were really great (all sorts of cakes, freshly pressed orange juice and hot chocolate made on spot out of Toblerone!). We also appreciated the one page news they make available in several languages (with news that interest persons from that particular language/countries). The location is very good, cannot complain about anything. One of the best hotel experiences I ever had!

Less ▲

camps258
Chicago, Illinois

Reviewer

5 reviews

Reviews in 3 cities

2 helpful votes

"Great location great hotel"

 Reviewed 23 June 2012 NEW

We stayed in this hotel our last night in Italy. We wanted to be within walking distance of the train station so we could take the Malpensa Shuttle the next morning. We had a group of 10 and the hotel was great to work with. I would recommend booking directly with the hotel via their web site. They will email you a few days prior to your arrival asking you how you would like your room prepared, ie temperature of room, extra pillows?, type of beverages inside your mini fridge,etc. their happy hour buffet is unbelievable, as is the breakfast. If you check out before breakfast, no worries, they'll pack you a breakfast to go bag!
The rooms are great. Nice size bathrooms. Free wifi and free use of public computers (printer as well) in lobby.
This hotel is a road warrior's dream.

celinatan68
Singapore, Singapore

2 reviews

Reviews in 2 cities

"Most thoughtful"

 Reviewed 19 June 2012 NEW

Location is very convenient as it's walking distance to the main central station and airport buses. The property makes an effort to ensure that you have a comfortable stay by asking you prior to your arrival on your preferences, eg: pillows, free non-alcoholic drinks in mini bar. We were pleasantly surprised when our free mini-bar was replenished everyday. This is definitely a plus as most hotels of this category do not provide free bottled drinking water, let alone sodas and juices. There are little gestures that they do to personalize your stay before, during and after. Breakfast was by far most extensive amongst the other places we stayed. Rooms were kept clean. Staff were very helpful and friendly. One of the male staff in the restaurant remembered that I had ordered a glass of latte for breakfast the day before and readily gave me another the next day without me requesting for it. That was sweet.
A couple of areas for improvement would be the noise along the corridor in the morning. As the rooms are not very sound proof, staff should be mindful of the level of noise they create, eg: talking too loudly, trolleys etc. The TV sports channel can be improved. There was mainly soccer and no coverage of Roland Garros, despite the fact that 1 of your female Italian tennis player got into the finals.
Overall, Berna has exceeded my expectations in some ways. I would definitely stay there again when I next visit Milan.

Less ▲

lin y
Shanghai, China
1 review

"excellent hotel for kids"

ⓞⓞⓞⓞⓞ Reviewed 30 May 2012

This is the only hotel that send email before hand for us to choose additional facilities that we need for our stay, including kid's shower head, kid's toilet, pillows, blanket etc. Sweet messages and small gift made us feel like home. Our son like the lobby kid's corner very much, enjoy his lego game and free candies.
The staff of reception and restaurant are very helpful and polite. They help me to solve the wifi problem even at midnight. However the printers in the lobby were not working properly, otherwise the stay would be perfect.

Less ▲

Source: www.tripadvisor.com, accessed July 2012.

cornerstone of a strategy for countering the threat of commoditization for boutique hotels. Hoteliers had to re-discover the essence of true hospitality—attention to the guest—and HGRM would help them to do so. The team was also convinced that the software could only be a part of the solution. This was evident when Fontana showed the system to a colleague, the GM of an upscale Hotel in Milan. While amazed by the potential of HGRM, the colleague confessed that he had bigger issues to take care of at the time. "I was there only three hours and I heard people quarreling and fighting in the back-of-the-house." He reasoned HGRM would not work in a hotel with operational or personnel problems. Despite being in the process of formalizing the new venture, Fontana was already in advanced talks with four hotels, two in Milan and two in Florence, seeking to adopt HGRM. Despite all the interest, sustaining growth at this point was no trivial task. Alberto

Capellini, articulated the challenge: "Today we have our own two hotels installed, with two somewhat different versions of the application, configured differently. We have been focused on growing the functionality and we have not systematized our approaches to software development, versioning and control. We can't go to market without doing that."

Despite all the uncertainty and potential difficulties, Fontana and his team felt that HGRM was a unique solution without any competition in the marketplace. As he had found when he sought to purchase a CRM solution in 2007, Fontana felt that the market was very specialized and no other firm offered a comprehensive solution spanning both customer relationships and internal operations. Moreover, as he put it: "HGRM is not software, it is a proven work system developed by hoteliers for hoteliers."

DUETTO: Industry Transformation with Big Data

We are not a revenue management software provider. We are a revenue strategy enabler.
— Patrick Bosworth, CEO and cofounder

We don't have any competition really.
Excel is our competition.
— Marco Benvenuti, Chief Analytics & Product Officer and cofounder

It was June 2010 when Marco Benvenuti and Patrick Bosworth decided to leave the Wynn Resorts in Las Vegas to create their own business, originally called Duetto Consulting. The two founders had a dream of revolutionizing hospitality revenue strategy and management to exploit the impending seismic shift in the industry due to the proliferation of data and digital data streams. Despite the fact that most lodging operations did not have specialized price optimization software, revenue management remained a critical element in their efforts to reclaim control over distribution and pricing (see Exhibit 9.1). Bosworth recalled the original thinking behind the new venture: "I don't know that we had defined the opportunity. Marco believed he could test some of his theories with a 'fancy excel spreadsheet.' We now call it open pricing, but at the time it was a hunch, an idea."[1]

With its product portfolio largely in place, Duetto was seeking a series C round of financing. The money would be earmarked for fuelling fast growth, both nationally and internationally. However, the large online travel agents (OTA) were beginning to take notice of new entrants in the revenue management space. The Priceline Group, the dominant OTA and owner of such properties as Booking.com, Kayak, Agoda and OpenTable, had just announced that it was acquiring

PriceMatch—a European online revenue management software provider. Thus, while working on four hours of sleep a night to run the business while also preparing to raise a further round of financing, the Duetto founders were evaluating their long term options. Should they stay true to the original vision of helping lodging and hospitality operators by offering a superior revenue strategy solution? This would entail focusing on organic growth and independent operations, leading perhaps to an IPO sometime in the future. Or should they seek an early exit selling to an established revenue management vendor or a major OTA with deep pockets?

Industry Background

By many accounts tourism/hospitality was among the largest global industries. The lodging sector, comprising hotels, resorts and casinos, was an important component (see Exhibits 9.2 through 9.6 for industry statistics) After centuries of stability, information technology (IT) had penetrated and transformed the tourism/hospitality industry. In the late 1970s and early 1980s the introduction of Central Reservation Systems (CRS), pioneered by Holiday Inn's HOLIDEX, demonstrated the power of distribution networks, which enabled the efficiencies and superior marketing needed to pursue growth through franchising. An era of consolidation and the emergence of large multinational chains ensued. As franchisors and management companies grew in size, they segmented customer markets and established strong brands in each market tier. A second major IT shock to the industry came in the mid-1990s with the emergence of the Internet. This time however hospitality operators were slow to adopt and new entrants with technology backgrounds and the strong entrepreneurial spirit of the dot-com era entered and grew quickly, capturing a substantial amount of the value created in the industry. The dominant players included Expedia, originally a business unit of technology giant Microsoft, and Priceline, the brainchild of technology entrepreneur Jay Walker. In early 2015, consolidation continued as Expedia purchased Travelocity for

---

1. This case was originally published as: Applegate, Lynda M., Gabriele Piccoli, and Federico Pigni. "Duetto: Industry Transformation with Big Data." *Harvard Business School Case*, 816–028, August 2015. (Revised October 2015.)

EXHIBIT 9.1. Revenue Management Software, 2014

Company	Headquarters	Properties	Managed rooms	Employees	Revenues	Funding received	Founded
SaS IDeAS	Minneapolis, MN	7,000	1,000,000	400	N/A	$3,5M	1989[a]
Rainmaker Group	Alpharetta, GA	155	>150,000	110	28M	$42.8M	1992[b]
EzRMS[1]	Solihull, UK	1,200	N/A	60	N/A	N/A	1999[c]
Price-Match[2]	Paris, FR	1,000	N/A	70	N/A	$10.4	2012[d]

Source: Table developed by casewriters.

Note:

[1] Acquired by Infor in June 2012 for undisclosed amount

[2] Acquired by Priceline for undisclosed amount—speculated $15–20M

[a] Data obtained from Crunchbase (https://www.crunchbase.com/organization/ideas accessed June 2015); IDeAS Corporate Overview brochure—2015 (http://www.ideas.com/files/brochures/corporate-overview/ accessed June 2015); LinkedIn company profile (https://www.linkedin.com/company/ideas-revenue-solutions).

[b] Data obtained from Crunchbase (https://www.crunchbase.com/organization/the-rainmaker-group accessed June 2015), Linkedin company profile (https://www.linkedin.com/company/the-rainmaker-group accessed June 2015), Rainmaker's GuestREV adds reputation module. Casino Journal, October 2014; The Rainmaker Group profile (http://www.inc.com/profile/the-rainmaker-group accessed June 2015).

[c] Data obtained from: Infor's acquisition press release, Company website (http://www.infor.com/company/news/pressroom/pressreleases/EasyRMS/ accessed June 2015).

[d] Data obtained from: Crunchbase (https://www.crunchbase.com/organization/pricematch accessed June 2015), Linkedin company profile, May, K. 2015, Priceline acquires PriceMatch, adds revenue management to hotel tech arsenal, Tnooz.com viewed July 2015 (http://www.tnooz.com/article/priceline-acquires-pricematch-adds-revenue-management-hotel-tech-arsenal/).

$280 million on January 23rd and Orbitz in February 12th for $1.34 billion becoming the world's largest OTA by total bookings. These new Internet distribution channels were introduced by new entrants—not by established lodging industry players (refer back to Exhibit 9.6 and 9.7). As Benvenuti remarked: "As a testament to the 'new order' introduced by Internet disruption just consider firm capitalization. Priceline is a $62 billion company. The major hotels chains are worth a lot less, Marriott is $22 billion, Hilton is $29 billion and IHG is $10.2 billion just to name the largest ones."

Large OTAs drove revenue through commissions and placement costs. However, unlike the use of fixed commission as in the "pre-Internet days," current arrangements created costs of acquisition through intermediaries ranging anywhere between 15% and 35%. OTAs weren't the only players in the distribution space. Metasearch sites, like Kayak, Skyscanner and Hipmunk were often the place where savvy travelers would shop first. Lodging operators and big brands sought to reclaim some control over their distribution with their website—so called "Brand.com" sites (see Exhibit 9.7). To further complicate matters, on the business travel front large travel agencies like American Express and Concur still served as intermediaries for a significant portion of hotel reservations. While the distribution landscape was complex, and many hoteliers yearned for the "simpler days of old" (i.e., before computing and the Internet), savvy operators sought to adapt to the new order.

The shift in bargaining power toward OTAs imposed high customer acquisition costs on hotels and an increasing dependency upon intermediaries in the distribution channels. In addition, given the strength of their cash flow, OTAs were able to invest in marketing and communication to attract consumers. They also

EXHIBIT 9.2. Largest Hotel Properties (by Revenue) and Room Supply, 2014

Company	Headquarters	Properties	Rooms
InterContinental Hotels Group	Denham, U.K.	4,697	686,873
Hilton Worldwide	McLean, Va.	4,115	678,630
Marriott International	Bethesda, Md.	3,916	675,623
Wyndham Hotel Group	Parsippany, N.J.	7,485	645,423
Choice Hotels International	Silver Spring, Md.	6,340	506,058
Accor	Paris	3,576	461,719
Starwood Hotels & Resorts	Stamford, Conn.	1,175	346,800
Best Western International	Phoenix, Ariz.	4,063	314,984
Home Inns	Shanghai	2,180	256,555
Carlson Rezidor Hotel Group	Minneapolis	1,079	168,961
China Lodging Group	Shanghai	1,425	152,879
Hyatt Hotels Corp.	Chicago	548	147,388
G6 Hospitality	Carrollton, Texas	1,100	104,018
Meliá Hotels International	Palma de Mallorca, Spain	397	99,566
La Quinta Inns & Suites	Irving, Texas	834	83,658
Extended Stay America	Charlotte, N.C.	684	76,219
NH Hoteles	Madrid	379	58,195

Source: Created by casewriters from data Baker, M. B. 2014, "Bucking History, Hotel Seller's Market Shows Few Signs Of Ending", *Business Travel News*, vol. 31, no. 8 (26 May 2014), pp. 25–34, Business Travel News—Business Travel Survey 2014, Northstar Travel Media. (http://businesstravelnews.texterity.com/businesstravelnews/may_26_2014). Accessed June 16 2015.

EXHIBIT 9.3. Projected Growth of Hotel Property Room Supply 2014–2015

Region	Hotels	Rooms
United States	3,127	381,503
Asia/Pacific	2,312	513,443
Europe	925	149,866
Middle East/Africa	573	137,193
Central/South America	390	63,780
Caribbean/Mexico	162	26,647

Source: Adapted from Baker, M. B. 2014, "Bucking History, Hotel Seller's Market Shows Few Signs Of Ending", *Business Travel News*, vol. 31, no. 8 (26 May 2014), pp. 25–34, Business Travel News—Business Travel Survey 2014, Northstar Travel Media on STR and STR Global data, http://businesstravelnews.texterity.com/businesstravelnews/may_26_2014, accessed June 16, 2015.

EXHIBIT 9.4. US Lodging Industry Profile, 2014

Properties	52,887
Rooms	4,926,543
Sales	$163B
Pretax incomes	$41B
Revenue per Available Room (RevPAR)	$68.64
Average occupancy rate	62.2%

Source: Data available from American Hotel & Lodging Association, 2014, *2014 Lodging Industry Profile.* https://www.ahla.com/content.aspx?id=3633, accessed June 16, 2015.

Note: figures are for year-end 2013.

EXHIBIT 9.5. Hotel Property Customer Acquisition Costs (2009–2012)

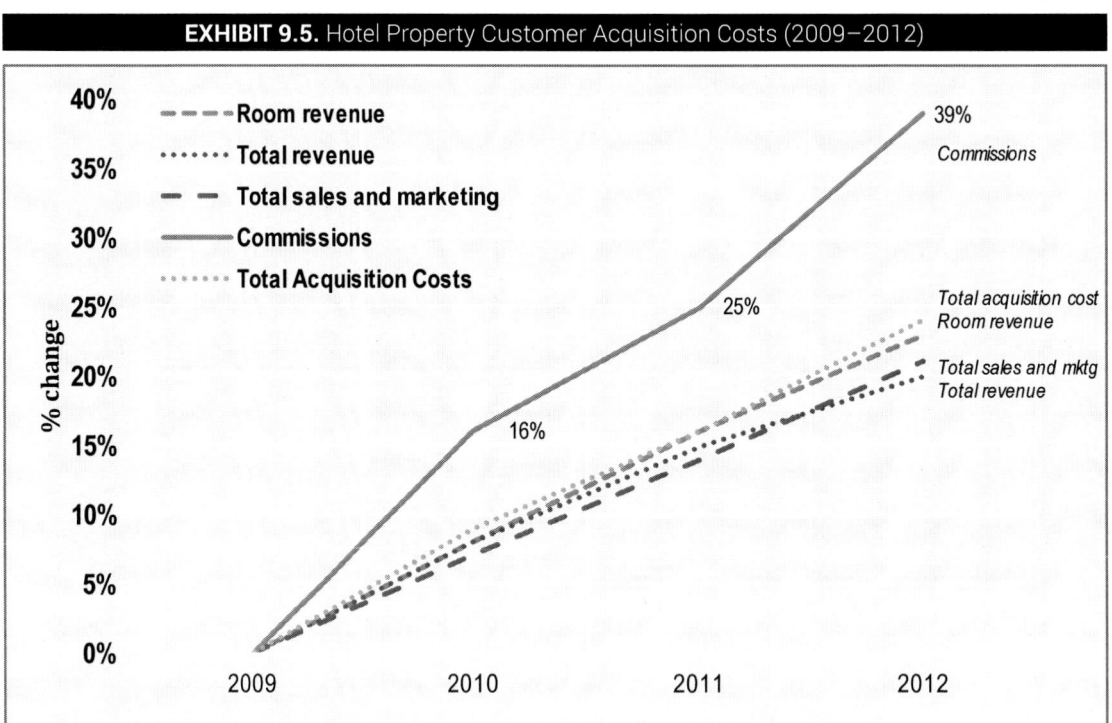

Source: Adapted from Kalibri Labs—HAMA Sales and Marketing Efficiency Study, 2014

Note: Kalibri Labs' definition of acquisition costs includes any cost incurred to generate revenue or acquire a customer. That could be a combination of commissions (OTA, retail, third-party meetings planners, etc.); transaction fees (GDS, website transaction fees, voice fees); sales and marketing expenses (from a TripAdvisor business listing to salaries for a sales staff); amenity costs to travel agents as part of contractual relationship (e.g. Virtuoso and Brand X); costs paid to branding or loyalty programs; digital campaign fees and commissions; and costs associated with hotel branding efforts.

EXHIBIT 9.6. Key Statistics: OTAs and Hotels

		Market Cap.	Revenues	ROA	ROE	EBITDA
OTAs						
The Priceline Group	USA	$59,683.57	$8,797.69	13.12%	28.87%	$3,266.21
Amadeus	Spain	$15,653.10	$3,663.58	10.12%	31.75%	$1,381.34
Expedia	USA	$13,948.91	$6,104.48	3.01%	29.40%	$705.84
Sabre	USA	$6,463.01	$2,736.06	6.04%	91.43%	$742.78
Hotels						
Orbitz Worldwide, Inc.	USA	$1,275.89	$933.50	2.37%	-21.07%	$106.82
Hilton Worldwide Holdings Inc.	USA	$27,204.22	$7,038.00	4.14%	13.51%	$2,315.00
Marriott International, Inc.	USA	$20,453.53	$2,848.00	12.30%	NM	$1,411.00
Starwood Hotels & Resorts Worldwide Inc.	USA	$13,857.14	$3,166.00	6.35%	26.24%	$1,101.00
Wyndham Worldwide Corporation	USA	$9,832.89	$5,406.00	6.52%	44.37%	$1,269.00
Intercontinental Hotels Group plc	UK	$6,058.77	$1,865.00	13.39%	NM	$739.00
Hyatt Hotels Corporation	USA	$8,163.11	$2,614.00	2.41%	6.08%	$637.00
Extended Stay America, Inc.	USA	$3,840.42	$1,249.15	5.13%	13.00%	$565.43
Choice Hotels International Inc.	USA	$3,124.13	$807.97	20.30%	NM	$220.27
La Quinta Holdings Inc.	USA	$2,989.03	$998.91	2.94%	1.32%	$327.34
Meliá Hotels International SA	Spain	$2,281.44	$1,599.15	3.35%	6.10%	$268.81
China Lodging Group, Limited	China	$1,520.16	NA	NA	NA	NA

Note: Market cap is as of June 2015. Revenue, EBITDA, ROA and ROE are calculated based on data from July 2014 to June 2015. Market Value, Revenues and EBITDA are in $M.

Source: Compiled by casewriters based on data from Capital IQ. Downloaded August 2015.

EXHIBIT 9.7. Hospitality Distribution with Examples of Major Players

Source: Developed by casewriters based on data available from Lynch, J. 2011, *Three things to consider in hotel distribution and marketing in 2012*, Available from <http://www.sabrehospitality.com/resources/hotel-marketing-blogs?id=three-top-trends-in-hospitality-marketing-and-distribution-to-consider-when-planning-for-2012&ccm_paging_p=3> accessed 22 May 2015.

continually innovated on their online offerings by introducing faster and better search and comparison tools and, more recently, a monitoring service that would rebook a reservation at a lower rate if the price dropped before the travel date. OTAs were also very aggressive on the contractual terms of agreements with property owners. Rate parity, a provision in all OTAs contracts, ensured that a hotel would not publish a lower rate than the one given to the OTA—not even on the hotel's online branded website. In September 2010 the provision had come under scrutiny by the UK Office of Fair Trading (OFT) on the contention that the practice infringed on both national and European competition regulations. Other European antitrust regulators followed suit but the matter had yet to be settled.

Hospitality operators seeking to combat the commoditization trend had two weapons at their disposal: revenue management and service differentiation through customer experience management.[2]

Revenue Management in the hotel industry

Sell the right room at the right rate at the right time to the right customer was the revenue management (RM) motto. An early form of predictive analytics, RM practices focused on price optimization. Born in the airline industry in the 1970s, RM was a mainstay practice in the lodging sector with hotels of any type and size engaging in some form of price optimization. Software providers were fairly consolidated with players such as IDeaS (owned by SAS since 2008), EzRMS (owned by Infor since 2012) and Rainmaker, focused mostly on casinos, dominating the hospitality vertical. Many of the larger chains ran their own proprietary systems.

RM systems had evolved over the years with each wave of IT innovation. Particularly transforming had been the introduction of the Internet, which drastically reduced data-sharing costs, and enabled greater visibility to competitor prices. For example, it was now standard practice for RM software to obtain regular updates of competitors' room rates, which enabled a hotel property owner to optimize prices based, not only on historical data, but also on current competitor's moves (see Exhibit 9.8).

Despite great technology changes, at its core RM remained a forecasting challenge. In the hotel industry

demand forecasting had centered on the analysis of historical transaction data extracted from the Property Management System (PMS) or the Central Reservation System (CRS).[3] Benvenuti captured the essence of the problem: "The math has not changed in 20 years. To manage revenue you need to know whether this request that you are getting is the best you can do or whether you will displace a customer willing to pay more at a later time if you have the courage and the knowledge to deny the request."

Building Duetto

Duetto Consulting, LLC: Two guys, industry knowledge and an Excel spreadsheet.

After graduating with a Master of Management in Hospitality from the Cornell Hotel School Benvenuti took a job in Revenue Management with Wynn Resorts. Promoted to the post of Executive Director of Enterprise Strategy in June 2008, Benvenuti focused on optimizing profitability throughout the resort. He recruited Patrick Bosworth—a 2007 HBS graduate—to head revenue management and analytics. Bosworth was an "outsider" to hospitality with the potential to bring a fresh perspective to revenue management. Exactly two years later with impending changes at the firm Benvenuti and Bosworth decided to leave Wynn to start their own company Duetto Consulting. Bosworth explained: "We had been thinking about going out on our own for some time, but everyone was telling us we were crazy. The exceptions were some of our long time mentors who understood the potential that new technologies and new sources of data could provide."

The duo from Duetto felt that none of the major commercial systems had been able to break free from their legacy restrictions and limitations. Benvenuti explained: "In 2010 revenue management systems were still basing their forecasts on data in a hotel's PMS. The rate decision was centered on the Best Available Rate (BAR)—a standard lowest available rate for each night

---

2. See Applegate, Lynda M., and Gabriele Piccoli. "HGRM: Bringing Back High Touch Hospitality." Harvard Business School Case 813–019, July 2012. (Revised January 2014) and Applegate, Lynda M., Gabriele Piccoli, and Arnold Peinado. "HGRM (B): Launching Hoxell, a New IT Venture." Harvard Business School Supplement 815–057, September 2014.

3. A Property Management System (PMS) is the "brain" of hotel operations. The software is used to maintain current room inventory (e.g., available rooms, occupied rooms, unchanged—or dirty—rooms), to check-in and check-out guests, to consolidate charges from various systems (e.g., minibar, restaurant systems, call accounting) and produce the guest folio (i.e., invoice). The Central Reservation System (CRS) is the computer application that supports electronic distribution of room inventory. Reservations coming in through the Web site, call center (i.e., 1–800 number), travel agents, and other channels flow to the CRS.

Traditional RMS	**Modern RMS**
Best Available Rate (BAR) pricing	Dynamic pricing
Increased occupancy as primary goal	Increased profit as primary goal
Manual or partial automation of pricing recommendations	Automatic pricing recommendations
Revenue management as silos	Revenue management integrated with marketing and sales activities
Manual propagation of rates to online channels	Automated channel management and optimization
Revenue management on rooms only	Revenue Management applied to all revenue streams (e.g., spas, restaurants)

EXHIBIT 9.8. Hospitality Industry Revenue Management Evolution

Source: Company documents.

of a multiple-night stay—with adjustments for forecasted and actual demand modifiers. Deals were kept open as room availability persisted, and closed when room availability decreased" (see Exhibit 9.9).

Duetto's founders felt that this was not the right approach to RM. They thought that, beyond accurately forecasting demand, a RM system had to have enough flexibility to allow the revenue manager to implement an optimal strategy. Such a strategy would allow rates to vary by day, but also to vary by room type, channel of distribution and any other relevant dimension (e.g., length of stay). In order to create a replicable process and some economies of scale in their consulting practice, Duetto Consulting sought to convince some of the dominant vendors to embrace their approach. Yet, progress was slow and Benvenuti spent many nights coding his ideas into an increasingly complex Excel model: "I coded my knowledge of the industry and my disdain for the BAR into the model! This made our work more scalable and also provided our hotel and casino customers with a 'product' to go along with our service, which helped to close sales."

In fact, the use of custom-designed spreadsheets to adjust room rates from the Revenue Management system was a common practice in the industry. What made Benvenuti's model unique is that it sought to price multiple records in the PMS independently, rather than produce a single forecast for the BAR. Benvenuti believed that this approach was far superior because it enabled revenue managers to price each room type independently for each distribution channel and customer segment. The drawback of Duetto's spreadsheet approach was a lack of scalability since the current spreadsheet required massive amounts of manual data

entry every time a rate was changed. A typical hotel would revise rates once a day, with properties in large markets doing so three or four times a day for high-demand travel dates. Bosworth recalled their dilemma at this time: "We had to decide if we were going to scale the consulting business, and start hiring employees under a traditional consulting model, or invest in building a much more complex system. The larger industry players would not license an excel model, they wanted a system. Truthfully, deep inside we agreed."

In June 2011 Duetto Consulting hired its first employee, AJ Jenveja, who would serve existing consulting clients while Bosworth talked with his professional and college network about the viability of re-launching Duetto as a technology startup. A recurring theme was that the cofounders needed a highly respected technical cofounder.

Leveling Up: Duetto Research, Inc.

Bosworth heard from Dan Scholnick that Craig Weissman was leaving his post as CTO of Salesforce.com—the cloud-based CRM solution. Scholnik was one of Patrick's former HBS section-mates, currently a General Partner at Trinity Ventures. Weissman was extremely well-known and respected for his technical talent in Silicon Valley. He had been the lead architect of the CRM software giant's cloud computing platform, Force.com, and was beginning a sabbatical as the Entrepreneur in Residence for Benchmark Capital. Chris Hemmeter, Managing Director of Thayer Ventures,[4] summarized the importance of a seasoned technical cofounder: "Beyond a large addressable market, a distinct value

---

4. Thayer Ventures later invested in Duetto's seed and Series A rounds.

EXHIBIT 9.9. An Example of BAR Pricing Decision

Source Company documents.

proposition and a sound business model, investors in technology startups need to mitigate technology risk. You need to ship products reliably and your technology needs to work and scale. You have a chance to do so only with an exceptionally strong technical cofounder."

After a few months studying the opportunity and discussing it over multiple meetings with Bosworth, Weissman agreed to become a cofounder of the company, which was now called Duetto Research, Inc. (see Exhibit 9.10). Duetto Research was incorporated in Delaware in Febraury 2012. Despite having multiple options for his "next tech start-up gig" Weissman was drawn to Duetto because of its vertical focus and the possibility of being at the very heart of operations for their clients. As Weissman put it: "While I did not know much about the hospitality/travel industry, I could see that it was a giant industry that was also a technology mess. The more I looked into it, the more the challenge appealed to me." Hemmeter stressed the importance of early decisions: "I often see business plans for ventures based only on a business model. They may work, but if the assumptions are wrong or the economics change, you are left with nothing. Great entrepreneurs have the skills and confidence to tackle a gnarly difficult problem. The venture may make more or less headway in solving the problem, but the challenge is real. It's not going to suddenly vanish."

With the expanded cofounding team in place Duetto began a phase of feverish work to bring its technology solution to market and raise the needed capital to grow. Product development was the first imperative and Weissman already had three engineers ready to start developing the platform. Within two months of launch, Duetto Research had attracted $2.1 million of seed capital. An

early testament to the quality of the team and the work done to date could be seen by the ability of the Duetto's cofounders to attract a strong investor group. For example, angel investors who participated in the seed round, included Marc Benioff, Founder and CEO of Salesforce. com, as well as Thayer Ventures, the first venture capital firm focused exclusively on technology in the hospitality sector. The first release of Duetto's new software offering was installed with a beta customer in August 2012 and the Duetto cofounders embarked on raising further financing. They closed a $10.1 million series A financing round in December 2012 from well known Silicon Valley venture capital firms, led by Battery Ventures. Duetto closed a series B round totaling $21 million in July 2014. (see Exhibit 9.11).

Duetto's Technology and Products

IT Infrastructure

Duetto clearly understood the need to develop quickly, ship often and iterate fast. However, Weissman knew that early infrastructure choices would create significant path dependencies constraining future evolution and flexibility. The technology infrastructure was built upon Amazon Elastic Compute Cloud as the platform, MongoDB as the core database engine,[5] and custom-written software for the logic layer and analytics. At the core the reservation data model included classic

---

5. MongoDB is an open source, No-SQL database management system that is document oriented rather than being based on the relational database model (https://www.mongodb.org/). Because of its architecture MongoDB is particularly well suited for integration of disparate data and big data applications.

elements (e.g., who is arriving, when do they arrive, what did they buy). But there were also many aspects of hotel operations, such as shared reservations or group blocks, which greatly increased complexity. Weissman commented: "Real-time synching with a third-party system is hard enough. In our case reservations are constantly changing and our customers use us for real-time business intelligence: historical and forward-looking. The numbers better match what they see in their PMS! When you add it all up, just creating a high-fidelity,

---

EXHIBIT 9.10. Brief Backgrounds of Cofounders

Patrick Bosworth, Chief Executive Officer

As Cofounder and CEO, **Patrick** drives vision and growth at Duetto. With over a decade spent in the hospitality, non-profit and government sectors, he has brought entrepreneurial insights to organizations and established them as industry leaders and innovators. Previously at Wynn Resorts, and with consulting clients, Patrick realigned strategic marketing functions to maximize profit. While in the public sector, he drove modernization of financial reporting standards, unchanged since the 1950s, making labor unions more accountable to their members.

Patrick holds an MBA from Harvard Business School and a BA in Political Science from the University of San Diego. He serves on the Hotel Sales & Marketing Association International (HSMAI) Revenue Management Advisory Board as well as the HSMAI Foundation Board, and recently as an advisor to the American Hotel & Lodging Educational Institute. He also advises Win-Win Entertainment, a non-profit connecting great causes with great entertainers . . . one show at a time.

Marco Benvenuti, Chief Analytics and Product Officer

Marco Benvenuti is Chief Analytics & Product Officer and Cofounder at Duetto, where he directs product vision, direction and implementation. Marco was formerly Executive Director at Wynn and Encore where he founded and managed the Enterprise Strategy Group, in which he led revenue management, data analytics, direct marketing and online channels. Prior to Wynn, Marco worked for Caesars Entertainment, Expedia and Four Seasons. Marco has patented two unique inventions: the Pricing Engine for one-to-one dynamic pricing and the Enterprise Value Algorithm for calculating the value of every customer. He holds an MMH from Cornell University, where he currently serves on the Board of the Center for Hospitality Research, and a Bachelor in Hotel Administration from UNLV. Marco is an avid college basketball fan and his favorite team is of course the UNLV Runnin' Rebels.

Craig Weissman, Chief Technology Officer

Craig Weissman is Chief Technology Officer and Cofounder of Duetto. He is a widely recognized leader in the field of SaaS software development and design. Before cofounding Duetto, Craig was the CTO of Salesforce.com where he was integral in the design and development of the Force.com Enterprise Cloud Computing platform including its scalable metadata-driven, multi-tenant design. Craig has a Master's degree in computer science and a Bachelor's degree in applied mathematics from Harvard University and holds multiple technology patents.

Source Company documents.

scalable data store in this environment is not at all a simple problem. That alone is enough for a new venture, but it's only 40% of what we do."

One decision was clear before the first line of code was ever written at Duetto: all offerings would run in the cloud. This meant that clients would not be installing any software at the property level, and that even the largest customers would not host Duetto products in their data centers. It was a pure Software as a Service (SaaS) model. Weissman's experience at Salesforce.com was invaluable. Salesforce had been an early pioneer of the SaaS model when it first launched in 1999,

Series	Investor	Investor profile	Notes
Seed Investment $2.1M Apr 19, 2012	Battery Ventures	Assets $4B, 300 Investments in 179 Companies, exits resulted in 10 IPOs & 48 acquisitions	
	Benchmark Capital	Assets $850M, 349 Investments in 183 Companies, exits resulted in 18 IPOs & 55 acquisitions	
	Rich Barton	Founder of Expedia, Inc., Cofounder, Executive Chairman of Zillow Group, Glassdoor, and Trover, 17 investments in 13 companies	
	Marc Benioff	Founder, Chairman & CEO of Salesforce, 59 investments in 45 companies	
	Steve Blank	Cofounder of Epiphany Inc., Zylog and MIPS Computers and other 5 high technology companies, 9 investments in 8 companies,	
	Brad Gerstner	Founder & CEO of Altimeter Capital, 3 Investments in 3 Companies	
	Parker Harris	Cofounder, EVP Technology of Salesforce	
	Trinity Ventures	Assets $325M 235 Investments in 136 Companies, exits resulted in 8 IPOs & 54 acquisitions	Led the round
	Thayer Ventures	17 Investments in 15 Companies	
Series A $10.1M Dec 11, 2012	Altimeter Capital	Assets $75M, 8 Investments in 6 Companies, 1 exit as IPO	Led the round
	Battery Ventures	Since seed investment	Led the round
	Marc Benioff	Since seed investment	
	Leland Pillsbury	Founding partner, Co-chairman and CEO of Thayer Lodging Group	
	Thayer Ventures	Since seed investment	
	Trinity Ventures	Since seed investment	
Series B $21M Jul 9, 2014	Accel Partners	Since series A	Led the round
	Altimeter Capital	Since series A	
	Battery Ventures	Since seeding	
	Leland Pillsbury	Since series A	
	Marc Benioff	Since series A	

EXHIBIT 9.11. Funding Duetto Timeline

Source: Compiled by casewriters. Data available from Crunchbase (https://www.crunchbase.com/organization/duetto-research, accessed June 2015)

and Weissman had been one of the key innovators who helped develop the multi-tenant SaaS architecture.[6]

The multi-tenants SaaS approach, while significantly more complex to build, offered a number of key advantages when compared to more traditional approaches (see Exhibit 9.12). For customers, a cloud solution reduced dedicated hardware and software investments, while providing them with upgrades whenever a new version was released. For Duetto the solution was infinitely and rapidly scalable, allowing it to also pool all the data in the database to power its forecasting algorithms. Weissman discussed the tradeoff: "As a startup you are running really fast, and there are many unknowns. You have to have the discipline to periodically refactor[7] to make sure your architecture is sound. Everyone asks for features, but you need to know when to invest in 'robusting' the code. If you don't have that discipline, soon enough the thing is unmanageable and your whole company is in peril."

A key advantage of the Duetto architecture was evident in its ability to "ingest" new digital data streams that could carry valuable information to improve forecasting. Duetto tapped into a number of data sources such as airline load factors, rates of hotels in the competitive set and the market, macroeconomic data, special events databases, weather forecasts and more (see Exhibit 9.13). This would amount to capturing over one hundred thousand data points per month for a typical client. But the digital data stream that Duetto felt most strongly about was real-time customer shopping behavior, including "regrets"—a room is available but the customer doesn't book it—and "denials"—requests for a room when no room is available.

The firm collected the data by placing a few lines of JavaScript code within the booking engine of its clients' public website. The forecasting value of regrets

and denials had been hotly debated in the industry. Benvenuti explained Duetto's stance on the matter: "Our competitors have contended for years that regrets and denials are useless because they are an unreliable signal. When I worked at Wynn I begged my call center operators to manually track them. But they were busy during their shift and I got incomplete data that was rarely credible. On the website the data is tracked by a computer, so it is accurate, complete and real time."

The Duetto Product Line

In the fall of 2012 Duetto officially launched its first product, or edition, as Duetto called the different versions of the application (see Exhibit 9.14). While the firm tailored subsequent editions to the needs of distinct customer segments, the core value proposition was that its SaaS offering produced precise, actionable pricing recommendations accessible directly through a hotel's PMS. Duetto rejected the BAR approach in favor of what it called *open pricing*.

Open pricing computed optimal rates for each date and room type independently and adjusted the price dynamically using real-time data. Moreover, rates could be allowed to vary dynamically by channel of distribution (for example, Priceline or Hotel Tonight). Instead of closing a channel and showing no availability when inventory was still available, Duetto's algorithms would simply increase the rate published to that channel on a specific date. In order to deliver at scale on the open pricing vision, having the data was just the beginning. Weissman and his team had to build custom forecasting algorithms that efficiently leveraged its unique, and growing, data stores. The output was a three-dimensional matrix of rates for each day in the next thirteen months, by customer segment and room-type. For a typical hotel a forecasting algorithm would analyze three years' worth of historical data, a few hundred thousand records, and produce a 400x15x8 matrix at least once a day. In addition, a client could also recalculate the forecast on demand. While general-purpose algorithms could produce forecasts for each property, individual hotels could take advantage of significant "local knowledge" by applying automated business rules. Weissman explained: "In a system like this you have to sprinkle in human intuition. Say the General Manager of a hotel property does not want to be more than $10 below the average of the competitive set because it would damage the brand. We would create a custom business rule for that property and enforce these extra constraints automatically." Business rules also helped in creating constraints around discounts and upgrades. For example, a discounted rate to AAA members could be limited to a range between 0

---

6. Multi-tenant SaaS is unique in that each customer has access to the same application and the same database. While data is secured and segregated, giving the illusion that each organization is using dedicated hardware and software, this architecture offers significant economies of scales and advantages. Chief amongst them are memory and computational efficiencies—dramatically increasing the speed of complex analyses—and delivery—with every customer always up to date running the only version of the software.

7. Refactoring is the process of taking existing code and rewriting it in an effort to streamline and optimize it. When a firm refactors its code it does not add any new functionality to its applications. Rather refactoring is necessary to ensure that the code is robust (i.e., efficient and scalable).

EXHIBIT 9.12. SaaS vs Cloud

Source: Microsoft, https://technet.microsoft.com/en-us/library/dn741581.aspx, accessed June 2015

and 15%. Thus, even if the forecast engine computed an optimal discount of 18% the suggested rate would be 15% (see Exhibit 9.15).

Beyond its sheer complexity, the reasons why open pricing had never been implemented in the industry on a large scale was the computational burden and the volume of rates that had to be transferred to the PMS. The industry had never standardized these operations and manual entry rapidly escalated team sizes and related costs—making it unfeasible. Duetto's architecture enabled it to cope with the computational requirements of open pricing but to efficiently transfer the data to the PMS it had to build interfaces to allow for record level rate access to each PMS. Weissman commented: "Integration is a technical challenge, but it has deep implications for your strategy. We debated this a lot. A new custom integration opens up a new addressable market, but integration is difficult and messy. There are some standards, but they are almost never fully implemented leaving you with substantial work to handle exceptions."

Particularly important in the Duetto philosophy was the role of the Customer Success team. The group, which in early 2015 was comprised of 17 professionals, was tasked with ensuring that customers would extract the maximum value from the use of Duetto products. Jenveja, who now led the team, explained: "Customer success is not customer support. The latter is reactive, customers open tickets and report bugs, and customer service representatives troubleshoot them. Customer success is proactive. We are the face of the company to the clients, it is our job to ensure that customers see the reason to stay with Duetto: they make better decisions and more money."

The role of the Customer Success team could evolve into professional services consulting for customers willing to pay for the additional service. Moreover, in an effort to educate the industry about the value of open pricing and of new data sources, Duetto engaged in significant thought-leadership. Hosting conferences, like its Revenue Strategy Summit and participating in panel discussions and university keynotes.

Early Results

Despite being a relatively young company Duetto's leadership felt that there was already much success to

EXHIBIT 9.13. Duetto External Data Sources and Processing

Source: Company documents

Note: DDS: Digital Data Streams

Extract Transform Load: The process of extracting data, integrating and rearranging it into a unified view and then loading it into a data warehouse.

Materialized Views: Replicas of a master data table or master site

OLAP: An approach to "Online Analytic Processing" that enables a user to extract and view data from different points of view.

Definitions: Accessed October 10, 2015 from:

https://www.simnet.org/store/ViewProduct.aspx?id=1537293;

http://docs.oracle.com/cd/B19306_01/server.102/b14223/ettover.htm;

https://docs.oracle.com/cd/B10501_01/server.920/a96567/repmview.htm;

http://searchdatamanagement.techtarget.com/definition/OLAP.

---

celebrate. As Benvenuti put it: "We have new offices in Austin, Singapore and London and grew our headcount by 300% in twelve months!" (See Exhibit 9.16). Duetto's cofounders were also very proud of their culture with an extremely flat organization where everybody had access to the leadership, and could feel free to bring any issue to their attention directly. Nobody had a private office, not even the founders; dress code was informal even at public events.

The firm had also applied for three patents. They covered several aspects of Duetto's Intellectual Property, from the use of regrets and denials in predictive price analytics, to system architecture, and the process Duetto employed to combine multiple datasets for forecasting. Moreover, in their contract with customers Duetto secured ownership of all the data their system collected. They felt that the way the application was architected, and the data sources they were able to collect put them at the core of hotel operations. Bosworth explained: "We started with pricing because it forces you to get good at some really hard things, like integration and data analytics. But we are poised to be the firm that helps hospitality operators leverage big

data to make optimal decisions in all aspects of their operations." The three cofounders knew that a tech startup was judged in terms of its customer growth and financial potential. This was particularly evident to Bosworth as he was preparing presentations for venture firms interested in Duetto's series C round of funding: "When you take top ten VC money, there are certain growth and return expectations. My job at this time is to make sure that we don't run out of oxygen before we fulfill our promise. We are hitting our major growth spurt and we have to keep that up for several more years."

In early 2015, Duetto had over 350 properties and 50 thousand rooms under management. It also had six pilots running with new customers and, with a track record of 100% conversion from pilot to client, believed it had a few sizable deals close to signing. However, the sales cycle could be long, averaging between three and six months. Despite attention to growth, the firm also had to ensure that current customers continued to be successful with the Duetto products. The firm needed strong references to continue to convert sales. As Bosworth put it: "That's easy to do when you have

EXHIBIT 9.14. Product Timeline and Key Events

Year	Date	Event	Type of Financing
2012	April 14th	Benvenuti, Bosworth and Weissmen incorporated Duetto Research in Delaware	Seed Investment: $2.1 million
	October 1st	**Duetto Edge launched** Features added: Open Pricing Regrets & Denials Integrations with Opera & Sabre	
	December 11th	───────────────────────▶	Series A: $10.1 million
2013	Spring	Features added: Group Displacement Pricing Experiments	
	May 21st	**Duetto Insight launched** for smaller and limited service hotels affordable price point	
2014	Spring	**Duetto GameChanger launched** specifically developed for casino hotels Features added: Reputation Comparison Airline and Weather Demand Data Smart Alerts Portfolio Manager	
	July 9th	───────────────────────▶	Series B: $21 million
	Fall	Features added: Financial Forecast Builder Tax Support E-mail Alert Notifications Restriction Management	
2015	Summer	Features added: Overbooking Enhanced Pricing Manager Rate Change Reviewer Auto Fixed Rate Restrictions Enhanced Pricing Algorithm	

EXHIBIT 9.15. Screenshot of Pricing Rules

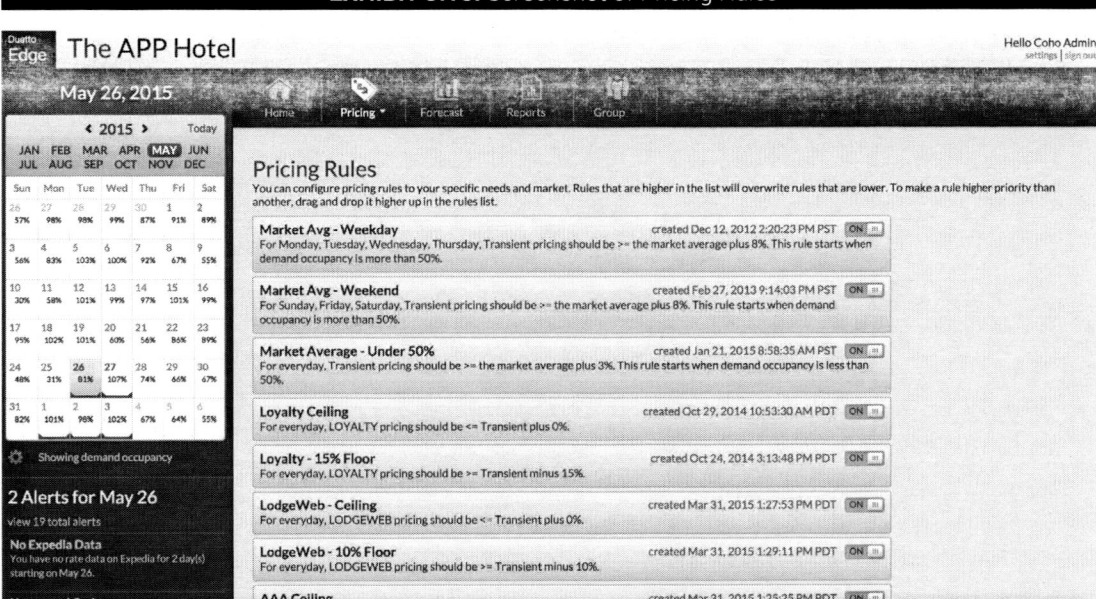

Source: Company documents.

Note: (Disguised hotel information).

EXHIBIT 9.16. Duetto's Growth

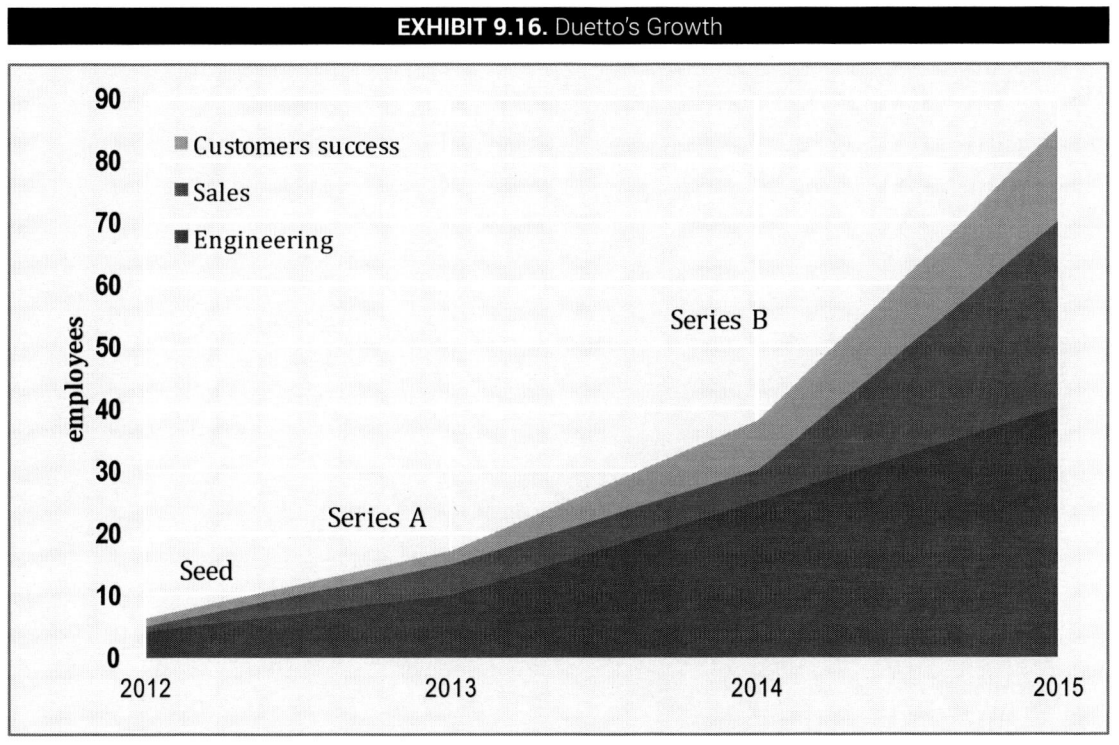

"Customers success" is the team in charge of proactive customers' support. The team is specifically created to support customers in appropriating of Duetto's platform features.

Source: Company documents.

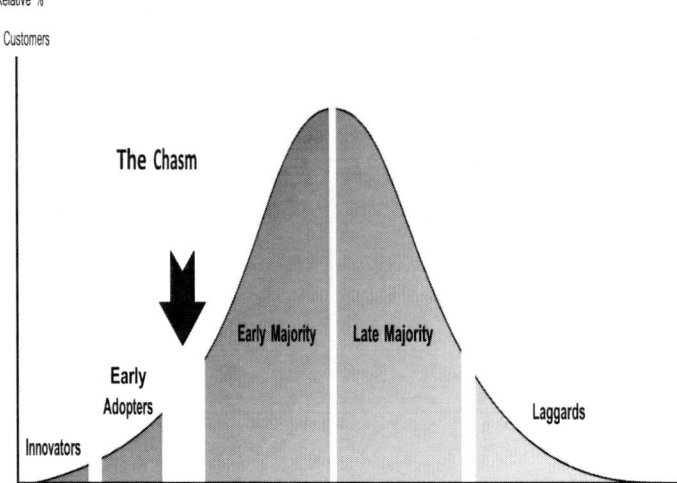

FIGURE 9.1. Technology Adoption Lifecycle
Source: Adapted Geoffrey A. Moore, *Crossing the Chasm* (New York: HarperCollins/Collins Business Essentials, 2002), p. 17.

a hundred customers, but as you ramp up fast you must architect the right sales force and Customer Success Team, training and performance management systems. And you better be efficient in how you do it." Strong references were also critical because Duetto was priced at a premium over competitors. Duetto's base system was priced at $15 per room per month. Prices were lower for the *Insight* edition and higher for the *Game Changer* edition, but discounts applied when a large number of rooms were contracted at once. (Refer back to Exhibit 9.14 for a list of Duetto Editions). Duetto justified the premium not only on the merits of its applications, superior data, forecasts and usability. But also on the level of support its Customer Success Team offered to clients.

The founders felt that Duetto was becoming stronger operationally as it matured. This was evidenced in the firm's ability to ramp up customers faster and faster. With properties using any one of the 25 third-party systems that Duetto had already integrated, the process of onboarding a customer would generally take between 30 and 60 days. When the certification of new interfaces was required the time could stretch significantly to over six months, and was complicated by the fact that Duetto was dependent on the availability of external partners (e.g., PMS or CRS vendors).

Despite the early success, preparing presentations for the next round of financing was a time for soul searching and reflection about the challenges ahead. Silicon Valley startups normally focused on the North American market before going overseas. However, travel was a global industry and being "born global"

was practically a requirement. Weissman summarized the cofounders' sentiment about the future: "I am convinced that our potential customers would readily agree that there is tremendous value in getting timely feeds from relevant data streams, producing forecasts based on the open pricing approach, and applying the business rules needed to put reliable timely information in the hands of the professionals making decision. If we continue to provide this, we will do well."

But only time would answer the bigger questions: Was Duetto on the right growth path? While customers enjoyed the product, the hospitality industry was notoriously slow-moving and still generally skeptical of technology innovations. Moreover, given the low margins of a typical hotel operation, negotiations could be painstaking. The firm was looking for two to three years of financing and hoped to raise $25–30 million to generate the hyper-growth necessary to become a billion dollar business fit for an IPO. But, given that the hospitality industry was slow-moving and generally skeptical of new technology, it was not clear whether they had simply attracted the early adopters. "Crossing the chasm" to attract the early majority pragmatists could prove much more difficult during Duetto's next growth phase (see Figure 9.1), and Duetto could settle into a more linear growth trajectory that would make it an attractive multimillion-dollar acquisition rather than a successful IPO. Duetto's founders knew that they would need to be prepared to address these issues during negotiations with investors in the next round of financing.

IT PLANNING AT MODMETERS

Brian Smith, CIO of ModMeters, groaned inwardly as he listened to CEO John Johnson wrapping up his remarks. "So our executive team thinks there are real business opportunities for us in developing these two new strategic thrusts. But before I go to the board for final approval next month, I need to know that our IT, marketing, and sales plans will support us all the way," Johnson concluded.[1]

Brian mentally calculated the impact these new initiatives would have on his organization. He had heard rumors from his boss, the COO, that something big was coming down. He had even been asked his opinion about whether these strategies were technically doable, *theoretically*. But *both* at once? Resources—people, time, and money—were tight, as usual. ModMeters was making a reasonable profit, but the CFO, Stan Abrams, had always kept the lid screwed down tightly on IT spending. Brian had to fight for every dime. How he was going to find the wherewithal to support not one but *two* new strategic initiatives, he didn't know.

The other VPs at this strategy presentation were smiling. Taking ModMeters global from a North American operation seemed to be a logical next step for the company. Its products, metering components of all types, were highly specialized and in great demand from such diverse customers as utility companies, manufacturers, and a host of other industries. Originally founded as Modern Meters, the firm had grown steadily as demand for its metering expertise and components had grown over the past century or so. Today ModMeters was the largest producer of metering components in the world with a full range of both mechanical and, now, digital products. Expanding into meter assembly with plants in Asia and Eastern Europe was a good plan, thought Brian, but he wasn't exactly sure how he was going to get the infrastructure in place to support it. "Many of these countries simply don't have the telecommunications and equipment we are going to

need, and the training and new systems we have to put in place are going to be substantial," he said.

But it was the second strategic thrust that was going to give him nightmares, he predicted. How on earth did they expect him to put direct-to-customer sales in place so they could sell "green" electric meters to individual users? His attention was jerked back to the present by a flashy new logo on an easel that the CEO had just unveiled.

"In keeping with our updated strategy, may I present our new name—MM!" Johnson announced portentously.

"Oh, this is just great," thought Brian. "Now I have to go into every single application and every single document this company produces and change our name!"

Because of its age and scientific orientation, ModMeters (as he still preferred to call it) had been in the IT business a long time. Starting back in the early 1960s, the company had gradually automated almost every aspect of its business from finance and accounting to supply-chain management. About the only thing it didn't have was a fancy Web site for consumers, although even *that* was about to change. ModMeters currently had systems reflecting just about every era of computers from punch cards to PCs. Unfortunately, the company never seemed to have the resources to invest in reengineering its existing systems. It just layered more systems on top of the others. A diagram of all the interactions among systems looked like a plate of spaghetti. There was *no way* they were going to be able to support two new strategic thrusts with their current budget levels, he thought as he applauded the new design along with the others. "Next week's IT budget meeting is going to be a doozy!"

Sure enough, the following week found them all, except for the CEO, back in the same meeting room, ready to do battle. Holding his fire, Brian waited until all the VPs had presented their essential IT initiatives. In addition to what needed to be done to support the new business strategies, each division had a full laundry list of essentials for maintaining the *current* business of the firm. Even Abrams had gotten into the act this year because of new legislation that gave the firm's outside

1. This case was originally published as: Smith, H. A., and McKeen, J. D. "IT Planning at ModMeters," #1-L05-1-008, Queen's School of Business, September 2005. Reproduced by permission of Smith School of Business, Queen's University.

auditors immense scope to peer into the inner workings of every financial and governance process the organization had.

After listening carefully to each speaker in turn, Brian stood up. "As many of you know, we have always been cautious about how we spend our IT budget. We have been given a budget that is equal to 2 percent of revenues, which seriously limits what we in IT have been able to do for the company. Every year we spend a lot of time paring our project list down to bare bones, and every year we make do with a patchwork of infrastructure investments. We are now at the point where 80 percent of our budget in IT is fixed. Here's how we spend our money." Brian clicked on a PowerPoint presentation showing a multicolored pie chart.

"This large chunk in blue is just about half our budget," he stated. "This is simply the cost of keeping the lights on—running our systems and replacing a bare minimum of equipment. The red chunk is about 30 percent of the pie. This is the stuff we *have* to do—fixing errors, dealing with changes mandated by government and our own industry, and providing essential services like the help desk. How we divide up the remainder of the pie is what this meeting is all about."

Brian clicked to a second slide showing a second pie chart. "As you know, we have typically divided up the remaining IT budget proportionately, according to who has the biggest overall operating budget. This large pink chunk is you, Fred." Brian gestured at Fred Tompkins, head of manufacturing and the most powerful executive in the room. It was his division that made the firm's profit. The pink chunk easily took up more than half of the pie. Tompkins smiled. Brian went on, pointing out the slice that each part of the firm had been allotted in the previous year. "Finally, we come to Harriet and Brenda," he said with a smile. Harriet Simpson and Brenda Barnes were the VPs of human resources and marketing, respectively. Their tiny slivers were barely visible—just a few percent of the total budget.

"This approach to divvying up our IT budget may have served us well over the years"—Brian didn't think it had, but he wasn't going to fight past battles—"however, we all heard what John said last week, and this approach to budgeting doesn't give us *any* room to develop our new strategies *or* cover our new infrastructure or staffing needs. Although we might get a little more money to obtain some new applications and buy some more computers"—Abrams nodded slightly—"it won't get us where we need to go in the future."

A third graph went up on the screen, showing the next five years. "If we don't do something *now* to address our IT challenges, within five years our entire IT budget will be eaten up by just operations and maintenance. In the past we have paid minimal attention to our infrastructure or our information and technology architecture or to reengineering our existing systems and processes." A diagram of the "spaghetti" flashed on. "This is what you're asking me to manage in a cost-effective manner. It isn't pretty. We need a better plan for making our systems more robust and flexible. If we are going to be moving in new directions with this firm, the foundation just isn't there. Stan, you *should* be worried that we won't be able to give our auditors what they ask for. But you should also be worried about our risk exposure if one of these systems fails and about how we are going to integrate two new business ventures into this mess."

Tompkins looked up from his papers. It was clear he wasn't pleased with where this presentation was headed. "Well, I, for one, *need* everything I've asked for on my list," he stated flatly. "You can't expect me to be the cash cow of the organization and not enable me to make the money we need to invest elsewhere."

Brian was conciliatory. "I'm not saying that you don't, Fred. I'm just saying that we've been given a new strategic direction from the top and that some things are going to have to change to enable IT to support the whole enterprise better. For example, until now, we have always prioritized divisional IT projects on the basis of ROI. How should we prioritize these new strategic initiatives? Furthermore, these new ventures will require a *lot* of additional infrastructure, so we need to figure out a way to afford this. And right now our systems don't 'talk' to the ones running in other divisions because they don't use the same terminology. But in the future, if we're going to have systems that won't cost increasing amounts of our budget, we are going to have to simplify and integrate them better."

Tompkins clearly hadn't considered the enterprise's needs at all. He scowled but said nothing. Brian continued, "We are being asked to do some new things in the company. Obviously, John hopes there's going to be a payback, but it may take a while. New strategies don't always bear fruit right away." Now looking at Abrams, he said pointedly, "There's more to IT value than short-term profit. Part of our business strategy is to *make* new markets for our company. That requires investment, not only in equipment and product but also in the underlying processes and information we need to manage and monitor that investment."

Harriet Simpson spoke for the first time. "It's like when we hire someone new in R&D. We hire for quality because we want their ideas and innovation, not just a warm body. I think we need to better understand how we are going to translate our five key corporate objectives into IT projects. Yes, we need to make a profit, but Stan needs to satisfy regulators and Brenda's going to be on the hot seat when we start marketing to individuals. And we haven't even spoken about Ted's needs." As the VP of R&D, Ted Kwok was tasked with keeping one or more steps ahead of the competition. New types of products and customer needs would mean expansion in his area as well.

Abrams cleared his throat. "*All* of you are right. As I see it, we are going to have to keep the cash flowing from Fred's area while we expand. But Brian's got a point. We may be being penny wise and pound foolish if we don't think things through more carefully. We've put a lot of effort into developing this new strategy, and there *will* be some extra money for IT but not enough to do that plus everything all of you want. We need to retrench and regroup *and* move forward at the same time."

There was silence in the room. Abrams had an annoying way of stating the obvious without really helping to move the ball forward. Brian spoke again. "The way I see it, we have to understand two things before we can really make a new budget. First, we need to figure out how each of the IT projects we've got on the table contributes to one of our key corporate objectives. Second, we need to figure out a way to determine the *value* of each to ModMeters so that we can prioritize it. Then I need to incorporate a reasonable amount of IT regeneration so that we can continue to do new projects at all."

Everyone was nodding now. Brian breathed a small sigh of relief. That was step one accomplished. But step two was going to be harder. "We have a month to get back to the board with our assurances that the IT plan can incorporate the new strategies and what we're going to need in terms of extra funds to do this. As I said earlier, this is *not* just a matter of throwing money at the problem. What we need is a *process* for IT planning and budgeting that will serve us well over the next few years. This process will need to accomplish a number of things:

- It will need to take an *enterprise* perspective on IT. We're all in these new strategies together.
- It will have to incorporate all types of IT initiatives— our new strategies, the needs of Fred and others for the new IT to operate and improve our existing business, Stan's new auditing needs, and our operations and maintenance needs.
- In addition, we *must* find some way of allocating some of the budget to fixing the mess we have in IT right now.
- It must provide a better way to connect new IT work with our corporate objectives.
- It must help us prioritize projects with different types of value.
- Finally, it must ensure we have the business *and* IT resources in place to deliver that value."

Looking at each of his colleagues in turn, he asked, "Now how are we going to do this?"

Discussion Questions

1. Develop an IT planning process for ModMeters to accomplish the demands as set out above.
2. What do you believe would be the optimal governance structure for the IS function at ModMeters. Why?

PROJECT MANAGEMENT AT MM

"We've got a real 'warm puppy' here," Brian Smith told Werner McCann. "Make sure you make the most of it. We could use a winner."[1]

Smith was MM's CIO, and McCann was his top project manager. The puppy in question was MM's new venture into direct-to-customer marketing of its "green meters"—a product designed to help better manage electrical consumption—and the term referred to the project's wide appeal. The strategy had been a hit with analysts ever since it had been "exposed" to the Street, and the company's stock was doing extremely well as a result. "At last," one had written in his popular news-letter, "we have a company that is willing to put power literally and figuratively in consumers' hands. If MM can deliver on its promises, we fully expect this company to reap the rewards."

Needless to say, the "Green" project was popular internally, too. "I'm giving it to you because you have the most project-management experience we've got," Smith had said. "There's a lot riding on this one." As he walked away from Smith's office, McCann wasn't sure whether to feel complimented or terrified. He had certainly managed some successful projects for the company (previously known as ModMeters) over the past five years but never anything like this one. "That's the problem with project management," he thought. "In IT, almost every project is completely different. Experience only takes you part of the way."

And "Green" was different. It was the first truly enterprise-wide project the company had ever done, and McCann was having conniptions as he thought about telling Fred Tompkins, the powerful head of manufacturing, that he might not be able to have every-thing his own way. McCann knew that, to be success-ful, this project had to take an "outside-in" approach; that is, to take the end-customers' point of view on the company. That meant integrating marketing, ordering, manufacturing, shipping, and service into one seamless process that wouldn't bounce the customer from one department to another in the company. MM had always had separate systems for each of its "silos," and this project would work against the company's traditional culture and processes. The Green project was also going to have to integrate with IT's information management renewal (IMR) project. Separate silos had always meant separate data bases, and the IMR project was supposed to resolve inconsistencies between them and provide accurate and integrated information to different parts of the company. This was a huge political challenge, but unless it worked, McCann couldn't deliver on his mandate.

Then there was the issue of resources. McCann groaned at the thought. MM had some good people but not enough to get through all of the projects in the IT plan within their promised timelines. Because of the importance of the Green project, he knew he'd get good cooperation on staffing, but the fact remained that he would have to go outside for some of the tech-nical skills he needed to get the job done. Finally, there was the schedule they had to meet. Somehow, during the preliminary assessment phase, it had become clear that September 5 was to be the "hard launch" date. There were good reasons for this—the fall was when consumers usually became concerned with their energy consumption—but McCann worried that a date barely 12 months from now would put too much pressure on his team. "We've got to get in there first before the com-petition," Smith had said to him. "The Board expects us to deliver. You've got my backing and the support of the full executive team, but you *have* to deliver this one."

Six Weeks Later

It was full steam ahead on the Green project. "It's *amaz-ing* what a Board mandate and executive sponsorship can do for a project," thought McCann, who knew how hard it usually was to get business attention to IT ini-tiatives. He now had a full-time business counterpart, Raj Sambamurthy. Samba, as he was known to his colleagues, had come out of Tompkins' division and was doing a fantastic job of getting the right people in

1. This case was originally published as: Smith, H. A., and J. D. McKeen. "Project Management at MM," #1-L05-1-009. Queen's School of Business, November 2005. Reproduced by permission of Smith School of Business, Queen's University, Kingston, Ontario.

the room to make the decisions they needed to move ahead. The Green Steering Committee was no "Mickey Mouse" group, either. Smith, Tompkins, and every VP affected by the project were meeting bi-weekly with him and Samba to review every aspect of the project's progress.

McCann had pulled no punches when communicating with the Committee. "You've given me the mandate and the budget to get this project off the ground," he had told them. "But we have to be clear about what we're trying to accomplish." Together, they had hammered out a value proposition that emphasized the strategic value of the project and some of the measures they would use to monitor its ultimate success. The requirements and design phase had also gone smoothly because everyone was so motivated to ensure the project's success. "Linking success to *all* our annual bonuses sure helped *that*!" McCann had remarked wryly to Samba.

Now he was beginning to pull together his "dream team" of implementers. The team had chosen a package known as Web-4-U as the front end of the project, but it would take a lot of work to customize it to suit their unique product and, even more, to integrate it with MM's outmoded back-end systems. The Web-4-U company was based in Ireland but had promised to provide 24/7 consulting on an as-needed basis. In addition, Samba had now assembled a small team of business analysts to work on the business processes they would need. They were working out of the firm's Cloverdale office, a 30-minute drive from IT's downtown location. (It was a shame they couldn't all be together but space was at a premium in HQ. McCann made a mental note to look into some new collaboration software he'd heard about.) Now that these two pieces were in place, McCann felt free to focus on the technical "guts" of the system. "Maybe this will work out after all," he thought.

Three Months to Launch Date

By June, however, he was tearing out what little hair was left on his head. He was seriously considering moving to a remote Peruvian hamlet and breeding llamas. "*Anything* would be better than this mess," he observed to Yung Lee, the Senior IT Architect, over coffee. They were poring over the project's critical path. "The way I see it," Lee stated matter-of-factly, "we have two choices. We can continue with this inferior technology and meet our deadline but not deliver on our functionality, *or* we can redo the plan and go back to the Steering Committee with a revised delivery date and budget."

McCann sighed. Techies *always* saw things in black and white, but his world contained much more grey. And so much was riding on this—credibility (his, IT's,

the company), competitiveness, stock price. He dreaded being the bearer of this bad news, so he said, "Let's go over this *one* more time."

"It's not going to get any better, but here goes," Lee took at deep breath. "Web-4-U is based on outmoded technology. It was the best available last year, but *this* year the industry has agreed on a new standard and if we persist in using Web-4-U, we are going to be out of date before Green even hits the street. We need to go back and completely rethink our technical approach based on the new standard and then redesign our web interface. I know it's a setback and it will be expensive, but it has to be done."

"How come we didn't know about this earlier?" McCann demanded.

Lee replied, "When the standard was announced, we didn't realize what the implications were at first. It was only in our quarterly architecture meeting that the subject came up. That's why I'm here now." The architects were a breed apart, thought McCann. All tech and *no* business sense. They'd lost almost three months because of this. "By the way," Lee concluded, "Web-4-U knew about this too. They're scrambling to rewrite their code. I guess they figured if you didn't know right away, there would be more chance of you sticking with them."

The chances of *that* are slim to none, thought McCann. His *next* software provider, whoever that was, was going to be sitting right here under his steely gaze. Seeing an agitated Wendy Chan at his door, he brought the meeting to a hasty close. "I'm going to have to discuss this with Brian," he told Lee. "We can't surprise him with this at the Steering Committee meeting. Hang tight for a couple of days, and I'll get back to you."

"Okay," said Lee, "but remember, we're wasting time."

Easy for *you* to say, thought McCann as he gestured Chan into his office. She was his counterpart at the IMR project, and they had always had a good working relationship. "I just wanted to give you a 'heads up' that we've got a serious problem at IMR that will affect you," she began. Llamas began prancing into his mind's eye. "Tompkins is refusing to switch to our new data dictionary. We've spent months hammering this out with the team, but he says he wasn't kept informed about the implications of the changes, and now he's refusing to play ball. I don't know *how* he could say that. He's had a rep on the team from the beginning, and we've been sending him regular progress reports."

McCann was copied on those reports. Their pages of techno-jargon would put *anyone* to sleep! He was sure that Tompkins had never got past the first page of any of those reports. His rep was a dweeb too—someone

Tompkins thought he could live without in his daily operations.

"Damn! This is something I *don't* need." Like all IT guys, McCann *hated* corporate politics with a passion. He didn't understand them and wasn't good at them. Why hadn't Samba and his team picked up on this? They were plugged into the business. Now he was going to have to deal with Chan's problem as well as his own if he wanted to get the Green project going. Their back-end processes wouldn't work at all unless everyone was using the same information in the same format. Why couldn't Tompkins see that? Did he *want* the Green project to fail?

"The best way to deal with this one," advised Chan, "is to *force* him to accept these changes. Go to John Johnson and tell him that you need Tompkins to change his business processes to fit our data dictionary. It's for the good of the company, after all." Chan's long suit wasn't her political savvy.

"You're right that we need Tompkins on side," said McCann, "but there may be a better way. Let me talk to Samba. He's got his ear to the ground in the business. I'll speak with him and get back to you."

After a bit of chitchat, Wendy Chan left McCann to his PERT chart, trying again to determine the extra cost in time if they went with the new technology. Just then, the phone rang. It was Linda Perkins, his newly hired work-at-home usability designer. She was one of the best in the business, and he was lucky to have snagged her just coming off maternity leave. His promise of flexible working hours and full benefits had lured her back to work two months before her year-long leave ended. "You've *got* to do something about your HR department!" Linda announced. "They've just told me that I'm not eligible for health and dental benefits because I don't work on the premises! Furthermore, they want to classify me as contingent staff, not managerial, because I don't fit in one of their petty little categories for employees. You promised me that you had covered all this before I took the job! I gave up a good job at LifeCo so I could work from home."

McCann had indeed covered this issue in principle with Rick Morrow, IT's HR representative, but that had been almost eight months ago. Morrow had since left the firm. McCann wondered if he had left any paperwork on this matter. The HR IT spot had not yet been filled, and all of the IT managers were upset about HR's unreceptive attitude when it came to adapting its policies to the realities of today's IT world. "Okay, Linda, just hang in there for a day or two and I'll get this all sorted out," he promised. "How's the usability testing coming along?"

"That's *another* thing I wanted to talk with you about. The team's making changes to the look and feel of the product without consulting me," she fumed. "I can't do my job without being in the loop. You *have* to make them tell me when they're doing things like this."

McCann sighed. Getting Linda on the project had been such a coup that he hadn't given much thought to how the lines of communication would work within such a large team. "I hear you, Linda, and we'll work this out. Can you just give me a few days to figure out how we can improve things?"

Hanging up, he grabbed his jacket and slunk out of the office as quickly as he could before any other problems could present themselves. If he just kept walking south, he'd make it to the Andes in three, maybe four, months. He could teach himself Spanish along the way. At least the llamas would appreciate his efforts! MM could take their project and give it to some other poor schmuck. *No way* was he going back! He walked furiously down the street, mentally ticking off the reasons why he had been a fool to fall for Smith's sweet talk. Then, unbidden, a plan of attack formed in his head. Walking always did the trick. Getting out of the office cleared his head and focused his priorities. He turned back the way he had come, now eager to get back in the fray. There were some things he had to do right away, and others he had to put in place asap . . .

Discussion Questions

1. Some organizational factors increase a project's likelihood of success. Identify these "facilitators" for the Green project.

2. Other organizational factors decrease a project's likelihood of success. Identify these "barriers" for the Green project.

3. Outline the things that McCann needs to do right away.

GIANT FOOD AND ELENSYS: Looking Out for Customers or Gross Privacy Invasions?

Introduction[1]

Russell B. Fair, Vice President of Pharmacy Operations for Giant Food Inc., was walking his dog early on a Sunday morning in February. As was his custom, he had brought the newspaper with him to read. When he unfolded the front section of the *Washington Post*, the headline leaped out at him: "Prescription Sales, Privacy Fears; CVS, Giant Share Customer Records with Drug Marketing Firm." The story began: "Using technology in a new way to market drugs, CVS Corp. and Giant Food Inc. are sending confidential prescription information to a Massachusetts company that tracks customers who don't refill prescriptions, a practice that some experts say raises new questions about medical privacy. The company, a computer database marketing specialist, uses the data to send personalized letters—written on pharmacy letterhead and sometimes paid for by drug manufacturers—that either remind customers to keep taking their medicine or pitch new products that will treat the customer's ailment" [O'Harrow, 1998].

The article quoted a noted physician, "It's a gross invasion . . . Do you want the great computer in the sky to have a list of every drug you take . . . all without your permission?"

"This is trouble," Fair thought to himself as he folded up the newspaper and headed for home. Within a few hours, he began receiving phone calls from the supervisors in the stores who reported they were receiving many complaints from irate customers. Fair knew immediately that Giant had a problem with the fledgling alliance Giant's pharmacy established with Elensys

Care Services, Inc. to run a patient education and prescription drug compliance program. When Fair reached Giant's CEO at home and explained the situation, the CEO asked him, "What do you want to do?"

The Companies

Giant Food, Inc.

In February 1936, N.M. Cohen and Samuel Lehrman opened the first Giant food store on Georgia Avenue in Washington, D.C. The store was based on a novel concept for the times: a large self-service store that could offer lower prices to consumers by substituting high volume for high markups. As of 2005, Giant operated 203 supermarkets including 174 full-service pharmacies in Virginia, Maryland, the District of Columbia, Delaware, and New Jersey. The Delaware and New Jersey stores operated under the name Super G. Giant also operated two large distribution centers, a bakery, a dairy processing plant, an ice cube processing plant, as well as a soda bottling plant, all in suburban Maryland. The company extensive private label line included as many as 9,000 products carrying the Super G label.[2] Giant was the market leader in the Washington metropolitan area.

Giant's reputation is a family business with a strong history of service to the community and innovation. In the late 1980s, Giant was the first supermarket chain to install front-end scanning in all of its stores, a feat which as of December 1991 had been duplicated by only a few others.[3] In 1970 it was one of the first food retailers to hire a consumer advocate, former Presidential advisor Esther Peterson. Giant's current Vice President of Consumer Affairs, Odonna Mathews was a familiar figure from Giant's newspaper and television ads,

---

1. This case was originally published as: "Giant Food and ElenSys: Looking out for Customers or Gross Privacy Invasions," by Culnan, M.J. © 2006. *Communications of the AIS*, (16) p. 317–328. Used with permission from Association for Information Systems, Atlanta, GA: 404–413–7444; www.aisnet.org. All rights reserved.

---

2. Giant Food. [1998]. Inc. Corporate Profile, May 1998.

3. Giant Food. [2005b]. The History of Giant

Table 13.1. Elensys Core Values

- Focus on patient health
- Patient confidentiality must be absolute
- Physicians are the focal point of all patient treatment decisions
- Pharmacists play a critical role in counseling and educating patients about their medications

---

in-store promotions and educational materials. Giant contributed more than $6 million annually in cash, goods and services to support charitable and community organizations in the markets it served.[4]

In 1964, N.M. Cohen, one of the founders, turned the reins of the business over to his son Izzy, who served on the Board of Directors since its founding. Izzy Cohen served as chairman, president, and CEO until 1992 when he tapped Pete L. Manos to serve in the role of company president. Izzy Cohen died on November 22, 1995. Cohen's commitment to the customer—"There is nothing too good for a Giant customer"—permeated Giant's corporate culture. Cohen's guiding principles endures today: quality, value, and especially service in a warm and friendly atmosphere.[5]

In October 1998, Royal Ahold NV, a Dutch grocery giant, completed a $2.7 billion cash purchase of Giant. Giant's stock was delisted on the American Stock Exchange on October 30. Pete L. Manos, Izzy Cohen's successor as Giant's Chairman and CEO, announced his retirement after four decades with the firm. In 2003, Royal Ahold announced it would merge Giant and its corporate sibling, Stop & Shop Supermarket Co., consolidating the corporate offices at Stop & Shop's headquarters in Massachusetts.

Elensys Care Services, Inc.

Elensys, located in Burlington, Massachusetts, was founded in late 1993 by Dan Rubin and Mike Evanisko. Evanisko was an executive with a management consulting firm. Rubin was also a management consultant with extensive experience in the pharmaceutical industry. Based on his experience, he saw an opportunity to address the health care problem of prescription noncompliance, primarily with chronic conditions such as hypertension (high blood pressure), asthma, diabetes, and high cholesterol. Rubin knew that more than half of all patients on these types of medications stopped taking their prescriptions prematurely.

The Elensys programs focused on the development and management of patient compliance programs that educated patients about their medications and reminded patients to refill their prescriptions. The services Elensys offered to its customers, retail pharmacies, included compliance program strategy and planning, communications design, program implementation and performance analysis to ensure maximum program impact. All of Elensys' programs were designed to provide clear therapeutic or economic benefits for patients as their core values illustrate.[6]

Better compliance potentially benefited everyone. For patients, it meant better health. For pharmacies and pharmaceutical companies, it meant increased revenues. Pharmaceutical manufacturers often earned very high gross margins on branded products. These companies made significant sales and marketing investments, typically focused on inducing doctors to write prescriptions for their products. For these firms, non-compliance resulted in billions of dollars in lost revenues. Retail pharmacies would increase their revenues through better compliance due to increased prescription refills plus whatever additional purchases their customers made in the stores with each store visit. As a result of managed care, gross margins in the retail pharmacy industry had declined from 35% to 17–20%. The health care system in general and the managed care system in particular would also benefit through reduced costs that resulted from better health of the public. The question was who should pay the costs of running compliance programs?

In developing his business model, Rubin spoke with a representative from a major managed health care organization but quickly learned that managed care was not likely to be a viable vehicle for implementing his idea. While increased prescription compliance would likely lead to lower overall costs for these plans, the head of pharmacy at most managed care plans was primarily concerned with controlling prescription costs (i.e. utilization); the programs Rubin envisioned running would lead to increased utilization of prescription medications and therefore drive pharmacy costs up for

---

4. Giant Food. [2005a]. Press release, April 19, 2005.

5. Giant Food. [1995a]. "Izzy," We News Special Edition, Giant Food publication, November 1995.

6. Elensys Care Services, Inc. [1998].

the managed care plans. Further, people switched health care plans approximately every 18 months, meaning the next plan would reap the benefits of the former plan's investment in the compliance program.

Rubin subsequently identified retail pharmacies as the potential partner with both a financial interest and a "professional obligation" to provide such services. This business model was attractive because pharmacies maintained an electronic record of every pharmacy transaction.

These data were needed to allow for timely communications with patients and to measure the effectiveness of these communications in improving compliance. The pharmacy data could help identify specific points or activities in a patient's therapy, such as missing a refill or obtaining their last refill without a new prescription. Further, many pharmacies did not possess the in-house information systems resources to develop the database and tracking capabilities needed to manage compliance programs. In the Gallup surveys of public perceptions of the most trusted professions conducted early in 2002 and 2003, the public rated pharmacists in the top ten.[7] Elensys' business model would build on this relationship between the consumer and the pharmacist by providing communication and prescription education materials about the consumer's specific medications to the consumer from their local pharmacy.

The Elensys compliance programs were funded in one of two ways. Many were funded by the pharmaceutical manufacturers who approached a pharmacy to run a compliance program for all of the pharmacy's patients for whom a specific drug was prescribed. Pharmacies could also pay Elensys themselves to run a program on their behalf.

The business was launched in July 1995 with two regional pharmacy chains as customers. Employees included two former Vice Presidents of Pharmacy at major pharmacy chains, and clinical pharmacists with both research and practical experience. By 1998, the firm grew to approximately twenty employees. At that time, Elensys received prescription data from approximately 15,000 pharmacies [O'Harrow 1998]. New customers were acquired primarily by making sales calls and by exhibiting at trade shows.

All communications to patients were sent on behalf of and at the direction of Elensys' customers, the pharmacies. Thus, nothing was ever sent to a patient that hadn't been previously reviewed and approved by the participating pharmacy chain. For example, once the

pharmacy decided to run a compliance program for a particular medication, Elensys would enable the mailing of personalized letters to a pharmacy's patients on the pharmacy's letterhead, educating patients as well as reminding them to refill their prescriptions. The format of the letter could be customized based on the patient's demographics using research on effective communication strategies for that demographic sub-group.

Pharmaceutical Industry Trends

In the 1990s, the move to managed care brought significant changes to the healthcare system and placed enormous pressures on the profits of the pharmaceutical industry. In the U.S., which constituted one-third of the world's pharmaceutical market, 80% of the population was covered by managed care in 1993. In 1995, managed care organizations controlled 75% of the drug purchases in the U.S. The majority of these organizations employed formularies, a list of approved medicines, as one method of cost control; the insurance company would only pay for drugs listed on the formulary. By the mid-1990s, the same price pressures had also reached Europe with governments imposing price reductions on many drugs.[8]

Further, by 1996, approximately 86% of health maintenance organizations (HMO's) routinely substituted generic products for patented drugs whenever possible, further reducing the profitability of the drug manufacturers. This trend away from the need to prescribe more expensive branded drugs was accelerated by the 1984 Waxman-Hatch Act that reduced barriers to entry in the pharmaceutical industry by accelerating the FDA approval process for bringing generic drugs to market. As a result of formularies, generics, and other cost pressures, pharmaceuticals appeared to be headed for commodity status. In an effort to combat these trends and to address a public health problem, prescription medicine noncompliance, the pharmaceutical companies initiated patient education programs.[9]

Patient Education Programs

During the 1990s, recognition of the importance of patient education concerning their conditions, their prescribed treatments, and their treatment options grew. This recognition was reflected in two regulatory programs:

1. In 1990, Congress required pharmacists to offer to discuss any information they deemed significant

7. Veverka. [2000]. In this survey, pharmacists ranked second, after nurses.

8. Harvard Business School. [1998].

9. Castagnoli. [1995]. p. 46–53.

with any patients receiving benefits under Medicaid. Subsequently, some states adopted laws requiring counseling for all patients.

2. In 1996, Congress required pharmacists to disseminate "useful written information" to all consumers about their prescription drugs. Pharmacists responded to this requirement with a variety of tailored printed materials that they provided to consumers in a face-to-face encounter when people received their prescriptions. Because of the costs associated with developing and disseminating this information in a format that satisfies the requirements of the law, the materials were often funded by pharmaceutical manufacturers.[10]

Pharmacies also engaged in three other kinds of direct-to-patient (DTP) messaging.

1. Compliance messaging encouraged proper use of prescribed medications. In particular, the pharmacy or the pharmacist might remind a patient to finish a course of treatment such as taking all prescribed antibiotics, or to refill a prescription. In developed countries, on average only 50% of prescriptions are taken as prescribed, and nearly half of all patients stop taking their medication within the six months of being prescribed.[11] Further, noncompliance, or the failure of an individual to take medication as prescribed, was estimated to account for over $100 billion in costs to the U.S. healthcare system.

   Compliance programs were particularly important for chronic conditions such as diabetes, high cholesterol, or hypertension (high blood pressure). For example, a study conducted by the University of Southern California School of Pharmacy found that non-compliant patients with high blood pressure cost the California Medicaid system $591.46 more per patient than those who maintained their therapy during a twelve month period.[12]

2. The second DTP program involved messages about treatment alternatives or adjunctive therapies. For example, the pharmacy might notify a consumer about a lower-cost generic drug that was equivalent to a more expensive brand name drug the patient was currently taking, or the pharmacy might notify the patient about alternative medications that were covered by the individual's health insurance plan. These types of messages were sometimes viewed as

controversial if they were sponsored by a pharmaceutical manufacturer. These messages also raised concerns about interfering with the doctor-patient relationship.

3. The third type of DTP messaging involved educating consumers about their conditions; for example, educating people with diabetes about ways to manage their disease. Pharmacists traditionally viewed this type of messaging as central to their professional responsibilities. However, these messages could also be viewed as controversial when they were funded by third parties such as pharmaceutical manufacturers.

The pharmaceutical companies were losing approximately $35 billion annually to unfilled prescriptions. DTP messaging programs potentially provided a way for pharmaceutical companies to reduce these losses. For example, prior research found that reminders, either by mail or telephone, increased prescription refill compliance.[13] McKesson, a healthcare supply management company, operated a Patient Care Enhancing Program (PCEP) in collaboration with 500 pharmacies nationwide. Compliance for Coumadin, a blood thinner from Dupont Pharma, increased 25% after patients received a PCEP reminder to refill their prescriptions.[14]

However, a letter from a physician to the editor in the Journal of the American Medical Association raised ethical concerns about compliance programs financed by pharmaceutical companies that only included consumers who were prescribed a specific drug from that manufacturer excluding the rest of the pharmacy's customers who suffered from the same condition. "It appears that the true motivation for this campaign lies in the drawers of their cash registers," the physician wrote.[15]

Privacy Issues

The use of DTP messaging also potentially raised privacy issues. In 1993, the *Harris-Equifax Health Information Survey* found that 60% of the public felt it was not acceptable for pharmacists to provide names and information of customers taking certain medications to pharmaceutical companies for direct marketing without first obtaining the individual's consent.[16] The Direct Marketing Association, a trade association that represented pharmaceutical companies through

10. National Consumers League. [2004].

11. World Health Organization. [2003].

12. McCombs, et al. [1994].

13. Stockwell and Schulz. [1992].

14. McLaughlin. [1998].

15. Hirsch, Sherwood and Denman. [1998].

16. Louis Harris & Associates [1993]

its healthcare marketing group, formulated voluntary privacy guidelines for marketing use of health and medical data. Because of the sensitivity of medical data, information derived from the patient-care provider relationship should never be used for marketing purposes. Other health and medical data voluntarily disclosed by the consumer should be treated as sensitive, and rented, sold, transferred or exchanged only where appropriate safeguards were in place. To participate in the McKesson PCEP for example, patients needed to register for the program and could "opt out" of the program at any time by calling a telephone number found in all mailings they received.

On April 14, 2001, U.S. Department of Health and Human Services (HHS) issued a Privacy Rule which meant that for the first time, the privacy of medical information in the United States was protected by law. HHS issued final modifications to the Privacy Rule on August 14, 2002. The Privacy Rule was required by the Health Insurance Portability and Accountability Act of 1996 (HIPAA) and covered health insurance plans, health care clearinghouses, and health care providers who conducted health care transactions electronically. The majority of covered organizations were required to comply with the Privacy Rule by April 14, 2003. Small health plans were given until April 14, 2004 to comply. Appendix 13.1 provides an overview of the provisions of the final Privacy Rule. A separate rule on information security took effect on April 20, 2005 for most covered entities. Small health plans had until April 14, 2006 to comply with the security rule. The security rule required organizations to "reasonably safeguard" protected health information from intentional or unintentional use or disclosure that violated the standards and further specified implementation standards for administrative, physical and technical standards.[17]

Rubin knew from day one that privacy would be an issue for Elensys. The following steps were taken to protect the privacy of the pharmacies' customers.

1. The database for each pharmacy was split into two parts: one part contained name and address information, the second part contained prescription information but no personally identifiable

information, so analysis could be done without knowing the patient's identity. To generate mailings, the two files could be linked through a unique I.D. assigned to each patient's records. The database had extraordinary security; even the CEO did not have access to the information.

2. Postcards were never used for mailings. Instead, all mailings were sent by first class mail using window envelopes so there was no chance of the wrong letter getting into an envelope. The pharmacy signed off on all communications.

3. Elensys considered itself a true partner and it would caution pharmacies not to accept any inappropriate programs to avoid potential trouble.

4. Patients could "opt out" of any compliance program at any time through a number of easy methods including a postage paid business reply envelope (BRE) and a toll free phone number included on all mailings.[18]

5. Elensys did not run marketing programs, it only ran compliance programs. It did not send coupons to patients nor did it run any "switch" programs where letters would be sent to patients taking one drug suggesting they ask their doctor to switch them to another drug or engage in other forms of direct marketing. These switch programs were a legal form of DTP communication and while other firms in this industry were running these types of programs, all of Elensys' programs provided information only about the specific drug prescribed by the patient's physician.

6. Elensys never provided or sold patient prescription information to pharmaceutical companies. Such an action would violate the contract between Elensys and the pharmacy.

Giant and Elensys

Giant began investigating the feasibility of providing a prescription compliance program in early 1997. In addition to the public health issues noncompliance raised, unfilled prescriptions resulted in lost revenue streams for Giant. The companies viewed compliance programs as benefiting consumers through better health in addition to increased sales for retailers and manufacturers.

Like other large chains, Giant was previously approached by pharmaceutical companies hoping to gain access to Giant's customers to do DTP marketing. Giant declined these offers because it was not comfortable with what the pharmaceutical companies wanted

---

17. See: http://www.hhs.gov/ocr/hipaa/ for complete information about the HIPAA Privacy Rule. A summary of the Rule is available at http://www.hhs.gov/ocr/privacysummary.pdf. The marketing provisions of the Rule are available at http://www.hhs.gov/ocr/hipaa/guidelines/marketing.pdf. Information about the Security Rule is available at http://www.cms.hhs.gov/hipaa/hipaa2 [accessed April 23, 2005].

18. The national "opt-out" rate for programs administered by Elensys was less than 3%.

to do and felt these offers were not appropriate. Giant also was concerned about mailing reminders to their customers. However, the trade publications suggested that everyone was running compliance programs, and no legal or other problems were reported with consumers. State Attorney Generals and consumer advocates had not raised any concerns about these programs. Russell Fair talked to other chains and found they were running similar programs. Further, Giant's own customers would bring in letters they received from competitors such as CVS. In short, nothing suggested that these programs raised a red flag.

Giant first investigated the feasibility of running a compliance program in-house. However, the information systems requirements were too large. For example, to develop the tracking database needed to monitor compliance would tie up too many resources versus partnering with an organization that already developed this technology. Giant decided to outsource the compliance program.

Fair learned about Elensys from reading articles about what other companies were doing in trade journals such as *Drugstore News and Chainstore Age*, and from attending trade shows where Elensys exhibited. He liked that fact that Elensys was the only independent company running compliance programs. The others all were associated with a pharmaceutical manufacturer. Fair didn't trust the firewalls these companies established between the compliance programs and the other parts of the business.

Fair decided to partner with Elensys. In his discussions with legal and risk management professionals all agreed the program raised privacy concerns. They were also concerned about other business risks. However, since so many other pharmacies were already participating in similar programs, they decided the downside risks were manageable. Giant's legal department negotiated the contract with Elensys. With many of its other customers, Elensys negotiated directly with the pharmaceutical companies for program funding. However, Giant chose to tightly control the environment by negotiating its own agreements directly with the pharmaceutical companies. Giant alone would determine what communications were sent to its customers. They would avoid offers for "controversial" drugs such as Prozac. Giant did not want to risk customers inferring that "Giant knows 'X' about me."

Once Giant negotiated with a pharmaceutical company to do a compliance program for a particular drug, the relevant consumers would be identified using Elensys' proprietary database software. Each consumer would be sent a letter introducing the program and inviting them to participate. An 800-number was provided for the consumer to opt out of the program. If no response was received, additional educational letters would go out on Giant letterhead. Separate letters were sent for each drug; no mass mailing was to go out to all Giant customers.

Elensys also provided periodic measurement reporting so Giant could assess the performance of the compliance program. Analysis was performed using non-identifiable data through proprietary techniques which used the Elensys database software, and could quantify the impact of the compliance programs statistically on increasing patient retention on their prescribed medications.

In December 1997, Giant began sending its pharmacy transaction data to Elensys to test the database design and so that Elensys could begin to identify trends. Each week, Giant would send the transactions for that week. Giant did not provide Elensys with its entire customer database (Appendix 13.2 lists the fields that were provided for each customer transaction). To track compliance, a baseline of 6–8 weeks of transaction data was needed. At Elensys, Giant's data were stored in a separate database that only contained data from Giant, running on hardware that was only used for processing Giant's data. Fair felt it was essential that no one else could gain access to Giant's customer data. However, as of mid-February when the article appeared in the *Washington Post* about the program, Elensys had yet to send out a single communication on behalf of Giant.

Dealing with the Impending Crisis

Fair arrived at work early Monday morning. He met with Odonna Mathews, Giant's Vice President-Consumer Affairs, who was not involved in the original Elensys decision. The two of them quickly agreed on a course of action.

Discussion Questions

1. What caused all the flap about Elensys? Dissect the information and money flows. Who pays whom for what? What information is being used and by whom? What is the business relationship between Elensys, the pharmacies, and the pharmaceutical companies?

2. Do compliance programs provide any legitimate benefits? If so, to whom?

3. Does the Elensys compliance program represent a compatible or incompatible use of Giant's prescription data? Based on your conclusion,

critique Giant's implementation of fair information practices.

4. Is there anything Giant could have done to salvage the situation, either from the beginning or after the fact? Consider the costs and implementation issues for your recommendations.

5. Is the Elensys program legal under the HIPAA regulations (see Appendix 13.1)? Is it ethical?

Acknowledgments

The author acknowledges the generous assistance of Russ Fair, Odonna Mathews, Dan Rubin, Rick Franks and Matt Glaser in the development of the case, and the helpful comments of Prof. William K. McHenry of the University of Akron on prior versions of this case. Editor's Note: This article was received on April 23, 2005 and was published on August 3, 2005.

References

Castagnoli, William G. (1995). "Is Disease Management Good Therapy for an Ailing Industry?" *Medical Marketing & Media*, January 1, p. 46–53.

Elensys Care Services. (1998). "Patient Compliance & Education Services: Description of Services?" Woburn, MA: Elensys.

Giant Food. (1995). "Izzy," We News Special Edition, November.

Giant Food. (1998). Corporate Profile, Giant Food, Inc. May.

Giant Food. (2005a). Press release, April 19.

Giant Food. (2005b). The History of Giant. http://www .giantfood.com/corporate/company_aboutgiant2 .htm (accessed July 25, 2005).

Harvard Business School. (1998). *The Pharma Giants: Ready for the 21st Century?* Case 9–698- 070, Boston, MA: HBS Press May 6.

Hirsch, Ronald L., L. M. Sherwood and J. Denman. (1998). "Merck-Sponsored Simvastatin (Zocor) Compliance Program for Patients Using Wal-Mart Pharmacy: Of Benefit to Whom?" *JAMA*, (279)23, pp. 1875–1876, (June 17).

Louis Harris and Associates. (1993). *Harris-Equifax Health Information Privacy Survey*, Atlanta: Equifax.

McCombs, Jeffrey S., et al. (1998). "The Costs of Interrupting Antihypertensive Therapy in a Medicaid Population," *Medical Care,* (32) pp. 214–226.

McLaughlin, Mark. (1998). "Pharmacy Database Program Helps Consumers Keep Their Refills Current," *DM News*, November 9, p. 10.

National Consumers League. (2004). *Health Care Communications Provided by Pharmacies: Best Practices Principles for Safeguarding Patient Privacy*. http:// www.nclnet.org/pressroom/pharmacy_privacy_ practices_report.htm (accessed April 23, 2005).

O'Harrow, Robert Jr. (1998). "Prescription Sales, Privacy Fears: CVS, Giant Share Customer Records with Drug Marketing Firm," *Washington Post*, February 15, pp. A1.

Stockwell, M.L. and R.M. Schulz. (1992). "Patient Compliance: An Overview", *Journal of Clinical Pharmacy and Therapeutics*, (17) pp. 283–295.

Veverka, A. (2000). "Gallup Poll Shows Fewer Americans Trust Accountants" Knight Ridder Tribune Business News, December 20, p. 1.

World Health Organization. (2003). *Adherence to Long Term Therapies: Evidence for Action,* Geneva: WHO. http://www.who.int/chronic_conditions/ adherencereport/en/ (accessed April 23, 2005).

Appendix 13.1. Overview of the Final HIPAA Health Privacy Rule[19]

The regulation established national standards to control the flow of sensitive patient information and penalties for the misuse or disclosure of the information. The regulation covers medical records and other individually identifiable health information related to treatment, payment, and health care operations held or disclosed by a covered entity (health care providers and health plans that transmit health information for standard transactions electronically). The regulation includes the following protections.

Consumer Control Over Health Information

Patients must be provided with notice of the patient's privacy rights and the privacy practices of the covered entity. Consent for routine health care delivery purposes is not required. However, treatment providers are required to make a good faith effort to obtain the patient's written acknowledgment of the notice. Consent is required for other uses of personal information.

Boundaries on Medical Record Use and Release

With limited exceptions, an individual's health information can be used or disclosed for health purposes only.

---

19. See: http://www.hhs.gov/ocr/hipaa/ for complete information about the HIPAA Privacy Rule. A summary of the Rule is available at http://www.hhs.gov/ocr/privacysummary.pdf. The marketing provisions of the Rule are available at http://www .hhs.gov/ocr/hipaa/guidelines/marketing.pdf.

Information about the Security Rule is available at http:// www.cms.hhs.gov/hipaa/hipaa2/

Entities covered by this regulation may disclose health information to a business associate, and may allow a business associate to create or receive health information on its behalf if the entity obtains satisfactory assurance that the business associate will appropriately safeguard the information. A business associate is a third party that may provide services on behalf of the entity on a contractual basis (e.g., outsourcing).

Establish Accountability for Medical Records Use and Release

Entities covered by the regulation must adopt written privacy policies, train employees, designate a privacy officer, and establish grievance processes for patients. The detailed policies and procedures for meeting the standards specified in the regulation are left to the discretion of each covered entity.

Health plans, providers and clearinghouses that violate these standards are subject to civil penalties. Federal criminal penalties apply if covered entities knowingly and improperly disclose information or obtain information under false pretenses.

Rules Related to Marketing

Health organizations covered by this rule (covered entities) must obtain the patient's written authorization to use or disclose protected health information for marketing. Marketing is defined as "communication about a product or service that encourages the recipient to purchase or use the product or service." Excluded from this definition are communications related to treatment, payment, or operations:

- That describe a health-related product or service that is provided by the covered entity;
- That describe health-related products or services available to health plan enrollees that add value to (and are not part of) the plan's benefits; or
- Are related to treatment of the individual including to direct or recommend alternate therapies, providers or settings of care.

Examples of communications that are not considered marketing include:

- A health plan sends a mailing to its subscribers approaching Medicare age with materials describing its Medicare supplemental plan;
- A pharmacy or other health care provider mails prescription refill reminders to patients, or uses a business associate to do so;
- A hospital uses its patient list to send a mailing announcing the acquisition of new equipment

For any permitted communications, a covered entity is allowed to disclose protected health information to a business associate to assist with the communication. The business associate is prohibited from using the information for any other purposes.

Protected health information may also be used for fundraising under a limited set of circumstances. In this case, the fundraising materials must describe how the individual can opt out of future fundraising communications.

Covered entities may not sell lists of patients or enrollees to third parties for the marketing activities of the third party without the individual's authorization. For instances where authorization is required, the authorization must disclose if the marketing involves remuneration to the covered entity by a third party. Simply put, an entity covered by HIPAA may not sell health information protected by HIPAA to a business associate or any other third party for that party's own purposes. Further, covered entities may not sell lists of patients or enrollees to third parties without obtaining authorization from each person on the list.

Appendix 13.2. Transaction Data Supplied to Elensys

Customer Name
Customer Address
Date of Birth
Gender

Prescription Components:

- Drug
- Prescription #
- Quantity
- Date Supplied
- Number of Refills
- Doctor

Elensys' proprietary database was structured in two separate parts. One part contained the patient's name, address information, and an indicator of whether or not the patient had "opted in" or "opted out"[20] of the program. The second part contained prescription and analysis information. This separation made it possible to do data mining operations on the prescription information without ever linking this information to specific patients. Data mining operations involved sophisticated analysis based on the unique medical and pharmaceu-

---

20. With "opt-in" the patient will not receive any mailings unless they have consented. With "opt-out" the patient will be sent mailings unless they object.

tical knowledge of Elensys employees, and went well beyond simple rules of the type "If patient X has prescription Y, send mailing."

Elensys did not own any of the patient data in their database. They were legally prohibited from selling or providing in any way any of the data they acquired from the pharmacies to pharmaceutical manufacturers or others.

Abbreviations

BRE: Business reply envelope

CRM: Customer relationship marketing

DTC: Pharmaceutical direct to consumer advertising

DTP: Pharmacy direct to patient messaging

HHS: U.S. Department of Health & Human Services

HIPAA: Health Insurance Portability and Accountability Act

HMO: Health Maintenance Organization

Index

CANADIAN EDITION

ACCOUNTING PRINCIPLES

WORKING PAPERS
Volume 1
Chapters 1-10

▶ **JERRY J. WEYGANDT** *Ph.D., C.P.A.*

Arthur Andersen Alumni Professor of Accounting
University of Wisconsin
Madison, Wisconsin

▶ **DONALD E. KIESO** *Ph.D., C.P.A.*

KPMG Peat Marwick Emeritus Professor of Accountancy
North Illinois University
DeKalb, Illinois

▶ **BARBARA TRENHOLM** *M.B.A., F.C.A.*

University of New Brunswick
Fredericton, New Brunswick

JOHN WILEY AND SONS CANADA, LTD
Toronto • New York • Chichester • Weinheim • Brisbane • Singapore

Canadian Cataloguing in Publication

Weygandt, Jerry J.
    Accounting principles, Canadian edition.   Working papers

Contents: v. 1. Chapters 1-10 – v. 2. Chapters 11-19.
ISBN 0-471-64308-4 (v. 1)   ISBN 0-471-64309-2 (v. 2)

Accounting – Problems, exercises, etc. I. Trenholm, Barbara A.
II. Kieso, Donald E. III. Title.

HF5635. W38 1998 Suppl. 1   657'.044   C99-930088-1

Production Credits
Acquisitions Editor: John Horne
Publishing Services Director: Karen Bryan
Developmental Editor: Karen Staudinger
Marketing Manager: Carolyn J. Wells
Design & Typesetting: Lakshmi Gosyne
Printing & Binding: Tri-graphic Printing Limited

Printed and bound in Canada
10 9 8 7 6 5 4 3 2 1

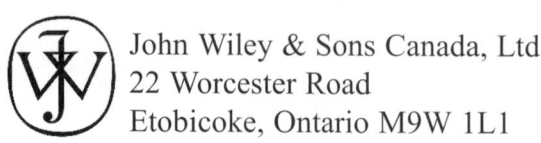

John Wiley & Sons Canada, Ltd.
22 Worcester Road
Etobicoke, Ontario M9W 1L1

Visit our website at: www.wiley.com/canada

E 1-1	Accounts payable	Assets = cash ✓
	Cash	a/c receivable ✓
	Cleaning equipment	cleaning equipment ✓
	Cleaning supplies	cleaning supplies ✓
	Accounts receivable	liabilities =
	Notes payable	notes payable ✓
	Salaries payable	salaries payable ✓
	H. Ace, Capital	A/c payable ✓
		owners equity =
		H Ace Capital ✓

E 1-2		
	1. ↑ assets ↑ owners equity
	2. ↓ assets ↓ owners equity
	3. ↑ assets ↑ payables
	4. ↑ assets ↑ owners equity
	5. ↓ assets ↓ owners equity
	6. ↑ assets (cash) ↓ receivables
	7. ↑ payable (liabilities) ↓ owner's equity
	8. ↑ assets (fixed) ↓ cash equity
	9. ↑ cash ↓ receivables

E 1-3	
	1. c
	2. e
	3. a
	4.
	5. e
	6. b
	7.
	8. f

(a) (1) ↑ Cash   ↑ owners equity

(2) ↓ cash (2000 to pd) ↑ office equip   ↑ payable

(3) ↓ cash   ↑ supplies

(4) ↑ cash   ↑ receivables   ↓ payables

(b)					
Investments				1 5 0 0 0
+ fees earned				8 0 0 0
− salaries	2 9 0 0			
− utilities	5 0 0			
− rent	6 5 0			

(c) Revenue				
Fees Earned			8 0 0 0
Expenses			
Salaries expense	2 9 0 0		
rent expense	6 5 0		
utilities	5 0 0		
Total Expense		4 0 5 0	
Net Income		3 9 5 0	

ROBERTA MENDEZ & CO.
Income Statement
For the Month Ended August 31, 1999

Revenue			8 0 0 0
Expenses			
Salaries		2 9 0 0	
Rent		6 5 0	
Utilities		5 0 0	
Total Expense		4 0 5 0	4 0 5 0
			3 9 5 0

ROBERTA MENDEZ & CO.
Statement of Owner's Equity
For the Month Ended August 31, 1999

Investments	1 5 0 0 0		
Net Income	3 9 5 0	1 6 5 0	
Less Drawings		2 0 0 0	
		9 0 5 0	

ROBERTA MENDEZ & CO.
Balance Sheet
August 31, 1999

Assets		
Cash		2 3 5 0
Receivable		2 9 5 0
Supplies / office Equipment		5 7 5 0
Total Assets		1 9 0 5 0
Liabilities		
Payables		2 0 0 0
Owner's Equity		9 0 5 0

cee pg 25

	Kate Cordova Company	Maxim Enterprises
Beginning of year:		
Total assets	9 0 0 0 0	1 3 0 0 0 0
Total liabilities	8 0 0 0 0	(c) 3 5 0 0 0
Total owner's equity	(a) 1 0 0 0 0	9 5 0 0 0
End of year:		
Total assets	1 6 0 0 0 0	1 8 0 0 0 0
Total liabilities	1 2 0 0 0 0	5 0 0 0 0
Total owner's equity	4 0 0 0 0	1 3 0 0 0 0
Changes during year in owner's equity		
Additional investment	(b) 4 0 0 0	2 5 0 0 0
Drawings	2 4 0 0 0	(d)
Total revenues	2 1 5 0 0 0	1 0 0 0 0 0
Total expenses	1 6 5 0 0 0	8 0 0 0 0

opening bal = 40,000 - 10,000
= $130,000
Net Income = 50,000
Drawings = 24,000

AS - OE = L

kate
bal = 10,000
Add In = 4,000
net Income = 50,000
Drawings = 24,000
End = 40,000

Max
OE - 95,000
+ 25,000 } = 140,000
net Income = 20,000
Ending Owner Eq = 130,000
Drawings = 10,000

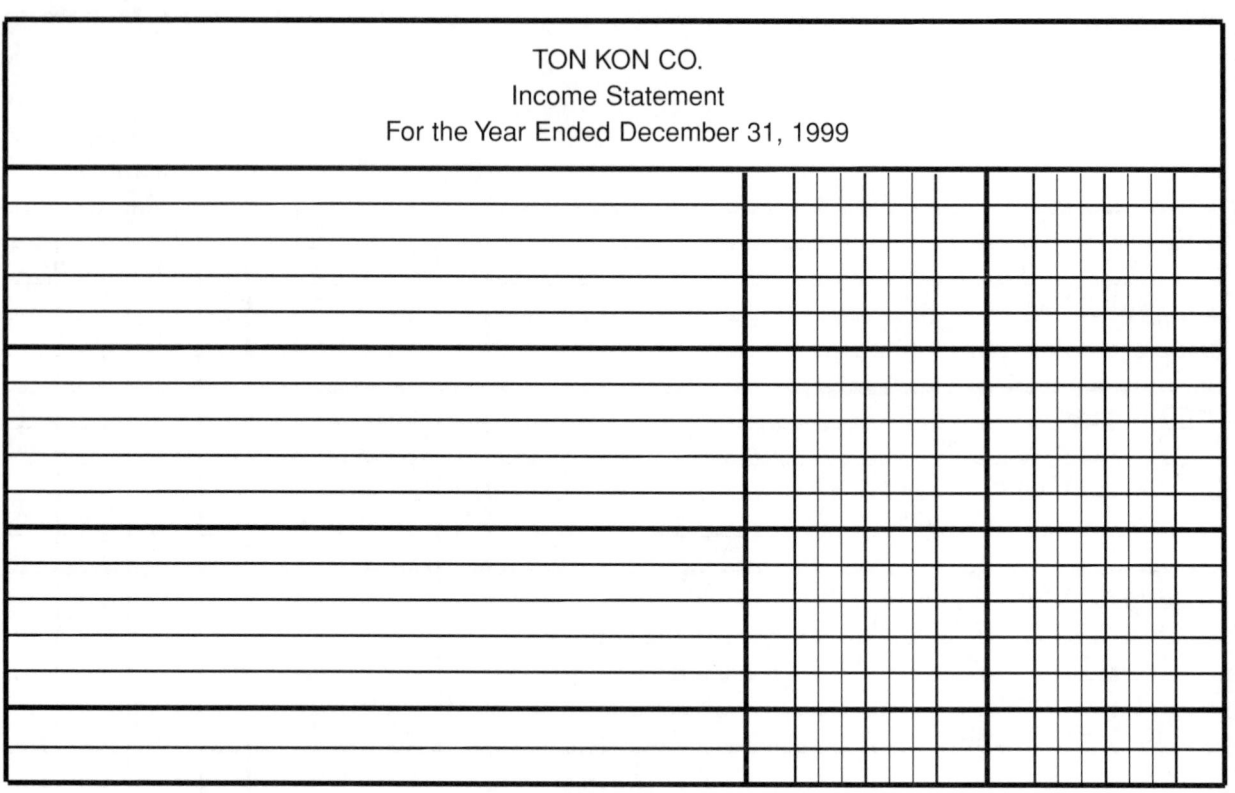

TON KON CO.
Income Statement
For the Year Ended December 31, 1999

TON KON CO.
Statement of Owner's Equity
For the Year Ended December 31, 1999

AURORA COMPANY
Balance Sheet
December 31, 1999

E 1-11

DUCHESS CRUISE COMPANY
Income Statement
For the Month Ended October 31, 1999

E 1-12

GRACE OLSEN, LAWYER
Statement of Owner's Equity
For the Year Ended December 31, 1999

Name FERN   Problem 1-1
Section Chap 1
Date 20/9/99   Seall Travel Agency

SEALL TRAVEL AGENCY

(a)

	Assets						=	Liabilities	+	Owner's Equity
Trans-actions	Cash	+	Accounts Receivable	+	Supplies	+	Office Equipment	=	Accounts Payable	+	Laura Seall, Capital
1 Investment	+ 20000									+ 20000
2 office rent	− 400								+ 400		− 400
	19600										19600
3 purchase of o/e	− 2500						+ 2500				
	17100										
4 advertise							2500		+ 360		− 360
	17100						2500				19300
5 purchase o/e	− 600						+ 600		+ 300		19300
	16500						3100		+ 1300		
6 comm. rec'd	+ 1000		+ 8000								+ 7000
	17500		+ 8000				3100		+ 300		22300
7 drawings	− 300		+ 8000								− 300
	+ 17300		+ 8000				+ 3100		+ 300		+ 28100
8 pay o/e	− 360								− 300		
	+ 17000		+ 8000				+ 3100		−		28100
9	− 1200		8000				3100		−		− 1200
	15800										
10	+ 8000		− 8000								

(b) Revenues:					9	0	0	0
Service Revenue	9,000				9	0	0	0
Expenses								
Salaries		1	2	0	0			
Rent			4	0	0			
Advt		1	3	0	0			
Total Expense					1	9	0	0
Net Income					7	1	0	0

IVAN IZO, BARRISTER AND SOLICITOR

(a)

Trans-actions		Assets				=	Liabilities		+	Owner's Equity
	Cash	+	Accounts Receivable	+	Supplies	+	Office Equipment	=	Notes Payable	+	Accounts Payable	+	Ivan Izo, Capital
Bal.	$4,000	$1,500	$500	$5,000		$4,200	$6,800
1.	+ 1400	– 1400					
2.	– 2700					+ 2700	
3.	+ 3000	+ 1400					
4.	– 460			+ 1000		+ 600	
5.	– 2750						– 2750
6.	– 550						– 550
7.	+ 2000				+ 2000		
8.	– 250						+ 250
	3750	1500	500	6600	=	2000	750	3250

(b)

IVAN IZO, BARRISTER & SOLICITOR
Income Statement
For the Month Ended August 31, 1999

Revenue			
Service Rendered			6 4 0 0 —
Expenses			
Salaries	1 5 0 0 0		
rent	4 0 0 —		
Adv	3 5 0 —		
utility	2 5 0 —		
		3 0 0 0 —	
		3 4 0 0 —	

IVAN IZO, BARRISTER & SOLICITOR
Statement of Owner's Equity
For the Month Ended August 31, 1999

Investment	6 8 0 0 —		
Net Income	3 4 0 0		
		1 0 2 0 0 —	
Less Drawings		5 5 0 —	
		9 6 5 0 —	

(b) (Continued)

IVAN IZO, BARRISTER & SOLICITOR
Balance Sheet
August 31, 1999

Cash			3750
A/c Recievable	1400		1500
Supplie			500
Office Eq	1650		6000
Supplies			
note Payable			2000
A/c Payables			12750
A/c Payable			
Owners Equity			3250
Ivan Izo capital			
Office Eq			
A/c Payables			
		0	
Income 12.			
	2950		
	50		
	50		

(a)

GLAMOUR COSMETICS CO. Income Statement For the Month Ended June 30, 1999		

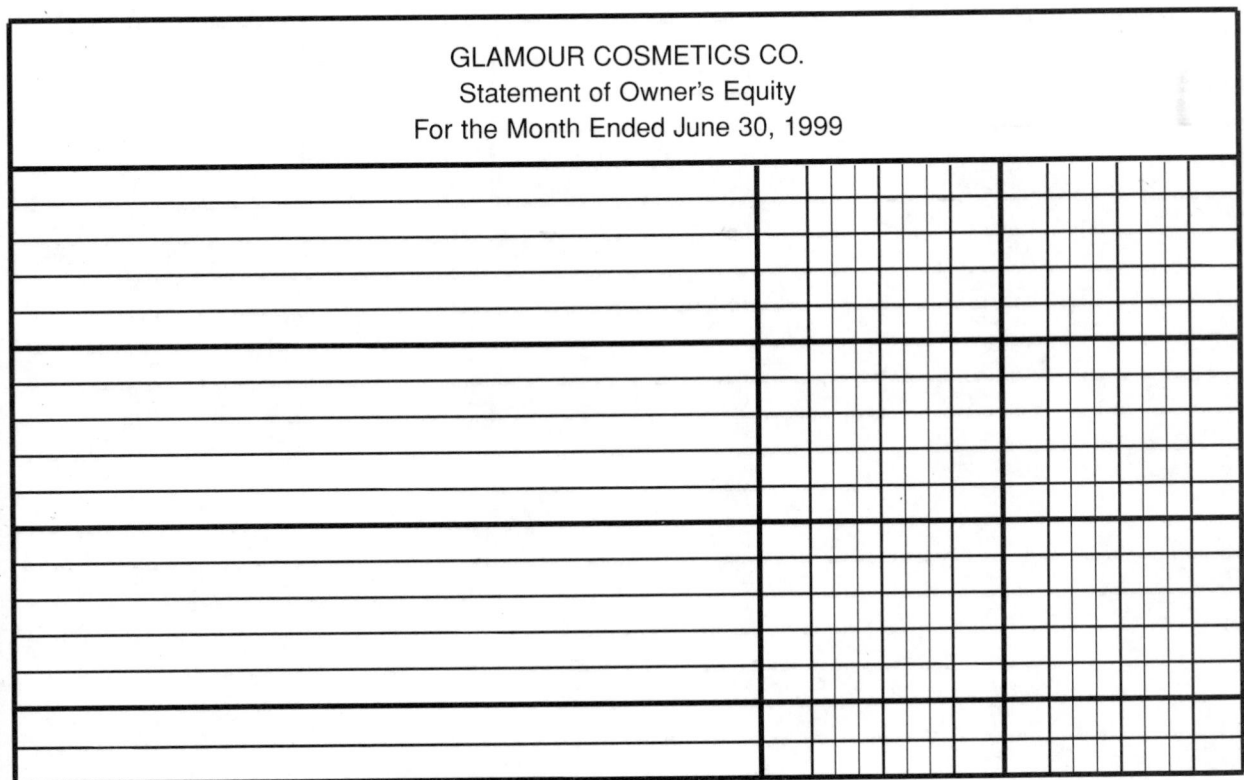

GLAMOUR COSMETICS CO. Statement of Owner's Equity For the Month Ended June 30, 1999		

(a) (Continued)

GLAMOUR COSMETICS CO.
Balance Sheet
June 30, 1999

(b)

(a)

UPTON CONSULTING CO.
Income Statement
For the Year Ended March 31, 1999

(b)

UPTON CONSULTING CO.
Statement of Owner's Equity
For the Year Ended March 31, 1999

(a)

	Baker Lake Company	Cambridge Bay Company	Dawson Company	Edmonton Company
January 1, 1999:				
Assets	80000	100000	(g)	150000
Liabilities	50000	(d)	75000	(j)
Owner's Equity	(a)	60000	45000	90000
December 31, 1999:				
Assets	(b)	130000	180000	(k)
Liabilities	55000	62000	(b)	80000
Owner's Equity	45000	(e)	110000	145000
OE Changes:				
Add'l investment	(c)	8000	10000	15000
Drawings	10000	(f)	12000	10000
Total revenues	350000	400000	(i)	500000
Total expenses	330000	385000	360000	(l)

(b)

BAKER LAKE COMPANY
Statement of Owner's Equity
For the Year Ended December 31, 1999

(c)

GOLDEN GUILDER COIN SHOP
Balance Sheet
April 30, 1999

Supporting Calculations:

(a)

CANADA COLA CORPORATION

Trans-actions	Assets					=	Liabilities			+	Shareholders' Equity
	Cash	+ A/R	+ Inventory	+ Furniture & Fixtures	+ Machinery & Equip.	=	A/P	+ N/P	+ LT Liabilities	+	SE
Balance	$102,000	+ $560,000	+ $870,000	+ $1,100,000	+ $3,000,000	=	$630,000	+ $160,000	+ $1,750,000	+	$3,092,000
1.											
2.											
3.											
4.											
5.											
6.											
7.											
8.											

(b)

CANADA COLA CORPORATION
Balance Sheet
January 7, 1999

(a)

JEANNIE WONG, LAWYER

| Trans- actions | Assets | | | | | = | Liabilities | + | Owner's Equity |
	Cash +	Damage Deposit +	Office Supplies +	Office Equipment +	Office Furniture =	=	Notes Payable +	Accounts Payable +	Jeannie Wong, Capital
1.									
2.									
3.									
4.									
5.									
6.									
7.									
8.									
9.									

(b)

JEANNIE WONG, LAWYER
Balance Sheet
March 31, 1999

(a)

(b)

PARMOR DRIVING RANGE
Balance Sheet
May 31, 1999

(c)

(d)

MEMORANDUM

DATE:

TO: Amy Joan, Bookkeeper

FROM:

SUBJECT: Balance Sheet Correction

MARY COMPANY
Income Statement
For the Month Ended July 31

MARY COMPANY
Statement of Owner's Equity
For the Month Ended July 31

MARY COMPANY
Balance Sheet
July 31

General Journal

Date	Account Titles and Explanation	Ref.	Debit	Credit

Trial Balance

	Debit	Credit

Trans-actions	Account Debited				Account Credited			
	(a) Basic Type	(b) Specific Account	(c) Effect	(d) Normal Balance	(a) Basic Type	(b) Specific Account	(c) Effect	(d) Normal Balance
1.	Asset	Cash	Increase	Debit	Owner's Equity	A. Mane Capital	Increase	Credit
2.								
3.								
4.								
5.								
6.								
7.								
8.								

Trans-actions	Account Titles and Explanation	Ref.	Debit	Credit

E 2-3

E 2-4

Date	Account Titles and Explanation	Ref.	Debit	Credit

(a)

CASH

NOTES PAYABLE

ACCOUNTS RECEIVABLE

J.L. KANG, CAPITAL

OFFICE EQUIPMENT

FEES EARNED

(b)

J.L. KANG, INVESTMENT BROKER
Trial Balance
August 31, 1999

	Debit	Credit

(a)

General Journal

Date	Account Titles and Explanation	Ref.	Debit	Credit

(b)

LUSH LANDSCAPING COMPANY
Trial Balance
April 30, 1999

	Debit	Credit

(a)

General Journal

Date	Account Titles and Explanation	Ref.	Debit	Credit

(b)

HOLLY CO.
Trial Balance
October 31, 1999

	Debit	Credit

(a)

General Journal

Date	Account Titles and Explanation	Ref.	Debit	Credit

(b)

Cash   No. 101

Date	Explanation	Ref.	Debit	Credit	Balance

Equipment   No. 157

Date	Explanation	Ref.	Debit	Credit	Balance

Accounts Payable   No. 201

Date	Explanation	Ref.	Debit	Credit	Balance

Shirley Basler, Capital   No. 301

Date	Explanation	Ref.	Debit	Credit	Balance

Shirley Basler, Drawings   No. 306

Date	Explanation	Ref.	Debit	Credit	Balance

E 2-9	(a)	(b)	(c)
Error	In Balance?	Difference	Larger Column
1. Credit posting of $400 to Accounts Receivable was omitted.			
2. $700 was debited to Insurance Expense instead of Prepaid Insurance.			
3. Collection on account credited to fees earned.			
4. Credit posting of $300 to Property Taxes Payable duplicated.			
5. Cash purchases of supplies understated $225.			
6. $465 Debit to Advertising Expense posted as $456.			

E 2-10

SPEEDY DELIVERY SERVICE

Trial Balance
July 31, 1999

	Debit	Credit

General Journal

J1

Date	Account Titles and Explanation	Ref.	Debit	Credit
1/8	T. cash Bus		50000 —	
	Inv on Bus			50000 —
3	Land Purchase			
	cash		38000 —	
	Purchase Land			38000 —

General Journal

J2

Date	Account Titles and Explanation	Ref.	Debit	Credit

General Journal   J1

Date	Account Titles and Explanation	Ref.	Debit	Credit

Cash   No. 101

Date	Explanation	Ref.	Debit	Credit	Balance

Accounts Receivable   No. 112

Date	Explanation	Ref.	Debit	Credit	Balance

Supplies   No. 126

Date	Explanation	Ref.	Debit	Credit	Balance

Accounts Payable   No. 201

Date	Explanation	Ref.	Debit	Credit	Balance
		201			

Unearned Fees   No. 205

Date	Explanation	Ref.	Debit	Credit	Balance

Patricia Perez, Capital   No. 301

Date	Explanation	Ref.	Debit	Credit	Balance

(b) (Continued)

Fees Earned   No. 400

Date	Explanation	Ref.	Debit	Credit	Balance

Salaries Expense   No. 726

Date	Explanation	Ref.	Debit	Credit	Balance

Rent Expense   No.729

Date	Explanation	Ref.	Debit	Credit	Balance

PATRICIA PEREZ, ARCHITECT
Trial Balance
April 30, 1999

	Debit	Credit

(a) Part (a) starts on the following page

(b)   General Journal   J1

Date	Account Titles and Explanation	Ref.	Debit	Credit

(a) and (c)

Cash   No. 101

Date	Explanation	Ref.	Debit	Credit	Balance

Accounts Receivable   No. 112

Date	Explanation	Ref.	Debit	Credit	Balance

Supplies   No. 126

Date	Explanation	Ref.	Debit	Credit	Balance

Equipment   No. 157

Date	Explanation	Ref.	Debit	Credit	Balance

Accounts Payable   No. 201

Date	Explanation	Ref.	Debit	Credit	Balance

Unearned Revenue   No. 206

Date	Explanation	Ref.	Debit	Credit	Balance

Jane Kent, Capital
No. 301

Date	Explanation	Ref.	Debit	Credit	Balance

Jane Kent, Drawings
No. 306

Date	Explanation	Ref.	Debit	Credit	Balance

Laundry Revenue
No. 426

Date	Explanation	Ref.	Debit	Credit	Balance

Salaries Expense
No. 726

Date	Explanation	Ref.	Debit	Credit	Balance

Utilities Expense
No. 732

Date	Explanation	Ref.	Debit	Credit	Balance

JANE'S LAUNDRY
Trial Balance
October 31, 1999

	Debit	Credit
Cash		
Accounts Receivable		
Supplies		
Equipment		
Accounts Payable		
Unearned Revenue		
Jane Kent, Capital		
Jane Kent, Drawing		
Laundry Revenue		
Salaries Expense		
Utilities Expense		

(a)

(b)

ALDOUS AUTOMOTIVE SERVICES
Trial Balance
December 31, 1998

	Debit	Credit

(a) Part (a) starts on the following page

(b)   General Journal   J1

Date	Account Titles and Explanation	Ref.	Debit	Credit

(a) and (c)

Cash   No. 101

Date	Explanation	Ref.	Debit	Credit	Balance

Accounts Receivable   No. 112

Date	Explanation	Ref.	Debit	Credit	Balance

Prepaid Rentals   No. 136

Date	Explanation	Ref.	Debit	Credit	Balance

Land   No. 140

Date	Explanation	Ref.	Debit	Credit	Balance

Buildings   No. 145

Date	Explanation	Ref.	Debit	Credit	Balance

Equipment   No. 157

Date	Explanation	Ref.	Debit	Credit	Balance

Accounts Payable   No. 201

Date	Explanation	Ref.	Debit	Credit	Balance

Mortgage Payable   No. 275

Date	Explanation	Ref.	Debit	Credit	Balance

(a) and (c) (Continued)

Frances Hill, Capital   No. 301

Date	Explanation	Ref.	Debit	Credit	Balance

Admission Revenue   No. 405

Date	Explanation	Ref.	Debit	Credit	Balance

Concession Revenue   No. 406

Date	Explanation	Ref.	Debit	Credit	Balance

Advertising Expense   No. 610

Date	Explanation	Ref.	Debit	Credit	Balance

Film Rental Expense   No. 632

Date	Explanation	Ref.	Debit	Credit	Balance

Salaries Expense   No. 726

Date	Explanation	Ref.	Debit	Credit	Balance

LAKE THEATRE Trial Balance April 30, 1999	Debit	Credit
Cash		
Accounts Receivable		
Prepaid Rentals		
Land		
Buildings		
Equipment		
Accounts Payable		
Mortgage Payable		
F. Hill, Capital		
Admission Revenue		
Concession Revenue		
Advertising Expense		
Film Rental Expense		
Salaries Expense		

General Journal   J1

(a) Date	Account Titles and Explanation	Ref.	Debit	Credit

General Journal

J1

Date	Account Titles and Explanation	Ref.	Debit	Credit

(b)

Cash

Accounts Payable

Accounts Receivable

J. Bablad, Capital

Office Supplies

Brokerage Fees Earned

Prepaid Rent

Rent Expense

Prepaid Insurance

Insurance Expense

Furniture and Equipment

Salaries Expense

Utilities Expense

(c)

Bablad Brokerage Services
Trial Balance
May 31, 1999

	Debit	Credit
Cash		
Accounts Receivable		
Office Supplies		
Prepaid Rent		
Prepaid Insurance		
Furniture and Equipment		
Accounts Payable		
J. Bablad, Capital		
Brokerage Fees Earned		
Rent Expense		
Insurance Expense		
Salaries Expense		
Utilities Expense		

(d)

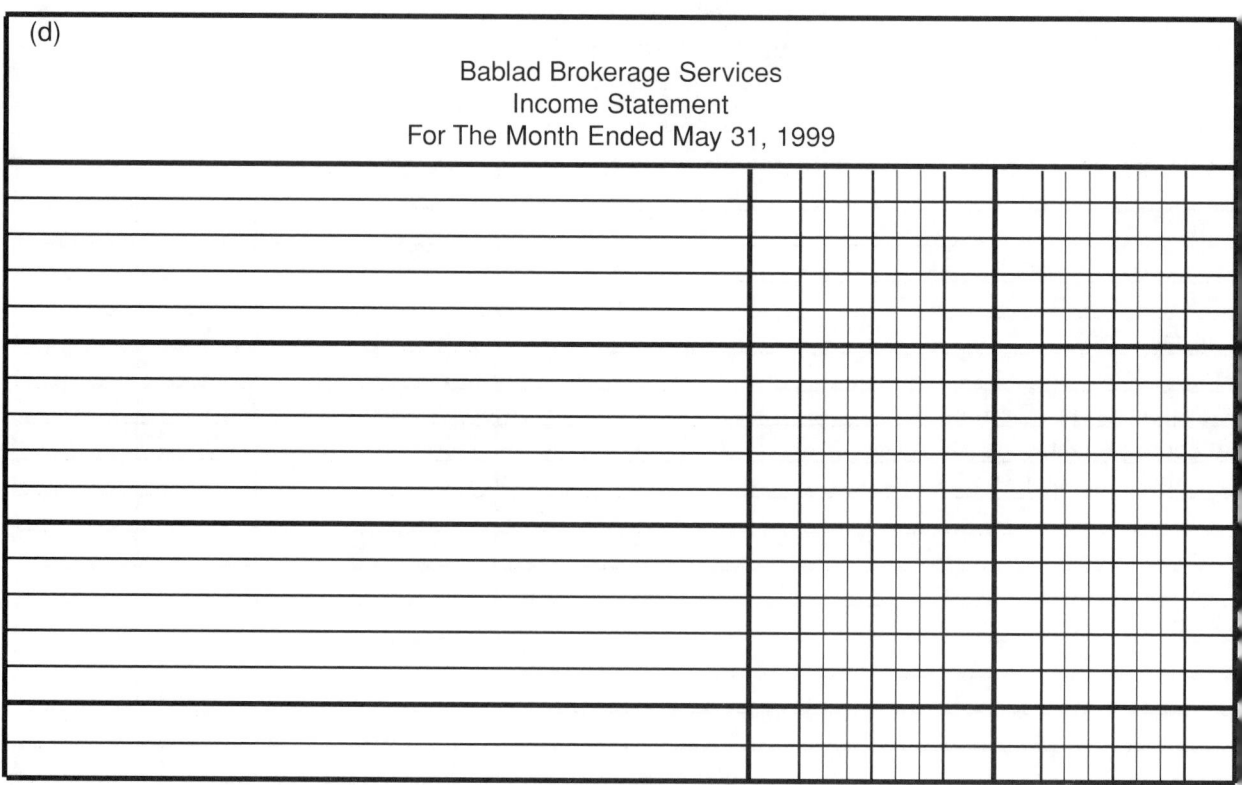

Bablad Brokerage Services
Income Statement
For The Month Ended May 31, 1999

Bablad Brokerage Services
Statement of Owner's Equity
For The Month Ended May 31, 1999

(d) (Continued)

Bablad Brokerage Services
Balance Sheet
May 31, 1999

Assets

Liabilities and Owner's Equity

(a) Explanation:

(b) and (d) T Accounts:

Cash	Mataruka, Capital

Accounts Receivable	

Parts Inventory	

Prepaid Rent	

Shop Equipment	

Accounts Payable	

(c)   General Journal   J1

Date	Account Titles and Explanation	Ref.	Debit	Credit

(e)

Byte Repair Service
Trial Balance
January 31, 1999

	Debit	Credit
Cash		
Accounts Receivable		
Parts Inventory		
Prepaid Rent		
Shop Equipment		
Accounts Payable		
L. Mataruka, Capital		

(f)

(g)

(a)

Byte Repair Service
Income Statement
For The Month Ended January 31, 1999

(b)

Byte Repair Service
Statement of Owner's Equity
For The Month Ended January 31, 1999

(c)

Byte Repair Service
Balance Sheet
January 31, 1999

Assets

Liabilities and Owner's Equity

Thom Wargo Co.
Trial Balance
June 30, 1999

	Debit	Credit

Calculations:

General Journal

Date	Account Titles and Explanation	Ref.	Debit	Credit
(a)				
(b)				
(c)				
(d)				

Memorandum
DATE:
TO:
FROM:
SUBJECT:

(a) Owner's equity, December 31, 1999

(b) Net income, year ended December 31, 1999

(c) Owner's equity, January 1, 1999

(d) Total expenses, year ended December 31, 1999

E 3-1	(a) Type of Adjustment	(b) Account Relationship	(c) Accounts before Adjustment
1.			
2.			
3.			
4.			
5.			
6.			

E 3-2

E 3-3			
E 3-4			

WELLER CO.
Income Statement
For the Month Ended July 31, 1999

E 3-5

E 3-6

BEOTHUK COMPANY
Income Statement
For the Year Ended August 31, 1999

BEOTHUK COMPANY
Statement of Owner's Equity
For the Year Ended August 31, 1999

BEOTHUK COMPANY
Balance Sheet
August 31, 1999

Date	Account Titles and Explanation	Ref.	Debit	Credit
(a)				
(b)				
(c)				

CASH   PREPAID INSURANCE

INSURANCE EXPENSE   SUPPLIES

SUPPLIES EXPENSE   UNEARNED FEES

FEES EARNED

(a)   General Journal   Ja

Date	Account Titles and Explanation	Ref.	Debit	Credit

(b)

Cash

Date	Explanation	Ref.	Debit	Credit	Balance
June 30	Balance				3000

Accounts Receivable

Date	Explanation	Ref.	Debit	Credit	Balance

Prepaid Insurance

Date	Explanation	Ref.	Debit	Credit	Balance
June 30	Balance				7200

Office Equipment

Date	Explanation	Ref.	Debit	Credit	Balance
June 30	Balance				1800

Accumulated Amortization – Office Equipment

Date	Explanation	Ref.	Debit	Credit	Balance

Buses

Date	Explanation	Ref.	Debit	Credit	Balance
June 30	Balance				140000

Accumulated Amortization – Buses

Date	Explanation	Ref.	Debit	Credit	Balance

(b) (Continued)

Accounts Payable

Date	Explanation	Ref.	Debit	Credit	Balance

Salaries Payable

Date	Explanation	Ref.	Debit	Credit	Balance

Interest Payable

Date	Explanation	Ref.	Debit	Credit	Balance
June 30	Balance				

Notes Payable

Date	Explanation	Ref.	Debit	Credit	Balance
June 30	Balance				62000

Unearned Fees

Date	Explanation	Ref.	Debit	Credit	Balance
June 30	Balance				15000

Eldon Kaplan, Capital

Date	Explanation	Ref.	Debit	Credit	Balance
June 30	Balance				70000

Fees Earned

Date	Explanation	Ref.	Debit	Credit	Balance
June 30	Balance				15900

b) (Continued)

Salaries Expense

Date	Explanation	Ref.	Debit	Credit	Balance
June 30	Balance				9000

Advertising Expense

Date	Explanation	Ref.	Debit	Credit	Balance
June 30	Balance				800

Gas and Oil Expense

Date	Explanation	Ref.	Debit	Credit	Balance
					1100

Insurance Expense

Date	Explanation	Ref.	Debit	Credit	Balance

Amortization Expense – Office Equipment

Date	Explanation	Ref.	Debit	Credit	Balance

Amortization Expense – Buses

Date	Explanation	Ref.	Debit	Credit	Balance

Interest Expense

Date	Explanation	Ref.	Debit	Credit	Balance

(c)

SCENIC TOURS
Adjusted Trial Balance
June 30, 1999

	Debit	Credit

(a)   General Journal

Date	Account Titles and Explanation	Ref.	Debit	Credit

(b)

Cash

Date	Explanation	Ref.	Debit	Credit	Balance
Aug. 31	Balance				196 00

Accounts Receivable

Date	Explanation	Ref.	Debit	Credit	Balance

Prepaid Insurance

Date	Explanation	Ref.	Debit	Credit	Balance
Aug. 31	Balance				5400

Supplies

Date	Explanation	Ref.	Debit	Credit	Balance
Aug. 31	Balance				3300

Land

Date	Explanation	Ref.	Debit	Credit	Balance
Aug. 31	Balance				25000

Cottages

Date	Explanation	Ref.	Debit	Credit	Balance
Aug. 31	Balance				1 25000

Accumulated Amortization – Cottages

Date	Explanation	Ref.	Debit	Credit	Balance

(b) (Continued)

Furniture

Date	Explanation	Ref.	Debit	Credit	Balance
Aug. 31	Balance				26000

Accumulated Amortization – Furniture

Date	Explanation	Ref.	Debit	Credit	Balance

Accounts Payable

Date	Explanation	Ref.	Debit	Credit	Balance
Aug. 31	Balance				6500

Unearned Rent Revenue

Date	Explanation	Ref.	Debit	Credit	Balance
Aug. 31	Balance				6800

Salaries Payable

Date	Explanation	Ref.	Debit	Credit	Balance

Interest Payable

Date	Explanation	Ref.	Debit	Credit	Balance

Mortgage Payable

Date	Explanation	Ref.	Debit	Credit	Balance
Aug. 31	Balance				80000

(b) (Continued)

Tina Leone, Capital

Date	Explanation	Ref.	Debit	Credit	Balance
Aug. 31	Balance				100000

Tina Leone, Drawings

Date	Explanation	Ref.	Debit	Credit	Balance
Aug. 31	Balance				5000

Rent Revenue

Date	Explanation	Ref.	Debit	Credit	Balance
Aug. 31	Balance				80000

Salaries Expense

Date	Explanation	Ref.	Debit	Credit	Balance
Aug. 31	Balance				51000

Utilities Expense

Date	Explanation	Ref.	Debit	Credit	Balance
Aug. 31	Balance				9400

Repair Expense

Date	Explanation	Ref.	Debit	Credit	Balance
Aug. 31	Balance				3600

Insurance Expense

Date	Explanation	Ref.	Debit	Credit	Balance

(b) (Continued)

Supplies Expense

Date	Explanation	Ref.	Debit	Credit	Balance

Amortization Expense–Cottages

Date	Explanation	Ref.	Debit	Credit	Balance

Amortization Expense – Furniture

Date	Explanation	Ref.	Debit	Credit	Balance

Interest Expense

Date	Explanation	Ref.	Debit	Credit	Balance

(c)

HIGHLAND COVE RESORT
Adjusted Trial Balance
August 31, 1999

	Debit	Credit

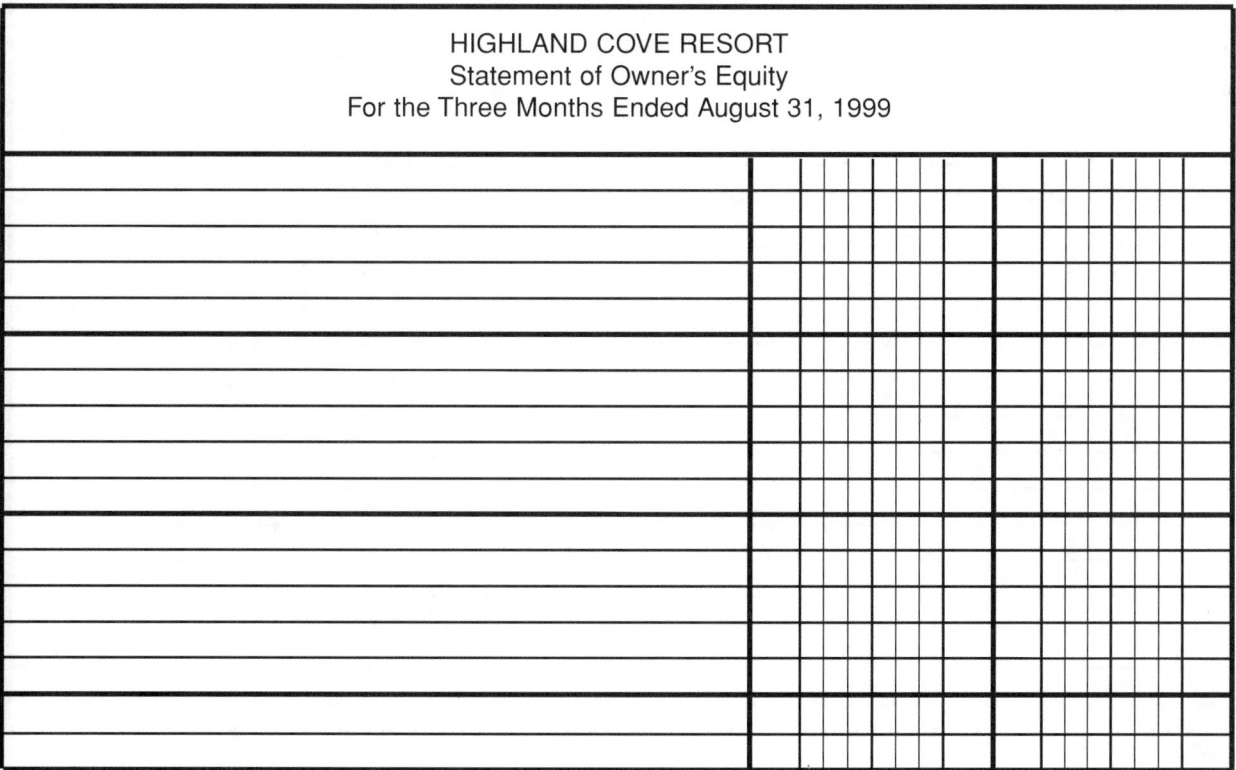

(d)

HIGHLAND COVE RESORT
Income Statement
For the Three Months Ended August 31, 1999

HIGHLAND COVE RESORT
Statement of Owner's Equity
For the Three Months Ended August 31, 1999

(d) (Continued)

HIGHLAND COVE RESORT
Balance Sheet
August 31, 1999

Assets

Liabilities and Owner's Equity

(a)

General Journal

Date	Account Titles and Explanation	Ref.	Debit	Credit

(b)

GRANT ADVERTISING AGENCY
Income Statement
For the Year Ended December 31, 1999

(b) (Continued)

GRANT ADVERTISING AGENCY Statement of Owner's Equity For the Year Ended December 31, 1999		

GRANT ADVERTISING AGENCY Balance Sheet December 31, 1999		
Assets		
Liabilities and Owner's Equity		

(c)

(d)

General Journal

Date	Account Titles and Explanation	Ref.	Debit	Credit

(a)

(b)

General Journal

Date	Account Titles and Explanation	Ref.	Debit	Credit

(a)   General Journal

Date	Account Titles and Explanation	Ref.	Debit	Credit

(b)

(a)   General Journal

Date	Account Titles and Explanation	Ref.	Debit	Credit

(b)

GLOBAL GRAPHICS COMPANY Adjusted Trial Balance June 30, 1999	Debit	Credit

(c)

GLOBAL GRAPHICS COMPANY Income Statement For the Six Months Ended June 30, 1999		

(c)(Continued)

GLOBAL GRAPHICS COMPANY Statement of Owner's Equity For the Six Months Ended June 30, 1999		

GLOBAL GRAPHICS COMPANY Balance Sheet June 30, 1999		
Assets		
Liabilities and Owner's Equity		

(a)

HOLIDAY TRAVEL COURT
Income Statement
For the Quarter Ended March 31, 1999

(b)

MEMORANDUM

TO: Mary Lee Virgil

FROM:

DATE:

SUBJECT: Adjusting Journal Entries

Type of Adjustment	Account Relationship	Accounts Before Adjustment	Adjusting Entry	Balance Sheet Effects of No Adjusting Entry	Income Statement Effects of No Adjusting Entry

Presentation Notes: _____

(a), (c) and (e)   Cash   No. 101

Date	Explanation	Ref.	Debit	Credit	Balance
Sept. 1	Balance				4880

Accounts Receivable   No. 112

Date	Explanation	Ref.	Debit	Credit	Balance
Sept. 1	Balance				3520

Supplies   No. 126

Date	Explanation	Ref.	Debit	Credit	Balance
Sept. 1	Balance				1000

Store Equipment   No. 153

Date	Explanation	Ref.	Debit	Credit	Balance
Sept. 1	Balance				15000

Accumulated Amortization — Store Equipment   No. 154

Date	Explanation	Ref.	Debit	Credit	Balance
Sept. 1	Balance				1500

(a), (c) and (e) (Continued)

Accounts Payable

No. 201

Date	Explanation	Ref.	Debit	Credit	Balance
Sept. 1	Balance				3400

Unearned Service Revenue

No. 209

Date	Explanation	Ref.	Debit	Credit	Balance
Sept. 1	Balance				400

Salaries Payable

No. 212

Date	Explanation	Ref.	Debit	Credit	Balance
Sept. 1	Balance				500

R. Rijo, Capital

No. 301

Date	Explanation	Ref.	Debit	Credit	Balance
Sept. 1	Balance				18600

Service Revenue

No. 407

Date	Explanation	Ref.	Debit	Credit	Balance

Amortization Expense

No. 615

Date	Explanation	Ref.	Debit	Credit	Balance

(a), (c) and (e) (Continued)

Supplies Expense

No. 631

Date	Explanation	Ref.	Debit	Credit	Balance

Salaries Expense

No. 726

Date	Explanation	Ref.	Debit	Credit	Balance

Rent Expense

No. 729

Date	Explanation	Ref.	Debit	Credit	Balance

(b)

General Journal

J102

Date	Account Titles and Explanation	Ref.	Debit	Credit

(b) (Continued)

General Journal

J102

Date	Account Titles and Explanation	Ref.	Debit	Credit

(e)

General Journal

Date	Account Titles and Explanation	Ref.	Debit	Credit

(d) and (f)

	RIJO EQUIPMENT REPAIR Trial Balances September 30, 1999			
	Before Adjustment		After Adjustment	
	Dr.	Cr.	Dr.	Cr.
Cash				
Accounts Receivable				
Supplies				
Equipment				
Accumulated Amortization				
Accounts Payable				
Unearned Service Revenue				
Salaries Payable				
R. Rijo, Capital				
Service Revenue				
Amortization Expense				
Supplies Expense				
Salaries Expense				
Rent Expense				

(g)

RIJO EQUIPMENT REPAIR Income Statement For the Month Ended September 30, 1999		

(g) (Continued)

RIJO EQUIPMENT REPAIR
Statement of Owner's Equity
For the Month Ended September 30, 1999

RIJO EQUIPMENT REPQIR
Balance Sheet
September 30, 1999

Assets		
Liabilities and Owner's Equity		

BE 4-1

	Total the statement columns, compute net income (loss), and enter it on the worksheet
	Enter the adjustment data
	Prepare a trial balance on the worksheet
	Enter adjusted balances
	Enter adjusted balances to appropriate statement columns

BE 4-3

Account	Income Statement		Balance Sheet	
	Dr.	Cr.	Dr.	Cr.
Accumulated Amortization				
Amortization Expense				
H. Khanna, Capital				
H. Khanna, Drawings				
Fees Earned				
Supplies				
Accounts Payable				

BE 4-7

BE 4-8

	Prepare a post-closing trial balance
	Prepare an adjusted trial balance
	Analyse buiness transactions
	Prepare a trial balance
	Journalize the transactions
	Journalize and post the closing entries
	Prepare the finiancial statements
	Journalize and post the adjusting entries
	Post to the ledger accounts

Account Titles	Trial Balance		Adjustments		Adjusted Trial Balance		Income Statement		Balance Sheet	
	Debit	Credit	Debit	Credit	Debit	Credit	Debit	Credit	Debit	Credit
Prepaid Insurance	4,200									
Fees Earned		58,000								
Salaries Expense	24,000									
Accounts Receivable										
Salaries Payable										
Insurance Expense										

BE 4-4

	General Journal			
Date	Account Titles and Explanation	Ref.	Debit	Credit

BE 4-5

Vivian Cheung Company
For the Month Ended April 30, 1999

Account Titles	Adjusted Trial Balance Dr.	Adjusted Trial Balance Cr.	Income Statement Dr.	Income Statement Cr.	Balance Sheet Dr.	Balance Sheet Cr.
Cash	13052					
Accounts Receivable	7840					
Prepaid Rent	2280					
Equipment	23050					
Accumulated Amortization		4921				
Notes Payable		5700				
Accounts Payable		5972				
V. Cheung, Capital		33960				
V. Cheung, Drawings	3650					
Fees Earned		12590		12590		
Salaries Expense	6840		6840			
Rent Expense	760		760			
Amortization Expense	671		671			
Interest Expense	57		57			
Interest Payable		57				
	63200	63200				

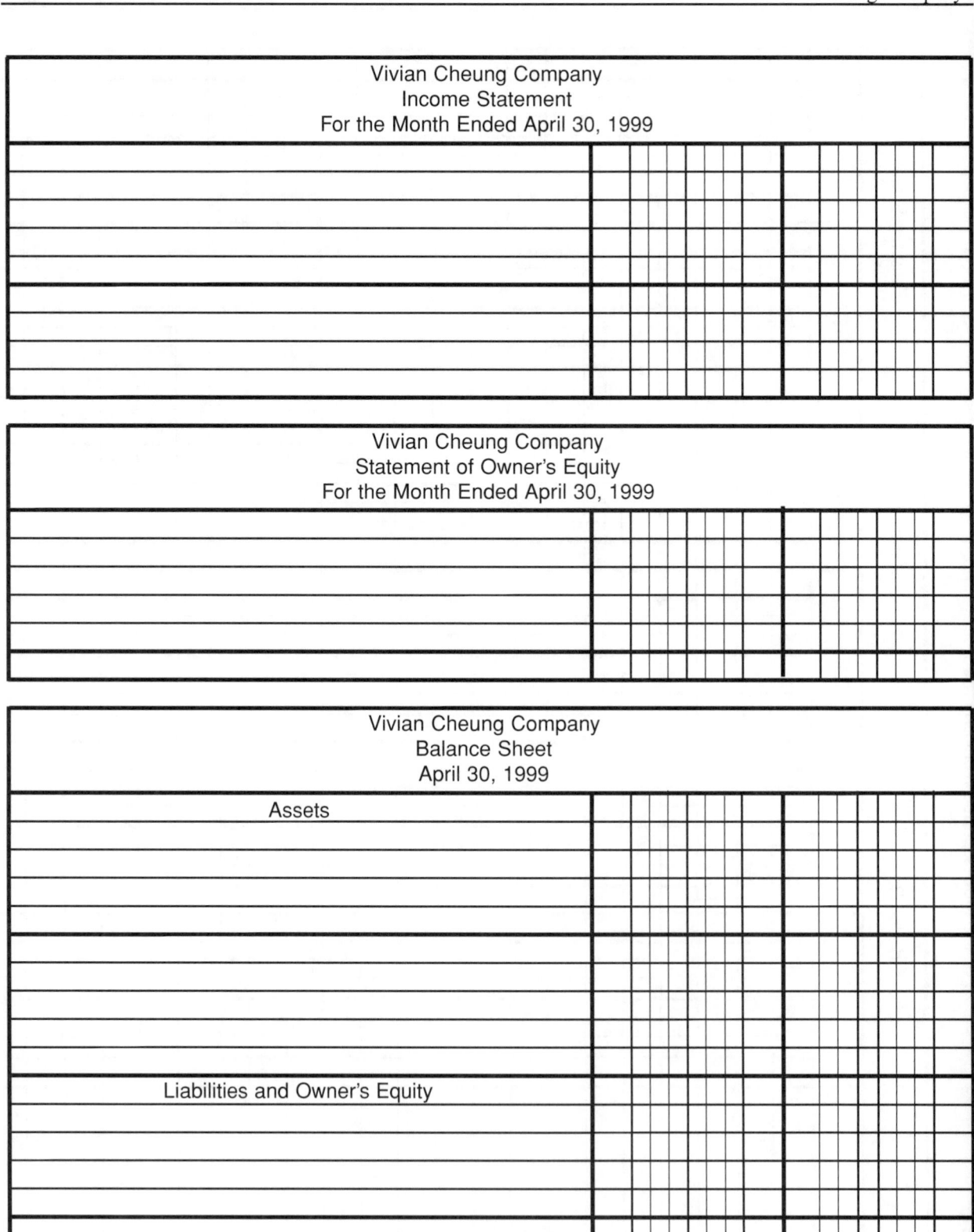

Vivian Cheung Company
Income Statement
For the Month Ended April 30, 1999

Vivian Cheung Company
Statement of Owner's Equity
For the Month Ended April 30, 1999

Vivian Cheung Company
Balance Sheet
April 30, 1999

Assets

Liabilities and Owner's Equity

(a)

General Journal

Date	General Journal	Ref.	Debit	Credit

(b)

V. CHEUNG, CAPITAL
33,960 Bal.

V. CHEUNG, DRAWINGS
Bal. 3,650

FEES EARNED
12,590 Bal

SALARIES EXPENSE
Bal. 6,840

RENT EXPENSE
Bal. 760

AMORTIZATION EXPENSE
Bal. 671

INTEREST EXPENSE
Bal. 57

INCOME SUMMARY

(c)

VIVIAN CHEUNG COMPANY
Post-Closing Balance
April 30, 1999

	Income Statement		Balance Sheet	
	Dr.	Cr.	Dr.	Cr.
E 4-4				
Accounts Receivable				
Prepaid Insurance				
Accumulated Amortization				
Salaries Payable				
Fees Earned				
Salaries Expense				
Insurance Expense				
Amortization Expense				
E 4-5				
(a) Accounts Receivable				
Supplies				
Accumulated Amortization				
Insurance Expense				
Salaries Expense				

(b)

(a)

General Journal

J1

Date	Account Titles and Explanation	Ref.	Debit	Credit

R. Batra, Capital — No. 301

Date	Explanation	Ref.	Debit	Credit	Balance
Aug. 1	Balance				45200

R. Batra, Drawings — No. 306

Date	Explanation	Ref.	Debit	Credit	Balance
July 31	Balance				14000

Income Summary — No. 350

Date	Explanation	Ref.	Debit	Credit	Balance

Commission Revenue — No. 404

Date	Explanation	Ref.	Debit	Credit	Balance
July 31	Balance				63100

Rent Revenue   No. 429

Date	Explanation	Ref.	Debit	Credit	Balance
July 31	Balance				6500

Amortization Expense   No. 711

Date	Explanation	Ref.	Debit	Credit	Balance
July 31	Balance				4000

Salaries Expense   No. 720

Date	Explanation	Ref.	Debit	Credit	Balance
July 31	Balance				58700

Utilities Expense   No. 732

Date	Explanation	Ref.	Debit	Credit	Balance
July 31	Balance				14900

(b)

BATRA COMPANY
Post-Closing Trial Balance
July 31, 1999

(a)

BATRA COMPANY
Income Statement
For the Year Ended July 31, 1999

BATRA COMPANY
Statement of Owner's Equity
For the Year Ended July 31, 1999

(b)

BATRA COMPANY
Balance Sheet
July 31, 1999

Assets		
Liabilities and Owner's Equity		

E 4-8

(a)

(b)

INCOME SUMMARY

E 4-9

(a)

SUMMIT'S BOWLING ALLEY
Balance Sheet
December 31, 1999

Assets		

Liabilities and Owner's Equity		

(b)

(a)

(b)

(c) and (e)

ACCOUNTS RECEIVABLE

COMMISSION REVENUE

INTEREST EXPENSE

INTEREST PAYABLE

(d)

(a)

EVERLAST ROOFING
Work Sheet
For the Month Ended March 31, 1999

Account Titles	Trial Balance		Adjustments	
	Dr.	Cr.	Dr.	Cr.
Cash	2700			
Accounts Receivable	1600			
Roofing Supplies	1100			(a) 650
Equipment	6000			
Accumulated Amortization		1200		(b) 200
Accounts Payable		1100		
Unearned Fees		300	200	
Jay Cambo, Capital		7000		
Jay Cambo, Drawings	600			
Fees Earned		3000		200
Salaries Expense	500		400	
Miscellaneous Expense	100			
Totals	12600	12600		
Roofing Expense			(a) 680	
Amortiz expense			(b) 200	
Salaries Payable				(c) 400
Roofing Supplie	1600	680		
Bal	420		480	1480
Roof Supplies Expense				
Adj	680			
Unearned Fees		300		
Adj	200			
Bal		100		
Fees earned		3000		
Adj		200		
Bal		3200		

14400
13700
700

Adjusted Trial Balance		Income Statement		Balance Sheet	
Dr.	Cr.	Dr.	Cr.	Dr.	Cr.
2200					
1600					
4200					
6000					
	1100				
	100				
	7000				
600					
	3200				
960					
700					
680					
	200				
14400	13700				

13200
12800
400

Owner's Equity
Capital/Invest = 7000
net Income = 1320
− Drawing = −600
7720

(b)

EVERLAST ROOFING
Income Statement
For the Month Ended March 31, 1999

Revenue			
Fees			3 2 0 0
Expenses			
Salaries		9 0 0	
Mis Exp		1 0 0	
Expense Roof		6 8 0	
Amortiz		1 4 0 0	
		2 0 8 0	
Net Income			1 1 2 0

EVERLAST ROOFING
Statement of Owner's Equity
For the Month Ended March 31, 1999

Capital			7 0 0 0
Net Income			1 1 2 0
less Drawing			8 1 2 0
			7 0 0 0
less Drawing			
		6 0 0	
			7 5 2 0

(b) (Continued)

EVERLAST ROOFING
Balance Sheet
March 31, 1999

Assets			
Current assets			
Cash		2700	
A/R		1600	
Roof Supplies		420	
Capital Asset			
Equipment	6	4600	
		9320	
Liabilities and Owner's Equity			
A/P			1100
Unearned Fees			100
Salaries Payable			400
Owner's Equity			7520
			9620

(c)   General Journal

Date	Account Titles and Explanation	Ref.	Debit	Credit
	Closing Entries			
1999				
31/3	Fees earned	1	3200	
	Income Summary			3200
	(to close rev a/c)			
	Income summary		1820	
	Salaries expense			900
	Misc expense			100
	roof			680
	amortization			1400
	(To close expense a/c)			
	Income Summary			
	Capital		7000	
	(To close net Income to k)			

)

MASON P.I. Income Statement For the Quarter Ended March 31, 1999								
Revenue						1 4 3 7 0	
Expenses							
salaries		1 2 0 0					
Travel		1 3 0 0					
rent		1 2 0 0					
misc		2 0 0					
Am		4 0 0					
supplies		3 0 0					
Int		2 0 0					
Insur		4 5 0					
		5 2 5 0			1 4 3 7 0		
						9 1 2 0	

MASON P.I. Statement of Owner's Equity For the Quarter Ended March 31, 1999								
Capital					2 0 0 0 0		
Net Income					5 2 5 0		
					2 5 2 5 0		
Drawings			6 0 0				
					2 4 6 5 0		

(a)

Account Titles	Trial Balance		Adjustments	
	Dr.	Cr.	Dr.	Cr.
Cash	12400			
Accounts Receivable	5620		750	
Supplies	1050			3 0
Prepaid Insurance	2400			45
Equipment	30000			
Notes Payable		10000		2 0
Accounts Payable		12350		
P. Mason, Capital		20000		
P. Mason, Drawings	600			
Fees Earned		13620		75
Salaries Expense	1200			
Travel Expense	1300			
Rent Expense	1200			
Miscellaneous Expense	200			
Totals	55970	55970		
ACC Amortization				400
Amortization exp			400	
Supplies ex			300	
Interest ex			200	
Ins exp			450	
				2100
			2100	
Ins payable		200		
ACC Amn		400		

| Adjusted Trial Balance | | Income Statement | | Balance Sheet | |
Dr.	Cr.	Dr.	Cr.	Dr.	Cr.
12400				12400	
6370				6370	
750				750	
1950				1950	
29000				29000	400
	10200				10200
	12350				12350
	20000				20000
600				600	
	14370		14370		
1200		1200			
1300		1300			
1200		1200			
200		200			
	400				
400		400			42450
300		300			9120
200		200			
450		450		52070	52070
57320	57320	9250	14370		
			5250		
			9120		

→ -400

(b) (Continued)

MASON P.I.
Balance Sheet
March 31, 1999

Assets				
Cash		12400		
A/C		6370		
Supplies		750		
Prepaid Ins		1950		
Equip		29600		
		51070		

Liabilities and Owner's Equity				
Note Payables				10000
A/c Payables				12350
Ins Payable				450
Am payable				400
Interest Payable				200
Supplies payable				300
Unearned Fee				23400
				750
Owners Equity				49120

) General Journal

Date	Account Titles and Explanation	Ref.	Debit	Credit
	Adjusting Entries			

) General Journal

Date	Account Titles and Explanation	Ref.	Debit	Credit
	Closing Entries			

Name   Problem 4

Section

Date   Diaz Compa

Diaz Company
(Partial) Work Sheet
For the Year Ended December 31, 1999

No.	Account Titles	Adjusted Trial Balance Dr.	Adjusted Trial Balance Cr.	Income Statement Dr.	Income Statement Cr.	Balance Sheet Dr.	Balance Sheet Cr.
101	Cash	14 600				14 600	
112	Accounts Receivable	15 400				15 400	
126	Supplies	1 500				1 500	
130	Prepaid Insurance	2 800				2 800	
151	Office Equipment	34 000				34 000	
152	Accumulated Amortization		8 000				8 000
200	Notes Payable		16 000				16 000
201	Accounts Payable		6 000				6 000
212	Salaries Payable		3 000				3 000
230	Interest Payable		500				500
301	C. Diaz, Capital		25 000				25 000
306	C. Diaz, Drawings	10 000				10 000	
400	Fees Earned		88 000		88 000		
610	Advertising Expense	14 000		14 000			
631	Supplies Expense	5 700		5 700			
711	Amortization Expense	4 000		4 000			
722	Insurance Expense	5 000		5 000			
726	Salaries Expense	39 000		39 000			
905	Interest Expense	500		500			
		146 500	146 500	68 200	88 000	78 300	58 500
				19 800			19 800
							78 300

4-28

b)

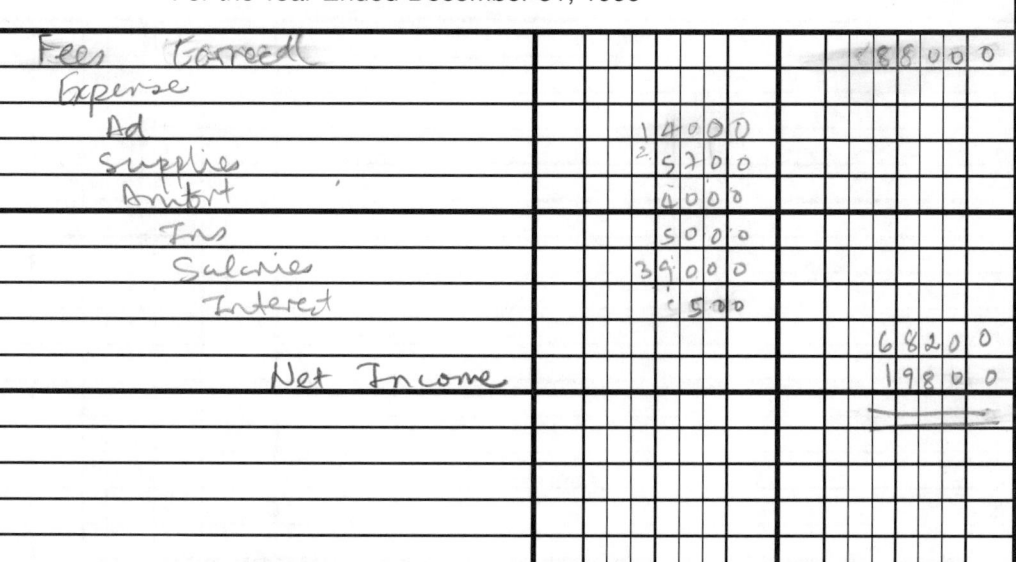

DIAZ COMPANY
Income Statement
For the Year Ended December 31, 1999

Fees Earned		88000
Expense		
Ad	14000	
Supplies	25700	
Amort	4000	
Ins	5000	
Salaries	39000	
Interest	520	
		68200
Net Income		19800

DIAZ COMPANY
Statement of Owner's Equity
For the Year Ended December 31, 1999

Investment	25000
Net Income	19800
	44800
Less Drawings	10000
	34800

Name   Problem 4-3 Continued

Section

Date   Diaz Company

(b) (Continued)

DIAZ COMPANY
Balance Sheet
December 31, 1999

Assets				
Current Asset				
Cash		14600		
A/R		15400		
Supplie		1800		
Pre paid Ins		2800		
Capital Assets				
Equipment (Less Am)		26000		
Total Assets		60300		

Liabilities and Owner's Equity				
Notes payable				16000
A/c Payable				6000
Salaries payable				3000
Ins payable				500
				25800
Owners Equity				24800
				60300

:) General Journal J14

Date	Account Titles and Explanation	Ref.	Debit	Credit
31/3/99	Fees Earned		88000	
	Income Summary			88000
	(To close Rev)			
31/3/99	Income Summary		68200	
	Advt ex			14000
	Sup ex			5700
	Amt ex			4000
	Ins			5000
	Salaries			37000
	Ins			500
	(To close exp)			
31/3	Income Summary		19800	
	Diaz Co capital A/c			19600
	(To close net income to k)			
31/3	Diaz Co.		1000	
	Drawings			1000
	(To close drawings to k)			

11) C. Diaz, Capital No. 301

Date	Explanation	Ref.	Debit	Credit	Balance
Jan. 1	Balance	J1		25000	25000
Dec 31	Closing entry	J3		19800	44800
Dec 31	Closing entry	J3	1000		34800

C. Diaz, Drawings No. 306

Date	Explanation	Ref.	Debit	Credit	Balance
Dec. 31	Balance		1000		10000
Dec 31	closing entry	J3		1000	0000

Income Summary No. 350

Date	Explanation	Ref.	Debit	Credit	Balance
Dec 31	closing entry	J3		88000	85000
Dec 31	closing entry	J3	68200		19820
Dec 31	closing entry	J3	19820		00000

(d) (Continued)

Fees Earned
No. 40

Date	Explanation	Ref.	Debit	Credit	Balance
Dec. 31	Balance			88000	88000
31/12	Closing entry	J3	88000		000

Advertising Expense
No. 61

Date	Explanation	Ref.	Debit	Credit	Balance
Dec. 31	Balance		14000		14000
31/12	Closing entry	J3		14000	000

Supplies Expense
No. 63

Date	Explanation	Ref.	Debit	Credit	Balance
Dec. 31	Balance		5700		5700
12/31	Closing entry	J3		5700	000

Amortization Expense
No. 71

Date	Explanation	Ref.	Debit	Credit	Balance
Dec. 31	Balance		4000		4000
31/12	Closing entry	J3		4000	

Insurance Expense
No. 72

Date	Explanation	Ref.	Debit	Credit	Balance
Dec. 31	Balance		5000		5000
31/12	Closing entry	J3		5000	000

d) (Continued)

Salaries Expense

No. 726

Date	Explanation	Ref.	Debit	Credit	Balance
Dec. 31	Balance		250 00		390 00
31/16	closing entry	J3		390 00	000

Interest Expense

No. 905

Date	Explanation	Ref.	Debit	Credit	Balance
Dec. 31	Balance		500		500
31/12	closing entry	J3		500	000

e)

DIAZ COMPANY
Post-Closing Trial Balance
December 31, 1999

	Debit	Credit
Cash	14 6 0 0	
A/R	15 4 0 0	
Pre paid Ins	12 8 0 0	
Equip	34 0 00	
Acc Amor		4 0 0 0
notes payable		16 0 0 0
Balance "		3 0 00
Ins		5 00
	68 0 0	

(a)

MELINDA COMPANY
Income Statement
For the Year Ended December 31, 1999

Fees Earned				54 0 0 0
Expense				
Repair		1 8 0 0		
Amort		2 6 0 0		
Ins		2 2 0 0		
Salaries		3 5 0 0 0		
Utilities		1 7 0 0		
Total				4 3 3 0 0
Net Income				1 0 7 0 0

MELINDA COMPANY
Balance Sheet
December 31, 1999

Assets				
Current Assets				
Cash		1 3 6 0 0		
A/R		1 3 5 0 0		
Prepaid Ins		3 5 0 0		
Total Current Assets		3 0 6 0 0		
Capital Assets				
Equipment (Less Acc Amor)		2 0 4 0 0		
TOTAL ASSETS		5 1 0 0 0		
Liabilities and Owner's Equity				
A/C Payable				1 3 3 0 0
Salaries "				3 0 0 0
Total Current Liabilities				1 6 3 0 0
Owner's Equity				3 4 9 0 0
				5 1 0 0 0

(a) (Continued)

MELINDA COMPANY Statement of Owner's Equity For the Year Ended December 31, 1999					

			Debit				Credit		
Capital							3 6 0	0 0
net Income							1 0 7	0 0
							4 6 7	0 0
Less Drawings		1 2 0	0 0				3 4 7	0 0

(b)

General Journal

Date	Account Titles	Ref.	Debit			Credit		
31/12	Fees earned					5 4	0 0
	Income Summary		5 4	0 0			
	(To close rev)						
31/12	Income Summary		4 3 3	0 0			
	Repair Exp					1 8	0 0
	Amor					2 6	0 0
	Ins					2 2	0 0
	Salaries					3 5 0	0 0
	Utilite					1 9	0 0
	(to close exp)						
31/12	Income Summary		1 0 7	0 0			
	Melind Co (K A/c)					1 0 7	0 0
	(to close net Income to c)						
31/12	Melinda Co		1 2 0	0 0			
	Drawings					1 2 0	0 0
	(To close drawing a/c)						

(c)

General Ledger Accounts

Ann Melinda, Capital, No. 301	
	Bal
	36000
	10700
12000	
12000	46700
	34700

Ann Melinda, Drawings, No. 306	
12000	12000

Income Summary No. 350	
43300	54000 54000 Bal
10700	10700
	Bal

Fees Earned No. 400	
54000	54000

Repair Expense No. 622	
1800	1800

Amortization Expense No. 711	
2600	2600

Insurance Expense No. 722	
2200	2200

Salaries Expense No. 726	
35000	35000

Utilities Expense No. 732	
1750	1750

(d)

MELINDA COMPANY
Post-Closing Trial Balance
December 31, 1999

	Debit	Credit
Cash	13600	
AR	13500	
Pre paid Ins	3500	
Office Eq	26000	
Acc Amort		5600
AC Paya		13300
Salaries "		3700
capital		34700
	56600	56600

(b)

SPACE AMUSEMENT PARK
Balance Sheet
September 30, 1999

Assets

Liabilities and Owner's Equity

(a)

SPACE AMUSEMENT PARK
Work Sheet
For the Year Ended September 30, 1999

Account Titles	Trial Balance Dr.	Trial Balance Cr.	Adjustments Dr.	Adjustments Cr.
Cash	37400			
Supplies	18600			1200
Prepaid Insurance	31900			2900
Land	80000			
Equipment	120000			
Accumulated Amortization		36200		6800
Accounts Payable		14600		
Unearned Admissions		2700	1700	1700
Mortgage Payable		50000		
L.A. Sparks, Capital		109700		
L.A. Sparks, Drawings	14000			
Admission Revenue		278500		1000
Salaries Expense	109000			
Repair Expense	30500			
Advertising Expense	9400			
Utilities Expense	16900			
Property Taxes Expense	18000		3000	
Interest Expense	6000		6800	
Totals	491700	491700		
Insurance Expense			2800	
Supplies Expense			17400	
Interest Payable				6000
Amortization Expense			6800	
Property Taxes Payable			3000	
Totals				51700

Adjusted Trial Balance		Income Statement		Balance Sheet		
Dr.	Cr.	Dr.	Cr.	Dr.	Cr.	
37400				37400		*Current Assets*
1200				1200		
3900				3900 →	42500	*Total current assets*
80000				80000		*capital Assets*
120000				77000		*TOTAL ASSETS*
	43000			199500		
	14600				14600	
	1700				1700	
	50000				40000	
	109700				6000	
14000					3000	
	279500		279500		65300	*Total current Liabilities*
109000		10900			10000	*Long term Liabilities*
30500		30500			25300	*Total liabilities*
9400		9400			164000	
16900		16900		9		
21000		21000				
12000		12000				
		28000				
28000		36800				
17400		115500	279500			
	6000		115500			
6800			164000			
	3000					
507500	507500					

4-39

General Journal

Date	Account Titles and Explanation	Ref.	Debit	Credit
(c)	Adjusting Entries			
(d)	Closing Entries			

(e)

SPACE AMUSEMENT PARK
Post-Closing Trial Balance
September 30, 1999

	Debit	Credit

General Journal   J1

Date	Account Titles and Explanation	Ref.	Debit	Credit

(a)   General Journal

Date	Account Titles and Explanation	Ref.	Debit	Credit

(b)	CAMPUS TV REPAIR Trial Balance April 30, 1999		
		Debit	Credit

Part A. (a)   General Journal   J1

Date	Account Titles and Explanation	Ref.	Debit	Credit

Part A (b)   General Ledger Accounts

Accrued Interest Receivable

Bal. 2,000	

Prepaid Insurance

Bal. 5,000	

Accrued Wages Payable

	36,000 Bal.

Unearned Sales Revenue

	40,000 Bal.

Part B   General Journal

Date	Account Titles and Explanation	Ref.	Debit	Credit
(a)				
(b)				

Part B (c)   General Ledger Accounts

Accrued Interest Receivable

Bal. 2,000 |

Prepaid Insurance

Bal. 5,000 |

Accrued Wages Payable

| 36,000 Bal.

Unearned Sales Revenue

| 40,000 Bal.

HELGA'S CARPET CLEANERS
Work Sheet
For the Month Ended March 31, 1999

Account Titles	Trial Balance Dr.	Trial Balance Cr.	Adjustments Dr.	Adjustments Cr.	Adjusted Trial Balance Dr.	Adjusted Trial Balance Cr.	Income Statement Dr.	Income Statement Cr.	Balance Sheet Dr.	Balance Sheet Cr.
Cash	(a)				1,200				1,200	
Accounts Receivable	4,400		(e)		5,000				5,000	
Cleaning Supplies	1,200			(i)	(m)				400	
Prepaid Insurance	(b)			(j)	1,650				1,650	
Equipment	7,000				7,000				7,000	
Accumulated Amortization		1,000		(k)		1,250				1250
Accounts Payable		1,200				1,200				(x)
H. Kohl, Capital		10,000				10,000				10,000
H. Kohl, Drawings	(c)				900				900	
Fees Earned		6,000		(l)		(q)		(u)		
Gas & Oil Expense	200				200		200			
Salaries Expense	1,500		(f)		(n)		2,000			
Total	(d) 18,200	(f) 18,200	2,300	2,300						
Amortization Expense			(g)		(o)		(s)			
Insurance Expense			150		150		150			
Cleaning Supplies Expense			(h)		(p)		(t)			
Salaries Payable				500		(r)				500
Totals					19,550	19,550	3,400	(v)	16,150	(y)
Net Income							3,200			
Totals							6,600 (w)	6,600	16,150	(z) 16,150

(a)

MOODY JANITORIAL SERVICE
Balance Sheet
December 31, 1999

Assets

Liabilities and Owner's Equity

(b)

MEMORANDUM

TO:

FROM:

DATE:

SUBJECT: Steps in the Accounting Cycle

		1999	2000
1.	Expenses paid in advance	_____	_____
2.	Revenue collected in advance	_____	_____
3.	Accrued expenses	_____	_____
4.	Accrued revenues	_____	_____

(a), (e) and (f)

Cash   No. 101

Date	Explanation	Ref.	Debit	Credit	Balance

Accounts Receivable   No. 112

Date	Explanation	Ref.	Debit	Credit	Balance

Cleaning Supplies   No. 128

Date	Explanation	Ref.	Debit	Credit	Balance

Prepaid Insurance   No. 130

Date	Explanation	Ref.	Debit	Credit	Balance

Equipment   No. 157

Date	Explanation	Ref.	Debit	Credit	Balance

(a), (e) and (f) (Continued)

Accumulated Amortization—Equipment   No. 158

Date	Explanation	Ref.	Debit	Credit	Balance

Accounts Payable   No. 201

Date	Explanation	Ref.	Debit	Credit	Balance

Salaries Payable   No. 212

Date	Explanation	Ref.	Debit	Credit	Balance

Jan Jansen, Capital   No. 301

Date	Explanation	Ref.	Debit	Credit	Balance

Jan Jansen, Drawings   No. 306

Date	Explanation	Ref.	Debit	Credit	Balance

Income Summary   No. 350

Date	Explanation	Ref.	Debit	Credit	Balance

(a), (e) and (f) (Continued)

Fees Earned   No. 400

Date	Explanation	Ref.	Debit	Credit	Balance

Gas & Oil Expense   No. 633

Date	Explanation	Ref.	Debit	Credit	Balance

Cleaning Supplies Expense   No. 634

Date	Explanation	Ref.	Debit	Credit	Balance

Amortization Expense   No. 711

Date	Explanation	Ref.	Debit	Credit	Balance

Insurance Expense   No. 722

Date	Explanation	Ref.	Debit	Credit	Balance

Salaries Expense   No. 726

Date	Explanation	Ref.	Debit	Credit	Balance

(d)

JAN'S WINDOW WASHING Income Statement For the Month Ended July 31, 1999		

(e)

JAN'S WINDOW WASHING Statement of Owner's Equity For the Month Ended July 31, 1999		

(b) and (c)

JAN'S WINDOW WASHING
Work Sheet
For the Month Ended July 31,1999

No.	Account Titles	Trial Balance		Adjustments	
		Dr.	Cr.	Dr.	Cr.
101	Cash				
112	Accounts Receivable				
128	Cleaning Supplies				
130	Prepaid Insurance				
157	Equipment				
158	Accumulated Amortization				
201	Accounts Payable				
212	Salaries Payable				
301	Jan Jansen, Capital				
306	Jan Jansen, Drawings				
350	Income Summary				
400	Fees Earned				
633	Gas &Oil Expense				
634	Cleaning Supplies Expense				
711	Amortization Expense				
722	Insurance Expense				
726	Salaries Expense				

Adjusted Trial Balance		Income Statement		Balance Sheet	
Dr.	Cr.	Dr.	Cr.	Dr.	Cr.

(d) (Continued)

JAN'S WINDOW WASHING
Balance Sheet
July 31, 1999

Assets																
Liabilities and Owner's Equity																

(g)

JAN'S WINDOW WASHING
Post-Closing Trial Balance
July 31, 1999

	Debit	Credit

e) and (f)   General Journal   J2 and J3

Date	General Journal	Ref.	Debit	Credit

ame

ction

ate

General Journal

Date	Account Titles and Explanation	Ref.	Debit	Credit

E5-3 (a)

CECILIE COMPANY
Income Statement (Partial)
For the Year Ended October 31, 1999

(b)

E5-4

	Debit	Credit

(a)

(b)

(a)		
(b)		

(c)

MERCHANDISE INVENTORY

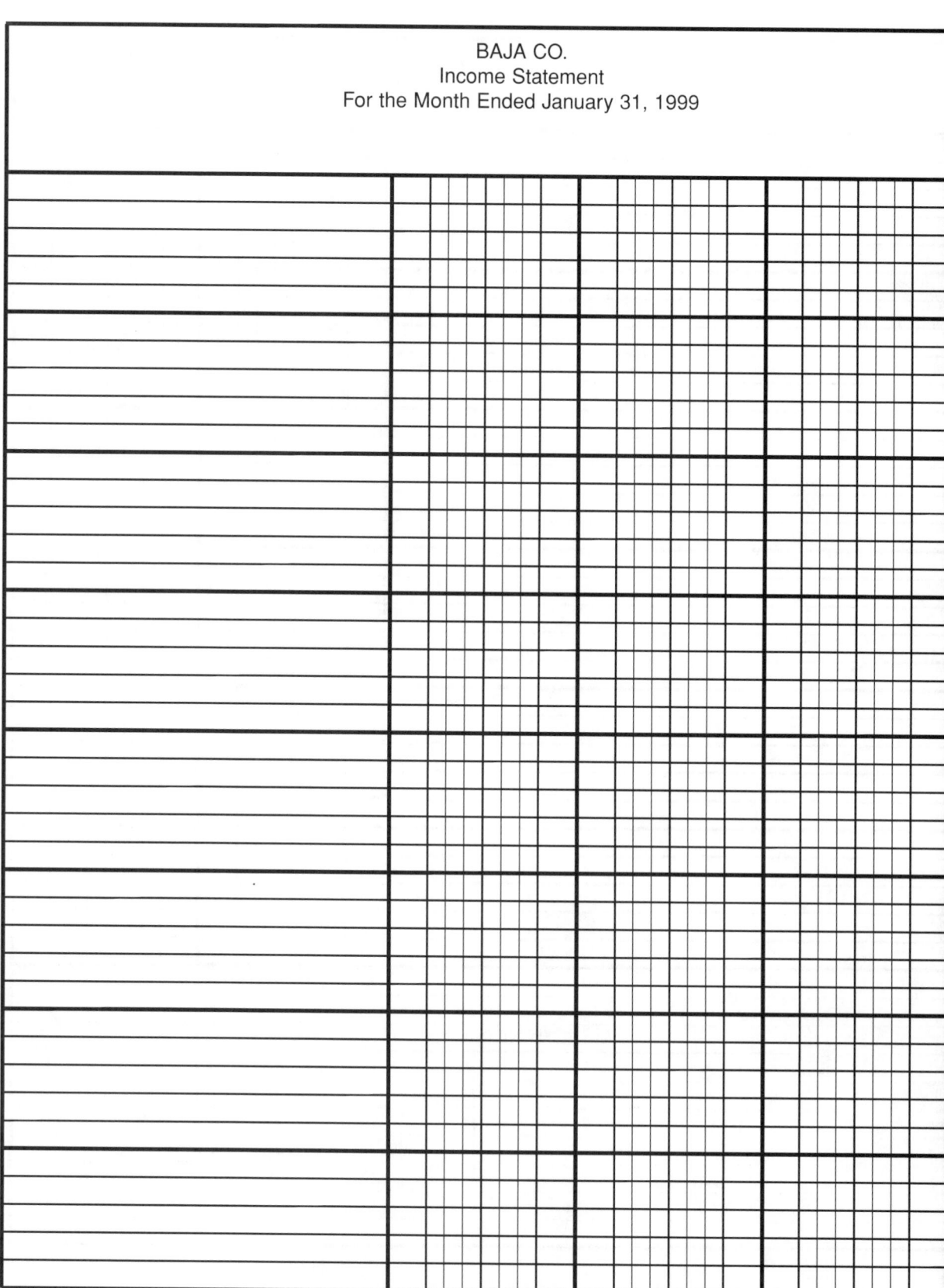

BAJA CO.
Income Statement
For the Month Ended January 31, 1999

(a) Sales Returns	
(b) Ending Inventory	
(c) Sales	
(d) Beginning Inventory	
(e) Purchases	
(f) Cost of Goods Sold	

MILIA COMPANY
Partial Work Sheet
For the Period Ended May 31, 1999

(a)

Account Titles	Adjusted Balance		Income Statement		Balance Sheet	
	Dr.	Cr.	Dr.	Cr.	Dr.	Cr.
Cash	9000					
Merchandise Inventory	8000					
Purchases	24000					
Purchase Returns & Allowances		3000				
Sales		45000				
Sales Returns & Allowances	10000					
Rent Expense	42000					

(b)

E 5-9

5-10   General Journal

Date	Account Titles and Explanation	Ref.	Debit	Credit

(a)

CHEVALIER COMPANY
Income Statement
For the Year Ended December 31, 1999

(b)

CHEVALIER COMPANY
Income Statement
For the Year Ended December 31, 1999

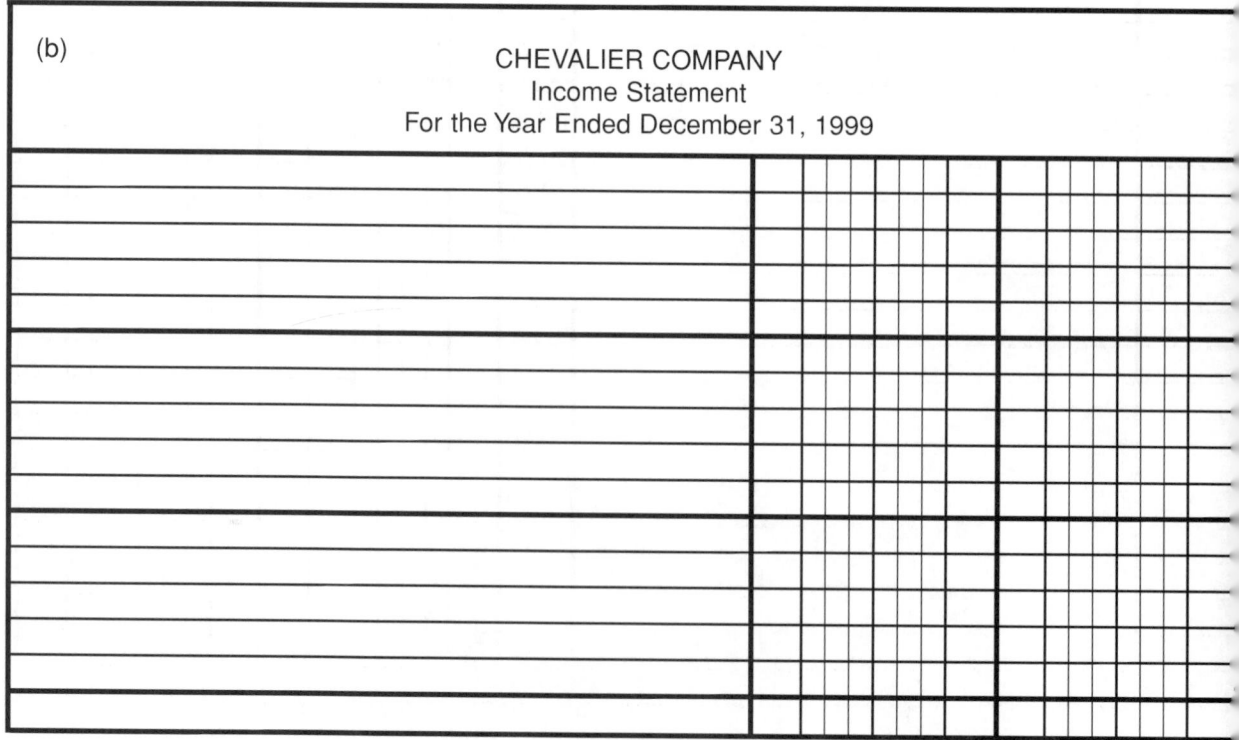

General Journal

Date	Account Titles and Explanation	Ref.	Debit	Credit

General Journal

Date	Account Titles and Explanation	Ref.	Debit	Credit
2/4	Merchandise Inventory	1	4900	
	A/c Payable			4900
	To record good purchased			
	on a/c term n/30			
4/4	A/c Rec'b	2	5000	
	Sales			5000
	To record credit sale			
	Cost of Goods Sold		4000	
	Merchandise Inv			4000
5/4	Freight In	4	200	
	A/ Payable			200
	to record freight charge			
6/4	Sales return + all	5	300	
	A/R			300
	Merchandise Inventory	1	300	
	Cost of Good Sold			300
14/4	Merchandise Inve	1	4400	
	Cash			4400
16/4	Sales return + all	5	500	
	cash (to rec all for refund)			500
18/4	Merchandise Inventory	1	4200	
	Cash			4200
20/4	Freight In		100	
	Cash			100
23/4	A/R Invent	2	6400	
	Sale			6400
	Cost of Good Sold		5200	
	Merchandi Inv			5200
26/4	Merchandise Inv.	1	2300	
	Cash			2300
27/4	A/P	6	4900	
	cash			4900
28/4	Cash	7	5000	
29/4	Sales return & A/		90	90
	cash			

a)   General Journal   J1

Date	Account Titles and Explanation	Ref.	Debit	Credit
1/4	Purchases	510	5000	
	A/Payable	201		5000
2/4	A/R	112	4000	
	sales	401		4000
5/4	A/Payable all	512	200	
	Purchases Return & All	180		200
7/4	Freight out	648	200	
	A/R	101		200
14	Supplies	126	900	
	Cash	101		900
12	Purchase	120	2400	
	Cash	101		2400
15	cash	101	230	
	Supplies refund	512		230
17	Purchases	510	1900	
	A/Payable	101		1900
19	Freight In In	516	250	
	cash	101		250
24	cash	101	6200	
	Sale	401		6200
25	Purchase	120	1000	
	A/Payable	101		1000
27	Cash	101	4000	
	A/R	112		4000
29	sales return + Allowance	412	100	
	cash	101		100
31			100	
30	A/P	201	5000	100
31	cash	101	600	5000

(a) (Continued)   General Journal   J1

Date	Account Titles and Explanation	Ref.	Debit	Credit
3/4	A/R		1600	
	Sales			1600

(b)   Cash   No. 101

Date	Explanation	Ref.	Debit	Credit	Balance
May 1	Balance	✔			5000
11/4				900	4100
12/4				2400	1700
15/4			230		1930
19/4				250	2180
24/4			6200		8380
27/4			4000		12380
29/4				100	12260
30/4				5000	7280

Accounts Receivable   No. 11.

Date	Explanation	Ref.	Debit	Credit	Balance
2/4		112	4000		4000
27/4		112		4000	0000
3/4		112	1600		1600
2/4			200		1400

b) Continued

Merchandise Inventory   No. 120

Date	Explanation	Ref.	Debit	Credit	Balance
31/4		✓			2400

Supplies   No. 126

Date	Explanation	Ref.	Debit	Credit	Balance
11/4			900		
13/4				230	670

Accounts Payable   No. 201

Date	Explanation	Ref.	Debit	Credit	Balance
1/4				5000	5000
5/4			200		4800
17/4				1900	2900
25/4				1900	1900
30/4			5900		6900

S. Dorn, Capital   No. 301

Date	Explanation	Ref.	Debit	Credit	Balance
31/3				5000	5000

Sales   No. 401

Date	Explanation	Ref.	Debit	Credit	Balance
May 1	Balance	✓			5000
2/4				4000	9000
24/4				6200	15200
3/4				1600	16800

Sales Returns and Allowances   No. 412

Date	Explanation	Ref.	Debit	Credit	Balance
27/4			100		100

Purchases   No. 510

Date	Explanation	Ref.	Debit	Credit	Balance
1/4			5000		5000
1/4			2400		7400
12/4			1900		9300
25/4			1000		10300

Purchase Returns and Allowances   No. 512

Date	Explanation	Ref.	Debit	Credit	Balance
5/4				200	200
15/4				230	430

Freight In   No. 516

Date	Explanation	Ref.	Debit	Credit	Balance
12/4			250		250

Freight Out   No. 644

Date	Explanation	Ref.	Debit	Credit	Balance
2/4			200		200

(c)

EAGLE HARDWARE STORE
(Partial) Income Statement
For the Month Ended May 31, 1999

Sales Revenue				
Sales				16800
– Sale return + All				100
Net Sales				16700
Cost of Good Sold				
Ending Inv		2400		
Purchases	10300			
– Purchase return + all	430			
Net Purchase	9870			
Freight In	250			
Cost of G Sold		10120		
– Ending Inv		12400		
				7720
Gross Profit				8980
Operating Exp				

(a) (1) Periodic   General Journal

Date	Account Titles and Explanation	Ref.	Debit	Credit
5/4	Purchase	J1	72000	
	cash	52		72000
13	Purchase	J1	56800	
	Cash	52		56000
17	Cash	J2	114000	
	Sale	S1		114000
20	Purchase		52000	
	cash			52000
22	A/R		26000	
	Purchase return + all			26000
24	Cash		102000	
	Sales			102000
28	cash		31000	
	sales			31000

a) (2) Perpetual   General Journal

Date	Account Titles and Explanation	Ref.	Debit	Credit
5/4	Merchandise Inv		72000	
	Cash			72000
13	Merchandise		56000	
	cash			72000
14	Cash		114000	
	M. Sale Inv			114000
	Cost of goods sold		96000	
	Merchandise Inv			96000
20	Merchan In		52000	
	cash			52000
22	A/R		26000	
	Merch In			26000
	Merchandise		26000	
	Cost g			26000
24	cash		102000	
	Sale			102000
	COGS		84000	
	Merch			84000
28	cash		31000	
	Sale			31000
	COGS		26000	
	merch In			26000

(b) (1) Periodic

	Purchases		Purchase Returns & Allowances
72 000			26 000
56 000			———
52 000			26 000
180 000			

(b) (2) Perpetual

Merchandise Inventory		Cost of Goods Sold	
72 000	96 000	96 000	00
56 000	84 000	84 000	
52 000	26 000	26 000	
180 000	206 000	206 000	

c)

VARSITY AUTO SALES
Cost of Goods Sold
For the Month of April

Sales Rev			
Sales			247000
Cost of Good Sold			
Opening Inv	23000		23000
Purchase 180 00	180000		
− Purch ret all 26 000	126000		
Nett to Purchase			154000
− Closing In	178000		
			206000
Sales		247000	
Income Summary			247000
In			

d) Income Summary

ask about n/30

(a)   General Journal

Date	Account Titles and Explanation	Ref.	Debit	Credit
4/4	Purchase +	510	600	
	GST recovery	114	42	642
	CA/P	201		
6/4	Freight In	516	60	
	Cash	101		60
8/4	~~Cost~~ A/R	112	1050	
	GST payable	214		63
	PST "	215		90
	Sale	412		900
10/4	A/R	112	428	
	Purchase Return + Rec	512		40
	GST recovery	114		28
11/4	Purchases	510	300	
	GST recovery	114	21	321
	Cash	101		300
14/4	Purchases	510	700	
	GST rec	114	49	
	A Payable	201		749
15/4	Cash	101	535	
	GST recov	114		35
	Purch ret	512		50
17/4	Freight In	516	70	
	Cash	101		70
18	Cash	101	936	
	Sale	412		800
	GST payable	214		56
	Pst "	215		80
2				
20	Cash	101	500	
	A/R			500
27	A/P		345	
			400	
	Cash			
30	A/R			400

) (Continued) General Journal J1

Date	Account Titles and Explanation	Ref.	Debit	Credit
27	P Sale ret re			70
	GST payable			21
	PST "			24
29	A/P		642	
	cash			642
30	A/R		1150	
	Sales			1000
	PST payable			80
	GST "			70

) Cash No. 101

Date	Explanation	Ref.	Debit	Credit	Balance
Apr. 1	Balance	✔			2500 00
6/4		J1		60	2440
11/4				300	2140
15/4			535		2675
18/4			1036		3711
17/4				70	3640
18/4			1036		4676
20/4			500		5176
29/4				642	4534
4/4			400		4834

Accounts Receivable No. 112

Date	Explanation	Ref.	Debit	Credit	Balance
8/4			1050		1050
12/4			425		1475
16/4				500	975
30/4			1150		2125
30/4				400	1520

GST Recoverable No. 114

Date	Explanation	Ref.	Debit	Credit	Balance
4/4			42		42
10/4				28	41
11/4			21	50	62
15/4				50	12

Merchandise Inventory   No. 12

Date	Explanation	Ref.	Debit	Credit	Balance
Apr. 1	Balance	✔			1700⁰

Accounts Payable   No. 20

Date	Explanation	Ref.	Debit	Credit	Balance
4/4				642	642
14/4				749	1391
27/4				345	2036

GST Payable   No. 21

Date	Explanation	Ref.	Debit	Credit	Balance
8/4				63	63
18/4				56	119
27/4				21	121
30/4				70	190

PST Payable   No. 21

Date	Explanation	Ref.	Debit	Credit	Balance
8/4				90	90
18/4				80	170
27/4				24	174
30/4				80	254

B.J. Evert, Capital   No. 30

Date	Explanation	Ref.	Debit	Credit	Balance
Apr. 1	Balance	✔			4200⁰

Sales   No. 40

Date	Explanation	Ref.	Debit	Credit	Balance
8/4				900	900
18/4				800	1700
30/4				1000	2700

Sales Returns and Allowances   No. 412

Date	Explanation	Ref.	Debit	Credit	Balance
7/#				30	30

Purchases   No. 510

Date	Explanation	Ref.	Debit	Credit	Balance
4/4			600		600
11/4			200		800
14/4			700		1600

Purchase Returns and Allowances   No. 512

Date	Explanation	Ref.	Debit	Credit	Balance
10/4				40	40
15/4				30	70

Freight In   No. 516

Date	Explanation	Ref.	Debit	Credit	Balance
6/4			60		60
14/4			70		130
14/					

B.J.'S TENNIS SHOP
Trial Balance
April 30, 1999

	Debit	Credit
cash		
A/R	4934	
merch In	1520	
A/c payable	1700	2036
Sale tax payable		4405
capital		4200
Sales		2700
Purchase	1600	
Purchase return + all	70	
Freight In	130	

(d)

B.J.'S TENNIS SHOP
(Partial) Income Statement
For the Month Ended April 30, 1999

Sales Revenue			
Sales		2700	
− Sales retu + all		30	
Cost Net Sales			2670
Merchandise Inv		1700	1700
Purchases	1600		
Purchase ret + all	70		
net Purchas		1530	
Freight In		1130	1660
COG Purchase			1660
COG ayβov Sale			2360
Gross Profit			1370
Operating Expen			
Selling exp			

General Journal

Date	Account Titles and Explanation	Ref.	Debit	Credit
2/9	Merchandise Inv	1	60000	
	GST recovery		4200	
	A/P			64200
4/9	Freight In		2000	
	cash			2000
5/9	A/R		7490	
	GST recovery			490
	Purch return + all			7000
6/9	A/R		23520	
	Sales			21000
	GST payable			1470
	CPST "			1050
	COGS		15000	
	Merchandise Inv			15000
15	Supplies		4260	
	GST recovery		280	
	cash			4480
18	Merchandise Inv		6000	
	GST recovery		420	
	cash			6420
22	A/P		32200	
	Sales			28000
	GST payable			1960
	PST "			2240
	COGS		20000	
	Merchandise In			20000
27	Purchases		32400	
	GST recovery		2100	
	AP			34500
28	A/P		56710	
	cash			56710

cash

cash

A/R

21,000

21000

(a)

METIS WHOLESALE COMPANY
Work Sheet
For the Year Ended December 31, 1999

Account Titles	Trial Balance		Adjustments	
	Dr.	Cr.	Dr.	Cr.
Cash	33400			
Accounts Receivable	37600			
Merchandise Inventory	62400		90000	
Land	92000			
Buildings	197000			
Accumulated Amortization—Buildings		54000		10000
Equipment	83500			
Accumulated Amortization—Equipment		42400		9000
Notes Payable		50000		57000
Accounts Payable		37500		
G. Metis, Capital		267800		
G. Metis, Drawings	10000			
Sales		902100		
Purchases	729700			
Freight In	12400			
Salaries Expense	69800			
Utilities Expense	9400			
Repair Expense	5900			
Gas and Oil Expense	7200			
Insurance Expense	3500			
Totals	1 353800	1 353800		
Acc Amor – Bldg expense			10000	
" " " payable				10000
Acc Amor – Eq expns			9000	
" " " payable				9000
Int expense			7000	
			26000	26000
			Net	

Adjusted Trial Balance		Income Statement		Balance Sheet	
Dr.	Cr.	Dr.	Cr.	Dr.	Cr.
33400				33400	
37600				37600	
90000				90000	
92000				92000	
197000				197000	
	64000				64000
83500				83500	
	51400				51400
	57000				57000
	37500				37500
	267800				267800
100000				100000	
	902100		902100		6800
725700		725700			
12400		12400		543500	543500
69800		69800			
9400		9400			
5900		5900			
7200		7200			
3500		3500			
		10000			
		9000			
11000		7000			
9000					
			18760		
		Less app			
7000					
1379800	1379800				
		Nett Income 65800			

current assets

capital assets

Inv

Purchases = 729780
            12400
          ─────────
            742100

net P 742100

COGA = 804500
     − EI
Salaries COG = 714500

80% S = 557840
             13960
20% A = ─────────
             69800

GP = 187600
     121800
   ─────────
Net Inc 65800

Expense
121800

5-33

(b)

METIS WHOLESALE COMPANY
Income Statement
For the Year Ended December 31, 1999

Sales Revenue			
Sales			902100
Cost of Good Sold			
Merch Inv		62400	
Purchases	729700		
Freight In	12400		
net Purchases		742100	
COGAS		804500	
End Inv		90000	
COGS			714500
Gross Profit			187600
Operating Expense			
Selling Expense			
Salary expense		55840	
Oil + gas		7200	
Amort.			
Admin Expense			
Salaries		13960	
utilities		9460	
repair		6900	
Ins		3500	
Am		19000	
Interest		7000	
Total Expense			121800
Net Income			65800
			0

(b)

IVANNA FASHION CENTRE
Income Statement
For the Year Ended November 30, 1999

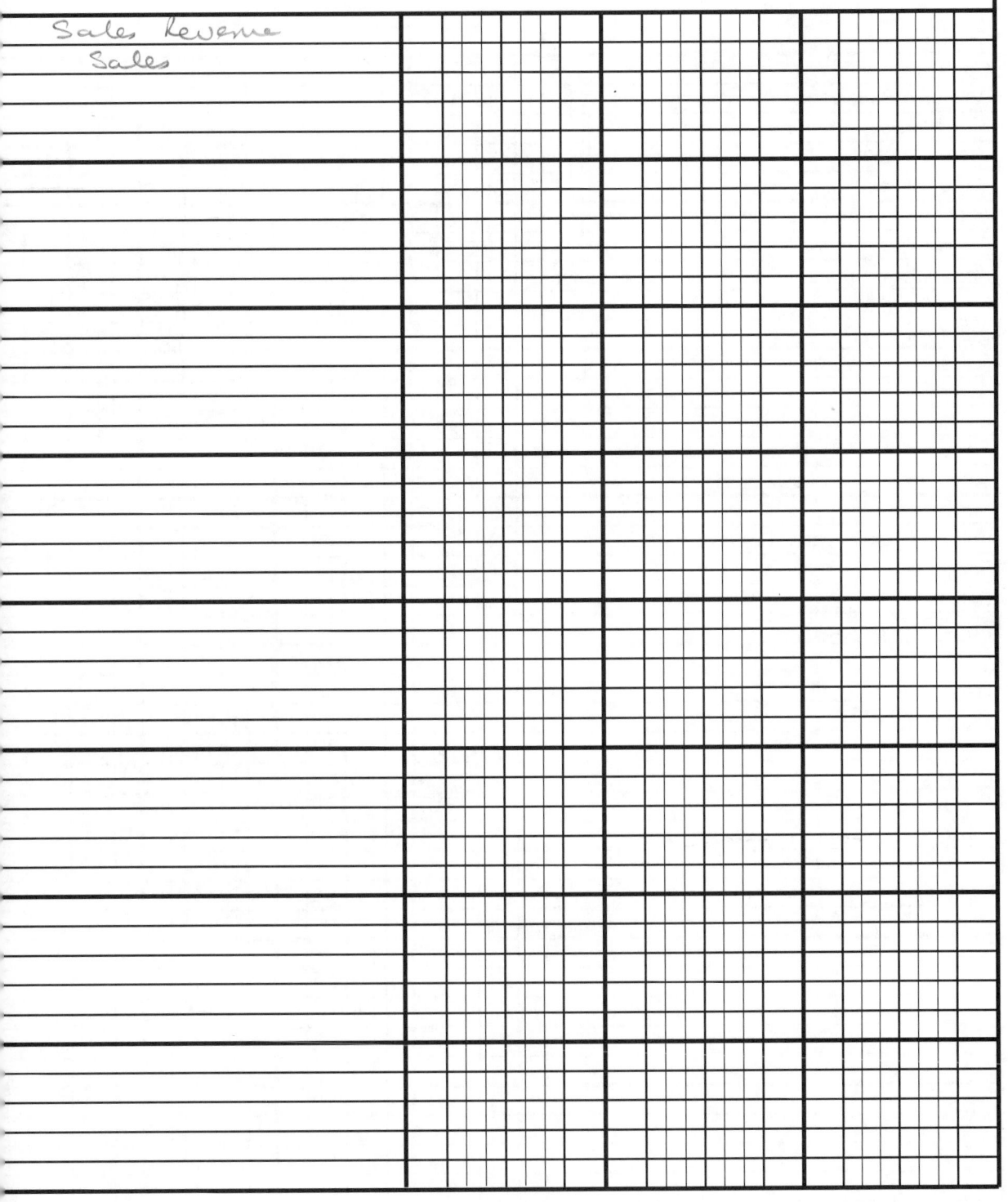

Sales Revenue

Sales

(a)

IVANNA FASHION CENTRE
Work Sheet
For the Year Ended November 30, 1999

Account Titles	Trial Balance		Adjustments	
	Dr.	Cr.	Dr.	Cr.
Cash	16700			
Accounts Receivable	40700			
Merchandise Inventory	38000			
Store Supplies	5500			2000
Store Equipment	85000			
Accumulated Amortization—Store Equipment		18000		9000
Delivery Equipment	48000			
Accumulated Amortization—Delivery Equipment		6000		7000
Notes Payable		51000		
Accounts Payable		48500		
Sales Taxes Payable		7000		
L.Ivanna, Capital		110000		
L. Ivanna, Drawings	12000			
Sales		750300		
Sales Returns and Allowances	4200			
Purchases	503600			
Purchase Returns and Allowances		6900		
Freight In	10800			
Salaries Expense	140000			
Advertising Expense	26400			
Utilities Expense	14000			
Repair Expense	12100			
Delivery Expense	16700			
Rent Expense	24000			
Totals	997700	997700		
Supplies expense			2000	
Amort expens – store			9000	
Amort ″ – delivery eq			7000	
Int expense			4000	
Ins payable				4000
			22000	22000

Adjusted Trial Balance		Income Statement		Balance Sheet	
Dr.	Cr.	Dr.	Cr.	Dr.	Cr.
16700				16700	
40700				40700	
38000		38000	45400	45000	
3500				3500	
85000				85000	
	27000				27000
48000				48000	
	13000				13000
	51000				51000
	48500				48500
	7000				7000
	110000			12000	110000
12000					
	750300		750300		4000
4200		4200			(49600)
503600		503600			
	6900		6900	250900	250900
10800		10800			
140000		140000			
26400		26400			
14000		14000			
12100		12100			
16700		16700			
24700		24700			
2000		2000			
9000		9000			
7000		7000			
4000		4000			
	4000				
1017700	1017700				

255200

146500

212600

Sales = 750300
S return + All = 4200
Net Sales = 746,100

BnI = 38000
Pur = 503600
Pur 6900
496700
Freight 10800
COGAS 507500
EI 545500
45,000
COGS 500500
G Profit 462500

GP = 275600
Expens- 253200
Net Income 18400

232950
35000
268950

167000
-6700
0300

232580

(b) (Continued)

IVANNA FASHION CENTRE
Statement of Owner's Equity
For the Year Ended November 30, 1999

Capital			1 1 0 0 0 0
Loss			4 6 0 0
			1 0 0 4 0 0
- Drawings			1 2 0 0 0
			8 8 4 0 0

IVANNA FASHION CENTRE
Balance Sheet
November 30, 1999

Current assets { Cash	1 6 7 0 0		
A/R	4 0 7 0 0		
Mer In	4 5 0 0 0		
Store Supplies	3 5 0 0		
Total Current Asset	1 0 5 9 0 0		
Eq	5 8 0 0 0		
Delivery Eq	3 5 0 0 0		
Total Assets	1 9 8 9 0 0		
Liabilities + Owners			
Current liab			2 5 0 0 0
A/P			4 8 5 0 0
Sales Tax			7 0 0 0
Total Current			8 0 5 0 0
Long - Term			3 0 0 0 0
Owners Eq			8 8 4 0 0
			1 9 8 9 0 0

General Journal

(c) and (d)

Date	Account Titles and Explanation	Ref.	Debit	Credit
(c)	**Adjusting Entries**			
	Income Summary		38000	
	Merchandise Inv			38000
	To close begin. Inv we used			
	Mdse Inv		45000	
	Income Summary			45000
	To record E I			
				7000
	Interest expense		7000	
	accrued			7000
(d)	**Closing Entries**			
	Sales		750300	
	Income Summary			750200
	Income Summary		759900	
	Sales Returns			500500
	Cost of Good Sold			4200
	All expense			255200
	(To close all debit Bal)			
	Income Summary		110000	
	Capital			110000
	To transfer net Income to			
	Capital		12000	
	Drawing			12000
	To close drawing to K			
	Merchand Inv End		45000	
	Sales		750300	
	Purchase return		6900	
	Income S (close Sales (+ Cr Bal)			802200
	Income Summary			

Perpetual

Period

(d) (Continued)

General Journal

Date	Account Titles and Explanation	Ref.	Debit	Credit

(e)

IVANNA FASHION CENTRE
Post-Closing Trial Balance
November 30, 1999

	Debit	Credit
Csh		
A/R		
M.I		
Supplies		
Eq		
Amortization		

(a)

METRO DEPARTMENT STORE
Income Statement
For the Year Ended November 30, 1999

(a) (Continued)

METRO DEPARTMENT STORE
Income Statement
For the Year Ended November 30, 1999

METRO DEPARTMENT STORE
Statement of Owner's Equity
For the Year Ended November 30, 1999

a) (Continued)

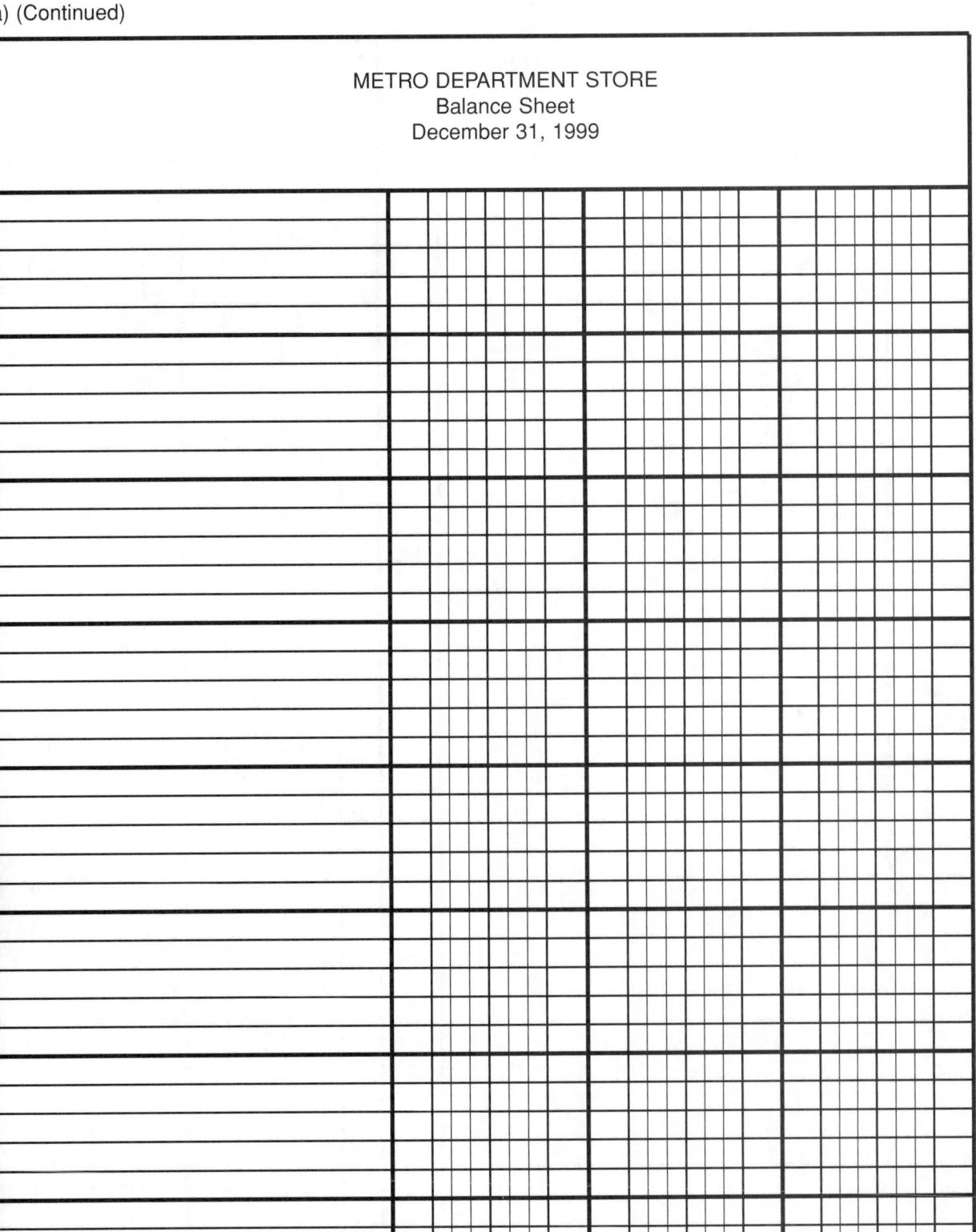

METRO DEPARTMENT STORE
Balance Sheet
December 31, 1999

(b)   General Journal

Date	Account Titles and Explanation	Ref.	Debit	Credit
	Closing Entries			

(a)

N-MART DEPARTMENT STORE
Income Statement
For the Year Ended December 31, 1999

Description	Col 1	Col 2	Col 3
Sales			6 2 4 0 0 0
– Less ref + all		8 0 0 0	
net sale			6 1 6 0 0 0
BI (merchan)		4 0 0 0	
Purchase	4 6 2 0 0 0	0	
– Pur ref + all	6 4 0 0		
Freight In	1 1 0 0 0 0	5 6 5 6 0 0	
COGAS		5 6 9 6 0 0	
– EI	7 5 0 0 0		
COGS		0 0	4 9 4 6 0 0
G Profit	–		1 2 1 4 0 0
Expense			(– 1 5 6 5 0 0)
Loss			(3 5 1 0 0)

(a) (Continued)

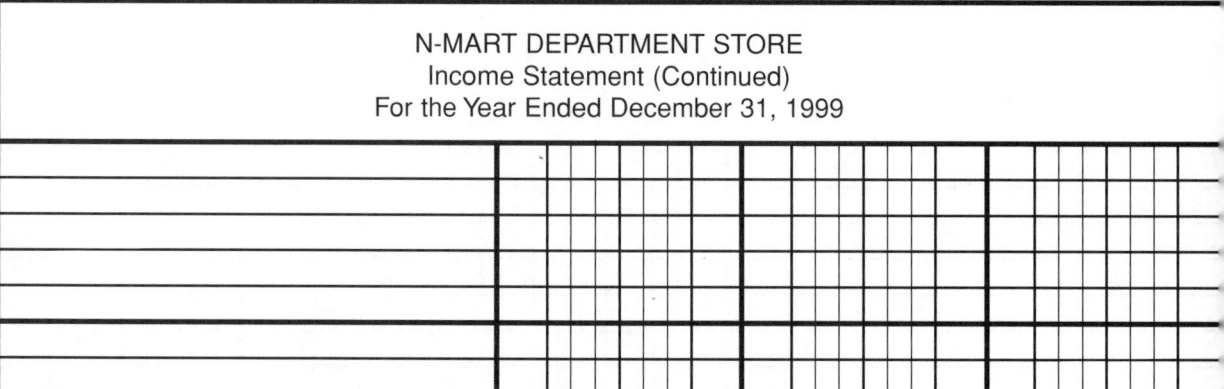

N-MART DEPARTMENT STORE
Income Statement (Continued)
For the Year Ended December 31, 1999

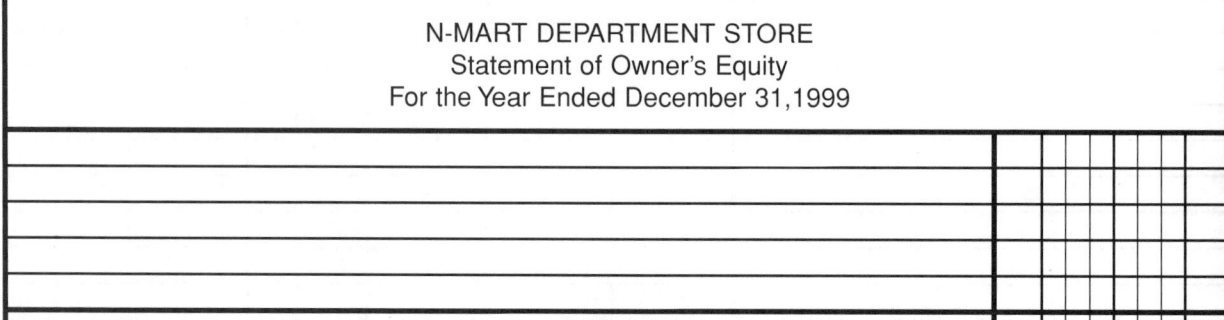

N-MART DEPARTMENT STORE
Statement of Owner's Equity
For the Year Ended December 31, 1999

(b)   General Journal

Date	Account Titles and Explanation	Ref.	Debit	Credit
	Adjusting Entries			
	Sales			
	Income Summary			
	(to close)			
	Income			
	CO G S			
	Sales ret + rev			
	all expense			
	Income Summary			
	capital			
	capital			
	draw			

a) (Continued)

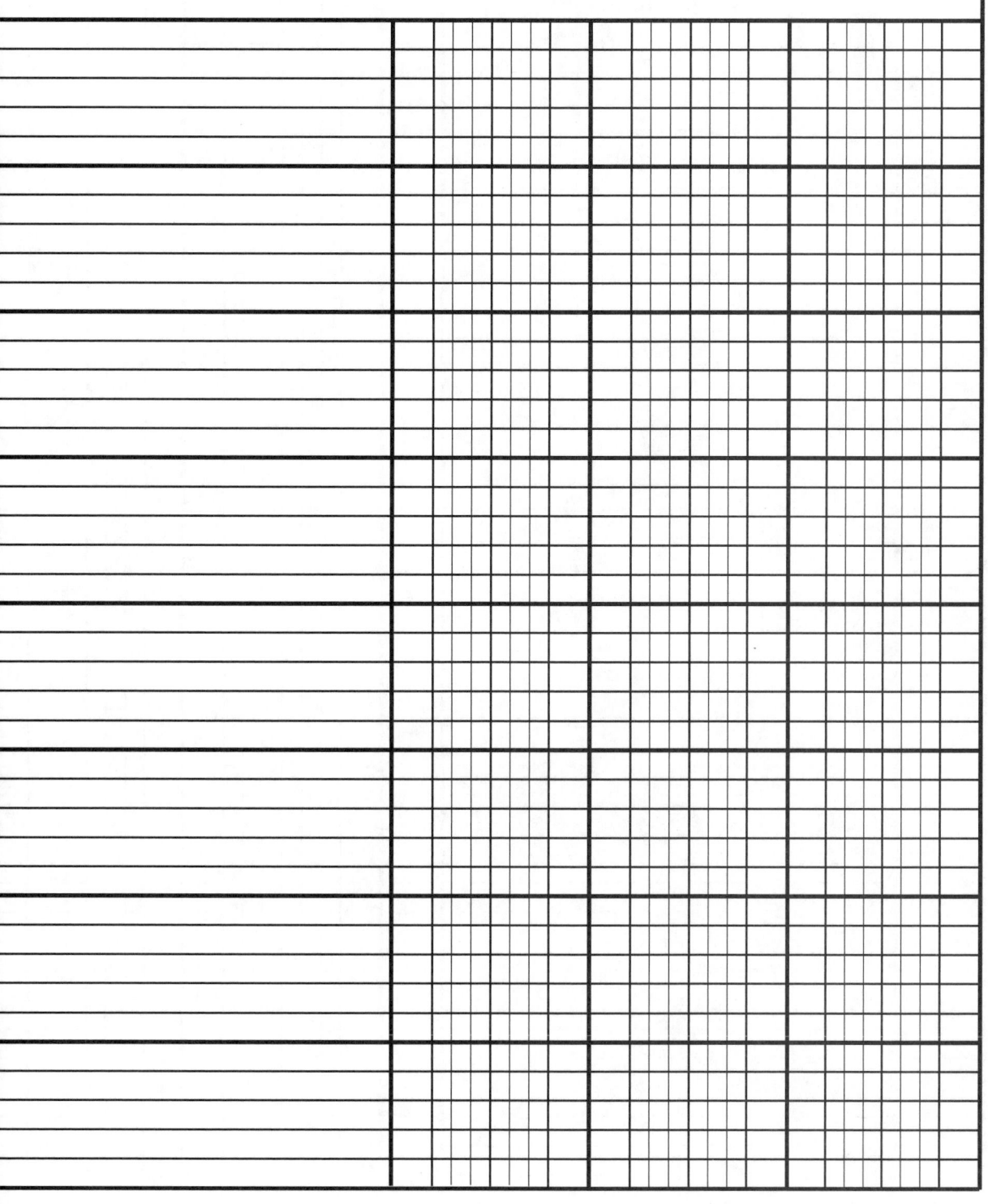

N-MART DEPARTMENT STORE
Balance Sheet
December 31, 1999

(c)   General Journal

Date	Account Titles and Explanation	Ref.	Debit	Credit
	Closing Entries			

a)

WORLD ENTERPRISES
Income Statement and Statement of Owner's Equity
For the Year Ended December 31, 1999

(a) (Continued)

WORLD ENTERPRISES
Balance Sheet
December 31, 1999

b)

General Journal

Date	Account Titles and Explanation	Ref.	Debit	Credit
	Closing Entries			

c)

MERCHANDISE INVENTORY

INCOME SUMMARY

(a) Detailed Single-Step Income Statement

ZAMBRANA COMPANY
Income Statement
For the Year Ended December 31, 1999

b) Condensed Single-Step Income Statement

ZAMBRANA COMPANY
Income Statement
For the Year Ended December 31, 1999

TAO COMPANY
Income Statement
For the Year Ended December 31, 1999

(a)

(1)	FEDCO DEPARTMENT STORE		
	Income Statement		
	For the Year Ended December 31, 2000		

(2)	FEDCO DEPARTMENT STORE		
	Income Statement		
	For the Year Ended December 31, 2000		

(b)

)

FEDCO DEPARTMENT STORE
Income Statement
For the Year Ended December 31, 2000

) Net Sales			
) Cost of Goods Purchased			
) Cost of Goods Sold			
) Gross Profit			
) Net Income or Loss			

Name

Section

Date

Name

Section

Date

E6-1

E6-2

(a) and (b)   *General Ledger*

Accounts Receivable

Date	Explanation	Ref.	Debit	Credit	Balance
Sept. 1	Balance	✔			10960

Accounts Receivable Subsidary Ledger

Bannister

Date	Explanation	Ref.	Debit	Credit	Balance
Sept. 1	Balance	✔			1440

Crowley

Date	Explanation	Ref.	Debit	Credit	Balance
Sept. 1	Balance	✔			2640

DeLeon

Date	Explanation	Ref.	Debit	Credit	Balance

Dotson

Date	Explanation	Ref.	Debit	Credit	Balance
Sept. 1	Balance	✔			2060

Seaver

Date	Explanation	Ref.	Debit	Credit	Balance
Sept. 1	Balance	✔			4820

-3 (c)

CRAMPTON COMPANY
Schedule of Customers
As of September 30, 1999

-4 (a) and (b)

HARIETT COMPANY
Sales Journal S1

ate	Account Debited	Invoice No.	Terms	Ref.	A/R (Dr.)	Sales (Cr.)	GST Payable (Cr.)	PST Payable (Cr.)

Purchases Journal P1

ate	Account Credited	Terms	Ref.	Purchases (Dr.)	GST Recoverable (Dr.)	Accounts Payable (Cr.)

E6-5 (a) and (b)

REESE ENTERPRISES
Cash Receipts Journal

CR

Date	Accounts Credited	Ref.	Cash Dr.	Accounts Receivable Cr.	Sales Cr.	GST Payable Cr.	PST Payable Cr.	Other Accoun Cr.

Cash Payments Journal

CP

Date	Ck. No.	Payee	Cash Cr.	Accounts Payable Dr.	GST Recoverable Dr.	Accounts Debited	Ref.	Other Account Dr.

E6-6

(a) Journal	(b) Journal Columns
1.	
2.	
3.	
4.	
5.	
6.	
7.	
8.	
9.	

Name

ction

te

(a)

(b)

E 6-8

E 6-9

ALPS COMPANY
Purchases Journal

6-10 (a)   P1

Date	Account Credited	Ref.	Purchases (Dr.) Acc. Pay. (Cr.)

)   General Journal

Date	Account Titles and Explanations	Ref.	Debit	Credit

6-11

LEMONT COMPANY
Cash Receipts Journal

(a)   CR1

Date	Accounts Credited	Ref.	Cash Dr.	Accts. Receivable Cr.	Sales Cr.	Other Accts. Cr.
1	F Lemont	101	6000			6000
4	smith	101	1600 —	1600		
5	North West Co	101	620 —	620 —		
6	cash sale	101	7245 —		7245 —	
10	Norris	401	900 —	900 —		
11	cash refund	802	550 —			550 —
23	Northwest	101	1600 —	1600 —		
25	Kerl		1200 —	1200 —		
			—			
			19715	5920 —	7245	6550 —

General Ledger
Accounts Receivable

No. 112

Date	Explanation	Ref.	Debit	Credit	Balance
1	S-t	S1	7200 —		7200
3(		CR1		5920	1330

Accounts Receivable Subsidiary Ledger

arris

Date	Explanation	Ref.	Debit	Credit	Balance
1		S1	1550		1550
10	Pymt on Inv 301	CR1		900	650

eri

Date	Explanation	Ref.	Debit	Credit	Balance
1		S1	1200		
29	Pymt Fr. Keri in full	CR1		1200	

Iortheast Co.

Date	Explanation	Ref.	Debit	Credit	Balance
1	'	S1	2900		
5	Pymt on In 307	CR1		620	2280
23	Pymt " " 310	CR1		1600	680

mith

Date	Explanation	Ref.	Debit	Credit	Balance
1		S1	1600		
4	Rec'd pymt in full			1600	

(c)   Accounts receivable balance: $ 1330

Subsidiary account balances:

Harris   = $ 650
Northeast Co = $ 680
Total   =   1330

(a)   Cash Payments Journal   4/64   CP

Date	Ck. No.	Payee	Cash Cr.	Accounts Payable Dr.	GST Recoverable Dr.	Accounts Debited	Ref.	Other Accounts Dr.
1	18	Purchases	700		49	Purchase	510	749
3	64	Purchase equip	864		56	Purchase	"	920
5	65	bal owed to Newton Co	1600	1600		Newton+Co	2✓	1600
10	66	Merchandise	2200		154	Eq	107	2354
15	67	Lein Co	1400	1400		Lein	✓	1400
16	68	Ins Premium	400			cash	101	400
19	69	Martin + Son	1400	1400		Martin+Son	✓	1400
24	70	Watson + Co	2300	2300		Watson Co	✓	
			10864	6700	259			4423

General Ledger
Accounts Payable

No. 201

Date	Explanation	Ref.	Debit	Credit	Balance
3(	~CPR	~R1	9200		9200
3(		CP1	0	6700	2500

Newton Company

Accounts Receivable Subsidiary Ledger

Date	Explanation	Ref.	Debit	Credit	Balance
1		PT	1600	1600	1600
		CP1	1600	1600	

Martin & Sons

Date	Explanation	Ref.	Debit	Credit	Balance
3(		Pn I		2500	2500
3(		CPI	1400		1100

llen Co.

Date	Explanation	Ref.	Debit	Credit	Balance
3(		P I		1400	1400
3(		CPI	1400		—

Watson Company

Date	Explanation	Ref.	Debit	Credit	Balance
		P T		3700	3700
		CPT	2300		1400

c) Accounts payable balance: $2500

Subsidiary account balances: Martin + Son = 1100
Watson + Co = 1400
2500

6-15

(a)

Purchases Journal

Date	Accounts Credited (Debited)	Ref.	Other Accts Dr.	Purchases Cr.	Freight In Dr.	Accts. Payable Cr.
2	Vans Co					8 0 0 0
3	Freight In				4 0 0	4 0 0
8	Golden Co					8 0 0 0
8	Don Co					8 7 0 0
10	Supplies					
16						
16						
17						
18						
20						
28						

Sales Journal

Date	Account Debited	Ref.	Acc. Rec. (Dr.) Sales (Cr.)
5	Penner Co		2 6 0 0
	Hendrix		2 7 0 0
	Nelles		1 5 0 0
23	Hendrix Bros		2 4 0 0
	Nelles Co		2 2 0 0
			1 1 4 0 0

a) (Continued)   General Journal   G1

Date	Accounts and Explanations	Ref.	Debit	Credit

General Ledger

b) Accounts Receivable   No. 112

Date	Explanation	Ref.	Debit	Credit	Balance
31			11400		11400

Supplies   No. 126

Date	Explanation	Ref.	Debit	Credit	Balance

Equipment   No. 157

Date	Explanation	Ref.	Debit	Credit	Balance

Accounts Payable   No. 201

Date	Explanation	Ref.	Debit	Credit	Balance

(b) (Continued)   Sales   No. 4(

Date	Explanation	Ref.	Debit	Credit	Balance

Sales Return and Allowances   No. 41

Date	Explanation	Ref.	Debit	Credit	Balance

Purchases   No. 51

Date	Explanation	Ref.	Debit	Credit	Balance

Purchase Returns and Allowances   No. 51

Date	Explanation	Ref.	Debit	Credit	Balance

Freight In   No. 51

Date	Explanation	Ref.	Debit	Credit	Balance

Advertising Expense   No. 61

Date	Explanation	Ref.	Debit	Credit	Balance

) (Continued)   *Accounts Receivable Subsidiary Ledger*

ndrix Bros.

Date	Explanation	Ref.	Debit	Credit	Balance

lles Company

Date	Explanation	Ref.	Debit	Credit	Balance

nner Company

Date	Explanation	Ref.	Debit	Credit	Balance

Accounts Payable Subsidiary Ledger

me Freight

Date	Explanation	Ref.	Debit	Credit	Balance

ll Advertising

Date	Explanation	Ref.	Debit	Credit	Balance

(b) (Continued)

Dorn Company

Date	Explanation	Ref.	Debit	Credit	Balance

Engle Supply

Date	Explanation	Ref.	Debit	Credit	Balance

Golden Company

Date	Explanation	Ref.	Debit	Credit	Balance

Vons Company

Date	Explanation	Ref.	Debit	Credit	Balance

Accounts receivable balance:		
Subsidiary account balances:		
Accounts payable balance:		
Subsidiary account balances:		

(a), (b) and (c)   Sales Journal

Date	Accounts Debited	Invoice No.	Ref.	Acc. Rec. (Dr.) Sales (Cr.)
4	Gilbert	371	126	7 5 5 0
9	Mays Corp	372	16	5 6 0 0
12	Amber	373	11	1 2 0 0
31	Gilbert Corp	374	157	9 3 3 6
31	G			
				2 3 6 8 6

Purchases Journal

Date	Accounts Credited	Ref.	Purchases (Dr.) Acc. Pay. (Cr.)
3	Pa Bell	510	8 9 0 0
8	Law Co		4 5 0 0
11	Hatch co		3 7 0 0
19	Johnson		5 5 0 0
23	Bell,		7 8 0 0
24	Levine Corp		4 6 9 0
			3 5 0 9 0 ✓

General Journal

Date	Account Titles and Explanations	Ref.	Debit	Credit
5	Cur A/c Payable (Bell Co)		3 0 0	
	Purchase return & all			3 0 0 ✓
15	Salary Payable Expense	726	1 4 3 0 0	
	Cash			1 4 3 0 0
31	Salary expense	726	1 3 2 0 0	
	cash			1 3 2 0 0 ✓

), (b) and (c) (Continued)   Cash Receipts Journal   CR1

Date	Accounts Credited	Ref.	Cash Dr.	Accts. Receivable Cr.	Sales Cr.	Other Accts. Cr.
4	Sales		3150		2150	
3	Sales		5340		5340	
15	Maya corp		5600	5600		
17	Gilbert		7550	7550		
20	Sales		3200		3200	
27	Sales		3730		3730	
			28570	13150	15420	✓

Cash Payments Journal   CP1

Date	Ck. No.	Payee	Cash Cr.	Accts. Payable Dr.	Accts. Debited	Ref.	Other Accts. Dr.
4		Supplies	80	80	Supplies	✓	
13		Bell	8900	8900	Bell	✓	
20		Law Co	4500	4500	Law Co	✓	
			13480	13480			

(a), (b) and (c)

Sales Journal

S

Date	Accounts Debited	Invoice No.	Ref.	Acc. Rec. (Dr.) Sales (Cr.)

Purchases Journal

P

Date	Accounts Credited	Ref.	Purchases (Dr.) Acc. Pay. (Cr.)

General Journal

G

Date	Account Titles and Explanations	Ref.	Debit	Credit

a), (b) and (c) (Continued)

Cash Receipts Journal

CR1

Date	Accounts Credited	Ref.	Cash Dr.	Accts. Receivable Cr.	Sales Cr.	Other Accts. Cr.

Cash Payments Journal

CP1

Date	Ck. No.	Payee	Cash Cr.	Accts. Payable Dr.	Accts. Debited	Ref.	Other Accts. Dr.

General Ledger

(a), (d) and (g)   Cash   No. 1

Date	Explanation	Ref.	Debit	Credit	Balance
26	Cash		48404		48404
31	Cash			47789	615

Accounts Receivable   No. 1

404

Date	Explanation	Ref.	Debit	Credit	Balance
26			26215		26215
	.			12305	
					13910

GST Recoverable   No. 1

Date	Explanation	Ref.	Debit	Credit	Balance
			2886		2886
			630		3516
			14		3524

Supplies   No. 12

Date	Explanation	Ref.	Debit	Credit	Balance
	Supplies		1000		1000

Equipment   No. 15

Date	Explanation	Ref.	Debit	Credit	Balance
			8000		8000

Accumulated Amortization—Equipment   No. 15

Date	Explanation	Ref.	Debit	Credit	Balance
				400	400

Accounts Payable   No. 20

Date	Explanation	Ref.	Debit	Credit	Balance
			48068		48068
				44023	

4043

, (d) and (g) (Continued)

GST Payable — No. 214

Date	Explanation	Ref.	Debit	Credit	Balance
				1715	1715
				385	

B. Taco, Capital — No. 301

Date	Explanation	Ref.	Debit	Credit	Balance
				30000	30000

B. Taco, Drawing — No. 306

Date	Explanation	Ref.	Debit	Credit	Balance
			1400		1400

Sales — No. 401

Date	Explanation	Ref.	Debit	Credit	Balance
				24500	
				5500	
					30000

Purchases — No. 510

Date	Explanation	Ref.	Debit	Credit	Balance
			41143		41143

Purchase Returns and Allowances — No. 512

Date	Explanation	Ref.	Debit	Credit	Balance
				200	

(a), (d) and (g) (Continued)

Supplies Expense   No. 6

Date	Explanation	Ref.	Debit	Credit	Balance
			700		700

Amortization Expense   No. 7

Date	Explanation	Ref.	Debit	Credit	Balance
				200	200

(b)

Purchases Journal

Date	Accounts Credited	Terms	Ref.	Purchases (Dr.)	GST Recoverable (Dr.)	Accts. Payable (Cr.)
2	S Healey			2243	157	2400
7	L Head			30000	2100	32100
16	Radley			2400	168	2568
21	Purchase			6500	455	6955
				41143	2880	44023

2243
157
2400

Cash Payments Journal   C

Date	Ck. No.	Payee	Cash Cr.	Accts. Payable Dr.	GST Recov. Dr.	Accts. Debited	Ref.	Other Accts Dr.
9		supplies	1020	1000	20	A/P		
12		Healey	2400	2400	157	A/P		
15		Eq	8560	8000	560			
17		L Head	32100	32100		A/P		
20		sly	1100			other a/c		1100
28		Radley	2568	2568				
			47998	46068	630			

Adams *Accounts Receivable Subsidiary Ledger*

Date	Explanation	Ref.	Debit	Credit	Balance
3			5350		5350
13				5350	—

Babcock

Date	Explanation	Ref.	Debit	Credit	Balance
			6955		
				6955	—

Chambers

Date	Explanation	Ref.	Debit	Credit	Balance
			7490		

Dawson

Date	Explanation	Ref.	Debit	Credit	Balance
			6420		

Able *Accounts Payable Subsidiary Ledger*

Date	Explanation	Ref.	Debit	Credit	Balance

Healy

Date	Explanation	Ref.	Debit	Credit	Balance
2			2400	2400	
12			2400		—

Held

Date	Explanation	Ref.	Debit	Credit	Balance
			32100	32100	
					—

(c) (Continued)

R. Landly

Date	Explanation	Ref.	Debit	Credit	Balance

(e)

TACO CO.
Trial Balance
February 28, 1999

	Debit	Credit
Cash	615	
Accounts Receivable	1 3 9 4 0	
GST Recoverable	3 5 3 4	
Supplies	1 0 0 6	
Equipment	8 0 0 0	
Accounts Payable		4 0 4 8
GST Payable		2 1 0 6
B. Taco, Capital		3 0 0 6 0
B. Taco, Drawings	1 6 8 4	
Sales		3 0 0 0 0
Purchases	4 7 1 4 3	
Purchase Returns and Allowances		2 0 0
	6 9 2 9 2	

Accounts receivable control account:	2 6 2 1 5	
Accounts receivable subsidiary accounts:		
	2 6 2 1 5	
Accounts payable control account:		4 8 0 6 8
Accounts payable subsidiary accounts:		

)

General Journal

G1

Date	Account Titles and Explanations	Ref.	Debit	Credit

)

TACO CO.
Adjusted Trial Balance
February 28, 1999

	Debit	Credit
Cash		
Accounts Receivable		
GST Recoverable		
Supplies		
Equipment		
Accumulated Amortization—Equipment		
Accounts Payable		
GST Payable		
B. Taco, Capital		
B. Taco, Drawings		
Sales		
Purchases		
Purchase Returns and Allowances		
Supplies Expense		
Amortization Expense		

General Ledger

(a), (d) and (g)   Cash   No. 1(

Date	Explanation	Ref.	Debit	Credit	Balance

Accounts Receivable   No. 1

Date	Explanation	Ref.	Debit	Credit	Balance
6	Hardy		175 00		675 00
				1490	
					3 00 0

Store Supplies   No. 12

Date	Explanation	Ref.	Debit	Credit	Balance
			600		6 00

Prepaid Rent   No. 1

Date	Explanation	Ref.	Debit	Credit	Balance
			6000		6 00 0

Accounts Payable   No. 2(

Date	Explanation	Ref.	Debit	Credit	Balance
8	Washburn		296 00		296 00
10	Lonusley			411 20	
					1 15 20

A. Pinckney, Capital   No. 3(

Date	Explanation	Ref.	Debit	Credit	Balance
				80 00 0	80 00 0

), (d) and (g) (Continued)

A. Pinckney, Drawing No. 306

Date	Explanation	Ref.	Debit	Credit	Balance
			2500		2500

Sales No. 401

Date	Explanation	Ref.	Debit	Credit	Balance
				17900	17900
				4000	400
					21900

Sales Returns and Allowances No. 412

Date	Explanation	Ref.	Debit	Credit	Balance
			170		170

Purchases No. 510

Date	Explanation	Ref.	Debit	Credit	Balance
			41120		41120

Purchase Returns and Allowances No. 512

Date	Explanation	Ref.	Debit	Credit	Balance
				450	450

Supplies Expense No. 631

Date	Explanation	Ref.	Debit	Credit	Balance
			460		

Rent Expense No. 729

Date	Explanation	Ref.	Debit	Credit	Balance
			500		

(b)   Sales Journal   S

Date	Accounts Debited	Ref.	Acc. Rec. (Dr.) Sales (Cr.)
	Hardy		6 4 0 0
	Wash		3 6 0 0
	Lowsley		4 9 0 0
	S Keen		3 0 0 6
			1 7 9 0 0

Cash Receipts Journal   CR

Date	Accounts Credited	Ref.	Cash Dr.	Accts. Receivable Cr.	Sales Cr.	Other Accts. Cr.
7	Sale		4 0 0 0		4 0 0 0	
	D Wash		3 6 0 0	3 6 0 0		
	Lowsley		4 9 0 0	4 9 0 0		
	Hardy		6 4 0 0	6 4 0 0		
	C/ memo					
			1 8 9 0 0	1 4 9 0 0	4 0 0 7	

)

Dixon   *Accounts Payable Subsidiary Ledger*

Date	Explanation	Ref.	Debit	Credit	Balance
4		II		6809	
5			6809		

Engel

Date	Explanation	Ref.	Debit	Credit	Balance
				7500	
			7500		

Gamble

Date	Explanation	Ref.	Debit	Credit	Balance

Hill

Date	Explanation	Ref.	Debit	Credit	Balance

Jacob

Date	Explanation	Ref.	Debit	Credit	Balance

(c) (Continued)

Hardy Co.

Accounts Receivable Subsidiary Ledger

Date	Explanation	Ref.	Debit	Credit	Balance

S. Kane

Date	Explanation	Ref.	Debit	Credit	Balance

L. Lemansky

Date	Explanation	Ref.	Debit	Credit	Balance

D. Washburn

Date	Explanation	Ref.	Debit	Credit	Balance

PINCKNEY CO.
Trial Balance
July 31, 1999

	Debit	Credit
Cash		
Accounts Receivable		
Prepaid Rent		
Store Supplies		
Accounts Payable		
A. Pinckney, Capital		
A. Pinckney, Drawings		
Sales		
Sales Returns and Allowances		
Purchases		
Purchase Returns and Allowances		

Accounts payable balance:		
Subsidiary account balances:		
Accounts receivable balance:		
Subsidiary account balances:		

(b) and (g)   General Journal   G1

Date	Account Titles and Explanations	Ref.	Debit	Credit

(h)

PINCKNEY CO.
Adjusted Trial Balance
July 31, 1999

	Debit	Credit
Cash		
Accounts Receivable		
Store Supplies		
Prepaid Rent		
Accounts Payable		
A. Pinckney, Capital		
A. Pinckney, Drawings		
Sales		
Sales Returns and Allowances		
Purchases		
Purchase Returns and Allowances		
Supplies Expense		
Rent Expense		

Sales Journal   S1

Date	Accounts Debited	Ref.	Acc. Rec. (Dr.) Sales (Cr.)

Purchases Journal   P1

ate	Accounts Credited	Ref.	Purchases (Dr.) Acc. Pay. (Cr.)

General Journal   G1

Date	Account Titles and Explanations	Ref.	Debit	Credit

(b) (Continued)

Cash Receipts Journal

CR

Date	Accounts Credited	Ref.	Cash Dr.	Accts. Receivable Cr.	Sales Cr.	Other Accts. Cr.

Cash Payments Journal

CF

Date	Ck. No.	Payee	Cash Cr.	Accts. Payable Dr.	Accts. Debited	Ref.	Other Accts. Dr.

(a) and (c)

General Ledger

Cash

No. 10

Date	Explanation	Ref.	Debit	Credit	Balance

and (c) (Continued)   Accounts Receivable   No. 112

Date	Explanation	Ref.	Debit	Credit	Balance

Notes Receivable   No. 115

Date	Explanation	Ref.	Debit	Credit	Balance

Merchandise Inventory   No. 120

Date	Explanation	Ref.	Debit	Credit	Balance

Equipment   No. 157

Date	Explanation	Ref.	Debit	Credit	Balance

Accumulated Amortization—Equipment   No. 158

Date	Explanation	Ref.	Debit	Credit	Balance

Notes Payable   No. 200

Date	Explanation	Ref.	Debit	Credit	Balance

(a) and (c) (Continued)

Accounts Payable   No. 2

Date	Explanation	Ref.	Debit	Credit	Balance

S. Garcia, Capital   No. 3

Date	Explanation	Ref.	Debit	Credit	Balance

Sales   No. 40

Date	Explanation	Ref.	Debit	Credit	Balance

Sales Returns and Allowances   No. 41

Date	Explanation	Ref.	Debit	Credit	Balance

Purchases   No. 51

Date	Explanation	Ref.	Debit	Credit	Balance

Purchase Returns and Allowances   No. 51

Date	Explanation	Ref.	Debit	Credit	Balance

) and (c) (Continued)

Freight In   No. 516

Date	Explanation	Ref.	Debit	Credit	Balance

Sales Salaries Expense   No. 726

Date	Explanation	Ref.	Debit	Credit	Balance

Office Salaries Expense   No. 727

Date	Explanation	Ref.	Debit	Credit	Balance

Rent Expense   No. 729

Date	Explanation	Ref.	Debit	Credit	Balance

Accounts Receivable Subsidiary Ledger

. Barton

Date	Explanation	Ref.	Debit	Credit	Balance

. Cole

Date	Explanation	Ref.	Debit	Credit	Balance

(a) and (c) (Continued)

S. Devine

Date	Explanation	Ref.	Debit	Credit	Balance

B. Senton

Date	Explanation	Ref.	Debit	Credit	Balance

S. Field

Accounts Payable Subsidiary Ledger

Date	Explanation	Ref.	Debit	Credit	Balance

R. Gilson

Date	Explanation	Ref.	Debit	Credit	Balance

D. Harms

Date	Explanation	Ref.	Debit	Credit	Balance

D. Lapeska

Date	Explanation	Ref.	Debit	Credit	Balance

S. Warren

Date	Explanation	Ref.	Debit	Credit	Balance

a)

GARCIA CO.
Trial Balance
January 31, 2000

	Debit	Credit
Cash		
Accounts Receivable		
Notes Receivable		
Merchandise Inventory		
Equipment		
Accumulated Amortization—Equipment		
Notes Payable		
Accounts Payable		
S. Garcia, Capital		
Sales		
Sales Returns and Allowances		
Purchases		
Purchase Returns and Allowances		
Freight In		
Sales Salaries Expense		
Office Salaries Expense		
Rent Expense		

b)

Accounts receivable subsidiary ledger:		
Accounts receivable control:		
Accounts payable subsidiary ledger:		
Accounts payable control:		

(b)   Sales Journal   S

Date	Account Debited	Invoice No.	Terms	Ref.	Acc. Rec.(Dr)	Sales (Cr.)	GST Payable (Cr.)	PST Payable (Cr.)

Purchases Journal   P

Date	Accounts Credited	Terms	Ref.	Purchases (Dr.)	GST Recov. (Dr.)	Acc. Pay. (Cr.)

General Journal   G

Date	Account Titles and Explanations	Ref.	Debit	Credit

b) (Continued)   Cash Receipts Journal   CR1

Date	Accounts Credited	Ref.	Cash Dr.	Accts. Receivable Cr.	Sales Cr.	GST Payable Cr.	PST Payable Cr.	Other Accts. Cr.

Cash Payments Journal   CP1

Date	Ck. No.	Payee	Cash Cr.	Accts. Payable Dr.	GST Recoverable Dr.	Accounts Debited	Ref.	Other Accts. Dr.

General Ledger

a) and (c)   Cash   No. 101

Date	Explanation	Ref.	Debit	Credit	Balance
Jan. 1	Balance	✔			395 00

(a) and (c) (Continued)

Accounts Receivable   No. 11

Date	Explanation	Ref.	Debit	Credit	Balance
Jan. 1	Balance	✔			15000

GST Recoverable   No. 11

Date	Explanation	Ref.	Debit	Credit	Balance
Jan. 1	Balance	✔			2800

Notes Receivable   No. 11

Date	Explanation	Ref.	Debit	Credit	Balance
Jan. 1	Balance	✔			42200

Merchandise Inventory   No. 12

Date	Explanation	Ref.	Debit	Credit	Balance
Jan. 1	Balance	✔			23000

Equipment   No. 15

Date	Explanation	Ref.	Debit	Credit	Balance
Jan. 1	Balance	✔			6450

Accumulated Amortization—Equipment   No. 15

Date	Explanation	Ref.	Debit	Credit	Balance
Jan. 1	Balance	✔			1500

Notes Payable   No. 20

Date	Explanation	Ref.	Debit	Credit	Balance

and (c) (Continued)

Accounts Payable   No. 201

Date	Explanation	Ref.	Debit	Credit	Balance
Jan. 1	Balance	✔			43000

GST Payable   No. 213

Date	Explanation	Ref.	Debit	Credit	Balance
Jan. 1	Balance	✔			980

PST Payable   No. 215

Date	Explanation	Ref.	Debit	Credit	Balance
Jan. 1	Balance	✔			1120

Marek, Capital   No. 301

Date	Explanation	Ref.	Debit	Credit	Balance
Jan. 1	Balance	✔			82350

Sales   No. 401

Date	Explanation	Ref.	Debit	Credit	Balance

Sales Returns and Allowances   No. 412

Date	Explanation	Ref.	Debit	Credit	Balance

Purchases   No. 510

Date	Explanation	Ref.	Debit	Credit	Balance

(a) and (c) (Continued)

Purchase Returns and Allowances

No. 5

Date	Explanation	Ref.	Debit	Credit	Balance

Freight In

No. 5

Date	Explanation	Ref.	Debit	Credit	Balance

Sales Salaries Expense

No. 7

Date	Explanation	Ref.	Debit	Credit	Balance

Office Salaries Expense

No. 7

Date	Explanation	Ref.	Debit	Credit	Balance

Rent Expense

No. 7

Date	Explanation	Ref.	Debit	Credit	Balance

R. Barton

Accounts Receivable Subsidiary Ledger

Date	Explanation	Ref.	Debit	Credit	Balance
Jan. 1	Balance	✔			2500

B. Cole

Date	Explanation	Ref.	Debit	Credit	Balance
Jan. 1	Balance	✔			7500

) and (c) (Continued)

Devine

Date	Explanation	Ref.	Debit	Credit	Balance
Jan. 1	Balance	✔			5000

Senton

Date	Explanation	Ref.	Debit	Credit	Balance

Accounts Payable Subsidiary Ledger

Field

Date	Explanation	Ref.	Debit	Credit	Balance
Jan. 1	Balance	✔			10000

Gilson

Date	Explanation	Ref.	Debit	Credit	Balance
Jan. 1	Balance	✔			18000

Harms

Date	Explanation	Ref.	Debit	Credit	Balance
Jan. 1	Balance	✔			15000

Lapeska

Date	Explanation	Ref.	Debit	Credit	Balance

Warren

Date	Explanation	Ref.	Debit	Credit	Balance

(d)

MAREK CO.
Trial Balance
January 31, 2000

	Debit	Credit
Cash		
Accounts Receivable		
GST Recoverable		
Notes Receivable		
Merchandise Inventory		
Equipment		
Accumulated Amortization—Equipment		
Notes Payable		
Accounts Payable		
GST Payable		
PST Payable		
Marek, Capital		
Sales		
Sales Returns and Allowances		
Purchases		
Purchase Returns and Allowances		
Freight In		
Sales Salaries Expense		
Office Salaries Expense		
Rent Expense		

(e)

Accounts receivable subsidiary ledger:		
Accounts receivable control:		
Accounts payable subsidiary ledger:		
Accounts payable control:		

me

tion

te

(a)   Sales Journal   S

Date	Account Debited	Invoice No.	Ref.	Acc. Rec. Dr. Sales Cr.

Purchases Journal   P

Date	Account Credited	Terms	Ref.	Purchases Dr. Acc. Pay Cr.

me

tion

te Hunt Co.

(Continued) Cash Receipts Journal CR1

ate	Explanation	Accounts Credited	Ref.	Cash Dr.	Accounts Receivable Cr.	Sales Cr.	Other Accounts Cr.

Cash Payments Journal CP1

te	Ck. No.	Payee	Cash Cr.	Accts. Payable Dr.	Accounts Debited	Ref.	Other Accts. Dr.

(a) and (e)

General Journal

Date	Account Titles and Explanation	Ref.	Debit	Credit

and (e) (Continued)   General Journal   G1

Date	Account Titles and Explanation	Ref.	Debit	Credit

General Ledger

(b) and (e)

Cash   No. 1

Date	Explanation	Ref.	Debit	Credit	Balance
Jan. 1	Balance	✔			35750

Accounts Receivable   No. 1

Date	Explanation	Ref.	Debit	Credit	Balance
Jan. 1	Balance	✔			13000

Notes Receivable   No. 1

Date	Explanation	Ref.	Debit	Credit	Balance
Jan. 1	Balance	✔			39000

Merchandise Inventory   No. 1

Date	Explanation	Ref.	Debit	Credit	Balance
Jan. 1	Balance	✔			18000

Office Supplies   No. 1

Date	Explanation	Ref.	Debit	Credit	Balance
Jan. 1	Balance	✔			1000

) and (e) (Continued)

Prepaid Insurance — No. 130

Date	Explanation	Ref.	Debit	Credit	Balance
an. 1	Balance	✔			2000

Equipment — No. 157

Date	Explanation	Ref.	Debit	Credit	Balance
an. 1	Balance	✔			6450

Accumulated Amortization—Equipment — No. 158

Date	Explanation	Ref.	Debit	Credit	Balance
an. 1	Balance	✔			1500

Notes Payable — No. 200

Date	Explanation	Ref.	Debit	Credit	Balance

Accounts Payable — No. 201

Date	Explanation	Ref.	Debit	Credit	Balance
an. 1	Balance	✔			35000

Interest Payable — No. 230

Date	Explanation	Ref.	Debit	Credit	Balance

(b) and (e) (Continued)

S. Hunt, Capital   No. 3(

Date	Explanation	Ref.	Debit	Credit	Balance
Jan. 1	Balance	✔			78700

S. Hunt, Drawings   No. 3(

Date	Explanation	Ref.	Debit	Credit	Balance

Income Summary   No. 3!

Date	Explanation	Ref.	Debit	Credit	Balance

Sales   No. 4(

Date	Explanation	Ref.	Debit	Credit	Balance

Sales Returns and Allowances   No. 4'

Date	Explanation	Ref.	Debit	Credit	Balance

and (e) (Continued)

Purchases   No. 510

Date	Explanation	Ref.	Debit	Credit	Balance

Purchase Returns and Allowances   No. 512

Date	Explanation	Ref.	Debit	Credit	Balance

Freight In   No. 516

Date	Explanation	Ref.	Debit	Credit	Balance

Sales Salaries Expense   No. 627

Date	Explanation	Ref.	Debit	Credit	Balance

Amortization Expense   No. 711

Date	Explanation	Ref.	Debit	Credit	Balance

Interest Expense   No. 718

Date	Explanation	Ref.	Debit	Credit	Balance

(b) and (e) (Continued)

Insurance Expense   No. 7

Date	Explanation	Ref.	Debit	Credit	Balance

Office Salaries Expense   No. 7

Date	Explanation	Ref.	Debit	Credit	Balance

Office Supplies Expense   No. 7

Date	Explanation	Ref.	Debit	Credit	Balance

Rent Expense   No. 7

Date	Explanation	Ref.	Debit	Credit	Balance

Accounts Receivable Subsidiary Ledger

) and (e) (Continued)

R. Dansig

Date	Explanation	Ref.	Debit	Credit	Balance
Jan. 1	Balance	✔			1500

J. Eaton

Date	Explanation	Ref.	Debit	Credit	Balance

B. Jaggar

Date	Explanation	Ref.	Debit	Credit	Balance
Jan. 1	Balance	✔			7500

S. Lowell

Date	Explanation	Ref.	Debit	Credit	Balance
Jan. 1	Balance	✔			4000

B. Sargent

Date	Explanation	Ref.	Debit	Credit	Balance

Accounts Payable Subsidiary Ledger

(b) and (e) (Continued)

D. Landell

Date	Explanation	Ref.	Debit	Credit	Balance

S. Lee

Date	Explanation	Ref.	Debit	Credit	Balance
Jan. 1	Balance	✔			9000

R. Mannon

Date	Explanation	Ref.	Debit	Credit	Balance
Jan. 1	Balance	✔			15000

D. Nordin

Date	Explanation	Ref.	Debit	Credit	Balance
Jan. 1	Balance	✔			11000

S. Walden

Date	Explanation	Ref.	Debit	Credit	Balance

d)

HUNT CO.
Income Statement
For the Month Ended January 31, 2000

(c)

HUNT COMPANY
Work Sheet
For the Month Ended January 31, 2000

Account Titles	Trial Balance		Adjustments	
	Dr.	Cr.	Dr.	Cr.
Cash				
Accounts Receivable				
Notes Receivable				
Merchandise Inventory				
Office Supplies				
Prepaid Insurance				
Equipment				
Accumulated Amortization—Equipment				
Notes Payable				
Accounts Payable				
Interest Payable				
S. Hunt, Capital				
S. Hunt, Drawings				
Sales				
Sales Returns and Allowances				
Purchases				
Purchase Returns and Allowances				
Freight In				
Sales Salaries Expense				
Office Salaries Expense				
Rent Expense				
Totals				

Adjusted Trial Balance		Income Statement		Balance Sheet	
Dr.	Cr.	Dr.	Cr.	Dr.	Cr.

(d) (Continued)

HUNT CO.
Statement of Owner's Equity
For the Month Ended January 31, 2000

HUNT CO.
Balance Sheet
January 31, 2000

ıme

ction

ıte

Hunt Co.

f)

HUNT CO.
Post Closing Balance
January 31, 2000

	Debit	Credit
Accounts receivable balance:		
Subsidiary account balances:		
Accounts payable balance:		
Subsidiary account balances:		

Name

Section

Date

Name

Section

Date

(b)

Recommended Change

Principle Violated

(a)

Weakness

1.

2.

3.

4.

5.

me

ction

te

(b)

(a)

Weakness	Principle Violated	Suggested Improvement
1.		
2.		
3.		
4.		
5.		

MEMORANDUM

TO:

FROM:

DATE:

SUBJECT: Suggested improvements in Internal Control of Cash Disbursements

E 7-5   General Journal

Date	Account Titles and Explanation	Ref.	Debit	Credit

E 7-6

(a)

ONO LOKO COMPANY
Bank Reconciliation
January 31

General Journal

(b) Date	Account Titles and Explanation	Ref.	Debit	Credit

7-7

7-8

a)

MOHAMMED COMPANY
Bank Reconciliation
July 31

General Journal

b)

Date	Account Titles and Explanation	Ref.	Debit	Credit

(a)

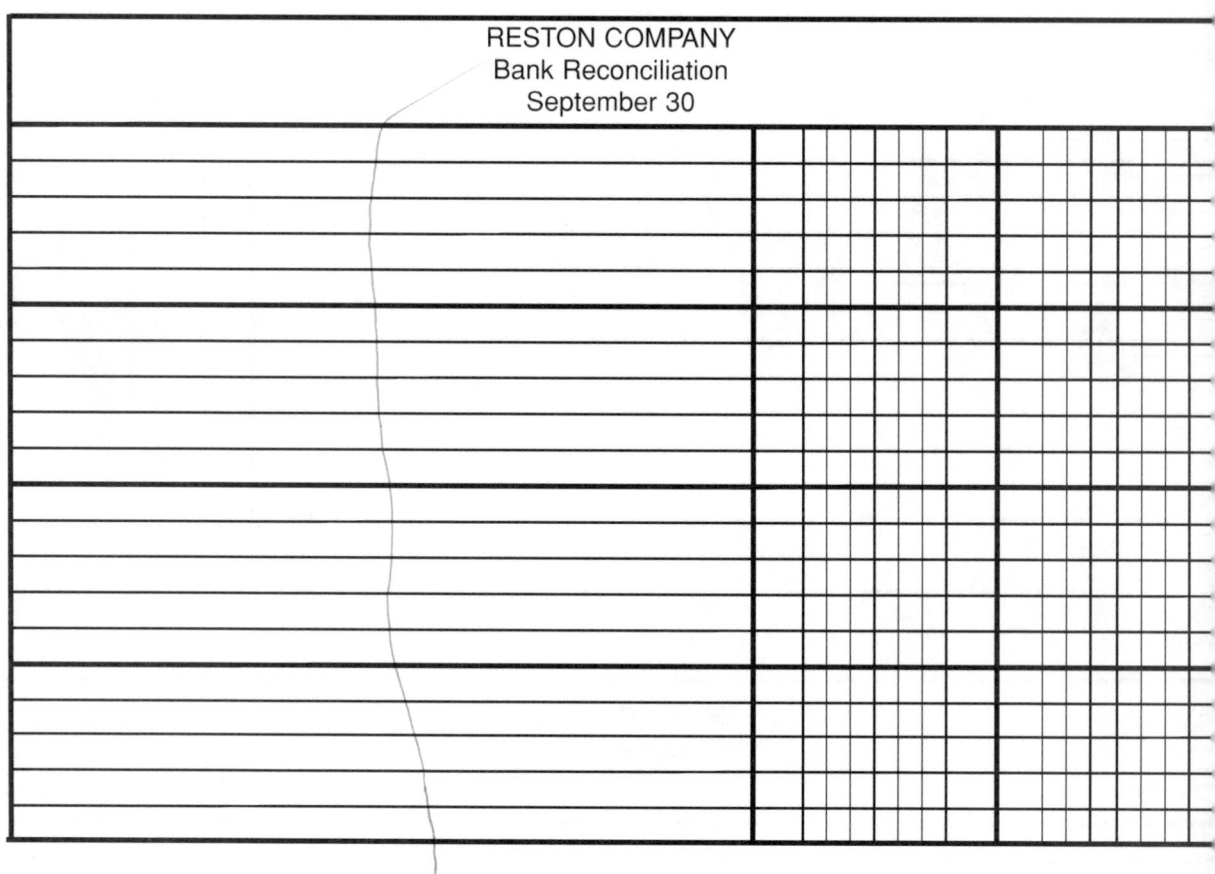

RESTON COMPANY
Bank Reconciliation
September 30

(b)

General Journal

Date	Account Titles and Explanation	Ref.	Debit	Credit

me
tion
te

(a)

Principles	Application to Cash Receipts

(b)

Principles	Application to Cash Disbursements

(a)   General Journal

Date	Account Titles and Explanation	Ref.	Debit			Credit		
1	Petty		2 0 0					
	Cash					2 0 0		
15	Freight		9 4					
	Postage		4 2 40					
	Ent		4 6 60					
	Mis ex		1 0 70					
	Cash over/Short		60			1		
	Cash					1 9 4 3		

Petty Cash

Date	Explanation	Ref.	Credit	Debit	Balance

2010

107 97.3 (a)

MALONEY COMPANY							
Bank Reconciliation							
May 31, 1999							
Cash per bank							
Add deposit in transit							
Less o/s check:							
# 3478 #84		538		1			
Adj 3481 3686		87 40		1 35 67			
Adj cash bal per bank				82 19			
Cash bal per books				1 05 96			
Add collections of note							
#2145 + interest of $160 – collection fee		22 90		12 08 63			
Less NSF		47 10					

(b)   General Journal

Date	Account Titles and Explanation	Ref.	Debit	Credit

LONDON COMPANY Bank Reconciliation November 30, 1999																						

General Journal

Date	Account Titles and Explanation	Ref.	Debit								Credit							

(a)

SANDRA COMPANY Bank Reconciliation December 31, 1999		

(b)   General Journal

Date	Account Titles and Explanation	Ref.	Debit	Credit

PALMEIRO COMPANY
Bank Reconciliation
July 31, 1999

Bal as per bank				24530
Deposit in transit				5000
Error in the deposit				100
Less o/s cheque				6600
Adj per bank balance				23530
Bal as per book				22700
Add: collections plus interest				2070
Less				09
error in Post cheque				90
Bank charges				40
				2460

2460

(b)   General Journal

Date	Account Titles and Explanation	Ref.	Debit	Credit

)

	MAYO COMPANY Bank Reconciliation August 31, 1999		

(b)   General Journal

Date	Account Titles and Explanation	Ref.	Debit	Credit

a)

ACURA COMPANY Bank Reconciliation October 31, 1999		

) and (c)

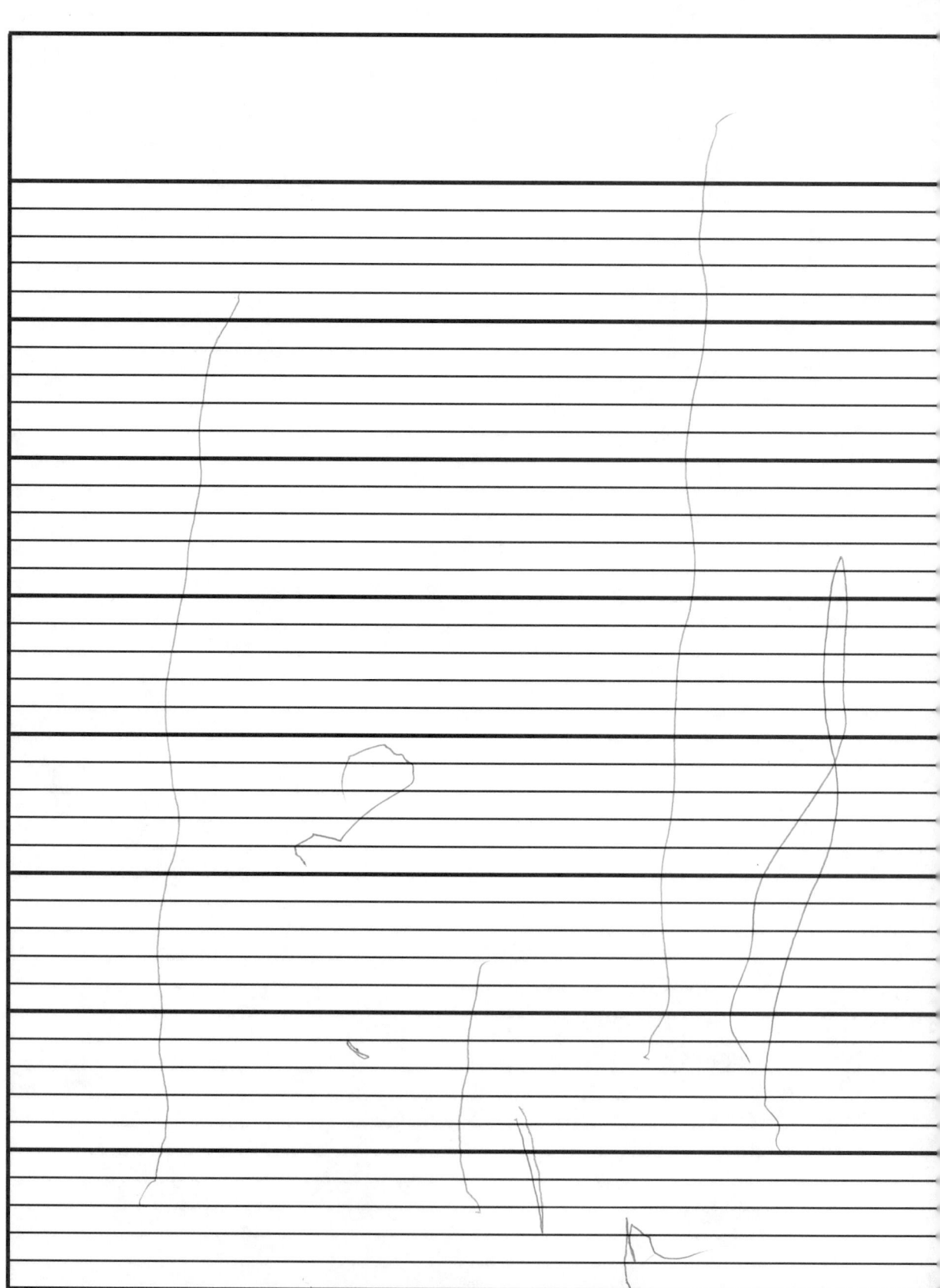

Material Weakness	Internal Control Principle

me
tion
te

General Journal

Date	Account Titles and Explanation	Ref.	Debit	Credit
8-1				
8-2				

E 8-3

E 8-4

ne
ion
e

General Journal

Date	Account Titles and Explanation	Ref.	Debit	Credit
8-5				
8-6				

General Journal

Date	Account Titles and Explanation	Ref.	Debit	Credit
E 8-7				
E 8-8				

me

tion

e

General Journal

Date	Account Titles and Explanation	Ref.	Debit	Credit
8-9				
8-10				

(a)   General Journal

Date	Account Titles and Explanation	Ref.	Debit	Credit
1.	A/R	3	3 200 000	
	sales			3 200 000
			. 0	
2	sales return + All		50 000	
	A/R			50 000
3	Cash		2 800 000	
	A/R			2 800 000
4	All for doubtful debt		90 000	
	A/R			90 000
5	A/R		35 000	
	All Doubtf			35 000
	Cash		35 000	
	A/R			35 000

(b)

ACCOUNTS RECEIVABLE		ALLOWANCE FOR DOUBTFUL ACCOUNTS	
96 000	50 000	90 000	70 000
320 000	2 800 000		35 000
35 000	90 000		
	35 000		
333 1 000			
			15 000

(c)   General Journal

3 331 000
2 975 000

Date	Account Titles and Explanation	Ref.	Debit	Credit

36, 000

credit sales   = $ 2000,000
      3%   =   2000 000 × ·03   = 60, 000

n / R   =   800 000
5 %   =   800 000 × ·05
       =   40 000
       =   40 000 − 3000
       =   37000

d)   40000 + 3000 < $7, 000
                    −   7 000
                       40 000

General Journal

Date	Account Titles and Explanation	Ref.	Debit	Credit

(a) and (b)

Bad Debt Expense

Date	Explanation	Ref.	Debit	Credit	Balance

Allowance for Doubtful Accounts

Date	Explanation	Ref.	Debit	Credit	Balance

General Journal

Date	Account Titles and Explanation	Ref.	Debit	Credit

(a) and (d)   General Journal

Date	Account Titles and Explanation	Ref.	Debit	Credit

Notes Receivable

Date	Explanation	Ref.	Debit	Credit	Balance
ct. 1	Balance	✔			23400 00

Accounts Receivable

Date	Explanation	Ref.	Debit	Credit	Balance

Interest Receivable

Date	Explanation	Ref.	Debit	Credit	Balance
ct. 1	Balance	✔			120 73

SELICA COMPANY
(Partial) Balance Sheet
October 31, 1999

Assets		
urrent Assets		

General Journal

Date	Account Titles and Explanation	Ref.	Debit	Credit

General Journal

Date	Account Titles and Explanation	Ref.	Debit	Credit

General Journal

Date	Account Titles and Explanation	Ref.	Debit	Credit

ne
tion
e

General Journal

Date	Account Titles and Explanation	Ref.	Debit	Credit

	1999	1998	1997

ne

tion

e

(a)

(b)

(c)

me

ction

te

9-6

E 9-1

E 9-2

Inventory Items	Total Cost	Market	Lower Cost and Market by		
			(a) Individual Items	(b) Major Categories	(c) Total Inventory

9-7	Women's Department				Men's Department			
	Cost		Retail		Cost		Retail	

9-8	1999	2000

(a)	1999	2000

(b) and (c)

Description	Purchased	Sold	Balance
(1) FIFO			
(2) Moving Average			

(a)   Cost of Goods Available for Sale

Date	Explanation	Units	Unit Cost	Total Cost

(b)   FIFO

(1) Ending Inventory	(2) Cost of Goods Sold

Weighted Average

(1) Ending Inventory	(2) Cost of Goods Sold

) Continued   LIFO

       (1) Ending Inventory   (2) Cost of Goods Sold

)

                                        FIFO   Average   LIFO

S: Ending Inventory

S: Cost of Goods Sold

)

(a)

		FIFO		AVERAGE	

REALTY NOVELTY INC.
Condensed Income Statements
For the Year Ended December 31, 1999

(b)

)

TUMATOE INC. Condensed Income Statements For the Year Ended December 31, 1999	FIFO	LIFO

)

Que how to det est gross profit

Gross profit rate = $\dfrac{\text{Gross profit}}{\text{net sales}}$

[Gross Profit = net sales − cost of goods sold]

(a) | | | | | | | | | | | | November |
|---|---|---|---|---|---|---|---|---|---|---|---|
| Beginning Inv | | | | | | | | | | | |
| Purchases | | | | | | | | | 2 2 1 0 0 |
| Less Purchase return & allowance | 3 1 4 9 7 5 | | | | | | | | |
| | 1 1 8 0 0 | | | | | | | | |
| | 3 0 3 1 7 5 | | | | | | | | |
| Plus Freight In | 4 4 0 2 | | | | | | 3 0 7 5 7 7 |
| Total Goods Available for Sale | | | | | | | 3 2 9 6 7 7 |
| Less Ending Inv | 2 9 1 0 0 | | | | | | |
| Cost of Good Sold | | | | | | | 3 0 0 5 7 7 |
| | | | | | | | |
| Gross Profit | | | | | | | 4 0 0 0 0 0 |
| Less Cost of Goods Sold | | | | | | | 3 0 0 5 7 7 |
| = | | | | | | | 9 9 4 2 3 |
| | | | | | | | |
| Gross Profit rate | | | | | | | . 9 9 4 2 3 |
| | | | | | | | 4 0 0 0 0 0 |
| | | | | | | | |
| Gross Profit rate = 25% | | | | | | | |

(b) | | | | | | | | | | | December |
|---|---|---|---|---|---|---|---|---|---|---|
| Net Sales | | | | | | | | 3 0 0 0 0 0 |
| Less est Gross Profit (.25 × 300,00) | | | | | | | 7 5 0 0 0 |
| Est cost of goods Sold | | | | | | | 2 2 5 0 0 0 |
| | | | | | | | |
| Beg Inv | | | | | | | 2 9 1 0 0 |
| Purchase | 2 3 6 0 0 0 | | | | | | |
| less Pur return + all | 4 0 0 0 | | | | | | |
| | 2 3 2 0 0 0 | | | | | | |
| Add Freight In (cost of good Pur | 3 7 0 0 | | | | | * 2 3 5 7 0 0 |
| Cost of Goods avl for sale | | | | | | | 2 6 4 8 0 0 |
| Less estimate cost of goods | | | | | | | 2 2 5 0 0 0 |
| Ending Inv | | | | | | | 3 9 8 0 0 |

Cost of goods sold = BI
+ = COGP
Cost of good AV =
− Ending Inv

	February

	March

(a)			Cost		Retail	

(b)

)

	Sporting Goods		Jewellery and Cosmetics	
	Cost	Retail	Cost	Retail
Beginning Inv	47360	74000	38000	62000
Purchases	620000	1066000	731000	1158000
Less Her returns	26000	40000	12000	20000
Freight In	6600		8000	
Good Av for sale	697360	1100000	765000	1200000
Net Sales		1020000		1167000
Ending Inv		80000		40000

ost to retail ratio
Sporting = 63 %

ost of retail ratio
Jew + Cost = 64 %

timate of End Inv
pmt good = $50 400

Estimate of sporting good
= 80 000 × 63·4 % = $ 50 727

Estimate Cost of Jewellery + Cost
= 40 000 × 63·7 % = $ 25 600

)

porting Goods = 80 000 × 60 %
= $ 48 000

Jewellery and Cosmetics = 40 000 × 65 %
= $ 26 000

Name _____   Problem 9-
Section _____
Date _____   Family Home Appliance Ma

(a)			FIFO					
(1) Date		Purchased			Sold			Balance
May 1	7 @ 150	1050					7 @ 15	1050
4				5 @ 150	750		2 @ 150	300
8	8 @ 170	1360					10	1660
12				5 @ 150	810		5	850
15	5 @ 180	900					10	1750
20				4	680		6	1070
23				3	530		3	
	20 =	3310		17	2770		3	540

(2) Date		Purchased			Moving Average Sold			Balance
May 1	7 @ 180	1050					7 @ 180	1050
4				5 @ 180			2 @ 150	300
8	8 @ 170	1360						
12				5 @ 166				
15								
20								
23								

(b)

(a)	FIFO		
Date	Purchased	Sold	Balance

)	(1) Sales			
	(2) Purchases			
)		1998	1997	
)				
)				

MEMORANDUM

TO: Joe Paisley, President

FROM:

DATE:

SUBJECT:

	EFFECT OF FISCAL YEAR	
	1999	1998
eginning Inventory		
nding Inventory		
ost of Goods Sold		
ross Profit on Sales		
come before Tax		
come Tax		
et Income		
nding Total Assets		
nding Shareholders' (Owners) Equity		

ne
tion
e

10-1

10-2

E 10-3

(a)

(b)	Computation			Annual Amortization Expense	End of Year	
Year	Units of Activity	x	Amortization Cost Per Unit		Accumulated Amortization	Net Book Value

E 10-4

ne

tion

e

10-5

)

)

0-6

Abner's Delivery Company and Wainright's Express Delivery

) Abner's Delivery Company:

Wainright's Express Delivery:

E 10-9		

E 10-10		

General Journal

Date	Account Titles and Explanation	Ref.	Debit	Credit

Item	Land	Building	Other Accounts	
			Amount	Titles
1.				
2.				
3.				
4.				
5.				
6.				
7.				
8.				
9.				
10.				
11.				

Year	Computation	Accumulated Amortization 12/31
a)	MACHINE 1	
1996		
1997		
1998		
1999		
	MACHINE 2	
1997		
1998		
1999		
	MACHINE 3	
1998		
1999		
b)	MACHINE 2	Amortization Expense
(1) 1997		
(2) 1998		

(a)   Straight-Line

| | Computation | | | Annual | End of Year | |
Year	Amortizable Cost	×	Amortization Rate	=	Amortization Expense	Accum. Amortization	Book Value
1999							
2000							
2001							
2002							

Double Declining-Balance

| | Computation | | | Annual | End of Year | |
Year	Book Value Beginning of year ×		Amortization Rate	=	Amortization Expense	Accum. Amortization	Book Value
1999							
2000							
2001							
2002							

(b) and (c)

)

General Journal

Date	Account Titles and Explanation	Ref.	Debit	Credit

(a) (Continued) and (b)   General Journal

Date	Account Titles and Explanation	Ref.	Debit	Credit

LAND

BUILDINGS

EQUIPMENT

ACCUMULATED AMORTIZATION—
BUILDINGS

ACCUMULATED AMORTIZATION—
EQUIPMENT

YOUNT CORPORATION
Partial Balance Sheet
December 31, 2000

General Journal

Date	Account Titles and Explanation	Ref.	Debit	Credit

General Journal

Date	Account Titles and Explanation	Ref.	Debit	Credit

Year	Amortization Expense	Accumulated Amortization
1997		
1998		
1999		
2000		
2001		
2002		
2003		

General Journal

Date	Account Titles and Explanation	Ref.	Debit	Credit

ne

tion

e

and (b)

General Journal

Date	Account Titles and Explanation	Ref.	Debit	Credit

) and (d)

Eikel Company
Capital Assets
December 31, 2000

General Journal

Date	Account Titles and Explanation	Ref.	Debit	Credit

(a) Tammy Company—Straight-line method

Year	Asset	Computation	Annual Amortization	Accumulated Amortization
1997				
1998				
1999				

Hamline Company—Double-declining-balance method

Year	Asset	Computation	Annual Amortization	Accumulated Amortization
1997				
1998				
1999				

(b)

Year	Tammy Co. Net Income	Hamline Co. Net Income As Adjusted	Computations for Hamline
1997			
1998			
1999			

(c)

MEMORANDUM

TO:

FROM:

DATE:

SUBJECT: Oil and Gas Accounting Disclosures

) and (b)